ORIGINALS

American Women Artists

ELEANOR MUNRO

SIMON AND SCHUSTER • NEW YORK

Designed by Eve Metz
Manufactured in the United States of America

1   2   3   4   5   6   7   8   9   10

Library of Congress Cataloging in Publication Data

Munro, Eleanor C
    Originals : American women artists.

    Bibliography: p.
    Includes index.
    1. Art, American.   2. Art, Modern—20th century—
United States.   3. Women artists—United States—
Biography.   I.   Title.
N6512.M78   709'.2'2 [B]   78-31814

ISBN 0-671-23109-X

The book *Originals—American Women Artists*
is an outgrowth of the television series
"The Originals/Women in Art"produced by WNET/Thirteen
and assisted by grants from the National Endowment for the Arts
and the Corporation for Public Broadcasting.

Grateful acknowledgment is made to the following for permission to reprint:
    The Archives of the Pennsylvania Academy of the Fine Arts, Philadelphia, Pennsylvania: for
passages from the Cassatt-Spartain correspondence.
    The National Gallery of Art, Washington D.C.: for passages from the Cassatt-Havemeyer
correspondence.
    Charles Scribner's Sons, New York: for passages from *Dawns + Dusks,* © 1976 Diana
MacKown.
    Harcourt Brace Jovanovich, Inc., New York: for lines from "Little Gidding" from *Four Quartets*
and from *The Waste Land* by T. S. Eliot.

    Portfolio of Color IV—*Jennifer Bartlett.* Day and Night/27 Howard Street, 1977. Private col-
lection, courtesy William Zierler, Inc.

ACKNOWLEDGMENTS

Credits are a writer's begats. For a woman who writes they can be extra-important, since so many names are concealed in the patriarchy. By calling to mind those with whom we are allied, we will them into form who are always, anyway, in our blood. Therefore, I begin back on the Isle of Skye, back in 1840, with my ancestor Janet Munro MacFarlane, in whose silence, cruelly misinterpreted by her husband, I seem to hear the suppressed artist's cry:

Janet is much depressed in her spirit [he wrote, explaining that he was not allowing her to emigrate to America with her brothers and sisters]. You know that she had but a weak mind, she did not expect but delight going through this wilderness. She did not anticipate any wormwood or gall, and she was not willing to drink the cup that was appointed from eternity for her. . . .

I call up others able to create their own lives: my paternal grandmother, Mary Spaulding Munro, an actress on the Chautauqua circuit, and my maternal grandmother, Berthe Clerc Nadler, who wrote sonnets and sewed many a fine seam as she followed her husband Westward and raised the three artist daughters whose names are on the dedication page of this book. Then there are my artist sisters: Elisabeth Munro Smith, a sculptor, and Olivia Kahn, a printmaker and ceramist. There are artist friends whose example I have admired over the years and women critics and connoisseurs whose dynamism inspired me—the late Aline Saarinen and Hilla Rebay, and Dorothy Norman and Katherine Kuh, still pioneers among artists and ideas in their seventies. There are also young artist-educators whose dedication is infectious. In my experience, Sheila de Bretteville of Los Angeles stands out among these. Writer Betty Jean Lifton and psychologists Margit van Leight Frank and Cynthia Beeker encouraged my impulse to turn this project into an experiment in discovery. And all who write about art must give credit to today's critics and historians like Dore Ashton, Ruth Bowman, Ann Sutherland Harris, Barbara Haskell, Hayden Herrera, April Kingsley, Lucy Lippard, Linda Nochlin, Barbara Novak, Barbara Rose, Phyllis Tuchman and Dorothy Seiberling among others.

5

Generous men, both critics and artists, also shared ideas and in some cases encouraged my writing this book: Thomas Hess, under whose editorial arm I studied art, artists and the art of writing about both; Harold Rosenberg, that rare humanist critic; B. H. Friedman, Eugene Goosen, Robert Motherwell, Sidney Simon and Jack Tworkov. That Hess and Rosenberg are to be called "the late" is a sad loss both for American culture and for friendship. I would also like to call back in memory that charismatic editor who nurtured both Hess and Rosenberg and gave early publication to many women writers including Saarinen (then Aline Louchheim), Betty Chamberlin, Dorothy Gees Seckler, Elaine de Kooning, Barbara Guest, Barbara Rose, Elizabeth C. Baker (now editor of *Art in America*) and myself: Alfred Frankfurter of *Art News*. And without pretending to academic parity, I should like to say that discussions heard through the years around psychohistorian Robert Jay Lifton suggested related ways of thinking about esthetics. To that subject, viewed according to his own discipline, my father, Thomas Munro, devoted his life. He bequeathed me, I hope, both his respect for the given evidence and his reach for conclusions beyond the expected ones. Not lastly, I speak in this book of models: my husband, E. J. Kahn, Jr., in his devotion to craft, grace and truthfulness, could be a model for any writer.

Specifically, Donald Cutler of Sterling Lord, Inc., and Frederick Jacobi of WNET-TV should be named midhusbands of this project. They made it possible for me to carry out an idea I had had in mind for some time. Perry Miller Adato's fine work for the TV series *The Originals,* as well as her literal sharing, were basic helps. As executive producer of that series and creator of three of the films (Cassatt, O'Keeffe, Frankenthaler), she has made a contribution to cultural history. This book is intended as a companion to the project of discovery and interpretation she and WNET-Channel 13 have launched. Editor Alice Mayhew took a chance my project would turn out worthy of its subjects. Her editorial support and overview of a large operation gave me encouragement all the way. Quotes by the artists not otherwise credited are from our conversations during '77 and early '78. These have been approved for publication by the speakers, in some cases after refinement. Beyond the stage of composition, there is the actual making of a book: in this I was helped by the sage judgments of editor John Cox, the good eye of designer Eve Metz, the interest of art director Frank Metz and associate publisher Dan Green, the scrupulousness of copy editors Sophie Sorkin and Vera Schneider, and the skilled know-how of editorial assistant Gwen Edelman and photo editor Vincent Virga, all Simon and Schuster. Afield, young women with special editorial skills—Laurie Bloomfield, Evelyn Lief, Maureen St. Onge, Carol Shookhoff—were much appreciated. Among dealers, I am especially grateful to Paula Cooper, André Emmerich, Rose Esmon, Xavier Fourcade, Millie and Arnold Glimcher, Jill Kornblee and Virginia Zabriskie. So too am I to Timothy Seldes of Russell & Volkening. Parts or all of the manuscript were read by Thomas Hess before his death, Barbara Rose and Katherine Kuh, by professor of philosophy Donald J. Munro, by Feminist artist Miriam Schapiro and by my husband. They each took time to make valuable suggestions in line with their special fields. I have made grateful use of these while also continuing on my own tack.

The project would not have seen the light at all if it were not for the Women's Movement in the arts that, paralleling earlier movements in politics and other areas of the culture, opened what had been a male enclave.[1] All women must therefore be grateful to the Feminist artist activists, some I have not otherwise treated in this book. Among them are Judy Chicago, Mary Beth Edelson, Harmony Hammond, Poppy Johnson, Joyce Kozloff, Ellen Lanyon, Brenda Miller, Patsy Norvell, Howardena Pindell, Carolee Schneemann, Joan Semmel, Sylvia Sleigh, Joan Snyder, Nancy Spero, Pat Steir, Anita Stekel, May Stevens, Faith Wilding and others. As the year 1978 unrolled, the number of strong women artists showing their work in New York galleries alone was remarkable, and I have no doubt that galleries in other cities coast to coast would report the same. I could not possibly claim to have done justice to what is a rising tide. May those many original artists not heralded here forgive me. As only one measure of my limitation, I have included only one practitioner of Performance Art, so rooted in the esthetics, politics and psychology of our time.

There are many artists and critics, including, but not only, Feminists, who have suggested that since "male" esthetic values predominated for centuries, it is impossible, and will be so for a long time, to know what "women's art" might be. I propose that the answer is at hand. The female voice was not lost, only not listened to. In that sense, my very evocation of Janet Munro Mac-Farlane can be considered the paradigm from which the interpretations in this book have evolved.

For my mother, Lucile Nadler Munro, a pianist,
and her sisters, Clara, a painter,
and Charlotte, a violinist

WOMEN ARTISTS

CONTENTS

*Gertrude has said things tonight it will take her years
to understand. . . .*[1]
—ALICE B. TOKLAS, *leaving a dinner party*

Methods and Matriarchs

Procedural
Notes

I had two interests in doing this book: one biographical or psychological, the other esthetic. I welcomed the chance to study the lives of a number of "successful" women artists to a rather missionary end: to show with what inner-directed commitment and sacrifice they kept to their goal long before success was a factor, and so possibly to offer models for other people (female and male) who find many of our society's goals inadequate. At the same time, I hoped to illuminate the work itself in an unconventional way. Since much of the art being made now has a look of dehumanized strangeness, I wanted to explore to what degree, in the case of these in no way average human beings who were artists, the work had still been drawn from commonly comprehensible life experience and so might be susceptible of interpretation, on at least one level, along humanist lines. It seemed to me, in other words, that these artists might have something to say of which even they (like Gertrude Stein) might be unaware.

As the work went along, however, a third interest took over. I began hearing the same theme rung again and again. Gradually, I began to feel as if it might be I myself standing in Toklas's shoes, hearing revelations whose significance outran my—and I felt the speakers'—first understanding. I began to feel that I was hearing certain clues to the operation of the mind itself from these artists sharing intimate memories and thoughts with me. What, I began to ask, is the nature of this "artist," and in what process, toward the creation of what structures, does that nature fulfill itself? The possibility of circling the question of what that procedure is occurred to me. I would have to work in much the same way the artists do, moving back and forth between raw material (in this case the data they provided me about their lives) and insights relating it

17

to the work, by both the artists and myself. I dared, I hoped not too preten-
tiously, to give this manner of approaching an old question a name that has
been often toyed with but not taken up. I offer this, therefore, as an essai, in
the dictionary sense of "trial," in psychoesthetics, one more of those ungainly
compounds, like archaeo-astronomy, sociobiology or psychohistory, by which
the imagination nowadays gropes ahead. These hybrids, I suggest, are the
mutters of a people, as my Alabama mother likes to say, whose "eyes are
bigger than their stomachs"—whose reach and curiosity exceed their methodology (perhaps a more hopeful condition than the reverse), who ask more
questions of experience than experience, conventionally seen, can answer.

I knew I was on precarious ground, however. Since Freud came to grief
interpreting Leonardo da Vinci's imagery by psychoanalytic methods, art critics
have been skeptical of non-art tools, especially psychological ones. That is, I
think, one reason for the dearth of biographies of visual artists, even of such
tempting subjects as Rothko, Still, Krasner, Neel, Bourgeois and so on, in a
period when writers, scholars, musicians, composers, conductors, dancers are
either lending themselves to biography if alive, providing such material for
researchers if dead or writing their own stories if they can. The potential art of
biography of visual artists, however, seems to have been cut short by this fear
of Freudian failure and also by the adoption of narrowly art-historical, formalist
or phenomenological categories in talking about the visual arts.[2]

The question of what is legitimate to include in writing about the arts is an
old one, however, and has been answered differently from time to time. Since
the nineteenth century, the originally Germanic object-centered view[3] pre-
vailed to a point where, in the 1960s, some artists and critics came to the
position that works of the imagination could be purified of "the personal, the
subjective, the tragic and the narrative, in favor of the world of things."[4] That
point of view paralleled the New Criticism in literature and a related style in
musical composition and criticism.[5] Yet, from what I infer after conversations
with these artists, even with such a one as the classic Minimalist Anne Truitt, it
is impossible to hold that even works as bare of representation as hers are
therefore empty of projected human content. To say that such a reading is
possible is to fall into the trap Harold Rosenberg describes:

. . . the net effect of deleting from the interpretation of the work the signs pointing to the
artist's situation and his emotional conclusions about it is to substitute for an appreciation of the crisis-dynamics of contemporary painting an arid professionalism that is a
weak parody of the estheticism of half a century ago.[6]

There was, as well, another perspective from which my own point of view might be criticized by some. Just as some critics say that only form and structure are worth taking seriously, others feel that the Women's Movement has been the most important event in history and should provide the basis for any discussion of women's art.

It is true that dramatic changes in the fortunes of women artists have taken place under the aegis of the Movement that since 1969 or '70 has been actively pushed forward, especially in New York, Chicago and Los Angeles. Women's art centers have provided a place to work and a forum for self-analysis and critiques of society. Pressure has been brought to bear on galleries, museums and university art departments to give better representation to women. Much has still to be done, and it is true also that here as elsewhere in life those who share the rewards are not always those who worked for them. There are women in this book who have kept out of the struggle,[7] while many who worked selflessly for the Movement are not included here. My criterion for inclusion in this study was not political. I selected a group whose work interested me and then narrowed my selection, as I unfortunately had to for space. Indeed, it was one of my aims to show what needs no argument: that women artists find their place in the cultural mainstream. Undoubtedly there is a "woman's truth" and "woman-art"—facts deriving from female endocrinology and certain handicraft necessities to which women were confined in days before spinning mills appeared along the New England river banks and the development of rolling mills led to the invention of tin cans for food. But these are intermediary truths. The women included here have shared with men the long, often cruel road to achievement. Men and women suffer alike from inequalities in the distribution of talents and so from degrees of injustice. Moreover, it can be said that every artist, essentially, is a member of a minority and that no community is caring enough to shelter the genuine original. Jackson Pollock's last shows were disdained by his peers; Barnett Newman's first ones were ignored by his. Artists on the rise of publicity and profit in one season will be put down in the next. As a matter of fact, one reason women's art has not been honored enough is that it has too often been considered just that—women's art—and not searched for revelations of the Zeitgeist. In this one respect, Feminism may even serve the enemy. To say, for instance, of Louise Bourgeois's work—as even so fine a critic as Lucy Lippard does—that "attempts to bring a coolly evolutionary or art-historical order to her work, or to see it in the context of one art group or another, have proved more or less irrelevant"[8] is to deprive her of the place she holds as a leading, if eccentric, American Surrealist today. To deprive the female of the background she shares with men is to show her

19

not more but less original. So I have not adopted Feminist perspective in discussing the work of these artists, while still, I hope, accurately describing the historical roles some of them played.

Given this, the question can be asked why write about *women* at all? I would give a simple answer: because it has not been done enough before, and because the times are ready for it to be done now.

In preparing these studies, which fall between and include elements of biography and autobiography, interview, profile and impression on my part, I spoke with each artist for from one to five or six hours. I asked the subjects, however short an interview we were going to have, to talk in a circular way beginning with early memories and ending in the present. In that way, the life took on an organic (esthetic?) shape in miniature, and correspondences between experience and the themes, images and even choice of mediums of the mature art emerged spontaneously. I have, in most chapters, removed myself from or simplified the give-and-take of our sessions, but it should be said that I did not present myself as an objective interviewer. My experience is not in the scientific but the esthetic field. Unlike professional psychologists who make bold to speculate about history, I am an art critic emboldened to say something about psychology. Or, I was a mutual searcher, if I may put it that way. Following that, readers will find that I have not adopted a formula for writing about the subjects. All issues are not covered in the case of each artist.

Some of the subjects talked well and openly, and I have let them speak for themselves. Others have less facility for consecutive self-analysis, or wished not to be quoted exclusively in the first person, or were otherwise better written about in essay form. Three whom I interviewed and would have included asked afterward not to be, and I respected their wishes while having by then a good understanding of what they wanted not made public. In each case, the content of the life was intimately and, in two cases, painfully revealed in the art, though, again, dramatically transformed in the process. In other words, these three cases were more rather than less in line with the thesis of this book.

I sought out women of three generations or four "waves" who work in various media. I include Mary Cassatt as an introduction and Georgia O'Keeffe as forerunner. It was my hope to get onto paper the thoughts of some of our leading elder artists as well as of some in the early phases of their careers. Inevitably, I hoped to be able to make some general statements about women's work at this time in history, and those appear in my notes on "A Century of History" and in the Afterword.

It may seem that we spent a disproportionate amount of time on childhood

20

memories. That is because, from the outset, I was interested in the roots of the impulse to become an artist and what influences reinforced the drive. Also, this material, I found at once, was fresh and in nearly every case of special, vivid interest to the speakers themselves. Information about all the turns of their professional careers is available elsewhere for the distinguished older artists, and the young may not yet be appropriate subjects for that treatment. Also, I should add that my purpose was not to arrive at critical judgments, though I have not hesitated to make some. Nor am I interested in ranking these artists as to their potential for immortality, though obviously I have opinions and am not averse to having them come through.

To begin with the matter of content and meaning, I found it fascinating across the board to learn how directly these women have worked with the content of their lives and how open they were, and knowledgeable, about the fact. I almost had the impression that some were asking for the right to have their work seen from this point of view, as if, having in most cases banished figurative subject matter from their paintings, sculpture or whatever, they wished even more to have the transformed elements of a projected self-portrait seen in the abstract forms. Not the conventional art-critical theory of an artist's relationship to subject, but one I heard distinctly. I suggest there is meaning in the formidable forms of contemporary art that might, if explored, join human beings on both sides of the object: the creator, and the audience. What the audience hungrily but mutely—because the impulse is discredited today—seeks in the visual arts, the artist, I found, is not so unwilling to provide as doctrinaire explicators would have us think. Extraordinary Fellow of Churchill College in Cambridge, George Steiner, recently wrote:

> . . . there is something to the widespread sentiment that ordinary men and women in their daily existence can no longer draw from the great springs of the imagination on the strengths, the delights, the bracing hopes they once did.
>
> Paintings are opaque scrawls; sculptures seem to be lumps of ugly matter; music banishes melody. Modern writing is often autistically demanding . . .[9]

My point is that the visual arts, at least, have assumed this appearance in part because some critics have failed to explicate them in other ways and some artists, bemused by hieroglyphic compliments, have gone on reiterating and building new self-serving theories on the opaque explanations.

By contrast, it became progressively more remarkable to me to find almost every conversation I had with these artists sooner or later bearing out Albert Camus's insight: "the work is nothing else than the long journeying through

21

the labyrinth of art to find again the two or three simple and great images upon which the heart first opened.''[10]

Since it is on perceptual stimuli that the eyes, mind and "heart" first open, it seems now unsurprising to me that these artists' imaginations are embedded in the physical world: land, light, growing things, wind, even the soil itself.[11] If male artists of another time returned obsessively to the female nude—that pleasant body there to be seen by the awakening child—as a source of renewed pleasure and so the fulfillment of the wish for permanence, these women find that paradigm in nature. I did not talk with one who claimed to have moved beyond the nature-self-art correlation to what critic Robert Pincus-Witten, for example, calls "epistemic abstraction," or purely intellectual content in art. There are artists like Dorothea Rockburne, Agnes Denes, Ruth Vollmer and others—whose work illustrates or explores series and systems of mathematics and pure logic—who might have given me other views. They might have supported the idea that there does exist an art today in no way based on remembered sensory experiences. But the subjects here each affirmed the presence of that content in their work, though of course transcending the germ of inspiration through wonderful mutations, so that however far removed in the end the work may look, it can still be more fully understood the more the observer knows about just that sensibility of the maker that some critics claim is irrelevant. In fact, in the experience of this book, the younger and more far-out the artist, the more innocent and obvious the connection, as my talks with Eleanor Antin, Connie Zehr and Patricia Johanson suggested.

But it was not merely a generalized "nature" from which these artists took off but often specific images. Memories of a first registered landscape, a first garden or sunset, memories even of such things as a story heard in childhood or a certain individual caught in a memorable moment, came back transformed by the process of art-making in the works of maturity. By noting the tagged-molecules of these images in their transformations one imagines how the imagination works on its raw material, in the Proustian sense, going forward, turning to reclaim the past, going forward again. When such memories surfaced and the connection was made with forms or other elements in the art, both the artist and I were surprised and sometimes moved.

Of course, I realize that the same artfully falsifying and fabricating process was at work backward upon the raw stuff of memory as, in the studio, acts forward upon random raw material. That is, certain memories will have been retained and emphasized because the artist had chosen, in maturity, a certain mode of work or focus. Moreover, just in recounting the trajectory of her life, the artist was, consciously or unconsciously, looking to impress form onto a past tangle of many conflicting impulses, to give her own version of the great myth by which artists and also many other human beings live: that they were, in some sense, "called" or "chosen," graced with a special mission, and then set single-mindedly upon the road to its fulfillment. As Otto Rank puts it:

. . . biography of an artist is as little an objective science as history is and would never fulfill its purpose if it were. . . . Always the starting point is the individual's ideologizing of himself to be an artist. From then on, he will live out that ideology as far as the realities of life allow him to do so. Insofar as they do not, the artist will fabricate those experiences for himself, search them out and give them form.[12]

Beyond childhood images, the raw material of the whole life invades the forms. Georgia O'Keeffe has spoken out clearly on this point. She explains she has painted particular events and also portraits that had a near-photographic verisimilitude to her eyes but which, misinterpreted, have passed into the public consciousness as abstract works.[13]

"The key is what is within the artist," Lee Krasner told me. "The artist can only paint what she or he is about." And again, "My painting is so biographical, if anyone can take the trouble to read it."[14]

"I never used to think that one's age, experience of suffering or joy got into the work. Now I'm beginning to think it does. I no longer believe that life and art are wholly separable," Frankenthaler has said.[15]

Male artists express the same thought. Arthur G. Dove: "We certainly seem to set down a self-portrait of our own inner feelings with everything we do."[16] Hans Hofmann: "You ask am I painting myself? I'd be a swindler if I were doing anything else."[17] Edward Hopper: ". . . the man is the work. Something doesn't come out of nothing."[18] Morris Graves: "One takes one's images during childhood . . ."[19]

There is nothing surprising about hearing the same from writers. Simone de Beauvoir says:

. . . nothing, I feared, would survive of [the child], not so much as a pinch of ashes. I begged her successor to recall my youthful ghost one day from the limbo to which it had been consigned. Perhaps the only reason for writing my books was to make the fulfillment of this long-standing prayer possible.[20]

And Virginia Woolf, naturally:

If life has a base that it stands upon, if it is a bowl that one fills and fills and fills—then my bowl without a doubt stands on this memory. It is of lying half-asleep, half-awake in bed in the nursery in St. Ives. It is of hearing the waves breaking, one, two, one two, and sending a splash of water over the beach; and then breaking one, two, one, two behind a yellow blind . . .[21]

23

I wonder whether it might not even be possible to generalize and say the successful artist is one who, among other things, finds by luck, labor, instinct or whatever a form and image to reflect in power (never in literal representation) the original sensory experiences that were received by the innocent mind. And by contrast, a failed or weak artist would then be one for whom, among other things, the way back is lost or confused or the reflecting image a counterfeit one or mechanically imitative.[22]

I observe, then, that to a degree at least, the creative mechanism works like this: the artist, probing into the unknown, adapts or invents novel stylistic and technical devices and modes, employing these as vehicles for material continually being probed up from memory.[23] "I had stored these fragments in my mind at one time or other, and I found them and pulled them from their clusters of memories," wrote artist June Wayne of her own working process.[24] In that way, I suggest, Mary Cassatt discovered "Impressionism" and used it as a carrier of feelings bred in childhood in Pennsylvania; O'Keeffe took "Japanism" and spoke through it of a mind tuned under the skies of Wisconsin; Nevelson used "Constructivism" to relive a personal night journey. Lee Krasner takes "Cubism" and makes of it a sending apparatus for the communication of love and rage and escapes from these, bred in Brooklyn, nursed in Manhattan and apotheosized in East Hampton, Long Island.

Just so, in her Surreal and abstract sculpture, Louise Bourgeois again traverses the dangerous night garden. Minimalist Anne Truitt stands again at the end of a lawn looking to where the violets grow. Abstract Expressionist Joan Mitchell walks again beyond "Paradise Pond," thinking, I want *more*.

Just so, I suggest, the "darkness" of Lee Bontecou's steel-and-canvas wall pieces has some connection with perilous mud flats and the fearful blackness of roots of trees torn out by a storm. The quiet space in the wood lattice of a sculpture by Jackie Winsor must have some organic link to the corner of a fisherman's "flake," where a child crouched amid drying fish on a quiet day. Patricia Johanson descends with the dancing princesses of Hans Andersen into the forests where the trees have gold, silver and crystal leaves.

The same surely holds for all artists. It enlarges my understanding of Rothko's veiled, glowing paintings to think of a fatherless child in Portland, Oregon, watching an inflamed sun disappear into westward-lying fog on its way toward the Russian homeland.[25] Just so, Robert Motherwell willingly draws the connection between the architecture and light of the South of France and his recent paintings with their empty fields of sky or sunset color, and I project backward to an innocent mind disposed to certain reactions by the sight of, again, vast, empty skies of Washington and California states. So, it expands my understanding of Don Flavin's white-light-sculptures to know that he was for a time a Dominican monk,[26] and of Carl André's identical objects scattered across the floor—rocks, stones, timbers, whatever—to know that he worked as a brakeman on railroads. I bring up these male artists' work and testimonies because some critics say it is sentimental or "womanish" to project experiential meanings into abstract art.

Also, we often forget the degree to which women artists, like men, are formed by images and sounds of literature gained in earliest childhood as well as later on: Biblical readings in church or synagogues (Lee Krasner), readings of fairy tales (Patricia Johanson), Dante (Isabel Bishop), Russian novels, Maeterlinck, Nietzsche (all Krasner, again), as well as images from the general cultural gestalt. For others, like Elaine de Kooning, Joan Mitchell, Mary Frank, etc., images and ways of handling materials were engendered by physical activities like baseball, ice skating, dance. For certain artists, like Louise Bourgeois, Helen Lundeberg, Beverly Pepper, etc., the "cool" disciplines of mathematics, science or mechanical drawing were fundamental influences on the later art.

In every case the imagery, in sum, is as much an inheritance from intimate subjective experience as, in other ages, the artist's store of Gothic, Renaissance or other "style" was. Only, instead of all artists possessing a shared style in these eclectic and fast-changing times, the content is private, hardly knowable until retrieved and explicated by the artists. How fascinating then to observe the inventions the mind works on the seeds of the art. "Art" does not suffer a diminishment in being read this way, but rather, at least to my mind, an enlargement. At the same time it is true—and I say again that I realize—that these works also can stand alone simply as formally composed objects, as a tree or a striated cliff can be seen for bark and strips of colored clay while revealing their more intricate inner machinery only to a knowledgeable observer. It seems primitive to argue an obvious point.

Beyond that, let anyone ask whether I think the last depths of these issues have been reached, and I would answer what those who know about trees or rocks would answer to final questions. The writer describes as best she or he can—and at a point description fails. My efforts to do justice to the mutating oeuvre of many artists here should make that point.[27]

To return to the place of departure, however: these women's lives also held another interest for me. For the women whose stories are told here, like others whom I regret I could not include, have been pioneers. Before them, because of a number of factors, few women artists surfaced, though many worked. And

25

in the future undoubtedly more women will achieve prominence, which means leaving historical traces in terms of followers. But the women represented here, in varying degrees depending on age and family circumstance, struggled alone to become what they did. Many others failed to keep moving toward goals to which instinct and intellect had pointed them. Some paid dearly for survival. How far did Mary Cassatt travel to find a home? How far O'Keeffe? Others live without the domestic support that males usually manage to provide for themselves in line with Flaubert's advice to would-be artists: to settle down in bourgeois style in order to be "violent and original in your work."

These pioneers, however, balanced losses and gains, changed and directed their lives—a use of personal power other women now are claiming. One critic in a moment of expansiveness has said that Helen Frankenthaler's paintings have the power to liberate mankind. It is true that a universal module, a template for future action, is embodied in these lives that have "come through," in D. H. Lawrence's words. In the narratives that follow, one finds a process of testing, renunciation, readjustment to some realities and forcing of others that men and women with different ultimate goals might be glad to imitate.

Indeed, these artists are linked by their common view of their lives as *Bildungsroman.* Nevelson has expressed the idea that it is often required to spend time in an antiworld to become conscious, free and powerful in the chosen one. It is striking how many of these women report near- or total breakdowns in their early years. The crisis, of course, is a result of unbearable conflict between the need for human contact and a recoil from the deadened life that often appears to be the price of Flaubert's recommended life style to the female in the equation. In the end, the power of that negative reaction helped drive the engine that propelled these artists out of one world into the new. My questions to these women tried to elicit memories of how "being an artist" came to be the overriding goal.

Why, however, if these few surfaced, did so many fail? In the aftermath of the epochal "Women Artists: 1550–1950" exhibition that toured the United States in 1977, that question has been often asked. One theory concerns the lack of educational facilities for creative women, particularly instruction in anatomy, during eras when the heroic nude figure was a major theme in painting and sculpture. But this issue seems to me exaggerated. Except for fig leaves, nude Greek and Roman casts were available in art schools, books of engravings were full of classic torsos, and from the late 1870s there were women's life classes in Philadelphia, New York and Paris.[28] More important, in the past most women lived close to the primal physical cycle of birth-sickness-death. The unclothed human body probably was no more a mystery to Victorian daughters than it is to city children today. And if the will had been there, women would have trained their eyes and hands in drawing naked infants, nursing mothers, ailing men and laid-out corpses.

More inhibiting seems to have been, and still is today, the taboo against women in male bonding places—bars, bistros, studios, artists' clubs, even whorehouses of the turn of the century—where night-long libated conversations take place out of which new ideas come. "I envied them, but I wasn't a part of it," says painter Isabel Bishop of that sort of social life in New York of the 1920s. "It was grim. I had no contact with artists—obviously I wasn't going to hang out at the bars," said one young sculptor recently come to New York forty years later. Louise Bourgeois spoke of the decades in between: "I had the feeling the art scene belonged to the men, and that I was in some way invading their domain. Therefore, my work was done but hidden away. I felt more comfortable hiding it. . . . Nowadays, I am making an effort to change."

Excluded from these forums, women did not become practiced in the craft of self-definition. They did not take the podium as prophets to define schools or movements. They did not know it would be helpful to put their ideas about what they were doing into packageable metaphors and slogans, partly for the media and historians to pick up and so use to identify them in the future, and partly so that by bringing their own themes into consciousness they could sharpen their sense of direction for future work. University art departments, criticized as a source of the depressing overintellectualization of art today, still serve a great need by putting pressure on women to get their minds together.

The Yale School of Art and Architecture is the leader here. Several women in this study are graduates of it. Yale educational style was set by Josef Albers, formerly of the German Bauhaus and then of Black Mountain College, who may have remembered that one third of Bauhaus teachers and participants were women. According to sculptor Barbara Chase-Riboud, the Yale experience affected her in this way: "It was *professional*. Professional implied a certain attitude toward work—no longer that of an amateur. What you do in life and with your art has to have clear and clean intellectual underpinnings. You have to be clear how and why you are working. Your technical training has to be impeccable in regard to color and design, but also in regard to your thinking. If you didn't master that, you never would do anything significant with your art, no matter how much talent you had, or how hard you worked. Maybe," she went on, "women are even more influenced by this kind of teaching than men because they are not used to the discipline."

27

Following from the matter of self-definition through rhetoric is the question of definition of one's work by a single, "trademark" image to be known by to peers, critics and marketplace. Adoption of the single image was an effective male modus operandi during the coming-to-prominence of the Abstract Expressionists. As an example, Harold Rosenberg told me that during the summer of 1946 he observed Mark Rothko working "with the most intensified fury I ever saw, turning out about a hundred paintings, every one of them different. Then when I went to his show that fall I was dumfounded to discover this tremendous variety had vanished and there was only one image left. He said that Barney [Newman] had the theory you have to have one image and stick to it and repeat it over and over. The idea came from Mondrian. It was that that bound those guys into a movement."

It is also possible that self-limitation can lead to a frightening impasse. Who was there to encourage Jackson Pollock's tentative, exploratory deviations from his trademark abstract drips, toward the end of his life? Women have often had the courage not to be pressured into molds, though theirs may be the courage born of helplessness because they were for so long without any hope of "success" in market terms. "For me," said Lee Krasner, who was married to Pollock but whose art followed a quite different course of development, "all the doors are open. One can't stand still. It takes enormous energy to keep growing and it is painful, the constant state of change. And yet I have never been able to understand the artist whose image does not change."

On the other hand, the Yale art school, especially under the direction of the painter Al Held, has pushed its students hard to this kind of self-definition. One artist told me, "A year after I graduated it was obvious I wasn't making major paintings. I was only showing I had learned my lessons well. So I began to consider other possibilities. I worked through many areas. We were voracious, tried everything. We were in the abyss out there on our own, agonizing. Then . . . I had an idea. A year and a half later, I had my show." The show "worked" to a spectacular degree and catapulted that artist to prominence, from which she can now do pretty much what she likes along other lines. Of those efficient first trademark pieces: "I destroyed them all. I didn't feel they worked."

An older (male) artist and teacher explained, "It's characteristic of the modern art scene. That young artist was ruthlessly ambitious, aggressive and determined to make it. She began to experiment wildly to find an identity, to attract attention."

Undeniably, however, the push toward this kind of professionalism has paid off.[29] Those who say the capitalist gallery system is near collapse are deceiving themselves. The art market exploits the capitalist corporate system, and vice versa. If Exxon or Ford or the United Arab Republic wants a tax-deductible work of art for its headquarters, its purchasing agents visit big galleries with rosters of stars, not small cooperative galleries. Fame is its own means to fame. And more women than ever are now being handled by the top galleries. Paula Cooper shows Bartlett, Benglis, Murray, Winsor. Cordier-Ekstrom has Grossman and Israel. André Emmerich now shows Frankenthaler, Pepper, Stone and Truitt. Max Protetch has Ferrara and Miss; John Weber has Aycock and Rockburne; and Holly Solomon shows Donna Dennis and Laurie Anderson. Schapiro is with Lerner-Heller, and even maverick Eleanor Antin has signed with the Feldman Gallery. Fifteen years ago there were not more than a few that handled women artists at all.

Part of the credit has to go to the women themselves who have won their status by tough measures. As much is due artists and researchers since the beginning of the Women's Movement in 1970. In the spring of 1972, Tamarind Lithography Workshop [30] published a 132-page booklet, *Sex Differences in Art Exhibition Reviews*. The conclusions startled even the reviewers concerned:

96.5 percent male shows reviewed in *Newsweek,* to 3.5 percent by women.
92.0 percent male shows in *Art in America,* to 8.0 percent by women.
78.6 percent male shows in *Art News* to 21.4 percent by women, and so on.

In 1976, Vandegriff Research published a pamphlet, *Funding a Future for Women in the Humanities.* Again the figures were astounding:

3.5 percent, only, of all grants in 1975 by foundations in the visual-arts, dance, theater, museum and historical fields went to women, both individuals and as project directors. This despite the fact that approximately a third of people in the professional work force in the arts are women.
24.6 percent of Rockefeller grants in the arts, in 1974, went to women.
18.4 percent of Ford grants, the same.
13.1 percent of National Endowment for the Arts grants, in 1975, went to women.

The conclusion was not only that the free-enterprise system worked against women, but that since the WPA ended in 1943 government itself had failed to divide funds equitably between male and female artists.

The WPA was, in fact, a singular success in drawing women into work projects involving organizational meetings, production programs and simple collaboration with male artists. Several subjects here worked on the Federal Arts Project: Helen Lundeberg in Los Angeles, June Wayne in Chicago, Alice Neel and Lee Krasner in New York. They all remember it as an exceptional, positive experience. "It was a great thing for artists," said Lundeberg. "And for me! I bossed a mural crew of six people, told them what to do, saw they kept at it. Most of us look back on those as the good days." Krasner told me, "I had to execute murals for people who left. What that experience did for me: it introduced me to scale, and none of this nonsense they call scale today." Krasner—like Alice Neel and June Wayne—was also involved with the Artists' Union during the disputatious late days of the project, and she sat on its executive committee from 1939. Wayne lobbied in Washington, D.C. These activities brought them into useful contact with male artists and future art critics, and taught them some facts of life about politics, the law and concrete possibilities of action.

There are other causes of women's failure to surface as artists for which it is hard to imagine a quick solution. If the quality of an imagination is inherited through the genes, then women will have to struggle to find their own frontiers of expression different from men's. That in some way genetics is a factor is unquestionable. There has to be some condition of hand-eye-nerve-muscle sensitivity that impels some individuals into work involving those parts of the body. Many women I talked with remember doing compulsive hand-eye play as children, repetitiously tearing paper, aligning scraps of colored cloth, making rows on rows of mud pies, dressing and undressing paper dolls. Too, nearly every woman artist included here had a mother or grandmother who sewed, and not just seams and buttons but obsessively, creatively, designing and making hats, coats, suits, dresses, embroidery, smocking and so on. At least two of these artists—Louise Nevelson and Barbara Chase-Riboud—even considered it a burden to have so many clothes made by these needle-happy relatives. If, over many centuries, the manual virtuosity of women was channeled into this time-absorbing work that was not frustrating and was, as a matter of fact, the source of competition and praise among peers, then it is no wonder few felt motivated to become "fine artists," given other social limitations.

The puzzle remains why many women make forays out of obscurity and sink back as if the machinery had stopped after a single turn.[31] Who today knows who was Virginia Diaz, who, it was said, "walked off" with one of the most important shows of her time in 1942, in which Jackson Pollock and Lee Krasner also exhibited alongside Picasso, Braque and de Kooning? And how long indeed did it take Krasner to get herself into a consistently productive condition? And who was Janet Sobel, whose drawings, shown at the Art of This

Century Gallery in 1944, caught Pollock's eye and may have struck the mark that led to the art that, as de Kooning has said, "broke the ice for us all"? She was, and apparently never became more than, "a 'primitive' painter (who was and still is a housewife living in Brooklyn)" when critic Clement Greenberg wrote that tantalizing line eleven years after the fact.[32] Many other women artists come to feel that the professional game is unrewarding, and go into periods of seclusion or work in other directions. Lee Bontecou, the strongest younger American sculptor of the '60s, has vanished from the scene. She explains why here. And after searching I found in California the sculptor Ruth Asawa, whose delicate hanging wire sculptures were praised in the late '50s. She is teaching in the public-school system. "What I do myself is relatively unimportant," she said. "I'm more interested in what we can pass on." Still, she is beginning to work with cast metal and "hoping to go back" to her art.

I propose that one reason for the often mentioned unsteadiness of women's commitment to their work is a lack of models for creative women that involve struggle and endurance: lives—to put it in mythic terms—that survive more than one death and rebirth. The pioneer woman earned such a reputation. The very words "pioneer woman" cause modern women to search their lives for deeds that measure up. But "woman artist" does not carry any such charge. Isabel Bishop has written:

In America art is an underground movement. . . . this explains the potency of the symbol those few artists and teachers become, whose almost saintlike unselfinterestedness and singleness of purpose give them the position of Chiefs of the Underground.[33]

But none of those Chiefs have been women, while myth-making on behalf of male artists is a lively industry. Here, for example, is an obituary of Barnett Newman, who died in 1970, written by Thomas Hess:

. . . Newman was a conscience to the art world, a powerful moral example. . . . First, foremost and always, he was an artist—the unique, individual creator. He felt that his was the highest calling. . . . Because be was dedicated to one universal principle, the triumphant creative force in man (*vir heroicus sublimis*), he was free to move across the whole spectrum of social and intellectual endeavor. . . . Many will not have the inclination or the strength to follow his sternly solitary example. . . .[34]

The passage was written by this sensitive critic who was also quick to praise women, but what is striking here is the exaggeration (the "zip"?) that runs through the passage, rendering the artist sublime, heroic, free. Also stern, and solitary.

To take, in fact, a span of time between Goethe and Jackson Pollock,

31

when the artist-hero has been a figure of consciousness, creative males have been described as complex, suffering, long-striving human beings who survive many defeats, renunciations and also sins. Tales of Van Gogh, Gauguin, Pollock, Rothko and many others comprise a mythos that turns on well-known passages: birth with special favors, wandering and waiting in a land of strangers, hearing the call and restructuring the life. There are other literary forms lying around [35] like empty shells on a beach: the daemonic genius, [36] the Dionysiac prophet, the reclusive sage, the depraved idealist, the criminal poet and the Don Juan. Alternatively, there is the Renaissance man, or the rustic who touches universal themes. There are also categories of myth that stem from fact but shed back on the heroes a glamorous aura: Impressionists tragically losing their vision; Post-Impressionists spaced out on absinthe; doom-haunted Abstract Expressionists. These men then become the sacrificial lambs of our industrial society, scapegoat seers, or see-ers.

Not only is fascination on the part of the art-buying public kept alive by these old tales coming back to life, but the artists themselves are given a range of options of styles of life as well as work. But women have no such latitude. There are only one or two templates for the female artist, and they shallowly have to do with social behavior and not with attitude toward work; the haughty princess, the awkward drunk, the asexual recluse or the "wife who also paints" [37] are a few. A sign of the need for more elevated and also deeper myths for their gender is the present idealizing of Georgia O'Keeffe and the posthumous devotion paid by women to poet Sylvia Plath and sculptor Eva Hesse (by contrast, a characteristically mythologizing male writer recently called Plath a "bitch-goddess" [38]). This, then, is an end to which I would be glad to contribute: to the substitution—for the future—of the myth of the female artist as *survivor,* instead of the past one, only too valid, of her as *victim* except in the role of Muse. It might be more efficient to create such a heroine in fiction, but most people today are fascinated by real lives—evidenced by rafts of books on women, professionals, executives, lovers and other categories of ourselves. So the real life, of the real artist, to return to my beginning, is of importance today.

It could be related, for instance, that women, like men, can experience the "call" I spoke of earlier, that afterward turns them into unliberated slaves to their chosen end. The psychology of the call is the same for males and females and as suprarational for both. One theory is that, faced with "existential despair" at some time, often in childhood (death of a parent, breakup of family, guilt about failure or error), some people reassemble their minds in a sudden electrifying flash. The result can be an intense feeling of reintegration and self-forgiveness. Becoming an Artist in this way (or a doctor, an astronomer, a rock star or a Born Again Christian), one might gain the feeling of being graced and also achieving a kind of outside-the-body immortality. In the religious revivals of the Great Awakening, thousands, women as well as men, saw the light. To achieve a "mode of transcendence" [39] is the Existential version of what is probably a universal longing. Therefore it cannot be enough just to feel called. The heroine must be seen to persist, suffer, grow through the work. In my childhood the only women I ever read or heard about who lived that way were Florence Nightingale and Helen Keller.

Stern? Solitary? Powerful moral example? The very words run counter to the view of women as flexible, social, forgiving.

But the women I spoke with in preparing this book often worked in painful solitude imposed by a critical outside world. To achieve their ends, they scorned the "powerful moral example" held up by males and followed their own compassless way. Portraits of women artists, then, should bring out the tenacious and willful features, though not with the bombast attending messianic self-presentations by male artists from Nietzsche to certain figures today. At the same time, the creative woman should be written about in a way that exposes her humanity, her obsessiveness, her bitterness, her guilt and her resilience. Her sullenness is her strength, her contempt for those who fail to meet her standards. Her refusal to be ingratiating. She has not necessarily (though sometimes she does have) the archetypal grace of her sister the dancer or actress, Calliope or Terpsichore, Isadora or the Duse. She hauls rocks, mixes oil and turp, wipes her hands with filthy rags. She blows on the coals and fires her kiln. Pygmalion, she calls to the mud to speak. Her hand shakes the dust— the great God's own prerogative. It was, in fact, particularly for the older women here, the coming to grips with their own outlandish proclivities that was hard at the beginning.[40] To come to the recognition that one is a "different" creature, maverick as that bearded fellow down the block.

"I was a creative freak, you might say," one of these artists told me. One defense is in obsessive secrecy about their background, loves, economic circumstances. I am grateful to these women who spoke to me about such things. Males do not usually have a fear of revealing their need for practical security and the measures by which they provide for it. But the gifted girl child was often the saboteur of a secure regime she abhorred,[41] and she plotted in private to escape it. She prayed in secret, acted out fantasy roles, doggedly went about her hand and eye training. She schemed, had tantrums, migraines, fainting spells, or evaporated into fogs. She was accused of being uncooperative, complaining, selfish. Her sister the poet could write at a desk in the corner, but this one pined for the mess, the turmoil, the suspicious profligacy and eventually the liberating fellowship of the studio.

Lifelong, these women testify, the creative will exerts its pressure. Nothing

33

human stops it, not deaths, losses, pain.[42] But *something* can send it under-ground, and when that happens the sense of frustration is unremitting until, by just as mysterious a mental reversal or a turn of events, the will is set free again. Many of these women, not having language to describe what may be basically as concrete a phenomenon as chemical action in the brain, talk about their "gift" as an independent agent creative *within* them. Sometimes, as Helen Frankenthaler says, "there will come this great sense of alarm. As if you have shocked yourself. . . . The gift had taken over." [43] Great athletes, scientific ge-niuses, psychotics and religious ecstatics talk the same way, which is to lend the feeling validity, not to denigrate it.

Eventually and just practically, the process of self-acceptance was made easier by the fact that all these women, including four who are black, came from educated middle-class or immigrant families with appreciation for the arts. That says something about our civilization but nothing we are not aware of. On the other hand, there were generational differences. The older women endured more suffering in the break with tradition than the younger ones. Women now in their early thirties have mothers young enough to have been affected by the Movement that might be said to have begun with the publica-tion of Simone de Beauvoir's *The Second Sex* in English translation in 1953. One group of these women comes from a surprisingly uniform background. Their fathers are men of a new professional class who have something to do with the land: rangers, trackers, artillery installers, rocket launchers, engineers. The daughters work a vein between architecture, engineering and exploration. Their fathers, in nearly every case, take a manful pride in their daughters' work.

Though there are a few generously gifted artists today who are daughters of artists, that pattern is not so exclusive as it was in history when, as Nochlin reports, nearly all were.[44] Prominent among them are the daughter and grand-daughters of Henry Varnum Poor—Anne, a landscape painter, and Anna and Candida, sculptors; Temma Bell, daughter of Louisa Matthiasdottir and Leland Bell; March Avery, daughter of Milton; Judith Shahn, daughter of Ben; and Emily Mason, daughter of Alice Trumbull Mason: all painters. In this book, I include a passage about the mother of sculptor Mary Frank—the painter Elea-nore Lockspeiser—and suggest that there may be a quality of eye and hand passed down by genes or example. But the subject is one to study at greater length.

Of whatever age and circumstance, however, there were two steps the future artist took to shape her life. One was a coming to grips, the other a breaking out. The first took place early, either a call or an easy natural move toward a way of life involving art instead of something else. The girl would go to art school instead of college, or make a trip to Mexico, or get a studio in Greenwich Village. She was on her way to becoming an artist, but not yet an "original."

The critical turn from which new conceptual attitudes spontaneously flowed, involved technique. By then the artist had chosen her medium and been trained. Then there came a specific problem to be solved. No known solution worked. She worried the problem again and again. Time went by. And then like that flash of light or bolt from the blue, or an unstoppable feeling of momentum and "rightness," the solution presented itself.[45] "From then on, I was home free," said Truitt. "And then it just hit me, like one of those light bulbs, and that was it," said Chase-Riboud. She was working at the time in solitude and freedom, probing the limits of her "unknown," confesses Georgia O'Keeffe.[46] "I began to live," said Mary Cassatt.[47]

What had been broken beyond were conventional solutions. What lay beyond was the possibility of working from oneself. I found fascinating the quiet, even secret diligence of the artists as they approached that turning point. There were, in those stages of trial, failure and error, no high-flown ambitions voiced, no rhetoric about theory, only a burrowing, nudging at the door, and waiting.

None of these possibilities would have been realized if it had not been for vigor and will to survive. Is it health, muscle, will, luck? "Many artists," said Helen Frankenthaler, "ironically since they are dealing with production and creativity—with life—have a special relationship to death. Some profound fear of dying. The positive side of this, for an artist, is here: that artists who survive often have an appealing magical energy. That's the dividend: that magic energy."

One way that will to survive expresses itself is in making use of opportunities. Nearly every woman I talked with had a relationship with a powerful male at some time early in her career or as an enduring marriage. Why not? These are charismatic women with a yen for experience and a deep capacity for love. However, where other women might suffer in such relationships, these profited by going their own way in the guise of following, or by sealing off areas of their lives or, eventually and in due time, taking the initiative in breaking off. There is a reverse Flaubertism at work here. The woman of potential knows where she wants to go and does not say No to help from wherever it comes, though one can expect that self-reliant women in the future may not gravitate to such external sources of energy and power.[48]

That life force that drives on in as blind a way as sociobiologists say the gene plasm does can create problems. A number of women artists told me of

35

having had multiple abortions, seven in one case, three or four in many others. The young on the Pill are far from invulnerable. Pregnancies occur in times of stress, loneliness or unhappiness. Between the gene and the creative imagination, there is not always agreement on how to reach what may well be existentially the same goal. There are also some lucky ones for whom both instincts come together. Patricia Johanson, awaiting the birth of her second son, wrote me, "Pregnancy is a magical time for me, during which I work hardest, am happiest and seem to get the most done." [49]

The issue of biology leads to that of female imagery in art by women ("vaginal iconography"), a topic of argument among artists, critics and Feminists.[50] That some artists paint genitalia for political reasons is a fact, though that choice of subject is no more indicative of esthetic value than any other literary message. It was during the 1970s, in the aftermath of Feminist turmoil in the art world, that a number of women began to employ imagery based on the nude body. As if in celebration of the unveiling of their own hopes to be artists and so to see the world through their own eyes, they focused with technical meticulousness on genitalia both female and male. Some of them claimed that the approach was a deliberate rejection of nonfigurative Conceptual Art, seemingly a more "male" esthetic. The idiom especially influenced Performance Art. Yvonne Rainer and Carolee Schneeman were the most daring of this group of artists who merged dance, theater, sculpture, costume, collage in expressionistic performance events that featured the nude body.[51] These theater pieces were only a more vivid example of a point of view that also affected more traditional painters from Alice Neel to Joan Semmel. Clearly, the works were considered political statements. They "reflected a development of consciousness. One looked to oneself—to one's own body—and heroicized it because it had been so defiled by others. Vaginal iconography was a true developmental stage" (Miriam Schapiro).

On the other hand, some critics and artists make more sweeping judgments. They hold that all women if left on their own will inevitably produce ovoid, centralized, "female" images. This view seems to me untenable. Anyone with knowledge of anthropology or psychology is aware of male and female sexual symbols in the arts. Tribal arts are full of them. It is also known that naïve artists, or the sophisticated when they doodle, often employ such motifs. Jurors for shows agree that many works by nonoriginal women show ovoid, centered compositions. On these perhaps genetically, perhaps socially conditioned tastes the entire "art" of advertising rests. Cigarette manufacturers, perfume sellers, purveyors of everything from Coke to motorboats know how to play interlocked and thrusting forms in illustrations to get the most out of audiences preselected by sex. Also, artists of consummate fastidiousness have used "female" and "male" compositional devices: the della Robbias and Raphael used the tondo form to suggest the embracing qualities of the Virgin, while artists from Uccello to David Smith picked vertical forms to express the spirit of male combat. But the idea that the developed artists in our eclectic society are deterministically bound into gender-derived imagery has to be rejected. Even artist Schapiro, one of the first to make policy of the idea, says today, " 'Vaginal iconography' was a way station for me. I don't use the term anymore. I wanted to move ahead. For me it was only a phase of my esthetics. For Judy Chicago, it held meaning for a longer time." We accept that a radical move forward is always accompanied by rhetoric and trumpet blasts. Abstract Expressionist language now sounds bombastic to our ears, while the Humboldtean ruminations of many young Earth Artists today has its own sound of innocence.

I have come to think, all the same, that there is something to be said about a "woman's art" at this point in time. The subject, however, has to be approached through history, not iconography.

A Century
of History
and the
New Woman
Artist

The artists here, distributed chronologically or else by point of entry into the art scene, span a century. Through them we witness the swings and transformations of American cultural life. Mary Cassatt's stable Protestantism uneasily merged with Parisian estheticism was the base. O'Keeffe signals the coming of internationalist Modernism to this country and at the same time, in her life and later work, prefigures a future mode of art and thought. In the First Wave of artists beginning with those "old as the century," as Alice Neel says, and including Realists, Surrealists and abstractionists, are several offspring of the massive immigrations, overwhelmingly Russian-Jewish, that in their way produced the American art of the '40s and the '50s. Others of that period were born in genteel suburban towns with a turn-of-the-century rusticity. In the great public schools of the time—Erasmus Hall in Brooklyn, George Washington and Washington Irving High Schools in Manhattan, the Armstrong Training School in Washington, D.C.—they gained a secret sense of gifts that set them apart from their people. Two World Wars and the Depression deeply changed their lives. In the decade of the Lost Generation they were not sophisticated enough to be lost; their struggles to survive, on the contrary, were painful. Only one of those here, Isabel Bishop, found a place in the pre–World War II art Establishment,[1] and she would undergo passing eclipse in the '50s. Louise Nevelson sold only rarely save to artists until she was nearly sixty. So for Neel and Lee Krasner. By then, deep and self-destructive angers had driven some far from their origins, but, tearing as these were, the break was not total. In their advanced age they talked about remembered things seen in childhood that seem somehow to have invaded their work. Late, they came into prominence in a men's world, ironic women with pride in what others may consider their

38

eccentricity, and a pithy sense of realism about the instability of fame.

Women of the Second Wave, schooled in the '30s of progressive education, political activism and cultural optimism, were raised to be winners. Early on, their gifts were praised by their parents. Tomboys, many were treated by their fathers as favorite sons. Their mothers were supportive but busy, writing, painting, running big homes, only a few of them still immigrant. The girls went to special schools, top art schools, colleges. Though many were sheltered from the Depression, World War II had a slowly darkening effect. Some traveled on fellowships to Europe afterward, encountered refugees, poverty, the heavy gloom of Existentialism. Gradually they woke up, lost a few illusions their optimistic parents had fed them. "I thought I would be married forever. I thought I would have babies. I thought my parents would always be alive." Or, to put it more down-to-earthly, "You got shows in those days through men. It was cutthroat between the women." In fact it was their sense of insult and peril when the reactionary '50s failed to see them for who they were that impelled them to roles they are identified by today. Some became swashbucklers, some solitaries, some—to put it one way—worldly. A handful made it as mavericks into a rare and liberated avant-garde of poets, theater people, musicians and critics, a true revival of the camaraderie of pre–World War I Paris. But as the leaders of the movement by then called Abstract Expressionist fell victim to car accidents, alcohol, premature heart attacks, the women of the "Second Generation" insulated themselves, fled the scene or bided their time. When the art-bedazzled late '60s to '70s would come, they would be there, survivors in their handsome middle age, ready to claim the top.

A Third Wave, of various ages and backgrounds, came into their own in the radicalism and free experimentation of the 1960s. In the crossroads of that decade, everything orthodox went out—easel painting, conventional sculpture, "crafts"—and everything unorthodox came in: plastics, latex, rope, rocks, objects that hung, swung, lay and crept. Women in the arts, lagging behind a Movement on the rails since the publication of Betty Friedan's *The Feminine Mystique* (1963), slowly took what they needed to begin their own move. Back behind, in the conservative '50s, a Fourth Wave had been born that came forward in the decade at hand. But since both of these groups rode the Women's Movement, I will say more about them later.

Of whatever age, however, these artists' dates of origin tell only part of the story, for all have worked without major interruption and changed with the times.

One of the deep themes of the century that lies behind us all has been the erosion of the comforting "sweet faith" of Christianity or the more somber one of Judaism and the various now hopeful, now hopeless ways men (I say "men" advisedly) have faced what might have seemed an existential break between themselves and the world. There were for a while two ways of reassembling a faith: the mystical or transcendental and the naturalistic. Visionaries, scientists and artists took one route or the other, inventing new imaginative structures— combines of data and intuition — in which they could have "faith." In that way, religious certainty gave way to Darwinian evolutionism and then, gradually in this century, to a phase of socioesthetics called Modernism which was simply one more way of expressing the same belief: that there is coherence and meaning within phenomena, that in the relationships between the forms of life, inanimate matter and, in this case, art, general laws about the nature of reality are embedded. The principle inevitably has to be seen and applied universally. Indeed, "Universalism" was the way "liberal" religious thinkers of the nineteenth century defined their position. And One World continued to be the dominant image for all three belief systems: the religious, the scientific and the esthetic. But we are now in a position to see how the global wars and traumas of the mid–twentieth century destroyed confidence in the immanent rational bond, and how social and ecological decay so obvious in the '60s and this decade have widened the break. Then there came to be, among other symptoms of anomie, a popular satiric stance on the part of some American pundits in the art world which was to say that the issue itself had no meaning. "Perhaps after all there is no message. In that case, one is saved the trouble of having to reply."[2]

Apropos of women, however, it seems to me that, for many reasons but above all their immersion in the life process of birth and their exemption from the killing process of war, they have continued to take the existence and continuation of that continuity between themselves and nature for granted, not as an exercise of intellectual theory but in mute confidence. The natural world *is* the ground of being, and all human life, as their own individual lives as artists and so their art itself, takes place within that natural order.

That condition is usually accompanied by a cultural conservatism.[3] It seems that traditionally women in the visual arts have stayed back with their sense of location and roots and worked along in existing movements. They have not looked to their art to take them to new metaphysical frontiers, or, being transported toward them willy-nilly, they have left it to the men to formulate new doctrines. As a sign of this fact, they have not been inventors of radical stylistic modes, new metaphysical statements in effect, as have their writing sisters like Gertrude Stein and Virginia Woolf.

Literal life-work patterns reflect this fact. The art world has not seen suicides of desperation among its female population (though many attest to periods of bitterness) like Plath and Sexton among writers, or Arshile Gorky, Rothko and Pollock, to name only three males. Nor do we see among female visual artists the kind of Divine Madness (though many use the term "ecstasy"—Simone de Beauvoir's "carnival elation"—to describe experiences basic to their becoming artists) that struck, to mention only three writers of a generation, Adrienne Rich, Francine du Plessix Gray and Gloria Emerson. I mean cases where the writer was so extra-blazoned by the fire of her life experience that her writing took off for outer moral spaces. Except for a couple of magnificently Quixotic examples, like Miriam Schapiro (viz.: her painting *OX,* '67, page 273) or Nancy Graves (viz.: *Camels,* '68, page 55), when the fire has lit on female artists it appears to have elected individuals of relatively coarse vision (viz.: Judy Chicago with her porcelain-and-needlework Feminist "Last Supper," or *Dinnerparty*⁴). One concludes that the materials-involved plastic arts have not attracted women of tenacious intellectual radicalism. On the other hand and more important, these artists are not nihilists. They lack the sense of detachment, the disdain for answers that mark a Marcel Duchamp in his public role, or a Cage or a Rauschenberg, and have conditioned much of the male art of the American 1960s and '70s. Not one woman I spoke with informed me that life is absurd—though many had much to say about absurd behavior by human beings. Women were uninterested in the Pop Art movement, for instance. "They didn't take it seriously," the dealer Betty Parsons said to me. Lee Krasner, Joan Mitchell and others confirmed their disdain for its tenets. By contrast, many important women artists were and still are interested in Dada, which in its absurdity embodied a quite rational attack on bourgeois hypocrisy. (Some exceptions might be noted: Rosalyn Drexler, Suzi Gablik, Yoko Ono, Marjorie Strider and, most famously, the sculptor Marisol. Her wood figures are superficially Pop, not at all Dada. But in some of her aspects, as her use of self-portraiture, she foreshadowed ideas that have become central to much art of the 1970s.

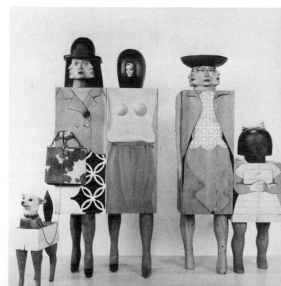

Marisol. Women [*self-portraits*] and Dog, 1964. *Fur, leather, plaster, synthetic polymer, wood. 72" by 82". Whitney Museum of American Art, New York.*

My point is that here may be the source of special promise for future work now that women have begun to seek original forms of expression for their own views. By their insulation from some of the psychically devastating circumstances of the past some creative women artists may have survived with their psyches intact to make a contribution now. And to repeat, a reason may be that women have been unescapably engaged in the cycle of cause and effect (love leads to birth leads to the need to nurture; birth leads, in the end, to death) and are therefore prevented (or saved) from seeing the life process as meaningless.

To return to the past: the medieval Catholic image of One World, expressed in paintings of circling orbs of many colors or in the sweeping metaphors of Dante, extended a unifying embrace to all living and also inanimate things. Protestant Christianity inherited the image and taught that within this embrace stood, specifically, the pious family (father, mother and obedient children, expanding in time through genetically pure offspring), and the Christian nation (law, church and shared values, expanding in space through ideologically pure colonies). Attacks had been made on the faith by rationalists and skeptics of various European schools, and the last blow was given by science in the mid–nineteenth century. Mary Cassatt lived through these years of change, and her art looks both backward and forward.

In the West and the Westernized East, science replaced mystic religious dogma as a form of faith and a source of the feeling of connectedness. In Cassatt's day, science-enlightened ex-evangelicals "believed" in science as their fathers had in heaven, and, as they contemplated its wonders, there even stirred in them from time to time and in spite of themselves that abandoned sense of the presence of a mystery—they called it natural law. All these discoveries—the beautiful theories of ontogeny-recapitulating-phylogeny, of stratification of rocks and organization of plants and animals, and finally evolution as the capstone—combined into a vast system again embracing all creation. At once, the system was seen also to extend to the creations of mankind. In the massive writings of Herbert Spencer that began to issue two years before Darwin's *Origin of Species,* evolution was projected into the forms of society and all mankind's arts. So the One World image was intact, only the focus had changed. What the church had been to Christianity, so now the institutions of a liberal society, its schools, colleges, its art museums and natural-history museums, were to the evolutionist: a place of illustration, celebration and study of the great laws of cause and effect, relatedness and correspondence, and progress through time.

The next transformation in the chain would be the emergence of Modernist esthetics as the vehicle of faith. That sense of a living bond between humankind and the natural world, and the power of art to reveal it, had been argued in different ways by the Transcendentalists and others whose ideas would be returned to by later artists and theoreticians, especially for our purposes, by members of the Stieglitz group in New York before and after a young Georgia O'Keeffe joined it. In much the same spirit, according to interpretations made today, some American landscape painters of the nineteenth century assuaged their longing for a deity they no longer contacted in church by seeing in the small leaf as well as the mighty waterfall a plasmic Spirit—rendered by these artists as golden sourceless light, sign of the presence of divinity since the Middle Ages. Apart from that loving rendering of nature in their paintings, however, nineteenth-century artists had not yet digested the new science—and soon there were the more disequilibriating discoveries of unseen rays, waves and particles to assimilate. Realistic art could *imitate* by illustrating it the nature that science was investigating, but not yet *investigate* that nature on its own. Only with time would the artist come to take his place beside the scientist in that place where the priest had once stood: in an intuitive relationship to Truth.

However, the idea that the arts could go farther than imitation and provide clues, even access to underlying strata of meaning had already been intimated by, among others, that same scientist-philosopher Herbert Spencer. In an essay "The Origin and Function of Music," he argued that song was the Ur-art and had begun as no more than a physiological reflex by which early people gave voice to feelings too impulsive for language. He described some Hungarian folk songs in precisely the terms some American explorers and landscape painters used to describe the effect on their sensibilities of geological wonders like Niagara Falls. Nature and art: both had the power to pierce the veil and release wellsprings of feeling. "The strange capacity," wrote Spencer in 1857, "which we have for being affected by melody and harmony may be taken to imply . . . that it is within the possibilities of our nature to realize those intenser delights they dimly suggest."[5]

In sum, there came into being this intent, that ran the course of the century and part of the next—reinforced by ideas from disintegrating American Protestantism and European Catholicism, from German Idealism and Asian mysticism—to pursue by science, logic or, gradually, art the laws and "intenser delights" concealed within random phenomena. It was in reaction against the failure of academic imitative art to play that new, heavy role that Modernism came into being. The conventional plastic arts of the late nineteenth century with their fainting maidens, pompous heroes and stiff set pieces appear false and shallow not because the technique is poor but because artists had lost belief in their goals. Their works appeal to sentimental memory of how once upon a time ancestors had responded with fresh interest to such images. A nostalgia, real to a viewer today as then, invests the works. They were already in their time backward looking, grounded in certainties vanishing behind the horizon in that golden Luminist glow. The Modernist perspective, only secondarily expressed in forms with a new "look," involved, firstly, a new content. Now the artist, like the scientist and the priest behind him, assumed the burden of asking essential and final questions about the structure of the world. Significantly, the new art began in several places at once—around the year 1911— in Russia, in Germany and in Paris, where one or two Americans caught the same wave. It was now to be Art, abstract art, that held the secret or, to put it better, *was* the secret: meaning incarnate in form.

Beginning with the Post-Impressionists, all advanced artists would work this vein, which would yield up Expressionism, many forms of abstraction, Surrealism and finally Abstract Expressionism. As the German Blue Rider Franz Marc would write: "I try to heighten my feeling for the organic rhythm of all things, to try to feel myself pantheistically into the trembling and flow of the blood of nature . . ."[6] And as the Russian Wassily Kandinsky would write: "Color embodies an enormous though unexplored power which can affect the entire human body as a physical organism. . . . color harmony can rest only on the principle of the corresponding vibration of the human soul."[7] And as the American Barnett Newman would write: ". . . the struggle is to bring out from the non-real, from the chaos of ecstasy, something that evokes a memory of the emotion of an experienced moment of total reality."[8]

There is a rhetoric still at work today that indicates the mystique that linked religion, science and art at that turning point. The term "light,"[9] used by Arthur G. Dove in the 1920s as by Helen Frankenthaler, Joan Mitchell, Robert Motherwell and others today, refers to some element inhabiting the colors and forms of the work that renders it, in Frankenthaler's term, quite unequal to the power of the work itself, "magical." And Modernist art, like those earlier categories of thought, was characterized by renewed seriousness about its subject matter and its goals. The first teacher a young Georgia O'Keeffe met who gave her the feeling there might be something beyond the defunct art of the Academy was one who told her art must be *interesting*.[10] An odd word but a clue, and it struck O'Keeffe deep. It is one of her key words today. Happiness goes like the wind, she has said, but what is *interesting* stays. And that teacher was not even from the formalist point of view very forward-looking. Nor does seriousness imply pompous solemnity, a frequent masculine art-world pose today. As Gertrude Stein keeps reminding us, the artists of her time were "gay." But they were absorbed by the universal significance of what they were doing. The solutions modern art was proposing were not local or parochial. Robert Motherwell stated the issue exactly when he said to me about the pioneers of his own generation, "We were like scientists trying so seriously to figure out which way to go."

There were only a few beachheads of Modernism in this country in the years before the First World War. One relevant to this book was Alfred Stieglitz' gallery at 291 Fifth Avenue in New York. When, around and after 1910, some American painters began coming home from Paris with news of new developments there, Stieglitz set out to exhibit the work of Matisse and Picasso, Fauvism and Cubism and exotic arts like African sculpture that provided new ways of seeing. The rhetoric of the Stieglitz circle was eclectic and most of all investigatory. All the currents were hashed over. Talk was of Bergson, Nietzsche, Whitman, about Japanese art and music and about the American machine age. Another beachhead was at Columbia University's Teachers' College, where, from 1904, the art educator Arthur W. Dow was head of the Department of Fine Arts. He had been influenced as a student in Brittany by the Post-Impressionist esthetic; back home, he worked in Boston in the years when Ernest Fenellosa was putting together the Japanese collections at the Boston Museum. Ardent Buddhist, Emersonian Transcendentalist, Spencerean evolutionist and also a foreshadower of the educational theories of John Dewey, Fenellosa would, through young Dow, transmit all these currents of influence to a young Georgia O'Keeffe as she moved into the stream of Modernism. The principle was that Japanese pattern art, reiterated leaf, petal, cloud and river patterns with contrasts of light and shadow, languid and rigid lines, colors and textures, has the power to tranquilize the mind, to elevate the appreciative viewer or doer to rare heights. And the Armory Show in New York in 1913, that epochal display of some sixteen hundred works of European and American Modernism, gave America its first look at the new esthetic. The major revelation of the Armory Show was Cubism as a new instrument for examining the world, and the single most anxiety-producing work, Marcel Duchamp's quasi-Cubist *Nude Descending a Staircase*. There would not be an American artist of serious intent until the late 1940s who would not have to tackle the issue of Cubism and how to move on beyond it. In 1916 Stieglitz put on a show of American artists, trying to refocus attention on the "excellent work" being done in this country, but the fact was that the progressive art movement here was rooted in international Modernism, as all the isms of our art since then until the 1960s were. Modernism was, in fact, a banner of *non-provincialism, non-nationalism*, in America of the 1920s and '30s. It was a manifesto of confidence by progressive American artists, critics and educators in an international cultural world of the future—that old Christian-Darwinian One World idea again, now in its third appearance—to be brought into exis-

45

tence through the new nonlocal art styles, through liberating art education that paralleled new social and political forms. It was an expression of trust in the future evolution of society toward what Spencer had foreseen as a richer variety in the works of man.

Modernism was, then, more than a style or a formal invention.[11] It was an ethic, a social philosophy, a science and a faith. Everything that had to do with mankind was grist to the Modernist mill: primitive arts, Japanese, Chinese and Indonesian arts; literature, tapestry, dance, industrial design and architecture. And it should be said that in Modernist criticism, formal analysis was only one of many ways of studying the arts, though since it dealt with the tangible and observable it was usually the starting point.

One more aspect of pre–World War II Modernism: there was not so much conflict between male and female practitioners of the arts as myth has it and as did exist in later years. Isabel Bishop says as much here. The social and sexual liberation of the 1920s with romantic looking to Whitman and Havelock Ellis gave many males a comradely view of women bold and gifted enough to break with conventionalism and become artists. Some of the singular figures of the European Modernist movements, especially around the Bauhaus, were women, and more American women were professional artists than one remembers today (though a close study of their lives would show they hardly enjoyed parity with their male colleagues). _____

The sense of optimism and belief in progress affected many who, during these decades, moved out through the United States to museums and university posts in the Middle West and the Far West, and so sowed seeds for the tremendous postwar expansion of the arts. Nearly all the women in this study were first awakened to the arts at Saturday classes for gifted children at local museums, a project set in motion by Modernist art educators of this period. That hope in progress through the arts even insulated liberal Modernists from the economic and political glooms of the 1930s and gave them confidence (though not necessarily joy) in American Realist and Regional art—Grant Wood, Thomas Curry, Thomas Benton and so on—that more advanced approaches would develop in time as the continents drew culturally closer. The two great European art movements of the time were Constructivism, which began in Russia in 1920 and then spread through all of Europe and America (where it would take the form of Precisionism) via the Bauhaus; and Surrealism, spawned in Paris in 1926 by artists and poets drawn to the world of dream and fascinated by the power of certain art activities, or "gestures," to release feelings. Fundamentally again, both movements implied a Rousseauesque hope— that humankind, if nurtured and channeled along the new paths, would still restore grace to a world that, year by year, was shaken by violence and the oncoming war. As the Bauhaus would end with the German upheaval of 1933, so the Surrealist movement was truncated in Europe by war in 1939; leaders of both movements found their way to America of the 1940s and helped stir into being art styles by virtue of which America would praise itself—in its postwar jingoism—for having "taken the lead" from Europe.

Meanwhile, even in an economically depressed United States of the 1930s, the WPA gave artists survival, encouragement and years of working experience. Later, after the war again, there would be hindsight mythologizing about the bitterness of those days, which were in reality not so bitter for some as some years to come. For one can go so far as to say that some Americans were so insulated from the political and social troubles of the 1930s by their faith in Progress through Art that when they confronted the traumas of the '50s and '60s their sense of disillusion would be crushing.

In the war years, America became the refuge of international Modernism. But there was little in fact that was "American" about an art scene in which charismatic figures were the Armenian peasant-poet Arshile Gorky with his fund of remembered peasant songs;[12] the German painter-teacher Hans Hofmann, here since 1932; the Dutch Piet Mondrian with his circle of American Neo-Plastic abstractionists; the Russian Kandinsky, represented with nearly his own entire museum—Hilla Rebay's Museum of Non Objective Art; and the French Surrealists with their literary brilliance and also their apparatus of publicity and social climbing. During the war years and after, the art called "new" and also "American" would begin to be formulated around those spots where the artists and talkers (male) gathered: the bars of Greenwich Village and The Club.[13] There old friends from the WPA and the Artists' Union, including the Russian-born Rothko and the Greek-born Baziotes, bonded in conversation with their European brothers including the Dutch de Kooning. The new art coming into being was, like other forms of Modernism, a matter of deep seriousness, as Motherwell said. The artist saw himself burdened with ethical responsibility: ". . . the subject is crucial and only that subject-matter is valid which is tragic and timeless."[14] And what else was that subject but the nature of the human spirit, female as well as male? For the shared belief, again, that extended an embrace around the believers, was, still, that humankind was capable of constructive good, and that the mind, if freed of its conventional concepts and habits, would conceive a dream of constructive reason (to misquote a less sanguine Goya).[15]

One of the "interesting" questions of modern art history, to be written about one day, is why, as this deep-dragging movement gradually coalesced and became a matter of increasing financial profit during the late years of the '50s and later, there came also a growing sense of fear and fatality, the intuition of a truly radical break preparing itself. And indeed eventually this art movement, rooted as much as any in history in international exchange of ideas and dedicated theoretically to exploring the nature of all human beings, would turn out in the end to be a movement of unparalleled parochialism, America-first jingoism and male chauvinism.[16] Then, as many women here attest—Alice Neel, Lee Krasner, Joan Mitchell and Nell Blaine among them—offensive aggressiveness and hostility among art factions took the place of that binding sympathy that had existed before. The suicide of a mortally depressed Arshile Gorky, in 1948, was the first portent. Meanwhile, there was surfacing the current of existential anxiety, guilt and fear for the future in Europe, while this country headed into the McCarthy era with the violence-charged decade of the '60s to follow.

Part of what happened was that, step by step, some of the more self-questioning of the artists began to feel the movement running away with itself, gradually even going amok, becoming a toy of a market beginning its gradual rise toward the manic expansiveness of the later 1960s. Some of the artists fought bitterly, as if their lives were at stake—and so it turned out they had been—against being included under such an imprecise and therefore the more misrepresenting while marketable rubric as "Abstract Expressionism." Some felt their control over their art draining away into the hands of dealers, collectors, the media exhorting from them, one by one, those trademark images by which they had become internationally famous. At the same time, there was a spirit of what one might call collaboration with the media on whose tides of print some of these artists were rising to prominence. As Lee Krasner wryly said, "They complained a lot, but they sure worked at getting there, so if it wasn't what they wanted in the end, that was another story."

Still, or perhaps therefore, swimmers with the economic tide or victims of it, the men of the First Generation of that school were fit bards for a human epoch that witnessed the Depression, the Holocaust, Dresden, Canterbury, Hiroshima, Nagasaki and, later, a divided Berlin. It is within this framework that the movement has to be seen that put an end to hopeful Modernism in America.

In any case, postwar, the media in America were bereft of good copy: no more dying soldiers or burned infants to sell issues. On August 8, 1949, *Life* magazine ran a spread on the new art. In January '51, one of the classic photos of all time appeared as a double spread: fourteen of the so-labeled "Irascible Eighteen" men, and one more gracefully philosophical than irascible woman, the Rumanian semiabstract painter Hedda Sterne, posed as they met to demand more attention from American museums. By then the original base was gone: Surrealism had nearly destroyed itself. Dali was excommunicated; Elouard and Aragon defected; the exiles in New York sailed for home as the offspring of their dalliance began to grow healthy. In the next decades, happily for a few stars, prices for works of art would mushroom from what might be considered a bottom line, the year 1950 when Jackson Pollock earned six thousand dollars from sales and Rothko not even three thousand.[17] Then, in a high tide of romantic messianism, the more verbal of the artists addressed the marketplace from high promontories.

. . . space and the figure in my canvases [wrote Clyfford Still in 1963] had been resolved into a total psychic entity freeing me from the limitations of each yet fusing into an instrument bounded only by the limits of my energy and intuition. My feeling of freedom was now absolute and infinitely exhilarating. . . .[18]

Meanwhile, Lee Krasner—who was Pollock's "wife who also paints"—had not even been asked to join the Irascible Eighteen.

Perhaps it was as a kind of self-defense or -insulation of the body esthetic that, at the end of the 1950s, a new art made its appearance. In December of '58 the cover of *Art News* magazine carried Jasper Johns's *Target,* bright, scumbled, fascinatingly surfacy, with a row of boxlike compartments lined along the top that held four identical heads truncated at the nose. A later version of this instant success went a step further. Now the boxes held parts of the body: nose, lips, penis, ear, hand—the human being dismembered, packaged. Meaning in terms of coherently structured relationship between the parts was discarded. Those parts were laid out in a line as a computer lays out its information. The work heralded a new age with a new cast of characters—boy-gods to replace the aging patriarchs—Johns, Robert Rauschenberg, Andy Warhol and their gurus, the gentle Dada-Surrealist-chessplayer Duchamp and the Zen-intoxicated composer-tinkler John Cage. Duchamp's famous rationalization for having given up making art altogether became a banner slogan for many in the next decade (he himself went right on working in private): "Every picture has to exist in the mind before it is put on canvas, and it always loses something when it is turned into paint. I prefer to see my pictures without that muddying."[19] Quickly a bandwagon of Duchamp idolizers without his Gallic irony got rolling. It would be the decade of the denigration of seriousness, of "de-mythologizing," of "evaporation of signficant subject," the era of analyses of the "thereness of the object," and cracker-barrel hokum of the kind long popular along provincial American byways: "I'm totally uninterested in European art and I think it's all over with."[20]

By the end of the '60s, Pollock, Franz Kline, David Smith, Ad Reinhardt, Mark Rothko, the Abstract Expressionist poet-critic Frank O'Hara and others related in other ways would be dead. There would also have transpired the years of assassinations, war in Vietnam and, eventually, the Kent State massacres, the breakdown of many social forms and the end, for many of the old Modernists and humanists, of an age. As earlier good men had bewailed the failure of colonialism and Christian missions to save the world, so now other good men mourned the death of the hope in art and art education to do the same.

Then there truly was a moment of crisis and emptiness. So-called Information Art would be an expression of this dislocation, with its patchy montages of unmeaningful and uninteresting photos, documents, notations.[21] Then, too, the manic gyrations and manipulations of an art market soon collaborating with multinational corporations with intricate tax-avoiding structures seemed to many only a venal side effect of a deeper discontinuity in the culture. All the effulgent, Roman-type expansion of public funding for packaging and purchasing the arts on through the early 1970s did not change the impression many had of a genuinely creative movement in process of winding down, like the Self-Destroying Machine that French sculptor Tinguely set into decline in the Museum of Modern Art garden in the spring of 1960. The sense of esthetic coming apart was vivid as fashion ground through the specialized isms of Pop, Op, Hard-Edge, Color-Field, Minimal, Conceptual and Object art (each one catching a rising market), those too frequently dry simplifications and dead "distanced" ends, each one exegetisized in turn by upcoming pundits of meaninglessness: "The absurdity of man's position in the world has become the guiding idea of many contemporary artists. The most meaningful act that can be performed, they insist, is to emphasize the meaninglessness of life."[22]

So exaggerated did the situation become that, as the 1970s went on, an issue quite beyond pure esthetics began to be raised by a few in the art world: the question, banished since the 1930s from discussions of art, of value in the larger human sense, of what the arts were, in effect, existing for. Considering what had been and what was, the thoughtful critic Barbara Rose began to write searchingly about the "difficulty the modern artist has experienced in finding a spiritual subject in a secular age."[23] That Target of Jasper Johns sold at auction in 1973 for $250,000, in a sale in which the then owner earned a total of $2,242,900 for works of art accumulated for a relative song in the past decade. That collector and others working with tax-exempt funds from personal or family foundations underwrote a series of heroic-scale and practically unvisitable earth works by artists like Robert Smithson, Michael Heizer and

Walter de Maria. In 1976, the artist Christo, after two years of energetic promotion and the forcing of the issue by actual litigation, erected his famous twenty-four-and-a-half-mile-long curtain of white silk that fluttered from an expertly built fence across the cattle ranges of California. The cost had been more than $2 million and there were many among Sonoma and Marin Counties' economically pressed and ecologically aware who did not find it the work of unarguable value that many in the professional art world did.[24] In 1977, the National Endowment for the Arts helped provide a grant to Object sculptor Carl André of $87,000 to transport a number of boulders from a quarry and arrange them, admittedly with a provocatively mysterious effect, in downtown Hartford, Connecticut. Again, there were those among the politically and economically responsible of Hartford who asked where was the value. A fee of $125,000 was proposed to sculptor Richard Serra in 1977–78 for one of his characteristic slab works to be part of the Pennsylvania Avenue redevelopment project in Washington, D.C. The artist produced a tentative model which was, in the end, rejected in a flurry of controversy with the project architect; still the artist received a payment of $41,655 for services rendered. Meanwhile, the Museum of Modern Art—funded indirectly with public tax monies—was offering through ads in *Business Week* an "Art advisory service . . . to corporations," presumably for the purchase of works of art out of corporate tax-exempt accounts, and other magazines were carrying ads like "Now finance a Rauschenberg the way you finance your car . . ." And meanwhile, too, high-level art criticism itself seemed to have gone berserk, so that now a Kenneth Noland was compared to Delacroix, Richard Diebenkorn to Rubens and Walter de Maria to Pythagoras.[25]

And yet . . . something else had happened in the meantime in the American art world, had begun and had been proceeding more or less on its own momentum, at first only infrequently visited by the media. Whether leaders of or benefiters from a new tide, women had begun to be active, demanding and influential as part of a Movement, not only as pioneers.

Of course, women had all along held powerful conserving roles in the cultural sphere, as collectors, patronesses, amanuenses. American women were notable in this regard: Cassatt, her friend Mrs. Havemeyer, Gertrude Stein; also Katherine Dreier, Gertrude Vanderbilt Whitney and Peggy Guggenheim in their times (that Guggenheim put on a show of Women's Art as early as '45 has been forgotten today). As a museum director, the German-born Hilla Rebay played a role in American prewar and postwar art that will be known only when the last vestiges of anti-Feminism are gone, for she was that anathema to many: an eccentric female elitist.[26] Dorothy Miller in New York, Adelyn

Breeskin in Baltimore, Grace McCann Morley in California, Agnes Mongen in Cambridge and Katherine Kuh in Chicago were pioneer women in various-level museum roles. Oppositely, women dealers for the most part reflected rather than opposed the bias against women. Grace Borgenicht, Rose Fried, Edith Halpert, Betty Parsons, Bertha Schaefer and Marion Willard in New York and Alice Roullier and Kuh in Chicago sought the best, but what they found was nearly all male. In the '60s, Eleanor Ward of the Stable Gallery, Eleanor Poindexter and Virginia Zabriskie began to turn the situation around. Now Paula Cooper,[27] Rosa Esmond, Miani Johnson (at Willard), Jill Kornblee, Holly Solomon and others in New York have joined them. In 1970, critic Lucy Lippard and Whitney Museum curator Marcia Tucker helped lead the Feminist attack on the Eastern art Establishment. Both are still in full steam, Tucker with her own foundation-subsidized exhibition gallery at the New School of Social Research in New York; Dextra Frankel and Jo Starrels are among many responsible for lively action on the Fullerton (California) and Los Angeles scene.

But so far as women artists as a working presence went, a real movement had begun only after the war, when the first of that Second Generation of Abstract Expressionists settled in New York. They were at the outset only a few. Unwilling to take No precisely because raised in those '20s and '30s of progressive education, these women were determined rather to exploit all possibilities, their talent, their beauty, their families' money insofar as it was forthcoming, to begin to do the work they felt capable of. They despised the idea of a female ghetto and refused to bond as sisters or to claim priorities on sexist grounds. At first they, like their elders, were isolated one from another, often in "cutthroat" competition. The men of the Abstract Expressionist movement they saw mostly in psychosexual terms: lovers, teachers, door-openers in the deep sense of the word, but not, except in rare cases, colleagues. Their art was not as doom-haunted, dream-loaded, not as fraught with radical conceptual matters, as the older men's. It was, in a word, more conservative. It was a matter of "light," color or gesture (in the work of Frankenthaler and Mitchell), or nature observed with a twist (Nell Blaine, Jane Wilson, Jane Freilicher), or figures splashed against walls of paint strokes (Miriam Schapiro, Grace Hartigan, Fay Lansner).

With the radical revolutions of the 1960s in other parts of the social system affecting the arts inevitably, women slowly, if still singly and under the heavy shadow of certain verborrhea-prone male artists of the decade, began to work new ground, joining in experiments with new materials. But they were clearly taking their own paths and were not to be heard praising the meaninglessness of their labors. The young German-born artist Eva Hesse, graduate of the Yale

School of Art and Architecture, influenced like many by Lee Bontecou and in turn like Bontecou influencing many who came after, worked with "non-art" materials to make objects that with excruciating visceral directness explored the human body. Now older women, long solitary, also began to tap new sources of subjective feeling and memory. Louise Bourgeois used latex, rubber and cement to continue her explorations of the sexual female. Lenore Tawney strung up an unconventional loom and drew from it ethereal phantoms far removed from yet derived from a human life history. Sylvia Stone took that cold industrial substance Plexiglas and turned it into a vehicle for poetic, if far removed, excursions into her own memory. Mary Frank, who had worked in deep privacy during the Abstract Expressionist decade carving wood, let the heavy and intractable go and began to use plaster and then clay to find her own language. The acclaim given her work showed how receptive a public was for art that spoke on a wavelength of sensibility without banality, that explored subjects by pseudoformalist orthodoxy appropriate only for poetry or song, or by the orthodoxy of meaninglessness, deserving of disdain.

"1970 was the tremendous watershed," says Lippard. "Before then there was no community of women in the arts." That Movement that had really begun with Simone de Beauvoir and Betty Friedan worked benefits of a total order. First for the future, the market began to look at women's work with new financial interest, making it possible for women to plan a realistic career. As Joan Mitchell put it, "I was successful in the '50s and then I was dropped in the '60s. It was the time of Pop, and I went on doing my 'little oil paintings.' Then, in the '70s, they had to dig up something new. So they came and dug my quote little oil paintings unquote. But the funny thing was, I hadn't ever quit." Also the sexual revolution, by then well won, made it possible for ambitious and still life-loving females to opt for a life of work without having to go through those tortured, rebellious and alienating experiences many of the older women endured. And then the Movement also shed benefits backward. A critical effect, and one that would set the direction of women's work apart from men's, was this: that daughters now looked on their gifted but voiceless mothers' sufferings with new understanding, pity and a will to "make it better" in their own time span. As June Wayne put it, "Well, kiddo, I'll make it up to you in the end." The new woman artist would not have to break with her past to become herself as, it seems, the creative male is impelled to overthrow his father by symbolically rejecting his art.[28] How important and special is this potential given women by the Movement for bonding to the communal human past I hope will become clear in the course of this book. So, bequeathed living connection with the past, some women may be now in a better position than some males to live without cynicism or desolation in a world from which all illusions of extrahuman salvation (through Christ, Science or Art) have drained away.

The 1970s, then, have been a decade of extraordinary and progressive flowering by women artists of all ages—some reported in this book—even during years of devastating political violence that also witnessed in the cellars of the art world such displays of nihilism as Vico Acconci's hiding his private parts between his legs to achieve a sex-change artwork, later offering a masturbation artwork from under the floorboards of his gallery.

Then, too, in addition to major work by Nevelson, Krasner, Bourgeois, Reynal, Frankenthaler, Mitchell, Frank, Tawney and many others, this decade has seen the emergence of a kind of endeavor one might with justice call a woman's new *use of art.* It was on the brink of the divisive '60s, in 1959, that C. P. Snow published *The Two Cultures,* arguing that science and the arts had fallen wholly asunder. I see these younger artists of the '70s, working in various mediums but coming from a remarkably similar background, returning to that earlier gestalt in which natural science and art were so closely enmeshed as to be aspects of the same imaginative, speculative process. For these women it was, rather, the Apollo landing in 1969 that gave a theme to the new era in which many of them set to work making art with a sense of coming home. In this light, I mention again those two quixotic and challenging works: Schapiro's *OX,* which she talks about here, and Nancy Graves's *Camels,* a set of life-size fur-covered Bactrian camels, a work of taxidermy-sculpture and a *succès* (or *chute*) *de scandale* when it was shown in the Graham Gallery in New York in 1968. Different as these works are, I take them both to signal the turning of a corner of rebellion. The rather obvious implications of *OX* are quickly seen, but the *Camels* may conceal a meaning not, as in Toklas's words, to be fully worked out for years to come. For Graves, born in 1940, had grown up a constant visitor to the natural-history museum established in 1903 in her town of Pittsfield, Massachusetts,[29] in just that spirit of humanistic devotion to science I spoke of before. There the walls are rich with diagrammatic paintings of flora, fauna and crystals and the descent of species. The cases are filled with models of animals, vegetables and minerals in all their amazing mechanical aptness, their fur and claws, feathers, scales and bones that together illustrate the evolution of life forms toward meaningful adaptation to the world. I propose that Graves's return to that vein of gold for such a witty amalgam of science and art signaled the turn of the tide. And though she herself quickly took refuge from the radicalism of that work in characteristic 1960s artspeak (". . . the psychological experience of confrontation with the camel is the oc-

Nancy Graves. Camels (left to right) VII, VI, VIII, 1968–69. Wood, steel, burlap, polyurethane, animal skin, wax, oil paint. 8' by 9' by 4'; 7½' by 12' by 4'; 7½' by 10' by 4'. The National Gallery of Canada, Ottawa. Gift of Allan Bronfman, Montreal.

casion to think about the nature of experience"[30]), what she was doing, I suggest, was to reclaim the natural world as a topic of *interest*. Indeed, there were critics who saw the point (". . . this is the most subversive thing that has happened to art since the early modernists abolished the subject altogether"[31]). There were also some who continued to draw a veil of words over it (". . . these works deal with perceptual problems of illusion and reality"[32]). In any case, the rightness of her attachment to her subject matter has been proved by Graves's subsequent work, much of it fascinating in the extreme and including variants and byplays on almost everything in that museum as well as newer naturalistic images like lunar maps and satellite photos of the seas. At the same time, she is expanding a joyous color sense in some latter-day Abstract Expressionist works from which nature is never wholly erased but lingers as a palimpsest for one who knows what to look for, as one might peer into a still pond for traces of the life that lives deep down.

There are many women working this old-new ground these days. With each exhibition season, I see the number growing larger and the work bolder with more direct grip on the matter from many vantage points of style. There is much to be said about the relationship between these women's world and their art. With some exceptions, all were born in the period of midcentury technological attack on the environment. Sputnik, Cold War rearmament, the development of computers and computer programming, television and space probes were the commonplaces of their childhood. Even more striking to me was the discovery that, again with only a couple of exceptions, all come from the same sort of family. Their fathers were almost all engaged in some kind of outdoor technological work, as contractors, mining engineers, engineers of celestial guidance systems or artillery installations. One is an agricultural economist, one a glider salesman and inventor of an aluminum canoe. Three, themselves, had fathers who led the same kind of life. They tracked the land and knew it well. They did not seek or find mystical Luminist emanations in the sky or the earth. It was the land itself, its layout, its compass points, its contained wealth and secrets, that held mystery and fascination enough.

The women's mothers too are of a kind not seen before in this book. Living in the far-flung corners of this country, often following their husbands in their restless professional moves, they harbored a poignant "love for art," most often ballet—that nonobfuscating form that turns on themes of longing and separations and was disseminated across this country by subsidized troupes from the late '50s on. These mothers themselves had mothers who were archetypes. One had run her own lace-making factory in Switzerland. One was a rugged homesteader-pioneer. One raised food, grafted trees, crossed flowers, made furniture. Their daughters, by a near-magical reach for integration, as I have come to see it, have staked their lives precisely in the region of synthesis: *art that probes the land,* and with an intent purely of this era that one would call romantic-scientific, not mystical. Rejecting the stiff disciplines of technology (only one I spoke with had a degree in architecture; the others claim disinterest), they still bring a naturalistic perspective to their subject whether it be rocks, bones, surfaces of the moon or the earth, the depths of the sea or the sky. They make literal use of subjects that Georgia O'Keeffe painted.

One category of works, taken as "art," is extraordinarily simple. Among the most interesting inventions of the late 1960s and '70s were those vastly expensive, foundation-financed Earth Works by male artists, interesting because they carried implications about the mind-nature bond, though many of the men were inclined to play down the literary suggestions. But the Earth Works as objects were exercises in awesome and even heartless futility. Located in flatlands, badlands, salt lakes of the West, they were inaccessible, hermetic, tragic or arrogant in their isolation. The women who make their own Earth or Site Works proceed differently. The structures they build deliberately engage an audience in exercises of contemplation of a strikingly primitive order. There is a quality of childishness to the works themselves, often made of boxes, crates, sticks, rocks, paper, ropes, twigs, saplings. Some works intentionally stir childish emotions of fear, blissful solitude, claustrophobia, fear of being lost, left in the dark. "I wanted to bring the vast space of the desert back to human scale," wrote Nancy Holt, one of the many—along with Susan Eder, Susanne Harris, Alice Aycock, Patsy Norvell and others—whose works fall into the category. "I just build houses everywhere," one of them says. Yet these works make their claim on the larger imagination too, with sitings offered off to distant horizons or the stars. In sum they are, one feels, in a real sense, "early works" in a mode of art that may have a long way to go.

And the impulse toward the future evolution of the larger idiom of which I speak is powerful. Such a backed-up reservoir of desire for expression one senses on the part of these artists! To change the metaphor, one wonders, in fact, whether the circuit (the simple work) is heavy enough to carry the voltage (so many ideas). These young artists display an appetite for encompassing the world's knowledge and feeding it through the meshes of their minds that one can only call Humboldtean.[33] "I wanted my piece to express geological and time change in the natural process," said one echoing many. Not in a thousand lifetimes, the listener feels, could they read all the books, follow all the paths down which their minds adventure. Their pretentiousness is at once touching and astonishing. They drop names like Gretel's crumbs through the woods of learning. Darwin, Heisenberg and Einstein, Merleau-Ponty and Lévi-Strauss are only a major quintet. They talk about the Uncertainty Principle, ice-age bone notations, Stonehenge, treatises on hormones and "disorder as a form of order." "Physical geography, how the earth rises and falls, winds blow, dolphins navigate" was a week's reading by one woman. Mythology, archaeology and the topography of the moon are all grist to their brains, as Japanese shadow plays and Zen gardens were grist to the 1920s and '30s.

University-trained, these young women have studied all art history and trekked many of the great sites of the world. Their touchstones are not style markers like Cézanne or Picasso but primitive archaeological monuments that, in early days, engaged human beings in ritual behavior or afforded them elemental shelter: Zoroastrian burial sites in Iran (for Alice Aycock), the loess caves in northwest China (Jackie Winsor traveled through China and was disappointed above all not to see these), the ruins of Tikal in Guatemala (Michelle Stuart). A gentle beginning of cash flow to these women from public subsidies makes some adventurous trips possible. In one six-month time, one of the women touched ground in Copán, Albuquerque, Mesa Verde, the Chillicothe, Ohio, serpent mounds, and several parts of Canada, exploring, collecting rocks and soil samples.

Back home, these artists find correspondences of form between what they have seen in person or in photos—the striated land and ocean currents, galaxies, bacteria swarms, the double helix—that the Humboldts only imagined. They project such cross-category works of grandeur for the future if asked: highway systems, city-nature environments, structures entered into and moved by wind, sunlight, sound and time itself, and structures to bury the dead. They pine, in a word, to establish their "presence in the continuum," as one artist put it. And then, on the edge of that mind-blowing sublime for the first time in history, this new *woman* artist often reacts as her frontier great-grandfather did before Niagara or the aurora borealis: with a flush of what Jacques Cousteau calls Rapture of the Deeps—"Don't you think the idea of Einstein is a little heartbreaking?" (see page 408).

A factor in the gathering momentum of this kind of art was the coincidence of our Bicentennial year, when many studies of the American ground, actual, historic and psychic, began to redirect attention to fundamental questions of who we are and what we have done with our heritage, the land. Landscape and the way it has been depicted by changing generations and from changing viewpoints, religious, scientific and esthetic, then became a subject for museum and literary surveys. In his earlier book *Landscape into Art,* Kenneth Clark suggested that "the best hope for a continuation of landscape painting consists in an extension of the pathetic fallacy and the use of landscape as a focus for our own emotions." [34] That is the direction in which I observe many of these women carrying their art. And if it is not the literal landscape as subject, it is the inner psychological landscape toward which the artist yearns. If painter Jennifer Bartlett and performance artist Eleanor Antin in their different ways reflect, on one level, the dismembering consequences of computer mentality—Bartlett by laying out her data along linear tracks, Antin by unweaving the human personality into a warp of singular personae—nonetheless both these artists told me of their attempts to achieve a holistic (One World?) view. For it is Bartlett's ambition to find a mode that would encompass subjective feeling, and Antin's to revive an "Eleanor who was" and "still is," in order to find an unbroken thread of consciousness that would connect past, present and future.

Many women are working this old-new ground of natural human experience in various degrees of abstraction and remove. I claim further that all the women in this book, of whatever age and style, are in the broadest sense to be considered part of the same tradition. In their conservatism or—to use a word more cumbersome but without negative political connotations—their *conservationism,* as I said at the start, may be the promise of their future. [35] Women artists of this transitional time, when the world is trying to salvage itself against an apocalyptic background, may have something to say that many males with their traditional rejection of the old, their dividing of the arts into national camps and their thrust to power and profit have not.

Relatedness, connection, continuity: these are words I heard the women of all ages use. If there is a "woman's art," perhaps it is here.

Mary
Stevenson Cassatt

BORN 1844, ALLEGHENY CITY, PENNSYLVANIA,
DIED 1926

*There's only one thing in life for a woman; it's
to be a mother. . . . A woman artist must be . . .
capable of making the primary sacrifices.*[1]

—MARY CASSATT

Mary Cassatt is the logical starting point for this survey: the statement above embodies the contradiction that underlies her life and her art, that makes her at once an end and a beginning.

It may seem odd that an independent woman at the culmination of a successful career, by then also a Suffragette and even, as she claimed, a Socialist, could have held so simplicist a view of the vocation of all women. But that paradox is at once a key to Cassatt's achievement and also to a certain containment one observes over the span of her work. Part of her genius was, to put it in contemporary terms, a conceptual one: to isolate and render with increasing mastery one single theme—the embracing mother and child—that was rooted in the substructure of belief in her time.[2] But the point is, that is not all there was to her. For she strained to the future too in her extraordinary technical virtuosity. And her work reveals the split temperament. The subjects of a majority of her oil paintings are those united mothers and children, icons of an unquestioned Protestantism,[3] while in her prints she apparently felt free of the claims of that image to follow to dazzling ends her feeling for the liberated line and the brilliant pattern, modes of seeing and working that might, if destiny had been kinder to her, have allowed her to become a true forerunner.

She was born—as were almost all the women artists whose life stories follow—into a strongly matriarchal family. Her own middle name, Stevenson, by which

59

she signed her first two submissions to the Paris Salon, was her maternal grandmother's; her elder sister, Lydia, was named for her father's mother; an older brother, for her mother's father. This latter was the Scots-Irish line of descent, in which clan and family relationships were considered the earthly equivalents of the heavenly hierarchies. In fact, the nineteenth-century middle-class Protestant family was a microcosm of the divinely ordained cosmos. If at the center stood the father, not far off were the mother and her babes, all these separate lives turning on a single axis like the meshed spheres of the heavens above. Bonded in love and absolute loyalty, family was a metaphor for permanence, for trust and hope in the small relationships as also in the larger, national political ones. In a nation of perpetual frontiers like ours, and of the kind of social unrest that characterized even the middle-class East in the nineteenth century (the Cassatts moved four times before settling in Paris, and then it was in their nature to be frequently changing residences and going off on journeys), the mother was the very principle of social organization. Her rootedness, her self-containment, self-mastery and sense of purpose were the structuring force in the family as in the nation and time eternal.

Toward the end of the century, as we know, that view of women began to change. The number of divorces rose, for instance, as the Women's Movement began to have an effect. With the advent of the eugenics and social-hygiene movements, even unliberated women began to take measures to limit the amount of mothering they would do. But in the decades of the 1880s and '90s, so fraught with change on all levels from scientific to political, Mary Cassatt came onto the scene, the last serious artist in history, with the exception of Picasso and Henry Moore, to do homage to the life-preserving mother as the ground of being.

That is, to be sure, the literary view of the artist. But it may be that we diminish the originality of her art by taking only the formalist view of it. It seems that she looms even larger in comparison with her literary peers and followers than she does with such fellow painters as Cecilia Beaux and even Berthe Morisot, both truly lightweight next to her. It is possible that in our admiration for her way of using brush, color and burin we have not said enough about the theme that is impacted into her forms, a theme also developed by writers like Cather, Stein and Virginia Woolf—of whom critic Ellen Moers has said that they

wrote of the power and grandeur of motherhood with an air of finality, as if what they were describing would never come again; as if there would never more be any mothers. . . . They [wrote] of mature, calm women of still, sculptural beauty . . . Their mothers are great queens, who impose order on the world. They have the power to create an ambiance, a drawing room, a whole landscape; they give access to the arts of civilization, the life of the senses.

These are mothers who "make of the moment something permanent."[4]

Before the daughter Mary Stevenson Cassatt, four other children had been born, nursed and nurtured, though the first, a girl, died after twenty-four hours. The second was another girl, Lydia; then two boys. In 1844, Mary.

When she was two there was a disaster of frightening proportions in their then residence of Pittsburgh. The city was nearly destroyed by a fire; together the family, mother, father and infants, watched from the far side of the Allegheny River the orange lights of flames reflected against the night sky. Later, another boy was born, cradled and died. Then another who lived: Gardner. Six years after that, while the family would be living abroad, the deaths of the ones who had survived birth would begin. Robbie, a twelve-year-old brother, would die of bone cancer. There was, one feels, a great deal of birthing, comforting and supporting in suffering for that mother to go through and the children to witness. And "my Mother's pride was in her boys," the one who became an artist would recall, somewhat ruefully, at the end of her life.[5]

Later on, after Cassatt had established herself in Paris and been joined there by her parents and sister, that sister Lydia whom she had painted over and over, her best and most loved model, died of Bright's disease at the age of forty. During the summer of Lydia's weakening, her sister did not paint at all but took over the nursing chores. After the death took place, Cassatt, who to that point had painted a fairly wide range of subjects—landscapes, fieldscapes with poppies, single figures of Lydia at the opera and genre studies of women drinking tea or riding in horse carriages—gradually narrowed her focus to the theme that then became dominant during the most prolific years of her career.

The real mother lived until the last day of 1895. By then, the painter was in her mid-fifties with three full decades of life ahead. For the first time, she was free of the burden of caring for dependents. Yet within a short time her zeal for painting apparently flagged, and she devoted herself more and more to helping her great friend from home Louisine Elder Havemeyer and her husband, Horace, put together what would be one of the most important collections of Impressionist art ever made. It is hard to avoid the conclusion that painting the maternal figures had some motivating meaning for Cassatt herself and that when the subject was removed her own interest dissipated. The question is, why did she not move on to new fields?

Nobody knows—for Cassatt left no memoirs—how the idea of putting her feelings down in line and color came to her as a child. From the reports of other artists in this study, one imagines her scribbling and drawing, being something of a drifter and dreamer, perhaps not focused until gradually her fascination with the mechanics of art impelled her to seek lessons. Then too, a spark may have been lit during the family's European trek that began when she was seven and went on until she was fourteen. The sorrow of the loss of Robbie marked that trip—as well as her life: in old age she would travel alone to his burial place in Germany to bring his body back to the family vaults in France. But the years were also undoubtedly made bright by her parents' pleasure in being abroad. Her father, the perfect Victorian male chauvinist, was also his daughter Mary's best riding and strolling companion and a restless, avid traveler. Her mother, fluent in French, a bookworm and the intellectual superior of her husband, also adored the life in the European capitals as long as she could find there a more or less settled life in a circle of Protestant friends.[6]

One great event in the life of the future painter would almost surely have been the Paris Universal Exposition in the year 1855, when she was eleven. Flags were flying, the streets thronged with festooned horses and crowds of tourists of all nationalities. The talk of the season was of the exhibition of paintings: forty canvases by Ingres, the grand old master of drawing and the cool portrait, and thirty-five by Delacroix, painter of color-soaked, exotic scenes of Arabs, wild animals and bloodshed. "I smell gunpowder!" Ingres is said to have muttered when he saw the works of his archrival.

The esthetic argument between these two engaged everyone in Paris those days who could muster an opinion, and in Paris, where art is at issue, everyone is engaged. Nor would the arguments have been dull even for a young girl. They struck to the heart of what art was about, and what life as well. To be forward-looking, adventurous and bold, or obedient to rules laid down in the past. For Delacroix, genius lay in "imagination" and "temperament." Ingres held the exact opposite: "There is nothing essential to be found in art since Phidias and Raphael . . ." Even a youngster might find something to say in a dispute between advocates of the old and the new! Most of all, she might gather the message that art was a matter of deep importance to both women and men, not just a pastime on Sunday afternoons.

Back home in Philadelphia, she must have begun to talk about getting some training in a field to which she felt lured. The idea, contrary to myth, did not scandalize her family. In fact, her elder brother Alexander took her seriously enough to begin to plan how he could make enough money to send her back abroad to study. Meanwhile, there was the Pennsylvania Academy of the Fine Arts, a respectable training ground and eventually to become the seedbed for the style of American Realism. Myth has it that Mr. Cassatt said he would sooner see his daughter dead than an artist, but if that was so, he soon changed his mind, for she was still in her teens when she began the course, starting with drawing from antique casts, working up through drawing from the live model and at the end copying old-master paintings. Another myth: it was not unheard of for a girl of good family to attend this institution, nor were the girl students shielded from studies of the human body.[7] Classes were segregated, but there were lectures in anatomy for both sexes and plenty of opportunity to study the partly undraped male figure in the plaster-casts studio. Nor is it a fact that drawing from casts was a worthless occupation, as progressive art educators of the future would hold. It was not. For the true artist, it could be the beginning of life, the beginning of seriousness. It marked the turn from hobby art to serious scrutiny of things in space, of mysteries of perspective, light and shade, proportion. Moreover, the very exercise of drawing from casts located the fledgling artist in her or his historic discipline. For generations, since the Renaissance, art students had sat as Mary Cassatt now would, charcoal in hand, in the dusky, dusty atelier, dressed in a smock, legs curled around the long legs of the high stool the better to see. And finally, what may have been most important of all for Cassatt's future direction as an artist, working from these relics of Greece and Rome conveyed a feeling for monumental form and for the timelessness of certain images throughout history, like perhaps the infants Bacchus or Dionysius or Romulus and Remus, or the Classical goddesses, Venus, Hera, Athena. Besides, a love of Classical things was in the air at the Academy. Girl students dressed up in floating Grecian tunics and wreaths of flowers for holidays, and in the school courtyard, shadowed by an immense hawthorn tree, stood a large figure of Ceres, mother of harvests.

After the Civil War came to an end, Cassatt, again contrary to the myth of the confined Victorian daughter, was allowed to travel alone to Paris, staying with friends, trying out various of the art academies that took foreign students. Her fellow Philadelphian and exact contemporary in age Thomas Eakins went to Paris the same year, studied in the academic École des Beaux-Arts and, discouraged with the brand of teaching there, went home to work out his own manner of painting the somber, earnest American faces and figures. But Cassatt took another path. She quickly determined she had had enough of conventional studio training and began to haunt the museums and the countryside copying masterpieces and making sketches from life. Her letters of those days are full of haughty, flighty, giddy comments that sound not at all like a constricted Puritan female. She was enjoying her liberty and the expansion of her skills, and she assured her family that "we professionals despise amateurs"![8]

She traveled also to Rome, which she came to know well, even to its cheaper hotels and restaurants, and by the time she was forced home in 1870 by the Franco-Prussian War she had also seen Capri and Naples, met a colony of Neapolitan artists and fallen in love with Spain.[9] One tends to forget what a network of expatriates and also helpful American consuls existed in Europe in those days through which sojourners could pass as if by osmosis without either peril or boredom. By contrast, the interim back home was intensely depressing. She wrote a friend that she was abandoning herself "to despair and homesickness, for I really feel as if it was intended that I should be a Spaniard and quite a mistake that I was born in America."[10] She was "ravenous for money" (to buy a return ticket) and "determined to try to make some."[11] "No amount of bodily suffering . . . would seem for me too great a price for the pleasure of being in a country where one could have some art advantages. . . ."[12] How wild I am to get to work, my fingers fairly itch and my eyes water to see a fine picture again . . ."[13] At a point, exhausted with the heavy Philadelphia summer weather, she even made desperate plans to escape to the American Far West but got only as far as Chicago, where, in the great fire, the second of her life, she lost all the paintings she had been trying to place with dealers—probably copies of religious works for sale to Midwestern Catholic churches. "The Madonnas of Murillo are great favorites with Catholics!" she had written.[14] Finally, later that year, she did get off and settled for six months in the city of Parma, under the supervision of an Italian printmaker, studying especially the work of the Mannerist artist Correggio.

Correggio was the Italian master she loved best, and one should look into his work for elements she would project into her own later. He was a supreme painter of the naturalistic yet idealized Madonna and Child, that contradiction in terms that defines Mannerist art. With what meticulous realism he studied and rendered the details of his Holy Infants with their wide-splayed legs and small hands reaching up to touch the mother's face, and then with what passion for communicating the Virgin's innocence he transformed her figure into the very image of girlishness. And simply as a painter, Correggio had much to teach her: those swaths and falls of textile that gave him plenty of space on which to exercise his brush. And though at first thought an element in Correggio's work that seems absent from Cassatt's is the hint of erotic feeling between even the holy figures that was part of the current of sixteenth-century Catholicism out of which Teresa of Ávila also drew her mystic-erotic visions, one should not be too quick to discount that element either.

From Parma, Cassatt went back to Spain, where she would set to work on the canvas she was going to submit to the Paris Salon; in it she introduced for the first and nearly only time in her oeuvre the head of a male, drowned in shadow and obscured by a wide-brimmed hat.[15] Outside of her father and brothers, she never painted another male except Degas, and that canvas she destroyed. There would be little competition in her mind for the central subject once she had grasped its nature.

Meanwhile, she had visited Madrid and fallen in love with Velásquez ("Oh! my man but you know how to paint!"[16]), and wished for a kindred soul to talk with ("beautiful, love, Oh! painting what aren't you?"[17]). And then she was in Seville, "gay, lovely . . . orange faces glowing in the streets . . . in the courtyard orange trees, aloes, a fountain sparkling in the sunshine . . ."[18] Already it is clear she was looking at both art and nature for clues about light and color that would enable her to read the Impressionist message when she saw it. And already she was talking about having her works accepted for major shows in Europe. Then Paris had accepted her, and she was aiming at Vienna and Milan. And she was packing off copies for sale in New York. And then soon her *On the Balcony,* fresh from the Salon, was on exhibit again in a gallery window in London, causing a number of newspaper comments. And by the summer of 1874 her mother had joined her for some travels to the Lowlands, where she became "enchanted" with Rubens and also quite satisfied with the numbers of her own sales to churches back home, with which money she could now pay for her own models, since her mother refused to do so. And soon, in Paris, she had begun to spot certain iconoclastic works in the windows of the Durand-Ruel Gallery and there would never be any question of ever going *back.* "How well I remember," she later said, "seeing for the first time Degas's pastels in the window of a picture dealer on the Boulevard Haussmann. I used to go and flatten my nose against that window and absorb all I could of his art. It changed my life."[19]

That year, 1874, she sent her third entry to the Paris Salon and the first one she would openly sign "Cassatt." The work itself shows that something had happened to her idea of what a finished piece was. This was no more a studio "set piece" of posed figures, but a face, a face alone and a face far from beautiful, its flesh and white-gold hair all dissolved by light. It was, to tell the truth, a sport among her own works of the time, the rest of which were still in the old manner, built up in heavy solid forms like sculpture transposed to canvas. But a person who had not seen her other efforts was Edgar Degas, who, walking through the Salon galleries to see what the conservatives were up to, stopped before this work and said, "There is one who feels as I do." By the next year, *light* had taken over. She submitted a work that the Salon jury found unacceptable. Cassatt knew why. With a feeling, one imagines, of both irony and diffidence, she repainted it, making it darker, sent it in the next year and, as she anticipated, had it accepted. But the next year she was again rejected and then never tried again.

The reason was plain. A mutual friend had brought to her studio that same Degas whom she so admired, who in turn invited her to become an exhibiting member of the group called Impressionists. "I had already recognized who were my true masters," she later remembered. "I admired Manet, Courbet and Degas. I hated conventional art. I began to live."[20]

Now, there were two sides to Degas, both to his art and to his theory. One captured Cassatt, let us speculate, and one held her. There was the radical Degas, a master of the technique of rendering the seen world in terms of its uncertain shimmer and reflection; a renunciation, if one will, of the plastic certainties of nineteenth-century academic art, and a moving forward toward the deep question that would preoccupy advanced artists ever after: what *is* the real, and how must it be rendered to be true to itself?

"What I want is difficult . . . ," Degas said. "The atmosphere of lamps or moonlight . . ."[21]

Then there was the classic Degas, who held fast to the monumental and timeless. "I show them stripped of their coquetry," he wrote of his ballet girls, "in the state of animals cleansing themselves." In this frame of reference, his masters were the masters of intellectual, controlled form, Giotto, even Ingres. Yes, he was the great synthesizer: he could love both Delacroix and Ingres. And this Degas urged and urged again simplification, reduction of one's scope so as to deepen the thrust. And repetition.

One must treat the same subject ten times, even a hundred times. Nothing in art should seem to be accidental. . . . One loves and endows with art only what one is accustomed to.

It is all very well to copy what you see, but it is better to draw only what you still see in your memory. Then you reproduce only what has struck you, that is to say, the essentials . . .

No art was ever less spontaneous than mine . . . of inspiration, spontaneity, temperament, I know nothing.[22]

In his person too Degas was a union of opposites in much the same way that Cassatt was, and that fact too bound them together. He was a renegade from conventionality only in the sense that he was an artist. But he had nothing of the bohemian hedonism of Monet, Renoir, Pissarro. He was an aristocrat, of a background quite as elevated as her own *haut-bourgeois* one. And he understood the matriarchy. He had adored his own mother and bitterly mourned her death. He was far from an easy man: learned, acerbic, critical, often morose, sometimes vicious. But his friendship for Cassatt was crucial in her development, just how much so one will never know because, in a fit of whatever moves people to do such things, she destroyed all his letters.

Obviously, however, they shared a grasp on the paradoxical and contra-dictory: the timeless, to be rendered in shreds of broken light. Neither was ever really an Impressionist, though both were freed by the Impressionist way of seeing. For him, there would be two great subjects: the dancer's body and the galloping horse, though he also painted many other things, including portraits and figure pieces. For Cassatt, there would be only the one.

What limited her so? She and Degas met in 1877, and, whether by coin-cidence or by plan after hearing of that encounter, that same year Cassatt *père* and *mère* and Lydia arrived to live with her, to chaperone, accompany and, eventually, in their sicknesses and deaths to burden her with work and respon-sibilities that cut deeply into her own time. One has to think they also burdened her with their perspectives on her own life style. "A woman who is not married is lucky if she has a decided love for work of any kind," remarked that intellec-tual mother. "And the more absorbing the better!" Likewise her father, over the years, sprinkled his letters to his children back in the States with comments about sister Mary's "female complaints," "gloomy spells," "fatigue" and "mis-eries."[23] She very often, as he saw it, was in bad need of "change of air and repose" and then would be afforded those things by being taken off on a trip, to Scotland or Switzerland, with him himself.

He was proud, however. She first showed with the Impressionists in their Fourth Exhibition in 1879, and one of her contributions was a ravishing portrait of Lydia in an opera box, wearing a pearl necklace and smiling with radiant self-possession. The painter Gauguin, seeing it, commented that Cassatt had as much charm as Berthe Morisot, the other female in the group, but "much more force." Her father informed the home side that she was "now known to the Art world as well as to the general public in such a way as not to be forgotten again as long as she continues to paint."[24] And, at the same time, she began to send her work to shows in New York, Philadelphia and Boston. Some of these were adventurous in their composition, with sweeping curving backgrounds— rings of opera boxes or backs of chairs—and figures viewed from a variety of angles, and showed a wide scale of influences of other artists, especially Manet. She was experimenting, but only to a point. Degas apparently made an effort to move her farther in the direction of a radical handling of space by giving her some "guidance," as she later said, with the background of *Little Girl in a Blue Armchair,* where four overstuffed settees have been pushed askew across an olive-green floor. By Degas's reckoning, one imagines, the real subject matter of that work would have been those bulbous shapes them-selves and the fishlike strip of floor. But Cassatt reestablished her own more conservative dominion over the work by making the subject plainly an indignant little girl, fancily dressed in Scots garb, flopped down on one of the chairs, her legs sulkily flung apart so that even the eyelet of her undergarments is visible (see page 73).

In 1880, Cassatt's brother Alexander and his wife and four children arrived to visit the expatriate members. During this time, Cassatt began the first of her paintings of mothers with children. At once, her handling of the subject attracted attention. In the Fifth Impressionist Exhibition that year, the French writer Huysmans singled out her works in that genre for praise. "Ravishing . . . only a woman can paint infancy," he said. And Degas agreed that what she had accomplished was "more firm and noble than what she did last year." Huysmans went on at more length. He found her maternal figures rather too Anglicized for his taste but wholly without that

sentimentality on which most of them have foundered. Oh! those babies, good heavens! How their pictures make one's hair stand on end . . . such stupid and pretentious poses . . .

[Now] for the first time, thanks to Miss Cassatt, I have seen the effigies of ravishing youngsters, quiet bourgeois scenes painted with a delicate and charming tenderness. Furthermore, one must repeat, only a woman can paint infancy. There is a special feeling that a man cannot achieve. . . . their fingers are too heavy not to leave a clumsy imprint, only a woman can pose a child, dress it, adjust pins. . . .[25]

And he went on to compare her, for the humanity of her subjects, with Dickens. In that, he was on the track. But in his comment that male fingers would be too heavy to catch the moment, he missed. In the long run it might, rather, be said that the maternal image, though provocative for a while, in the end would be limiting on her not because it was for her too light a matter, but because it was too heavy.

As Cassatt deepened her hold on the theme in the great maternal paintings of the 1890s, gradually she moved to universalize their poses and even their costumes and coifs. And then it is that, as the children's faces become steadily more particularized, their vividly real gestures of touching, caressing and leaning rendered with uncanny empathy, so do the mothers become more mute, grave, inward, in a word, more archetypal. She began to choose her models from among peasant women or servants instead of the society mothers whom she might have found in her own or other drawing rooms.[26] She found the villagers more natural in their nurturing gestures, more patient in their quiet sitting. Their bodies assumed the protective, embracing pose with an unstudied, habitual relaxation: child on the lap, arms around its body, the two faces pressed together, the hands gently laid one upon another.

Mother and Child. *Oil on canvas. 36⅛"
by 29". The Metropolitan Museum of
Art, New York. George A. Hearn Fund.*

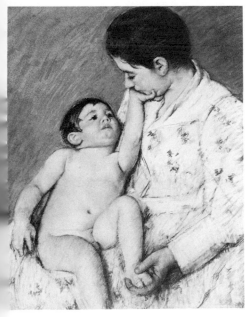

First Caress, *1891. Pastel on paper. 30" by 24". New
Britain Museum of American Art, New Britain,
Connecticut. Harriet Russell Stanley Fund.*

Mother and Child, *1889. Oil on
canvas. 35⅜" by 25⅜". Wichita Art
Museum, Wichita, Kansas. Roland P.
Murdock Collection.*

Touching, touching: it is the *touching* of these pairs of figures that distinguishes Cassatt's works from those of any of the other Impressionists. Degas's figures are always isolated, each one sunk in its own preoccupation; even his firelit whores are solitary, and the dancers literally look away from one another. The unifying device is nonhuman: it is light, glancing off arms, toes, hair, from parallel uplifted arms. In Berthe Morisot's works there is even less relationship between the figures. They often stand quietly side by side and stare passively out at the artist. Only with Daumier is the human bond sometimes rendered so poignantly, as in a work like *The Laundress,* where two figures merge into a single dark blur. In respect to this theme of physical contact, Cassatt's iconic mother-image may be the portrait of her own mother, painted the same year as Lydia's death, 1882. She is rendered as the quintessential matriarch, nearly majestic in her concentration on what she holds in her lap. One imagines she will always be there, clocking the passing hours, never moving on, making idle talk or drinking tea. And, according to her daughter's concept of her, she must be shown holding on to some *thing,* even if now no longer some*one*. And so what does the daughter show her holding in her lap, there where other mothers place, the better to enfold them, their infants? Why, the morning journal—*Le*

Reading "Le Figaro," 1883.
Oil on canvas. 41" by 33".
Privately owned.

The Lamp. *Dry-point and aquatint printed in color. The Metropolitan Museum of Art, New York. Gift of Paul J. Sachs.*

Figaro!—through which the world filters into her secluded corner and which, therefore, can be read as a symbol both of her immersion in her existence as Mother and of her portentous reaching out to the world beyond.

In 1890 there was an exhibition of Japanese wood-block prints at the École des Beaux-Arts. Cassatt and Degas went to it together, and she later bought quite a few, by Utamaro and his followers, those who specialized in figures of bending, swooping, posturing geishas in kimonos of limpid, contrasting colors. The next year, Cassatt began work on the series of prints—drypoints and aquatints—that represent a movement beyond the architechtonic content of her oil paintings. As early as 1879, she had collaborated with Degas on some graphics, and she confessed later that she had taken the medium up to discipline her use of line. The technical challenge inspired her, as other women in this study report having broken out of old molds by concentrating on technical issues. Every evening, after working all day in her studio on the oil paintings, she would sit down in the family circle under the lamplight and work at her graphics. Technique, on the one hand, and, on the other, the Japanese esthetic opened a door in her art for her to move ahead.

The flooding of Europe and America with Asian arts and ideas is a tale often told, but it bears retelling because it helped bring on the world in which Cassatt's followers, notably Georgia O'Keeffe, were to be formed. For centuries, little Asian artifacts had come filtering to the West by camelback and sail ship—silks, ceramics, ivories, an occasional bit of carved jade—that influenced artists from Rembrandt to Thomas Chippendale. And then, from India, along with teas and printed cottons, had come ideas relating to the worship of Brahma, the transcendental spirit of the universe, that influenced many Ger-

71

man philosophers and also Emerson. But it was not until China and then Japan were forced to open their ports to foreign traders in the 1840s and '50s that the great influx of graphic works began that would produce such a transformation in Western art and esthetics. In 1856, a French printmaker and friend of Degas found some of these colorful wood-block prints stuffed into a crate of dishes sent from Japan. Soon similar ones were on view in Parisian art shops. In 1867 there was a group displayed at the Paris Exposition. Degas and Manet were captivated. Whistler eventually would buy some examples and take them back to London, and Monet, Gauguin and others would pin them up in their studios. Gradually there commenced that commingling of East and West that would become a flood tide in years to come.

How curious it is, then, that after the turn of the century, when this ferment of ideas was going on both in Europe and in America, Cassatt stopped developing as an artist, nearly in her tracks. Her eyes, which later failed her, did not do so for many years. Why, one wonders, did she not press forward in the direction of her graphic designs, their counterpoint of arabesques and slanted lines, their luxuriant, sensuous contrasts of flowers and stripes, paisley and crosshatchings? There is little left here of the iconic stillness and gravity of the great oils; it is as if another artist brilliant but different came forth, worked for a while and then, for whatever reason, laid down her tools.

Cassatt's mother died in 1895. There was then, if one may put it that way, a substitute ground and refuge. Three years before, the artist had bought a villa outside Paris. Now that her mother was no longer there to be cared for in Paris, Cassatt gradually transferred her residence to the country and lived there, reigning there as a sort of matriarch herself except for short travels and the years of the First World War, until her death in 1926. Home, all that time, was the pinkish-red brick hunting lodge with a glassed-in gallery that gave a view over a wide green lawn. There hung her collection of Japanese prints and also the Persian ones she bought after the epochal show of Muslim art in Paris in 1893. Outdoors, there were forty-five acres of land, great chestnut and poplar trees, roses, two hundred varieties of chrysanthemums and all the vegetables including American corn. In this ambiance of studied, cultivated luxury and beauty, she lived as a proper Philadelphian unhampered by her spinsterhood, entertaining such eminences as Clemenceau, Mallarmé and the art dealer Ambrose Vollard.

Mary Cassatt's adventures as a collector belong to another chapter. As she relinquished her passion for making art, she lived more in her intellect. She fought the battles of her time at least in words, broke with Degas over the

Little Girl in a Blue Armchair, 1878. Oil on canvas. 35" by 51". Collection Mr. and Mrs. Paul Mellon, Upperville, Virginia.

Dreyfus case, argued for a Fenellosean brand of art edification for the under-privileged, called herself a Socialist and wrote passionate letters home in favor of woman suffrage. She railed against the "state of anarchy" in the interna-tional art market[27] and vented spleen on the aging artist peers of her youth. She detested the late Monet, Cézanne and Matisse. Rodin struck her as "humbug."[28] She found the aged Renoir courageous but a failed artist. She mourned Degas's death in 1917 but had been estranged from him for years. It was a moral objection she had to Rodin. "Why will he make his figures crawling on all fours? Humanity has grown up . . . humanity does not take that posture."[29] Meanwhile, she deepened her love for the writers and painters of naturalism: Tolstoy, Courbet; she had no toleration for Edith Wharton or Henry James. She was appalled at the scene at Gertrude and Leo Stein's, and the only time she went there she demanded to be taken home at once.

Her horror and sadness at the First World War and the "moral disintegra-tion" of Europe that followed overwhelmed her last years. She wrote with anguish about the bombardment of Reims, for it had not seemed possible to her that men would fling bombs out of airplanes. In the end, she could find only a single hopeful thought. Once again, she turned to the image of the saving woman.[30]

73

With the slaughter of millions of men, women will be forced, are now being forced, to do their work, and we have only begun. . . .[31]

One begins to feel the dawn and to see the reasons of this awful war. The emancipation of women one of the results . . . perhaps the greatest . . .[32]

After the war . . . there will be a great revival and surely a new view of things. It is then that the women ought to be prepared for their new duties, taking part in governing the world. . . .[33]

Had her life early on not been so confined to family and deformed by the dependence of those nurturing but also smothering parents, had her eyes not begun to fail around 1910 until at the end she was nearly blind, had . . . had . . . had, most fundamentally perhaps, there been open to her the model of die-and-become to which her male peers could turn along the course of their creative lives, reinforcing them in their power and freedom to abandon the old and renew themselves while continuing to force their art through transformations . . .

Degas said of her, "She had infinite talent," and the words, as one hears them today, sound sad, for she outlived that talent by so many years. What might she, then, have done? One imagines two directions: one, the way of the graphics and the esthetics of spontaneity and free expression of feelings. And the other?

In 1911 she made a trip to Egypt. "I am crushed by the strength of this Art," she wrote afterward. "I wonder if ever I can paint again. . . .[34]

"All strength, no room for grace, for charm, for children, none, only intellect and strength. How are my feeble hands to ever paint the effect on me?"[35]

At the end, she had come to think of Degas's sculpture as his greatest work. The thought, then, of the monumental stones of Egypt weighed in her hands. Is it possible that she might also have tried her hand at sculpture, not like Degas's, of course, but perhaps along the line of one whose work was reaching its maturity in those same years but who was, as far as we can tell, unknown to her: Maillol?

To be radically original in the visual arts seems to mean both possessing and abandoning certain parts of the past conceptually as well as technically; giving up those preoccupying subjects and symbols that focus the intellect and by so doing limit the eye and the hand from carrying their inventions to unforeseen ends. It was the source of Cassatt's genius when it worked and also of her containment within its first insights to have been grounded upon an image of such compelling power that she could not move beyond it. Any more than did her age.

Georgia O'Keeffe

BORN 1887, SUN PRAIRIE, WISCONSIN

ALBIQUIU, NEW MEXICO, 1977

I could hardly stop looking back at her. She was standing there behind the heavy red-brown adobe gate, wearing a long white dress partly covered by a sky-blue smock (that artifice of costume that falls between Dominican habit and Japanese kimono). She was smaller than I had expected. So was her house. Smaller and plainer, literally made out of earth, with walls of packed earth one yard thick. On her feet were little gray shoes like pads, and she stood leaning on a cane with a rubber knob. And as I looked back, I had the flash of an impression that she was holding a pose by the door so that I would remember her, carry away with me the memory of a face that is part of the mythology of our time, even if veiled by her ninety-some years and a pinned-back fringe of gray hair. But then I recalled that her eyesight was not what it had been and of course she was standing there for another reason, probably waiting for her red chow dog to be rounded up and brought home.

And I thought, that is the way it has always been with O'Keeffe. People are always projecting their own thoughts into her words and works. For this she has scoffed at them and drawn the barriers tighter around herself in the isolation of her extraordinary fame. But also, I wondered, is it not a measure of this artist's power and validity for our time that through so many changes of style and ideology she has lent herself to this kind of evolving interpretation?

In the beginning of her career, for instance, there was Alfred Stieglitz, the photographer and her husband, both an old-fashioned romantic and a Modernist, who conceived of her as Womanhood that he might capture with his most up-to-date instrument, the camera. He pursued his vision of what that might be through five hundred still photos of every line of her body,[1] and then had to watch while her spirit (the word would have been his, not hers) evaporated from before his lens and went to inhabit the Ghost Ranch where it could be itself.

Then in the 1920s, when she began painting blown-up images of dark-tissued iris and flesh-white jimson weeds, she announced she was doing so to make people stop and look hard at art in a time when everyone was rushing somewhere.[2] And still people went on reading sexual meanings into the paintings as they were inspired to do by the just-published works of Freud, and as we in our skepticism about Freud still find it inconceivable not to do today. The painter Marsden Hartley even found those flowers "shameless" revelations of things never before exposed.[3] Soon, however, the shameless revealer was turning her attention to whitened bones in the sand and knobs of wind-smoothed obsidian, at which point critics versed in Surrealism found their own meanings in those, which she in turn denied. Nowadays too, critics are placing her in one stream of cultural history or another. Art historian Barbara Rose, who probably knows as much about her mind as anyone else alive, maintains she is a latter-day Emersonian Transcendentalist.[4] By contrast, Eugene Goosen, who also knows O'Keeffe well, calls her a proto–Color Field artist,[5] a judgment which, since it involves colors not ideas, she is more inclined to allow. Beyond that, a visitor finds evidence that her spell over the general public is awesome. Letters pile up on her tables from people asking if they can bring her loaves of home-baked bread and show her their photos and paintings. The cult over which she has, unconsentingly, now been made matriarch is, I suggest (entering my own interpretation into the record), the one of Process-in-Nature that has replaced nineteenth-century Christianity with its sweeping correspondences between Family, Nation, Nature and Deity. Out of that four-legged system that in its fading days, as we have seen, gave a theme to Mary Cassatt, now in our faith-depleted age only one leg is left. Georgia O'Keeffe's paintings of the relics of natural evolution (rocks, cliffs, skulls), her Western landscapes with their clefts and mounds, their Black Places and flesh-brown hills, their mountains we instinctively call "ribbed," are our icons of the mystery of how, from its origins, human life has been integrated into the natural world, just as once Christian icons served as icons of mysteries of the supernatural.

Her own very latest paintings may suggest even more personal meaning.[6] I saw them at the Ghost Ranch, where she is still at work though always indoors now. There were three canvases—she still works in series as if there were always another view to be caught—showing a gray sky framed by slanted blue curtains. Those curtains, I leaped to think, might be the edges of the same blue smock she was wearing, and the sky her dress, and so the whole image a projection of the artist facing the abstraction of old age. To which reading, if I had voiced it, O'Keeffe might have reacted with her customary dry denial.

She went out of her way, as she habitually does, to keep deflating a guest's fancy ideas. She took me around her house, beginning with the famous rocks. They lay on the windowsill next to some plants in pots. One of these was the "Blood of Christ." My pen flew to my notebook with deep ideas, but she stopped me with the news that it was merely a weed that grows by the road. Then there was a cattle horn and a Mexican jar, and outside a window a table with yet more rocks. Those hard, natural shapes are her treasures. So is a tiny fireplace for piñon wood that she instructed a laborer how to build brick by brick, and an aged tamarisk tree outside a window, and a weathered wood boddhisatva in a niche. And a black door.

That black door in the patio wall at Abiquiu has perplexed and fixed her for thirty years.[7] We went out, sat down and looked at it. She has painted it— twenty times? a hundred? She told me what she has told a hundred others: that the door had a horrible fascination for her, nearly a sickness. You find a door, and you're bound to it.

I offered a theory again. Stieglitz had an outdoor darkroom in his Adirondacks home, so dark inside, in fact, that when the door was open it looked shut or vice versa. So "black door" could be a link in time and space, between life past and life today. O'Keeffe was not inclined to accept that reading. She pointed with her cane at the blue sky overhead and gave me to understand it was nice out here at night too.

Again, one does not require that the artist have the last word about meanings, as Alice Toklas inferred. For was it not by the same process, of letting correspondences breed, that this artist first came through to herself as an original? Letting her feelings about landscape and certain individuals come through on paper? After that breakthrough, too, O'Keeffe had the key to painting abstractions with the flowing movements, tonal colors and also feelings of the art she likes best next to her own: music. Her love for music goes way back in her life, back to the time when she was a girl on a Wisconsin farm. The household she grew up in was torn between loyalties to three religions. Her great-aunt, whom she disliked, frequently took her to the Congregational church, where there was neither music nor color. Her mother belonged to the Episcopalian church patronized by the rich and social. But there was another church in town with stained glass, the fragrance of incense, long white and black robes and crimson vestments, paintings on the walls, and music. The ensemble enthralled the youngster. It was her father's church, and though he was not a practicing Catholic, his brother, her uncle, was and would come around occasionally on a Sunday with his horses and buggy and take her off.

Following from such memories of O'Keeffe's, one can suppose that her sensitivity both to the land and to lines and tones of music and painting may have been alerted back in that experience of an awed child beset by what Paul Tillich calls the "sense of the unknown" in a Dominican Catholic church on the plains of the American Midwest. And if so, she must take her place as the perfect link between the religious and the Modernist and, now, Post-Modern eras, a connection not usually recognized because of her dislike for historical self-analysis. As far as she will go in describing what she has been after in her life work is to suggest, in many of her published writings, that there is some intangible quality to the natural landscape that stirs feelings in her and keeps luring her back to try to capture it in paint.[8] That is the landscape of O'Keeffe's mind and the minds of the American women artists of the late 1970s with whom I spoke, who stand square upon the real. There, too, is where one who wishes to ascertain how all their lives moved toward their art must begin. And if in the process of understanding O'Keeffe we must pass, as she did, through a more complicated gestalt of Modernist ideas, then at the end, as she did, we will come back to the land again.

In the beginning was the prairie: wheat country of southern Wisconsin, and a farmhouse that looked out upon a yard and six hundred acres of farmland extending on all sides toward what later O'Keeffe would find again in the Southwest—wind and emptiness.

Now, the thing about emptiness is that one can fill it: an empty landscape, an empty paper. One can make one's own mark. And in a wide, flat, empty landscape, one is centered wherever one is. As the French ambassador said to his hostess, "Where I sit is France." Beyond are only these other elements, two steady, two in constant motion: the earth and the sky always still, and light and the wind always changing. And black crows that swoop down from nowhere, to take the corn.

O'Keeffe's first recollections, as she has written in the memoir she published in 1977, are of her impression of light as she sat among heaped pillows on a quilt on the grass, and those extra-large white pillows themselves, like clouds brought down from the sky. Later on, she began to notice how in harvest time, as the twilit sky turned red, hay wagons would lumber in from the fields almost like elephants so ungainly and heavily laden on their small wheels. Later on, in the Southwest, she would paint humps of eroded hills in the distance like backs of elephants.

The family house was oriented to the outdoors. At some point her father, whose family house it had long been, attached to one corner of what was otherwise a standard, large white Colonial structure an architectural flourish:

a tall sort of tower with a cupola on top and big picture windows on two stories. The downstairs windows were filled with flowers and ferns, O'Keeffe remembers. Upstairs behind the other window lived that Congregational great-aunt, Jennie, whom she did not like but who pretty much ruled the household. Jennie was an old-timer of prickly fortitude. She had gone West by wagon in the old days, then traveled back East by ship long before the Panama Canal was built, and then ended up in the West again in the O'Keeffe household helping to raise seven children.

Though Mrs. O'Keeffe's face and manner do not come through very distinctly, there was one thing she had that comes through clear in all of her daughter's written and spoken memoirs: her love for adventure stories. She had energy left over, even on a full day, to read aloud for hours, that mother of seven. She read stories about Hannibal and Horatio, and Romulus and Remus, and the Leatherstocking Tales of the pioneer days, and stories of Kit Carson and Billy the Kid.

The tales of heroes, however, were all about men and boys. "Art," it was considered in those days, was for girls; indeed it was standard practice in many a family for the girls to paint a bit. So three sisters went off periodically to the nearby town of Sun Prairie for lessons. The Irish grandmother had had a gift for that kind of thing. There were, O'Keeffe has often recalled, two of her paintings in the house, one of two plums, done with a tiny brush, very neat and finished; the other of a moss rose alone on the canvas. Young Georgia found that extraordinary. She had never seen such a flower. That grandmother had quite a lot of other wonders on shelves between her windows: shells and things, some of which came from one ocean, some from another, some off the land beyond the oceans, all to be picked up and closely studied by an inquisitive child.

About those early art lessons, O'Keeffe has written: how she was set to work copying the perspective of a cube, shading a sphere, painting copies of horses and roses, standard art education of the time. At home, however, she began to try some harder problems. A sun, for example: how with yellow and pink to make a sun appear really to "shine"? How, with black, blue and lavender, to evoke the reality of a moonlit grove of trees? Something about these preoccupations, and working out these equivalents between colors and things seen, was so engrossing that by the time Georgia had finished eighth grade, at thirteen, she flushed a bird—to drag in a country metaphor—and brought it down with a shot. She asked a girl about her age what she was going to be when she grew up, and when the girl said she hadn't any idea, Georgia, who was already known in her family for wild notions, said *she* was going to be an artist.

That same year, her father fell ill, and the family sold the house and moved to Virginia, leaving the older two children behind to finish high school. Georgia was sent as a boarder to a Dominican convent offering the best instruction in the area.

Whatever else she learned from the nuns, we know O'Keeffe took a way of thinking about drawing that would become fundamental. The drawing sister set down the cast of a baby's hand and then scolded the student severely for rendering it too small. Not only too small but too dark. Too dark meant with too soft a pencil. With a soft, heavy black pencil, the artist can let the line flow. With a hard pencil, one has to go slowly, always in control. The sister gave her a hard pencil. It would take her a long time to break out of the hard-pencil kind of drawing, and even then the clear, cool mode of drawing would usually win out. Another lesson was learned the next year, though a curious child would have already found it out for herself. A teacher held up a jack-in-the-pulpit and folded back the purple hood to reveal the jack in all its rigidity, pointing out the colors inside, black-violet to greens and browns. From that exercise one deduced there was always another level or recess of nature to explore.

And then O'Keeffe was off to Virginia, leaving Wisconsin forever and the emptiness for a long time, and boarding in an Episcopal girls' school this time—her mother's faith—painting occasional studies of lilacs and corn, and taking tremendous long walks in the hills, looking always off toward the ridge of the Blue Ridge Mountains. She considered that after that point in her teens she never really lived as part of her family again, but was already on her own road. It led next to the Art Institute of Chicago. Here she was vividly impressed by exercises in figure drawing, especially nude male torsos with no arms, only the ribs, back, shoulders and shadows she would later discover in the land. No need for face, arms or legs to prove its identity. At that point, she contracted typhoid fever and went home to be nursed for many months, so that when she finally got going again she was twenty, with her hair cropped close and curly from the fever. That year she went to New York for the first time, to take courses at the Art Students League.

It was 1907, the year a twenty-seven-year-old Picasso, in Paris, put the last strokes on the *Demoiselles d'Avignon,* that crucial work in the evolution of Cubist Modernism. In America, a conventional nineteenth-century tradition still held: genteel dark paintings with glistening, surfacy brushwork, smoky shadows and golden auras, and characters in perspective and scale that imitated things as seen. Here and there was an eccentric working in obscurity: Ryder, a recluse in Manhattan; Eakins, in isolation in Philadelphia; Blakelock, in and out of mental institutions; Eilshemius, practically unknown. There was pride in the by now honored expatriates Whistler, Cassatt and Sargent, but still whatever there was of new in American art seemed to be being produced by the artists of the Realist group—Henri, Luks, Bellows.

Hardly visible were a few individuals whose idea and work would in time become a real bridge: in Paris, a small community of artists like Max Weber, Arthur G. Dove and Alfred Maurer, working in pre-abstract, pre-Cubist styles influenced by Matisse, Derain, Picasso. And in New York there was Stieglitz, home since 1890 from studies in Germany. The year Georgia O'Keeffe arrived in New York, he opened, in his Little Galleries of the Photo-Secession at 291 Fifth Avenue, his first exhibition not of photos but of paintings—by a woman artist, the mystic-romantic Pamela Coleman Smith.

For the time being, little radical talk would reach O'Keeffe in her classes at the League. She took anatomy from Kenyon Cox, apostle of old-school drawing techniques. Six years later, after the Armory Show, Cox would go on tour across the country protesting what he called the "cheap notoriety" given advanced European art. O'Keeffe's painting teacher was William Chase. In years to come he too would take off against the Modernists, especially Matisse, whom he would call a "charlatan and faker." But at the time he seemed a good enough teacher. First, he was the perfect model of a dandy-artist, wearing spats, gloves and a silk hat to class and so broadcasting the news that artists might have style in their bearing as well as in their brushwork. Next, he loved thick, glossy, rich application of paint and encouraged his students to lay it on vigorously. Third, he kept urging his students to make their works *interesting*. "Interesting" meant visually concise and striking: a composition with impact. O'Keeffe never would forget that word or the principle.

She was also already attracting attention for her own interesting looks. One student who would turn out to be a conventional portrait painter asked permission to sketch her, and when she said No he retorted that there was no point in her working so hard, that all she could hope to be was an art teacher, while he was going on to great things. That was Eugene Speicher, and while he was finishing the portrait that she finally consented to his doing, another student came into the room and asked them both to come along to the 291 gallery. Stieglitz, it happens, had been persuaded by Max Weber, just back from Paris, to show works by Matisse. The ship was delayed, the paintings were held up, so in the interim Stieglitz hung a group of watercolors of dancing figures by the sculptor Rodin.

Off the students went, and in the end O'Keeffe was doubly put off by the experience. The drawings were just lines and scratches to her. Quite as odd was the personality of the man the students had gone to bait: Stieglitz himself, volatile, either irascible or passionately enthusiastic, one could never tell in advance. That day the bait worked. Stieglitz became heated, and the sound of arguing voices drove O'Keeffe to an inner room to sit by herself till it was time to go home.

Teaching was indeed the career she was considering in those days. In Chicago she had taken courses in art history and lecturing, and her graduating report from the Art Institute said she would make an excellent teacher. As for the question of being an "artist," it seemed remote. There were only a few times she caught sight of something worth trying to get down in paint. One night she sat by the Hudson River, the water flowing black before her. Patches of black sky and pinpoints of stars shifted and vanished as branches of trees moved overhead. Another time, visiting in the Adirondacks, she looked across mist and cattails toward a stand of birches. Something about those white lines against fog also touched a chord.

Then it was time to go to work, and she put such thoughts out of her mind. "I began to realize that a lot of people had done this same kind of painting before I came along. It had been done and I didn't think I could do it any better. It would have been just futile." [9] She got a job drawing lace and embroidery for ads. It may be surprising to hear that she was not frustrated at that job. She learned a lot, especially how to work fast and turn out attractive patterns. Also, those linear designs for lace, repeated curves, scallops, stitches, were not so far off from petals of flowers as one might think.

It was not until the summer of 1912 that O'Keeffe sat in on a class at the University of Virginia given by Amon Bement, one of the progressive art educators being trained by Arthur B. Dow in his Teachers' College laboratory. Through Dow, who had been a student among the Post-Impressionists in Brittany and then assistant to Ernest Fenollosa in Boston, and through Bement, who read and was impressed by Kandinsky's *On the Spiritual in Art* when it appeared in English in 1914, O'Keeffe would be plunged into the gathering mainstream of Modernist esthetics.[10] A basic principle was that certain formal patterns of flowing lines and lights and darks placed in certain relationships could attain a harmony and power never found in nature and could play on the human nervous system their pure, passionless music. O'Keeffe's relief and pleasure was immediate at finding a kind of art that spoke directly to the senses and was rid of a sentimentality she had already learned to shun. She accepted an invitation from Bement to be his assistant the next summer and then took advantage of a job offer to get some teaching experience first. The post was in Amarillo, Texas. O'Keeffe was then twenty-five and had not yet painted a line she considered original or perhaps even "art."

Going to Texas provided the way forward, but it also provided O'Keeffe with a first return to the landscape of her memory. The country was wide, windy and empty, dusty and brown. Along the long lonely rails going east, west and north, cattle were transported, and the sound of their lowing and breathing and shuffling was a song-of-the-plains never ending.

She left the next summer, as agreed, and returned to Virginia. From that first summer of work with Bement dates the first work we know by her hand. It is simply a view out a tent door at night: five angular passages from midnight blue to pale blue, and a tent pole (ca. 1913, watercolor. In the museum of the University of New Mexico). Already she was ranging the countryside with friends or alone, setting off by train, getting off where the spirit moved her, walking all night if it pleased her, then painting when she got home.

The next year, O'Keeffe took Bement's advice and went to New York to study with Dow himself. She lived in a single student's room for four dollars a week, with only a single pot of red geraniums to bring the outdoors in. She took painting workshops and made some new friends; one of these was Anita Pollitzer, her favorite correspondent in years to come. She and Pollitzer apparently were already outstanding. While most of the class went on drawing from casts, these two took themselves off to a corner behind a screen, set up their own still lifes and flower arrangements and painted from nature.

Then one day she had an experience that affected her deeply, that she has often described to friends and that may have returned her for a moment, whether she was conscious of it or not, to those early Sundays of combined music and color in church. She was walking down a corridor and heard music coming from a classroom. She went in and found Bement playing records on a Victrola for his drawing students, who were trying to interpret the music with charcoal on paper. While O'Keeffe watched and listened, he played "The Volga Boatmen" with its solemn repetitions, then "Land of the Sky-Blue Waters," up in the treble. She joined the others in their drawing and later turned the matter over in her mind. The idea struck her, she has often said, with a particular sense of promise. One might go so far as to suppose she was possessed by one of those lost images "on which the heart first opened," here brought back to life and proffered to her, again, in the form of musical lines.

That idea of correspondences between past and present, remote and near, was a favorite subject with Alfred Stieglitz in those days. His 291 gallery, like the rest of the Eastern Seaboard, was still reverberating from the effects of the great Armory Show of the year before. O'Keeffe, teaching in Amarillo, had missed the event, but she had heard about it and was now receiving the Modernist message in her own way. As if to drive home the lesson that Cubist lines and angles were not only a radical avant-garde language but a universal human way of seeing the figure, Stieglitz mounted that year the first exhibition in this country of African primitive sculpture. O'Keeffe confided to her friend Pollitzer that if ever he should see and be interested in a work by her own hand, it would be the best thing she could imagine. For meanwhile, she had reached another impasse. "One day," her most oft-quoted quotation goes,

I found myself saying to myself . . . I can't live where I want to . . . I can't go where I want to . . . I can't do what I want to. I can't even say what I want to. I decided I was a very stupid fool not to at least paint as I wanted to and say what I wanted to when I painted, as that seemed to be the only thing I could do that didn't concern anybody but myself.[11]

Once more she returned to Texas and there, now twenty-eight, apparently exhausted with false starts and artificial solutions, set out to work in a way that would please only herself.

All day, she taught classes of Mexican children. The Dow-Bement method was simple in the extreme, indeed as used by some teachers might become a mere rote enterprise. Draw a box. Decide where to put the door. Where the windows. Let the instinct move the pencil. Was the idea not, though a decade in advance of it, approaching that of Surrealist automatic writing? Then O'Keeffe would shake off school and walk for a couple of hours. Eventually she would come back to her rented room, sit down on the floor with a drawing board propped against the closet door (a closed door with darkness behind, that was also an opening) and begin to draw. This, then, was the way to go.

She put aside color. That was Dow's first step. Charcoal first, to bring the mind down to basics. And then, as she sat there, there came the feeling of what O'Keeffe and other artists have described as a shape in the mind.[12] There were forms that coalesced in her imagination so instinctively and intimately "hers" that she had not thought of putting them onto paper. Gradually, as she has written, an extraordinary feeling of working in tune with herself took over. She was working into her own unknown, unhurriedly, increasingly confident of the rightness of her direction, at once fearful the gift might evaporate and full of elation. She wrote all this to Pollitzer and has described her feelings of growing mastery in her memoir of 1977.

She began sending the charcoals to New York and to Pollitzer, who wrote that they were filled with strong emotions and finally that the last batch, which arrived New Year's Day 1916, were so powerful they made her cry. These Pollitzer took to 291; the rest is art history. Still, it did not happen quite as some books say. It was winter twilight and the small rooms were quiet and gray. Stieglitz, who remembered Pollitzer as one of the many students who visited the galleries though more vivid and quick than most, agreed to look at the drawings. He took a long time, then began to speak. He told Pollitzer that he found them genuinely fine and that he would have known the artist was a woman because of the sensitivity of her arm motions. She was unusual, bigger in spirit than most, he said, and broad-minded as well. He instructed Pollitzer to relay the word that they were, as he put it, the purest, finest, sincerest things he had looked at in 291 in a long time, and that he would not be at all ashamed to show them. What he apparently did not say were the famous words, "Finally a woman on paper."[13]

It was spring by the time he actually hung them up, and by then O'Keeffe herself was back in New York with Dow. Informed that "Virginia O'Keeffe's" work was on view, she went down—one can hardly suppose as angrily as the stories say—and asked him to remove them, but since they were on the walls among examples by two other artists, both men, she agreed not to disturb them. When she left the city soon after, her correspondence with Stieglitz began. He also sent her prints of the first photos he had made of her, the first of the famous five hundred.

That winter she moved from Amarillo to the West Texas State Normal School in the small town of Canyon. The landscape was still emptier. Auto headlights would appear at night from over the horizon, vanish and reappear as they wound through low hills. Daytime, one saw trains coming from afar, lost then seen again between the hills. Elsewhere the land was so flat one could lose one's sense of direction. It was like an ocean with things cast upon it, rocks, sticks, bones, like the shells other oceans deposit on other beaches and a grandmother had gathered. She painted many watercolors that season, the famous *Blue Lines* that, thirty years later, historian F. S. C. Northrup would use for the frontispiece of his work on cultural correspondences, *The Meeting of East and West*. Some of the works, in vivid, naturalistic hues, showed the working out of abstract themes over four or five sheets, a fascinating novel idea. A red-and-yellow snail of an evening star might uncurl over a green-blue ground; borealislike arcs of blue might pulse over the horizon. There was a sense of flow and change to these works, an innocent directness, a relaxation in handling the brush. There was a softness of outline, a luminosity of color, a variety of image and stress and an evolving tension within each series that one would not, to tell the truth, see again in O'Keeffe's oeuvre, though it is possible some of the hundreds of abstract paintings she has gone on making but, for the most part, refused so far to exhibit may have some of these qualities.

Stieglitz hung the watercolors in the spring of 1917 and wrote her that he had done so. It was, at the same time, the swan song for his gallery. The war had begun, there was little interest in looking at modern pictures. His magazine

Camera Work folded. The last copies were loaded out onto the sidewalk to be blown into the gutter and walked over by soldiers marching up Fifth Avenue.

When O'Keeffe heard both pieces of news, she bought herself a railroad ticket and embarked. Stieglitz met her, took her to the empty gallery and rehung the show for her. As he himself wrote later, he had only one consolation in that season of disappointment: he had given the world a woman. And for her part, when she got back to Texas for her last season of teaching, she wrote Pollitzer that she had gone North for the sole and inescapable reason of seeing him.

A review in the last issue of *Camera Work* discussed her watercolors in Modernist terms. Other artists, the reviewer said, had tried to render the emotions usually aroused by music in terms of line and color, but they had failed. Here at last was one who succeeded.

"Stieglitz was the most interesting center of energy in the art world just when I was trying to find my way," O'Keeffe has said in an interview. "To have him get interested in me was a very good thing." [14] It was in fact the opening she was ready for. In the summer of 1918 she left Texas for good, returned to New York, joined the Stieglitz circle and applied herself to becoming what she had promised herself at the age of twelve in Wisconsin—a professional artist.

When they met, if O'Keeffe was at a turning point, so was he. His early life focused on Europe, and a first marriage had ended. He never crossed the ocean again (whether the fact that O'Keeffe did not do so until long after his death was due to her own diffidence or to his unwillingness to put her "Americanism" to the test is uncertain). The war put an end to his 291 gallery and to his hopes for *Camera Work,* but later he found other places to exhibit and promote his artists, and from 1929 until his death he dominated the scene from An American Place Gallery. A cosmopolitan, dramatic small figure of a man with flowing hair and penetrating eyes, Stieglitz had long sought a woman artist in whom he could believe. Several times, he thought he had found one. There was the poet-photographer Anne Brigman, a romantic pioneer who posed nude female models in the High Sierras for works she titled *Soul of the Blasted Pine* or *Cleft of the Rock.* [15] Stieglitz also promoted the work of the gifted Gertrude Käsebier, who specialized in atmospheric shots of mothers and children and like tender domestic groups. His other tastes were of a kind: romantic music, grand opera, Baroque art. His favorite painting was Rubens's *Portrait of Hélène Fourment in a Fur Coat,* that figure at once voluptuous, seductive and girlish. His own photographs reflected the same sensibility. The greatest were made in charged atmospheres, mist or snow, rain or fog, or streaked clouds. So in life he liked crowds and emotional relationships, impassioned patronage of artists he admired, excited conversation with his "American children," John Marin, Arthur G. Dove, Marsden Hartley, Paul Strand, Max Weber and others, and now Georgia O'Keeffe.

They lived first on Fifty-ninth Street; Stieglitz soon took her to his family summer home at Lake George, always full of family and guests. In 1924 they married and moved into the Shelton Hotel, from which she painted the bold, even phallic views of skyline tower-totems that, she has noted, made even the males look twice. Quickly she gained prominence in a world in which she was sheltered and admired as her work went through the fast-paced evolution so well known, beginning with a series of pale-colored, sky-vast abstractions, continuations from the Bement days rapturously received by reviewers: *Music, Pink and Blue, Blue and Green Music* and others. Around 1924 she began to do the marvelous flower paintings that caused such havoc in the responding machinery of her public. Inspiration for these may have been flower paintings by Joseph Stella or Francis Picabia's exploding Cubist flower forms, the works of Synchronist S. MacDonald Wright or close-up photos: Paul Strand's *Round Forms* or Imogene Cunningham's magnolias with erect stamens (or the moss rose and window flowers, close up and framed in a glass, of another day). But they spoke powerfully to the Freudian Zeitgeist and seemed to many to reveal for the first time the true nature of that perplexing creature, the Suffragette.[16] That her works brought high prices from the start, only ever to be rivaled by Marin's among the Stieglitz group, was a source of pride. However much her fortunes may have turned on the initial patronage of Stieglitz, that she was self-supporting was a measure of her own independent worth.

So that when her role at Lake George as house-organizer began to pall and certain other events perhaps made her feel not so primary as before, O'Keeffe made her move. In 1929 she traveled West for the first time in years. Though she was swept instantly into the madcap circle of Mabel Dodge Luhan in Taos, along with D. H. Lawrence and Frieda and Brett, she could look beyond the confusion of that household to see that the country still held for her what all the cosmopolitan riches of the cultural capital had not: a seductive emptiness.

She was not the first Easterner to be drawn to that scene. By 1915 there had already been some hundred artists painting away in Taos, escapees both from the city and from hackneyed European birch forests and Alpine fields.[17] John Marin took to the windswept slanted hills with brio and painted more than a hundred watercolors there, though what he caught—the multiple storms, gathering and dissipating aerial electricity—would reveal another desert from the one she saw. She knew it, and when he was there in 1929 and there was a question of her going out with him to paint, she would go at the same time but not to the same spot.

She went there a painter, one might say, but still in search of subject. There had been painters in the Stieglitz circle whose influence meant something: Hartley, whose landscapes with high horizon and wide, simple ground structures were close to those she would come to one day. Dove was always closest to her.[18] He too went the great round from nature to abstraction and then back to nature again, desperate, he said, for the infusion of life it afforded him. And she took in other ideas during the New York seasons that continued until Stieglitz' death in 1946. There was her fascinated discovery of early music with its polyphonic repetitions and overtones of solemn religious mood. There was the Asian-Indian fervor of the '20s and '30s when the Indian dancer Shankar opened the eyes of the West to his grave, stylized, awesomely ritualistic art form. Collections of Japanese art were being formed then; one of the best belonged to O'Keeffe's friend, the poet and Japanophile Louis Ledoux. With him, she spent hours over rare seventeenth-century black-and-white woodblocks and volumes on the stark, tragic Japanese Noh theater. Traces of all this eclectic experience would appear in years to come not only in her art but in the growingly stylized figure she would cut in the public eye. But none of this gave her her subject. That she would seek on her own. It was a long way home.

She worked outdoors there every summer until Stieglitz' death; thereafter, she lived only in the West. In her younger years, winter and summer, she went out painting for days on end, camping in the hinterland in winds so fierce they lifted the coffee out of her cup or carried off her easel, in sun so hot she had to creep under her car for shade, or air so cold she had to paint in gloves, standing on a rug. She painted the Black Hills and the Red Hills, red sunsets and black rocks, roses and crosses, death's heads and bones.

Eventually, in her great landscapes of the '40s and '50s, she found a way back behind Stieglitz' misty romantic atmospheres, to a world empty of all but light, stars, umber, black and gray cliffs. It was Willa Cather land, where our pioneer grandparents put down roots in the last days of the frontier.[19]

Was it a conscious intention on O'Keeffe's part to seek to rediscover so as to make art of their or other shadows in the West? One of the first paintings she made there was the famous *Black Cross*.[20] She has described how she walked out on one of her first evenings there, saw it silhouetted against the sunset and later painted it against an imaginary backdrop, a streak of blood-red light with blue above and a few stars, those pinpoints she often puts into her skies as if she has taken a stabilizing fix on them. "I might have been a Catholic if the

Single Lily with Red, *1928. Oil on canvas. 12" by 6¼". Whitney Museum of American Art, New York.*

Church had got to me early enough," she said once, "but my father was unpracticing and religion as practiced here is a thin black veil of sorrow covering everything. So somber, mournful and filled with tears."[21] Again it seems possible that a factor in O'Keeffe's psychology and so in her art has been that double childhood sense of isolation on the planet and alienation from once-

The Mountain, New Mexico, 1931. Oil on canvas. 30" by 36". Whitney Museum of American Art, New York.

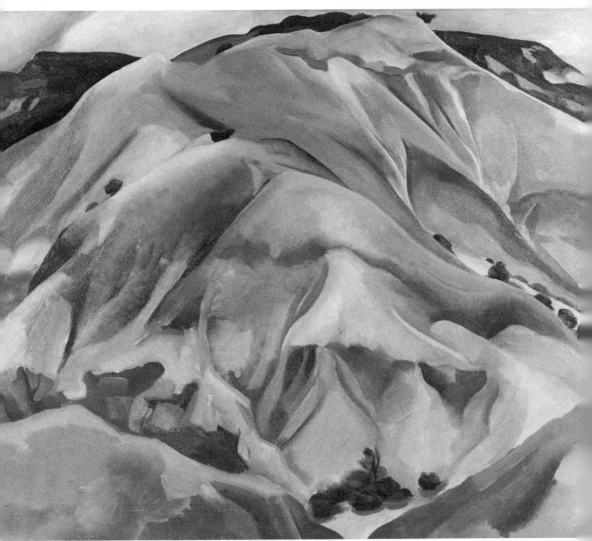

binding traditions and even individuals, so that when later she would catch a glimpse of that "something" that seems alive on the desert she would go out to meet it as inevitably as some forms of life seek light. And in that way she would have come to be the Teacher for many today who seek a reunion not necessarily mystical, but still not explainable in words, in the natural world. For such seekers, especially the young who make up such a proportion of her devotees today, she seems to have provided both a personal image and works that touch upon two fundamental human intuitions about the nature of reality. These are that there exists motion (in the case of her person: a life of action, self-determination, will; in the case of the world: changing lights, shadows, wind, forms in mutation, music and the breath of life) and that there exists a permanent ground (in the case of her person: ritualistic, timeless costume, silence, the austerity of her isolation and manner of life; in the case of the world: stars, earth and bones).[22] And in this way, Georgia O'Keeffe has provided for a world in need of such things both an active model and a reassurance of the permanence of some values and ideas.

All the same, even considering all she has offered our time, there is a certain distance of radical experiment that O'Keeffe never went (unless, again, those still unexhibited canvases tell another story). In that respect she is no different from Mary Cassatt. Even in the '30s and '40s there were critics who saw her oeuvre for what it was: personal and full of nuance but not outstandingly original. During the years of radical adventure of the New York School, she stayed aloof from it. Her "rediscovery" was to come with her exhibition at the Whitney Museum in 1970, when the young seekers I spoke of above and Color-Field artists looking for American antecedents to their own esthetic fell on her work with joy.

Those works, for one thing, are always "finished," combining her characteristic cool drawing with color intimations of a sourceless white light, symbol in past times of eternity but now simply a quite literal description of what she calls the far away. These works are not put into paint until the image is clear in her head. She may jot down some notations no more than an inch high before she begins to work. But to start right in with the brush as she did in those restless watercolors of 1917 and '18 is a procedure she no longer follows.

Are there recesses of feeling and intuition she has not searched for her precious lines, I wondered? In my opinion, no later work of hers has equaled in power the Black Iris of 1926, so shocking and also tragic in its dark-fringed anatomy. What about Penitente music, I wondered, indigenous to her region, that seems as laden as the iris with mortality and cannot even offer the alleviating stayingness of the flower or the hilltop cross? She has never drawn or painted that music, though once a year the flagellants assemble on a hill behind her Abiquiu house and come down three or four times a day, chanting over and over their four bars of dirge. When they march, she is no casual observer of the scene. She stays indoors, behind the curtains. That music has power to hurt. Only once or twice she tried to get it down on paper, she told me. But she got only as far as a few lines of pencil.

"Do you wish you had done more?" I asked. "Are there things you wish you had done?"

She looked at me with her eyes plenty sharp at age ninety and asked whether there were things in my life *I* wished I had done.

And I said, "Of course."

Women
of the
First Wave:
Elders
of the
Century

INCLUDING

HEDDA STERNE

AND

SARI DIENES

Alma Thomas, eldest of this group, like Georgia O'Keeffe was born as the frontier era in America was coming to an end. Child of a black family in the Deep South, she was the most vulnerable of all the artists here to that first break in the national fabric, the Civil War. Yet she lived into, was open to and, indeed, came into her creative own only in the present decade in the idiom called Color Field. So the threads are woven between which women artists, like their male peers, have their location.

All the women of this group were formed in that era of cultural growth and idealism that saw the United States opened to migrating populations from Asia and Europe, to be melded, here, into One People. But we know that cultural expansion, tending toward a universal community of arts and ideas, was paralleled by political expansion that, having fulfilled itself on land in that same frontier-building, reasserted itself in the Spanish-American War the year a number of these artists were born, only finally to exhaust itself in the Indo-chinese adventure of the 1970s. That countercurrent expressed itself also in early exclusion acts against Asians, then Eastern Europeans and finally, during the McCarthy era, against political radicals of all stripes. Meanwhile other disintegrative forces operating in the world—wars, depression, class struggle, poverty, lack of education—also had repercussions here. These tumultuous events, as I have suggested, did not always have upon women artists the same impact they did on the males. Memories these women share today are of those early trials but also of other things: the world of colors and shapes into which they awakened with a sense of special giftedness, from which they were driven into psychic exile during painful years of struggle, but into which they have at last found not only reintegration but a new life of the imagination on a scale hardly anticipated.

Many distinguished Americans still living today, whose careers began before the great mid-century turning point of War and Bomb, might have added their tales to those told here. Among them are Janice Biala, Minna Citron, Dorothy Dehner, Ethel Edwards, Ruth Gikow, Dorothea Greenbaum, Loren MacIver, Agnes Martin, Maud Morgan, Ethel Schwabacher, Charmion von Wiegand and others. Hedda Sterne, for example, was born in Bucharest in

1916 and made her way here after apprentice years in Paris and Vienna. In New York she showed first in 1941 at Peggy Guggenheim's Art of This Century Gallery and had the first of a long career of shows at the Parsons Gallery in 1943. Her account of a solitary and unshakable determination might be echoed by the others.

"I spent my days drawing, years before I knew there was such a thing as art. I was given books on the great painters before I could read. The one thing I wanted was to be a great painter. In my childishness, I thought of it as one word—*greatpainter*.

"I drew on any scrap of paper I could find. One day my father brought me some large pieces of white paper. To this day I am awed by a piece of beautiful white paper." Is this perhaps one of those "first great images" of which Camus spoke, that after many permutations offered itself up in new form as Sterne's purified mature idiom? I take "beautiful white paper" in some way to be the source of these cold snowfields lit by pale lemon suns; these arctic glacier fields flecked with pin-high dark trees; and these, her most beautiful works— drawings of lettuce on white canvas, whorls and skeins of leaves, rippled, ingathered and outward-flowing at the same time, full of correspondences like Leonardo's studies of hair and water, or photos of galaxies.

This artist's life, dress, living space and use of materials are marked by the same rule: to shun or discard the nonessential. She has parables to tell that may reveal the cost in pain of her kind of discipline. "From my earliest days, my interest was in training myself. In my teens, I did a lot of backpacking. One time we were hiking and came down terribly thirsty. Finally we came upon a stream and everyone else drank. But I kept my thirst and suffered one hour more waiting for the good beer ahead. Also it was to steel myself. . . .

"A legend I heard as a child: There was a master builder who built a beautiful church. For the church to stand, he had to wall his sweetheart into the foundations. He did so, even as she was weeping and begging to be spared. And all the time, his heart was breaking. . . ."

Like many of her contemporaries, Sterne found New York of the '40s, that melting pot of Surrealism, Expressionism and Neo-Plasticism out of which the "new" American art was to come, a place of inspiration. "It was brilliant. I met many of the refugee immortals. I went to the Museum of Modern Art and saw the Calder hanging in the stairway. Like a child's dream! I was beside myself with delight. In this country, I thought, *they*—meaning the Establishment— take such a thing seriously!

"The first time I went to Peggy Guggenheim's house it was in November of 1941 in the forenoon. She came into the room wearing a pink satin negligee trimmed with maribou. 'Do you want to see Max Ernst?' she asked after a

A PORTFOLIO OF COLOR

Part I

The black-and-white passages of this book explore events in time. These color pages can be said to make time stop. For in this cross section of works, all save two made in the last few years, all are wrenched from their makers' lives, as it were, to be grouped with others with which they bear formal relationship. And so if, in the text portions, we pursue however indirectly the issue of "women's art," in these color pages it is possible to regard the works "merely" as products of mainstream Western art. For that reason, we have felt free to add examples by a few important artists not elsewhere discussed at length in this book.

This diversified, free-flowing mainstream has been watered by many springs in this century—Post-Impressionism and Cubism; Non-Objective abstraction and Constructivism; Dada, Surrealism and Abstract-Expressionism; and isms still not given textbook titles. Theories about the nature of light, space, human anatomy, the human mind, the forms of human society; evidence about events on the nuclear and cosmic scales, about the moon's surface and dwellings of primitive peoples—all these make up the present gestalt in which these works are founded. Of steel, Plexiglas and the earth itself, as well as the age-old mediums of oil paint, wood, fiber and clay, these are the works of American artists—gender aside—whose reach, power and grace have expanded dramatically to fit the circumstances of their liberated environment.

Mary Cassatt. First Caress, *1891. Pastel on paper, 30" by 24". New Britain Museum of American Art, New Britain, Connecticut. Harriet Russell Stanley Fund.*

LIGHT: Hardly an artist in this century has failed to deal in some way with the uncanny effects of light on solid bodies in space—light that both dissolves and clarifies the contours of forms. For Cassatt to paint light frazzling the surface of flesh or cloth was an adventure into an esthetic unknown. Bishop, who came along later, could employ the more advanced tool of Cubism to describe light-broken space. But both artists begin with and return with tenderness to the human figure in its classic, anatomically correct appearance.

Isabel Bishop. Nude Reaching, 1963. Oil on canvas, 28" by 35". Indianapolis Museum of Art, Indianapolis, Indiana. Gift of the National Academy of Design. Henry Ward Ranger Fund.

Georgia O'Keeffe. Yellow Calla, 1926. Oil on fiberboard, 9⅜" by 12¾". National Collection of Fine Arts, Smithsonian Institution, Washington D. C. Gift of the Woodward Foundation.

NATURE REDUCED TO ESSENTIALS: Though O'Keeffe was a painter mostly of the outdoors, and Lundeberg has preferred to work in her studio, neither has forsaken the persistent search for correspondences between shapes and hues in the world of nature—flower, mountain, plain, sweep of shining air. For Lundeberg, in her Post-Surrealist days, that list would include images that reveal the mind of the artist (see cover and page 174). For O'Keeffe, it would include the tones of music (see page 83) and, perhaps only unconsciously, forms of anatomy.

Helen Lundeberg. Desert Coast, 1963. Oil on canvas, 60" by 60". Collection the artist.

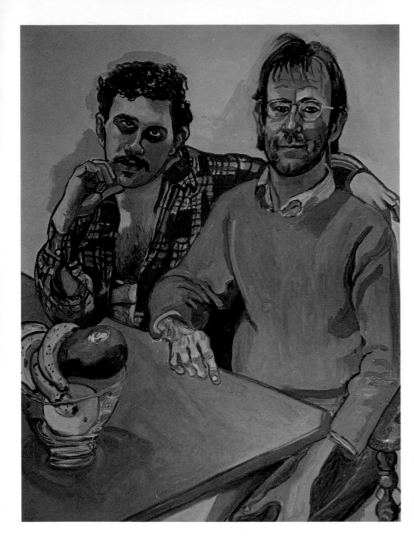

Alice Neel, Geoffrey Hendricks and Brian, 1978. Oil on canvas, 44" by 34". Collection the artist.

Joan Semmel. Hand Down, 1977. Oil on canvas, 44¼" by 62¼". Museum of Fine Arts, Houston, Texas. Gift of Christine Connal.

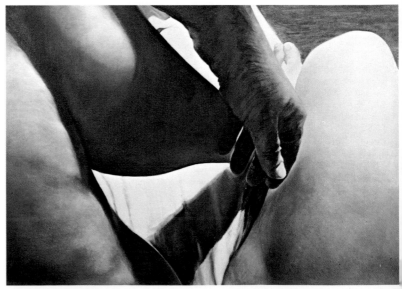

A PORTFOLIO OF COLOR

Part II

If pundits of another time proposed that to make works of heroic scale or triumphant outline, one had to have the wings of the male (some used other terms), then one might say that the makers of the works that follow are wingèd for victories of their own. These aggressive, grandiose, gaudy or glamorous works, these steel trees, soaring rainbows of paint and cloth, huge light-defined circles and tunnels, are all modes of reaching out and taking a grip on the natural world. They are the visible expressions of strong feelings: ambition, longing, command. They are the tokens of dominion over land, wind and light. If they are rooted, as in some cases we know, in intimate memories (Nevelson's Russian birch trees, Truitt's spot of sun on a ceiling, Stone's vanishing houses), they also can challenge the public at large unaware of those private meanings, simply by their presence on the urban horizon or in the deeps of a snowy landscape.

Since Japanese prints taught the Post-Impressionists to draw what the eye in its queer focusing and rejecting "sees," many artists have followed that mode. Here, anatomy, furniture, space and color are all given a twist by Neel's powerful distorting lens (top left). Semmel works changes not on her subject—still drawn in classically "correct" form—but on the observer, who is drawn into the aperture of the artist's own eye.

STEEL TREE, MOUNTAIN PEAK AND RAINBOW: Three images on the contemporary horizon: Louise Nevelson's complex of seven black-painted Cor-Ten steel figures (opposite), called *Shadows and Flags,* constitutes the new Louise Nevelson Plaza in the Wall Street area of lower Manhattan, 1978. (Detail shown, 71' high.) Beverly Pepper's *Pi* (above), 1974–75, displayed upon a hillside in her workplace in Umbria, Italy. Stainless steel, 5'9" by 14' by 3'3". Now owned by the Indianapolis Museum of Art, Indianapolis, Indiana. Gift of the Alliance of the Indianapolis Museum of Art. Since 1971, Corita Kent's *Rainbow* (below), on the Boston Gas Company's liquefied natural gas storage tank, has been a landmark on the skyline outside Boston, Massachusetts. 158' high; 73,374 square feet of painted surface.

Nancy Holt. Sun Tunnels, 1973–76. Each tunnel 18' long, weighing 22 tons. Concrete on buried concrete foundation. Great Basin Desert, Utah.

Patricia Johanson. Ixion's Wheel, 1969. Acrylic on plywood, 1300' in circumference. As installed, State University of New York, Albany, New York.

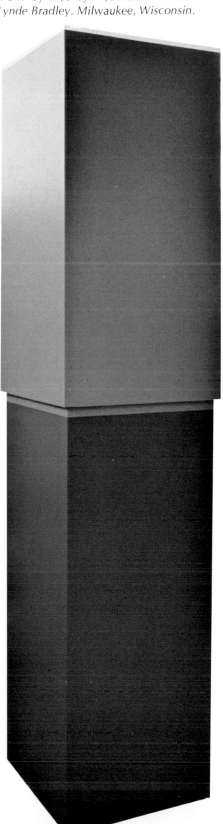

LIGHT: These artists literally draw light into their three-dimensional structures. Through the ends and pierced sides of Holt's Stonehenge-like work, sun and stars alternately beam their rays. Johanson's sunlit round refers to the Greek myth of Ixion chained to a fiery wheel in Hades. *Summer Sentinel* might be the essence of a green forest: Truitt would have us see it changed hour by hour by circling daylight (see page 324).

Mary Miss. Perimeters/ Pavilions/Decoys, 1978. Project includes three towers—18' high (left), 15½' high, 13' high; underground structure with 16'-square opening, 7' deep, 40'-square space underground; wood and earth. As installed, Nassau County Museum of Fine Arts, Roslyn, New York.

Donna Dennis. Station with Lighted Interior, 1974. Wood, cellulose compound, paint, electric light fixtures, 74" by 43" by 32". Holly Solomon Gallery, New York.

Jackie Winsor. #1 Rope, *1976. Wood and hemp. 40" by 40" by 40". San Francisco Museum of Modern Art, California. Purchased with funds from National Endowment for the Arts, and the New Future Fund Drive.*

MEMORIES MADE THREE-DIMENSIONAL: Entering the ground, walking through a tunnel, standing under an opening to the sky; or wrapping and wrapping hemp around wooden stakes—actions like these are pantomimes whose meanings we may learn from the artist's own reminiscences (see page 436). And then, enlarging on private experience, many artists invoke a Humboldtean richness of other sources. In her catalogue for this project, Mary Miss quotes texts on military fortifications, North American Indian games, Kansas homesteads, Islamic courtyards and English gardens (see page 393; also note 33, page 486).

Hedda Sterne. Lettuce
Metamorphosis, 1967. Ink on
cotton.

while, which for me was like asking, 'Do you want to see Dürer?' She took me
upstairs and there in bed, under a cover made of the same pink maribou, was
Max, holding a lorgnette, reading and looking like a bird of prey.

"Another time I told her I was a little lonely. 'Come tomorrow!' she said.
I did so and found a party for about five hundred people. I sat on a chair in the
corner. In my experience in Rumania, parties were only given for weddings
and funerals. I had no small talk at all. But soon a quiet middle-aged man with
glasses came and sat beside me. It was Mondrian. The party was for him. And
like me, he was completely bewildered.

"Then there were the '50s—the period of getting off the shoulders of these
giants. The so-called 'Americanization' of American art. I believe, however,
that isms and other classifications are misleading and diminishing. What entrances me in art is what cannot be entrapped in words."

There is, also, the artist who evades being trapped not only in words but
in the lineaments of a single theme. "I had four big shows with the Betty
Parsons Gallery," says Sari Dienes, age eighty, her white-gold hair standing
out around her face like a nimbus."And at the end, Betty said, 'Sari, you
haven't created an image.' And that's my situation in the art world. These
things are factually so, but I am not bitter. If I were, I couldn't work as I do."
Dienes has made too much: prints and collages, ceramics and, in the '50s,
famous rubbings of gravestones, manhole covers, gratings and the cracks in
city streets that set off much new interest in that kind of work. Dienes elabo-
rates instead of purifying. Through her mind and hands, images and
materials—shiny gold Mylar, burnt wood, broken bottles, color Xeroxes, as-

Sari Dienes. Bone-fall, *1973. Bone and string. Collection the artist.*

semblages of bones—keep up a steady flow like time that only now and then compacts into a "moment remembered."

She was born in Debrecen, Hungary, came here in '39, worked once in Paris and London with Ozenfant but better said has been a part of all the avant-gardes: of art, music, poetry. Most fervently today, she is part of the Women in the Arts Movement, which in the autumn of '78 feted her birthday with a film by the much younger Feminist artist Martha Edelheit, called *Hats, Bottles and Bones*. But it may be in a walk around Dienes's house in the Catskill Mountains outside New York that one gets closest to her nature. Here is her *Rock River,* fed by a *Bottle Stream* that runs by a *Musical Gazebo* to the foot of a *Fuji*—a brick volcano with a pine tree on top. Her output of years swells the confines of the house itself. One of her favorite works is *Bone Fall.* "I collected bones for years. Twenty years! Then all of a sudden, I strung them all up. I'd like a museum to take *Bone Fall.* That's the kind of thing you make only once in your life. You can't go on making bone constructions over and over.

"When I was a little girl, I was going to be a pianist. At fourteen I got a touch of TB and the doctor said a pianist's life would be too hard. I'm glad. Now I still make music, but of another kind.

"The first time I read a book on Zen I said, This is how I've felt all my life. You can't learn Zen. You have to have it in you. Then I met John Cage. I said, I had to come to America for no other reason than to meet John Cage.

"I went to Japan to live in a land where Zen is fundamental. You can do anything in Zen. You can go right. You can go wrong. There is no Way. There is no How. There is no Where.

"Through Zen, I became disinterested in psychology, in looking for motives. Why and How are not fruitful. Why that? Why that? It's an endless chain going nowhere."

Dienes' epiphanal works? *Snow Paintings.* "You pour the paint on the snow and take photographs while it melts. All the time it melts, it changes."

Here, then, are others who have changed yet kept their nature, as water does when it freezes, mists, melts, then courses.

Lee Krasner

BORN 1908, NEW YORK CITY

*I am never free of the past. I have made it crystal
clear that I believe the past is part of the present
which becomes part of the future.*

—LEE KRASNER
East Hampton, New York, 1977

Lee Krasner, Abstract Expressionist painter, collagist and survivor, at seventy-plus talks that way: pushing ahead, driving to a new end. It is her mode of operation, in person and work. The life force, whatever that may be, reasserts itself even over its own past to get where it has to go.

She works in concentrated spells, then for a time does little but take care of chores and wait for a return of the fire. Those postwork, postexhibition fallows are not especially enjoyable. When I visited Krasner one summer day after the winter of her 1977 show at the Pace Gallery in New York, she was in the throes of one. I asked whether it felt good to have done a good job and to let down now.

"I'd give anything to get back. That's the height. Life is beautiful at moments like that."

I asked whether it felt good to have been recognized, at last, as one of the major figures of the Abstract Expressionist movement, twenty years after Jackson Pollock's death and as many of fighting her way out of the box of identification with him.

"No, it doesn't make me feel great. It's thirty years late. Too bad it didn't happen thirty years ago. It would have been of help then. But I have had obstacles and I have dealt with them. And I have come through."

Krasner has come through with works that are not easy—any more than their maker with her heavy voice, her sullen, frequently contemptuous evaluations and ironic summings up, is an easy person. There are few who admire her who have not been scathed by her, as her enemies are continually. Hypocrisy and any kind of limiting prejudice or provincialism affront her. For some

100

younger women artists she has little regard: their roads to success were easy compared to hers and she names and dissects them with sarcasm. "But there are not many men I'm chummy with, either." But then when that mood passes, the same force drives Krasner on to a new agreement, a motherly feast tendered to a batch of friends, for example, or a pursuit of thoughts, sitting on the porch of her East Hampton house looking out over the marshes. At such times, one feels that the bitterness that has boiled up in her is no irrational reaction but a voicing of desolation that things so frequently fall apart, that the center—of art, friendship, the community of artists—has failed again to hold. It is a matter of need with Krasner that certain forms created by human beings be held together or reforged when they fail or self-destruct. Therefore, not to give up the past, to carry it along whether it is a burden or a light, is a fundamental of the belief which amounts to a religion with her: in continuity.

Continuity is the rule in Krasner's home in East Hampton. There is the Victorian clapboard house in a small field backing up to marshes and then the bay. Mimosa saplings planted when she and Jackson Pollock bought the place are full-grown now, and in July the lawn beneath is covered with their yellow-fringed mauve brushes. On a sight line from the back steps to the marsh is a clump of boulders Pollock hauled there to create a middle distance; wildflowers spindle from between them. There are differences from what used to be, however: indoors, hanging in the living room, facing the immense dining table (English eighteenth century; to seat fourteen in a circle), are works not by Pollock but by Lee Krasner: two self-portraits from her youth; collages from the 1950s; and *Fragments from a Crucifixion* from 1962, an enormous burnt-umber-and-white violence painted in sweeping strokes so wide and rapidly applied that their edges are furred with spray. The whole surface is drawn into the turmoil, yet in the four corners the strokes bend inward, rushing back upon themselves into a vast oval, enclosing the storm and the deed.

Another way of stating her belief might be: in rebirth. Much has actually been lost of her past work. Most of her early drawings and paintings were destroyed in a fire. Twice she has gone back into what survived and torn or cut the work up for collage. In '51, not liking the reception given her first exhibition, or perhaps not liking the work itself, she cut up the canvases, combined them with black shards of cloth and torn paper, and turned out a number of fiercely vertical compositions with titles expressive of a will not to lie down: *Milkweed . . . Burning Candles*. Pollock died in '56, and, much as Krasner would like to avoid it, it is not possible not to see her subsequent work except as catalyzed by will to go on. There was a sudden burst of life-proclaiming works: *Earth Green . . . Upstream*. Then an antiphonal swing back to incorporate the past

Present Perfect, 1976. Collage on canvas. 50" by 38¼". The Pace Gallery, New York.

(*Fragments from a Crucifixion* falls here) before another surge forward: *Bloom . . . Primeval Resurgence . . . Palingenesis.*

Was it from that last title, with its linguistic trace of "palimpsest," that, when she found a cache of drawings done thirty years before, she took her next theme? The works she turned out in '73, in collage, may have been the most ruthless declaration of the right to life of this era. The early Cubists used collage to play a metaphysical game upon the card table of a picture-surface, dealing out bits of the "real"—cigarette papers, bits of type, photos, textiles—to combine with the unreal. Robert Rauschenberg considered he was doing a great deed of deviltry in 1955 when he erased a de Kooning drawing to show that the past was effaced. Pollock himself, in '51, took some old drawings on Japanese paper and tore them up to make a papier-mâché sculpture. And many artists now use collage in a didactic way, to declare the continuation of certain concepts like, for example, "women's work" with cloth. But for Krasner in this instance, collage was both sword and plowshare, a handle to savage, and salvage, the early works by cutting them into lots and rooting them into new compositions. Enormous, full of action, these have something of the character of that banner of a rejuvenated civilization, Paolo Uccello's *Battle of San*

Romano—a painting, incidentally, admired by Gorky, Krasner, Pollock and others in the early Abstract Expressionist days.

Two very great figures of that time paid her the compliment of confidence if there were others who failed to reckon with her refusal to stay submerged. One was Piet Mondrian, who, in New York in the early 1940s, stood in front of one of her paintings and said, "You have a very strong inner rhythm. Never lose it." The other was Pollock. When she was suffering, as she sometimes did in the years when she was married to him, from a plenitude of troubles, he said to her more than once, "Think of it as a storm, and that it will be over eventually." And then would come her time.

It is amazing, today, to hear Krasner talk about her childhood. Every house is in place. The name plates bear the old names. Trees lift their branches where they did. The flowers still bloom in the fields.

She lived in Brooklyn, but not the Brooklyn of stereotypes.

"Where I lived there were beautiful flowers. I loved it. A back yard with irises. My fleurs-de-lis—my favorite flower. And wild daisies. Bridal veil. And lilac. And roses on the fences, and in all the back yards.

"I would walk to school through the lots filled with buttercups. There was a farm with a pail and cows. Smells. Warm milk in the bucket. I hated the taste, but for Mother and the family it was a treat. So I would go through the fields to get there.

"Or we would walk over a little wooden bridge.

"There were old houses—traditional saltboxes. Miss Reagen lived in one with a picket fence. Across the street, the Millers', with a vegetable garden. Trees? Not so many. An oak in our front yard. Next door, where Cissy and Mabel lived, a chestnut. I loved that chestnut, especially when it was in bloom. Ruth Jacobsen lived in the last house. I can't seem to see what tree her house had, but that chestnut! Every time I see another one, I remember that chestnut.

"That is what it was like. Rural. Not a city. To say East New York now is to mean the biggest slum area. But my early recollections of it are different. Not until I went to Washington Irving High School in Manhattan, on the subway, did I have contact with a 'city.' "

It was a Russian immigrant family from a forest village near Odessa by the Black Sea. Lenore was the fifth of six children, the first one born in this country. The household languages, when she was growing up, were Russian and Yiddish, only gradually English. Life was hard. "Yes, we were poor. Everyone had to work. Every penny had to be dealt with." The mother, herself an orphan, and father worked in the family fruit, vegetable and fish store. An elder sister cooked and was the caretaker of the young.

103

"Mother—she gets up and goes to work, and comes home at night. On Sundays she's tired and resting. She was loving but not demonstrative. She would back what I wanted. Father—I adored him. But he was very remote. He told stories. Marvelous tales! About forests. Beautiful, beautiful stories, always like Grimm. Scary things. The sleighs in winter going out with the dogs, and there would be someone standing in the road to stop them. The forest, and always the snow, and sleighs. A foreign world to me. I'm in Brooklyn, remember!

"I'd sit close to him and he'd tell the stories. Oh, I was terribly scared at night, scared of the dark, still am. Maybe those stories . . ."

One of the few family legends concerned an old aunt of his who had come from the city to their village in the forest, to help celebrate their wedding. She was so great a personage the bridal couple had to give up their bed to her. She was tough, dominant and nearly immortal. When she died at 103, she had outlived four husbands. Krasner is fond of that story; she also recalls hearing about her paternal grandmother who could tell fortunes and prophesy the future. Something of both fear of darkness and instinct for prophecy combined at a point to produce a Proustian complex of event and memory in Krasner's mind. Once, she was about five, she was standing in a dark hall, she thought she saw something jump over the banister and land on the floor beside her. She was so frightened she could only say, "Half man half beast . . ." Years later, at a bad time, she would paint a very strange work titled *Prophecy,* and only then, when events drove her into analysis and she began to question the meaning of the painting, would she remember the vision and the words she had used to describe it.

Whatever there was of classical culture was carried into the house by Krasner's elder brother, a student of chemistry and surrogate father for the young ones. He liked music and brought Caruso records. Eventually he brought books Lenore would read, Dostoevski, Gogol, Gorki, and her first literary passion, Maeterlinck. But her first impressions of literary and musical form and solemn heightened feeling were undoubtedly gained in the synagogue. It was an Orthodox family with all that that implies in patriarchal law and matriarchal dominion over the household. Religion was the tie that bound this family, literally rootless, to ancient times.

"I went to services at the synagogue, partly because it was expected of me. But there must have been something beyond, because I wasn't forced to go, and my younger sister did not. So some part of me must have responded. On the High Holy Days you fasted. Yom Kippur. I fasted. I didn't shortcut. I was religious. I observed.

"And then in the house there were plenty of Hebrew books, Bibles, the books you took to the synagogue. I was going to Hebrew school and working with those books. I don't remember clearly, but there may have been gold margins and big letters. Today, my orange and alizarin orange is my involvement with manuscripts and illuminations. Way, way back my involvement with them began."

Somewhere Krasner saw ancient Scriptural texts with decorative illuminations; later on, her taste for these was reinforced by Persian manuscripts with Arabic calligraphy. Eventually, as she says, the love she felt for those compositions with streaks of color blazing through gray-black fields of handwriting would come out in her work.

At the time, she was pugnacious in defense of what she believed. In high school she adamantly refused to sing a traditional Christmas carol. Some years later, on the other hand, events had destroyed her orthodoxy. She was an art student then, on a high of German philosophy. Nietzsche and Schopenhauer showed her the way to go. She arrived home on a Sabbath when her parents were sitting having tea with a friend, "came in like a charging banshee," and declared she was through with religion. There were, as she sees it now, two reasons for the defection, which was not only a turning away but the beginning of a search for another source of emotional richness. One was the reading. The other was anger about the place of women in Judaism.

"The beginnings were there in the synagogue, and I am told to go upstairs. I have never swallowed it to date. Much later, I had a running bout with Barney Newman about my objections to the role of women in Judaism. We battled till he died; he said I misunderstood and I said I understood loud and clear but I objected. Then one time he asked me whether I had seen the plans for his synagogue. I asked why I should see them.

" 'Because it'll settle the argument,' he said.

" 'Well, and where are the women in your synagogue?' I asked.

" 'You'll see! You'll understand!' he said. 'Right on the altar!'

"And I said, 'Never. *You* can sit on the altar and get yourself slaughtered. I want the first empty seat on the aisle!' "

School, on the other hand, provided that weaning away of a younger generation from the previous one's ethnic identification for which the American educational system was set up. One activity useful for the making of good citizens was making maps, making the American terrain concrete and seeable.

"Every time I see a Jasper Johns map, I remember how crazy I was for doing that thing. We had to figure out what each state was known for. I got tiny empty capsules and filled them with wheat or whatever and glued them onto a piece of beautiful blue paper. I had drawn the states in colored crayon.

And I just loved that blue. It's a strange thing, but later in life it became very hard for me to paint a picture using blue. It just doesn't come easy."

That map, and a teacher named Wollrath, are what Krasner remembers of those days. He was eccentric enough to think girls should be allowed to play baseball with the boys. "Togetherness like that was my kind of thing!"

Why Krasner decided about then to be an artist she has no idea, but it was to that end that she applied to the all-girl Washington Irving High School in Manhattan. There she majored in art, and there again what caught her imagination was a project that involved putting together elements from nature.

"We drew big charts of beetles, flies, butterflies, moths, insects, fish and so on. We would get models of a fly or butterflies in boxes with glass tops. Then it would be up to us to pick the size of sheet or composition board and the range of hard pencils and to decide how many to put on the page. And we would get anatomical assists from books. I loved doing those!

"Much later, when I was in the WPA, the very first job I was given was to assist a geology professor doing a book on rocks. There I was with a hard pencil, and what came to me was the memory of all those butterflies and beetles, only now in more abstract form. I was happy as a lark doing that stuff!" All those happy early drawings were part of the collection destroyed when her parents' house burned down later. "I was just developing my hand by drawing. It felt normal. It didn't feel like making 'art.' "

In 1926, at eighteen, she went on to the Women's Art School of Cooper Union, where she studied traditional drawing from life and casts and excelled so that a teacher asked her to do plates for a text on the subject. "At both those schools there had only been women, so there didn't seem anything unusual about being an artist and a woman."

The next step, however, was her first away from the easy givens of school days. Krasner chose the conservative National Academy of Design, where she was a square peg from the beginning. Was it as a challenge that she presented, in fulfillment of an assignment, one of the self-portraits that hang in her house today? It shows no conventional salon image but a stalwart, muscular young woman in overalls, painting outdoors in a grove of trees. Onto one she has nailed a mirror. The idea of painting oneself in the open air was a surprise. She was suspected of having trumped up the outdoor background and was put on probation.

In 1929 the Museum of Modern Art opened and began to show Picasso, Matisse, Braque and other Advanced French artists. "It was an upheaval for me, something like reading Nietzsche and Schopenhauer. A freeing . . . an opening of a door. I can't say what it was, exactly, that I recognized, any more than some years earlier I could have said why it was I wanted to have anything to do with art. But I know one thing, beyond the esthetic impact: seeing those French paintings stirred my anger against any form of provincialism. When I hailed those masters I didn't care if they were French or what they were. Nowadays again, when I see those big labels, 'American,' I know someone is selling something. I get very uncomfortable with any kind of chauvinism—male, French or American."

Krasner went back to class and turned out a picture in light bright colors; her teacher Leon Kroll told her to go home and "take a mental bath." Painting light when convention and the males ordained dark had landed both Mary Cassatt and Georgia O'Keeffe in trouble before her—a minor example of the relevance of psychology to esthetics. Beyond issues of esthetics, however, it was clear from that and other evidence that, as Eugene Speicher had long before informed Georgia O'Keeffe, males held the prerogatives. A student who wanted to paint a still life with fish at the Academy, for example, had to work in the basement; no women were allowed belowstairs.

"That was the first time I had experienced real separation as an artist, and it infuriated me. Your not being allowed to paint a . . . fish because you're a woman. It reminded me of being in the synagogue and being told to go up not downstairs. That kind of thing still riles me, and it still comes up.

"Well, you don't just have a few Feminist meetings and resolve the issue. It takes slow patient years. It's not a political revolution fought once and then it's over. I think it will take a long time for woman to find her proper place."

In '32, with the Depression under way, Krasner left school and went to work. Ahead were the bitter years of bank failures and of forebodings from abroad. She took a job as waitress in a Greenwich Village nightclub where artists and intellectuals gathered, among them Harold Rosenberg, who would survive the years along with Krasner and remain a friend until his death in 1978. There was a lot of sitting around and talking politics and art in these coffee-drinking days. It was 1933 when Krasner painted another of the self-portraits she keeps on her wall today. Her left eye, heavy-lidded, looks out from just above the center of the canvas. Beneath reddish-gold bangs it gazes with a certain irony. Later on, that same "eye," reduced only to a pair of intersecting arcs, would become a disturbing motif in many of her abstract paintings and in Pollock's as well.

The next year, the WPA began to operate, and Krasner, along with Rosenberg and so many others, began making art for a nation trying to rescue itself. The kind of work turned out was far from advanced; Social Realism and Regionalism were now given government stamp of approval for public building projects; but the essential was that the artists were working and earning enough to live.

"There was no discrimination against women that I was aware of in the WPA. There were a lot of us working then—Alice Trumbull Mason, Suzie Freulingheusen, Gertrude Greene and others. The head of the New York project was a woman, Audrey McMahon.

"It was my job eventually to execute murals for people who left the project. One was by de Kooning. He worked on it and then was fired because he wasn't a citizen, so I was called in to do it. He gave me a life-size sketch and he'd come unofficially to my studio and see what I was doing. It was Hard-Edged for de Kooning and very abstract. Later, I did someone else's *History of Navigation* for Brooklyn. That mural seemed to be two or three miles wide. I worked from the original small sketch and blew it up. I had assistants and we worked on a pier over the river. Eleanor Roosevelt came to see us working there.

"That whole experience introduced me to *scale*—none of the nonsense they call scale today. So by the time I came to do a mosaic in the Uris Brothers building in downtown Manhattan, eighty-six feet long, that scale was nothing new to me. Long before I met Pollock, too, I had been working that large.

"Beyond that there was the camaraderie instead of isolation, and that led eventually to other feelings. But basically, it was a living for us all."

During the years of political activity when the Spanish Civil War was going on and the greater one preparing itself, the battle lines were drawn here too. The Project was attacked by conservatives; there was counteragitation from the artists. Krasner became a leader in the Artists' Union set up to fight the issues. She was fired and rehired twice and more than once jailed for illegal activities. At those times, she booked herself into prison as Mary Cassatt. And why Mary Cassatt, that Philadelphian abroad who would hardly have taken to the streets under any circumstances? Probably because in those days Krasner was studying with the German artist and teacher Hans Hofmann, who once paid her the same compliment Degas paid Cassatt: "This painting is so good you'd never know it was done by a woman."

A radical move forward in art of the kind Krasner would participate in during the rest of the decade of the '40s takes place on two levels. There is a burden of feeling that accumulates until it cannot be contained in handed-down forms, and there is the human limb (hand, foot, arms or literary mind, depending on the medium) that must be freed to invent the new forms. All through the prewar and war years and their aftermath, the sense of pressure grew among artists not enjoying patronage from the Establishment but bonded by their work for the WPA and their common psychic situation. Many of them, like Krasner, came already charged with what Harold Rosenberg, speaking of Arshile Gorky, later would call "fractured memories": consciousness of childhood immigrations and moves, and abandonments of old ways. To these reasons for guilt and anxiety, history contributed its burden as the world moved toward war, and horrors mounted with movements of refugees, revelations of torture and Holocaust, eventually atom bombs to come. Fundamentally, then, as many artists saw it, it was the dialectic between power and slavery, death and life, that seemed a fit symbolism for the times. Darkness and light, black and white, might be considered the esthetic terms of the dialectic. But for a while the means of making a new art on the basis of that symbolism evaded the artists' reach.

Since its invention in Paris around 1910, it was Cubism that had provided the basic means and metaphysics for Modernist artists. It was a rational analytical tool that seemed scientific, endlessly flexible and true to nature. But the French brand of Cubism, particularly, was cool and objective. Characteristically, the Cubist line was a clear-cut, short, specific one, more a notation of the position of a shape in space than a means for the discharge of feeling. But these artists in New York brought to their work a hunger for emotional depth and an appetite for form capable of expressing it: shapes internally cadenced, lines long and sonorous, at once dense and also linear as lines of Biblical poetry or, in Arshile Gorky's words, "the songs in the fields." Some years later, when the artists would have found their individual voices, some of them would put into apocalyptic words the nature of their search.

We seek the primeval and atavistic. [Rothko]

Only that subject matter is valid which is tragic and timeless. [Rothko]

Let no one underestimate the power of this work for life, or for death if it is misused. [Still]

Krasner herself said to me, "It is possible that what I found later on—art—would be a substitute for what religion had been for me earlier."

But in the early '40s the form the emotion would take was still not apparent. "We must admit we are defeated," said the Gorky of the Armenian shepherd songs after a meeting of artists including Krasner had failed to come up with a formula to advance their cause.

There were, all the same, a plethora of sources of suggestion available in the eclectic art world of New York. There were various forms of Expressionism—German, Russian, Middle European—being worked and exhibited. Theories of psychoanalysis and anthropology offered clues for the freeing of buried feelings. Surrealism provided theory and technical apparatus. The paintings and writings of Kandinsky were catalysts. "Color," Kandinsky wrote, "embodies an enormous though unexplored power which can affect the entire human body as a physical organism. . . . Therefore, color is a means of exercising direct influence upon the soul." There was also the abstract ideology preached by a group of artists of the Constructivist-Bauhaus mode. Krasner was a member of the Abstract American Artists group, which was established in 1936, and a number of gifted women including Perle Fine, Alice Trumbull Mason, Charmion von Wiegand, and Nell Blaine were active. But its orthodoxy soon displeased Krasner, and she left them in '43. "The AAA wouldn't allow a Surreal breath to pass the door. They were provincial like any groupie. I tried to keep it open. I tried for example to get Calder invited and was told No. Tried to get Hofmann to lecture and was told No. On the other hand, they did invite Léger and Mondrian."

For Krasner, the important sources would be Hans Hofmann's classes in drawing and painting, and the ideas of the Russian Surrealist-mystic John Graham. Hofmann, an immigrant from Munich in 1932, would influence two generations of American artists and critics, most of whom today are hard put to describe the gist of a doctrine from which realist landscapists got as much as future Abstract Expressionists. What he projected was a Germanic feeling for nature imploded into the rational structure of Cubism. An engineer and inventor in his youth, he may have kept a tough, pragmatic feeling for balance of stresses: a work of art, drawing or painting, was to have its own internal life as a system of pushes and pulls acting across the whole surface. Then these interrelated thrusts would generate an all-over field of energy. Physical nature—a still life, a figure, a landscape—was always the model, not to be copied but to be referred to. It was there that these charged relationships between shapes were to be studied.

For Hofmann's classes in the late '30s, Krasner made dozens of charcoal drawings, plotting the lines of force of figures in standing or seated poses, carving the forms down to essentials with long, full-arm slashes and curves, pulling the farthermost reaches of the paper into the action with planes of rubbed shading. These were the works "so good" they seemed to be done by a man. "I got his message," says Krasner. "It was basically Cubism and I got it." Meanwhile she was reading Graham's book, *System and Dialectics of Art*, that echoed the Surrealist line: the intellect was a "useless tool . . . the things we know impede us from seeing things we do not know." Pure feeling could be rendered "automatically in terms of brush pressure, saturation, velocity, caress or repulsion, anger or desire." Krasner, de Kooning, Gorky, David Smith and others, including the Jackson Pollock still unknown to her, read the work. Krasner's own charcoal drawings, seen when she turned them into collages in

1977, were no mere intellectual Cubist studies of forms in space. She was making intensely expressive semiabstract works in which line was the conveyor of feeling as it would be in Pollock's work to come. The difference between her work and his was in scale and in degree. She remained with the figure and the still life, with the fragment of sky or architecture, while some of her male peers were to make the leap that would carry them into another dimension of radicalism.

Since her arrival, in her own time, at that point, it has been asked why Krasner did not make the transition earlier. The answer, as I have already suggested, may go to the heart of the issue of women as artists. There may be a personal reason and, from that, a more general one.

It seems there was a burden of feeling accumulated during those years of the late '30s and early '40s that Krasner's tales of her WPA activities and her work with Hofmann do not fully explain. The message lay in four lines of poetry by Rimbaud that she lettered in black paint on her studio wall:

To whom shall I hire myself out? What beast must I adore?
What holy image is attacked:
What hearts shall I break?
What lie must I maintain? In what blood tread?

Rimbaud translator Louise Varèse—also a member of the New York art world in those days and wife of the avant-garde composer—wrote in her introduction to Rimbaud's *Illuminations*: "No one who has read *Une Saison en Enfer* will, I am sure, deny that it is a *mea culpa*—a heartbreaking confession not of faith but of failure."[1] When Tennessee Williams visited Krasner's studio and argued with her about the lines, she asked him to leave. When I suggested they were odd touchstones for a woman who believes in her own worth, Krasner disagreed emphatically.

"They express an honesty which is blinding," she said. "I believe those lines. I experienced it. I identified with it. I knew what he was talking about. How much more reality do you want? Those lines have to do with reality—not lies."

She is not about to go back and expose those feelings now. But clearly there was a bond felt during those fraught and frustrating years with another artist who had begun in full hopes only to find himself negating his gifts "in the hell-fires of disgust and despair."[2] Whatever the source of the despair, it existed. Transmuted by time into a creative impulse, it may have been what impelled her first to destroy, then to remake the drawings of that time into the

111

collages of '77. Rimbaud himself, we cannot forget, did something of the same sort. After writing his *mea culpa* and farewell to art, he made sure the manuscript was delivered to a printer for publication and his own immortality.

The meeting between Krasner and Pollock has been described often: how in '42 John Graham was putting together a show of French and American artists; how he chose works by Virginia Diaz (who *Art News* said "walked off with the show"), Lee Krasner and Pollock among a number of other Americans to hang with Picasso, Matisse, Braque and others. Pollock had been in New York since 1930, gradually hewing a style out of elements from Thomas Benton, Albert Ryder and the Mexican Siqueiros with input, too, from a Jungian analysis and his own undoubted genius. Krasner, who was contributing a Picasso-esque still life, went around to Pollock's studio to meet him before the show. She walked in, saw one canvas that "just about stunned me," and then others. "I saw a whole batch of early work there, finished paintings not drawings. He had already moved to that point. I was confronted with something ahead of me. I felt elation. *My God, there it is.*

"I couldn't have felt that if I hadn't been trying for the same goal myself. You just wouldn't recognize it. What he had done was much more important than just line. He had found the way to merge abstraction with Surrealism."

Thirteen years after his death, Krasner would put it into moving words: "You do have an individual who . . . appears on the horizon and opens a door wide. We all live on it for a long time to come, until the next individual arrives and opens another door."[3]

The following year, Pollock had joined Peggy Guggenheim's stable and painted his "breakthrough" work, a twenty-foot-wide mural done in one working session: a continuous chain of vertical curling strokes that covered the whole surface. Krasner, who had moved into his studio by then and was working on an easel at one end of it, was also helping out in the gallery, folding and addressing announcements.

"After I met Pollock, it took a long time for me to absorb the kind of work he was doing, just as with Cubism earlier. But we equalized in some sense. In fact, once we asked ourselves hypothetically what would have happened if it had been me who came through first. But I wasn't earning a living in those days, and we had to concentrate on what would bring in some money. If I had had to be a teacher as so many of the artists' wives who supported their husbands were, I wouldn't have painted at all. I maintain I never gave up. I kept a corner for myself. And I always painted."

It was after meeting Pollock that Krasner made what was, she later felt, a mistaken decision to abandon working from nature, as Hofmann taught,[4] in order to take on the canvas as a "thing in itself," to "work it up" in Surreal automatic gestures. The experiment seemed at the time a failure. Giving up the impulsive nature-derived line in which she had been strong, she seemed to have short-circuited her gift. Her attempts to create an "all-over" image out of random upsurges from the unconscious led only to an accumulation of thick, granular impasto with a nervous, vibrating intensity (it was not until the "Abstract Expressionism: The Formative Years" show at the Whitney Museum in '78 that Krasner's work of that time was revealed as the strong, individual passage it was).

So few of her early paintings are left today it is hard to know what she gave up at that juncture. A still life of 1938 may hold a clue. It is a Cubist composition, linear and light, with a patch of blue, spacy sky breaking through the upper left as if "weather" had blown open the confines of the canvas. From this example, one might deduce that she too had been on the brink of a breakthrough in those days, one that would have been rooted in direct experience of nature, rendered in terms of the freighted line but also open space and light. That is possible. But then one would also have to say that in her bargain with destiny and that unfashionable quotient, love, Krasner probably emerged at the end with a deeper apprehension of the themes of life and death, fear, struggle and regeneration for which she had already shown an instinct.

In '45, Krasner's father died and she married Pollock in the Marble Collegiate Reformed Church—a final break with the world of the synagogue. "I didn't want to marry until he died," she says. "Then I did a reverse, a total swing of the pendulum." They bought a house in Springs, Long Island, and spent a couple of years cleaning it out, discarding old farm tools and moving a barn out of the direct view to the bay. That done, Pollock took over the barn as his studio and Krasner set to work in an upstairs bedroom. There she would paint for the next eleven years. The first motif to "appear" in her new work was what she called the Little Images. These were fields of coiled lines, a shallow tide of variant eye-forms poured in thick viscous paint and aligned in tight parallel rows. "I was working on the floor then because of the technical problem. Jackson was working on the floor for different reasons." For a few years, his work expanded season by season in size, control, expansiveness. There was a lyricism and natural easeful energy to those first Easthampton Pollocks spun in circular handpourings like insects circling in the grass between the house and the bay. Krasner meantime, looking out on the same meadow, was going through hard times, threading out her skeins of inward-spiraling lines coil within coil.

But what is coil but that which will uncoil one day?

113

Meanwhile, they isolated themselves from the art life in the city. "We were not Club people. We left the city in '45 when The Club was at its heyday. We are not belongers. Physically, we are not there." Where they were and what they belonged to, instead of the quickening politics of the art world, was their work and certain introspections Krasner is not averse to talking about. In fact, sitting on her porch today, she returns to a level of feeling that seems undiminished.

"One thing Jackson and I had in common was experience on the same level . . . feeling the same things about landscape, for instance, or about the moon. He did a series around the moon. He had a mysterious involvement with it, a Jungian thing. I had my own way of using that material. Very often I would get up at two or three and come out on the porch and just sit in the light here.

"We had a helluva lot in common—our interests, our goal. *Art* was the thing, for both of us. We focused on it, zeroed in on it, because our backgrounds, though different, were not so different as all that. Cody . . . Brooklyn. Not so different.

"With Jackson there was quiet—solitude. Just to sit and look at the landscape. An inner quietness. After dinner, to sit on the back porch and look at the light. No need for talking. For any kind of communication.

"If we found we couldn't sleep at dawn, we might drive the little car and park it and go walking in the woods, for hours. That was the big thing to do. Or—let's go swimming at night.

"Common responsibilities. They infuse a life. How to achieve that again?

"The fact that he drank and was extraordinarily difficult to live with was another side. But the thing that made it possible for me to hold my equilibrium were these intervals when we had so much."

By the end of the '40s her own work, she felt, had opened and changed. In '51, her debut was held at Betty Parsons'. These large-scale canvases were marked by what Pollock himself said was a "new freshness and bigness" for her. One rare remaining work of the time, not exhibited, is a bold ink drawing of two tumbling white forms on a black field, as if a buried pod or seed were beginning to turn in its track. But the show was poorly received. Pollock left Parsons for the Janis Gallery, and Parsons, in direct reaction, Krasner feels, let her go.

It was the following year that Krasner's old friend and by then the well-known art critic Harold Rosenberg wrote an article on "The American Action Painting."[5] "After a certain moment," he pointed out, these artists, each in his own way, had decided to abandon conventional art-making to take to the canvas "as an arena in which to act." The gesture on the canvas had been one of liberation from traditional standards of operation not only esthetic but moral and political. "The American vanguard painter," he declared, "took to the white expanse of the canvas as Melville's Ishmael took to the sea."

Rosenberg claimed for the new art a content universal as human nature yet also personal: "A painting that is an act is inseparable from the biography of the artist. Anything is relevant to it. Anything that has to do with action— psychology, philosophy, history, mythology, hero worship." The following year, Krasner herself took to the material of her past as, one might say, Ishmael took to the sea. She took the old canvases, cut them and pasted them together with fragments of rejected work by Pollock for her first collage series. *Milk-weed* was one: razor-thin pods shearing upward across several torn black shapes that lazily orbit from the lower right, up to the left, and then begin to fall toward the ground.

By then, in point of fact, the movement's creative ascent had been accomplished. During the years of country life for Krasner and Pollock, the movement had coalesced around the Artists' Club, first in its location on Eighth Street, later on Tenth Street, in Manhattan. It was there that the idea of amalgamating themselves into an official group with a name was pushed for by some members, including a few critics and museum officials enamored of labels, and opposed by others, mostly artists, who valued their single eccentricities. The namers won. Not unexpectedly, once that loose affiliation of idiosyncratic originals had been melded, they began to want a piece of the action from an art Establishment long aloof. In 1950, the famous challenge to the Establishment was made by the Irascible Eighteen, photographed more at a simmer than a boil, for *Life* magazine. Jackson Pollock was prominent among them; Hedda Sterne, always exhibiting in a prominent gallery, was the only woman. Krasner had not been invited to sign the petition, an honor afforded a few women of whom Louise Bourgeois was one. Two years later, the challenge had paid off. The Museum of Modern Art gave the Abstract Expressionists its official imprimatur in a show of "Fifteen Americans," again not including Krasner. By then, Barnett Newman, for example, had begun to show his enormous fields of single blazing colors including the megaphonically patriarchal *Vir Heroicus Sublimis.* Clyfford Still, Kline, Rothko and others began consolidating their individual abstract idioms, rid of any remnant of Surreal, Cubist or other figurative elements, narrowing them to the marketable single images by which they would, before long, become world-renowned.

The suicide of Arshile Gorky in 1948 had perhaps been the first intimation of the end to come, though still for some years there would be a period of second growth as the budding tip of the movement opened to include a new generation of painters, poets, theater people, flocking to the city. Meanwhile, there were some who did not hide their belief that after 1951 Jackson Pollock, by moving in a tentative way back to figurative material, had "repudiated his progress of the past years." Soon it was said he had lost his touch. After 1954, he did not paint at all. Troubles mounted. "He brought me terror of another kind," said Krasner of those years of the mid-'50s. "I was paralyzed with fear about his well-being and safety. I never knew if he would come home unhurt."

It was 1956 when she turned out the work she titled *Prophecy,* a brooding and bunched figure half man, half beast. The image troubled her and she asked Pollock to come look at it. (By agreement they visited each other's studios only by invitation.) He liked the work, but he pointed to the upper right-hand corner where there was one of those unmoving, chilly eyes and said, "I'd take that out." She did not.

"The image was there, and I had to let it come out. I felt it at the time. *Prophecy* was fraught with foreboding. When I saw it, I was aware it was a frightening image, but I had to let it come through. Some people might not have been afraid, but I was. So I allowed it to happen, but I didn't pursue the meaning at the time.

"Later Eleanor Ward of the Stable Gallery came up, and saw it before I had intended her to. She said, 'God, that's scary.' I didn't really know what it was then."

In July Krasner made her first trip to Europe. While she was there Pollock was killed in an automobile crash.

"I came back and came into the studio and found that painting standing there. It was some years, until I was in analysis, before I made the connection between it and that memory of being so frightened as a child by something that jumped over the banister."

In the first eighteen months after his death, Krasner painted seventeen big canvases. That fact alone tells a story, but the titles tell an even more poignant tale: *Earth Green, Springbeat, Upstream.* In *Listen,* the artist signed her name in enormous brown calligraphy that then spills across the whole field to bind up fuchsia, green and mauve leaf and flower forms, clouds and falling streams. The works were shown at the Martha Jackson Gallery in 1958 and praised. But there was still a return to make.

"After Pollock's death I came back to New York, rented an apartment and then abandoned it after two years. I couldn't stand it. So I went back out to Springs. The second attempt was very beautiful. I wasn't depressed at all. Then, at a point during that time, I took over the barn. There was no point in letting it stand empty. Meanwhile I had the difficulty of also trying to reestablish myself in New York. I couldn't live in the country all the time alone. So I had to try also to get back into New York."

An avid New York art world was hanging on the widow's progress. Her costudent at Hofmann's classes, Clement Greenberg, then moving into a position of power at the French & Co. Galleries, offered her a show on the basis of the "earth green" works. Neither he nor she calculated what the move back into the barn might produce. What came next was a great wave of dark-umber and white works: *Charred Landscape, White Rage, Cobalt Night, Night Birds* and *Fragments from a Crucifixion*. Greenberg was "disappointed" by the turn the work had taken, and he said so. Angered, Krasner canceled the show and went on working the vein. She worked until she was felled by a serious

At right, the artist shown with The Gate, early state, from the umber and white series. Above, final state, 1959–60. Oil on canvas. 7'8¾" by 12'. Collection the artist.

operation in 1963. By then the assertion of dominion over the charred land-scape seemed done. There has been no return to that palette or that content.

The works of the decade '64 to '74 established Lee Krasner as a painter of power and feeling. The swinging arcs of color in these works clearly based on nature all but overflow the confines of her large canvases. She returns to yellow-green, dark green, raspberry and alizarin orange as touch colors for a sense of impassioned connection with growing things (bridal veil, lilac, fleurs-de-lis?). In '65 she was given a major show at the Whitechapel Art Gallery in London, and in '73 one at the Whitney Museum. From '67 she has divided her time between the city and the country and need have no fears now about not being honored in both places as the original she is. The collages of '77 were a kind of coda to what went before, yet imply no termination.

I asked Krasner whether there were other meanings to those works than the ones drawn.

"No. I don't know what they're about. I created them, but that doesn't mean I can read them yet. I have enough confidence in myself to accept what came out, even though I can't rattle off a definition.

"Obviously, I'm hauling out work of thirty years ago. Obviously pulling that out. Dealing with it. Not ignoring, hiding it. I'm saying, Here it is in another form. This is where I've come from: from there to here. It gives me a kick to be able to go back and pick up thirty years ago. It renews my confidence in something I believe. That there is continuity."

Krasner's survival out of a movement so heavy-burdened and in the end fated bears on our theme. In his first description of the Action Painters, Rosenberg said that "based on the phenomenon of conversion, the new movement is, with the majority of painters, essentially a religious movement." It seems that Lee Krasner's saving grace may have been, paradoxically, her rejection of conversion, her ironic detachment from—even hatred of—totalism or Rim-baud's "holy image" that she first developed long ago in a religious orthodoxy that held women less than equal. From this experience, reinforced by other painful ones of a lifetime, would have come her skepticism about all closed ideologies, her resistance to joining any one of them, and also her reliance on instinct to endure long periods of waiting in the confidence that her prophetic gift would assert itself eventually. By this interpretation, her "failure" to go along with Pollock on his leap into the conceptual future would have been due not to a block, as some have suggested, but to the endurance of her life force, her rejection of the consequences that lay ahead for some who went the other way.

For the convert, the past has ceased to exist. It is annihilated. To use

Mysteries, 1972. Oil on canvas. 69½" by 89½". The Brooklyn Museum, Brooklyn, New York. Dick S. Ramsay Fund.

Rosenberg's phrase, the imagination afterward is "fractured" and reset. "I am never free of the past," Krasner says. "I believe in continuity. I have made it crystal clear that the past is part of the present which becomes part of the future."

Notwithstanding, she determined to deal with the dark side of the dialectic, that fund of foreknowledge, fear and anxiety, "that element Jackson got and I feel no one else uses today." She would be no lady bountiful providing "beautiful" pictures for a market, though she has remained open also to the lighter side and waited for the life process to return her, from time to time, to it. Rejecting dogmas, or their parallel in art, closed images, in favor of an esthetic that alternates between the poles has been the condition of her rejuvenations.

"If the alphabet is A to Z, I want to move with it all the way, not only from A to C. For me, all the doors are open. One can't stop growing though it takes enormous energy to keep growing and it is painful. Yet I have never been able to understand the artist whose image never changes.

"The *Stations of the Cross* [by Newman] doesn't interest me. Rothko too took a single image and stayed with it. I have never understood that. My images are always open.

"I believe in listening to cycles. I listen by not forcing. If I am in a dead working period, I wait, though those periods are hard to deal with. For the future, I'll see what happens. I'll be content if I get started again. If I feel that alive again. If I find myself working with the old intensity again."

Alice Neel

BORN 1900, MERION SQUARE, PENNSYLVANIA

For all I know, my human images originate in terror.

—ALICE NEEL
New York, 1977

How many masterworks make a master? Alice Neel, I propose, has painted one, *TB, Harlem, 1940* (page 128), that might stand for time to come as witness to the world she knew: an age of massive social failure. There is, I think, only one other portrait of the American early midcentury that can rival this hopeless figure dying on a pale-mauve pillow, half wrapped in a sheet soon to be shroud, with dark Christ eyes softly engaging the viewer. That is Franz Kline's mad, dying Nijinsky, no more than a skein of black naked nerve ends drawn at the very turning point of the painter's leap from figurative art to abstraction.[1] Indeed, it was just during those middle years of Alice Neel's life, when her social conscience was moved and her hand released, that most other advanced painters in New York began to formulate an esthetic of transcendence over human suffering (another word might be "escape") through Abstract Expressionism. But for whatever reasons, nervous, psychic, ideological or all three, Neel stayed with the human figure. And if few of her later works have equaled this, it is perhaps less her failing than that of the subjects she portrayed later on: no more the faces of the barrio but a spoiled American cultural "elite" which, taken in a series, looks like a strip from the old Katzenjammer Kids cartoons that struck revulsion into her when she saw them as a child.

Still, the newer works, portraits of Pop artists, rock musicians, critics, collectors, etc., retain a fascination partly as reflections of the Zeitgeist, as Neel likes to say, but also as direct translations into line, color and image, of one woman's coping with a life of extreme stress. For her art began and was

120

reforged at a point, as she tells us here, as a means of salvation. Therefore, deep and so far unanswerable questions can be raised in connection with it. How, for example, does mental condition alter precept and then artistic expression? What is, say, the correlation between anxiety and color—witness Neel's extraordinary palette of sour greens, magentas, citrons? What is the relationship between apprehension, even panic, and the sweeping waves of dark line and shadow that disturb some of her early work as well as works of Blake, Van Gogh and Munch? Bearing these questions in mind makes listening to Neel's life story less a matter of scandalous eavesdropping than a provocative foray into our field of psychoesthetics.

Even without such rationalizations, Neel's confessions are held precious by many in the Women's Movement today who consider her a model of rare courage and openness. She also projects, in person, a rosy sweetness and optimism that belie altogether the desperate-eyed, spring-fingered personae who leap onto her white canvas time and time again.

After long years of deprivation and relative obscurity except for the constant friendship of a few art-world regulars, Neel began her ascent to prominence in the early '60s, has exhibited widely nearly every year after and in '74 was given a one-person show at the Whitney Museum. That is not to say she has not suffered—as who of the individuals here has not?—atrocious insult from time to time, as we shall read. But now she speaks her piece. As she said when I asked her one question, "I haven't ever told anyone that because I didn't want the world to snub me. But now I don't give a damn. I'm getting so famous it won't make any difference."

"I had what it takes to make a good artist: sensitivity and tremendous will-power. Hypersensitivity—because in order to be an artist you have to react intensely. And then you must have the will. What is it, really—character, belief? The power to stick with what you believe? I had a very strong, adamant self. That is proved by the art I have produced. Now, I don't know how you arrive at that. But in my case I believe it came about because other people had such a strong effect on me.

"I was hypersensitive as a child. If a fly lit on me, I'd have a convulsion. A real convulsion. There was a stuffed cat I lived in terror of. For all I know, my human images originate in terror. It may be I need to exorcise something.

"Other people loomed too large. Everybody could knock me off base, so that it was hard for me to be myself. I'd make such an effort to be what they wanted, a pretty little girl, that I wouldn't be myself at all. As for that, I doubt if I was really myself until my mother died, when I was fifty-four. I was extremely attached to her. She had a strong, independent self, a stronger character than

121

I, but she was terribly nervous. She could have done anything, run a big business establishment. She was very well read, very intelligent, and she had a terrific capacity, but she couldn't compromise. This made her marry a man who, while he had wonderful manners and was very kind and even the most philosophical one in the house, nevertheless allowed her to run the roost. I grew up in a mother-dominated household.

"My father's family were opera singers in Philadelphia. They had money when he was a child, but they made no provisions for the future and none for him. So he worked all his life as a clerk for the Pennsylvania Railroad. His heritage was Irish, but my mother's was English. Her name was Hartley. We're old, old Americans.

"She didn't know anything about art, but she wasn't against it. When we were both older, she would say, 'Oh, Alice, I could never have a life like yours—always striving.' But that striving is innate. It's not something I 'do.' What drives the artist? Well, that's the mystery. Once my mother said, 'None of us will ever be remembered.' And my father said, 'Well, I'm not so sure about Alice.' Even as a child, I was sure there were three things I could be: a writer, a painter or a sculptor.

"I wasn't then as I am now, however. I hadn't any direction. I never knew what I wanted in the small things. My mother would say, 'Coffee or hot chocolate?' and I wouldn't know, but not only would I not know, I'd go into a fever of trying to decide. My whole life was a matter of never knowing what I wanted. Why? Because I didn't give a damn for any of it. But later on, on white canvas, I was free. That was my world. It was mine.

"In the little town I grew up in [Colwin, Pennsylvania], there were no artists, no writers, but there was material for everything. My street had once been a pear orchard, so there were still three rows of pear trees. That was lovely. I was just a child then, but I remember all the flowers, what they looked like: elephant ears, and four-o'clocks and scarlet sage. Once in 1973, I set my brain back to 1915 and I managed to remember flowers—and paint them—as I had seen them then. Quite a feat. And the flowers were fresher. The pansies. The gloxinia, and lilacs. It was a wonderful feeling. I remember, too, the paint book I got one Christmas, the one with apples and flowers. I was a romantic, and that was the most exciting thing for me. Not like the one they gave me one year, with the Katzenjammer Kids. I hated that.

"That was part of the fears. When I was very small, at night I'd turn on my side in bed and look out the door at the gaslight in the hall. With one eye I could see the light, and with the other I couldn't, and I thought the eye that couldn't see was blind. I was always afraid of going blind. The minute the light went out, I thought I was blind, so I was terrorized at night. There's a poem by

W. H. Auden that says people with night fears never will become nice people. I had these fears, but I wouldn't tell anyone. Even by the time I was three or four, there was already a wall between me and the reserve of my mother.

"I internalized everything. Mother and my older sister were different. They were elegant ladies. They didn't make any noise, but their emotions went outward. Mine went all inward."

"I went to Darby High School, where I was a whiz at mathematics. But because I was worried then about my family's financial condition, I thought as a responsible person I should take the commercial course and learn to be a stenographer and type. The superintendent of schools came over to see the family and told them it was mad for me to take that course, because I was so bright. But I did, and then I took the Civil Service examination, and since I was so good in math I got a very high mark and a job right away with the Air Force. I held that job for three years, from 1918 to '21, but all the time, I was going to art school at night. I took some courses at the School of Industrial Art, and then for a while I went to a downtown school run by a very famous man.

"One time he said to me, 'You don't need to make the hair just the way it grows; just put on a tone.'

"I said, 'But I prefer to do the hair the way it goes.'

"He got very angry and said, 'Young woman, before you can conquer art, you'll have to conquer yourself. And anyway it will be forty years before you paint anything decent, so I advise you to give it up.' I wasn't learning much in those days anyway. You know why? Because I was too tired.

"I had a small nervous breakdown when I was seventeen, only a small one but I remember not being able to hold my head up for a couple of months. It came from repression, from growing up in a very puritanical atmosphere. Nowadays, when I hear of boys and girls living together, I love it! In any case, in 1921, I quit those jobs and went full time to art school. I'd answered an ad for a very good job and got it, but suddenly I had a vision of myself just going along working that way, so I turned it down. Instead, I applied to the Philadelphia School of Design for Women. I paid one semester, and after that they gave me scholarships.

"The reason I went to the School of Design for Women instead of the Museum of Fine Arts school was that in the museum they were teaching Renoir and picnics on the grass and yellow lights and blue shadows. I didn't want to learn that. The School of Design was badly run, but you could do as you pleased there, and since I thought it was going to be a struggle for me to find out what I wanted anyway, that suited me better. All I wanted was to learn to paint. I just wanted that. Why do we want anything?

"I was very beautiful then and all the boys chased me, but my life wasn't happy. I chose a women's school so there wouldn't be anyone there to distract me. I hated the '20s. I hated all that forced gaiety, jumping up and down dancing. Now I have a grandchild who is a morbid little thing and she said to me, 'Alice, I hate people who laugh,' and I thought that was the greatest thing, because it was what I hated.

"I hated America. The American idea. I hated the conformity. I hated the factories. During World War I there had been a man in my town whom I heard say, 'I don't care how long the war lasts. I'm making a profit.' I had despised him for that.

"Well, at school I worked very hard. There were all these rich girls who went there as a finishing school. At the start I went out to lunch with them, but I realized that wasn't what I was there for, so I gave up everything and became a grind. There was one good teacher there, who taught anatomy. I've never forgotten what she taught: the mouth is a rubber band. That's why when you get old, your mouth frizzles in.

"For three years I worked so hard I nearly destroyed my own talent. I worked so hard because I had a conscience about going to art school, not for my own family but for all the poor in the world. Because when I'd go into the school, the scrubwomen would be coming back from scrubbing office floors all night. It killed me that these old grayheaded women had to scrub floors and I was going in there to draw Greek statues. One of the rich girls told me, 'I don't think you'll ever paint a good picture, because you stretch the canvas too well.' But I can't paint as a slob. I can't paint on a floppy canvas. And not one of those girls lives as an artist today.

"My third year in the school, I was so sickly from overwork and going to the theater with boys every night that my family sent me out to the summer art-school extension of the Pennsylvania Academy over in Chester Springs. I went out there to spend six weeks, but in the end I left after three. Because at Chester Springs I met Carlos.

"That was the first time I really fell in love. I'd always had a difficulty. If I liked a boy physically I didn't like him mentally, and if I liked him mentally I couldn't stand him physically. That was partly my mother's fault. Those Hartley girls were hell on wheels. They were too domineering in some terrible way. After I met Carlos, I went back to school, and although I worked hard it wasn't like the other years. So he went back down to Havana where he came from and got a job, came back up, and I married him the following June. But then I refused to go back down with him. Now, by then I'd had too much experience of a kind, but never the real thing. I was terrified of the whole business. He thought I was a normal American girl. I had every appearance of being utterly

124

normal and beautiful. But I couldn't go. I couldn't go. It was the worst agony, because I really wanted to go. So he came back in February and got me, and I finally went down, and got pregnant right away. I'd eaten my heart out all those months, and then afterward I had no rest.

"So I had this baby. They're more animal than we are, in Havana, and for them to have a child is the most normal thing in the world. For me, it was a major event. They don't give anesthesia there. Now, I couldn't stand Anglo-Saxons; I couldn't stand their soda-cracker lives and their inhibitions; I loved Latins. But I wasn't a Latin, and for me to have a baby without anesthesia was frightful. In the end, it had been eight hours of agony. And then when I came back to New York, even my father only said, 'Oh, well, anybody can do that.'

"I had had that child in Havana, and she died in New York just before she was a year old, of diphtheria. There's a picture I made, three years after, that's a distillation of that and so much else: *The Futility of Effort*. Into it went the amount of effort you put into having a child. Pregnancy. All the rest. Then the tragedy of losing it. Everything. Everything. When we were together, all we did was paint, Carlos and I. In Havana that's all we did, and in New York that's all we did. In 1927, '28, '29.

"When I was pregnant with the second child, we didn't have any money, so I got a job in the National City Bank. And then friends told Carlos he was being a petty bourgeois trying to have an apartment, a wife and a child. So he ran off to Paris. He was a weakling. Neither he nor I had any money. Nothing. If I'd had only five hundred dollars, I wouldn't have had the nervous break-down. I had gone every day and worked in my studio and realized all these great paintings. If I'd had a few hundred dollars, I could have had a show. But as it was, three months after he went away, I had my first nervous chill."

EM: "What is a nervous chill, Alice?"

AN: "If you've never had one, never have one. It leads to dreadful things.

"I had one on August the fifteenth, 1930. It lasted about six hours. I had Freud's classic disease: hysteria.

"Your senses are never more acute than before you have a nervous breakdown. You're hyped up. In three months of June, July and August, before the middle of August, I painted some of my best paintings.

"Then I went to the hospital and there I fell into the hands of the enemy. Because you know what psychiatrists say: 'Well, it seems you've had a rather bohemian life. But you see it hasn't gotten you anywhere.' They didn't under-stand that where I wanted to go was not where they wanted to go. It was another voyage.

"Eventually Carlos came back from Paris and took me home from the

125

hospital. But just the ride in the taxi was too much for my nerves. When I got home I had about a half hour of normality. Then I fell asleep. When I woke up, I thought I heard my mother and father talking in the next room. But when I went in, they were sound asleep. Then for the first time, it occurred to me the breakdown wasn't just nervous, it was mental. So I went downstairs and put my head in the gas oven and committed suicide. I stuffed up all the holes, but I forgot the cellar door, and some little air came up through there. The next morning my brother found me on the floor. After about four hours, when I hadn't come to, they sent me to a hospital and gave me Adrenalin, and then sent me to another hospital, where they chained me to the bed. My brother made a significant remark. He said, 'I didn't know if it was Mama or Alice,' because we used to hear our mother say, 'I'll turn the gas on.' She used to say that to our father because she was so dissatisfied with life. Her sisters had all married successful men with big cars and all that.

"Well, they took me back to the hospital. Carlos came and said we could go out to the country somewhere, but it was too late for me. I was beyond that. I was finished. I just had to sit it out, you know. That was January of 1931. Later I decided to commit suicide by swallowing glass, so when they brought my dinner I smashed the drinking glass, but they heard me and came. Next they sent me to the Philadelphia General Suicidal Ward. I thought of every kind of suicide there, but the windows were barred. I can still see the schizophrenics standing next to the blank walls pushing imaginary buttons to go down in the elevator. They accused me of having a Napoleonic complex because I said I was an artist; they said I had never drawn a picture.

"It was nearly a year later when I looked up and saw a woman who had been sent to a state hospital and came back, made pregnant by a guard. I thought, 'My God, this is going to be my fate.' So then and there I decided to get well.

"If I could put into my work this moment the energy it took me to get over the nervous breakdown, I would be a real genius, you know.

"A nice young social worker came along about then. She gave me a pad and pencil, and of course I began to make drawings of the patients. I'd been incontinent for about three months, so just for me to hold my urine long enough to make a drawing was torture. But it was the drawing that helped me decide to get well. The social worker saw my efforts and called my family, and they moved me to a private sanatorium. And there, slowly, I worked at getting well. It was a deliberate process. Even intellectual. For instance, I read a very ordinary American novel published in installments in a magazine. Waiting for each issue, looking it up, reading the sections in order, made me exercise my brain. Later on, when I left the sanatorium, I even forced myself to make a dress, though I had always hated sewing.

"Soon after I had arrived at that place, a woman doctor had said to me, 'If you want to get well, you have to get over the habit of worrying.' For the first time, that made me think of worrying as a habit and so something one could get rid of. I began to try to explain it to myself. That I never had been able to ask for room for my nervousness. I'd never been able just to say, 'Look. I'm frightfully nervous.' I had swallowed everything. And I'd had that pathological need to keep people happy, so even when I was talking to an idiot I felt I had to sink to his ground. I'd had to keep my mother happy as well. She was so superior, so sensitive. She couldn't bear anything. And she'd been doomed to live in that sappy little town."

"Back when I was drawing the patients in the Philadelphia General Suicidal Ward, I had forced myself to notice everything about them. To begin with, the mentally ill, I realized, are usually physically ill as well. They are physically depleted. I was analyzing them all the time. I even studied the psychiatrist while he was analyzing me. I would look at his hands and think he was probably impotent. They looked old and frizzled enough for him to be impotent. While I was working there, one crazy patient tore my drawing up. She said it was the work of the Devil and tore it up. There were many such characters to observe. At the sanatorium, I shared a private room for a while with an old woman who put her corset to bed every night in her bureau drawer and patted it off to sleep.

"How strange that I remember when I entered that sanatorium, I heard played over and over again on the Victrola the old song, 'Just a gigolo . . . everywhere I go . . .'

"In the summer of '31 I came home. Shortly after that, I went out to visit a friend in the country, and there was a sailor. An addict, but an interesting fellow. So the next year, I returned to live with him in Greenwich Village. By then I was known about as an artist. One of the important social documentary paintings I did at that time was the *Russell Sage Investigation of Poverty*. Out of that investigation came, later on, both the welfare system and Social Security.

"In 1933, I got a letter from the Whitney Museum asking me to come see them. They asked whether I would like to earn thirty dollars a week just painting. The Public Works of Art Project was prepared to pay recognized artists that to keep them alive and working. I said, 'Of course.' So I worked for the PWAP for the six months it was in operation. During that time the sailor

127

TB Harlem, *1940. Oil on canvas. 30" by 30". Collection the artist.*

suspected I was seeing someone else, and he got high on cocaine and destroyed all my work. It was a holocaust. He burned all my clothes, all my
paintings. Sixty of them, and three hundred drawings and watercolors. He
burned up a fortune. I never recovered from that.

"Later on, I joined the real WPA. In ways, that was a good experience.
You had a world of your own. We had our own gallery, and once I showed my
street scenes there along with some writings by Mary Heaton Vorse. She wrote
class-conscious literature. But, you see, I was always class-conscious. By then
I had been everything: rich, poor, everything. In Havana living with Carlos's
family we had seven servants, a chauffeur, car, lots of money. Then I had been
in New York starving to death. And Carlos took that other little girl away when
he finally left. My second child. By the time I got on the WPA, I was convinced
that no one on earth should suffer. That anyone who wanted to paint should
be able to do so.

"In later times, I lived in Harlem for twenty-five years and had my sons
Richard and Hartley. And I painted all those years. I never followed any school.
I never imitated any artist. I never did any of that. I believe what I am is a
humanist. That's the way I see the world, and that is what I paint. And I have to
be myself. I think this strange life I've had has been a search for experience,
and that all the experience you can have is good for your work because it

128

Jackie Curtis and Rita Red, *1970. Oil on canvas. 60" by 42". Collection the artist.*

makes you more of a person. It forces you to have a broader view of life. Provided it doesn't kill you."

EM: "What's the theme of your work, Alice?"

AN: "Life. All life."

EM: "Why portraits now?"

AN: "I didn't think anyone had done good portraits in our time. They looked wooden. Too formal. They were not living, and not of this era."

EM: "And how would you describe yours?"

AN: "I am only showing the barbarity of life."

EM: "Really? Is that your intention? I hope you'll let me say that: *I am only showing the barbarity of life.*"

AN: "I'd love you to say that. I hope you say it. Because I think it's a wonder people survive. It is an inhuman demand made on them."

EM: "Does all that show in their faces?"

AN: "Everything shows. The face is the center of the senses. Life, history, the environment shows. Everything.

"I'll tell you what you can see. Their inheritance, their class, their profession. Their feelings, their intellect. All that's happened to them. You see everything in their faces. I like to think, too, that I have reflected the Spirit of the Age. I have painted faces of the '50s, the '60s, the '70s. Each of those decades is so completely different."

EM: "What would you say about your recent subjects?"

AN: "They're driven. Well, a certain amount of driving sharpens them up, but at a price. Less time to dream. When I look at a cemetery today it gives me a wonderful feeling of security, because those people were decently preserved, with a stone and all. Some of them even thought they were going to heaven. But now you're just ashes in a jar, that's all. Life, the quality of life, has suffered tremendously.

"Old age, for instance, is hard. You lose all your escapes. I can't drink much now. You can't unless you want to be really ill. There are supposed to be compensations. In China, your seventy-fifth year is the Year of the Mountain. That year, you are supposed to look back over your entire life.

"I was down in SoHo a while ago and I bumped into Henry Geldzahler. He'd just put on a big show at the Metropolitan Museum. Now he's just opened a big show of figure painting in Russia. Nothing by me in it. Nothing by me in the other show.

"That time I met him, I said, 'Look, Henry. When you give these shows, why don't you include me?' (I'd painted him in 1967.)

"He looked at me, and guess what he said. 'Oh. Now you want to get professional?' "

Louise
Nevelson

BORN 1899, KIEV, U.S.S.R.

I like my houses well enough. They accommo-
date me. But they're not my concept of the way
I would have chosen to live. . . . So then this is
a projection of what might have been.

You say, What's in it? People. The King and
Queen, if you wish. I'm a Queen to myself. I'm
probably even a King to myself. I don't mean to
say I'm the Queen of England. I think it's enough
to be Queen of myself.

—LOUISE NEVELSON,
New York, 1977

If "art" substitutes for "religion" today—the museum standing for the cathedral, the art gallery for the chapel where a few coins in a saucer are not
disdained by the monk in charge, and the critic for the evangelist—then it
follows that a work of art can offer the same instruction in metaphysics as a
religious vision. It also follows that there are qualities common to both the
esthetic nature and the religious nature. Louise Nevelson's latest work—her
awesome and dazzling twelve-foot-high walk-in *Palace*—and her life, laid bare
in many published and spoken revelations of the past years, are a case in point.

She intends that consummate work to be seen not as art but as a metaphysical proposition. "Begin with the premise that I didn't want to make a
'thing,' " she said to me. "I don't call it a 'sculpture.' It pleases me to know
that I can project, from within myself, a statement, a statement that stands. That
stands like the Rock of Gibraltar. All of one piece. As if a million people were
here and I would say: This is one body of people. This is my kind of thinking.
I could put a million pieces together but they would make one piece.

"On this earth," she went on, "are many philosophies. We search. We
have formal religions, which are fine. Religions are essences of thought, not

131

made by one person. You know how many times the Bible was changed until it became an essence. Then we have Indian philosophy, Chinese, Japanese. Now, for my survival on earth, I have to dig. From these philosophies I have taken things that sustained me. I don't ask whether they are true or false. When great philosophers tell me they're searching for the truth, I think there's a screw loose in their heads. They're on the wrong track. But what then?

"What then is that each of us has our own truth. Each of us is looking for a structure. Take a canvas. White. Pure. Now, you can have the most beautiful passages on it, but you must take them out because they don't harmonize with the whole. That means: I use truth or lie as it suits my canvas. I may use certain ideas that are not 'true,' because I need them for my survival. And one of these ideas is that life is an illusion.

"In my reading, I have also found the idea that what has been crystallized can be decrystallized. So you can take a work in three dimensions and say, for example, This is wood, or This is marble. But in the fourth dimension the work may be no more than grains of sand in time. And it may be that in the fourth dimension it has its eternal existence.

"That is why I say the *Palace* is the fourth dimension of the fact that I have never lived in a house I would have chosen. I like my houses well enough. They accommodate me. But they're not my concept of the way I would have chosen to live. In seventy-eight years I have lived only in three-dimensional houses. So then this is a projection of what might have been.

"You say, What's in it? People. Two people on the left. The King and Queen, if you wish. I don't need an outside King or Queen. I'm a Queen to myself. I'm probably even a King to myself. I don't mean to say I'm the Queen of England. I think it's enough to be Queen of myself."

This moon-palace, the Queen's home, is, then, a formal disquisition on the idea of the One behind the Million, a religious theme since Abraham left Ur. It is a walk-in structure of pieces of wood tacked together in the artist's usual manner and airbrushed, as usual, black. One of her indicative fascinations is the play between formal (and so metaphysical) truth and lie, substance and illusion. The *Palace* is rich in such conundrums. While clusters and patches of wood suggest false doors, false panels, false windows, and the walls bend to offer illusory corridors, they also present real shadows and real substance and—since the structure floats on a black mirror—real reflections. By the back door is a significant row of real barrels. All bound up by black. Black, indeed,

Mrs. N's Palace *(detail), 1964–77. Black-painted wood, black mirror floor. 140" by 239" by 180". The Pace Gallery, New York.*

serves the thesis. Does black denote tragedy or death? I asked her, bound by my inherited Manicheanism.

"Black is not death. Black is harmony," Nevelson instructed me, reflecting the Tao. "The word 'harmony' is as it is in music or in poetry. You use black because it is a strong statement of harmony."

She explained more fully in her book:

I give the work order, by one tone. . . . Black means totality. It means: *contains all* [italics mine]. . . . We will continue on black because I think if I speak about it every day for the rest of my life, I wouldn't finish what it really means. You see, the human mind must have some rest. . . . We see something and we want that fleeting thing for eternity. . . . You had a moment of joy and you say, "I want to remember this forever." You arrest it, and it's your tool forever.[1]

Black, then, is a reach to arrest time. The *Palace,* floating on its black plinth, is time stopped, memory incarnate, as well as a projection into future time-space. It is Louise Nevelson's Old Testament of what she has lived through and her New Testament of what she believes today. Let us number its ways:

It is a seasick scow with barrels of sea biscuits on its decks, wallowing west toward America seventy-five years ago with the Berliawskys aboard, mother, son and two daughters.

It is a float on wheels fifteen years later, carted down the Main Street of Rockland, Maine, for the Lobster Festival, with the Lobster Queen—but not the one who earned the honor—standing in the prow with the usurped crown on her WASP-bright hair.

It is Shakespeare's Barge where stands the Rightful Queen. It is the stone boat of the Empress of China, beached on its root in the Summer Palace Lake. It is Luxor and Nara, Konarak and Cluny, any rock-cut, stone- or wood-posted temple with hieroglyphs in its forecourt and night-dark passageways leading to the sanctum sanctorum. "Through my own consciousness, I've experienced all the ages," says the Architect of Shadows, as she calls herself. "How is it that when you go to Egypt you know certain things? There is something inside us that knows." That "something that knows," like one form of the Buddha, knows itself only by contemplating its creations. "The core of my being, from the earliest days, is this: that I have a great search within me. I'm seventy-eight, and I'm still on the track of understanding what this so-called living world is about. And it's only through projecting myself beyond myself, out into the visual world, that I have a concept of what the world might be." And so it is that *Palace* is both a work of sculpture and a religious vision, of what the world might be.

What, then, are the qualities common to the esthetic and the religious nature? I propose there are three major ones, shared and discussed here by all the artists I interviewed.

There is, first, the capacity for a heightened nervous sensation many call "ecstasy," that alights such an appetite for its repetition (as animals subjected to certain brain stimuli press a button till they die) that no single sight or insight, achievement or technical procedure satisfies but the artist (like the religious devotee) must be back working the lever tomorrow. Naturally the sexual rhythm comes to mind. But so does the life force itself—"energy," or "magic energy" as various artists here call it—that propels biological matter to higher degrees of structural complexity in defiance of the law of entropy and seems simply more upward-aspiring in some individuals than in others.

The weaver-sculptor Lenore Tawney, for instance, put it this way: "I remember my first ecstatic experience, working all day on a sculpture. It was reaching a state of being where there is nothing but the work. . . . Later, I realized I couldn't continue working at that level if I wanted to have a personal life, an emotional life, and I wasn't ready to give up life. And so, since I couldn't give everything to the sculpture, I gave sculpture up. It had to be all or nothing" (see page 325). That confession and what it implies of pain and struggle, both then and later as the decision to give her "whole life" to art was reached, is characteristic. I am speaking of the artists' recognition that there is only one recompense for the sacrifice: a return of the state of transcendence. "I'd give anything to get back," says Lee Krasner (see page 100). "That's the height. Life is beautiful at moments like that." ". . . no matter what one does in life," says Nevelson, "it hasn't got the vitality or the excitement of really living [as much as] when you're really working. . . . When you're creating there's an added energy that surpasses anything else."[2]

Is the fire set in childhood, or does it come already lit, adding its smoke to Wordsworthean clouds of glory? Nevelson's first experience of that sort took place, as often happens, against a background of fear, turbulence in the mind and even physical illness. She was only two when her father left his family behind in Russia to find a foothold in this country. Louise was traumatized; for six months she forgot how to speak. Then, when she was four, there came the long voyage, palimpsest of all later voyages, actual and ideal. Halfway here, halted in midpassage, she contracted a communicable disease and was quarantined in Liverpool. Memory breaks through to a single scene. Louise Berliawsky is playing with some children also quarantined. They show her a doll that shuts and opens its eyes. Those eyes with their fringe of stiff lashes—what child doesn't know them, hasn't brushed a thumb along the naturalistic yet artificial rows of little bristles? They stick out from the plaster of the face. Even the hair, sculptured curls under a pasted-on wig, is not half so tactile, so intriguing as those eyes that shut, and their lashes. "That was almost the first thing to make me an artist," said Nevelson. "Because of the wonder of it." Another experience came soon after. "The thing that I think really established me as an artist was in the station in Liverpool. On the shelves were jars of colored candies. To me, they were like a Christmas tree. They didn't seem real. I thought we were in heaven. I remember the vision. It was magical. I don't think I've ever met anything on earth that, from a standpoint of my own reaction, was more important to me." She also remembers the joy of foraging in barrels for sea biscuits on the way.

These moments of extraordinarily vivid seeing or touching merge, as the artist matures, into a habit of seeing or handling external reality. The artist focuses on certain images, caught by stimuli to which she is idiosyncratically sensitive, and which will then become elements in her conscious esthetic: for Nevelson, lights, shadows, reflections, patches.

A white lace curtain on the window was for me as important as a great work of art. This gossamer quality, the reflection, the form, the movement . . . it has its own life. It is constantly in movement. A breeze gives you new forms, and the glitter is like a river or an ocean really.[3]

Or the sight facing her house in New York:

I can sit right here in the dining room of 29 Spring Street, looking at the enormous school building across the street. Hundreds of windows with the sunset reflected on them like molten gold . . . then the moon will come over and give it another light, then the windows at night would be totally black, and one window with one tiny light will appear . . . for me. These are the keys to my existence.[4]

Even in the subway, that place of contemporary horrors:

I would go into the subways and see the black supporting columns and recognize their power and strength standing there. They did something to me . . . as if they were feeding me energy.[5]

These are the confessions of an ecstatic, a potential sister of Teresa, though couched in the language of vision as is natural to an artist. In a 1977 televised film about her, she says, "Some people that are writing books on art . . . say, 'But look at the ecstasy,' or they'll say, 'Well, what in the hell did she do it for?' They'll have different answers. I'm not writing what they're writing. I'm talking about what happened to me to come through to this."[6] But "what

Essences #5, 1977. Softground etching. 41" by 29¼". Pace Editions Inc., New York.

happened'' to her was exactly ''the ecstasy''—the power to ''come through'' to her own mode of vision that draws in from the world and returns what it takes in the shape of a work of art. Those curtains, for example. They found their way into three great series of etchings, in 1950, in 1963 and in '77, for which the artist invented her own method of pressing real lace onto copper plates before immersing them in acid. The prints of '77 are very large works, gatherings of black tissue, crumpled, redolent of steamer trunks and whispers (''A whisper can be louder than thunder,'' Nevelson said about them). She calls them *Essences* and thinks of them as among her best work or at least her most favorite. ''I never felt gladdened in my life, but there's something about those . . .''

A second quality common to certain artists and certain devouts is a nakedness of the nerves: how else describe a condition scientists have not explained? I questioned a distinguished neurologist after hearing a like description of a state from many artists (and corroborating it from my own experience). He said there was no such thing, but added, ''I know what you mean. My wife's an artist.'' A sexist remark? Or an intuitive one? It is as if the body were skinned alive, laid

137

open to painful sensations others might be not bothered by. It involves a vulnerability that often lands artists, both male and female, in nervous collapse, since there are no monasteries or convents to shelter and heal them. Was it not Santayana who said that if it were not for the cloister, the insane asylums of the world would be fuller? And indeed as the cloisters have emptied, the asylums have filled to overflowing, as have museums. "I feel the *Palace* is both highly sophisticated and highly primitive," says its maker, "and there, I feel, is the meeting place of genius and insanity. Insanity has something to do with the primal, and I don't make much distinction between primal and sophisticated."

Louise Nevelson's books and confessions are full of episodes of anguish. Other women's stories are, too, though not all women are as open about revealing them, sharing the superstition that mental confusion is related to inhabitation by sinister powers. We are still medieval in that respect.

I didn't say life was easy. For forty years, I wanted to jump out of windows. . . .[7]

I was running south and here came five hearses. One big one for the father. Then the oldest child next. The other three next. The black hearses and this quiet procession moving . . . I must have been fourteen. When I got in the house, I shed a ton of tears. My mother couldn't believe it. She was overwhelmed to see my power of feeling . . .[8]

I was desperate. I was going through a tough time emotionally, and it broke. Everything broke . . . so many psychological problems, motherhood and separation and the struggles within myself. . . .[9]

. . . the guilts and the weights of separation . . . the guilts of motherhood were the worst guilts in the world for me. . . . That struggle blinds you. That's the price, the great price.[10]

. . . I saw *darkness* for weeks. I was alone and struggling . . . in a great state of despair. And I recall that my work was black and it was all enclosed . . .[11]

It is a night. And then you *have* to fight for the day. And the darker it is, the further your drives.[12]

She recalls her life in packets of emotion—joy or pain—materialized in images: those candies, those hearses. Then came high school in Rockland, Maine, where her father had gone into the lumber and real-estate business, and became a success for his business acumen and also for his affable personality. Her mother, however, was something else. "She would not mix with the WASPs. She was a great beauty and she used rouge and wore fancy clothes. She was no farmer. She loved style. We were dressed. Never anything but the best clothes. Overdressed! And she wouldn't mix with the people. She was almost a recluse.

138

"I was the tallest girl, and I was shy, so I sat in the back. I didn't recite a great deal. My hand didn't go up too much. Why was I shy? I wish you'd tell me. Partly because I was the tallest. Partly because—if I may say so—I was the most attractive girl in Rockland. But I wasn't a WASP. So I couldn't get the prize.

"Every year we had a Lobster Festival. There was a Lobster Queen. And every year, everyone said, 'Oh, you're going to be Queen,'[13] since you're the captain of the basketball team.' Every year they said that, since I was a little girl.

"I've never talked about this. Should I?

"All right, we'll go into it."

EM: "Did you suffer every time the Queen was announced?"

LN: "Yes. Not only that. I suffered every day. I wanted to commit suicide."

EM: "Was there a ceremony when they announced the Queen?"

LN: "I don't know. I didn't go. But I think they had cars, floats going through the streets . . ."

EM: "And you were never chosen."

LN: "Never. But I knew I was going to have a big stage. Now I have to be frank. I knew I was going to be what I am today. If it came sooner or later, it didn't matter. I take the whole credit for moving myself. Look, if you want to go to Washington, you get on a plane. Someone has to take you there, but it's your voyage."

It was much the same with her studies: "I wasn't a great reader, but when I got into Shakespeare it was as if I had created him. I see it today as a red line, telling me exactly what the meaning was. In *Hamlet*, when he says, 'Oh God, I could be bounded in a nut-shell and count myself a king of infinite space. . . .' And then no one had to say anything to me about the passage in *Macbeth*, 'I look'd toward Birnam, and anon, methought, the wood began to move. . . . I say, a moving grove.' "

That predilection for Shakespeare, of course, was not an expression of pain, but of empathy: the finding of touchstones that alleviate the feeling of isolation.

A third capacity shared by artists, religious visionaries and indeed to ·some degree by all human beings is a cerebral one but no less mysterious. There exists a dynamic machinery in the brain that drives it to weld unities of what others might let remain multiplicities. It is that structure-making genius (Kant's "transcendental unity of apperception"?) that some individuals possess, by genes or grace, to a greater degree than others. In the end, it may be what drives the artist to keep returning to the past all her or his life and then, in the climactic years, to bind up the whole span in an image or idiom that returns to the paradigm.

At an early age, Nevelson had already determined to be an artist. At eight or nine, she said as much to a librarian who posed the question. She replied, in fact, so forcefully that she intended to become a *sculptor*—"I don't want color to help me"—that she burst into tears. When she spoke that line, standing in the library as she recalls today, her eyes were fixed on an imposing plaster figure of Joan of Arc. Whether she was moved by the heroic and tragic image, the plastic form of it or the striking colorlessness of it one does not know. Enough that some part of Louise Berliawsky knew.

The tale of her progression toward her destiny has been often told: how she married for escape and security, had a son, regretted the marriage and suffered for the child's suffering when she abandoned him to go to Munich in 1931 to study with the already famous teacher Hans Hofmann. She was thus among the first of many hundreds to work with Hofmann, who would become docent to two generations of American abstract artists after his arrival here in the following year.

Back in the States in the early '30s, she drew and painted in a linear style derived from Matisse via Hofmann. In those years, she met and was a friend of many in the gathering clan of still unrecognized, advanced artists in New York, a galaxy added to as war loomed in Europe and famous refugees began to come to this country. Her sculptures were stolid, volumetric figurative pieces derived from Cubism, though in the early '40s she made and exhibited a group of Surreal wooden circus clowns and animals that were harbingers of future work. However, in one of her frequent fits of destructiveness, she burned all these in a vacant lot behind her house soon after they were exhibited.

French Surrealism, in fact, was the esthetic that spoke to her. Like Lee Krasner, who also was swimming in the New York milieu of immigrants, expatriates and WPA artists, Nevelson never subscribed to the America-firstism of the late '40s and '50s. "So the war brought these people to our shores, all these creative minds. . . . Kenneth Hayes Miller [for one] felt that great art could only come from a person that came from a particular country. He felt if a European came here, he could never really give us the feeling of this country. Well, I don't believe that. I think in our time you recognize that it really is one world."[14]

Through the early '40s, Louise (now Nevelson) showed some not especially commanding groups of wood objects in Constructivist manner; then one of those debilitating periods of depressive "waiting" took hold, and it was the mid-'50s before she got back to work. Her 1955 show at Grand Central Moderns Gallery marked the beginning of her recapitulation, one might say. The title of the exhibition, *Ancient Games and Ancient Places,* rang a mythic note, gathered all the works together into a unity that struck deep into the past.[15] Two years later, she came forward with *Royal Voyage of the King and Queen of the Sea,* even more a single conceptual structure embodying two themes never again to be wholly abandoned: the royal pair and their black night voyage, by sea, by float, by dream, by pain. This time, for the first time, matte-black paint bound the population of the gallery-floor-deck-of-ship into a unit. In '58, her *Moon Garden Plus One* incorporated the work that marked her achievement of her own idiom, never to be relinquished: *Sky Cathedral,* an eleven-foot-tall assemblage of boxes filled with found fragments of wood, the whole painted black, to be seen under blue light filling the gallery. "Appalling and marvelous, utterly shocking in the way they violate our received ideas on the limits of sculpture . . . yet profoundly exhilarating in the way they open an entire realm of possibility," was the way critic Hilton Kramer reviewed this work in *Arts* magazine that season.[16] Hans Arp saw it and compared it to Karl Schwitters' famous Constructivist room *Merzbau.* Alive with shadows and half-lights gleaming from the rounded ends of dowels, the points of splintered crates, the arcs and orbs of knobs and handles, the work encompasses a universe of random happenstance, finding, and juxtaposition and, by the single sweeping maneuver of *black,* binds it all into that "harmony" the artist twenty-five years later would still come back to.

The following year, '59, she exhibited *Dawn's Wedding Feast* at the Museum of Modern Art. This time, white was the unifying veil of Maya that covered fragments of not-so-virgin wood. ". . . when you've slept and the city has slept you get a psychic vision of an awakening. . . . between the dream and the awakening it is like celestial. . . . The black for me contains the . . . essence of the universe. The whites . . . move out . . . into outer space."[17]

In the early '60s came the gold pieces, now moving out on a wash of reflection and Day-Glo: *Royal Tide, Royal Winds, Night Flower, Royal Fire.* About gold, too, Nevelson has written: how it first struck her eye, then appealed to her mind.

Every nail we use gives off a light that is almost gold or silver. Look how many millions of people open cigarette packages . . . look at the light from this paper . . . how many millions of people are opening this and never see . . . that's reflection . . . as pure light as the most choice gold and silver in the world. Gold . . . reflects the great sun.[18]

Apparently everything in her life is subject to the same devouring hunger for the unified statement. She wears, she says, "only cotton" so that she can sleep or work in it (though the world knows the glitter and reflections of the

141

Transparent Horizon, 1975. Black-painted Cor-Ten steel. 28' high. At the Chemistry Building, Massachusetts Institute of Technology, Boston, Massachusetts.

cloths-of-gold she wears over the cotton). She lays out her tools and her supplies in a ritually purist manner each night "so when you get to the studio it's like kneading bread or doing anything. You start working. Everything is clean, is nice. You are very happy."[19] She has taken all her possessions, her numerous Mexican, Indian, Asian, African works of art, and either disposed of them or put them away out of sight behind shutters in her plain work-living space. She has pared down her life itself: "I've lived alone for years and I slowly cut out a social life. I just do my work. I like to work."[20] It is, clearly, easier to achieve "harmony," that harmony that is beyond all things, if one dispenses with them all. "Look, darling," she has said, "I can't afford to look back. That goes for houses and furniture and I don't know what not. Because I've destroyed so much. If I had looked back, I would have destroyed myself."[21]

Since then, there have been shore excursions into Plexiglas with floating nails, into aluminum and Cor-Ten steel. Plexi was fascinating for a time because of its reflective surfaces and the potential it held for revealing a multiplicity of inner chambers unified in this case by light: silver lines circumnavigating pierced holes in the surface. But there was also something unbending about the material. In the early '70s, Nevelson moved on to steel. She floundered for a time because of the need to translate her wishes via the foundrymen. But she learned to use their arms and machinery as extensions of herself—Queen's mates, to coin an awful pun—and began to turn out the massive "environmental pieces" that now frame cityscape views of Boston, Cambridge, San Francisco, New York and other places in their monumental, rust-weeping embrace.

Then, in 1977, the year also of the *Palace,* Nevelson unveiled a work that, to my mind, is not a success: the all-white Chapel of the Good Shepherd, in St. Peter's Lutheran Church in the Citicorp Center, New York. The trouble is not really Nevelson's. It is in a disjunction between the medium and the message. The person at fault may have been the pastor of St. Peter's, if he failed to explicate Protestant doctrine to the artist.

Nevelson's esthetic is built upon an Eastern mystical platform: the one behind the many, a million pieces as a single piece. Protestantism preaches the opposite principle: acceptance of diversity, the equal reality of and war between good and evil, white and black.[22] In Protestant Christianity, there is no solution to the often anguishing struggle by—in her words—a "lie as it suits my canvas." Good and bad are not illusions, says the Lutheran dogmatist in a whisper that indeed often sounds like thunder. The past may be black. It shall be made light one day. But it is real. Art that fails to impose that heavy message fails to convey the Christian view of truth. Matisse's Dominican chapel, for example, silences us by the power of his black lines, meager as they are, to

Chapel of the Good Shepherd, *north wall, St. Peter's Church, New York, 1977.*

spell out on pure-white walls the human alphabet in its postures of both devotion and woe.

No, the chapel remains, as some critics have said without explaining why, a Constructivist artwork, not a Christian religious statement. Nevelson's masterpiece, one of the masterpieces of this time, remains the *Palace*. In that work, she completes her visionary binding up of the years. There, as we have seen, is the nutshell, the moving grove, the float and the barrels. And as a viewer listens to her talk about it and observes her, there, famous as any of her sculptures, are the mesmerizing eyes with their bristle-lashes borrowed from those dolls seen long ago, whose gaze turned a traveler lost to one not yet arrived but sure of the goal. Still seeking today, at seventy-nine, a way to the Essence, she confides, "I am coming closer. . . ."

Isabel Bishop

BORN 1902, CINCINNATI, OHIO

Without my conscious knowledge, somewhere along the line I had become committed. This commitment to being an artist had, I realized, come on me even without my being aware of it. . . . then I realized that, no matter how awful I felt about everything I had done to that point, the decision was made. I was prepared to do anything to keep myself painting. Anything.

—ISABEL BISHOP
New York, 1977

The painter Isabel Bishop has been one of the luminaries of the American art world since the 1930s; in '46 she became the first woman officer of the National Institute of Arts and Letters; in '75 the Whitney Museum in New York gave her a major retrospective. All that is to say she is not only one of the singular survivors of a phase of American Realism that now seems far in another world, but also one who has continually enlarged her work so that it seems, today, most contemporary. For while no American has painted the female nude—a most traditional subject!—with more poetry than she, in pearly tones crossed with light-shot striations that dissolve flesh into insubstantial fields of energy, she has also in recent years evolved a new theme, of crossing, walking figures, intersecting but never meeting, that could be icons for this age of anomie and the search for the real.

Bishop received a classical training in the historic tradition of Rubens, Fragonard and Renoir. Her paintings, in their classic stillness, that paradoxical arrest in the flow of time, may also make one think of certain works by Piero della Francesca. The theoretical basis of her art is not far from that of Goethe, who, in his book on color, proposed the idea that there is no such thing as unbodied light; that, as he wrote, "images originate when light falls on dark

145

edges; light must somewhere strike edges that make it visible." Following this observation of a natural phenomenon, Bishop rejects, for her own purposes, an esthetic of pure abstraction—the handling of pure-light or pure-color—preferring what is, for her, a painfully frustrating, never solved problem of rendering the material and the immaterial as they intersect along the contours of the human body. Then, in the sea of light that breaks across them, her figures can be said to come into their only visible existence. By laboring this technical and metaphysical issue, Bishop departs from conventional Realism to join the ranks of artists since the Impressionists who have questioned the nature of vision and the problem of rendering the insubstantial real.

In person, Bishop is a fervently articulate woman with darting glance, long strong hands and a body that seems about to break into a run at any moment. For a half century, until she was sadly forced to move in 1978, she always worked in studios overlooking Union Square in New York (her new eleventh-floor-rear space is a melancholy exile). The last was her pride and delight and also her link with her own past. Through its windows, she looked down on an angular view of tilted green park and intersecting boulevards filled with cars and the crisscrossing of walkers. "Look how they swing their arms!" she said, peering and pointing. "How people swing their arms in the street!" That studio was filled with studies of those walkers and of walking models. The paintings themselves are built up laboriously, slowly, with much backtracking, achieving their final state only after months of labor. How painful that labor is, and how discouraging, even after so long a career, Bishop tells us here.

On her studio wall was a piece of paper with lines by Henry James:

We work in the dark.
We do what we can—We give what we have.
Our doubt is our passion, and our passion our task.
The rest is the madness of art.

I asked the artist how she came to elect the "madness of art." "Ah . . . that matter of commitment!" she said. "I've thought about it a great deal. In my case, it just happened gradually, anything but deliberately. One simply found oneself in a state of commitment. And after that, there wasn't any choice except jumping off a roof."

The process of commitment—whatever it implies—would take place in the 1920s in New York, but long before then circumstances must have begun to work upon her, laying the ground for what would become the imagery of the paintings. Isabel was the youngest by thirteen years of five children; ahead of her were two sets of twins. Coming and going back and forth, from and to schools, colleges and eventually jobs, these older siblings would pass her by in pairs—much as the walking figures in her paintings cross paths again and again, never quite to meet. So infant impressions come back in time to haunt. "They would go off here and there. Whichever was at home would take an interest in me, decide what kind of person I should be, what I should wear, and then go off again. One sister had me in Eton collars and tunics. Then another came and said, 'Oh, those terrible dull clothes!' and put me in fancy things. Everyone was trying to do something to me, except my mother. She was quite indifferent."

Mrs. Bishop was a Feminist and a Suffragette, with an independent mind and a taste for writing; though she was rarely published, she wrote continually. She learned Italian in order to make her own translation of the *Inferno*. Her feeling for that work of Christian dogma was something of a contradiction, for she was also one of those militant anti-Christian religionists of the early twentieth century. Her opinions, in fact, clashed sometimes with those of her churchgoing Episcopalian husband. "There was a time," their daughter recalls, "when I was about eight, when some event caused Mother to testify in court. She stood up and refused to take the oath because she didn't believe in God. It caused a scandal in the Detroit of that time, and I felt desperately sorry for my father."

Bishop *père* founded a boys' preparatory school in Princeton, then moved to Cincinnati, then on to Detroit, becoming, for a while, principal of a large high school. In the end, he returned as putative dean of faculty to a boys' military academy in Peekskill, New York, where his learning was barely appreciated. His plight touched his daughter, but she was relieved of having to experience it firsthand by being sent off to New York—thanks to a cousin—to study art.

"The only thing I had any aptitude for was drawing. I'd been at Saturday classes in Detroit, where the teacher was so radical as to have even young children drawing from life. When I was twelve, walking in for the first time to find a great fat nude woman posing was something of a shock! But at least by the time I got to New York I felt I had been initiated.

"I was sent to the New York School of Applied Design for Women, and I convinced the school that I was already an experienced student. So I went immediately into the life class. This was 1918. In November, we students marched, in our smocks, in the Armistice Day Parade. The Armory Show had been a long time before, in 1913. But the end of the war triggered a renewal of the excitement of it. I felt the excitement, remote as I was. And so I began learning about modern art.

147

"There was the Société Anonyme, where Katherine Dreier held forth on some evenings. I never met the lady herself, but the place was an inspiration."

Dreier indeed was one of those formidable art patrons, powers and personalities of the time, a Suffragette and a supporter of advanced European arts and artists. Her pet was a young Marcel Duchamp, and Dada and Surrealism were her causes. After the Armory Show and until the opening of the Museum of Modern Art in 1929, her Société Anonyme was the liveliest group propagandizing modern art in its headquarters, a house on Manhattan's East Forty-seventh Street.

After a couple of years at the School of Applied Design and in the Dreier ambiance, Bishop decided to follow the march to the Art Students League, where O'Keeffe and so many others had had their first taste of the professional creative life.

"And that was exciting! The students were arguing in the lunchroom. The teachers were having feuds, not speaking to each other. And you could study whatever you wanted, pay for a month and go where you wished. I tried out Max Weber's class in late Cubism and thought it was great at first, but then I couldn't make headway with him. I felt he was arrogant. But I found Kenneth Hayes Miller interesting and I could relate to him. He had had work in the Armory Show and was open to new developments, though he himself was concerned with a concept of classic—not academic—form. Guy Pène du Bois was another influence, and I formed a close friendship with him, though he and Miller were antipathetic.

"It didn't occur to me then to wonder whether I was committed to being an artist. Miller was so dedicated himself he just assumed any serious student would be, too.

"Another thing: there was absolutely no feeling, in those days and in that place, about my being a girl. It just didn't come up. It is surprising to me now to find the issue being raised. Though it's true that I did come to the League just.in time to be admitted to the first mixed life class!"

Miller and du Bois, unlike in temperament, were important figures in the American Realist school that seemed to be a mainstream current in the decades of the '20s and '30s. Du Bois had lived in Paris, and he painted New York café night life in a richly satiric, "Continental" manner. Miller based his paintings on studies of the forms and palette of the old masters, especially the Italians. What he achieved, with his glazes, golden tones and carefully composed groupings of figures in clothes of the moment, were oddly self-contradictory works: textures so refined, subjects so banal. All the same, he was one of the most influential of all American art teachers and reigned over a generation that came along in between those two other radically unlike yet equally catalytic teachers, Robert Henri of the Ash Can era and Hans Hofmann of the Abstract Expressionist era.

Bishop studied at the League and, for a while, lived like a lady in one of the many "chaperoning establishments" on the Upper East Side along with other provincial but well-bred art and music students. Then she decided she was ready to be on her own and moved to the Village to work alone. All went well for a time. "And then I began having a terribly *hard* time.

"I was only in my early twenties, and, working by myself, I got into a bad state. I couldn't manage it as a person, I see now, and I drifted into an extreme depression, stayed up all night, couldn't do anything all day.

"Then, just at that point, Miller offered an 'Advanced Composition Class' back at the League, and I went and enrolled in it, to make my life livable again. And in fact taking that course did give my life a structure again by allowing or obliging me to work alongside my peers. So I stayed with that class for another two years.

"And then I had another severe jolt. I woke up to realize that I had misinterpreted Miller's teaching. That I had been trying very hard in a completely wrong direction! Working all by myself, in my isolation, I had lost my nerve as an artist; coming back to the class, I had thought that by following Miller's methods I would arrive, again, at a point of confidence. But that hadn't happened.

"The School of Paris was dominant at that time in the '20s among all the more interesting artists. But Miller took the exact opposite direction. I thought he was teaching that as long as you used a rational method, rendered figures solidly and firmly in formal relationships, the works would have meaning. But they had *no* meaning, no personal expression! I had lost track entirely of the idea that to be an artist is to say something for oneself. It was du Bois who opened my eyes. He came into my studio for the first time in a couple of years and said, '*What* are you doing?' And the moment he said that, I realized my error. I felt those years had been a mistake.

"In 1975, cleaning out my studio, I found some of those pictures. When I looked at them, I saw they were so terrible! I had to take an ax to them! Literally—physically; they were on gesso panels and so tough I had to break them up with an ax.

"All the same, another thing had happened during that wrongheaded period. Without my conscious knowledge, somewhere along the line I had become committed. This commitment to being an artist had, I realized, come on me even without my being aware of it. And that made the feeling even worse, because then I realized that, no matter how awful I felt about everything

Nude, 1934. Oil on composition board. 33" by 40". Whitney Museum of American Art, New York.

I had done to that point, the decision was made. I was prepared to do anything to keep myself painting. Anything.''

In 1927, the year she began to paint "out of myself," Bishop moved into the first of her two studios on Fourteenth Street. It was a different New York from the one that young art students and artists encounter today. "I'd come into the Miller class in the next wave after Alexander Brook, Kuniyoshi, Peggy Bacon, Katherine Schmidt. There are classes where a number become known and classes where no one does, and not much mixing between them. The group about four years older than I had a lively time. They went bowling at Teutonia Hall Tuesdays and did many social things together. I envied them, but I wasn't part of that group. In fact, I had no artist friends. No art life. Eventually, however, the Whitney Studio Club run by Gertrude Whitney was a resource. Du Bois recommended me, I became a member and showed my still lifes there. A lovely place to go. Aside from that, I just went on working in my studio on Fourteenth Street." Eventually, Bishop would marry a research scientist, have

150

a son, and move her living quarters to Riverdale, but she never abandoned Union Square and still commutes there daily today.

This area became, in the late '20s and the '30s, as much a center for Realist painting as, in the '40s and '50s, Eighth Street and then Tenth Street would for the Abstract Expressionists. Miller and Reginald Marsh, the brothers Soyer and Bishop became the bards of the quarter. There were figures and faces of orators, immigrant shoppers at Klein's, "bag ladies," sleeping bums. And if one's studio was high enough, fascinating perspectives and vistas opened up beyond the bright lights and tacky shopfronts, on toward impersonal ranks of skyscrapers.

"As time went on, I began spending more and more time down in the square sketching. I'd been abroad (my cousin again, bless him) to see the museums. I remembered sitting in the Green Park in Antwerp with my pen and sketchbook. When I came back to Union Square, the difference in the people on the benches from those in Holland fascinated me. It was the first time I registered the *particularity* of what I was looking at, the genre aspect of the scene. For example, after seeing a certain sleeping bum a number of times, I took courage, waited till he woke and then approached him and explained I would like him to pose. He asked whether I wanted him to take his clothes off. I assured him not. In the end, he came to the studio, more frightened then I was, and returned many times. A dreadful man. He once threw an easel through the window. Then Raphael Soyer got hold of an older man and persuaded him to pose and he did so for everyone. That made my bum furious and he beat up the other man in the Bowery. In the end, these subjects made a whole epoch for me—my interest in these people. They had for me what I had been seeking: subjective reality."

For a time, Bishop went on making her studies of the population of the square: overcoated commuters and bums, and girls with graceless hats and slumped, cross-legged posture. Then, in 1932, she painted a work that struck a new note. The theme was the same one that had, in another form, captivated her mother, but Bishop drew it into her own "subjective reality": *Dante in Union Square*. The painting shows a crowd of figures in 1930s costumes; behind them rise the epochless ranks upon ranks of New York architecture. Real and unreal, anecdotal and abstract seem to intersect in this odd work, struck here and there by a glow of cold sunlight as if to announce that the passing scene is not one viewed out a window on any particular day but seen in the mind's eye. "It struck me as a subject—the multiplicity of souls." Whatever the source out of which the image came (the absent twins in their crossings?), it was one Bishop could return to again: those crowds that, in T. S. Eliot's words (apropos

151

of Dante, again), "flowed over London Bridge, so many, I had not thought death had undone so many . . ." [1]

"Then I began sketching down in the subway under the square. There was a time I thought it was so beautiful down there. You could stand and see two levels of floor, with all the columns and vaults exposed. I spent a whole summer trying to draw that, and finally I saw I was failing because when I put the people in, it seemed to turn into a prison. But that was the opposite of what I wanted! The station was, after all, a place of movement, of going and coming. Gradually I decided that the only way for me was to make the people ephemeral, transparent. Not fixed.

"So I had a model move along in a series of walking steps and I stopped her, as in the Muybridge photos.[2] And so I drew a sort of frieze of gestures that I introduced into the scene as only the vaguest impression. Later, I thought of using the frieze of figures themselves as the motif for a painting.

"And that was my first walking picture": *Under Union Square,* a combination of Piranesiesque arches and vanishing perspectives in a golden Italianate light.

Many more followed, showing women, women and men, and, recently, young people walking back and forth. Light moving across and through the figures becomes almost a theme in itself in these studies of figures seemingly adrift in a strangely glimmering underworld. So her work has moved from Realism to a kind of Conceptualism, while the central technical problem—and it has been an unrelenting one—remains to achieve that light-shot "seamless web" Bishop speaks of as a metaphor for continuity: an atmospheric plasma in which forms hover on the very edge of appearance. She wrote, in 1945, an explanation partly of form, partly of content, that seems partly to elucidate while also leaving much in shadow:

When I see . . . an elderly man . . . engaged in such a private occupation [as] sitting on the Union Square fountain enveloped in the morning light, the man, his action and the fountain seem all of one piece and somehow alone and remote. Unable to convey the magic of that light and atmosphere, I have tried to give the sense of oneness by weaving the figures and the surroundings together.[3]

Had she ever, I asked Bishop, thought of going a step further, dispensing with figures and dealing only with that light she uses as Turner did, as an instrument for the dissolution of forms into colors in motion?

"Oh, no! Figures are for me the central subject! And *is* it light they are walking in? That would be nice to think. But it's such a dilemma. It has to be *all air* in some way, or *all material,* and that is the dilemma. To carry the solution further in some unknowable way.

"I have nightmares every night about the work. It seems to me so lacking, so terribly lacking. And at this point I don't want to fall down on it. I want it to be not weaker and less, but more. And I backtrack so much. Only one painting out in the last year. So little!

"No, I don't think all artists have so much trouble. There are others so fecund, able, prolific. I know they do not succeed altogether without struggle, but there are some who have a most enviable genius.

"My ability is so small! And yet the pursuit never stops engrossing me entirely."

Recess #3, 1976. Oil on canvas. 31¼" by 45¼". Collection Mr. and Mrs. Lawrence Brinn, New York.

Louise Bourgeois

BORN 1912, AUBUSSON, FRANCE

Once I was beset by anxiety. I couldn't tell right from left or orient myself. I could have cried out with terror at being lost. But I pushed the fear away—by studying the sky, determining where the moon would come out, where the sun would appear in the morning. I saw myself in relationship to the stars. I began weeping, and I knew that I was all right.

That is the way I make use of geometry today. The miracle is that I am able to do it, by geometry.

—LOUISE BOURGEOIS
New York, 1977

I sat with sculptor Louise Bourgeois one evening on the stoop of her house. She lives on a quiet street on the West Side of Manhattan. South, behind other houses, lay the sea; to our right the sun was setting behind the river. It seemed that we too were suspended in geometry for a while, to follow memories leading back to early days in France and also thoughts leading to some programs for future work. In her conversation and her work, Bourgeois looks both ways, to the shadows and to the clear. She takes material from both worlds and works it into sculpture of radically different sorts. That sculpture, in fact, can hardly be ordered chronologically, because of her constant crossing back and forth, picking up again and transforming her images as the years have provided new materials and ways of using them.

The 1940s, for instance, saw frontier work in stone and metal being made by Calder, Noguchi, Smith and others. Bourgeois chose those years to work in raw wood. In the experimental 1960s, she took off on all sides: latex, plaster, wire, rope, rough-hewn wood for the shadows; polished marble for the light. Anxiety and geometry: the poles between which she balances. It is probably because of its diffuseness that her work has sometimes puzzled instead of seducing a public avid for quick esthetic jolts. But from that ambiguity, as well as from her extraordinary dexterity with materièl, comes her power to disturb and intrigue.

She is terse, lucid and searching in her conversation, and, occasionally, when an insight leaps ahead of words, she breaks into a shy and pleased smile, looking down into her lap and folding her hands on her knees. For Louise Bourgeois is also gifted with gentleness: a paradoxical manner for one whose art has touched dark issues. "I would love to be articulate," she says, "because of this optimistic, way-down streak in me that believes *if* people knew me, they could not fail to love me—I do believe that! And that is why I try so hard to be articulate." She has, as a matter of fact, opened a dialogue with nearly everyone living on her street. As we talked, they came strolling by and greeted her. One neighbor, however, was not of the same mind.

"Frost says good fences make good neighbors, but I take the exactly opposite position: good fences are obsolete! Therefore when the people next door decided to take down their old fence and build a much, much higher one to keep the local children out of their garden, and dumped the old fenceposts into my yard, I determined to make a Conceptual sculpture out of them. I decided to illustrate the obsolescence of fences in the twentieth century by processing them as a work of art. Very carefully, very elegantly. I bought a strapping machine and strapped them into groups with strong iron tapes. You see the extreme deliberateness of the process. You cannot just throw things out casually. We have the means of eliminating waste in a most elegant fashion today.

"Obviously, the art was in the eliminating of a fantastically painful subject—and also the *damn fence*." Today, the strapped posts lie in her garden in a romantic pile twined with a blue flowering weed that has sowed itself around them. Mutely, the straps rust in the rain.

Irony is not, however, Bourgeois's usual style. She is in earnest about her motivation. "That's what I always talk about," she says. "Because I'm really concerned about the reason an artist works, and specifically about my own reasons. Because of the compulsive, repetitive quality of the work." The theme binding that work is a heavy one that would have been unthinkable for a Cassatt and undesirable for an O'Keeffe (though not so far from what her early critics thought about O'Keeffe): the troubled theater of men and women bound by their sexual identity, which can be a prison unless it is an area of trust.

Her sculptures are phantoms from the past—father and mother, brother and sister—who stroll and recline as they did in life or sometimes appear only as parts or abstractions of themselves. On the other hand, "geometry," the work in stone—those reiterated shapes placed on the floor in groups, like bulbs about to open (or stalks, truncated)—then is still what it was when she studied Euclid as a young woman at the Sorbonne in Paris: reassurance that a set of more rational, Platonic relationships exists in the mind. She talks about the notion in double entendres. Take that word "triangle," for example—a term with unsettling overtones when applied to human beings in love. But "triangle" can also be a reminder of the grace she says she received in the midst of panic when she realized she was standing in a certain place, on firm ground, and looked up to see the moon *there*.

Her own life has moved through three points of orientation. There was her childhood by the River Bièvre near the famous Gobelin tapestry works. There were years in Paris as a mathematics, then an art and art history student in the Montparnasse bohemia of the 1930s. Then in '38 she married and came to this country. Here, in the cosmopolitan ambiance of emigré French artists, many of them founders and "gods," as they seemed then to her, of Surrealism, she gradually found herself as an artist. At that juncture she took her own route not only as an individual but as an American.

"Duchamp, Ozenfant and I had met before, but we met again when we were investigated by McCarthy in 1951. We had different fates. Duchamp had powerful friends, so he was safe. Ozenfant was a very awkward person, original and independent. When he was attacked he would attack back like a child. So he was kicked out of the country. But I defended myself. I was interrogated several times after I made application to become a citizen. My defense was that I had no connection with or knowledge of what the men I was involved with were doing politically. And fortunately by this time women had come into their own to this extent: that I was not considered merely someone's wife or friend. I was Louise Bourgeois. And I always have been."

Artist and citizen, Louise Bourgeois still did not promote her work publicly until the Feminist Movement gave her what felt like a mandate to do so.

"I have had a guilt complex about pushing my art, so much so that every time I was about to show I would have some sort of attack. So I decided it was better simply not to try. It was just that I had the feeling the art scene belonged to the men, and that I was in some way invading their domain. Therefore the work was done and hidden away. I felt more comfortable hiding it. On the other hand, I destroyed nothing. I kept every fragment.

"Nowadays, however, I am making an effort to change."

Bourgeois was born three years before the outbreak of the First World War. Her father went into the military, and her mother, who adored him, followed him from city to city; since Louise was her youngest child and also the one who looked most like the father and was therefore his favorite, she was taken along though only a toddler.

The restless moving and worry of those days made an impression that has not faded. At night, she and her mother would wake up to see the trains going by under their windows, slowly passing on their way back from the front laden with wounded and dying. Her mother would weep at the sight. And indeed eventually it was her father who was wounded and mustered out, and eventually he and his wife settled down to the work her family had done for generations: making tapestries.

Bourgeois's mother was born in Aubusson in central France, a mountain town on the Creuse River, whose waters are rich in tannin and other chemicals useful for dyeing wool. As a child, Louise heard stories of that matriarchal society on the Creuse, a world of women weaving, dyeing, gossiping, working the shuttles of their looms, the vertical ones and the horizontal. The work was monotonous, and to make time go by one woman would be appointed to read to the others, like nuns in a convent. And so while the women worked, they were being filled with romantic tales, stories that repeated the fictions that novel-readers of the time fed on: that lovers are always true, that husbands are faithful and kind, that kindness is returned and hurts are made better. And while the women were working and being worked on by these emotional fables and half-truths, the men were out in the granite quarries nearby cutting stone blocks for house lintels and foundations. So the generations went by. And then, at the turn of the century, a maternal uncle decided to better his situation and learn architectural drafting, and, to keep him company, the family moved to Paris. It was there that Bourgeois's mother met her future husband, and one supposes she felt herself as lucky as the heroines of the stories. "In my mother's eyes, he could do nothing wrong. He was a sportsman then. His great love was gliding. He would glide, and she would admire him." And that was pretty much the way it would be all their lives, as Bourgeois recalls. Her mother adored him, forgave him his glidings, and he in the end complimented himself that though he had frequently slipped he had never failed to come home in the end.

But to return to the beginning, they eloped; a daughter was born and died. Later there was another daughter and then Louise. "I was called Louise because mother was a Feminist and a Socialist; her ideal was Louise Michel, the French Rosa Luxemburg. All the women in her family were Feminists and Socialists—and ferociously so!" Her father had wanted a boy, but his wife soothed him by pointing out how much little Louise resembled him, and after the war a son was born. By then, with a full complement of children, the couple decided that his literal airborne days were over.

157

They found a factory complex on the Bièvre near Paris, a few miles from the Gobelin tapestry works. And here again, on a cold-flowing, chemical-rich river, the whole workshop setup was put in motion, with the looms and the women sitting at them talking and gossiping. Only now there were the two small daughters of the family to observe the work and the idleness at first hand and hear the women talking about the age-old subjects, love and sex, men and babies, infidelities and happy endings or not so happy ones. And since all the workers, men and women, spent their days in close communal quarters, there was a good deal of flirtation and covert sexual activity. The father apparently took pleasure in exposing his children to the facts of life under his roof. And it is there, at the very root of memory, that as Bourgeois talks one encounters the first statement of the duality that underlies her esthetics today: between science and clear structure—and that turbulent mix of anxiety and passion which is also human nature.

"Each of us, my sister, my brother and I had a garden and we tried to make the most of it, learning the art of cutting trees, espaliering pears and apples. They were formal gardens, with roses in certain areas marked off by boxwood. I was hard-working, interested in that garden. And I had a passion for rock collecting. I began with granite and moved on, through studying geology, to other kinds of rock.

"But that garden had another importance for me. We had a tent at the bottom of it, and sometimes we would sleep there. Often we took our meals there, and then we had to carry all the food out from the kitchen and back. Dinner was served late, and night would surprise us as we were eating. Then you could look back and see the light of the kitchen, only far away through the trees.

"And then our father would often say, 'Now, I don't want to have children who are afraid, so you are going to go to the kitchen and bring the salt shaker.' So my brother and I would run, terrified. We would take different ways back, and I would end at the kitchen door. There was always a man there, the man who took care of the sheep and the pig. He would say, 'You are not supposed to come into the kitchen!' The reason was that he had been kissing the cook. Then both of them would say things to make me blush. It seems to me now that our father did this to test us, knowing, among other things, that we children were afraid of the dark."

At the same time, there was inner discipline of a sort that later would condition the artist. There were designers and painters in the atelier, and there was the family tradition of the granite-lintel makers and the uncle who became an architectural draftsman. And Bourgeois's father took the business in a modern direction: since new tapestries were not so much in demand anymore, he went around the countryside buying old ones from old houses. He brought them home for cleaning, restoration and eventual sale to museums. Often these works of the fifteenth and sixteenth centuries had been long since relegated to the stables to keep the livestock from freezing in winter. Over the centuries, the lower portions of the weavings had been rotted by animal urine. So Louise, whose talent was precocious, was assigned the job of drawing in the missing portions of the design—most often, under the circumstances, feet. Pointing in or out, frontward, backward, never quite touching the bottom border, but invariably slender and flipperlike in traditional slippers, the feet had to be drawn to match the upper bodies, sometimes twelve or fourteen pairs in a single work.

Monsieur Bourgeois communicated his concern with the authenticity of works of art. In his ramblings he also collected antique lead garden statues. These broken lead figures, or parts of them—arms, legs, torsos—lay around in the grass of the gardens while he studied them and made plans for restoration. "There was always a moral aspect to the issue of authenticity for my father, since one of his sublimated urges was to be a moral man. A tapestry, for instance, had to be *authentic*. He was able to touch a piece of furniture and tell whether it was an authentic antique. Naturally this translated, in time, into the importance of a person finding and keeping to his or her own personal style."

The atmosphere in the house, then, was charged with hard work and constant discussions of techniques and style. Bourgeois's mother ruled the establishment and was the supervisor of the dyes. "When my mother said something, the building shook and my father fled. She had a lot of women working for her and she had to be forceful. Even today I am still afraid of what I think of as the 'Angry Mother.' " At the Gobelin factories, cheap chemical colors were being used; she insisted on making her own out of natural sources—cochineal shells for red, and indigo for blue. All over the house were little color charts with threads wound around in somber earth hues. Some of these muted tones find their place now in Bourgeois's paintings and graphics. For example, a drawing in colored inks for a lithograph has soft rose, green and gray-blue globules rising out of dusky blue waves; eventually a set of these prints is to be sold as a long frieze to circle an entire room like tapestries.

In addition to the unusualness of their work, the Bourgeois family diverged from their neighbors in their anti-Catholicism. A religious family in a religious community enjoys a sense of balance. Guilts can be expiated and anxieties set right by priestly advice or friendly example. There was no such leeway or forgiveness offered to Louise Bourgeois, no escape from emotional involvement, from the feeling that any time, around the corner, in the next room at the end of the garden, one might come on something that would be better not witnessed. Uneasy feelings were stirred in the family and left to build that would break out in various forms according to the sensitivity of the person. By that time, however, Louise Bourgeois would be on the way to becoming an artist and so have a means of salvation. "I didn't have the security of any kind of religion," she says today. "So in the end, that is how I became an artist—to find a mode of survival."

School years, at the Lycée Fénélon in Paris, marked the transition into the world. There she trained her intellect, not her eye, by majoring in philosophy. She received her baccalaureate in '32 and went on to the Sorbonne. That year, her mother died. Studies were therefore a refuge from grief, and it was there, at this turn in her life, that she discovered mathematics. That a subject so logical and free of emotion existed was a revelation.

"I learned that it was possible to study subjects where all the rules were known. Studying geometry, I learned a system in which things proceed without surprises. One is, essentially, safe. That was a revelation: that it was possible to anticipate! You could predict the position of the stars. The sun would rise where it was supposed to. It never failed you. Never betrayed you.

"Principally, it was a world of order that I wanted. I had been in a state of anxiety and needed reassurance. Solid geometry and cosmography—the dynamics of the stars. That was paradise. It lasted several years, my happiest time." Paradise lasted as long as the subject was solid geometry, but next came calculus and algebra, and "the thing died on me." There was only one trace of the old passion left, for the time being, a transposition from mathematics to life and also that play of language Bourgeois takes pleasure in:

"I was still interested in triangles. Now, with the mathematical triangle you can actually do something. For instance, if you want to measure a plot of crooked land all you have to do is divide it topographically into a series of triangles and measure each one. But triangles also have to do with the relationships between men and women. And about the triangles that I was aware of in real life, there was not a thing I could do."

After graduation, there was the question of what Louise Bourgeois was to do with her life. The natural thing was to study art, and Paris had many well-known teachers, each at the head of his own atelier, most of them working in quasi-Cubist styles. She sampled a number, beginning with Otto Frieze, then moving to André L'Hôte, whose classes were especially popular with expatriate American students and where the stress was on color theory. Eventually she settled down with those two powerful post-Cubists, Ozenfant and Léger.

Ozenfant liked to demonstrate how to draw solid forms by pinning a curl of wood shaving to the wall so that the students could render it in light and shadow. That assignment reminded Bourgeois of solid geometry, and she made a couple of stone carvings of the rising spiral in three dimensions. One of these was accepted for a Salon d'Automne, no mean accomplishment for a student. Later when she explained to Léger how hard she had worked to be mathematically correct, he lectured her in words she still remembers. "He told me, 'But, Louisine! You don't have to be so rigid and precise. You can push geometry around a bit.' He gave me a key by saying that." Another day, listening to Léger stress and stress again the desirability of building up solid forms, sculptural in appearance on the flat surface, she decided it would be more sensible to make the sculpture itself.

And all the time, as a student still in her early twenties, Bourgeois was getting to know the bohemian life of the quartier, enjoying some freedoms while she continued to commute back to the family house, now presided over by her father alone, but also finding out some things about what lay ahead. "When I was at the École des Beaux-Arts we had a nude male model. One day he caught sight of a woman student and suddenly had an erection. I was shocked at first. Then I thought, What a fantastic thing to reveal one's vulnerability so openly!" At the Grande Chaumière, the famous workshop of generations of art students, Bourgeois was given the honorary job of overseer of the models. They were all prostitutes, she remembers, figures out of a Fauve dream, with white, white skin, lips painted red or purple, and hair in amber or jet curlicues. Like the loom women of her childhood, they delighted in making a fuss over her and teasing her for her innocence. She in turn was fascinated by many things about them, including their fixation on hygiene. "Louisine," they would call out, *"tu t'es lavée aujourd 'hui?"* and then turn to one another and break into smiles. "Very strange creatures" were these females without fears or modesty.

Then it was the beginning of the '37 Paris Exposition, and she got a job as translator-guide for foreigners at the Louvre. All day the Americans would come in with their odd manners and way of saying, "Oh! Gorgeous!" at everything. "This was the word I heard all day long." But she was becoming something of an expert in pictures and also a wage earner, so she moved out of the family house into rooms in a Left Bank building owned by Isadora Duncan's brother Raymond. Around the corner was the gallery Gravida, run by Surrealist André Breton as a showplace for "all kinds of crazy Surrealist objects." Bourgeois stopped in to look often enough, but in those days she was too shy to introduce herself, Breton was such a "god." And then, as one more activity in the art field, she decided to do a bit of buying and selling. So she went to an auction house, bought early works by Bonnard, Vuillard and Villon. But then when she took the Bonnard and the Vuillard to the artists to have them authenticated, it turned out that neither one was genuine.

"Vuillard took the picture out of my hand, tore it in two and threw it in the fireplace and said, 'I never want to see you again!' But Bonnard did not get angry. He was very tall, taller than people believe. He leaned down and said, 'My child, let's not talk about that. Let's talk about you. And then afterward you go take the picture back where you bought it.' So that is what I did."

So there were disappointments, but at the same time she was learning that artists were not necessarily gods but accessible human beings. This was an important lesson for a young woman who was unsure of herself; even more reassuring was the fact that she was becoming expert in English, in demand as a translator. And there were Americans in Paris in those days who made a stir about her as a real daughter of Gaul. One of these was the American art historian Robert Goldwater, who was in France finishing his book on primitivism in modern painting. In 1938 she married him and came to America, and though as a Feminist she kept her career apart from his until his death in 1973, she is willing to say something about the quality of her feeling for him.

"I had met someone who was kind. I felt all was well and that I was safe with Robert. And that left me free to begin. When I got here, my old anxiety was transformed into *manageable loneliness.*" Eventually there were three sons, and them too, since they all have their own lives today, she prefers not to discuss when she is talking about her art, though her interest in them is shown by the examples of their work and ideas in her studio. "The kids were a fantastic amount of physical work, but I was quite strong. And when women tell me they don't want children—well! I just don't believe it."

The year after Bourgeois arrived in New York, war was declared in Europe and the migration of artists to this country began with the arrival of Surrealists Yves Tanguy and Matta. In '40, Dali and Léger joined them. In the next two years, Max Ernst, André Masson, André Breton and Marcel Duchamp found haven here. Many of them found a platform at the Art of This Century gallery started in 1942 by Peggy Guggenheim. The small, tunnellike space of this gallery, designed by the sculptor-architect Frederick Kiesler, provided a breeding ground for the abstract and Expressionist styles to come after the war. There in 1943 Jackson Pollock made his debut.

In those early years of a New York to a large extent taken over by the French, Bourgeois was one of a few who were bilingual and could move between the worlds. The immediate challenge, however, was accommodating herself to her new role in life. Her first works here explored this not altogether agreeable subject, by a series of drawings called *Femme Maison,* "House Woman," little stick figures of women whose bodies were houses, or who hide their heads in houses. The uncomfortable novelty of finding oneself revealed to the world as a sexual object was the not too concealed message.

"In those days I only sensed it, but now I understand clearly. If you ask a person, 'Are you male or female?' what should that person do? Should one simply die of embarrassment that such an intimate personal matter has been revealed to the whole world? The woman I was drawing in those days—the *femme maison*—did not yet have enough poise or objectivity simply to say, 'Don't ask me such a question!' No. She fled, and hid herself away."

The drawings were charming, wistful, Klee-like. In 1943, a number were shown at the Museum of Modern Art along with works by Calder and Masson; that marked her first appearance as artist, not house-woman, in her adopted country. Four years later, she published a suite of engravings in the same manner, illustrating poignant little fables about missed meetings, accidents and lost treasures. Again the images were lonely little structures—skyscrapers, towers without windows, spiky cabins on stilts—a city seen by a stranger. One story contained only two words, but two such sad ones: "Leprosarium, Louisiana." About those works the Surrealist writer Marius Bewley wrote:

The problem is simply that of loneliness and isolation presented in terms of a cultural failure as it impinges on the individual. . . . This problem is one which every modern artist has had to deal with after his own fashion. . . . The personal tragedy is by no means disqualified in this process. It remains the prime motive in the final product.[1]

Meanwhile, Bourgeois had begun to work in sculpture again, now reaching back toward memories of pain. Her first exhibition in 1949 was an extraordinary assemblage of forms for that or any year.[2] Wooden constructions with knobby heads, tall and thin as giant asparagus, stood together or walked across the gallery floor in clusters. As if to point up the reality of those phantoms, she dispensed with bases for the sculptures. They simply *were,* as people in a room. A six-foot-tall group of wood beams, painted the purplish red of tapestry backgrounds and joined at the craniums by one wooden lintel, clumped unsteadily across bare floor: *The Blind Leading the Blind,* on one level a deliberate comment on McCarthyism. Other groups were hung and gingerly touched the floor on pointed buds of toes, like those acid-worn tapestry feet of long before. The gallery was lit to suggest a "tragic mood, as if people were coming back from the past—people who were missed, badly missed presences." As for that tentative toe-touching to the floor: "The object of that was to show their fear of touching, their uncertainty about where to put their feet." The groups together created a "social space," or a world of their own. "They stood

163

The Blind Leading the Blind
*(detail of lintel, above right),
1948. Wood. 7' by 7⅓'. The
Detroit Institute of Arts, Detroit
Michigan.*

for my intense desire to have my family with me again, even that father of mine, my brother—all of them.''

The following year, yet another group was shown, this time figures with the most commonplace of titles, simple folk one might meet walking down a road in a country village: *Figure qui apporte du pain; Figures qui supportent un linteau; Une femme gravit les marches d'un jardin* . . . The show caused a stir. Alfred Barr bought one work for the Museum of Modern Art, *Sleeping Figure,* seven feet tall, a black wood chrysalis held upright between two poles. Around the same time, Bourgeois designed sets for the dancer Eric Hawkins; these too were wood environments of several figures, all black. ''But, Louise, everything is black!'' Hawkins commented.

164

"And I said, 'Yes, because the world is in mourning. It is the black of missing people, as simple as that.' Whereas now, certain people are showing only the black of the black. . . . But I was less interested in making sculpture in those days than I was in creating a past that I could not do without. And not only recreating the past: also controlling it."

Other wood groups have followed; for a major piece at the Whitney Museum in 1958, she created a *Garden at Night,* clusters of black and white forms like shoots, bulbs or asparagus again, leaning against one another, sprouting and jostling. These, one has to think, grew from the unknown but feared population that lay in the grass before the lighted kitchen in France so long before.

Bourgeois also was then making single works of stone or plaster, evidently parts of bodies. One of the oddest is *Femme Couteau,* "Knife Woman." She appears as an elongated marble shape with anatomical folds and apertures. In another incarnation, she is bulbous and birdlike, with a droll little projection that might reflect a nubile girl's puzzlement about what precisely she owns. Giacometti and Duchamp dreamed up such disembodied bits of anatomy, but their *Disagreeable Object* and *Pointe de Malice* make one shudder; Bourgeois's are both sweet to the touch (the marble) and tender (the little bud). Of this one she says:

"People say it is an aggressive form, but it is *not.* She is harmless, armless, but very afraid! She is in a defensive period of her life. She is a girl who has

Femme en colère, 1969.
Travertine. 6' high. Xavier
Fourcade Gallery, New York.

found a knife but doesn't know what to do with it. It is a beautiful thing, shiny, but wasted on her. After all, she is only a little bird defending her nest."

In fact, Bourgeois is full of sympathy for the victimized woman. Her Feminist concern extends to women's professional and social lives in a half-liberated world. "Women are losers," she told me, "they are beggars, in spite of women's lib. Because our fate is conditioned by our gifts. That is a very cruel thing. If you have no gift, have only a third-rate education, no manners, no self-restraint, then what are you going to do with your life? So it is a serious matter, life. It is often tragic. And yet, beyond the tragic, there is Black Humor. There is Dada."

When black humor takes on psychic depth and plumbs memory and the theater of dreams, then Dada turns to Surrealism. At a point in the 1950s, Bourgeois went to the Lascaux caves and came away moved by the sight of those great hollows of darkness, eroded by millennia of rainwater. Returned from Lascaux and furnished with that visceral '60s material, latex, Bourgeois began to make a series of what she called *Lairs*. She would build a wire mesh, cover it with latex, then with papier-mâché and plaster. One, four feet tall, was cast in bronze. Rough and ragged outside but warm and completely "safe"—that favorite word—within, these quite plainly were a "benevolent mother, a place to put a baby." Then came the ultimate *Lair*, focal work in her 1975 exhibition. This was a seven-foot-wide Surreal theater-tableau in latex and dark space, presenting *The Destruction of the Father*. Bulbous shapes were suspended from the roof of the claustrophobic space. Two more humped forms loomed from the floor. Around them lay the debris of a giant gluttony: animal limbs cast in latex. The colors of the forms were malignant. As Bourgeois tells the story, it is a scary tale out of the night of time.

"There is a dinner table and you can see all kinds of things are happening. The father is sounding off, telling the captive audience how great he is, all the wonderful things he did, all the bad people he put down today. But this goes on day after day. A kind of resentment grows in the children. There comes a day they get angry. Tragedy is in the air. Once too often, he has said his piece.

"The children grabbed him [she is talking now in the past tense as if of something that happened long ago] and put him on the table. And he became the food. They took him apart, dismembered him. Ate him up. And so he was liquidated.

"It is, you see, an oral drama! The irritation was his continual verbal offense. So he was liquidated: the same way he had liquidated his children.

"The sculpture represents both a table and a bed. When you come into a room, you see the table, but also, upstairs in the parents' room, is the bed.

Those two things count in one's erotic life: dinner table and bed. The table where your parents made you suffer. And the bed where you lie with your husband, where your children are born and you will die. Essentially, since they are about the same size, they are the same object.

"And all those things of latex are actually casts of animal limbs. I went down to the Washington Meat Market on Ninth Avenue and got lamb shoulders, chicken legs and cast them all in soft plaster. I pushed them down into it, then turned the mold over, opened it, threw away the meat and cast the forms in latex.

"I built it here in my house. It is a very murderous piece, an impulse that comes when one is under too much stress and one turns against those one loves the most."

From art of that kind, she tells us, there is always the accessible relief of geometry. More than a relief, it is a means of transcendence. "Once I was beset by anxiety," the artist confessed. "I couldn't tell right from left or orient myself. I could have cried out with terror at being lost. But I pushed the fear away by studying the sky, determining where the moon would come out, where the sun would appear in the morning. I saw myself in relationship to the stars. I began weeping, and I knew that I was all right.

"That is the way I make use of geometry today. The miracle is that I am able to do it—by geometry."

From that discipline, with its virtue of affording a distinct sense of location in space, the artist has drawn many of her strongest works. An especially rarefied one, made recently, is *Ongoing Dialogue*. Two stone components of a large xylophone are placed on opposite sides of a room to be played back and forth, producing tinkles and chimes allusive and elusive as notes in a work by Satie or Cage. This characteristic product of one side of Bourgeois's nature offers us the pure Platonic essence of a dialogue burdened by neither anxiety nor love.

The little geometries do not, however, always manage to keep wholly free of the agitations of this world. Several times Bourgeois has presented whole gallery shows of marble cylinders (actually cores of vases discarded by an Italian marbleworker) arranged on the floor by the hundreds, sometimes lopped off diagonally as if with saber blows, sometimes topped with little pentagon and hexagon hats—perhaps "a family," as she suggests, or perhaps also those jostling, shouldering, muttering lines of marchers in the '60s peace demonstrations she passionately supported: beings on the move but not dangerous; rather, "safe," or marching to ensure our own safety. And recently she has returned to wood for compositions of geometric arcs and circles in pale grays and white, leaning against the walls.

"I think of them as classical landscapes, permanent; I have bound the pieces together, you see, or they would slip apart. These things tied together by me are an immense symbol, too, for the loosening of relationships that takes place in time. As long as you have tied the elements together, things are *not* going to slip away from you."

For the future, Bourgeois has much to do and much not to let slip away. She has achieved the eminence to which her work destined her if it had not been for those burdensome years of "shyness" laid upon her by an old world. Two exhibitions of her work were held simultaneously in New York in the fall of 1978, at the Fourcade and Hamilton Galleries. The latter featured an immense and powerful new work called *Confrontation.* There was a long float, table or palanquin, draped with blue cloth. Movable wood barriers were set all around, creating an unbridgeable, perhaps holy space within. On the table was a rambling arrangement of those latex globular shapes out of *Destruction of the Father,* lifted out of that gruesome setting and spread forth here like the relics of some barbarian event whose horrors have been tranquilized by the passage of time.

The year before, Bourgeois had been given an honorary doctorate by Yale University. She recalls the presentation ceremony with some amusement. "They said I got the degree for having explored 'the human condition and the relationship between men and women.' They were trying to pay homage to my sex, I imagine, and also to my French background. I suppose they figured any Frenchwoman would know about 'the human condition'!"

The human condition continues to fascinate her. She has just finished a major commission for a federal building in Manchester, New Hampshire. The basic theme had to do with conservation of energy. But in a characteristic flight of association, Bourgeois engaged a multiplicity of ideas relating to intimate human relations. The piece consists of a rough geometry of those triangular barricade forms that surround *Confrontation,* only here made of steel. By slight turns of their reflecting surfaces toward the sun, these forms snare and shine forth beams of sunlight. For what myriad meanings is this action a metaphor? Begin with the old French country sport of snaring swallows in nets. Take the eye of a swallow, a mere facet turning to the light. Skim on to the image of a person, attracted, then captured by the light in another's eyes. Ah! The piece has to do with desire. And with the capturing, by whatever means, of what one most yearns for.

And so it seems that by the alchemy of time and the sense of self-worth that derives from her growing eminence in the art nowadays, Louise Bourgeois

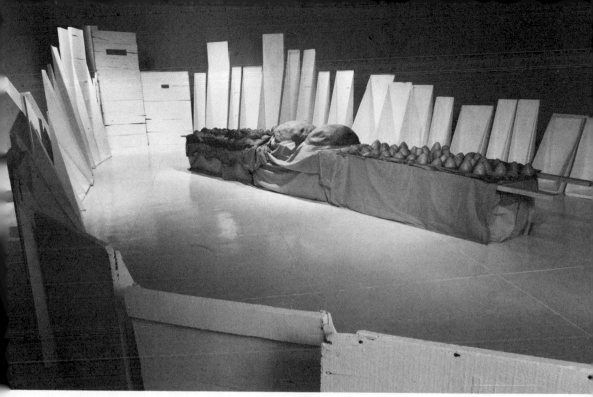

Confrontation, 1978. Wood, cloth and latex. Installation in the Hamilton Gallery, New York.

has begun to leave behind some of the heavy preoccupations that once burdened her. I asked her whether those troubling images still stayed with her in the hours when she is not working, or whether they are loosening their claim on her.

"No, I do not carry them away with me. I am in my studio all day working, often in that deep and violent way, and when evening comes and family life reclaims me, then I feel stabilized and become—a nice person!

"It may seem strange to live in this world of imagery and also to have a normal life. But I sleep like an angel. Never a nightmare. It is a great privilege to be able to work, and I suppose to work *off,* such feelings through sculpture."

Helen Lundeberg

BORN 1908, CHICAGO

... a friend of my mother's suggested I take a course at the local art school, since I was at loose ends. ... Well, I began and that was it. I felt I had found something I wanted to do and could do. So I plunged deeper and deeper.
—HELEN LUNDEBERG
Los Angeles, 1977

There are dreams of reason and dreams of monsters. Renaissance religious paintings with their serene symbols are the sweet visualizations of good dreams. French Surrealism, born in the economic and political turmoil of the 1920s, proposed a more modern operation: to confront the monsters and draw them into the light of consciousness. There was also, however, during those decades of the '30s and '40s when French Surrealism was being propagated around New York City, a contrary idiom being advanced by a few artists in Los Angeles.[1] "Post-Surrealism" returned to the Renaissance mode of rendering the dream. One of its original exponents, who then by natural evolution moved in the decade of the '50s into another, related forerunning position, Hard-Edge painting, was Helen Lundeberg. Always an original, often a pioneer, she has been insufficiently praised because of her distance from the center and her diffidence about fame. Now at last, in the wake of the Women's Movement, she has begun to receive her due: a retrospective exhibition at the Los Angeles Municipal Art Gallery in January '79 and, in the fall of '79, a double show with her late husband, Lorser Feitelson, at the San Francisco Museum of Modern Art.

Surveying her oeuvre of nearly fifty years and listening to the untraumatic events of a lifetime, one wonders finally how much of an esthetic attitude is inherited, how much invented. For something essential in Lundeberg's art and personal style seems carried over from the childhood she describes. Her parents were Swedish Lutherans, born in the famous town of Galesburg, Illinois, that also produced Carl Sandburg and the American Surrealist painter Dorothea Tanning. Within that town was an inturned religious community to which all four of her immigrant grandparents belonged. Her paternal grandfather was a deacon in the church, and though both her parents reacted against Lutheran strictness and moved to nearby Chicago, where their two daughters were born, it is hard not to read that influence into her studious, introspective career. She is Swedish in appearance, a tall woman with an extremely courteous manner that can be drawn aside—like the curtain she literally painted into many of her Surreal works of the '30s—to reveal a mental landscape of clear-cut foreground and of background depths not to be fully revealed.

"My father was brought up so strictly he couldn't read anything but religious books on Sundays. As a result, he turned against the whole thing. But I went to Sunday school and I enjoyed the music. When I was about twelve, I began thinking my parents should go to church, too. Church or not, on Sunday afternoons in our house you could have heard a pin drop. Everyone was reading. I still remember the atmosphere. I don't think I ever knew such a quiet, peaceful time. Nothing disturbed it.

"In those days I had no ideas at all about becoming an artist. I wasn't aware there was such a thing. But I do think now that my turn to art came about, strangely, from those Sunday afternoons reading. I began to read everything, but especially novels and travel books. I became such a daydreamer! And then, from being so interested, I began doing some scribbling of my own, mostly oriented to nature. I was always a great gazer too. I loved landscape. But with so little background in the visual arts it seemed more likely I'd become some kind of writer."

When Lundeberg was four the family moved to California, where her father went into business. "I couldn't bear economics and paid no attention to what he was doing," she remembers. All the same, it seems he once had had a feeling for things she would come to find important.

"All through my childhood, a picture he painted when he was twenty hung in the living room. It must have been a copy, though he had taken some painting lessons. It was sad. A gray picture of a girl in a boat on a marshy lake. She looked lonely, melancholy. Sad and gray. But painting wasn't considered a career for a young man, and he never talked about it. It was my mother who seemed to be the artistic one. She made all our clothes, and they were beautiful! Dresses, coats, hats. She might well have been an artist under different circumstances.

"And of most of our houses out there, I remember only the outdoors. Once, we lived in an English-style cottage with an enormous pepper tree in the back. There was a lawn, a rose garden and a fence I'd climb to look off into the mountains after the rain."

In high school, Lundeberg was chosen one of the "gifted children" in a research program conducted by Dr. Louis Terman of Stanford University. The project involved reports at five-year intervals. One result of this focus on long-term development was that her family did not hurry her to make career plans. "It's possible they put up with my vacillation about what I was going to do because they thought they had a budding genius on their hands—better let her alone." In 1930 she graduated from a junior college, intending to go further and major in English, but it was the Depression and there was no money.

"It was at that point a friend of my mother's suggested I take a course at the local art school, since I was at loose ends. She offered to pay for three months. Well, I began and that was it. I felt I had found something I wanted to do and could do. So I plunged deeper and deeper.

"The first classes were in life drawing by the Bridgman method of constructing the figure in a series of boxes. It's a good thing there were only three months of that. Then Lorser Feitelson took over the class and stayed on. He not only got me over Bridgman but explained in such a way that everything began to make sense. I was enchanted.

"In grammar school, I'd been poor in math, but high-school algebra and geometry had made marvelous sense to me, they were so logical. I could learn the rules. Probably that same peculiarity of mine was what led me to like so much Lorser's lectures on composition, illustrated with diagrams on the board. He was a wonderful teacher. When he sensed talent in a student, he urged the student to work seriously, not be 'just a student.' "

Feitelson, that influential teacher and Lundeberg's husband, was a pioneer American Modernist who had lived in Paris, known the Dada, Surreal and so-called Metaphysical artists like de Chirico and also studied the Italian Renaissance masters. Back in California, beginning in 1933, he and Lundeberg would invent and propagate their own version of Surrealism.

"I got deeply into something that I feel was really Lorser's brainchild, though I was involved from its very beginning and wrote the first theoretical 'manifesto,' published about the same time as the first public showing of our paintings in 1934. We called the style New Classicism, or Subjective Classicism, with Post-Surrealism as a subhead—but everyone who wrote or talked about it called it Post-Surrealism, and that's the name that stuck.

"We were trying to do something with certain principles of Surrealism, but based on the normal functioning of the mind. There was nothing 'automatic' about our paintings; each composition was very consciously planned." [2]

172

Works by both Lundeberg and Feitelson of this period locate fragmentary gatherings of objects in cool, articulated space—instead of the shifting perspectives and ambiguous space of East Coast Surrealism—in a deliberate effort to achieve a tranquil and elevated effect. Instead of imagery drawn from a turbulent night landscape of mutating forms, like those of Gorky and Tanguy, the New Classicists disposed their symbolic images—flowers, stars, clocks, books and so on—in conceptual, even narrative frameworks, so that each work, like a Renaissance tableau, presented an arcane but to a degree legible meaning.

The epiphanal work of this genre was Lundeberg's *Double Portrait of the Artist in Time* (acquired in '77 by the National Collection of the Fine Arts, Washington, D.C.). The work could be a graphic illustration of themes in this

Double Portrait of the Artist in Time, *1935. Oil on Masonite. 48" by 40". National Collection of the Fine Arts, Smithsonian Institution, Washington, D.C.*

book, for autobiographical, Feminist, social and even metaphysical meanings are suggested by this curious image of two figures—the blue-eyed child full of expectation and the "daydreaming" adult—bound into a single space-time warp by the long shadow that lies upon a wall. In other works of that period, Lundeberg returned to a number of basic image themes: a road ascending distant mountains; seashells; a single greenish light bulb reflected in a dark mirror. It was on the purely formal basis of works like these—with their clear drawing and contrasts of light and shadow—that, in the decades of the '50s and '60s, Hard-Edge painting, with its conscious rejection of subject matter, would build.

Meanwhile between '33 and '41 Lundeberg worked with the California WPA doing Italianate murals in Los Angeles public buildings as well as lithographs and easel paintings. The work was good training for hand and eye, but, as for women across the country, it was even more liberating psychologically.

"I'd still been living at home, but then I moved away to live near the project headquarters. For a while I bossed a mural crew of six people, told them what to do, saw they kept at it. I even had a chance to drive a truck. No man in the group had a driver's license and I did, so I took a work crew out to a nearby town. Altogether, it was a great thing for most artists. And for me! My being an artist had been a worrisome thing for my family. But the project saved the day. It gave me enough to live on, and also made just being an artist okay."

It is sometimes claimed that some Los Angeles painters, because of the outlandish look of their city, turned their backs on it early on and so arrived ahead of Easterners at flat, cool abstraction as a mode of utopian escape. As early as the mid-'40s, the Los Angeles painter John McLaughlin was making geometric, apparently emotionless black-and-white abstractions, flat to the surface: icons of contemplation for which he credited his studies of Zen Buddhism in Japan before and during the war. Lorser Feitelson showed canvases in that mode as early as 1952, calling them "Musical Space forms." By the late 1950s Los Angeles critic Jules Jangsner was describing the style by the name that stuck: "Hard-Edge." During these years Lundeberg and Feitelson worked alongside each other, as they did for nearly half a century until his death in '78, sometimes sharing an esthetic interest but as often diverging. In the late '50s and early '60s, Lundeberg herself as she says "dropped out all those 'charming objects' " to create her own flattened compositions of arches and other architectural forms in low-keyed blue and umber (for sunlight and shadow). Pictorial structure was a prominent interest. "I wanted to keep the sense of literal space and perspective, but with the least possible means, and to work for the harmony of the flat shapes themselves." Feitelson meanwhile developed his own

Icarus Bay, 1970. Oil on canvas. 60" by 60".

powerful idiom involving fluctuating space activated by flowing tendrillike streams of color.

In the decade since then, Lundeberg, in spite of protests about her disinterest in painting landscape, has moved toward a feeling-rich rendition of things observed: still life and landscape, mountains, sea, plains and gullies of shining light.

"I tried painting outdoors once or twice in my student days. It's so messy! The wind blew. Everything flew away. I work better from memory, and imagination. The days of outdoor landscape have passed. But I am looking all the time, so I have a repertory of landscape effects in the back of my mind.

"In fact, I always play with some notion of illusion. Nowadays I like to do works flooded with a pervasive light in a single hue—blue or green, for in-

175

stance. To key a painting to one color. That can give a moonlighty, dreamy quality I like."

Blue Calm is one of these works; it hangs on the wall of the studio-house she shared with Feitelson. Suffused with blue-gray light, it is a seascape seen from a far distance with flowing striations of sand shoals in the foreground in a delicate tonal scale from darker blue-gray to silver. "The lower part gave me horrible trouble! In the end, though, that's the part that pleases me most, getting the luminosity from these gray slivers of form. But whatever you do, don't use the word 'nostalgia' to describe these!"

So I will not. In fact, whatever there might be of the nostalgic—meaning the still-regretted, or the painful—in Lundeberg's work is so webbed in tranquility that it might be there only as a hidden motive power never to be revealed. Nor does she express regrets for experiences she has not had in her life. Her husband, for example, had finished his travels before they met. She, who based so much of her early work on the Italian painters like Piero della Francesca, has never been outside the United States. There is a measure of acceptance of that and other facts that parallels a quality in her work.

"I never had your young girl's normal ambition to get married, to have a nice house and children. I was too daydreamy, full of romantic notions. And no, I've never traveled, though as an adolescent I read travel books all the time, books especially about women traveling! And everything of Conrad's over and over. But now I feel as if I'd been everywhere."

Working so closely in apparent harmony over years, Lundeberg and Feitelson might, I thought, have something to reveal about psychoesthetic differences between the sexes. "He's a more conceptual painter than I am," she said to me at the time, "and his mind is more analytical, but that may be an individual rather than sexual difference. My colors never come from color theory; color, it seems to me, is a perceptual affair. We agree on that.

"Perhaps men do have more tendency to intellectualize, but for so long women were tied to the male view of what art is that it's hard to know just what differences really exist. I am not, for example, an impulsive painter. Though there is a point in painting, getting the first thing on, when it looks so marvelous you don't want to touch it. It's a temptation to leave it. And sometimes you do!"

Is it a female response, for example, while exploring cool abstraction, also to have made paintings where color plays on the sensibilities through tonal nuances subtle (and unfortunately as unreproducible in black and white) as a piece of diaphanous tissue?

There is also in Lundeberg's work, however, another, surely non–gender-

176

linked intuition. In 1947, she painted a picture called *The Wind That Blew the Sky Away.*

"I was walking home from the market. The clouds and sun were so beautiful. I went home and made a little sketch. First it was greenish, with a blue sky. Then, I don't know how it happened, the idea of blowing the sky *aside* came to me. The wind blowing the sky aside! I went on to conceive of the idea that the wind might even come blowing all the way from outer space and pull back the sky-illusion and show the darkness that lies behind." And indeed, in this canvas, such a blackness is revealed behind the sky. A blue-black and brown vortex into which the wind sucks as if into a black hole, while a tiny tree at the edge like a harried weathervane describes the direction of the whirl.

Is it possible to propose, taking off from this work, that it is not nostalgia these works contain but the recognition that "harmony," set forth as an esthetic ideal back in the '30s, is achieved only at the price, also, of letting break through, in some pictorial even if not formal sense, the contradictory disorder behind things—as metaphors for which Lundeberg gives us, from time to time, the shadow on the wall, the darkness in a mirror, the black door that screens the sunlit vista? "Most people don't recognize the influence of Mannerist art on painting today," she commented. "The role of tension as opposed to harmony. Imbalance, incompleteness." It is a mark of Helen Lundeberg's originality to have implied this recognition, paradoxically, in the course of an oeuvre of extraordinary outer quietude.

Jeanne Reynal

BORN 1902, WHITE PLAINS, NEW YORK

Being an artist meant being myself, errors, warts and all . . . establishing myself within myself . . . So finally, in the end, there comes a day when it's all what it's meant to be. A certain realization of what one has attained.

—JEANNE REYNAL
New York, 1977

Mosaic: one of the oldest arts, old as weaving, as architecture. Possibly older: don't bowerbirds adorn their nests with bits of mica, shells, flowers?

Jeanne Reynal, one of the leading mosaicists of her time, has written that her art is "not painting with stones and not sculpture, but an art the essential quality of which is luminosity. . . . mosaics do not belong to a time but a human need of exceptional duration, a need for a new variety of flower, for the spirit of man who has in his heart a stone, the universe." [1]

To make the stone bloom! That was what the earliest mosaicists had in mind, in Mesopotamia in 5000 B.C. when they sank glazed clay cones—red, black, white—into mud plaster walls to reflect the desert light. The Greeks and the Romans, less interested in paradoxical effects, used flat black and white pebbles for their floors. Byzantines went back to the original idea, setting tiny, shining tesserae, often backed with gold leaf, one by laborious one at slightly varying angles to multiply the dim light of candles. So set, mosaic tesserae can literally "give forth light," as Reynal puts it, as the flower comes breaking out of the dry mud.

But the technique fell on hard times after the sixteenth century when Baroque painters learned to simulate the effects of light and when architects learned to build soaring domes that would scoop in their own measure of real light through pierced windows. By 1928, when Reynal began to work in London as apprentice to the then famous academic mosaicist, the Russian Boris

Anrep, the craft had reached a low point. Conventionalized Renaissance-type pictures were made by pressing preglued tesserae into cement and peeling off the backing to make quick-applied decorations for banks, railroad lounges and so forth. Her story, then, is unique: the choosing of this ancient medium as her own and then the carrying it forward as a major art form. Her mosaics, no mere decorative panels, are related to relief sculpture, even in certain cases to free-standing sculpture, and are created in a direct gestural process expressive of the artist's temper and thought, in a style close to Surrealism and Abstract Expressionism.

In another way too, what Jeanne Reynal confides about her life strikes a singular note in this assemblage. For though from her front window, as she pointed out to me, she faces tangible proof of her place in a continuous heritage, her memories of that heritage include a rupture still painful and now to be eternal since those who insisted on it are on the Other Side of time. How strange and moving it is, then, to come, midway in the span of her adult career, upon a work that foreshadows a shift in style by a full decade and is also a vivid illustration of the thesis of this book. It is a structure mysterious perhaps as Stonehenge, set up in a certain field in Millbrook, New York. In this case, however, the artist herself provides the key to the reading of the secret of the stones.

I visited Reynal one spring day in the Greenwich Village home she shares with her husband of nearly twenty-five years, the painter Thomas Sills. She had been ill, and we could not talk long. But I wanted to see and hear what I could.

Through the tall windows at the front of her house she looks directly across the street to another eighteenth-century building with which Reynal feels kinship. It is built of "old Verplanck bricks" bearing a lovely pinkish cast, manufactured by her Dutch immigrant forebears when they came here in the seventeenth century. Those Verplancks from whom she apparently inherited a feeling for *ground,* and for small modules set into it, settled around Storm King Mountain on the Hudson. There they turned that dulcet pinkish earth to such admirable ends—as she in her time would do in her way—that they became rich and converted from Judaism to the Church of England. One of their descendants was painted by John Singleton Copley as *The Boy with the Squirrel,* now in the Metropolitan Museum. Another descendant, the artist's mother, had their energy, their ambition, their flair, but perhaps not their sense of organization. As Jeanne Reynal wryly remembers, "She thought she was Queen of the Earth. She loved to gamble and she loved to drink. But she lost her money and her mind in the crash of the '30s. I wasn't close to her, and she never accepted my being an artist." That extraordinary Queen of the Earth had, her

179

daughter implies, an imagination of her own: she loved going about in Indian costume, the finest of Sioux trappings she bought at a costume store. Mad or merely madcap, she cast a shadow that lay darkly in her daughter's mind. "Repeatedly, I had a dream about her and later about my sister Adele. I dreamed they were half buried in the ground and that they condemned me for being childless. It was with that kind of feeling that once, I made a mosaic sculpture called *Woman Coffined, Cribbed, Confined.*

"Oh, but I was a scandal at times, from being overconfined myself, when I was a girl! I could always tell when I'd behaved scandalously, because then we'd all set out on a trip to hide the trouble—really the impending *birth,* as my mother invariably leaped to fear.

"On one of those trips, however, she took us out West. It was a portentous trip. I was about seventeen. There I saw Indian sand paintings for the first time. Years later, when I went back to the Indians with the Surrealist André Breton, I decided to work with my stones as though they had the quality of sand themselves.[2]

EM: "And your father and others of the family—what were their roles in your life-to-be?"

JR: "My father's father was a poor but noble Frenchman, descended from French Huguenots from Normandy. He came north to this country from the Martinique—Jules Reynal Roche Fermoy de Saint-Michel—a fine shot with small arms, rifles and shotguns. My father inherited those skills, along with his father's taste for hunting hounds, riding horses and hunters, and polo playing. He was small, blond and handsome, and shy, with a fearful temper. He would beat up the stableboys for the least infraction. He was rich, and not at all artistic, though he was fond of showing us his tight, correct drawings. But he was good with animals, and I adored him."

Jeanne Reynal was the second of five offspring and, like many other women who became artists, a solitary. "I didn't play with the others except a younger sister whom I thought of as my own child. The others were forever playing togetherness games. Swiss Family Robinson in a tree house. Baseball. And skating. I was remote. I read a great deal. The tree house was too cooperative for my taste. In fact, all the games were too cooperative. I've always been a person who did things by myself.

"I didn't live in a child's world, it seems. In fact, I feel now the others disliked me and were even afraid of me because I was different. That includes my brother Eugene, who became the founder of Reynal publishing company. They all grew up to have the conventional opinions, marrying right, living right. They lived for what other people thought."

But, in secret and solitude, the artist was forming herself, not only technically but from the standpoint of those never-to-be-forgotten attachments, never to be transcended in the lifetime.

"There were two things I loved doing when I was a child. One was picking up stones I called 'feelies.' And I was always doodling and scribbling. By the time I was six, I had fallen in love with Rosa Bonheur's *Horse Fair* from a print on the nursery wall and made drawings of all the parts of the animals, ears, hoofs, necks, eyes. Much later, when I was working for Anrep, he had to design a Saint George and the Dragon. No one in the studio could draw a hoof. But I—I knew the structure by heart!

"There was another thing that set me apart from my brothers and sisters. I never went to school. I was thrown together with my father and his friends, all hunting people. That was because when I was about nine Mother and Father separated. He left the home they shared and went to live in Millbrook, New York, where he built himself his own house. For whatever reason, it was me he chose to take along, with a governess, to live with him.

"Many a morning those days, he would come in and say to the governess, 'It's a lovely day! Much better for Jeanne to come riding with me than to study!' My father's lovely animals! I adored them. And I myself had a pony twenty-seven inches high who would follow me like a dog.

"But my father too, in the end, couldn't accept what I wanted to be, and then also that I wanted to live on my own. After I moved to Paris and a whole new world opened up for me, he literally cut me off, and I never made it up with him. I would come through New York on a visit and see him and my mother. He and I would go for a drive and ride side by side in absolute silence. It was that conventional idea about the arts and a lover. In my family it was all right to tinker on the piano.[3] I'd been escorted into the city to see the Armory Show when I was eleven, by a governess. But don't take it seriously! And the trouble was that from about the age of twelve I had accepted that I would be an artist."

EM: "How did you go about getting there? Step by step, or by one leap?"

JR: "I think art grabs people. I don't think I just leaped into it. This was how I met Boris Anrep and my life began. I was twenty-four. Mother took all of us—that is, two sisters and two brothers—to England, France and Italy for the summer. While we were in London, two friends, older, one an architect, the second a painter, arranged for me to see the famous Courtauld collection and have tea with Mrs. Samuel Courtauld. Roxane, my younger sister, and I had arranged to see a pack of harriers who were willing to sell their stud; this was to be a present for Papa. Mrs. Courtauld was so intrigued by American girls who were interested both in art and in dogs that she arranged a dinner with Boris Anrep and other English notables to look me over, for the Courtaulds were included in the famous, infamous Bloomsbury set and were very chic hosts. Anrep, a very large Russian, intimidated me more than a little. Though he sat at my right at dinner, we hardly talked. But I had a curious feeling he was going to play a part in my life.

"The next day we met and he took me to see his pavements at the Tate Gallery and the two large floors at the National Gallery. The following day, we left for Paris, and then again Anrep was at the door, so to speak. We went to Chartres and Les Halles and Russian nightclubs. When we left for Venice and then Rome, there he was again. And then my life commenced. I began to be 'in myself.'

"Two years later, from a return trip to America (Anrep insisted that I see my parents every year or they would forget me, which began to be true), I stopped at London. Anrep took me to the Bank of England, where he was laying the floors, which pictured the coins of the realm in gold on black. He asked me if I would like to help, and of course I said I'd love to. The big sheets of paper with the tesserae on them had been sent over from Paris, and it became my job to glue back the stones that had fallen off. The workers told me I'd ruin my hands doing it, but I stayed on and worked with him, every night, down in the vaults under the bank with the sheets spread out on long tables, while the guards walked back and forth. I *loved* it!

"So I returned to Paris to work with Anrep. He had signed a paper guaranteeing that the Bank of England mosaic would last three thousand years, but already some of the tesserae were beginning to fall out. That's when I drew the horse's hoof. And later on there were decorative borders he had done for the Greek Orthodox church in Bayswater that had to be carefully reconstructed, eight hundred running feet of a border of flowers and swags in the Byzantine style. The other women workers did it by rote, as you'd sew a button on. But when there was a part that had to be drawn in by hand, no one could remember how the design went. I did. I drew it from memory. And Anrep said, 'If you can do that, you're a mosaicist.' At that, I began experimenting with some designs on my own. I remember thinking that maybe *line* would be a new way of looking at mosaic, so I did one based on Picasso's *Two Women*.

"It was at that time, when I realized how much I was *grabbed,* that I broke totally with the family. Being an artist meant being myself, errors, warts and all. Mother was so appalled she actually tried to have me committed to an insane asylum, but I got a lawyer. She died around 1940 and my father about the same time, both of them of broken hearts. But I was an artist by then and there was no turning back."

EM: "You left Paris for good in 1937. You had, it seems, lost the way or the possibility of returning to a stable old world among your family. Was that, then, a painful time for you?"

JR: "I should perhaps answer that question by bringing up the question of children. I have not regretted being childless. From time to time, friends have left their children in my care when they were little, and these boys and girls are still my friends. And still that may not have been enough. I dare say my careless ways more than hint that, with some part of me, I would have liked a child of my own. In fact, with my fourth pregnancy, during those Paris days, I toyed until nearly the fifth month. I even persisted in the idea of leaving Anrep and bringing up his child by myself. But about that time my father cut me off without a cent, and when he heard this news Anrep announced he could not 'afford' me. He took up instead with a wealthy Englishwoman who supported him until his death some forty years later, in his eighties. I saw him only once after that break.

"I had a terrible dream about that time. I dreamt I put my head in the oven and turned on the gas. But then while I was still dreaming I said to myself, 'This is not the way to end. You will live. And you will not regret it.'

"I was in shock. I think it true to say that I suffered a nervous breakdown then that has lasted a lifetime, though by now I have learned to live with it. And still, before leaving Paris, I did have the good fortune to meet a charming Californian who had come to Paris with a group of Socialists and Communists, to aid the American young men who formed the Abraham Lincoln and George Washington Brigades in the Spanish Civil War. Soon after his arrival, he was told that his son, a member of the Abraham Lincoln group, was missing in action. He with his sorrow and I with my disaster made suitable companions, so I lived with him until my father's death.

"Eventually, I returned to the U.S. for good and went out to California. I worked in a potting shed in Marin County for a while. That was the time of experimenting for me. I tried all kinds of things in mosaic—copying drawings, copying Picassos, learning everything I could. And there were plenty of artists in San Francisco then.

"Shortly after my father died, my mother's death liberated me by a rather handsome amount of money, which was really my grandmother's endowed-for-three-generations funds. At that point, I met a young man who had been on the WPA and also had worked with the Italian crew imported to work on the mosaics at San Simeon. He was of great help in acquiring supplies of smalti, the glass used in my work, and in teaching me the use of various cements necessary for the installation of reverse-method mosaics on walls and floors. We became friends and soon moved to the High Sierras, where I built a house and a studio. Other friends visited, but it was lonely. Fourteen feet of snow every winter. Warm summers with a thunderstorm every afternoon. I longed for New York.

"In the winter of 1946, I closed that house and returned to New York, where I lived in an apartment until I found a house in Greenwich Village large enough to have a studio. I still live in this same house, and in May 1978 I will have been here thirty years. It is in this house that I was able to entertain my many American artist friends and to bring them together with the Surrealists."

EM: "In any case, you'd have left Paris at the beginning of the war. And you did come back to the U.S. at the same time as the Surrealists. Gorky was a close friend, too, in those days. Can you say how those artists affected your way of working?"

JR: "Ah! The Surrealists only talked about sex. Art was what you *did*. The idea was always 'Try another! See what happens. See how it works.' That was a wonderful viewpoint! Following from that principle I did lots of automatic drawings, and that helped to loosen my feelings. So that at a point I threw away the prepared drawings and the reverse technique I had been used to and began working directly. I began, in other words, setting stones right into the cement. Later, it was Gorky who told me I was using stones that were too big. So I tried smaller ones, and that was better. Then Marcel Duchamp suggested the use of Pointillist methods. So I tried even tinier sparkling stones set according to a color program. But that manner was too organized for me. I like things to happen by accident, the happy accident.

"Then I met André Breton. It was 1945. He and Elise Claro were in Reno for six weeks waiting for divorces. My ski lodge in the High Sierras was forty-five minutes away, so I saw them often. My friend and I chauffeured them through the Indian country on a six-week tour greatly enhanced by the marvelous sensibilities of André. He spoke very little English. Elise spoke Spanish and a little English. I spoke English and French. My friend had no languages and a speech impediment. It was a difficult companionship for the duration but marvelously maintained by the splendid goodwill of Breton, who never let it sag. For instance, he loved picking up semiprecious stones. We'd all go out walking and looking for them. He liked the sparkle, the richness. So I tried to make use of them, but the results made me think of the French saying 'Ça fait riche.' I had to temper down the sparkle!

"Well, in those days I was putting in at least eight hours a day at mosaics, not doodling but living. I was establishing myself within myself. Then there came the time when I began to do the pieces that really worked—loosely woven together, with the tesserae scattered like abstract brushstrokes. So finally, in the end, there comes a day when it's all what it's meant to be. A

Great Field of Hands, *1941. Mosaic floor, in situ. Private collection, California.*

certain realization of what one has attained. What one has to accept is that by the time that happens, it often is the case that nearly half one's working life already lies behind one."

Jeanne Reynal's first original work, done in this country after her return from Paris, had been a mosaic floor for a house in California. It illustrates two lines of poetry by the English Surrealist Hugh Sykes Davies, "I see a field of hands like flowers/When the sun will shine, these hands will open." There are closed fists of political protest, and a fan of opening hands like the prints of prehistoric palms pressed to the walls of the caves in France and Spain: a moving opening statement of her own. But it was in New York in the Abstract Expressionist days that Reynal came into prominence, turning out those fields of stars, those tumultuously grounded ramparts of obsidian, jasper, flint and common pebbles, glinting dully in opalescent beds, on which her reputation was founded. In those days, she showed her work regularly in New York and widely in museum exhibitions.

In 1953 she married Sills; and their travels to far parts fed her imagination. She tracked a number of rivers—the Rio Negro, the Amazon, both Niles; she studied Hispano-Indian churches with their black Virgins and weeping saints, and took something of the primitivist feeling of those sanctuaries for her own works, incorporating more blacks, crystals, white marble, mother of pearl. In

185

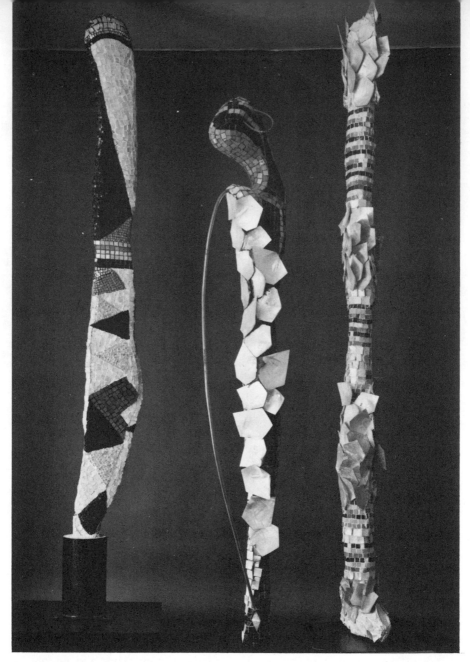

Totems: Emperor's Greys, 1969–71. Mosaic. 5'5" to 10'8". Collection the artist.

the 1960s she made a number of architectural mosaics: for Our Lady of Florida monastery and retreat house in Palm Beach; for two state office buildings in Lincoln, Nebraska; and for the Church of Ss. Joachim and Anne in Queens,

New York. But her nonecclesiastical works, which stand on their own and draw their meaning from private sources of imagination, are more distinctive.

Many of the finest of these, however, stand unseen in Jeanne Reynal's Village house today. There is not much demand for her work now, and pieces unpurchased wait in the shadows like festival banners for a parade that has gone on ahead. There are several eleven-foot-tall pole pieces, shown in a group at the Parsons Gallery in 1971. They take their aura of barbarism from memories of things seen in the Honduran and Guatemalan jungles and in Africa. *Emperor's Greys* is Reynal's return, then, to mornings in Ethiopia, watching from her window as the royal horses were brought out to exercise in a courtyard. She watched them wink their ears as they drank, then raise their heads and shake them. The top of the *Emperor* pole is alight with broken, angular shards of pearl shell, set points up like fluttering leaves. Below, rings of red, yellow and green tesserae gleam like a bandleader's baton, or the Lion of Judah's regalia (or a polo player with flying fair hair, on a tall horse on a sunny day?).

It was in 1961 that Reynal made that work of mute intuition that anticipated Minimal art of a decade later. It was a somber structure, six large wheels of gray cement with a sparse scatter of tesserae on either side. She set them up on edge, in a Stonehenge-like alignment, in a field in Millbrook where once

she rode to the hounds on her father's horses. *La Ronde des Heures,* she calls it. But it did not survive the hours to come.

"The idea was good," she says today, "but we didn't understand about the heavy weight of the cement. The wind knocked several down. One is still lying out there in the bushes." Others lie on their sides in her garden today, grown over by falls of roses.

A tall window overlooks that garden. It is filled with an immense cage holding flocks of birds, flickering modules of bright color in a gray window-pane: cockatiels with yellow heads, peachfaces from Africa and finches descended from an aged yellow-feathered patriarch who disconsolately ruffles and broods below. In the rooms behind are works of art by Reynal's many artist friends: the first oil Jackson Pollock ever sold, purchased in 1941; paintings and sculpture by Gorky, Rothko, de Kooning, Hare and others. For years, the house was a kind of reunion place for artists both European and American and of many styles and persuasions. The isolation visited upon Reynal today by the rounds of time and fashion is not to her liking. Still she is the realist about this destiny of hers, if she must be now, as she always has been, somewhat eccentric to the mainstream.

"My work isn't liked," she said to me. "Mosaics aren't liked. I said to Rose Slivka the other day [Slivka is her good friend and editor of *Craft Horizons*], 'I'm well-known—but I'm not liked.' And Rose said, 'That's right.' "[4]

"Nevertheless," says Reynal, "as I look back on my life as it was given its start by Anrep, then recreated by me slowly, over forty years, I can see that at a point I was transformed by my determination to succeed with my art. So I reversed the trend of resentment toward him which would have been so destructive.

"Let me put it this way. What was inside is now outside. I believe my work shows it. I have, I feel, created my best work in the last ten years. And there is more ahead."

Alma W. Thomas

BORN 1892, COLUMBUS, GEORGIA
DIED 1978

I have remained free. I paint when I feel like it. I didn't have to come home. Or I could come home late and there was nobody to interfere with what I wanted, to stop and discuss what they wanted. It was what I wanted, and no argument. That is what allowed me to develop.
—ALMA THOMAS
Washington, D.C., 1977

Alma Thomas died in February of 1978 at the age of eighty-six. *Hors concours* in many ways, she did not find herself as a painter until the decade of the '60s, when she was in her seventies. Also she was black, came from the Deep South, and spent most of her life teaching in the public-school system of Washington, D.C. But what she turned out in the last years of her life won her one-person shows at the Whitney Museum and the Corcoran Gallery in 1972, smaller annual shows here and there afterward and national recognition.

Her handling of color was what revealed her as the artist. The fact that her emergence as a colorist coincided with the flowering of the Washington-based movement of Color-Field painting gave her canvases their look of contemporaneity. Under these circumstances, how misapplied was the parochialism by which Thomas was repeatedly included in shows of Afro-American artists. She saw a world of things in many hues with no ethnic twist.

I visited her two months before she died, still at work in her little house in Washington crammed with paintings and an orderly richness of books, papers, artists' announcements. She liked to keep in touch. The front rooms were lit through tall Victorian windows—old District of Columbia architecture. A central bay window was full of dark-green leaves of a big holly tree that pushed

189

against the glass from outdoors. One saw through those leaves a flicker from behind, a sense of space, sunshine, flashing cars. When I came that late-autumn day and looked around as I do to find what the artist's eyes rest on in working time, I saw that window-tree (as Robert Frost would say) and thought to myself: *there*. It was one of my better insights. An hour later, Thomas had explained exactly what that tree had done for her eye, her imagination and indeed her life.

And in fact some of her works look as if a dark glassene surface had been stretched and stretched till it broke in many places to let a luminous underneath layer show through. Mauve breaks to reveal green-golden; scarlet breaks to white; dark blue to yellow. These fields of color were her impressions of natural phenomena. Spring flowers break through the crust of earth. White azaleas break through the dark woods. On a blue-black Washington night, stars break through in the same crystalline patterns a young Georgia O'Keeffe saw one Texas night sixty years ago. Other Alma Thomas works are wheels of color—garden banks of scarlet sage or chrysanthemums; still others show fields of warp and woof like bright dyed weavings held up to a lamp. Complex formalist interpretations were laid on her work, relating it to French Divisionism or Tachism, or Bauhaus color theory or Kenneth Noland's targets. But all that seems forced. She used her eyes to see with, and studied work by other painters as well as photos from outer space and her own garden. What she took from these sources, and how she transformed them in her original way, was not directed by formalist doctrine. She was, as she says here, "free," while also "of this day in time."

There is also, in that regard, a metaphorical digression to be made from those dark-surfaced paintings with colors within. I find a bitter pathos in the lives of the people this artist grew up among. Alma Thomas, like her mother and her aunts, inherited tenacity, imagination and will. She dreamed of being a "great architect," or of building bridges. She had about as much chance of developing herself in those directions as she had of going to the moon alongside the astronauts she admired. Instead she spent thirty-five years teaching art. "I devoted my life to the children and they loved me," she says here with a beautiful humanity. The irony, of course, is that it was "color," for which, for a long time, she says she felt no special affinity, that turned out to be the passport to a life of mainstream cultural prominence she had not known before.

"I was born in Columbus, Georgia, in 1892, in a Victorian house that stood high on a hill a little off from the city. At night you could look out and see the lights of the town. It was the first house built in that vicinity; later it became a desirable neighborhood, so white people came and built houses all around and there was a white school two doors away from us. I didn't go to it, of course.

"Summers we spent with my maternal grandfather, who lived across the Chattahoochee River in Alabama, about twelve miles downriver in a place called Fort Mitchum. He had about a thousand acres there, a marvelous plantation. He had a white half brother he looked after all his life. They went to the Civil War together; then after they came back and settled in Alabama, their plantations were right next to each other; in the beginning his brother even allowed some of Grandfather's children to go to school with his own children. My mother was too young for that, but the oldest boy and two or three of my aunts went, and later they went on to college at Tuskegee and Atlanta University. It was just like *Gone with the Wind:* when the brother came back from the war he didn't know what to do with himself and he became a drunkard. So my grandfather just watched over him and eventually buried him.

"I remember the times we went to their plantation. It was a beauty. I remember the gorgeous sunsets; I remember the lovely fowl, every kind of fowl. There were peacocks. In the afternoons we would sit on the front porch while they came and put on their display for us. And there were beautiful pigeons, fantails, and ducks. And every kind of animal, pigs and goats, horses and ponies.

"Then, too, I would go wandering through the plantation finding the most unusual wildflowers. And the cotton—oh, that was a gorgeous sight: as far as you could see, beautiful flowers, white with a bit of pink, bell-shaped. I haven't painted that yet, but I do want to someday—paint my memories of that cotton.

"Then there was my grandfather. He raised horses and sold them; gorgeous horses. He was much respected. He looked after the community, helped the old people who lived on the farm when they became ill, always wanted to make the people around him live better. And we saw we were fortunate to get a few minutes for him to speak with us. In the mornings, he would go down to the post office and get the papers and come back. And then we would all sit in the sun and he read the paper. Then he discussed politics—all the affairs of the world. Something that interested him he would tear out and put aside to be read again and discussed. We would be hanging around him, around his neck; my younger sister in his lap. He had very gorgeous hair, and some would be patting his beard and some his hair, and he would go on discussing what was in the paper. And when he got through, he would line us up for a spelling bee or some game. He would give us the words, and after a while he would make one up and of course we had never heard of it. We loved our grandfather! And meanwhile, our aunts would be sewing or knitting or combing the cotton out, weaving or spinning on the wheel."

191

EM: "Did you paint or draw in those days?"

AT: "No. We didn't know anything about that in that day and age. But there was one thing I did. There was a little brook running down below our house, and water tripping down the hill. That water had some kind of acid that changed the clay to different colors. I would get little cans and put the separate colors in separate cans. Then I'd take them home and make things out of it. I had never seen anyone do that at all. Little cups and little plates. The truth is, I was always building something."

EM: "Who else was in your family?"

AT: "Three other girls, younger than me. Then, my mother was a dress designer, outstanding in colors. Everything she made was like a painting. She sat at the sewing machine, and at night we would hear her singing as she sewed. That's why I am as I am. So that young people come around me, those who want to be painters and those who love art. I got that from my grandfather and my mother.

"And my father. He gave his soul to us. He looked Italian; like my mother's father, he had a white father. His white half brother built houses; that's how we got the one on the hill. So we lived in the best place, you might say, for a Negro at that time, where there were the blacksmith and doctors' offices and the post office and the coal yards. And in our house we always had books and papers. My aunts who were teachers had cultural clubs. White professors from Atlanta would come to lecture once or twice a month. I still have the books today that were bought at that time. Latin books and Shakespeare and the history of the world."

EM: "And history of art? Did you go to museums?"

AT: "Museums! They had none way back in that day. There was nothing like that. Mercy, this is back in the beginning of time! There was only one library in Columbus, and the only way to go in there as a Negro would be with a mop and bucket to wash and scrub something.

"But there were people then who painted on velvet—you put in the petals and other patterns, and all those paints were around when I was little. I loved to use the paints, and to make things. But education was the important thing. I was aware early on that one of the ways to get ahead was to become a professional, like a lawyer. But I was born with a hearing and speech impediment, so I couldn't go that way. My mother always thought that was because, before I was born, a lynch party came up the hill near our house with ropes and dogs, looking for someone. They got to the top and found my father there. They recognized him for the most respected Negro in Columbus and didn't bother him, but it frightened us, and Mother said it caused my deafness.

"Eventually, my aunt and uncle who lived in Washington invited the whole family to move up here so we children could finish our education. So we came and stayed.

"I went to Armstrong High School, a new trade school. When I entered the art room, it was like entering heaven. A beautiful place, just where I belonged. I stayed three or four years and took all the art courses as well as sewing, millinery, cooking. The Armstrong High School laid the foundation for my life.

"Later I went to the teacher-training school, but I didn't do so well there. There were many smart ones who could express themselves better than I. But I went into kindergarten training and found again I could make things. From my architecture studies at Armstrong, I learned to construct little buildings out of cardboard. I made a little modern schoolhouse, for one, that was shown at the Smithsonian in 1912.

"Later I went down to Delaware and stayed for six years running a kindergarten and a settlement house. And then the war was over, and there came a turning point. There was no more of the old ways of teaching. Now they used the Montessori method. I told my mother I would have to change my life, that technology was taking over. But at the same time I had developed an interest in costume design. So in the end, I went to Howard University to get a degree in costume design. And the first year there I happened to meet Professor James Vernon Herring. He opened the first art department at Howard, and he asked me to be his student.

"He became my mentor and took me under his wing. He had beautiful books. In my leisure time, I would go to his home. He would take the books and explain the artists to me. And so I came to know the great artists.

"After graduating, I taught art here in Washington, thirty-five years in one room. I enjoyed those thirty-five years. I devoted my life to the children, and I think they loved me, at least those did who were interested in art. Even after I retired in 1960, I devoted my time to the children who lived nearby. Rounding my neighborhood were the slums of the world. On Sundays those children would be running up and down the alley. So I got them to clean up and come to my house and we made marionettes and put on plays."

EM: "And you were moving then toward becoming an artist."

AT: "Yes. Back at Armstrong I was known as being excellent in architecture. I wanted to be a sculptor, or a great architect. I always said I'd have loved to build beautiful bridges. At Howard I began doing sculpture, and later on, when I went to Columbia University for my master's degree, I worked in sculpture again. And then during the 1950s I studied painting at American University and made a trip abroad.

"I was doing representational painting. But I wasn't happy with that, ever.

I watched other people painting abstractly, and I just kept thinking about it, turning it over and over in my mind. Then, in 1964, I had a terrific attack of arthritis. I thought, This is the end, I'll never be able to move my arms again, or walk. Just then I was offered a retrospective of my paintings, at Howard University. I thought about it. I recovered my health. And I said, 'I'll try.'

"I decided to try to paint something different from anything I'd ever done. Different from anything I'd ever seen. I thought to myself, That must be accomplished.

"So I sat down right in that chair, that red chair here in my living room, and I looked at the window. And you can see exactly what I saw, right before my eyes, from where I was sitting in the chair. Why, the tree! The holly tree! I looked at the tree in the window, and that became my inspiration. There are six patterns in there right now that I can see. And every morning since then, the wind has given me new colors through the windowpanes.

"I got some watercolors and some crayons, and I began dabbling. And that's how it all began. The works have changed in many ways, but they are still all little dabs of paint that spread out very free. So that tree changed my whole career, my whole way of thinking. I never even go to the other windows anymore. I used to, but then they put up houses and cut off the view. When they put in those high buildings, I said to the other trees, 'Goodbye.' I was sick when I couldn't see them come in red in the spring and go out red in the fall. But through that one window I could see the light, how gorgeous it is.

"I've never bothered painting the ugly things in life. People struggling, having difficulty. You meet that when you go out, and then you have to come back and see the same thing hanging on the wall. No. I wanted something beautiful that you could sit down and look at. And then, the paintings change on you. All you have to do is put natural light on them. In the mornings, I come in here when the sun comes up, and the pictures change. Light is the mother of color, and no place stays the same. Look in that corner. It's dark. Look over here, and you see light.

"And then—since we're not living in the horse-and-buggy days—I began to think about what I would see if I were in an airplane. You look down on things. You streak through the clouds so fast you don't know whether the flower below is a violet or what. You see only streaks of color. And so I began to paint as if I were in that plane. And at that time I hadn't ever been in one!

"From then on, I just painted. The next year, in '67, there was a show of black art at George Washington University and I was included. My banner year was 1972. My breakthrough. I presented my pictures at the Whitney Museum in New York, and about twelve New York art critics wrote about my

Wind Tossing Late Autumn
Leaves, *1975. Acrylic on
canvas. 72" by 52". Martha
Jackson Gallery, New York.

work. Later on, Harold Rosenberg wrote in *The New Yorker* that I brought joy to the '70s!

"It's strange how it all came about. I never really thought about being a painter. I didn't even understand about color, until all of a sudden it came to me. But you never know what you're going to do unless you keep working. People come to me and say, 'Tell me how to paint.' I say, 'I can't. It comes from inside you. You have to expose yourself. Nobody taught me how to paint. I had to do it myself.'

"I don't know how it happened, but it seems to me that I've conducted my life so that every time I came to a crossroads I took the right turn. I never married, for one thing. That was a place I know I made the right choice. The young men I knew cared nothing about art, nothing at all. And art was the only thing I enjoyed. So I have remained free. I paint when I feel like it. I didn't have to come home. Or I could come home late and there was nobody to interfere

195

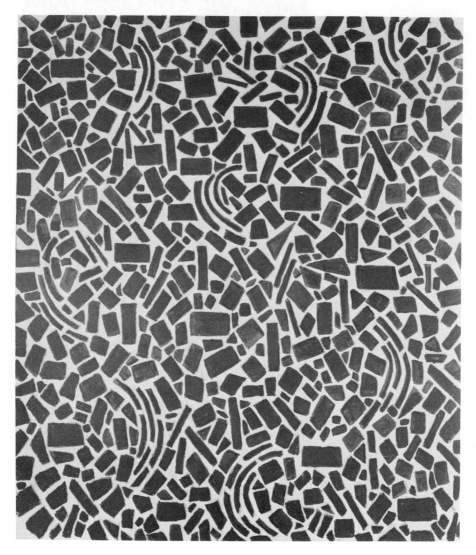

Garden of Blue Flowers: Rhapsody, 1976. Acrylic on canvas. 60" by 50". Collection Harold Hart, New York.

with what I wanted, to stop and discuss what they wanted. It was what I wanted, and no argument. That is what allowed me to develop."

EM: "Do you think of yourself as a black artist?"

AT: "No, I do not. I am a painter. I am an American. I've been here for at

196

least three or four generations. When I was in the South, that was segregated. When I came to Washington, that was segregated. And New York—that was segregated. But I always thought the reason was ignorance. I thought myself superior and kept on going. Culture is sensitivity to beauty. And a cultured person is the highest stage of the human being. If everybody were cultured we would have no wars or disturbance. There would be peace in the world."

EM: "Tell me how you work on a painting these days."

AT: "I make a lot of little color sketches. I have hundreds of them. And I keep up with what's going on. I buy all the art magazines, and many of the new books. And I go to exhibitions. I like to feel myself part of this day in time.

"I also visit places like our arboretum here in Washington, not to paint but to get impressions. A friend of mine goes there and gets every leaf. I said I'd go crazy doing that. I told him, 'Just go and look. It settles in you, and then you don't need to look at it anymore.' My painting *Washington in the Springtime,* for instance, shows the city putting out all those gorgeous tulips, pansies and jonquils in the spring. But it's only an impression. I leave behind me all those artists who sit out in the sun to paint. I leave them back in the horse-and-buggy times when everything moved slowly. I get on with the new."

EM: "And where do you get your amazing titles: *White Roses Sing and Sing, Reflections of a Brilliant Sunset Shimmying in a Lake, Wind Dancing with Spring Flowers?*"

AT: "Singing and dancing to rock 'n' roll music! Or out of my mind, just like the paintings. I look at them and look at them, and change them and change them, and all the while I'm getting titles for them. Some I have done from my memories of my grandfather's place. *Grandfather's Pond.* And *The Spring Awakening.* And there are more I'm going to do of those. And one of my works is called *Earth Sermon: Sun, Beauty, Love and Peace.* That is what I paint. I paint the earth. I paint the sky."

EM: "Are you a religious person, would you say?"

AT: "I think the religious part is helping people. Always being out to help somebody. To help the children. But my real belief is in my art, in beauty. I say everyone on earth should take note of the spring of the year coming back every year, blooming and gorgeous."

Women of the Second Wave: Mavericks at Midway

INCLUDING
GRACE HARTIGAN,
JANE FREILICHER,
FAY LANSNER

It is not usually remembered that men of the First Generation of Abstract Expressionism and women of the Second began to show in commercial galleries and so to begin their rise to prominence at the same time. Nell Blaine, for example, began exhibiting in the '40s, that decade of esthetic turmoil explored in the "Abstract-Expressionism: The Formative Years" show at The Whitney Museum in 1978. It was indeed as late as 1950 that Franz Kline and Barnett Newman had their first shows; that was Jackson Pollock's greatest year of work—thirty-two huge canvases, including *Autumn Rhythm,* in a single summer. One year later, Joan Mitchell, Grace Hartigan and Helen Frankenthaler had their first shows; that same year, Newman painted *Vir Heroicus Sublimis.* In '52, Frankenthaler "broke through" to her staining technique; that same year, the Museum of Modern Art gave the first official imprimatur to the "new" art with its "Fifteen Americans" show that included Pollock, Still, Rothko and others. It may seem, therefore, that the very labeling of "First" and "Second" generations carries as much implication of gender as of primacy. For only considerably later did women of the "First" Generation come into public prominence. It was not, for example, until '55 that Louise Nevelson showed, and was acclaimed for, her first environment work, *Ancient Games and Ancient Places.* Only in '58 did Lee Krasner break through with her "Earth Green" series. The early to mid-years of the decade of the '50s, then, were irradiated by the sense of portent and momentum, the intuition that the movement was literally catching on season by season. All there was, in those days, of a New York art world—a few galleries, bookstores, off-Broadway theaters and studios of some fifty or so artists—shared in the adventure, which was, in a genuine sense, a multimedia one contributed to by dancers like Merle Marsicano and Merce Cunningham; actors like Judith Malina and Julian Beck; musicians like Lucille Dlugoszewski and Morton Feldman; poets like Barbara Guest, John Ashbery and Frank O'Hara; and critics like Elaine de Kooning and Thomas Hess.

But the ascendant phase was swifter and sooner ended than one might have wished. If Gorky's suicide in '48 tolled the first bell, deaths of Pollock, Tomlin, Jan Müller foreshadowed the decimation of the movement that would steadily take place, perhaps only to end with the deaths in 1978 of Hess and

Harold Rosenberg. Meanwhile, the '50s were marked also by revelations of an exploitative commercial spirit underneath this cover of a burgeoning American culture. There was the Wildenstein-Knoedler Galleries wiretapping scandal, showing that art dealers were not above crude illegalities; there were the $64,000 quiz show scandals, showing that the media were learning to feed on the charisma, the innocence and also the ambition of artists and intellectuals. And meanwhile, some surviving male heroes of the Abstract Expressionist movement moved to positions remarkable in the history of art discourse, preaching a chauvinism both male and American. The honored German-born teacher Hans Hofmann was one of a few who made fervent pleas for an international cooperative spirit, but even he was to be heard claiming that only men had the "wings to be artists" (see note 16, page 484). By the decade's end, that power-conscious ideology had bred its antithesis: the increasingly popularizing, some thought vulgarizing, art market that exploited the boom of Pop Art.

In years to come, some of these women of the '50s, bred on the principles of the prewar progressive-education movement, would go underground, some flee, some enter long procedures of self-transformation, while a few would ride the "fabulous '60s" to unprecedented heights. Their futures depended to a large degree, then, on their relationship to the mainstreams: whether they participated in or opposed the Abstract Expressionism that was, then was not and now has again become a kind of esthetic standard. Many gifted and articulate women might have contributed tales to this chapter: among them Pat Adams, Anne Arnold, Ruth Asawa, Alice Baber, Joan Brown, Gretna Campbell, Rhys Caparn, Mitzi Cunliffe, Lois Dodd, Claire Falkenstein, Sonia Getchoff, Ilse Getz, Leslie Jackson, Buffie Johnson, Corita Kent, Ellen Lanyon, Marisol, June Leaf, Marcia Marcus, Mercedes Matter, Louise Matthiasdottir, Vita Peterson, Lil Picard, Anne Poor, Leatrice Rose, Judith Rothschild, Joan Snyder, Yvonne Thomas, Jane Wilson and others.

Grace Hartigan, for example, was one of the prime, gifted swashbucklers of the Second Generation. Born in Newark, New Jersey, she arrived in Manhattan in '46 and by '50 had been tapped by Clement Greenberg and Meyer Schapiro for a New Talent show at the Kootz Gallery. The next year, her one-person debut baptized the new "younger" gallery, Tibor de Nagy. Bold, gestural, splashy, her colorful canvases veered in idiom from abstraction to semi-realism and back again. So intense a fixation on a realist idiom had to have had a time and place of origin. "My first impression? Nature. I spent most of my childhood sitting in an apple tree looking at Gypsies camped in a field next to our house. Real itinerant Gypsies, with golden earrings and long satiny

Grace Hartigan. Grand Street Brides, 1954. Oil on canvas. 72" by 102½". Whitney Museum of American Art, New York.

skirts. Men sharpening their knives. Caravans. Bonfires. And me, sitting up in the tree, staring at them.

"I spent so much time looking at this fantasy world, I had to bring it into my painting. Living on the Lower East Side of New York, I found the same thing. Pushcarts. Jewish peddlers. Barrels of pickles. So I took the "overall" manner I learned from Hofmann and painted my "City Life" shows of '54 to '58.

"But pressure from Kline, Guston and others made me drop this subject. They made me feel it wasn't serious. Subject matter must come from the act of painting, they felt." So, after her marriage in '58 and her removal to Baltimore, Hartigan spent the next years teaching and painfully hammering out a style of her own. "It was a personal battle to come back out of that esthetic. I didn't break through back into imagery until the end of the '60s. Since then, these ten years have been a constant investigation of imageries observed from life. My studio. Lyrical nature. My own 'art roots'—medieval manuscripts, myth, the Lascaux caves." In the fall of '78, Hartigan had her most organic, vivid show in years. She interwove collage passages with passages of the loose "wrist" painting of Abstract Expressionism to build images wholly *hers,* from history and memoir.

203

Jane Freilicher, by contrast, still paints the intimist, quirky landscapes, still lifes and cityscapes she first experimented with under Hans Hofmann's aegis in the early '50s. Labels can be applied to her work, however, without ever fully explaining the hard, meditated willfulness of her search for the particular intersection between shapes and colors that might give a feeling of what she calls "exaltation": "I remember feeling exaltation over bits of nature available in Brooklyn, where I was born. A bouquet of flowers. On Brighton Beach, picking up stones. Some chrysanthemums growing in two inches of dirt in a yard. Without feeling that I had any specialized talent, I thought I might do

Jane Freilicher. Casement Window, 1974. Oil on canvas. 24" by 20". Collection Dr. Jeremiah Barondess, New York.

Fay Lansner. Sacred and Profane Love, 1960–61. Oil on canvas. 76" by 96". Collection the artist.

something in art, not for fame or achievement, but out of a romantic inclination to beautiful things. A free-floating feeling that something was creative *in me*."

"Romantic" and "free-floating" qualities do not, however, mean a trite gentility to Freilicher. She speaks of the very act of painting as "vigorous" and "athletic" and her touch upon the canvas as "not gentle." It is a persistent, exploratory obsession she confesses to: "I am relearning to paint with each new canvas. Always a new beginning, even if the subject matter remains much the same. Only now there is a higher percentage of resolved works. Works that seem in some way to have completed themselves. I'm not particularly interested in Feminist esthetics. I don't look at art from that point of view. A still life before a window: now, that's a complex thing. The intimacy of the interior . . . the jumble of the city or a country landscape behind."

Fay Lansner, on the other hand, is one whose paintings, nominally Abstract Expressionist, took a long time to be seen for what they are: statements in a powerful Feminist idiom to be justly regarded only in the 1970s. Her enormous, part-figurative and narrative canvases show a theater of women of classic monumentality encountering tangles of calligraphy or blazing Fauve color fields that must be in some way symbolic of obsessions Feminism does not shrink from making explicit.

"I was not a rebel against my background," Lansner says today. "I loved the people I grew up among. I thought they were great and beautiful. Their world was Russian-Jewish culture, history, literature. To be 'an artist' was my only act of rebellion against them.

"My problem later was to work out my identity as a woman. Becoming a mother, having a family—and painting. I had to fight my way to a sense of myself. First, I was immersed in Hofmannesque abstraction. Living in Paris [in the early '50s], I became interested in Existentialism. Then I grew tired of the philosophical postures I observed around me. I conceived the idea that my experience could be a universal one. So I gave up abstraction and began instead to paint works that traced my struggle to become a woman. Some of them concerned my relationship with my mother, a thread that runs through my life. Some concerned the process of moving from darkness to light. I reasserted the eruptive self of my youth in black images of despair. Gradually the psychological drama lessened, then all but disappeared. I feel that somberness gives way, eventually, to light.

"Lately, I've taken new directions—the freshest, freest things I've done. I don't want to have to interpret them. Ah! But I always push to have things mean something. That is so Russian. My heritage!"

Perhaps, *our* heritage.

Helen Frankenthaler

BORN 1928, NEW YORK CITY

Many artists, ironically since they are dealing with production and creativity—with life—have a . . . profound fear of dying. The positive side of this, for an artist, is here: that artists who survive often have an appealing magical energy. That's the dividend: that magic energy.

—HELEN FRANKENTHALER
New York, 1977

Frankenthaler's studio in Manhattan is a whitewashed brick structure that was once a garage. Its arched double portal is big enough to let in a coronation carriage. Space is important to her. She says as much of her paintings. "Many have to be bigger because that is where I live. The gesture is that size, in relation to the thought, the arm, the body. You need that many feet of flat surface for the illusion, for the light."

That scale speaks on many levels: of ambition and an earned freedom; of will and that self-replenishing energy; of New York, where Frankenthaler was born and has lived; of her esthetic forefathers, the Big Boys—Jackson Pollock, Mark Rothko, Clyfford Still, Barnett Newman. In the shades of difference between their use of scale and hers, however, is a key to the difference between their generation and hers and a first clue to a meaning of her art.

"Scale equals feeling," said Newman, who had read up on the historic controversy between artists and philosophers about how best to render the true nature of things: by art that is "beautiful" or art that, ignoring beauty, reaches for the "sublime." Superhuman feelings require sublime spaces, Newman claimed, space in which to render "the chaos of ecstasy." Nature also plays the dialectical game between the Beautiful and the Sublime, now running along in a state of controlled amiability with beings living within it, now erupting with death-dealing violence of all kinds. A poetically inverted way of putting the notion is what Frank O'Hara said of Jackson Pollock's painting *The Deep:* "an abyss of glamour encroached upon by a flood of innocence."[1] For what is "glamour" but control over the ancient arts of persuasion and seduction perfected in the abyss of time; and what is "innocence" but artless uncontrol? It is the acceptance of both these light and dark sides of nature as well as of human nature that links the two Abstract Expressionist waves: Newman's and Pollock's, and Frankenthaler's. And again it is in their different emphases that their difference is revealed. For while Frankenthaler is Pollock's heir in the technical sense, she did not inherit the First Generation's sense of sublime excess, infernal spinning energy, linear turmoil, psychic contradiction and oncoming doom—all that made their work epiphanal for a time nearly past when she came on the scene.

Her work, so far at least, has mostly explored the other arm of the dialectic, though she seems to be moving out of the tranquil and into deeper waters today. Still, the feeling-tone her paintings have projected has been the serene and beautiful, achieved by insightful control over the elements of form: floating areas of color; occasional fountains, spurts, jets of color thrown against bare canvas; hard-edge panels or curtains of bright flat non-naturalistic color; and—more recently—fields of warm earth color pulsating on a languid cycle like red stars or stains of strange phosphorescent hue hovering like mirages at the edge of a world. Canvases like *Eden, Arcadia, Arden*—Frankenthaler titles of '57 to '62—have seemed to speak for an era yearning to put an end to chaos. By its marshaling of light (the ancient metaphor for infinity)[2] and color (which is light given in the terms of this world), her art has addressed the human longing to rise above the street corner. It implies there is a mode of relief or transcendence that does not mean abandoning the visual or sensory world and its pleasures. To return, then, to the question of scale: though Frankenthaler's work sometimes approaches the First Generation's in sheer size, there has been no trace in it of that other element historically implied in the sublime: the terrifying. The terrible was, on the other hand, very much an ingredient in the work of some of her predecessors. We may suppose, therefore, that what Frankenthaler means to invoke is something more like that vast natural ambiance which normally neither dwarfs nor terrifies: the sky.

Skylight, electric light, real light, not the metaphorical element she refers to when she is talking about her paintings, fills her Manhattan studio. It leaves no shadows where the racks of canvases on stretchers are aligned row on row. Her work area is at the rear. She moves around in it with a sense of concentration and command, somewhat like a ballet mistress of mesmerizing self-possession.

I was there in her studio one spring day for a surveying and titling of new

Arden, 1961. Oil on canvas. 87½" by 120¼". Whitney Museum of American Art, New York.

paintings, some twenty of them, an average good working season's output. The ancient Chinese had a ceremony for launching new statues, called "Opening the Eyes of the Buddha"; that morning in the studio unrolled with a comparable ritualistic pace, and applying a title to a work of radiant color but indistinct image often "opened the eyes" of the observer to its meaning.

Frankenthaler's assistant—she employs a changing series of young assistants who lay out supplies, stretch canvases, etc.—pulled out the canvases and displayed them. The artist stood back against the opposite wall and regarded each one quite a long time. Sometimes she would point and ask for it to be turned upside down or on a side. Eventually the top was decided on if it had not already been done. Then the title. A notebook lay on a counter. Potential future titles were listed there, and the list grows. In some cases, the name jumped off the page. *Caravan* was natural for a large canvas with a golden-brown stain on pale-yellow ground, and an anchoring blue streak at the base. *Orion's Belt* fit. *Warming the Wires* was preassigned. "I hadn't been working for ages and then I really got going one day, and my assistant said, 'Hey! Warming the wires!'"

209

A large horizontal canvas streaked in glowing umber was pulled out and pushed back into the rack almost before anyone could see it. It was *Into the West*. "I don't want to part with it, because it means so much to me and I need it with me to go on from."

One unstretched canvas, *Midday*, was laid on the floor to be cut down the middle.

"I worked and worked on it. I worked till it got heavy and wet. I worked on the wall, then on the floor. Then I took it off the stretcher and went all the way to the bare edges of the canvas trying to save it. But it kept getting more and more *beautiful* in the wrong way and looser, instead of working in its space. It got deader." A part of it could be saved by cropping, and the failed area would be thrown away.

Afterward goblets of Muscadet were served around, again a sort of tea ceremony for purposes of unwinding. The unwinding space in the studio is a square blocked off with a table, a leather couch and some chairs. Facing is a tiny kitchen. Overhead on a shelf stands a row of splits of Moët and Chandon for visits of another order. Frankenthaler offered pistachios from a five-pound bag. She likes some supplies in quantity, and there was something solacing about this big sack.

On the wall over the couch, one new painting or another is usually hung to be analyzed. One day some months before the naming ceremony, *Caravan*, still titleless and then the other side up, held the spot. Seen that way, the blue streak was on the top. The work was breathtaking: a flight of birds across a sunset sea?

I was there that earlier day to pursue some flights of my own with the artist's cooperation. Frankenthaler is used to talking about her work. Prominence has brought many demands on her to speak about technique and esthetics. But she is less confident talking about intangible issues, and her fears of being misunderstood are intense, probably because she feels she has not mastered the movie star's manner of fielding questions and disguising her feelings. Rather, her way with an interviewer is not unlike her way with paint. Waiting, she assumes a posture of wary sizing up. The question I put to her was what it had felt like, in the beginning, to be in possession of a "gift." After some complimentary small talk on both sides, she began to warm to the topic. Talk took on its own momentum, and she broke through her guard to release a flood of self-impelled insights.

"If you have a gift, it is your halo and your cross. There is no choice. You are what you are, what you have been born. And what is inherent in that condition is the loneliness that goes with it.

"It was first manifest in me not as objective talent but as a sense of specialness, both inner and outer, both negative and positive. That is, I was a special child, and I felt myself to be. Also, I received special attention from the outside. All my infancy and childhood, my parents treated me this way. I had the genes . . . intelligence . . . talent . . . the 'gift.' Who knows what it is, really? But it was a positive thing. The condition was my destiny.

"On the other hand, what is hurtful in the long run is if a child with those qualities is made to feel fragile or in peril . . . that the child must be especially careful, or live up to standards of perfection.

"The child is alone, isolated. The child cannot know, at first, that the gift is *creative within*. So there was this constant state of potential crisis, of excitement, of things driving toward perfection, of impatience with the obvious, easy solutions. Things were in a constant state of exhilaration.

"Well, one learns eventually that life cannot be lived that way. One will have to learn, eventually, to make certain compromises with life, as opposed to art—to force oneself to be socially adaptable, for instance, in the years to come. But the truth is, you are different.

"You will learn, if you become an artist, not that you can do anything you please, but that what you do do is not mad or destructive. It is simply different.

"Then sometimes, when the artist is working along and free, once in a while there will come this great sense of alarm. As if you have shocked yourself. You combined certain elements in such a way as to work something new and puzzling. *It* ran ahead of you and did this *to* you.

"The gift had taken over.

"Eventually, of course, you will have to judge what you have done. At that moment, the artist becomes the critic."

Frankenthaler was born in upper Manhattan, and one of her early memories is calling her mother to the window of their apartment and asking her to come watch the light of the setting sun.

"My first awesome experience with the natural world, ridiculous and surreal as it sounds, was this: at an early age I would call my mother to the window of our apartment in New York and beg her to watch the sunset with me."

It was she, youngest of three daughters, who was usually given the room with the sky view when the family traveled—to Maine in summers, for instance. She would retain her love for the long view of land, sky and sea—not inland ponds or rivers but the open sea: Atlantic City, Cape Cod, the sea from shipboard.

"I would spend time looking out my window in the early morning, and what I saw was connected in my mind with moods or states of feeling. There is an early-morning light, for example, that can remind me of the time of my worst school days—a feeling that the war is on, the dimout. Ahead lies the day. A tight time schedule, and I am failing. I feel that in the pit of my stomach.

"Or else it is a feeling of marvelous energy. There is nothing like the beginning of day!

"Or in certain arduous work periods, I will get up at dawn and feed the birds on the terrace. Then morning means that the night with its dreams is over, even if still with you."

This artist was very young when she was picked out as a gifted child in a talented and highly motivated family. Now, specialness can be nurtured or ignored and the child let grow up like a cabbage. In her case, circumstances combined to give her a sharp insight into her own condition. At the same time, destiny provided a counterpoint between favors and painful events that, by destroying some certainties while establishing others, may have conditioned her to take leaps when fate offered them.

"Laced with my parents' recognition of my mental and physical agility and specialness (and sometimes my tantrums) was also their feeling of pride and overprotectiveness. Their fear *for* me.

"So, you have certain lucks: body strength, good schools, good teachers. You travel well. You have an ally in a sibling. But on the other hand, I was never allowed to be alone, for fear something would happen to me. So there was this double thing: to be alone—*the gift* not yet clearly understood by me—and then at the same time to be the focus of fearful attention from people around."

Frankenthaler's father was a judge of the New York State Supreme Court and became a figure of stature during the Depression when he came to the legal rescue of many people whose small inheritances were in jeopardy.

The judge adored his city and knew it block by block. It was one of his joys to walk the streets with one or another of his daughters, pointing out architectural and historic monuments. He was, one might say, a good guide, and his family were beings to be guided. He was, one gathers, like many powerful men, a worrier about those he loved, but as a harmonious man he wanted to be informed of none of the discords that normally agitate the flow of life in a family. When he suspected he had developed cancer, he would not go to a doctor, because he did not want to face interrupting his life in midstream.

Frankenthaler's mother was as striking-looking as he, "a classic knockout, with great energy, style, humor," and as tall—both of them were over six feet. Like most women of her time, she lived through her family, though she possessed a never-tested gift for painting. After Helen would have her first show in

212

a professional gallery, in 1951, her mother would paint a series of tiny oils rather like the watercolors Georgia O'Keeffe made when she was a young teacher in Texas.

"She said to me shyly, 'Do you think I can be an abstract painter, too?' Sort of a combination of camp and talent on her part. And in fact many of hers had a great feeling. The light. Something touching and honest, though limited.

"She had painted before. I have a bunch of violets on a green ground that she did years before she was married, the way women painted then. But the later painting was, I think, her way of trying to show she wasn't threatened by the life I had chosen. Showing she acknowledged it and appreciated it. She had an inkling of quality—and a very little bit of competitiveness!

"It was her way of saying, and she expressed it very beautifully, 'See. I can speak that language, too.' "

School years were good years for a while. There was a "marvelous kindly kindergarten—one of the first progressive schools for very little children that showed the teachers' faith in the realities of young minds." Then she went to Horace Mann, "an experimental, progressive and great school," and was a student there the year her father died. That year, 1939, is probably the year she feels she goes back to in certain foreboding morning lights. For a number of reasons, she was moved to another school. And the war began in Europe.

"His death was a terrible blow, one I consciously registered, but the full extent of the psychological loss didn't make itself felt till much later. But the tragedy, the shock, my loneliness and my efforts to resolve that loss later on are painful to remember.

"I was eleven, and the girls in my class at the new school were thirteen. I couldn't hit a hockey ball. I couldn't master logarithms. Everyone else was in silk stockings. And I had begun to suffer from migraines."

Four years of deep unhappiness followed, in a bleak and uncomprehending school environment, with the additional trauma, for a child, of great family suffering. If there are dark memories and fears that alternate in Frankenthaler's life and working procedures today with periods of "magic energy," they are probably rooted here. She was rescued by being sent to the Dalton school, where Charlotte Anne Durham, the famously kind, Deweyesque educator had created a model progressive school based on learning-through-doing.

Frankenthaler was no book person then or now. What she had an instinct for but no means, to this point, to express was the visual. At Dalton the Mexican painter Rufino Tamayo was in charge of the studio classes. He worked in a broad, semiabstract, post-Picasso style, but, more important, he was a professional artist who exhibited in New York galleries and communicated to the students the fundamentals of a professional attitude toward art. It was during her one year at Dalton that she made her decision to go ahead with art.

"I was fifteen or sixteen, and for the first time I seriously felt I wanted to be an artist. A sixteen-year-old can recognize and seize talent and go ahead. Before then, the childish thing is often only a gift many kids have. I would say, too, that the recognition did not mark a radical change for me.

"Later on, after I graduated from Bennington, I had become aware that being an artist implied being a kind of renegade. By then, too, I had the idea I didn't want to repeat the patterns I had come from—certain parts of a domestic package that didn't attract me."

Much of the weight of the previous years may have seemed to lift during Frankenthaler's time at Bennington, a college in the Green Mountains of Vermont, where the arts, especially dance, theater and painting, were stressed. Head of the art department then was the California painter Paul Feeley. The college had a system of nonresident semesters, and during these periods Frankenthaler worked at various jobs in the art world or took studio courses, one at the Art Students League and one with painter Wallace Harrison, a Hofmann-esque teacher. She also worked for a time with a mini-newspaper-flyer in New York, *MKR's Art Outlook,* that published reviews of shows. This job gave her her first quasi-professional view of the inside world of Fifty-seventh Street. After she graduated, she would keep close ties with the college, help set up an active traffic of New York artists coming to lecture and demonstrate. She sits on the board of trustees today.

Instruction in art there had been along the line of dark Cubism in the manner of Picasso, Braque or Max Weber, so that Frankenthaler was turning out figure paintings and still lifes in this mode when she arrived back in New York—dark, thickly scumbled images with heavy black outlines around the forms. It was a style that had not been considered "advanced" for decades but was a sort of academic passageway through which most art students had to go before finding their own way. There were, in fact, a few months of wavering: Frankenthaler spent some time at Columbia University taking art history and living in her mother's apartment, but then she made the break, moved into an apartment in Chelsea, eventually sublet the Tenth Street studio of the Surrealist sculptor David Hare, and set out to see whether she could become more than simply a gifted student.

New York in 1950 was, in fact, a threshold in many ways. All during the early years of the decade, as the first postwar generation of career-seeking young people came into the city, one could feel the exhilaration that attended the Abstract Expressionist movement in its formative phase. Behind the art and the artists, too, there was a critical apparatus warming up in those years that not only would help make the movement famous but also would in a real sense shape some of the work and ideas to come. A surfacing issue was the rivalry between Paris and New York. The second was the beginning of rivalry between certain artists and their critical advocates. Most partisan of these then were Harold Rosenberg and Clement Greenberg. Greenberg and Frankenthaler became friends, and through him she was drawn into the turmoil of the art world. It may have seemed, at first, a rather terrifying place to be.

"Through Clem I met everybody, the whole cast. I was terrified. I was just coming out of a Cubist academe. But seeing pictures by de Kooning . . . Gorky . . . Pollock . . . it was thrilling. And Clem never said, 'You must like . . .' He just opened it up to me. What he gave was the ability or the hope of feeling and experiencing painting. In this, he was a giant."

One whom Greenberg introduced her to was John Bernard Myers, a Buffalo-born literatus and esthete who had grown up as a hinterland Surrealist and was on the point of opening his own gallery in New York. He might have gone the Dada route (his first idea was to show some works in fluorescent lace that lit up in the dark) if Greenberg had not proposed to bring around some better young artists. That way, he gathered his first roster of the Second Generation—Grace Hartigan, Larry Rivers, Harry Jackson and the two Janes: Jane Freilicher and Jane Wilson. Most of them were making figurative paintings in a loosely Abstract Expressionist vein. These younger artists had missed the years of sociopolitical bonding during the WPA and the war. They were less ideologically burdened; there was, perhaps, less sense of moral urgency. The major doctrinal breakthroughs had been made in the tougher '40s. Nor was there the day-to-day sense of grinding economic peril that had made those older artists' choice of their life work a genuine risk. It was not that art was a minor thing for them: this younger generation was ambitious, and the females were not prepared to closet themselves even temporarily in domestic situations as some of their elders had done from time to time. But there was a feeling that art need not necessarily be a vehicle for the expression of Sturm und Drang. Landscape was a favored mode; the potato fields and lawns and east-facing skyscapes of Long Island, where most of the artists summered, were frequent subjects. For the other generation, "painting landscape" had been a metaphor for exploring the complex equation between a human being and the world, but of the Second Generation only two, Frankenthaler and Joan Mitchell, would deliberately lift it to that level of interpretation.

Frankenthaler was not on John Myers' first slate: she had been in New York too short a time; she was younger than the others and could wait. But after a few months he proposed a show, so she made her debut at his gallery in the spring of 1951, with works on themes that even in a more evolved phase would never lose their hold on her: *August Weather, Great Meadows, Cloudscape* and so on. That spring, too, there was the famous "Ninth Street Show," organized by senior members of The Club—Kline, Pavia, Leo Castelli and others—and introducing a few of the younger generation. There was some muttering about whippersnappers taking up all the space with untactfully big canvases, but there were also, as there would always be, some who said, "Let's go by the art and not the age."

"Hindsight is always easy, of course, but it seems to me now those days were fruitful, and we were all living in the young, lively, active nucleus of an 'art family.' It was lucky and wonderful to be in one's early twenties, with a group of painters to argue painting with.

"It was a relatively trusting and beautiful period . . . there seemed to be little that was motivated, threatening or contaminating . . . so few of the decisions of the ugly kind we are often forced to make today. It seemed far more trusting, pleasurable and very productive. There was judgment, but not so much the judgment that goes with power or with moralizing. It didn't have to do with self-righteousness."

She was, at that point, someone who "had looked very hard at Gorky, de Kooning, Pollock." In fact, she was painting fluently in an eclectic and graceful manner absorbed from various sources:

Gorky's graceful line and active, organic forms . . .
Miro's amoebalike shapes in flat, unreal space . . .
Kandinsky's fast-moving, swirling forms . . .
Hans Hofmann's, or Pollock's, over-all, activated canvas . . .

Abstract Landscape was done about that time. The scene is tipped up vertically until a line of mountains nearly brushes the top of the canvas, and the middle distance is alive with dancing, extruding, fingering shapes. Already the painting has something of a topographical map as if one were looking both into and down into a world. In the flat portions are naturalistic but intensified colors— golden yellow, turkey red, sandy tones of a burnished molten intensity. All over, passages of land laid out flat and land in perspective shift and alternate. Line is the hoyden: it plays where it will.

But this was still not an "original" work of art.

In the spring of '51, Frankenthaler visited the Pollocks. She spent time in the tall, light-filled barn-studio where some fifteen big works for his autumn show were piled on the floor. Lee Krasner was working in her upstairs bedroom-studio in the house, preparing her first one-person show in the fall. She had put behind her the gray, tight imagery of her own transitional period and was developing a freer, more personal hand. Both Krasner and Pollock felt that. To the younger visitor, the Krasner-Pollock ménage seemed impressive in its cloistered dedication to work and to craft. There were features of Pollock's craft that were unique: not only the pouring of the paint but the artist's "spread" as he worked, the dancelike way he engaged his whole body, his arms and legs in motion, as he circled the work on the floor in the center of the studio. Then, after he had poured and otherwise swept, dragged and pulled his work to a condition of approximate synthesis, his encounter with it as judge and critic would take place. He hung it on the wall, studied it, discussed it with Krasner, decided which side should be up, down, where the signature and what the title.

In the spring of 1952, the Museum of Modern Art finally gave the new art its official stamp of approval in a large show. That year, Harold Rosenberg, for whom humanist interpretations counted, published his article on the American Action Painters that took note of a psychic process: each of the painters had, "after a certain moment," decided to abandon his earlier methods and take to the canvas "as an arena in which to act." Moreover, "a painting that is an act is inseparable from the biography of the artist. Anything is relevant to it. Anything that has to do with action—psychology, philosophy, history, mythology, hero worship." [3]

The opposite point of view had been expressed by Greenberg since the early 1940s. He had predicted the emergence of an American art devoid of "religion or mysticism or political certainties. . . . Integral efficiency is as lofty an ideal as any other—that complete and positive rationality which seems to me the only remedy for our present confusion." [4] Modern painting would inevitably develop toward "the over-all 'decentralized,' 'polyphonic' picture that relies on a surface knit together of identical or closely similar elements which repeat themselves without marked variation from one edge of the picture to another . . . it comes very close to decoration." [5] Painters he admired were John Marin, for his play of watercolor washes against bare ground that achieved near-miraculous "fidelity in the registration of evanescent sensations," [6] and Pollock, in whose works "every inch of surface receives maximum of charge at cost of minimum of physical means." [7]

There was a moral imperative to Greenberg's esthetic, too. A Modernist might hope to have "the sublime lightness of [in this case, Milton Avery's] hand on the one side, and the morality of his eyes on the other, the exact

217

loyalty of these eyes to what they experience." [8] Failing that degree of loyalty to experience, an artist might "betray his gifts" or "misunderstand himself." Much, therefore—far more than the success or failure of an individual painting—hung on esthetic decisions.

The high, cool and blue skies of Nova Scotia, its wide-rolling hills and the northern sea light around that island were in Frankenthaler's memory when she returned to New York in the autumn of '52 after a vacation there painting and drawing landscapes. There was a good deal of looking and talking about Pollock that season. Greenberg was organizing a show to travel to Bennington College. And Pollock's show at Janis was discussed, including *Number 12,* which contained passages of stain-thin paint suggested by Mark Rothko's method.

It was October when Frankenthaler set off on an eclectic tack inspired partly by Pollock and also in part by Marin. She tacked a seven-by-ten-foot piece of unsized, unprimed cotton duck to the floor and, working with oil paint thinned nearly to the consistency of watercolor, poured and pushed it in its meanderings. By this method, she abandoned the potential for slow, gradual overpainting that workers in oil had had since the invention of the medium in the fifteenth century. But she gained what watercolorists had always had— freedom to make her gesture live on the canvas with stunning directness.

Mountains and Sea was the first major stained work of '52. "I took the floor of the studio for my easel," she explains. "From the very first, there was one side of the canvas I conceived of as 'bottom,' and though that day I walked around it and worked it from all sides, the 'bottom held,' and in the end I signed and dated it, that same day, on the edge I had signaled out in the beginning." Though the viewer today may find certain ambiguous spatial features—a centralized Cubistic image that might be flowers—the work still reads vividly and instantly as landscape. As if to reiterate the fact, Frankenthaler marked a horizontal blue sky-stain at the top with swift Futuristic streaks. "I had the landscape in my arms when I painted it," she has said. "I had the landscapes in my mind and shoulder and wrist." One might say the technical step had taken her at once to Marin's level of seeing. It let waterlight fill her work—that engulfing envelope of reflected illumination that fills the sky even when one is standing behind mountains (or high in a Manhattan tower?).

The technical breakthrough led to new categories of procedure and eventually new levels of meaning: Frankenthaler now paints invariably on canvas spread on the floor, pouring color into pools that bleed outward under their own momentum but that she can control to a degree by using sponges, wipers and so on to steer the flow. The battle line of her work is that place of intersec-

Mountains and Sea, 1952. Oil on canvas. 86⅜" by 117¼". Collection the artist, on loan to the National Gallery of Art, Washington, D.C.

tion between the controlled and the accidental: the edges of forms. These bled and creeping edges have proceeded according to their own laws, with the artist as cooperative guide. "I was guiding the red—and the red was guiding me," she said of her biggest work, the thirty-three-foot-high accurately titled *Guiding Red.* She has also said, "I think accidents are lucky only if you know how to use them. People who hope for a tool of accident without having had real limits or a 'self-censor'—a discipline—often wind up with a mess."

Against the blind-outward-creeping edge of the stain, then, there plays another counterpoint: everything done by hand or, as Sumi ink painters say, the "wrist" that controls the line that reveals the artist's sensibility through variations of thickness, stress, motion, breath. Frankenthaler's chosen favorite masters are those whose line was vital and vivid: Dürer, Degas, Matisse, Gorky. She speaks of "wrist" as a kind of mystique, an element equal in value to "light." It is her insistence on wrist that, whatever their differences, aligns

219

her in the end closer to the Abstract Expressionists than to the 1960s Color-Field painters, who tried to eradicate all subjective handwriting to achieve the Greenbergian model, efficient, decorative and cool, "a remedy for . . . confusions."

"Light" is the other element that connects her to a past tradition,[9] in this case a historic landscape school beginning with the Flemings and Venetians, then the sky-land painters of the French seventeenth century. The mode reappeared in the American nineteenth century, particularly in the hands of artists of the backwaters who, according to some interpretations, assuaged their longing for lost religious certainties by imagining that the divine spirit was still findable in the tones of light-streaked skies.

That once-mystical idea—that visible nature is a scrim concealing the face of reality—has passed down, through the understanding of exactly what "ancient being" (as Emerson referred to it)[10] was concealed there has changed, as we have said, from a deity to various naturalistic abstractions like natural law, correspondence between forms in the material world and so forth. Frankenthaler inherited the vocabulary as well as the concept. I asked her to define it.

"It's more than light as an element. It's a metaphysical, esthetic light. Every work of art that works, on paper or canvas, happens to have that common denominator. It is a combination of the artist, the medium and the magic—elaborate magic. As a word used by me, I became aware of it when I was looking at pictures for the first time, back in the 1950s, at Pollock or Hofmann or Gottlieb—or traveling through the hill towns of Italy, or the Prado or the Frick. Some Corots, for instance, have it, some more than others. Or you can see a certain Courbet that makes other Courbets go dead.

"By 'light' I don't mean not dark. It is as if an overall workingness emanated from the surface of the picture. It takes off at once on its own. For sculpture, it could be called 'poise.' "

However defined, "light" has to imply an embodiment in the natural world. "It used to be water—oceans, not so much rivers or ponds. I'm more of a horizon person than a valley person," Frankenthaler said to me. Therefore it seems possible to say that the technique she adopted and perfected to her own ends, that gave her access to "light," also inevitably determined her subject matter: nature, subjective and without.

Nineteen fifty-seven was one of Frankenthaler's most productive years, and then, late that year, she met Robert Motherwell, Europeanized and literate member of the elder Abstract Expressionists. They were married in '58, and her life took a new turn. She lost touch with the downtown scene to a degree but extended her connections in the international art world. Her days at Tibor de

Nagy ended—most of John Myers' artists would move sooner or later to more prestigious galleries—and she joined André Emmerich, who helped organize shows in major international cities. In 1960 she had a one-person show at the Jewish Museum in New York. In '67, *Guiding Red* hung prominently in the United States Pavilion at Expo in Montreal. In 1969 she was given a full-scale retrospective at the Whitney.

Between her and Motherwell there were undoubtedly influences, but, as in all artistic ménages, they are risky to try to document. Perhaps as instructive may have been his language. He writes undogmatically and with epigrammatic intuition about the meaning of art in his time and also about the artist's character:

To modify one's art is to modify one's character. An artist whose work develops represents character growth, either slow and steady like a garden, or in leaps. . . . The problem is to seize the glimpse.

If life were longer, one could express more. Since it isn't, stick to essentials.

. . . it is light that counts above everything. Not colored light, but color that gives off light—radiance!

The supreme gift, after light, is scale.[11]

Their lives expanded to include a house and summers for painting in Provincetown on Cape Cod Bay, where the water came up to the piers of their deck and in a high wind would spray and clatter against their windows. There were children—Motherwell's daughters by a former marriage and daughters of the welded-steel Abstract Expressionist sculptor David Smith, who was nearly a member of the family—and years of the good life, travel, friendship and work. But Motherwell was confessedly a man at war with himself, and some of the contradictions, in which were implicit the ending, were perhaps summed up by his recollection of his old friend, who had by then, like Pollock, died in an automobile accident.

He [Smith] and I both loved a *ménage,* with women, children and friends and a bountiful table and endless drink, and we could do it unselfconsciously with each other, which is perhaps the deepest relief one peer can give another. . . .

And we both knew damned well the black abyss in each of us that the sun and the daughters' skin and the bounty and the drink could alleviate but not begin to fill, a certain kind, I suppose, of puritanical bravado, of holding off the demons of guilt and depression that largely destroyed, in one way or another, the Abstract Expressionist generation, whose suffering and labor was to make it easier, but not *realer,* for the next generation. And if they liked it cool, we liked it warm, a warmth that is yet to appear in the art of the young. . . .[12]

In '71 they were divorced, and since then Frankenthaler has lived alone. Her paintings, if anything, have extended the measure of those essences: light and a sense of the wide-open view. Some titles convey the state of mind: *Passage, New Paths* and *Sound of the Bassoon; Royal Fireworks, Kingsway; Newfoundland* and *Caravan.* Statements of a life in a festival midcareer.

She also has begun recently to try her hand at other media, and then occasionally to talk about her experiences to student audiences. She speaks well, always in that characteristic alternation of precision, letting go and then self-correction:

On working in clay: "Once I touched the clay, I was flooded with ideas and couldn't move fast enough. Madness—I wanted to make boxes, towers, landscapes, colored arrangements; looking out the studio window, everything became sculpture."

And afterward: "Were they any good? Were they beautiful? Did they take off? Did they have that essential thing that contributes to any sculpture I like: a certain kind of poise, balance-of-off-balance, light?" [13]

On working in prints: "The artist's wrist is of crucial importance. I believe that wrist, that sensibility must be in and on the whole concept of the making of the print . . . the artist of quality [creates] a beautiful graphic that 'bleeds' his sensibility—his feeling, magic, head, heart—within the felt embrace of a sensitive workshop." [14]

On lithographs: "It was hard. A stone seems to weigh tons. It's not like drawing—it was like learning a new language, knowing the meaning of the words, but not being able to phrase the sentence. . . . It was remote, but it had to do with my orbit." [15]

On woodcuts: "[They] made me ecstatic, furious, frustrated, ready to give up and ready to solve the problem. *Savage Breeze* went dead like a lead balloon. . . . I couldn't get the light. I knew the drawing was right. I knew the scale was right. Then I thought—why not whitewash the paper first and then print? We did, And it glowed." [16]

There have, inevitably, been influences between her and her contemporaries. While the Washington School artists Kenneth Noland and Morris Louis took the stain technique from her, she has learned something from Color-Field artists like Jules Olitski and Larry Poons. However, Frankenthaler has used her influences well. If in her youth she took a magic trick from the masters Pollock and Marin and plied it in an original way to make works of freedom and beauty but perhaps less profundity than theirs, today she has taken stylistic manners from artists more limited than she and used them to move her art toward a searching statement. And it is true that a new element—a fitful, expressive

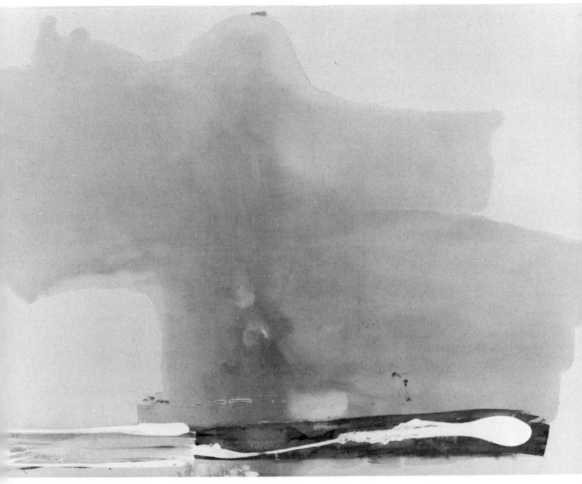

Caravan, 1977. Acrylic on canvas. 7' by 9'6". Collection Mr. and Mrs. P. Leibowitz.

darkness, metaphor for a new level of feeling?—has begun to deepen the shadows in some of her recent works.

She went West in 1976 and again in '77. A Western light and air—though not the clear skies of Georgia O'Keeffe—found their way into her new work. *Natural Answer* and *Into the West* seem to be offerings of sections of red earth turned up so that one faces into its rich, granular depths while golden or calcified light suffuses from "somewhere beyond" through dark-umber striations. A dislocating upturning of *ground,* until one remembers that these works were painted on the floor, as of course was *Floor,* a watery-green spill that, if

223

it were laid down flat, could be a pond. These works, then, seem more and more to be not simply paintings but *places*. That early sensation of having the landscape in her arms has held—that echo of Pollock's "I am nature . . . " and Hofmann's "I bring the landscape home with me . . ." [17] But it seems that there is an even more personal emotional burden in this new work than that conceptual one.

Thirty years ago that early guide Clement Greenberg wrote about the art he foresaw coming:

The over-all may answer the feeling that all hierarchical distinctions have been, literally, exhausted and invalidated; that no area or order of experience is intrinsically superior, on any final scale of values, to any other. . . . It may express a monist naturalism for which there are neither first nor last things . . . [18]

Let us take a different reading than that from Frankenthaler's latest work. If her way of painting has bred a concept to embrace both art and the natural world, and the artist in relation to both, it may be the simple but open-ended belief that a *Natural Answer* is contained in nature, inexhaustible and valid, knowable in all its colors and textures in their hierarchical distinctions. That confidence alone might have a liberating effect from the doctrines of meaninglessness.

And also that even in a "monist naturalism," if that is what the physical world is, there can still be, on the scale at which human life is experienced, first and last things. That to return to the natural ground is to experience the restoration that past ages found in some of their consoling rituals. For the lights and colors as well as the obscuring darkness of nature have a power—which we little understand but acknowledge in our works of art—to stir back to life moments of the past, perhaps even those Emersonian ancient beings, we have left behind.

The root of the meaning for this interpretation would lie back in the time of innocence, before the caravan ever set out, in sunset skies seen from a high window.

A PORTFOLIO OF COLOR

Part III

The works in this section belong to the historic category of "bringing the landscape home" (as Hans Hofmann, teacher of many of these artists, put it), or "carrying the landscape around with me" (as Joan Mitchell puts it), or "having the landscape in my arms" (as Helen Frankenthaler puts it). "Bringing," "having," and "carrying" are actions, and the vivid gestural brush strokes on these canvases are, more or less, expressive abstractions of the hues and shapes of nature. So one can say correctly that these are products of Action Painting or Abstract Expressionism. But there may be more to be said than that. For there is a literalness to some of these works that seems to push beyond the conventions of that American ism of the '40s and '50s. Frankenthaler's works, in this ambiguous sense, may be said to aspire to "be" experiences of sky (see page 208) and Mitchell's may "be" walks in the country (see page 235). A work by Graves "is" a moonscape as photographed by satellites, while Stuart's works literally are made out of earth. So if on the one hand this is an idiom well rooted in the past, on the outer edge of invention it may be probing new forms of relationship to nature.

Lee Krasner. Palingenesis, *1971. Oil on canvas, 82" by 134". Collection the artist.*

THE ARM CREATES THE LANDSCAPE: Sweeping upward to fall back upon themselves like growing things in the natural cycle, Krasner's brush strokes could be read as a survivor's claim on experience in time: all things, in due course, are gathered up again and incorporated into the body of the work. For Mitchell, the symbolic language can be read another way. Each brush stroke here is a step into landscape, the definition of a location, as if one read "I was here" (see page 235).

Joan Mitchell, Posted, *1977. Oil on canvas, diptych 110" by 157½". Xavier Fourcade Gallery, New York.*

Helen Frankenthaler. M, 1977. Acrylic on canvas, 6½' by 9½'. Collection the artist.

LIGHT: These artists do not "use" light to describe bodies on a flat canvas as Bishop does. Nor do they engage moving lights in their structures, like Holt or Truitt. Instead, they give us light as an emanation from a radiant source far behind the picture-plane, that wells and breaks through its cover, be it clouds, autumn leaves or high mountain peaks. In paintings of the medieval and classical landscape tradition, this light from the beyond was a symbol for divinity. Even today, one can perhaps still infer a private preoccupation with the far-off, the unreachable and longed-for (see note 9, page 482).

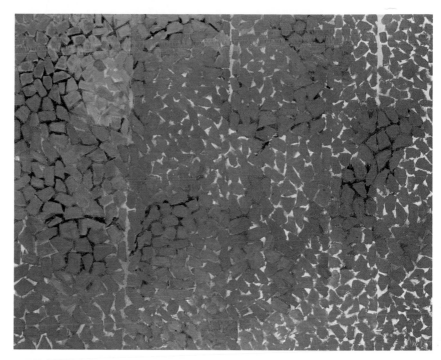

Alma W. Thomas. Autumn Leaves Fluttering in the Wind, *1973. Acrylic on canvas, 40" by 50". Martha Jackson Gallery, New York.*

Alice Baber. The Bridge to the White Mountains, *1974. Oil on canvas, 58" by 77". Collection the artist.*

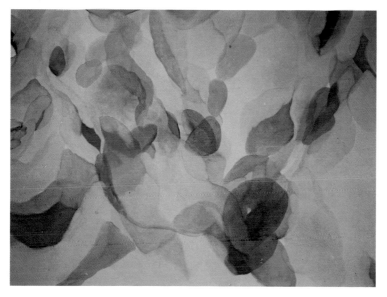

Nell Blaine. Old Lyme Bouquet, *1973. Oil on canvas, 27½" by 23¾". Collection First & Merchants National Bank, Richmond, Virginia. Virginia Artist Collection.

Jane Freilicher. Still-life with Two Fish, 1973. Oil on canvas, 47" by 50". Collection Mr. and Mrs. Arthur A. Goldberg, New York.

EYE, WRIST AND "EXALTATION": The slightly askew-eccentric images of two realists who persistently twist the world to their own enamored view of it (see pages 261, 204).

THE MYSTERIOUS REAL: *(see page 471): (Above) Nancy Graves.* Part of Sabine D, Region of the Moon, Southwest Mare Tranquilitatis, *1972. Acrylic on canvas, 6' by 6½'. La Jolla Museum of Contemporary Art, La Jolla, California. Purchased with funds from National Endowment for the Arts (see also page 55). (Below) Michelle Stuart.* Sayreville Strata, *1976. Each panel 144" by 62". Sayreville, New Jersey. Earth and rock indentations on rag paper, muslin mounted. Droll-Kolbert Gallery, New York*

A PORTFOLIO OF COLOR

Part IV

The "real" has many faces. The works in the pages that follow announce themselves on two levels, one before the eyes and under the fingertips, the other invisible but no less real. Some of these complicated objects in wood, clay, metal, paper or whatnot stir the memory and evoke presences from long-gone times. Other works make visible such a mystic image as "waters above the firmament" that might, at some forward time, shine out between the commensense threads of this world. Then there is that same commonsense world of here and now, engaged in for itself. Here are works so plain in their reality one can describe them in a few words: folded paper, paint drops in a grid, the simple image of an animal. But as one considers how these were made and, more to the point, why, one becomes aware of that enigmatic creature whose tracks *are* the work. Like the bowerbird, the artist provides for the future by picking up things cast out in the past to fix them, now, in formal structures. We know that all human beings, male and female, and many forms of life and non-life are driven by the same necessity to a degree. It seems to be what several artists in this book refer to by the vague term "rhythm of nature" and celebrate in such words as "relatedness, connection, continuity . . ." (see pages 58, 472).

Louise Bourgeois. Structure III—Three Floors, 1978. Painted wood and steel, 74" by 45" by 31". Xavier Fourcade Gallery, New York.

Betye Saar. Indigo Mercy, 1975. Mixed media and assemblage, 42" by 18" by 17". Collection the artist.

Margaret Israel. Seven Temperaments on Pillars, 1975. Clay, 58" high. Various private collections.

(Above opposite) There are three floors to this house-person. On each, are glinting eyes that tilt to catch the light. The house-person stands upon thin, unsteady legs but holds the floor. On a ledge inside is a little stick painted red: the light of awareness. Or else, this is "merely" a formidable assemblage of angular shapes. (Above) The *Temperaments*—asleep or adream—stand on roots that might drive down into tombs of antiquity, Greek, Mesopotamian, Chinese. (Opposite) The black furniture of a specific beloved person; also of a race; also of a period in history.

Miriam Schapiro. The Anatomy of a Kimono *(detail, see page 279), 1976. Collage and acrylic on canvas, whole, 80" by 56' 10". Collection Bruno Bischofberger, Zurich.*

The unseen presence here is the anonymous handworker—quiltmaking grand-mother, Islamic tilemaker, Persian carpetweaver. "Pattern artists" of today frequently speak of their wish to rectify historical injustice done their forebears. Their works, then, are not "only" bold, colorful designs but political statements of a new order.

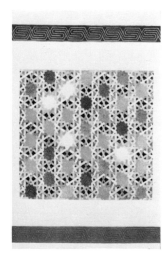

Joyce Kozloff. Pictures and Borders I, 1976–77. 16-color lithograph, 29" by 18½". (Detail shown in color.) Tibor de Nagy Gallery, New York.

Mary Grigoriadis. Persian Steep, 1977. Oil over gesso on raw linen, 12" by 12". Collection the artist.

Dorothea Rockburne. Roman I, 1977. Craft paper, varnish, glue, blue pencil and rag board, 44⅛" by 43⅞". John Weber Gallery, New York.

HORSE, HOUSE AND PAPER PATTERN: Such are the subjects, at first glance, of these deceptively simple works. A less tangible subject is the field of energy inside each work. By shifting angles and edges and making adjustments in texture and color, the artist manipulates the charge of the whole field. Or the artist varies the scheme of paint drops in the squares of a grid. In sum, it is the artist's mind—figuring, calculating, counting and perhaps aspiring to larger intuitions —that is the deep subject here (see page 408).

Susan Rothenberg. Two hand-colored versions of an untitled lithograph, series 1977, 12" by 15½". Willard Gallery, New York.

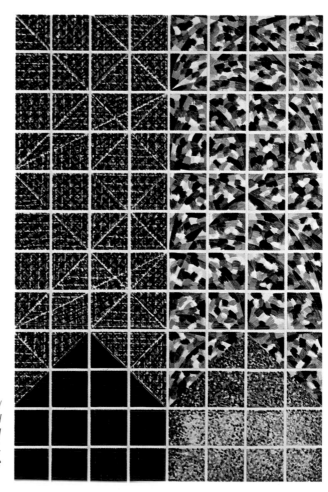

Jennifer Bartlett. Day and Night/ 27 Howard Street, 1977. Baked enamel on 96 1-foot-square steel plates with silk-screened grid, whole 12' 11" by 8' 7". Private collection, New York.

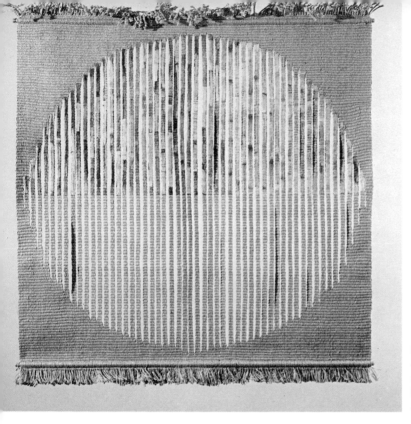

Lenore Tawney. The Waters Above the Firmament, 1974. Linen, collage, manuscript print, 83¾" by 70¾". Collection the artist.

Weaving may be the oldest art, contrived by insects out of blind instinct, and raised to a high craft by women of the age of myth and oracle. The rhythmic back-and-forth motion of shuttle through the warp threads gradually builds out the Ur-grid (a structure many artists take today as their starting point), out of whose criss-cross, according to mystical lore, the whole universe is born (see page 331 and note 1—Tawney section, page 498, for more personal interpretations of these works).

Agnes Martin. Whispering, 1963. Watercolor on paper, 9" by 9". Betty Parsons Gallery, New York.

Lila Katzen

BORN 1932, NEW YORK CITY

I had always been the artist, since I was a child. But during some of my early years I had no room of my own. I could never go through that again. Therefore, later on, I always managed to have my own place. It was where I lived. It was inviolate.

On the other hand, when I had a family, the kids were easy for me to handle. I'd work till two A.M. and nap when they did. I found them a source of invention and creativity, never debilitating, never in my way. A lot was due then to my husband too. If I was down he'd say, "You have no right to think like that . . ."

For all these reasons, I feel marvelous now when my works find a home. They are like my children. They are my links to the past. They are what I am.

—LILA KATZEN
New York, 1977

Lila Katzen, sculptor, has the tall stature, the red hair, the gray-green eyes and probably the vigor of her Russian maternal ancestors, whose lives she describes: their triumphs, migrations, voyages and deaths. All that lies behind her. During her own life as an artist she has pushed ahead from idea to idea. In this way, beginning in childhood, she produced drawings, plays, costumes, commercial art, paintings and sculpture. Although she was first known as a painter, she won acclaim in the 1960s with her plastic assemblages and environmental sculptures involving ultraviolet lights and fluorescent liquids, suggesting the mystery of forms flashing into existence. Then, as had happened before, she found she had come to the end of that exploration. Next she turned her attention to steel. An ambitious progression! Now in her loft in SoHo are a

225

number of daunting pieces of steel-rolling and fabricating equipment. This equipment is used for works she can make in her studio. For the major works, she goes to industrial rolling mills.

Some critics see an austerity in Katzen's steel pieces compared to the luminosity and fantasy of her light works. But in the very qualities of the metal and her way of bending it to her will lie the mystery and also the meaning of these works. Take one of the most important of her many new public installations, which was commissioned to stand in front of the new East Wing of the National Gallery of Art in Washington, D.C. (It may be eventually located in the Sculpture Garden instead.) Its title too is instructive: *Antecedent*. For what is the antecedent but that which lies behind? The work is a single monumental wall of two-inch-thick cold rolled steel, sliced in three places to create apertures or gateways, with the cut elements rolled back like bridges or curtains. Open spaces on one side, those backward-bending elements on the other: expressive in its obduracy. It is as if in its very recalcitrance, its normal refusal to bend, *steel* here acts like time or the past itself, which cannot be bent or trespassed into, except by magic or art.

Katzen has been a part of the New York art world for many years, sharing ideas about materials, images, ways of working and goals with other artists. In the materials fever of the 1960s, she was an innovator with her step-in environments. In the mid-'70s, she is working for a tougher, more permanent image than Plexiglas and disembodied color could give. That search—or drive—conditions her view of her life as well: that stress she lays on her family's survival and well-being, and also that fascination she retains with the process of binding up the past with the future.

"My maternal grandfather was a court artist in St. Petersburg. He painted ceiling frescoes, cupids with fruit, gilt reliefs, that kind of thing. He left ahead of his family, at the time of the pogroms, and came through Tashkent near the Chinese border, wandering alone toward what he thought of as 'civilization.' Eventually he came here via Germany.

"I was his favorite, and he reveled in my early drawings. From the age of two, I was the drawer. To me, he was a magician, a huge man, six feet four, with red hair and blue eyes. I marveled especially at the fact he would drink glasses and glasses of hot tea holding pieces of sugar between his teeth. In this country, he did fresco murals in municipal buildings, schools, post offices, and even in private mansions. He painted false marble with feathers as a brush, and when I was about six he taught me to paint fake wood, just like Braque's father. He taught me to work with gold gilt as well. He would take thin sheets of gilt, create a magnetism by rubbing them with a stick, then lay them down

onto a surface he had prepared with glue. He would take the gilt, flick it in the air, attach it all in a second. It was an incredible visual moment!

"His wife, my grandmother, had come from a so-called 'noble' family in Russia, and no matter how many honors her husband had won there for his work, she always thought he was a bum. An artist was a bum! She married him for love—that was unheard of—but in the end she regretted it because she had to leave Russia. But the real horror was on the ship coming over here. Cholera broke out, and of the thirteen or fourteen children she had, every single one except my mother died. They were traveling steerage, and as Orthodox Jews they wouldn't eat any food except what they had brought with them. They even refused to come up on deck and stayed down below, though my mother would sneak out for a breath of air now and then. My grandmother always said she had 'left a palace for a walk-up.' In the end, the tragedy made her bitter.

"My mother should have been an actress. She had tremendous flair. When she walked into a room, they knew she was there! She was married a total of five times and accumulated a lot of furs and jewels and dramatic clothes. She was a great lady. Although she didn't always understand what I was doing, she came to all the openings and always said she did understand. In the end, though, I think she felt trapped between her father and me, her daughter.

"The Depression wrought upheavals in our lives. I had always been the artist, since I was a child. But during some of my early years I had no room of my own. I could never go through that again. Therefore, later on, I always managed to have my own place. It was where I *lived*. It was inviolate.

"On the other hand, when I had a family, the kids were easy for me to handle. I'd work till two A.M. and nap when they did. I found them a source of invention and creativity, never debilitating, never in my way. A lot was due then to my husband too. If I was down, he'd say, 'You have no right to think like that . . .'

"For all these reasons, I feel marvelous now when my works find a *home*. They are like my children. They are my links to the past. They are what I am.

"My father died in the late '30s, when I was about three and a half, and my grandfather's work went into an eclipse. Mother had nothing. She was left a widow with three children. What could she do? There was no recourse. She put us three into an orphanage. There I lived until I was seven, drawing and decorating whatever area was mine. I never had a room of my own. Grandfather and Mother came to see us on Sundays and brought glass jars of sour balls of different colors, but they were taken away from us and doled out. My two older brothers turned rebellious and I don't blame them.

"Finally Mother got a job and took a house in Brooklyn, and we were all carted out. It was a happy day when we all gathered there. But then it turned out to be such a strange, dark, mysterious house. It had a *succah* in the yard, covered with vines, a lattice thing like a gazebo that Jews use to celebrate the harvest time. It wasn't supposed to be left up, but these people left it up all year. I played and drew and worked in it from the age of eight.

"I was alone a lot, Mother working and my brothers at school. The house seemed enormous, completely vacant because there wasn't too much furniture. The rooms were scary, empty and dark. I could hear my own footsteps. As a contrast to the garden, choking with plants and vegetation. A strange contrast. I notice now in my living quarters I like all the space to be filled up with things!

"Later we moved to a place near Kings Highway, a walk-up over a shade store. All I remember of that was that Mother was very keen on my looking just so. I would be dressed and told not to get dirty. My hair absolutely straight, cut in a Buster Brown. One time I was standing in front of the house with my doll, and the shade-store family's son teased me and pulled my doll out of my arms. I was angry. Methodically I unbuttoned my dress, took it off over my head, hung it on the doorknob and then beat the hell out of him. I cleaned up and put the dress back on, and he went screaming to his mother. She came out and there I was all dressed up, holding my doll. She looked at him and yelled, 'Liar!' and socked him. Those were the days when I was playing with dolls and paint sets and a woodburning set, and my brothers had Erector sets. I would steal them, because I liked to build more than they did.

"And then life changed for me. At ten, I was thrust into a situation I loathed. I was expected to clean the house.

"Mother was working, my brothers were working. I would come home from school to a disheveled, messy house. Mother came home about six and expected the table set, dinner on. It was not unreasonable, but in those days it seemed incredible. I couldn't play without feeling guilty. I had to give up puttering around, drawing, working with wood or clay. I was overwhelmed by all I had to do. In those days I was drawing everything. Everything I owned, all my possessions. Making sculptures of everybody. There were constant fights, screaming, aggravation. I had loved cooking because I like to mix materials, but I wasn't allowed to do that. That job was given to one of my brothers. So I figured out a plan. I got my playmates to come help by setting up theater games. It was the Tom Sawyer idea. Eventually, of course, the parents realized the kids were cleaning our house, and they read the riot act to Mother and she read the riot act to me. And from this I developed a weird system that has helped me deal with life ever since. I learned to work with many things simultaneously and not lose track. Thus I would make time for myself. I would draw for a half hour, leave it, do a chore, return, draw a half hour, do a chore, begin a sculpture and work forty-five minutes, do a chore. The problem was, God help me if I became so fascinated I couldn't stop.

"One summer I got involved in an environmental sort of thing. We put on plays in the back garages. I wrote all the scripts, designed all the costumes and scenery. I was about fourteen. We made money. But it was so successful I didn't want to do it again.

"Because of that experience, I thought I would be a costume and set designer. When I was fifteen, I sold some theater designs to Brooks Costumes. By that time I was at Washington Irving High School.

"We had already had a marvelous fine-arts program in junior high school, using reproductions from the Metropolitan Museum. Early on, I admired Rosa Bonheur—a woman whose work I could identify with. I knew the prints came from the Museum and I'd never been there, so one day when I was about eleven I played hooky and went into Manhattan and spent the day there. By the time I went to Washington Irving, Brooklyn no longer interested me and I began spending all my time wandering around New York. I was hungry for it. I went to the old Whitney on Eighth Street, the Met, the Frick, the Non Objective, the Modern. Not the galleries—I didn't know they existed. But by the time I graduated at seventeen, I'd had more courses and experience with art history than many a college grad. I'd had a good sculpture teacher and learned classic techniques: to build with the armature, cast and do built-up sculpture, and painting. I also took a job as assistant to a commercial artist for five dollars a week, working from three to six every day. I did her pencil drawings and she would ink them in later. I also had a job with Paramount Pictures making composite photographic renderings. I was the only woman in the bullpen. I'd select the stills and lay them out and make the posters. I received good training there, too, keeping my pencils absolutely sharp, my table neat and clean. I developed a certain precision, organization, and was fortunate to have access to materials. But I was getting no encouragement from my family then at all. Although Mother, who was a saleslady, would get me fabulous French magazines from customers of hers interested in art, she never thought art would be more than a hobby for me.

"And then the art director suggested I try out for Cooper Union. It was very hard to get into. You had to take IQ, sculpture, art history and topography examinations. I was accepted, and it became another world for me. Cooper Union absolutely jelled everything that was going on. I spent about six months taking night classes and working during the day. Then I quit my job and went full time. I lived with Mother and her new husband, who gave me five dollars a week for carfare, lunch, stockings and supplies. But I won lots of materials scholarships and stayed up until two or three every night doing the work. I had found what I wanted.

"All the hotshots were at Cooper Union then. Alex Katz tells the story that we were all so hot we couldn't wait till the first life class to show off. Each one picked up charcoal and worked and then looked around and got sick because everyone else was doing so much better!

"I was interested in sculpture by then. I had to take architecture and I couldn't see the benefit. It infuriated me to have to work out the mathematical steps. It's odd, because now I use math all the time and it gives amazing insights into what I'm doing.

"Hovannes was my sculpture teacher. Our first project was to carve a lion out of a log. At the same time, we had to make a Constructivist sort of thing out of cut wood. Now, I knew exactly what I wanted and I made detailed drawings for the lion, but then I was bored stiff with doing all that carving. So I made a deal with a fellow student who enjoyed carving. I would cut the wood for him—a job I enjoyed. I knew all about tools, circular saw, jigs and so on. And he would do the undercarving for me. I went to Hovannes so as not to do it behind his back, and he was furious and horrified. 'Where's your feeling?' he asked. He said I was too facile and ended by telling me I was a *painter*. He meant it as an insult. The result was I went into painting and stayed with it a long, long time, doing abstractions.

"Hans Hofmann had his school on Eighth Street then, but I knew nothing about it. Those were the days of the '50s, when I met Morris Bernstein, who later became Morris Louis, at an Artists Equity meeting in Baltimore. He was intense and talked about artists and how they should be more independent. He was very political then, perhaps a Socialist. He was doing flower paintings. I was great for new materials, and I introduced him to Magna, the oil compatible acrylic. Later I became aware of Pollock and started pouring and staining. One summer I went to Provincetown to work with Hans Hofmann. He opened a new way of seeing, of getting past the limitations of the object, or transforming the object into a new reality, dealing with totally abstract concerns.

"By the time I was in Provincetown, I was painting with fluorescent paints on sheets of plastic. In 1960 I met George Segal there. He saw these sheets of plastic with paintings lit from underneath with black light. I was trying to get the images to leap forward, to make them three-dimensional. He said, 'It's very important what artists say to one another. We must always listen carefully. I think you are, or what you want to be is, three-dimensional.' And hearing him say that was as if, at last, I had been given permission to put the painting away.

"By 1968 I had set to work anew, and worked big. I made the *Light Floors* with

Antecedent, 1975. Weathered mild steel. 6' by 25' by 8'. Temporary site, Rawlins Park, Washington D.C. The National Gallery of Art, Washington D.C. (presently not on display).

a grant from the Architectural League of New York. These were three total environments of acrylic floor constructions, eight inches deep, lit with fluorescent tubes. Changes would take place in them as you walked across them. There was *Diamond,* with clear silver walls, lit from underneath with ultraviolet and golden fluorescent light. It was in a room walled with mirrors. *Horizontal Slide* was in a black room with a mirrored ceiling. The ceiling was made of uneven aluminum sheets so that when you looked up you would see a double or triple ghost image of yourself. *Oblique* was in a room with a mirror on one wall. The mirror reflected both you and the floor backward, which gave a sense of illusionistic space. The three matte black walls and the matte black floor area gave you the sense of falling into an abyss if you stepped off the floor. In '69 I had a show at New York University's Loeb Center: *The Universe as Environment: Moon-Markers.* There were large color transparencies of the

231

moon. Green and red transparent plastic shapes, colored sands, mica and fluorescent materials.

"Then, in '70, I was one of the artists to represent the United States in the São Paulo Bienniele. I did a sixty-five-foot octagonal tunnel filled with fluorescent liquids in vinyl pouches. The critics said it was like looking into an opal. After this, I exhibited at the Max Hutchinson Gallery in New York in a show titled "Liquid and Solid," and first introduced curvilinear steel forms. It was then that I realized I had *done* it. It culminated what I wanted to do with light. I somehow needed to move on, and this was a transition to my next stage.

"Now I'm working in steel. Steel pulled out of itself, keeping a memory of where it came from. The steelness of the steel. I like the physicality of the work. I also like the fact that though the work consumes me when I am at it, when I see it later I have a feeling of mystery, a sense of my own existence in a way— something beyond the work—hard to put into words."

EM: "Let me ask, Lila: Could there be a connection between these shining steel forms, the way they glint and bend, and those gilt sheets your grandfather the magician worked with so long ago?"

LK: "Yes! A tremendous connection!

"The sheet of gilt was so delicate, so precarious, you had to work with it immediately. You had to have immediate knowledge of what you were doing. No chance for mistakes. Neither is there with the steel. You can't reroll it. It'll lose its elasticity.

"And the tension is so similar! Such a preordained sense of what the shapes are going to do. So little room for accidental transformations. You can learn from piece to piece, but not in the course of working on any single one.

"These are surfaces that become more than surfaces. . . .

"Nothing here is found, discarded, used before. It's all pristine material. Never touched before except by me. And you couldn't touch the gold. I loved those sheets of gilt. Yes! That is the gleaming of the foil, and the transformation of the flat sheet . . . "

Joan
Mitchell

BORN 1926, CHICAGO

I think of white as silent. Absolutely. Snow. Space. Cold. I think of the Midwest snow . . . icy blue shadows . . .

I remember the yellow cornfields . . . Saugatuck in summer . . . oaks . . . dark birches . . . wild pines . . . . Those things cohere.

—JOAN MITCHELL
Vétheuil, France, 1977

They cohere, but they divide too. Between them the struggle takes place and the art is its expression: between white and green, snow and wild pine, ice blue and the saffron of late-summer cornfields that, even at the moment of being seen, are breaking back into the bluish ground and announcing the antiphone: "I think the white will probably return. The white is in me. It might come back."

This is the landscape of Joan Mitchell's Abstract Expressionist paintings and the landscape of a Protestant mentality. There is no "magic" in these paintings, any more than one hears mystic explanations from Mitchell herself, but there is the real: in nature, which is her essential subject, and in the psychic struggle for which we take the natural one as symbol. That concept has given the work its striking cohesiveness over the last twenty-five years, as the artist intimates without spelling it out. But what is even more real, in the tangible sense, is the most voluptuous pure oil paint to be seen on canvas in the recent time span.

That oil painting began on a "violent" (the word is hers) high when Mitchell was a precocious and affirmative ten-year-old in Chicago. "I never painted so bright again. All those reds and yellows!" Then, as she wryly says, she "Cubed it up" for a few years as a newcomer to high art, at the Chicago Art Institute, in Mexico and for a couple of unsettled years in New York and

233

Paris: dense, thick-angled fields of darkish paint with figures "mushed" into the background, then abandoned for good. Around 1953, at that point a committed expatriate from hinterland provincialism in the tradition of Wisconsin's O'Keeffe and Kansas' Pollock, she found her own idiom in the Big City, in the specific tradition of those masters of the loose brush and the giant black-and-white stresses: Kline and de Kooning. "Then the white really came in," she says of her work of the time. The paintings of Mitchell's first professional decade introduced the white ground—never after to be wholly absent—broken by athletic, slashing strokes of colors of the seen world: umber, green, brown, wide as two arms' reach. They "worked," as examples of quintessential Abstract Expressionism, as powerful shadow projections of the artist, who she was and what she came from. They made her reputation. She showed nearly every year in those days.

During the haywire '60s, when an Establishment antithesis rose up and laid low the Abstract Expressionist movement, Mitchell suffered along with many others. Though she survived as many (many men) did not and a few (notably women) did, she has no love for the memory of those times and no qualms about saying so: "I was successful in the '50s and then I was dropped in the '60s. It was the time of Pop, and I went on doing my 'little oil paintings.'

"Then, in the '70s, they had to dig up something new. So they came and dug my quote little oil paintings unquote. But the funny thing was, I hadn't ever quit. I hadn't done anything else in the meantime. I had never gone over to the Hard-Edge stuff. I was still doing them."

Even before "they" came to dig up her work, however, she had opened up a new territory of imagery and gesture. Then, against that acquiesced-to, white metaphysical void, she began to create passages (in individual canvases and also in whole episodes of work) lit by a fiery orange: palpitating walls of alizarin extracted from the memory of sunshine, sunflowers, broken fields of cornstalks. These she set into play, working with patches of deep blue and tangles of the old green-brown, streaked, raining and scumbled impastos in remembrance of past skies and thickets. There were also some paintings that confronted and even celebrated whatever it is we shall learn "white" stands for, with blue shapes blooming upon it like morning glories upon melting ice. In '76, her work took yet another turn. *Quatuor II* heralded the new idiom. The work is twenty-two feet wide, four panels of trunks of trees, vines and sky, pressing vertically forward against the surface of the canvas, while in the climactic panel on the right hand, the place of "heaven" in old church reliefs, is a bunching of "white" in an alternate incarnation: as Proustian hawthorns in bloom, or the blossoming chestnut of Yeats. What these paintings are ac-

Quatuor II for Betsy Jolas, 1976. Oil on canvas. 9'2" by 22'4". Xavier Fourcade Gallery, New York.

tually, then, beyond cadences of paint, are works of a kind of epic anecdote. Like a walk through landscape, the surfaces are stalked, each stroke a step and a declaration: I was here; here I stood, saw, felt, laid down this bar of color; I was here.

Here I am, but where am I? The perennial question of the provincial in exile, pilgrim on the road. Mitchell is three times self-exiled: from her birthplace of Chicago; from New York ("If I belong anywhere it's New York") and from metropolitan Paris, which she left in 1968 to live out in the Monet and Van Gogh countryside. The issue of removal from and attachment to whatever "home" may be is relevant, in a way useful to explore, to Mitchell's art. The question is one of the acceptance of loneliness, anomie. The acceptance, in the end, let us suppose, of "white."

"I'm an isolated person. But how to put that? I'm very interested in people. But for some reason, I remain isolated, no matter how I try (that's why I like dogs)."

Or: "I may have painted myself into a corner out here . . . "

Or: "I carry the feeling of being displaced around with me all the time. I've never really unpacked here. I used to have paintings hanging around me all the time. Now I don't have any on the walls."

EM: "Do you feel you've gone a long way just to come back to Saugatuck [in the northern Michigan forest-wilderness]?"

JM: "I don't think I've gone anywhere. It's all with me. Sort of packed in the suitcase. Only, the suitcase gets bigger."

The suitcase stands now on a hillside in Vétheuil, a town one hour outside Paris by suburban train. The house is halfway up a hillside toward the very field of poppies where Monet caught them in scarlet bloom one sunny afternoon just over a century ago. A taxi brings visitors to a blue iron gate at the far end of a twisting, gray-walled village street. A winding gravel path leads uphill through trees. Dogs bark from pens in the distance. Others lope around indoors all the time, are fed in orgiastic bouts in midafternoon, drowse on couches while the humans work. George and Isabelle, Bertie and Marion—those are the dead dogs who live on in the titles of some of her paintings. In Mitchell's latest show is *Posted: No Trespassing*. Amid a welter of green-blue strokes is a new, clear overhead yellow, shining through the top branches. "You know, the light you see through the trees . . . .It's a place I don't want anyone else to walk in. It's for me and the dogs." A visitor may find the dogs fairly scary, a Dantesque outer ring of defense. Cross it at your peril. But once inside, relax. You too are inside the Close.

The whitewashed stone house is dark in front, overshadowed by an immense spreading linden tree in the courtyard. One goes through the dark halls and out the back, to come upon the artist and her high-up panoramic view over village, Seine and distant lake. Mitchell stands in a doorway, a Lautrec figure these days, extremely lean and angular, closed off by brown bangs that meet the top edge of her Chinesey-horizontal dark glasses. She smiles, greets happily, then folds her arms in a defensive posture across her chest. Now and then she gives an ironic laugh—mostly at herself—and pulls herself up abruptly. Then, unannounced and inexplicably, she frequently also swoops into a remembered affection, shedding a wide grin. She is not fond of being interviewed, much as she warms to company. Much is useless to try to put into words, even for one who once played with the thought of becoming a writer.

That view, for instance: it has gone straight into the work. Standing on the balcony, one looks out, at one's very feet, over the roof of the house where Monet lived, with its ranks of terra-cotta tiles, provocatively similar in alignment to the thick strokes of tree trunks in the bottom portions of her recent works. Below and beyond is the middle ground: a street, little provincial dwellings, domesticated trees, their leaves so meticulously picked out in the clear air that one can read them at a distance—locust, pine, willow, pear. Then there is the blue-black river, flowing left to right. Boats glide by, barges with laundry flapping on their decks. The sun lights on patches of grass and broom, on yellow sand rimming the water's edge. Genre scenes unfold: dogs race, housewives mount bicycles. But Mitchell says,"I don't even see that middle section. The town. Le Lavacourt. That's Monet's territory. I see only trees and sky and the lake in the distance. An immense overturned bowl." It's a style of seeing that determines the art: a long glide to the place where the colors are clear.

Mitchell's studio is an outbuilding, wood-beamed and whitewashed, with carved fruitwood doors and a powerful smell of oil paint and turp. Dog-food cans stand all over the floor, stuffed with brushes. The hi-fi plays music when she is working, Mozart to Verdi.

EM: "How goes your work day, Joan? Get up in the morning?"

JM: "Not always. [A short laugh.] Lunch at one. With Hollis [her young American assistant and friend] or by myself. Afternoon, I do the crossword puzzle and listen to a couple of shrink programs."

EM: "To *what??*"

JM: "Oh, people call up with their problems, and that sort of makes you feel better you don't have *that* problem.

"Then, winter, the light goes down around four-thirty. I dog-feed then, or I can't see in the kennel. Later, in summer. Then Jean-Paul [Riopelle, the French-Canadian painter she has lived with since '55] comes home around seven-thirty to nine for supper. We eat. Look at television. Then I might paint. Or I might *not* look at television—and paint. Ten to four I paint. Something like that. Except the bad times."

EM: "What are the bad times?"

JM: "Bad times? When I don't feel anything. Everything looks the same no-color. I fight it. It's not a cyclical thing—seems to be my water level. I don't play around with it, though. I hear music, try to be active, walk to town. If I get into the work, then it's not there. That's the only fun I have. When I'm in it, I don't think about myself." (A long night's journey into day, that 10 P.M. to 4 A.M. working span. "Jean-Paul calls me Rosa Malheur. *Rosa Malheur!*")

EM: "If it's so tough, then how explain the marvelous expansion in your work, say, the last couple of years?"

JM: "Longer than that. Since we moved out here to the country in '68. Oh, the first winter was difficult. We bought the place by chance. I never thought of myself as a country person. It was Cedar Bar or Montparnasse. And there I was, isolated. A totally different approach. You're not going out to parties or having people around. And I liked it!

"So it was an unconscious change. At the same time, I knew what was happening. A lot had to do with a practical question too: space. I had a lovely studio before, but I couldn't get the paintings down the stairwell. You're con-

237

scious of that kind of thing without being. You know, if you paint thick, and you're going to have to roll the canvas to get it out the door, it's going to crack. So you don't put it on. Absolutely.

"Now I can leave the paintings out, not always turn them to the wall when people are around. It's having them in the separate studio. A lock on the door. And I don't have to roll them to get them out. That's made a great change.

"Then, the color is right here, outside my door. That helped, too.

"Then something else. You know *Quatuor*. That painting was a key. A change. It began when I was in Jean-Paul's studio one day, waiting for him. I was looking at the trees out his window. I did a drawing, just a few lines on a piece of paper. Then I made the picture. Worked on it for a year, changing it, switching the panels around.

"The greens are trees. Trees rather than lakes or fields. Marvelous trees. And that was the beginning."

EM: "Beginning of . . .?"

JM: "Maybe there aren't other words. I'm not sure there are other words. Except . . . trees . . . and fields . . . and whatever."

The beginning was in Chicago in 1926, in an era when the city was more a literary than an art frontier. It was not the center anymore of enthusiastic artistic experiment it had been, say, thirty years earlier, in 1893, when Mrs. Potter Palmer engaged Mary Cassatt to paint her murals for the Women's Building of the World's Columbian Exposition. Nor was it yet as exciting a place for the visual arts as it would be thirty years later, when a band of former Bauhaus artists and architects—Moholy-Nagy, Archipenko, Mies van der Rohe and others—would settle there and establish the famous Institute of Design. But still, like many provincial centers, Chicago did have a constant love affair with a farther world, in this case not New York but Paris. The bond had been created by the great gifts of French painting given to the Chicago Art Institute by the Potter Palmers and also Mary Cassatt's friends the Havemeyers—the Renoirs, Monets, Van Goghs and Delacroix among which Joan Mitchell grew up. Pride in that nucleus of French civilization located in their city was reinforced by the feeling many Chicagoans have that their nearest neighbor is really not part of the States but the land to the north: Canada, source of wind and snow.

Much has been written about other aspects of the American landscape, but not enough about the cold that, coming down from the Canadian plains, blankets the Midwest and farther West each winter. From the windows of her family's apartment in Chicago, overlooking Lake Michigan, Mitchell as a child learned as much about the ramifications of cold upon the soul as Ahab knew of the Polar Bear, the Whale and the White Shark. When she read that chapter of Melville it struck a chord. "That lake looked vast. No, infinite. Bleak. In winter it was icy, broken ice. Sometimes it's very blue. It has a lot of quality to it. It's changing, alive. Not just a dull body of water. Even summers, it's very dangerous. Not wide enough, and the wind changes.

"I remember when I was very little, my father pulling me on a sled along the edge of the lake. Somehow I fell in through the choppy ice. The waves were coming. He pulled me out, of course, but I was very, very cold. One didn't complain about being cold, with my father."

Cold had another dimension as well. Mitchell's mother was deaf and used an ear trumpet in the days before electronic aids.

EM: "Did your mother's being deaf strike you as isolating, sad?"

JM: "I felt she was very alone. I was very aware of that. I often tried to imagine what kind of silence must be inside a deaf person."

EM: "You thought about that a lot?"

JM: "Oh, yes."

EM: "Is there a connection between silence, white, cold and the lake?"

JM: "I would not have thought of it. But it's true I think of white as silent. Absolutely. Snow. Space. Cold. I think of the Midwest snow . . . icy blue shadows . . .

"Have you been North, in the snow? In that silence you can almost hear?"

There was a way away from the silence of cold: Mitchell was a figure-skating champion in her school days. That sport, or rather art, is a favorite in the Midwest, and a sight common on cold days is the indoor rink, blue-white and crossed with streaks where blades have cut their figure eights and threes, while between and across go the girls in short bright gored skirts, flaring out like morning glories or sunflowers on white fields, or holding still with their arms wide outstretched, whirling.

"I was mad at a reviewer who reviewed my first show back in '51 and said it was like figures on ice. I thought skating had nothing to do with painting, and I didn't want anybody to know about the painting-skating thing. Well, I've come around now. I admit you can't get me away from the television when the skating things are on. I love skating. If you use your body as you do in any sport, that's all part of your coordination."

So one might say a way out of the silence of cold was by mastery of an art, which involved, among other powers, the knowledge that after the skating season comes spring again, melting ice, pale green, then gold fields turning burnt orange ("I remember the yellow cornfields . . ."), then dark reds turning near-black, black-green.

As for trees, whether red or green, non-Midwesterners hardly know what they mean there, either: high elms caught at the tips in the sighing flood of "terrible" winds off the Canadian plains, or, in summer, sugar maples, ash, birch and sycamores in tangled Courbet glens, mattings of uncleared second growth choked in vines, all so steeped in humidity that those leaves, stems and trunks sometimes seem drowned in green water. There is no sign, there, of the spindle poplars or pristine fruit trees of Monet country, the neatened forests of Barbizon, the dulcet small hilltops of New England or, either, the desolate untreed plains of the farther West. "Green," or "green trees" in the Great Lakes region, then, can be a metaphor for so much coming up from underneath that the top layer of things can hardly sustain the pressure.

The summers of her seventeenth and eighteenth years Mitchell spent in a forested part of Michigan in an art colony run by the Chicago Art Institute. "I have a hard time enjoying things. I don't enjoy easily, because I'm always hedging against enjoyment. I'm afraid it will go away, so why . . . why enjoy? But the best time? Saugatuck in summer, maybe. I haven't thought of that for so long.

"You walk a mile to take a little ferry over to the town. It was wild, no electricity. There was sand. Dunes. Marvelous oak trees. Sort of an Indian mound, with trees in a circle. They must have had some kind of rite there. Oaks . . . dark birches . . . wild pines.

"We painted outdoors, in the field with the trees behind. A very strange experience, painting the nude outdoors. Exciting and beautiful. There was a model, Cleo, with a marvelous body, like a Renoir. She posed by the lake.

"Afternoons, the landscape. Evenings, we sat by kerosene light and did lithography.

"My teacher from the Art Institute was there. He talked about decisions. My decision to leave college was the decision that time is short. Time to become a painter. I felt one doesn't paint by being an English major. One paints by painting. Full time."

Thereafter, Mitchell left Smith College, where she had spent two fairly restless years, won a scholarship from the Art Institute and moved back into her parents' apartment overlooking Lake Michigan. From her windows, she was there that first art-student year to watch it turn cold, freeze, turn blue, turn to ice again.

Mitchell had begun life in a civilized orb in Chicago, devoted to the arts, poetry, music. Her mother, Marion Strobel, was the daughter of one of those American tycoons of the early 1900s. He was of German extraction, trained as an engineer in Stuttgart, who returned to this country to become an inventor of structural-steel elements for bridges designed by himself. He was a formal man and a moral one, and he impressed his granddaughter greatly. Until he died, he donned striped morning trousers to pay family calls, and he left journals in which he recounted his meetings with Carnegies, Fricks and Freers with reports of their ethical shortcomings. Joan Mitchell saved those journals and his drawings and keeps them as her special link with the past. Marion Strobel herself aspired to the life of a poet but settled for something possibly less, possibly more realistic: the "mother business," as her daughter puts it. After boarding school, she had renounced college and stayed home to write her lyric verses and even for a time to work as co-editor with Harriet Monroe of *Poetry*. But her amateur status displeased her, and it is possible she took out some of her dissatisfaction by resolving not to do more of that mother business than was absolutely required. She was rather more a cultural force than a traditional maternal one. To the Mitchell house came from time to time Thornton Wilder, who read poems to Joan and her sister at bedtime, T. S. Eliot and Dylan Thomas. "Aunt Harriet," frequently there, was not so impressive to the young. Joan, at least, was always "worried her false teeth would come out."

Mitchell's father was a self-made and successful doctor, an orphan from age six whose father had fought in the Civil War and whose grandfather had fought in the Revolution. By his late forties he had achieved eminence and then, on the late side for easy adaptability, married and had his family. He did not forget his origins: he never took vacations, and he worked in clinics for the poor. Also, he doted on his daughters, especially perhaps sportive Joan, and spent many "snowy Sundays" with her at the Art Institute and the Field Museum of Natural History. At six, she had picked out Van Gogh as her favorite painter; her feeling for Cézanne came a little later. Her father was also that unconventional thing: a male nonartist who liked to draw. Summer days, they went sketching. "It's funny, I can see the watercolors he made very, very clearly, but I can't remember the ones I made at all. He would paint a red barn and a blue sky and green grass." At the zoo, they drew elephants and lions. In the country, it was trees and clouds. He also was a music lover. But mainly he was competitive, tough and driving, and had a fondness for wise saws: "Desserts are only for women and children," "Jack of all trades, master of none" . . . Or that business about not complaining about the cold. "I did feel a pressure to become, quote, a professional. I began very early feeling I had to excel."

All that apparatus of ancestry, culture and striving for excellence would have, in a way, insulated a person from conforming to the life of the greater inland city. There was, to tell the truth, a peculiar island-sense of isolation about a nucleus of culture in the American provinces in the decades before TV massified the nation. Those who participated in it were sheltered from the inanities of their surroundings but were without an organic connection to the

241

wider cosmopolitan world except through visitors (or those art tokens) from beyond. They had a tendency to develop inwardly and pine for a more congenial ambiance. They might want to get going, get on the road. But to where? They might suffer, then, anomie and earn by it a desperate integrity: consider Hart Crane, Sherwood Anderson, O'Keeffe, Pollock. "I was split," says Mitchell. "I was split right down the middle. There was culture in Chicago, but it depended what you were born into. I knew I did not want the social scene. Mother too was split, of course. My father, because he was a self-made man, was not. I went to a marvelous school, but then we went to a ghastly summer place in Lake Forest, ninety-nine percent Social Register people. Everything I did later, I did on my own. I didn't want to use my family's influence. When I went to the Art Institute, I didn't want anyone to know where I lived. I felt that coming from the background I did, I would not be taken seriously by anyone."

There is also often a hapless innocence about the provincial, a Julien Sorel–ish propensity for foolishness, for risk-taking, rebelliousness and an ungovernable appetite for elected wicked enjoyments. From that inclination to fall has come the provincial's conflicted view about Vanity Fair. The Big City versus the Natural Paradise. O'Keeffe fled; Crane and Pollock took more desperate ways out. For an artist the conflict can be acute, since art percolates fastest in the capital cities. The artistically aspiring provincial is drawn to them but gets into trouble there, avoids the country like death until one day the country is all around and then "I rather like it!" Growing up beyond the fractious egalitarianism of the capital melting pot, where a maverick kid finds herself or himself swiftly out of one stream and swimming in another, the provincial's Way can be a very long one.

"I remember, around the seventh or eighth grade, thinking, I've got to be something. What is it? It's going to be either painting or writing, and it can't be both. I mean, Jack of all trades, master of none. So it was paint. After that, that was just what I was going to do. My great hope was to be, if I worked very hard, an Ann Ryan. Why? Look—she was a lady painter I admired. How many are there? I mean, women couldn't paint—and women *didn't* paint." From second grade, she had attended Saturday classes at the Art Institute; for high school, Mitchell attended one of those famous Deweyesque progressive institutions that grew up in the nation around the '20s: Frances Parker, where there was a memorable teacher, Malcolm Hackett. "He opened such vast visions to the few of us who listened. He gave us the message: to become an artist, you had to go through poverty and passion. At the age of fourteen, working for that teacher, I knew more about painting than most people do today.

"He'd come into school through the back door. He thought that school was for fancy, rich kids, and he couldn't bear most of the people there. But there were about six of us who would have followed him to the ends of the earth. It was partly because of him, but partly, too, just because of the way I was, that I turned my back on all the conventional social business. He had laid down certain principles, like wearing blue jeans instead of evening clothes. Remember, blue jeans weren't a uniform in those days."

The war came midway through high school. "I was very moved by it; all the kids going off; boys only a couple of years older getting killed. It was a *real* situation," and one that penetrated the isolation of the provinces even while at the same time fading into the background in cities enjoying the economic boom of war industries. When Mitchell went off to Smith College in 1943, there were still WAVES marching on the green, and the Navy Language Group was at Amherst College down the pike. Students were doing war volunteer work, and there was a more mixed, professionally oriented population than a later decade would see. She studied a couple of years of painting with the studio teacher George Cohen, in those days a fairly derivative semiabstract painter, who gave her one of her rare marks below an A. And she spent time painting outdoors. There were the lovely fields and mountain valleys around Northampton. Behind the college flowed a stream dammed to make a lake where in spring the girls boated and in winter skated. "Paradise Pond," remembered Joan Mitchell. "I'd always go farther than Paradise Pond."

It was perhaps the same impulse she records today, asked about some of the "beautiful" painters she has known. "But I always wanted *more.* I wanted more."

The hard years began when she came to New York, in '48, after finishing with the Art Institute. "I had to get out of school and work and live." For a few months, she lived under the Brooklyn Bridge—shades of Hart Crane, shades of her bridge-building grandfather—on the Brooklyn side, on Fulton Street, on the first floor only a step from the water. "I've almost always lived on water. Later I went to Paris and I could see the Seine. After that I went to the South of France and I could see the Mediterranean. And now I can see the Seine again"—shades of the lake. She heard about Hans Hofmann's school, and tried one or two classes, but "I couldn't understand him and he scared me so I didn't go back.

"Then I had to go somewhere, so I went to Paris. I had won a traveling scholarship from the Art Institute. You had to go somewhere. So I went to Paris. And that was . . . depressing. I arrived in Le Havre. I'll never forget it. The sun was setting and there was all the devastation. I remember sailing toward the

243

coast, seeing the Liberty Ships lit by the setting sun. Red. You felt there had been a war. Maybe other people didn't think about it, but it's all I thought about.

"Then I got a little place just off the Seine next to St.-Julien-le-Pauvre, in sight of Notre Dame. A fantastic place. But I had no heat. Just one little stove. In Chicago at least we had heat. In Paris I was cold. Really cold. So was everyone else. Frozen."

There was rationing in Paris; shortages of everything; expatriates and drab refugees in the streets, at the university, in cafés. Her toilet was a black hole beside the stairs; you flushed it with a bucket of water. There were rats. In July, Gorky committed suicide back home and the news quickly reached the Americans in Paris. It was "the horrible year. I thought, Why don't I quit this stuff, be strong enough to kick this? But there wasn't any other way. It was the only thing." She was self-rescued by illness and was obliged to go south to the Mediterranean, but there the Mistral was blowing its deranging blast. "It was a strange period."

She retrenched to New York, a brief marriage with Barney Rossett, founder of Grove Press and a friend of childhood from Chicago, and half a decade in a New York gradually heating up around the Abstract Expressionist movement. "I had painted terribly that year in Paris, semiabstract stuff. I remember the last figure I did. I knew it was the last figure I would ever paint. I just knew. There were no features, and her arms were . . . rudimentary. I knew that was it. After that, I just removed the figure and kept on Cubing it up."

Women on the wave of the Second Generation came in swinging and frequently—one hears the word from many sources—"cutthroat." There were "greaters" and "lessers" jockeying for the pitifully few gallery spots for women. Mitchell began at the New Gallery in '51, then showed regularly at the Stable between '53 and '65. She went on working, Cézanne and Kandinsky her historic models now. Van Gogh of the sunflowers not in the forefront yet. More white. Something of bridges. Much of skating. Her present models were ones she discovered on her own. "I met Kline in '51 and went to his loft on Ninth Street to see his work. I walked in and there were brick walls with paintings, not on stretchers, tacked all over them and all over the floor. And those drawings he made on telephone book pages. I was overwhelmed. I thought they were the most beautiful things I'd ever seen in my life. We talked . . . or he talked . . . until about seven-thirty in the morning. Double-talk . . . a lovely sense of humor. What about? Oh, one never knew exactly what Kline was talking about."

Another was de Kooning. "There was a painting, a big black-and-white painting, at the old Whitney. I'd never heard of him, but I wanted to meet him.

The artist at work on Bridge, 1957 (destroyed). Oil on canvas. 90" by 80".

Who is he? I thought; I have to find a way. I found him in his studio over on Fourth Street. He worked on one single painting all that winter long. I'd go up there and say to myself, Why doesn't he stop? It's finished! But it wasn't, and he didn't.

"Well, it was exciting. You had this feeling of a group against the world, against dealers, even against Artists Equity. This seedy, exciting group of people."

Not that it wasn't tough. The feeling was that women couldn't paint. Hofmann himself said as much, one time, to the sculptor Lila Katzen, or implied it, saying that only men had the wings for art.[1] Louise Nevelson heard another version: to sculpt, you had to have balls. Still there were women in the famous Ninth Street Show, as we know. Leo Castelli had asked Mitchell to submit a picture, offering even to carry it over. "And when we got there, de Kooning and Hofmann and Kline all said, 'What a marvelous painting!' and hung it in the best part of the show." And Mitchell, Elaine de Kooning and Mercedes Matter, the painter and daughter of Arthur B. Carles, were among the few female members of The Club.[2] The sculptor Philip Pavia "was the one who allowed [!] me to become a member in '51.

245

"Well, you got shows in those days through men. In fact, the people who encouraged me were always men. They inspired me and encouraged me."

It was in those days of the early '50s that Mitchell coined her own version of the famous Hans Hofmann phrase "I bring the landscape home with me."[3] He was fond of saying that after standing on the dunes at Provincetown watching the sun set behind Plymouth Bay in a fiery display whose reds, gray-greens, yellows and lavenders found their way eventually into his abstract paintings. Helen Frankenthaler's version was "the landscape was in my arms as I worked," a statement that more concerned process, the wrist gesture from which her image naturally derives. "I am nature . . ." said Jackson Pollock, voicing a symbiosis so engulfing it was unendurable for long. The fact that O'Keeffe paints outdoors, *in* the landscape, explains the difference between herself and these four related artists of the Abstract Expressionist idiom, all of whom distill the landscape through the agency of memory in their studios and therefore paint their own search for place as much as the place itself.

"I carry my landscape around with me" was Joan Mitchell's way of saying it, meaning more than *having* the landscape in her arms, and less than *being* nature entirely, but rather, I suggest, that she possesses it as Everyperson possesses, or carries within, according to Protestant tradition, heaven and hell and also the long walk that leads from one to the other. So Mitchell too in her way does more than "paint nature": she externalizes the nature that is within, human selfhood, the alternating dark and light that Transcendentalism tried to mist over but could not for long in the face of visible facts—the fields, yearly broken on the wheel of the real. Yet in spite of the pain of it, artists of that bent drive themselves to return again and again to the real as source of inspiration, as Arthur G. Dove did after wandering into pure abstraction for a while, and finding then that both his work and he himself had "gone dead." ("After Father died," said Mitchell, "I kept going home and making Christmas for Mother until her death, just the way she had done when we were small. With a tree.")

The 1960s were of all the years perhaps the worst for some artists of the Abstract Expressionist waves, victims of the shift in taste and power that many remember as "terrible." The bitterness remains, even for one who weathered the time abroad. "If you have a little success," says Mitchell now, "and then hard times, nothing much matters afterward. That's what happened to me. I knew then that I would do my own thing no matter what came. You do derive a certain sense of assurance. The reinforcement comes from yourself."

Coming out of those years, she painted, in 1972, one of the "coldest" works of her career: *Canada,* with floating panels of blue upon white. A con-

Mitchell before works in progress, 1974.

fronting of the absolute in one of its polar incarnations: Canadian Riopelle's ground? "Jean-Paul's always up there. Last fall he went all the way to the North Pole."

EM: "Have you been there with him?"

JM: "Too cold for me! But he's painting beautifully these days. Enormous, just black-and-white paintings."

Can one say that Joan Mitchell, for her part, works the ground between "just black and white," is driven back and forth like the seasons themselves between those poles, always back to the natural "more"? A faint blur of green pigment on the snowfields of *Canada* heralded spring. Soon would come the day she would see the trees through Riopelle's window. "I think now of the Lake, and of Saugatuck. Those things cohere. They form a continuity. The Lake is with me today. The memory of a feeling. And when I feel that thing, I want to paint it.

"I wouldn't say that solaces my loneliness. . . . But it replaces loneliness."

247

Elaine
de Kooning

BORN 1920, NEW YORK CITY

I struggled with the pose for a year. I came to understand the struggles Ingres had with Monsieur Bertin! Many of the tries were failures. They kept getting worse and worse. I began to feel desperate. Now and then I'd feel I was closing in, but then the image would freeze. . . . At one point I had thirty-six canvases going at once, all at different stages. . . .

Then the assassin dropped my brush.

—ELAINE DE KOONING
Paris/New York, 1977

Elaine de Kooning, painter, critic, teacher, lecturer, came along midway in the Abstract Expressionist era. By inheritance a Feminist, by training an articulate explicator of thorny esthetic matters, she quickly came into her own in that fractious group. Though she married the future Abstract Expressionist master Willem de Kooning—Bill—in 1943, she thereafter and more so since their amicable separation in '56 steered pretty much her own course. Her manner of handling paint in raking, pleated, balanced-in-tension strokes was learned mainly from him with traces from others she admired, particularly Arshile Gorky. But her imagery was her own. Her theme, one that other women have nearly universally ignored in their art, has been the image of the Towering Male. As male painters through history pursued the nymph-goddess-virgin-queen down the corridors of dream and esthetic mannerism, E de K (as she signs her paintings) has followed her romantic, over-life-size grail, posed now as a portrait subject, now as athlete, now as President, now as Bacchus. Now he appears with a recognizable face, now without features at all, sitting knees apart, those jutting knees a child might see first foremost when facing a grown person. *He* appears even, in some works, as the bull at its moment of truth.

248

E de K's most taxing commission was to paint President Kennedy. That was a living father-brother figure she could not come to grips with. Although one of the series of portraits is now in the Kennedy Library collection and another in the Truman Library, she felt that she had not accomplished what she set out to do. Death released her from the commission but set her off into a period of compulsive portrait painting. Finally, recently, she has found two liberating new variants of her old idol, aspects at once heroic, adorable and carnal: one the painter Aristodemus Kaldis, long a figure of the New York avant-garde, with floating hair, vivid dark eyes and barrel chest; the other, a figure from a statuary group in the Luxembourg Gardens in Paris: a naked Bacchus elevated on a rocky plinth, with tublike belly, splayed legs and wickedly gleeful countenance.

For herself, E de K is a disarming figure in the art world, a lively backer of liberation movements of all kinds—old artists, young artists, out-of-town artists, female artists. She is not one to deplore women's work done in whatever hinterland obscurity. "I find that women can be creative in total isolation. I know excellent women artists who do original work without any response to speak of. Maybe they are used to a lack of feedback. Maybe they are tougher. Men, unappreciated, tend to wither on the vine. But then again I know many male artists who work in the same kind of isolation. It's dangerous to generalize."

She is also a popular teacher and speaker and divides her time these days in presenting one- or two-week workshops at museum schools in different parts of the country. "It turns out that teaching art—which, ideally, is shop talk—fills the gap left by the disappearance of The Club and the Cedar Tavern and, before then, the cafeterias of my pre-teaching days."

"My mother was a mighty figure to contend with. Irish, and fanatically so. Her father, Peter O'Brien, came to New York from County Mayo, became a bartender and eventually owned his own bar at Twenty-eighth Street and Eighth Avenue. Her mother's father, Patrick Murphy, came a generation earlier and was a cobbler. In Ireland, they were all farmers, with a priest or a nun in every generation. My father's family were farmers from Bavaria. He was born on a farm in upstate New York, but his father, Conrad Fried, gave up farming when my father was eight years old to build houses and barns. He was a fantastic carpenter. My mother had just begun to study law when she was 'delighted to discover' she was pregnant. From then on, her children (we were all born, four of us, within five years) were the central interest in her life.

"She and my father moved to Brooklyn to have a back yard for us to play in. He was a CPA and had to commute an hour each way to his office, but he didn't mind because he had his garden—all sorts of flowers, particularly roses, different kinds, some tiny ones that I've never seen since. He was great with animals too. We had chickens and ducks and rabbits and cats and dogs and white mice and flying squirrels. When he took us out, it was to Madison Square Garden to see horse shows, rodeos, the circus, sporting events. When my mother took us out it was to the opera, the theater and restaurants. She had tickets for the theater every week, and, being the oldest, I got the lion's share of the outings. I got to go with her every other week, not one in four.

"She was contemptuous of Brooklyn, but we loved it. Its tree-lined streets, its lawns, hedges, gardens and its marvelous, dangerous places to play—lumberyards, excavations and half-built, abandoned constructions, some of them two and three storeys high. And the hills leading up to elevated 'subways,' empty lots. And the great, gnarled, hundred-year-old trees to climb.

"Mother filled our house with large, framed reproductions of paintings, and she would talk about them to me. There was a Raphael *Madonna and Child* that I thought was a picture of the two of us. And I remember a Rembrandt that frightened me because I saw faces in the shadows. There was also a Vigée Le Brun *Mother and Daughter* and, most impressive, Rosa Bonheur's *Horse Fair.* I began life with the assumption that half the painters in the world were women.

"She also gave me opulent art books. I remember a purple book of Biblical paintings—Michelangelo's Adam and God, Moreau's *Salomé.* She took me to the Metropolitan Museum when I was five, and I recognized the difference between paintings and our reproductions under glass at home. From the first instant, the Met was drenched in glamour for me. When we got home my mother made a primitive little sketch of me. I was immediately galvanized and thought I could do better. From then on, I began to spend hours drawing, copying comic strips, making up pictures—scenes of covered wagons or Spanish women with mantillas (I loved to draw lace). Other children began to ask me for my drawings, teachers praised them and I lapped up the attention.

"I began to spend Saturdays and Sundays in museums—the Met and the Brooklyn Museum—drawing from statues, and I became interested in the lives of artists, how old they were when they made certain paintings. By the time I went to high school, I didn't have a doubt that I would spend my life painting.

"I went to Erasmus Hall High School, where you could major in art. We had geniuses for teachers there, elegant, mostly spinster ladies: Virginia Murphy, who later founded the High School of Music and Art, and my favorite, Regan (Miss? Mrs.? I never knew), who had studied with Hans Hofmann when he came to this country in 1932. There were reproductions of Cézanne, Picasso, Matisse, Degas on the walls. The emphasis was on modern art. Regan took us to the American Place Gallery, to the Museum of Modern Art, and—a great event for us—to *Four Saints in Three Acts*. She adored Gertrude Stein, whom I read reverently but without understanding until the dance critic Edwin Denby read a page aloud to me a couple of years later, making its meaning clear in terms of its rhythms. But my mother was my chief reading guide until I was sixteen. She was marvelous about introducing me to authors at the right time—Dickens when I was twelve, Shaw at thirteen, Proust at fourteen, Henry James at sixteen. As with the painters, when women appeared—George Eliot, Jane Austen, the Brontës, Emily Dickinson—she made no special point of it. It was just the natural order of things. She did put emphasis, though, on the relationship of Sappho and her daughter, and Madame de Sévigné and her daughter.

"The only male chauvinism I ever encountered was, however, hers. She told me how disappointed she was when my sister and I were born and how delighted she was with my two brothers; how little girls were smarter than little boys, but that men were smarter than women. On the other hand, she made me feel that 'firstborn' was an exalted position. I reacted, of course, against my mother's ambivalent but fierce anti-Feminism by being competitive with boys, and my way of competing was to join them. I played with boys exclusively until I was thirteen—baseball, football, field hockey, handball. And I was just as competitive with girls. It was important to excel, to get high marks, to concentrate. I had women idols—Babe Didrikson and Amelia Earhart. When I was twelve, a teacher told me I looked like Earhart; no compliment could have pleased me more. I also had heroines among dancers. I began to take dancing lessons when I was seven—ballet, tap dancing, acrobatics, the whole smorgasbord they used to give children (the dancer Merce Cunningham told me he started with the same kind of lessons). I adored dancing. I was on my way to being professional, but I knew I had to make a choice in terms of time. I opted for painting. From then on I kept on taking dance lessons, but I knew it was 'on the side.' "

"I graduated from high school in '36 and went to Hunter because that's where my mother went, but after a couple of months I knew something was wrong. I didn't feel in control. *I wasn't choosing what to do.* I was never near a paintbrush. I was miserable. One day I heard about the Leonardo da Vinci Art School on Third Avenue and Thirty-fourth Street. I rushed there that same evening, carrying a pad, ready to start work. The atmosphere was free and easy, artists and students milling about in the hallways, sculptors carving stone or modeling clay in one room, students drawing from the nude in another. The prospect of drawing from the nude was exciting. The model's stillness seemed intimate and variable, different from the frozen, public contours of a statue. I showed my drawings of sculptures and was enrolled at once and began to draw immediately.

"I felt I had entered a charmed circle. During the rest periods, I found out that some of the faculty were employed by the WPA. Then someone took me to a show of the American Abstract Artists, and I was thrilled. I had thought all abstract artists were European, that American art was exclusively 'commercial' or 'realistic.' I studied the paintings and the names of the artists (within a year I met most of them). 'But,' my friend said, 'the two best abstract artists in America are not in this show: Bill de Kooning and Arshile Gorky.' A week or so later, we met Bill in a cafeteria and he invited us to his studio to hear some Stravinsky. I was dazzled by the immaculate space of Bill's studio, the gleaming gray linoleum floor, white walls, spare furnishings and the wall of windows in his work area. There was a painting of a man on his easel, unlike anything I had ever seen, in strange tones of yellow ocher with taut, quivering contours. I thought it was the most mysterious painting I had ever seen.

"Then one day the painter Milton Resnick told me about an even bigger and livelier place, the American Artists School on West Fourteenth Street. So I brought work to show them, got a scholarship and began working there day and night, from ten in the morning until ten at night. I took sculpture with Milton Hebald and learned to work in clay and cast in plaster. I studied watercolor painting with Ben Wilson, oil painting with Tchachbasov. I had classes in lithography, etching and silk-screening. And we sat in on stormy Artists' Union meetings, listened to boogie-woogie at Café Society Downtown, saw Betty Comden, Adolph Green and Judy Holliday at the Village Vanguard, went to foreign movies at the Rialto on Forty-second Street, went dancing at Webster Hall or to dance halls up in Harlem. Now, at last, every minute of my life was chosen by me. I was free of constraints. I loved the conviviality of the school, the endless arguments over politics after class in cafeterias or parks. I had been brought up as a Roman Catholic, but I felt at home with members of the Young Communist League or the opposing Trotskyite groups. Our discussions would rage on and on, night after night.

"Mexican artists were the big influence then—the murals of Orozco and Diego Rivera, the Duco enamel paintings of Siqueiros—and political consciousness was the prevalent content of painting. Abstract art was considered 'ivory tower,' elitist, unfeeling. Art should be concerned with the problems of the world. Goya and Daumier were the giants. I was swept along with it. I began to paint scenes of the Spanish Civil War—women reaching toward the sky with blood running down their arms.

"Then one day, out walking, I met Bill on the street again and invited him to come see my paintings, which were gorier than ever. It was embarrassing. He just stood there a while and then said, 'Why don't you just paint a still life?' And I realized that Social Realism had pulled me off the track.

"He suggested I come and set up a still life in his studio and paint along with him. I spent two days arranging objects he gave me—a coffee pot, a large shell, a yellow cup, an old blue cotton shirt and an army blanket. I set up that still life with Cézanne in mind. I'd been aware of him since I was thirteen, that he was in some sense clumsy but that he was doing something original. It was the same when I read Gertrude Stein the first time. I knew something was there. I worked on the painting for three months. Bill would talk to me about it. He'd talk about the space between the objects in that intense way he had of scrutinizing a tiny area. He'd say, 'See this curve here, of the bottom of this object, and how it relates to this, and the distance between them . . .' Everything was a matter of tension between objects or edges and space. The tension extended to every part of the canvas. Wherever you looked, there were these tensions.

"He'd say, 'Look how this sits there . . .' He'd use that term often, and it would be as if you had never seen a cup before. He'd explain that the object could expand or contract in all possible ways. We'd both be looking at the same still life, and he'd be pointing out the space that the object occupied and displaced.

"Sometimes he'd paint on my canvas a little bit, and every stroke was freighted with meaning. As dancers make a single step over and over to make the leap work. When he talked, it was as if I were lifting weights. Not as if he were giving an opinion, but as if he were demonstrating something that was absolute and true, but that I had never seen before. As if he were telling me what $E = MC^2$ means. I had to strain. It was that kind of consciousness. Tremendous. A working out. Not dodging things. It was making it as hard as possible. See this . . . see this ellipse . . . see this object. After he finished, after an hour, I'd have to go lie down. I was brain-tired.

"When I finished that still life, I began another, then another. I finally gave up my studio and just worked at Bill's. We were married in December, '43.

"Chelsea, where we had our studio, was full of artists then. You couldn't go out at any hour of the day or night without bumping into someone and getting involved in a discussion. Gorky lived a few blocks away near Union Square, and there were visits back and forth or excursions on Saturdays to the Metropolitan with concentrated examination of particular works of art. There was always something specific Gorky wanted to see. There were composers in the neighborhood whom we met through Denby. I knew his book of poetry, *In Public, In Private,* by heart. And he was writing his extraordinary dance criticism for the *Herald Tribune.* I often accompanied him to performances and tried putting my own impressions into words afterward. Then I would study his reviews in terms of my own responses. In 1945, the Museum of Modern Art had a retrospective show of Stuart Davis' work. It fascinated me and I wrote an article about it—ten typewritten pages—to record my perceptions for myself.

"Then in 1948, the same month that Bill had his first show, I began writing reviews for *Art News*. No collectors were buying his paintings then—just a few sales to friends, Denby, the photographer Rudy Burckhardt, painters Alain and Biala, and Fairfield Porter. We were always broke, and I had this ludicrous idea that I could make money writing reviews. *Art News* paid two dollars a review, but I often spent ten hours on one paragraph. The reviews were, at most, two hundred words, and I was very conscious of the fact that I was covering a year or two of someone's hard work in that short a space, so I had to make every word count. I found it a challenge. I'd jot down notes on one show after another, and when I looked at each set of notes in the evening the entire show would come back—the colors, the sizes, the juxtapositions. Writing reviews taught me a lot. Before then, if I saw a show I didn't like, I'd just dismiss it. Now I had to examine it, analyze it, describe it. The revelations that even bad art offered were a surprise. After a year, however, I wanted to write only about art that interested me, not just whatever came along, so from then on I wrote just an article or two a year—Josef Albers, Edwin Dickinson, Gorky, Hofmann, Andrew Wyeth, David Smith, Jeanne Reynal." [1]

EM: "Your own portrait painting and figure painting began in the middle '40s. How?"

EdK: "I visited Fairfield Porter one day while he was making a portrait of his wife, Anne. I thought she had a terrific face, very strong and beautiful with wonderful shapely eyes. I made a very careful drawing of her that evening and then two small paintings from the drawings. After that, the painter Joop Sanders and I posed for each other. I'd spend a day drawing and then make a painting from it the rest of the week. Then I began to make drawings of my brother, Conrad, and the paintings from them kept getting larger and larger until they were life-size. I worked on them for months. I became fascinated by the way men's clothes divide them in half—the shirt, the jacket, the tie, the trousers. I worked with just a few stylized poses. Some men sit all closed up—legs crossed, arms folded across the chest. Others are wide open. I was interested in the gesture of the body—the expression of character through the structure of the clothing. I centered the figures; I thought of them as spinning—'gyroscope men,' isolated in space."

EM: "Tell me about some of the other themes: the basketball players, the bullfight and so on."

EdK: "Time and time again as I was going past a newsstand my eye would be caught by a particular abstract composition and it would turn out to be a sports photograph. So I began to collect them and make drawings from groups of them—a figure from this photograph, a pair of arms from that. The drawings suggested another scale, and I worked up to seven- and eight-foot-high canvases, with elongated figures that were a reversion to my adolescent passion for El Greco, with colors flowing through and across the reaching forms.

"In '57 I made my first trip west of the Hudson, and it was a revelation. The ruddy earth, the naked musculature of the Rockies, the brilliant colors of the sky behind them at twilight, the massive horizontality of the environment—it was all overpowering, and my painting responded. I went to Juárez to see the bullfights, which immediately struck me as a heightened image of the Southwestern landscape—the panorama of the arena, the heraldic colors. I

Sunday Afternoon, 1957. *Oil on Masonite. 36" by 42". Collection Ciba–Geigy Corporation, Ardsley, New York.*

255

worked with this theme for three years on wider and wider canvases until finally I found myself face to face with a canvas twenty feet wide and ten feet high. Milton Resnick told me that he was extending his brushes with six-foot aluminum pipes. I found that a useful device, but still it took me a month to work up the nerve to start. I didn't want to ruin that glorious piece of canvas! And after working on it a couple of months, I felt I had achieved what I was after.

"When I had my show of the bullfight series in 1960, few of the stretched canvases would fit through the door. Most had to be taken off their stretchers and rolled on cardboard cylinders used for pouring cement columns, and then restretched in the gallery. Seeing the brush strokes flying around the columns started me off on a year's work on cylindrical paintings ten and twelve feet high. Working on a curved surface was curiously exhausting, and after I showed them, in '61, I returned to portraits—influenced by the columns—a series of tall, standing men. These vertical portraits were shown the following year at the Graham Gallery, and John Canaday, art critic of *The New York Times,* attacked them in two and a half columns in the Sunday paper.

"Two weeks later, a representative from the White House came to my studio carrying the *Times* article. He pointed to the reproduction of one of my standing men. 'We'd like a portrait of President Kennedy painted in this way,' he said. The commission was for the Truman Library.

"I worked eleven months on that project, from December '62 until November 22, 1963. I went to Palm Beach, where the President was vacationing. I made charcoal, pen-and-pencil, casein and watercolor sketches of him in the mornings while he went over papers various assistants brought to him. He had papers in his lap or in his hands in every one of these sketches. Afternoons and evenings and way into the night, I worked in a huge studio in the back of a theater, on canvases of different sizes, trying to crystallize my fleeting impressions. After a week's work, I made a very simple, life-size charcoal drawing on canvas of the President in shirt sleeves. Although I had made the drawing as a guide before starting to paint, it had caught a very characteristic pose. He was resting his weight on one hand on the arm of the chair. I decided to keep that one without working on it anymore, as a kind of shorthand notation, a key. I was struggling with other poses too. One morning, the President sat sprawled with one foot up, resting on a beach chair. 'Is this pose all right?' he asked. 'Well,' I said doubtfully, 'it's supposed to be an official portrait.' He smiled and left his foot there. I thought, OK, I'll take what I get. I smiled and nodded back and went to work on a small casein sketch. I liked the informality of the pose, and after I got back to my studio in New York I concentrated on paintings made from that sketch. When the representative from the White House came

E de K before studies of Bacchus, *1977.*

by after a month, he looked at these paintings and gasped. 'That's not a Presidential pose!' he said.

"I returned to the pose of the large charcoal on canvas, but then there was another problem. All my drawings showed him in shirt sleeves, and I wanted to paint him in a jacket. So I began to make drawings of him in a jacket whenever he appeared on TV. In the end, I struggled with the pose for a year. I came to understand the struggles Ingres had with Monsieur Bertin. Many of the tries were failures. They kept getting worse and worse. I began to feel desperate. Now and then I'd feel I was closing in, but then the image would freeze. I began to work from friends with a similar build to get the sense of working directly from life (by now it was six months since I had seen him). At one point I had thirty-six canvases going at once, all at different stages.

"Finally, by September, I had made a painting that had the spontaneity I was after. In the following week I made another that was even more successful. I was hitting my stride. But the painting I felt closest to was a standing figure of the President wearing a sweat shirt, sailing pants and sneakers, squinting in the sunlight—the way he looked when I first caught a glimpse of him. 'A glimpse' was what I wanted to capture in the portrait. I returned to work on that painting.

"Then the assassin dropped my brush.

257

Drawings of President John F.
Kennedy, 1962–63.

Charcoal on paper. 18" by 14";
17 ½" by 14".

258

Portrait of President John F. Kennedy, *1962–63. Oil on canvas. 61" by 46". The Harry S. Truman Library, Independence, Missouri.*

"I was traumatized. I had identified painting with painting-Kennedy. For a full year, I couldn't paint at all. I had agreed to teach at the University of California at Davis beginning January '64. I wandered into the foundry there on a day they were pouring bronzes. It was medieval. It was magic. The sculptor, Tio Giambruni, explained the process to me in minute detail, and I was hooked. I immediately saw a way of working in a kind of three-dimensional collage—

tearing, bending sheets of wax, tacking them together with a torch. It was as if all the drawing and painting I'd done in my life was preparing me for this.

"The first sculpture I made was a head and shoulders of Kennedy—the last image the world had of him, above the rim of the car. Then I made some crucifixes. I didn't want them to be recognized as crucifixes but as floral forms reaching up in growth or flight. Then I made some images of swirling cloth, which led me back to the bull image. I cast fourteen bronzes that one year.

"I returned to my New York studio and went straight back to painting portraits, but this time directly from life without preliminary drawings. Some artists, of course, cling to one way of painting. I try to avoid that. That's why I keep changing media, sizes, subjects. Now I was after a spontaneous image that looked unstructured. One that might seem 'blown on.' For a time I found it interesting to paint strangers as well as friends or family. Knowing people intimately affects my way of painting them. Memory imposes curious simultaneous images onto the image of a person you are looking at. And of course I work differently with different people. I didn't see the painter Gandy Brodie in the same space as Alex Katz, even though they posed in the same part of my studio, or enclose Robert De Niro in the same kind of space as the poet John Ashbery. At the same time, the way I approach the *Bacchus* is a return to the way I worked on the basketball series years ago. I like the way the gray light shimmers all over the form of that statue. And the pose: from one angle, you see a single female nymph supporting that enormous male figure.

"In '76, I went to Tamarind Workshop for two weeks and did six lithographs, many of them huge, on the *Bacchus*. And I'm still at work on the theme. The last canvas is nine feet tall, with leaves all around the figure, yellow-green leaves with the blue-green of the bronze. Everything is in motion. But frozen motion. The limbs pouring over one another, as in those paintings of athletes. In a real sense, it seems to me there's only one single idea running through one's life, even if we find an infinite number of ways of expressing it."

Nell
Blaine

BORN 1922, RICHMOND, VIRGINIA

"Organic" is a word I'll stick by. It means the work is an extension of your blood and body; it has the rhythm of nature. This is something artists don't talk about much and it's not even well understood: the fact that there exists a state of feeling and that when you reach it, when you hit it, you can't go wrong.

—NELL BLAINE
New York, 1977

"Nellie Blaine was the first real artist I'd met. She infused me with zeal," says landscape and still-life painter Jane Freilicher, yet another in the Hofmann-influenced Second Generation of the Abstract Expressionist school. Mutual influences and kindnesses weren't frequently attested to in those days of the early '50s. But Blaine had come to the city primed for a positive experience: A fleet-foot hoyden rebel from an old Southern town—Richmond, Virginia, mother city of the Southern Baptists—she came bursting into New York in '42, eager for all the stimulations and discoveries home could not provide. Within a month or two, she was deep in the scene: Dixieland jazz, Hofmann's classes and the beginning of a swirl of companionship that would see her through hard times to come: first the rampantly divisive macho and politicized late '50s of The Club and then, after disastrous illness in Greece in '59, years of struggle against the effects of polio. A right-hander who had loved to "zip around" big, light-dazzled, dispersive paintings of interiors, rooftops, harbors, she then had to cope with left-handedness and far less physical latitude, but in so doing she sharpened her focus on a world she now could not go out to explore. She tells here how the long way went, beginning with her early awakenings to all that "modern" meant in Virginia, on to first intimation of her own gift and direction, then a prolonged wandering in a somewhat alien esthetic and, at last, the return that was also a going forward. Financially it has been rocky all the way. Blaine, while painting, has also worked at carpentry, free-lance designing, house-painting, delivering, ticket-taking, and teaching. There was a time she painted flamingos on neckties.

A short amiable marriage to a French-horn player was annulled in '48, and in the '50s she lived with pioneer modern dancer Midi Garth, doing costumes, sets and posters for her performances, as well as the same kind of artwork for Artists' Theater performances of those years by John Ashbery, Frank O'Hara, Kenneth Koch and others. For the past decade, she has shared an apartment and a Gloucester summer house with painter Carolyn Harris. On a sunny terrace or before a table crowded with glasses, cups, books, snap-dragons, geraniums and beach grass, she paints the compacted, brilliant-hued, slightly askew-eccentric still lifes that have made her the strongest American painter in this idiom today. From time to time, too, Blaine will cajole her helpers into portaging her wheelchair to a high point overlooking dunes out to the sea, where wind blowing and colors shifting in the flickering sun engender a parallel turmoil in her brush.

Blaine's case is one, however, that must keep Feminists from self-congrat-ulations about territory gained in the art world. Though she lives to a degree upon grants and awards, inexplicably she has not yet had a one-person show at the Whitney Museum. Her living expenses—for around-the-clock aid and extra sums for travel, etc.—require her to receive special consideration from sales middlepeople. Therefore, her new New York gallery, Fischbach, will promote her work while Eleanor Poindexter, with whom she showed from '56, will continue to act as a private dealer. For the rest, collectors, like friends, make the trek to the Blaine-Harris apartment overlooking the Hudson River. There, as she puts it, "I paint all night, with a rest in between, building up to it, sort of a collapse thing. If I do a really ambitious painting, it nearly kills me.

"And I try to work all over the canvas at once, because I feel that the forces of nature are unpredictable. To tell the truth, I could work with one flower forever.

"A haunting and major image from my childhood is the backwoods of Virginia, where we had relatives who were farm people. The life was different from the one I knew in Richmond. Lush trees and, in the backwoods, wooden-slat and white-sand roads, with people selling melons and other incredibly beautiful fruits in abundance. I loved those old areas!

"Our cabin was extraordinarily beautiful, too, on Mobjack Bay. It was roughly built, and the spaces between the floorboards were so wide I could lie and watch snakes crawl under the house. The pines around were extremely tall, with foliage way up at the top. We would put planks between the trees to clean the fish on. It was a way of life as well as beautiful country, a magic place in my memory. I've always felt I'd like to go back, to see it again. But it would probably be changed or not even there at all—any of what I remember so well.

"I was often sickly as a child, and I had astigmatism and crossed eyes, as well as being nearsighted.[1] For two years no one recognized the severity of the problem. Then when I was two I was given glasses, and I was so thrilled. I went around exclaiming, 'What a treat!' and naming everything. 'Tree! House! Water!' The world opened up. Something about the deprivation, I think now, made me feel that visual things were extraordinary.

"Because of my health and also certain problems with my family, I was thrown on my own a lot. My mother was a former schoolteacher and a dominant figure. My father had been a farmer as a child; his people were puritanical and hard-working. From the age of eight he ran a farm with his mother and his younger brother. Then, in his teens, he left the farm and went into the lumber business in Richmond. He excelled in that, and he also kept his feeling for flowers and plants and the out of doors. When I was a kid, he took me with him on buying trips to forests. But I was, to tell the truth, afraid of him. He had a frightening temper when he got out of control. A couple of times he nearly killed me by accident. On the other hand, he could be very gentle.

"Mother was a provincial Southern lady, very domestic and fiercely religious. Things were always clean and spotless. Compulsively so. So I had these bumpy times to go on. I tell you these things because I think they all helped shape me as an artist. Early on, I became a little rebellious. Either you go under or you fight back. I reacted by doing wild things, climbing on rooftops, taking chances, fighting with boys even though it would be three to one. Or I'd be a bully, or else protect some kid from a bully. Once, I climbed out of the window and ran for many blocks up the alleys chasing some boys. In my memory, I ran so fast I was hardly touching the ground.

"There was a certain notion in Virginia about 'culture': that art was a genteel thing, prissy, and somewhat bland. That was the kind of 'proper taste' I absorbed from the 'art lovers,' and in a way it was a hindrance, an inhibiting thing.

"But I began drawing on my own very early, and Mother later told me that at the age of five I expressed a very firm feeling that I wanted to be an artist. A painter. I had a cousin, Ruth, who came over one day bringing some watercolors. She made a little sailboat. I liked the way the watercolors sat on the picture, and I said, 'If only I could do that!' I had another cousin who was an artist, and my mother's sister painted—all of them as women did in that time: deer in the deep woods with a little sunset behind. They had a certain feeling for nature, and their paintings, though timid, aren't as bad to me now as I once thought they were. But I can't say their example set me off, because I was already interested, how is a mystery. I just know visual things were important. I liked making things, creating things. I wrote poetry too. Mother read to me a lot when I was sick, nature books and adventure books. I loved the part in *Swiss Family Robinson* where they were independent and could make do on very little, make their own candles and live in the wild. So I began to build things too. I'd get old boxes and knock them apart. Once I built a clubhouse with a neighborhood boy until someone came and snatched us apart.

"They taught art in public school. I had one very good teacher who hung pictures of Egypt around the classroom and made us think about art seriously. She was also the first one to assign us to draw from nature. When she set up a little still life, it was thrilling to me. By that time, I was already considered 'the artist.' I'd do portraits in class, to the teachers' annoyance, and sell them for twenty-five or fifty cents.

"But it was really my mother who helped me in terms of lessons, though when it came down to it she opposed my becoming an artist, partly because she thought it wouldn't be remunerative. Much, much later she finally accepted me, and then to a degree so did the other relatives. I had an uncle in Baltimore, for instance, who was interested in art, in literature and in gardening. He had a brilliant mind and a photographic memory. He didn't exactly encourage me in art, but he was the one I would tangle with intellectually, because like the rest of the family he was conservative, and, as I say, I was already rebellious.

"I went to college at sixteen, in 1938, at what is now Virginia Commonwealth University, as an art major. The little skill I'd developed in that closet fashion seemed academic, and the teachers didn't know what to do with me. I didn't fit in, and I felt miserable and cut off, and yet I obviously wanted to learn. It wasn't until the second year, when the painter and teacher Wörden Day came, that I began to understand. She had studied at the Art Students League with Vaclav Vytlacil, who had talked about studying with Hofmann in Munich. That's how I first heard about Hofmann.

"Before then, I'd had only teachers in the American genre. Then along came Wörden, who talked about things they never mentioned: bringing forms to the surface, concern with the two-dimensional, space and so on. She stimulated my interest, and since I was already dying to get away from Richmond,

I determined to get to New York. I'd made a trip there once with a school club and it absolutely knocked me on my ear. I don't think I slept more than two hours the whole three days. I remember seeing an exhibition of abstract painting with works by Mondrian and Carl Holty. I didn't know what to do about the ideas, but abstraction was entering into me. That whole New York trip I had felt like a bird. I'd been ripe for it. I began at once doing little abstract studies out of my head, with horizontals, verticals, triangles, very decorative and not very structural or organic. I knew that even then, but I kept struggling with it.

"Wörden did something even more important. She took me out to look at my own home town in a way I'd never seen it before. I'd get up early in the morning and go out onto the hills and other old parts of town. I did lots of big watercolors influenced by her. I must have had enormous energy then, because I'd be out on my bike by six in the morning, then home for breakfast and then rush off to a job I had, clean across town. Evenings I'd ride the bicycle back across town and visit with Wörden. We'd talk, talk, talk. She'd tell me about New York and say I should go there with her. The whole idea was magic. My mother, however, was getting more upset by the moment, knowing she was going to lose me. She fought to the point of hysteria, but she couldn't stop me. And ultimately, reluctantly, she helped me pack my suitcases.

"It was the fall of '42 when I arrived. All that hot Southern summer before, I had saved every nickel till I had ninety dollars. I went right away to Hofmann with a portfolio, asked him for a scholarship, and he gave it to me. He was very, very sweet. He looked at this work that was so tight and pointed out that the oils had a leathery look. I was very crestfallen. Secretly I thought I was a genius. But he was taken with my sincerity and enthusiasm, so he made me a monitor and I worked there two years. Right away I met Al Kresch and, through him, Leland Bell and Dixieland jazz. I was wildly excited by it all!

"And as for Hofmann himself, I thought him a kind of jovial, intellectual Santa Claus. He demanded you regard him as a master, and I gave him what he wanted in that way because I was a real disciple. I had feared his teaching would be scary and obscure; but that wasn't so. I never even found him hard to understand. To me he was clear.

"He was simply trying to be extraordinarily explicit about where things were positioned in space. He would say, 'Where is this? And tell me where this is.' And then, it's true, he'd be annoyed or bored if you didn't know, if you weren't dealing with the problem, because he had worked so hard to set up the still lifes. I'd watch him. He spent hours putting them together, those setups, using cloth and objects to delineate movements into space. They were rhythmic, never stiff or academic. His teaching was fluid, too. It changed through the years according to his interests, sometimes more related to Cézanne, sometimes, as the year I went, more to Mondrian. The only picture I ever saw hanging in the classroom was Cézanne's *Boy with a Red Vest*.

"In those days, I had a miracle of a studio with beautiful north light on West Twenty-first Street, for only twenty-five dollars a month. I never had such light again as I had those first nine years. I gave some sketch classes there in the studio, and ran little model sessions. I felt confident that I knew what Hofmann was talking about; a lot of students seemed confused, and perhaps it was arrogant of me, but I began to try and help them out. There was, in fact, a cultist atmosphere at the school that a lot of us objected to, but I still felt he gave so much to the people who could use it, treated everyone as an individual, saw your needs and really had the insight to know what you were trying to do and help you with it. That was the great gift he had.

"Those were the years of the early '40s. It was wartime. There were some austerities, I'd say, but not having any money was bearable for a young painter. I earned twenty-four or twenty-five dollars a week. We'd eat forty-cent dinners, terrible food though not as horrendous as what some of my friends had experienced during the Depression, eating only oatmeal. It was so cold in my studio you could see your breath; even colder than the outside. I had a kerosene stove I carried around with me.

"But I met a lot of interesting people and, in fact, got married in '43 to a French-horn player. He and Leland Bell hit it off, and so did he and Al, so it was these three guys and me, and in a way I was like the fourth fella. We were young in spirit and very fond of each other. And through him I met Jane Freilicher, whose husband was also a jazz musician, and we'd go to a lot of jazz sessions. Eventually I had big parties in the studio, and all kinds of things went on then. I don't know how we managed to keep afloat.

"Of them all, Lee Bell was the most articulate, dogmatic and aggressive and the first artist I'd met who really stuck his neck out, lived on nothing and went through hell to achieve. The first time he saw my work, he told me the only painters were Mondrian and Arp and that I was following Matisse and Picasso. He insulted me terribly, and that piqued me. So I became influenced by him and his ideas, because I had already tried to do those pure abstractions back at home in Virginia. After Mondrian died, I went to his studio and that affected me enormously, and then there were two major exhibitions of his work. And at that point I became totally influenced by Mondrian.

"My first show was in 1945. By this time there had been a turning point, yes. It was at Hofmann's in '43 or '44. One day I was working on a drawing

Lester Leaps, 1944. Oil on canvas. 24"
by 13". The Metropolitan Museum,
New York.

from a still life, and suddenly I found myself dividing up the page in a way that was interesting to me. It worked spatially, and yet was kind of witty and inventive. I went right home and made a painting that was larger than anything I'd done before, and fresher. There was a big white shape that looked almost like a cigarette coming up from a boatlike base outlined in black with a kind of washy green background and a big red shape. I guess it was influenced by Hofmann, but the influence came through in a healthy kind of way. I felt liberated by that painting. It was funny-looking, but people came to see it and were excited, and suddenly I felt I was an artist.[2] For the first time, I think.

"From then on, I had enormous confidence. The kind of confidence that came, I felt, from making contact with my own feelings. From knowing that I could pull them out at will. For the first time, and even though I was still very

267

young, I felt that I was in touch. It was Hofmann who had helped me to that point. It was his gift to help you see what was false, to know the difference between organic and static. 'Organic' is a word I'll stick by. It means that the work is an extension of your blood and body; it has the rhythm of nature. This is something artists don't talk about much and it's not even well understood: the fact that there exists a state of feeling and that when you reach it, when you hit it, you can't go wrong. The work carries a body rhythm. You can't do the slick and you can't do the gimmicky or dishonest. That may sound like a naïve religion, but I've had faith in it ever since. And with that particular painting, it came into being. Afterward some of the work was less good, obviously. But everything I've done since has been in touch, in that way.

"Back to the '40s!

"I was very dogmatic, in those days, about purist abstraction. I thought it was the only way to work. It was very narrow of me. But it was also very much in the air, that we were pioneers of American Neo-Plasticism. At twenty-three, I was the youngest member of the Abstract American Artists. Then I joined the Jane Street cooperative, the first serious one of its kind. There were about ten members; we put our money into the operation and each spent time sitting in the gallery. It wasn't a moneymaking thing, however; it was ideological. Hyde Solomon, one of the pioneers, invited me to join. Later on, Larry Rivers would have his first show with us, and Clement Greenberg would say it was the best gallery in New York. We had very strong principles. In fact, we threw out members who were working figuratively and gave the place the homogeneous character we wanted. I felt that my own work then was very pure in spirit and structure. Very much influenced by Mondrian. Yet it always had some sensuous interest too. Later on I began to dare to use a little bit of paint quality: it was a big thing if you made a little scumble in the paint, or a little modeling.

"By that time I'd met de Kooning and many of the artists of the other, Expressionist tendency. We liked them personally and we were stimulated by them, but felt, in our arrogant way, that we knew what structure was and that they were going up the garden path. For our part, we felt an allegiance to the European influence—Mondrian and Arp and Jean Hélion. Eventually, the schism became very deep. Those artists who retained a connection with European ideas were treated with hostility by the others. We, on the other hand, felt we wanted continuity. That we weren't unfresh or lacking in the 'American spirit,' but that this talk of 'American art' as superior and cut off from European was not only a distortion but also silly. Hélion was very articulate about these issues, and so was Leland Bell.

"By the early '50s, that schism had become a serious issue at The Club. I went there frequently, but I felt that we were outsiders. I remember one evening Max Ernst was invited to speak. I cared least for the Surrealists, but I felt Ernst was an authentic and interesting artist. He talked about the common experience of artists in Europe, how they had helped each other and worked together, and he said he didn't feel this in New York. The audience turned hostile. People threw questions at him, asking what he thought of Jackson Pollock and whether he didn't think so-and-so was the greatest. I felt they showed a terrible belligerence, attacking a man of that quality and someone they had invited to speak.

"By that time—even more later—the atmosphere was one in which the Abstract Expressionist idea only was being promoted by various cliques. The idea was America the Great. I thought this view was destructive. But I suppose it's the same as with any minority group: American artists had had such an inferiority complex they needed to feel a sense of independence and at the same time create their own heritage. But I never wanted to break with the past.

"Meanwhile, in my work I had been moving gradually away from the pure abstract idiom. I began to draw from the model again and even out in the street. At first it was simply that I didn't want to deny myself using witty shapes based on animal or natural images. According to Neo-Plastic ideology, shapes shouldn't come from nature but from pure reason. Even to think about changing something that seems so basic gives you a pain in the stomach!

"Then, in 1950, I went to Paris, and though I still felt the influence of Hélion and Léger, I began drawing outdoors. The new landscape excited me. I found myself noticing movements, proportions again. Before, I'd been trying to impose the abstract canon onto nature, almost like a device: taking the weight of the Léger line, for instance, or organizing what I saw in terms of an abstract structure. But when I got to France, it was like opening a window. Suddenly a lot of sunlight came in. So I decided to let myself go and become a kind of hedonist, to enjoy painting again, loose painting. Even *too* loose.

"I liked working on the banks of the Seine. I liked going to the villages. The fact that the landscape was different from home helped me make the transition. My love affair with the past had something to do with it, too, especially the Impressionists. Theirs seemed a natural way of painting, and I was always trying to find the natural and honest way, looking to be more direct and clearer, with less artifice.

"It was really only after I came back from Paris that I went through a difficult transitional period. I didn't meet my own standards anymore; I felt I'd been doing more competent paintings in the purist mode, that I'd worked with that idiom for some years, refining and refining it, and that I could handle it.

View from the Ledge: Gloucester, 1975. Oil on canvas. 35" by 45½". Collection Mr. and Mrs. Donald Cooper, Elizabeth, New Jersey.

Now I was sticking my neck out and the work didn't look as confident. But there was no turning back. I had to go that way.

"By the mid-'50s, the paintings had improved, become more natural; since then it's been all of a piece. Gradually, I became interested in natural light; trips to Mexico in '57 and to Greece in '59 only heightened that feeling. And always, since '54, there have been working trips to the shore in Gloucester, Massachusetts, where I spend every summer now.

"Something about Gloucester connects with my childhood, with those trips into the backwoods of Virginia. There's a wildness to the scene. I found a spot by the shore with lots of trees, crazy rocks and water in the distance. The house has old beams and doors from the Shaker times. And then I had the roof raised up so there's that beautiful Gloucester light and an open feeling of clouds and sky.

270

"For me, that matter of rejoining the past is important. I don't mean in an academic way. The idea now is that everything has been started from scratch. Critics like Clement Greenberg have preached novelty to a point where people are suspicious of any art that seems to bear a connection with the past. That's had a bad effect on the public and therefore on artists in terms—simply—of bread. And it seems to me it has shut the door on what I think of as genuine creativity. A freely creative person ought to be able to move out in any direction. There ought to be a feeling of encouragement for paintings of many kinds. Critics walk on dangerous ground. The balance for painters is a delicate one, and they need encouragement.

"Not that they need undiluted praise! I remember when I was coming along, I never felt any doubts about being a painter. It was as if I'd been born one. I might have doubts about what I was achieving, but never my identity. No matter how disheveled or disorganized life became, painting was so big in my life and so important that I'd paint all night, drag through the next day, sleep through any job. Whether I was sick, without money, whatever, I always went on painting.

"Now my physical limitations may have affected the style I work in, but I'm still moved by the pleasure it gives me, the old hedonistic consideration. If I'm not excited by the way two colors work, I just don't use them. The colors are even more brilliant now than they used to be. I used to love to draw with a big brush—zip around. I can't do that anymore. Instead, I suppose, I enjoy the more striking aspects of nature. I simplify things more, work for a simpler image. In the end, it's hard to talk about. So much is instinctive. In the end, what affects your life most deeply is things too simple to talk about."

Miriam Schapiro

BORN 1923, TORONTO, CANADA

My God, as an artist I was given the right to do it as I wanted. . . .

—MIRIAM SCHAPIRO
New York, 1977

Schapiro is a restless social force as well as an experimenter in several esthetic idioms and the strongest practitioner today in Pattern, or Decoration, Art. She sees the evolution of her work from orthodox Abstract Expressionism to cloth collage as a steady self-liberation from the male-dominated esthetic of Cubism. Feminist instinct, she argues, has impelled her toward the use of these bright, printed, woven or sewn fabrics with their multiplicity of patterns and historic overtones, while a "male" power of conscious control enables her to employ them in visually impressive structures. It is Schapiro's involvement with this ongoing dialectic that "gives life to my art, I believe." It was also this impulse to "humanize" or inject a greater Feminist sensibility into her work that, as she explains below, underlay her most argued socioesthetic projects: *Woman-house* and *The Dollhouse,* made in California in 1971–72. Passionate, vocal and also of a strong maternal bent, Schapiro changed her life as she changed her art and has encouraged a wave of younger women artists to do the same.

She began her career in New York in the 1950s, drawing the themes of her sweeping abstract paintings from landscape and the female body. Already, however, it was the question of identity or self-knowledge that concerned her. In that decade, Surrealism, Cubism, psychoanalysis and Existentialism provided the esthetic and philosophical ground. An activist approach was called for. Schapiro took to the activist road early on, abandoned what some considered the High Church of Abstract Expressionism and moved step by step toward another Zeitgeist: Women's Liberation.

For a while, she painted bright, beckoning, standing shrines of symbolic self-portraiture: atop, a golden arch signifying Aspiration; below a bit of the past, for example a copied fragment of a Cézanne; at the base, a symbolic egg and mirror. She moved on to the Constructivist, Hard-Edge idiom called Abstract Illusionism, later expanding her repertoire in this mode with images projected by a computer. Meanwhile, her life changed literally. She moved to California, where she encountered the tide of Feminism. In an episode of hard psychic travail, as she explains here, she produced a portentous Abstract Illusionistic painting, with an O and an X superimposed, that became a banner for the Women's Movement and a masterwork, if it can be called that, of "vaginal imagery." Now back in New York, in the carnival of cloth and color that fills her workrooms, she is engrossed in her new medium with political overtones: collage, or, as she calls it, "Femmage." Doilies, laces, handkerchiefs, aprons, shawls and antimacassars, costumes and quilts—these are her raw material. Using a canvas base large as her Abstract Expressionist works, she cuts and applies fabrics in exploding, swinging compositions that embody the volumi-

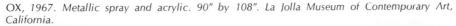

OX, 1967. Metallic spray and acrylic. 90" by 108". La Jolla Museum of Contemporary Art, California.

273

nous energies of that earlier idiom but have the added "feminine" character and connotations of cloth. In this way, in 1976, she assembled *Anatomy of a Kimono,* a fifty-foot-wide collage based on the motif of a Japanese robe, stretched out flat with outstretched sleeves—a fit image of that flamboyant and imperious *persona* a liberated woman might be moved to assume. That work, shown in New York at her long-time gallery, André Emmerich, marked a turning point of a sort, however. She now shows at Lerner-Heller Gallery.

About the commercial-gallery scene Schapiro is not sanguine. "I'm moody. I change. I shift. I wouldn't take a signature piece and work on it for a decade. But the dealers say, 'They just got used to your new style and now you change again.' " It's a complaint that many artists have voiced but not all— since all artists are dependent on that system—choose to voice aloud. It is characteristic of Schapiro's missionary determination that she does.

Part of that belief in truth-saying and the license to evolve was bred into her by her Utopian-Socialist parents. Part, too, was art-world ideology in New York of the '50s. "We believed in the Picasso myth," she says. "We believed in changing. We felt impelled to do so." She has taken risks, lost points and gained others to go her own way. For example, she is presently raising funds for a proposed Feminist Art Institute she hopes will one day be located in New York—among other things to gather oral histories of women workers in the needle trades and other hand industries. For this kind of socioesthetic program she wryly notes that Al Held of the Yale School of Art and Architecture has been heard to say she "gave up the true faith."

"My father was a dreamer, keen on education, self-educated and sensitive. He never finished high school, but he had passions: books, art history, esthetics. He kept files of reproductions of works of art; he painted and photographed the city he loved. Beyond that, he worked hard to make a living. He began as a designer, worked with the WPA. At a point, he stopped making and wrote. He wrote about the Renaissance, the history of art, the Golden Mean, Dynamic Symmetry, not methodically but as his passions moved him. Then he would turn to me, as his only child, and explain. In the '30s, he was director of the Rand School of Social Science, an anti-Communist, Socialist school pioneering in adult education. He ran for Congress on the Socialist Party ticket. He was interested in cultural education, in the democratic-Utopian-Socialist tradition.

"I often think of myself this way: that the outside of me is my father; the inside, my mother.

"She was also self-educated. Her interior world? You ask . . . I remember: *home.*

"She had a taste for folk art, paisley shawls over the tables. She painted cigar boxes and varnished them. Her father was in the toy business and invented the first movable doll's eye in America. Her mother was the only daughter among eight children, and the last-born. She did wonderful needlework, crocheting and tatting the edges of pillowslips, hems of sheets. These became our heirlooms. But also my grandmother was a powerhouse. She would waggle her finger and tell Mother, 'Remember, your DUTY is to that child.' It was a strong matriarchal line, from that grandmother to my mother and her sister, my aunt, who had no children and helped bring me up. Three powerful women."

EM: "Did they bring you up to be an artist?"

MS: "They were aware of my gifts and it was assumed that I would be an artist. I studied modern dance with the Rhom sisters, refugees from the Weimar Republic who taught the Dalcroze method. During the Spanish Civil War, I wrote poetry about the Loyalist cause. Earlier, as a child, without friends or siblings, I played with my dolls and paper cutouts, and with Dixie Cup tops with pictures of movie stars on them. At night, after I was put to bed, I would lay out these ice-cream covers and, by the light from the street in my window, make up a world of my own.

"I bridge two worlds, the traditional one my father knew and taught me about and the modern one I discovered. I went to Victor D'Amico's Saturday classes at the Museum of Modern Art, for example. I remember once he spilled a box of thumbtacks out on a table. They fell into a random pattern he called a 'composition.' This was a different idea from what I had been taught was the Golden Mean."

Schapiro spent two years at Hunter College in Manhattan in 1941, then transferred to the University of Iowa, where she met painter-critic Paul Brach and married him. When they returned to New York, he taught at the New School and reviewed for *Art News,* while she sold books at Brentano's and worked as a secretary: a fairly standard division of labor at the time. Their lives encompassed Long Island summer art-colony seasons, The Club and the Cedar Bar. Schapiro has often expressed herself on the isolation of those years when each woman artist was "making it" for herself. "Those were lonely years, when I was training myself to be an artist. We went to The Club every Friday night, but I had no sense of camaraderie with the men; there were women whom I counted as close friends, but we rarely talked about painting." In 1957 she made her debut in the "New Talent Show" at the Museum of Modern Art. Then there came a time when, as she has written,

pressures came to a head and I lost the ability to work . . . not knowing HOW to make a painting, as if everything I had ever learned had washed out of my brain.

275

[So] I developed a ritual that allowed me to start work again. I talked to myself as if I were reborn, totally new on this earth. "You have to have turpentine. You have to have your paints laid out. You dip the brush in the turpentine. . . ." I repeated this litany . . . I began to work again.

A totally new image surfaced in this period of renewal, a painted image based on a new self-image. I finally came out of the jungle of Abstract Expressionism.[1]

Her "Shrine Paintings" were exhibited in New York and in circulating shows until, in '67, Brach was called to the University of California in San Diego to start an art department there. "I had just had my most successful show at the Emmerich Gallery. My husband said he didn't want to stay in New York. I suppose the choice was up to me. Finally I said that since I had opted for marriage and a family I would go to California and we would be together. In return, Paul told the university that since I was an artist too I would have to have a job that would connect me to the art community. That's the kind of support I've had all my life from my father and my husband."

The Southern California scene was full of a new kind of action. Schapiro became assistant professor in San Diego, then in 1970 followed Brach to Los Angeles, where he became dean at the new California Institute of the Arts. By the time she arrived in that city, her conversion to the Feminist cause would have taken place.

"I had felt, as the decade of the '60s went on, that something in my nature was restless and undefined. I was getting older, yet *something* hadn't happened. I was, possibly, too gifted, too experienced. I felt I had spent the longest possible waiting period. I began to ask myself whether it could be the case that I simply didn't have to wait any longer.

"One day in 1967 I began to work on a particular painting. I felt a tremendous need to do it. As I was painting, and even immediately after I'd finished it, I didn't know what the image—*OX*—meant. I only knew that the work seemed overpowering to me. It was so powerful, in fact, that the first thing I did was to turn it to the wall. I had to wait until I was secure enough to deal with its strangeness.

"And then, eventually, I understood what it was about. The meaning of the motif was revealed to me. It was about vaginal iconography. About myself, in sum. The image, you see, was clearly a passageway. It was up to me to accept, literally, that this physiological entry was—in the realest sense—*me*. My impulse, when I began to work and as I continued, had been simply to paint a space that was tender and inviting. Space a person could enter into. But as the concept developed, it became embodied in the most clean-cut, powerful, Hard-Edge of images.

"Later I said to Judy Chicago, '*That's what it's all about.*' And hundreds of women I later came in contact with, all over the country, showed me similar images, all of them confessing they had been making them privately for years and had also been afraid to interpret them."

Fifteen years younger, also an ideological painter using Hard-Edge imagery to communicate Feminist intuitions about female nature, Judy Chicago[2] was then on a powerful consciousness-raising bend. She introduced Schapiro to a circle of bright, even "scary" young Feminists.

"When I came West," Schapiro recalls, "I had been the sheltered person. I had stayed pretty much in the bosom of my family with my husband and child. I wasn't a mover and shaker. I'd read de Beauvoir and Lessing, of course, but I didn't understand the political process.

"Judy and I got it together. We talked about the world as we could really affect it. To one meeting we invited every woman in the California art world: curators, art historians, artists, critics. We exchanged our life stories. I remember one curator saying, 'All my life young men were calling up and saying, "Come for a studio visit." And all my life, no woman artist ever called and suggested it.' I thought to myself, God, is *that* how they do it? I had always thought one had to be pleasant and wait. That was the way I was taught by my mother and father. So in the beginning Judy and I simply reinforced a side of each other's personality, the side that wanted to shake things up. We gave each other courage.

"In the end, we shook the whole West Coast up. We were organizing, teaching, talking about women's art, getting women to show their slides. And meanwhile, Lucy Lippard and others were shaking it up in the East."

Schapiro and Chicago, both hired by Brach and teaching at the California Institute of the Arts, initiated a Feminist art program and took steps toward politicizing the female art community. They visited studios and discovered that while most New York artists had big lofts and assertively spent time, money and energy on their work, the West Coast style was anonymity. Women worked at home on dining-room tables, shielding themselves behind the cover of domesticity. Schapiro and Chicago initiated a process of consciousness-raising in the art professions that in the next few years would engage women all over the country in casting off that cover. The intent was to feed the energy of the "unseemly emotions," as Schapiro calls them—jealousy and anger—back into the process of growth. In 1972 Schapiro and Chicago set up the West Coast Women Artists Conference. In 1973 they collaborated on an article on sexual iconography, published in *Womanspace Journal*. Schapiro and eventually her students produced two important Feminist documents, *Anonymous*

Was a Woman and *Art: A Woman's Sensibility,* collections of biographies and statements from artists from coast to coast.[3] But the most controversial and in the end enduring project was launched from Cal Arts by Schapiro and Chicago with a number of their students and women artists from Los Angeles: *Womanhouse,* the first "all-female art environment." Inspired by this experiment in socioesthetics was Womanspace, the first cooperative woman artists' gallery on the West Coast, and finally the Woman's Building, which still functions as a busy art center there.

"Judy and I wanted to find a way beyond just talking. We consulted Paula Harper, a historian, and she suggested we put together a literal House that would embody all our ideas.

"We felt we were embarking on an adventure. We wanted to find out everything we could about this new race, this new culture: women. We wanted to understand their art, their fantasies, their limitations, their powers. How long could they keep at a task or project, for instance? And how would they react to pressure? It was like building the Parthenon: we were working out every step anew as we went.

"I went into all this with agony in my soul. In New York I had painted assertive paintings. I had, I suppose, the type of personality the Feminist sculptor Lynda Benglis calls 'macharina.' I'd been a professional for a long time. I'd shown consistently and successfully. In a sense, I'd been a token woman— taken seriously but not seriously enough. Now I decided that if I wanted a genuine 'female' art experience, I would have to take on the anonymity most women at that time felt most of the time.

"There were two kinds of women I wanted to reach: those inside the home and those outside. The outside ones traveled long distances, as I had done and was doing. They had moved toward points of power. They were tougher. Token women. But the inside ones, the anonymous ones, worked alone in their kitchens and bedrooms. I tried to decide how to address these. It seemed to me that to do so effectively I would have to behave as if I were a child again. I asked myself what I could make for Womanhouse that would come out of that experience. I went back to my own childhood and, working with Los Angeles artist Sherry Brody, I made *The Dollhouse.*"

Dollhouse was just that: a meticulously crafted tiny family dwelling with six rooms appointed with political implications: a nursery, a seraglio, a male artist's studio and a female star's bedroom. Building the miniature *Dollhouse* went along at the same time as the building of the macrocosmic *Womanhouse.* An abandoned house was found and rented. Its windows were replaced; walls and floors were restored and painted; wiring was redone. The very process of salvaging the house from disuse and disrepair and making it work was symbolic. The women involved considered it a therapeutic and effective endeavor even if some who visited the finished house-environment questioned its esthetic value. Mannikins of domesticated females stepped out of linen closets; a kitchen with fried-egg breasts on the walls was the "nurturing center"; performances by live participants in Surreal rooms illustrated women's historic bondage to cosmetics, to lassitude, to their menstrual cycles and to their generalized fears of attack (a plastic sculpture group including snakes, dinosaur, spider and crocodile). In any case, the finished project marked the end of a process for Schapiro and a new release of energy. "I went back to my studio, and new work just came pouring out of me."

In the years since *Womanhouse,* Schapiro, now back on her home turf in New York, has continued her efforts to synthesize politics with esthetics in those visually striking collage works of which *Anatomy of a Kimono* was the major one. "I had just come from California," she says today. "It was my first show back in New York. I wanted to take a stand. To create something so bold that when people saw it not one of them would just take a look and go away. I worked in a fury. I worked sixteen hours a day for three months. I wanted the work to move symphonically through tender and soft areas, on to hard, flat, decorative ones.

"I was working for all women who want to be bold and strong, who want to traverse space. The *Kimono,* in essence, had to fit *me.* To be a surrogate for me. A universal form. Generous. You could make a tent of it. And then I

Anatomy of a Kimono, 1976. Collage and acrylic on canvas. 80" by 56'10". Collection Bruno Bischofberger, Zurich.

realized that men wear kimonos, too. And so I realized it was even a more universal symbol than I'd thought.

"I wanted to create a heroic work. And I did.

"My God, as an artist I was given the right to do it as I wanted. . . ."

EM: "Tell me, how do you feel about the ongoing issue of Feminism today—eight years after the Movement began? Have you any qualms about being labeled as much an advocate as an artist?"

MS: "What makes you ask that question makes it clear that I'm on difficult ground. Women of my generation were conditioned to believe that an artist could only function making art. If she did anything else, she would be suspect as an artist. Well, Rubens managed to paint and also to be an ambassador at court. I paint, make my collages, prints, drawings. And I am also a political being.

"I had to grow into my new role. But as time went by I became comfortable with the diversity of my new life: making art, teaching, mothering, cooking, having shows, lecturing. Now I feel that we socially concerned women are setting an example of a possible new life for the artist. It's about time!

"Now I feel integrated in this new life style. I don't separate life and work. The meaning of my art today, for example, is in its origins in woman-life of the past. The collage elements in my paintings are the needlework of departed and

forgotten women. Often, as I recycle and revive these women's arts, I wonder what, exactly, we are saying together. We are speaking in covert language, one still to be deciphered, but the connection is there.

"Every move I've made has been in the direction of that kind of connection. With other parts of my life, with motherhood, with my parents, with my husband, with the sisterhood. My connection with the women in my collective—Heresies—is a rich one. My work with other women artists in New York is rewarding: Joyce Aiken, Ida Applebroog, Nancy Azara, Lynda Benglis, Louise Bourgeois, Judy Brodsky, Diana Burko, Marty Edelheit, Harmony Hammond, Paula Harper, Ann Harris, Valerie Jaudon, Joyce Kozloff, Ellen Lanyon, Lucy Lippard, Pat Mainardi, Melissa Meyer, Lee Ann Miller, Cynthia Navaretta, Linda Nochlin, Barbara Novak, Irene Peslekas, Carrie Rickey, Elloise Schoettler, Dorothy Seiberling, Judith Stein, May Stevens, Carole Stronghilos, Michelle Stuart, Phyllis Yes. What a gold mine! Knowing them makes me feel part of the world I didn't realize could exist.

"I cherish the past while wanting the most out of the present. If I am afraid of anything today, it's of going back to the place where I was before. In isolation. I come from a background of optimists and idealists. I do not cultivate loss. I connect. That is the basis of my life."

June Wayne

BORN 1918, CHICAGO

You reach a point where you know what you think about life. . . . You've had enough experience, finally, to have a reasonable and regular expectation of success. . . . And now when I start something, . . . I expect to carry it off.

—JUNE WAYNE
Los Angeles, 1977

June Wayne has had several lives. The most heralded of these has now been relegated to the archives as far as she is concerned, though whether history will let her out of it is another question. It would be impossible to make a study of the art of lithography in America that did not include Tamarind Lithography Workshop, this country's first big experimental print laboratory, which Wayne put together in Los Angeles in 1959–60. For a decade it flourished under her direction. She raised over two million dollars in four epochal grants from the Ford Foundation, a bonanza for tax-exempt Tamarind and also a straw in the wind marking the debut of the Ford Foundation as a subsidizer of the arts on a massive scale. It was the debut of the Fabulous '60s, as Wayne calls them, the era of cultural explosion. She achieved her ends by arguing that this country, while rich in artistic talent and trainable technicians, had no print facilities to equal European ones. "Lithographs here were made so poorly I used to pick them up like dead mice."

During the heyday of the Workshop, artists were brought from all over the world to spend two months mastering the delicate and difficult procedures of the medium. "We set out to restore an art form and also all the social elements it would need to survive without subsidy. And it worked in most respects. The big question at the start was whether kids would be willing to go into a métier where they would be working as artisans, not genius-artists. I was sure a lot would if the goals were high and there were peer recognition and jobs as there are in the film industry right here in L.A. So we set high standards for excellence and offered young people the chance to do a job marvelously well. And they worked their asses off. We trained dozens of printers, using that Ford money to prime the pump. We validated the idea of collaboration, and made it work." Meantime, Wayne's own energies and time had also gone to scouting for new stones, inks, papers, and publishing dozens of manuals on making, classifying and preserving prints. Something had to give. What gave was her career as a painter.

Wayne had had her first show as an eighteen-year-old expatriate in Mexico City. By the postwar '40s and '50s she showed consistently, but when Tamarind got going she stopped cold. "During those ten years I took my work off the market because I think corruption begins at the top. I couldn't speak for my own art and also for Tamarind. Finally, after the project ended in 1970, it took me four or five years of working full steam to reestablish my own art."

Tamarind is now the Tamarind Institute at the University of New Mexico in Albuquerque. It amuses the founder to survey the whole experience as an example of Conceptual Art. "One rarely has an idea where everything falls into place so neatly.

"I'd thought we'd give it a flyer for a couple of years. I really didn't count on success, but the timing had been right. In the end, my problem became how to get myself out without killing Tamarind off. So I began removing myself as new people came along who could replace me. In effect, I Stalinized myself—turned myself into a nonperson—by suppressing references to my own name, excising myself out of its life as much as possible. I rarely refer to it anymore in press interviews. In the end, the fact that it works without me is a contribution I can make to lithography."

Another channel for Wayne's organizational power was the Women's Movement in the arts as it began rolling in the early '70s. Her career as an activist had begun long before. Daughter of Russian immigrants, she dropped out of high school in the Depression to go her own way toward books, music, art. After Mexico, she surfaced in wartime Chicago, working with the WPA and lobbying in Washington for the Artists' Union. It was three decades later that the delayed Women's Movement tapped a deep source of impatience. In the fall of '71, she gave a seminar in Los Angeles on business and professional problems of women artists that was so galvanizing it was quickly dubbed the Joan of Arc Seminar. She led round-table discussions, set up role-playing games. As she had lobbied and lectured for the union and for lithography, now she was in demand for nonhazy talks on women's opportunities in the arts. From the outset, she saw her stake in the Movement. "It was a blessing for me to be direct instead of smiling to get my way and being careful about my language. Before, I was called a feisty little blonde or I was cast in a maternal role, and the males would write articles about what good housekeepers we were and how clean the Workshop floor was. But when the Movement got under way, I could do away with the bullshit."

Wayne has now come back to her starting place. She is being her own artist, painting, making prints, designing tapestries, with an expanded sense for the possible and also for certain mysteries beyond reach. "The human tragedy," she recently wrote,

is said to derive from the ability to understand our own mortality, but such understanding seems inadequate to the fantastic scale of depersonalized data crowding in upon us. What does it mean that our molecules are no different than those in a doorknob? If that is true, what about the assumption that each of us is unique—and all that implies about our values and our arts?[1]

Though she prefers her unknowns in concrete form as practical challenges, Wayne can be persuaded to ruminate on insubstantial things. In that same article, which wryly debunks the concept of "creativity," she still made a try at capturing in words a phenomenon this book is also concerned with:

. . . sometimes, like the "flash of inspiration" described in all the literature, my way opens before me. I have retraced the details of such "flashes." Each time the same thing happened: a number of disparate "messages" drawn from the reservoir of my experience arrived in the interval. One cluster of "messages" included a phrase out of *Axel's Castle* . . . , the pattern of freezing rain on a train window in the winter of 1939, the flare of a match which almost singed my hand. These fragments were unrelated in time, mood and character. But all three were needed for the painting then in progress. . . . I had stored those fragments in my brain at one time or another, and I found them and pulled them from their clusters of memories . . .[2]

To reach back among those clustered memories and make a work of art that seeks to bring them back to life almost literally: can it be done? Recently, Wayne was inspired to try. She set out to make a series of collage prints that might do as much for the span of her mother's life.

"My mother was a private person, very prideful and vulnerable. She had come from Russia as a child, married, had me, her only child, when she was eighteen and then was divorced when I was an infant. From then on she was the wage earner and she supported me and my widowed grandmother. My view of her was almost as though she were a father and my grandmother were the mother.

Dorothy, the Last Day, August, 1960. *Four-color lithograph. 22 ¼" by 30".*

"To be a wage earner and divorced in those days was tough. All my life my mother was 'Miss Kline,' because divorcees were apt to lose their jobs or not be hired at all. She lived and died as Miss Kline, and very early on I saw her as a separate person from me, one who happened to be eighteen years older than I was. She died in 1960, five days before Tamarind opened. My first print for Tamarind was about her death: *Dorothy, the Last Day.* She would have hated being seen as I showed her in that print. When I realized that, I thought, 'Well, kiddo, I'll make it up to you in the end.'

"Thinking of the difficulties of her life and our all-female household made me realize, quite early in my life, that there are many ways to skin a cat; that the usual way to do things is not necessarily the only way. That gave me considerable objectivity and also a sense of possibility.

"For instance, in doing this series, I have tried to suppress my personal hand in order to let *her* come through. It is an interesting esthetic problem, to reveal her life from her point of view, not mine. Can I re-create her aura simply through collaged prints that make use of actual things that belonged to her? Report cards, photographs, garments, documents? Once, I was examining a family photograph under the enlarging glass and I noted a miniscule wedding picture on the upright piano. There was a man in it beside her. It had to be my

285

father. I blew it up, and there I had a picture of the father I had never seen. Curiously, to me it was just part of the research. But will the result mean anything to people who did not know this woman? Writers often assume such a distance from the subject, but can it be done with images?''

The White Knight: Dorothy Series. *16-color lithograph. 21½" by 17¼".*

That mind that works to provide what the art "needs" takes its own way, however. The "creative process" is not mechanical or literal. It does not *represent* those images that Camus spoke about. It works changes on them until they are sometimes so removed that only the artist can read them, and sometimes they are even better read by another person. Was it by that process, then, that Wayne achieved, perhaps without knowing it, a memorial to her mother that strikes me as more evocative than any assemblage of "things that belonged to her" could be? Miss Kline was in life a saleswoman of pinks and silks and gauzy underthings. Knowing that, I see the artist's feelings for her mother revealed here in a technical feat that possibly no other lithographer in the world could duplicate. To bind the individual prints into a single oeuvre, Wayne has chosen a melting color-ground for them all, a tone cool yet somehow radiant, dimensionless yet enfolding, that shades off from pale peach

Genetic Code Series: Burning
Helix, 1978. Two-color
lithograph 38½" by 23½".

through uncanny blurred rose-oranges. This is a color at once flesh and cloth, a virtuoso performance by the artist, a conceptual statement and an expression of daughterly care. And so one might answer the question of whether the works succeed in bringing the subject to life by recalling that, in the old tale of the Juggler of Notre Dame, it was not the things juggled that made the Lady smile, but the perfection of the juggling, which revealed a loyal heart.

Wayne's other works open not to the past but, as I said, to the unknowns of science. Her imagery comes from astronomy, microbiology, lunar exploration, shapes of the sea. Like many women artists of the '70s, she is haunted by Humboldtean correspondences between the mind, the world and the still be-yond-phenomenological. "There are things going on now in space, with astro-physics, with molecular biology, that imply extraordinary dimensions of

287

thought and feeling. Everything is called into question. It's impossible to reconcile the new science with old assumptions, however familiar they may be, about ethics, religion, family, economics, falling in love, crime in the streets, being a woman, death . . .

"John Donne expressed feelings we have today: 'the atomies of which we are made . . .' I'm working on a series of prints based on the winds, on tidal waves, on the genetic code and DNA, and on fingerprints that look like maps. What an irony, that fingerprints, that denote our individuality, are also the one sure way of keeping track of us in a computerized world!"

An esthetic based on correspondences of form has to deal with both the miniature and the vast. The mind skids easily from swirls of protoplasm under a microscope to swirls of stars in a galaxy. I found it interesting that, as a technical parallel to this theoretical interest, Wayne works in two mediums, lithography and tapestry, where multiple copies can be turned out by procedures of a very close, detailed, even scientific kind.

"But I've always been fascinated by science. As a child I was always wondering *why* things were as they were. And *what* were they? And *who* is this? And what *is* the situation? I remember looking at comic strips and discovering that the green was made out of yellow and blue dots. That was impressive.

"And then, I was nearsighted. I had to move in very close to see at all. There was a time in the '50s when I was painting optical works, playing with focal and peripheral vision. I worked and worked on one painting. I painted it fifty times, and still it was wrong. I went to a new eye doctor, who prescribed new glasses, and when I went outside I saw the leaves on the trees for the first time. Then I went back to the studio and looked at the painting. It was finished! And quite brilliantly I thought. It must have been finished for months. To this day when I put my glasses on, I smile with pleasure. That may be a reason I like to get in on things, close up to details.

"But also, as you've gathered, I share an impulse toward the grandeur implicit in our times. I want to do monumental tapestries. Seven stories high! I'm ready for that. And my images would hold, I know. Whether from the micro- or the macrocosm.

"You reach a point where you know what you think about life. It's not frozen in place, but you've had enough experience, finally, to have a reasonable and regular expectation of success. Now I have a curious, even idiotic belief that my art can and should reach many people. Be hung in public places. And now when I start something, I expect not to teeter on the edge of failure. I expect to carry it off."

288

Mary
Frank

BORN 1933, LONDON, ENGLAND

There are times when I can't work, can't do any-
thing. I can't concentrate, I get scattered, feel I'm
dying. . . . I have thousands of ideas I don't ever
get to. I see them all as a huge soup kettle. . . .
Day and night I could work and still wouldn't do
it all. . . .

The important thing is to keep producing
. . . to be tenacious. Keep working it up. It's like
mixing up the old clay. . . . I let it dry, then break
it into little pieces. Put them in water, stir. Labo-
rious! Let it dry . . . pound it . . . put it into the
buckets. Just to get a hundred pounds of new
clay, such labor!

—MARY FRANK
Lakehill, New York, 1977

A perennial question for lovers, critics and philosophers: Can one really know what goes on in another mind—that reservoir of static and confusions out of which, from time to time, an image, a form, a structure is extruded? There are artists who bring their works to a clear finish and disguise the primordial illogic of the process, making us think we "know" what they "knew" they were about. There are also artists who expose and celebrate the other condition, whose works trail clouds—as Wordsworth might put it—of their origin in formlessness. One who accepted the imagination as it is—transitional, glancing, metamorphic—was the poet Marianne Moore, for whom mind was no more stable an instrument than "glaze/on a katydid-wing." Mary Frank is another who lets us see what is mysteriously coming into being. Her works of the last few years, in clay, drawing and monotype, reflect the very flicker and leap of a mind in extraordinary play.

The sculptures are, among other things, figures of lovers, nereids, nikes and fallen, leaf-winged angels, assembled out of sections of baked, hollow stoneware, stretched out on the floor or walking on the ground without pedestals. Students who look for artistic sources here must look to all history. Nearly every person and people who treated the human figure as a thing of dignity and fragility might have had a hand in this work. There are traces of the Classical and the Cubist, the Surreal and the Expressionistic. There is something of the Egyptian and the Hellenistic, the whip-movement of Tanagra and the stillness of Karnak. Rodin and Matisse, Picasso and de Chirico have breathed into Mary Frank's memory bank. A shadow of Max Ernst, of the women-turning-into-plants, may be somewhere there. So is Brancusi of the *Sleeping Head,* Giacometti of the walkers, Reuben Nakian and Constantino Nivola. So are memories of films and plays and the dance, in the forms of fabric that blow around her figures. And yet despite all this drawing on the past, the oeuvre has originality because the artist does not draw from these models in a planned or conceptual way. The models—things seen in passing—form a rich drift of debris in the mind which the memory is continually sifting while the hands are seeking ways of concretizing them again.

"I love the torn clay . . . the weight of the clay as it tears or cuts. You can see where the fingers go fast, into wet clay. Mostly, I rip quickly. But you can also do it slowly.

"I love the gesture of work, watching someone do work they do well or with experience, with certain essential gestures, nothing wasted. Watch someone washing clothes, lifting things, even cooking. Stirring or sifting. There is a grace, that Whitman writes about . . ."

Or: "I began using cut paper—a lovely thing to do. You're drawing with scissors. You're inside out and upside down. You don't know where you are and you get lost. You have to go by trust. The light, to see that play of shadow . . ."[1]

The same for other things Mary Frank makes: drawings, prints, notebooks, tiny carved cylinder seals showing reverse patterns dug out with a needle, to be rolled across wet clay, "so I can make a whole migration of birds, for example. You could print them for miles if you had enough clay."[2]

Or as a notebook will say:

. . . sculpture could be just a deepening impression like a fossil . . . also drawings in charcoal or ink [could be] sculptures risen to the surface, colors flaking off—swept on and raked off. A gardening of the paper.

Some things, forms, take root. Others are more like passing air . . . the bird's shadow . . .

Notes are interspersed with sketches of leaves; of the nude model, male and female, in quick poses; of cranes in flight; sketches in a darkened theater during rehearsal; of Vietnamese "tiger cages"; sketches, in wash and pen, from the American Museum of Natural History, the Bronx Zoo and the New York Botanical Garden; and translucent watercolor drawings of waterlilies and fish from her pond in the country.

The drawings are not studies for sculpture but follow their own sifting and searching process. They are modes of perceiving things in motion, trees in the wind, birds in flight, figures on beaches; and things in the process of impossible metamorphoses: deer into humans, birds into humans, heads of figures born out of leaves. She works from the model, but not from set poses. Sometimes, but rarely, one of these quickly drawn images is transferred into clay. A model one day by accident cupped her hands beneath her breasts in a gesture of archetypal grace. That moment found its way into a full-size clay figure, winged, walking through wind.

Also, Mary Frank is one who will talk about her dreams, maybe because many of them are so innocent. "I was floating in the universe, a night sky full of stars, inky blue-black. And who appeared but a pink angel, the one in Rousseau's painting who comes floating by with a trumpet like an amaryllis.

"And then she held out the whole world, an incandescent globe, and offered it to me.

"It was extremely beautiful—an arrogant dream! . . .

Head in Ferns, 1975. Stoneware. 11½" by 19½" by 17". Collection Mrs. Albert List, New York.

"I dreamed that outside my country house there were unicorns, zebras, giraffes, all together like the Peaceable Kingdom. I said, 'Look what's there!' But they were behaving as if it were the most natural place to be, especially the unicorn. . . .

"Once from the Truro bluffs I saw whales. Their spouts were fantastic, and when they turned over I could see their underbellies white with calcium. And in the country, the hills are white with mountain laurel in June.

"I dreamed the whales came up onto the bluffs and danced in the dark green of the laurel. . . .

"Every year, in the spring, or even before spring comes, I have the same dream: I dream of early-spring water running everywhere, in colors unbelievably luminous."

On the other hand, there are frightening passages through a kind of creative overdrive.

"I'd been in the Museum of Natural History. As I left and walked down the stairs, I seemed to lose whatever it is that keeps things in the mind separate. All my ideas and images began to flow into a mesh.

"I started thinking about space . . . about meteorites. I went on to the earth, and fossils, and moved up through spores to seeds and plants, dinosaurs and fish, on to the lower mammals and the ice age. Every form of evolution went through my mind, on many levels. I was frightened, as if I were on some sort of borderline, or as if I'd taken LSD.

"It went on, I couldn't stop it . . . to man with his inventions . . . the knife, the wheel, the needle . . . on to society, language, to art . . . to refrigerators. . . . And all the time, I was walking along Central Park West. It was all in an incredible rush; as if I were being attacked by my own mind.

"I thought, if only I could stand still and write it all down, but I couldn't. The experience lasted around twenty minutes. All that time I was out of touch with clock time, and in the end there was nothing at all that I could draw."

The experience of imaginative flight (ecstasy?) has its reverse: "There are times when I can't work, can't do anything. I can't concentrate, I get scattered, feel I'm dying. I could work on twelve sculptures at once, but of course I can't, so they just sit around, and the clay dries up. It's an experience not unrelated to the one outside the museum. Horrible.

"I have thousands of ideas I don't ever get to. I see them all as a huge soup kettle. There are the books, the notebooks. Day and night I could work and still wouldn't do it all.

"Working is failures, and parts and pieces. I could do fifty and not get one right. Some big pieces begin as small ones. Or I begin with a foot or a torso. Or they may remain only thoughts.

"I need the tangible thing to hold on to. It's only once I make a work that I can think of going forward and making another one like it. Only when the object exists can I think clearly about it. It's the same with everything I do—gardening, cooking, playing music.

"The important thing is to keep producing. All artists have that quality. You have to be tenacious. Keep working it up. It's like mixing up the old clay. If I have a piece to throw away, I let it dry, then break it into little pieces. Put them in water, stir. Laborious! Let it dry . . . pound it . . . put it into the buckets. Just to get a hundred pounds of new clay, such labor! And the older the clay, the better. Clay a hundred years old would be the best."

Her country house in the Catskills is the best place to find Mary Frank at work. One crosses a rattling bridge, walks between flower beds, by cut-down trees bearing "stump gardens" or assemblages of rocks and plants created by her son Pablo. Beyond is the house; indoors, rooms are lined with drawings, prints, maps, sketches, letters. Farther on is the studio with tables and racks of clay figures and parts of figures; behind the house, the kiln yawning empty; behind that, the rocks and knolls where she deposits the sculptures after firing and later displays them. Behind that rises a hill where she has thinned back the trees and bushes to find the *edge*. Together with her friend of six years, the architect and planner Barry Benepe, she has undertaken an ambitious land-scaping project, including that moving back of the woods to open up vistas that can provide an odd effect of paradox: you sit on the porch and see wind *there,* feel stillness *here*—or see daylight here, and over there nightfall already gathering between the trees.

Up the hill and through the trees, Mary Frank and Benepe have made covered walkways by tying the tops of witch hazel boughs together. The arches lead to a spot where a century ago masons at work cut slabs of stone, leaned them against what were then saplings and went away, never to come back; now mature trees hold the stones in paws of bark. This is, all in all, a place where nature is ever overrunning its boundaries, being cut back, pressing to assume a new shape. The ground itself stands in vats in the studio, covered with damp cloths, waiting to be given a form.

An epiphany of the mind's behavior under pressure may be the firing of the kiln. Twice a season or so it takes place, and it is a time of nearly traumatic anxiety. "If it will survive the firing . . ." Mary Frank keeps saying about works in her studio still unbaked.

Packing the oven is the trickiest part. The pieces have to be stacked just so. The sense of possible disaster hangs over it all. An explosion could ruin a

293

dozen pieces. Haphazard juxtapositions on the shelves take on an unlucky air. Some artists put into the furnace what they call "kiln gods" that have already survived a number of passages. Mary Frank adds not one but nearly a dozen. "I need all the help I can get."

The actual process takes over ten hours, at the end of which time a column of fire three feet high rises from the chimney, singeing the leaves on trees overhead. Then a day and a half to cool. Then the pieces are laid out on the grass. "You get so frantic," she wrote in a notebook. "I'm in a sort of continuous ecstasy with the trees and the leaves and the air . . . hopefully the firing will become less traumatic." But it never does.

The artist in person is soft-spoken, physically large and light on her feet, with a mop of brown hair that in damp weather thickens to a mane or a pharoah's coif. She has made some erect little plaster figures mounted as walkers turning their backs on threatening waves at the seashore. Sometimes these are described as sea goddesses or women out of myth, but they could also be simply the image she sees in her mirror.

She is the daughter of a painter and once was puzzled by her mother's painting obsessively, "as if her life depended on it." Events have now moved Mary Frank too to work as if life depended on it. Getting out of the way of the breakers is also achieved through reading: *Leaves of Grass* ("The most beautiful title I know, because he accepts everything without judging—counts it as much to be a loser as to be a winner."); Proust ("I could spend a lifetime with it, the passages on photography, music, flowers, architecture, people's relationships, games. You could destroy the work completely by taking each thread apart that way!") . . .

And through music: she plays a rapturous recorder whenever she can muster a couple of fellow musicians. She listens to records of Rumanian and Peruvian panpipes, music for the lute and the guitar as well as Bach and Mozart. At parties she is a mesmerized dancer. She likes to go sit in darkened theaters at rehearsal time and draw. One of her friends is the dancer Henrietta Bagley, who works with crushed-paper forms, lengths of cloth and other movable, sculpturesque props. Translation of a single piece of material into many forms is the idea: the body too can be "material" to be translated. Another friend is Gwen Fabricant, who paints meticulous studies of plants and rocks with an intense inner energy restrained in grid structures. The conflict between things in motion and those restraining edges is the idea. Mary Frank's mother, Eleanore Lockspeiser, who once painted for dear life, is still doing so. "It's intuition and struggle," says Lockspeiser today. "Make a shape, tilt it a little . . . the color could be warmer, cooler . . . lighter, deeper. The struggle is with

(Above) Henrietta Bagley. Dancers in cloth. (Left) Gwen Fabricant, Cowbone, 1975. Oil on canvas. 30" by 20".

the color, its power, its glow. Or the lack of it. Go back and correct? Almost impossible. Make *one change,* you can never go back. Live a million years and you wouldn't finish the variations."

One change made the difference for Lockspeiser and her daughter, and they never went back. In 1940, when Mary was seven, they sailed from London to the United States in a refugee-evacuation ship, leaving behind Edward Lockspeiser, a well-known music critic and specialist in Debussy. Already, Mary had learned to sing to his accompaniment, and for some time after the separation he went on sending little impressionistic tunes written for her. But the years made the break permanent, and by the time he came over to visit them his wife had made her life as a painter and Mary, fifteen, was absorbed in dance classes with Martha Graham. There was another try at reconciliation a year later when he invited Mary to meet him in Paris, but she spent most of her time with Robert Frank, the Swiss-born photographer and the man she eventually married, so that her father, who was not up to understanding the ways of American girls, even had her hospitalized.[3] "I was fearless in a way and very romantic," says Mary Frank today, "and I didn't think into the future. The hospital was one of the oldest in Paris and it had a beautiful garden. They said I could sit in it. I did so for a half hour, and then I was put into a room by myself and kept in it. When Robert came, they told him I had gone back to America." Eventually Mrs. Lockspeiser had to rescue her daughter, and that was the final break.

Mary's memories of the first seven years of her life, the years in England, are sparse at first, not much more than "hills with sheep and hedgerows, and coming to a place with a smell of rotted apples and a huge wood cider press." But then it was wartime. Mary was evacuated along with other London children to a series of country boarding schools. Here the memories are more vivid. "I was homesick, but I didn't want to say so, so I didn't. There was a lot of stiff upper lip.

"I remember children in blazers and gray tunics, tie, hat and knee socks running with butterfly nets to save the cabbages from being eaten by moths. To help the war effort—horrible for a seven-year-old! It was hard to make us see that the war made this slaughter of the butterflies necessary. We were supposed to put them into boxes with laurel leaves. The boxes were orange and red, and the leaves gave off a poison that killed them. We would get a farthing for each dozen moths we killed.

"But I loved the moths. So I decided not to eat any cabbage at meals. . . .

"The air-raid shelter was in the garden, underneath the rose bed. There was an entrance that led beneath a sort of hummock or rampart of earth all covered over with roses.

"We went down in there nearly every night and sat in our nightgowns with our gas masks on. We sat facing one another in two rows with the masks on, some of them hanging on their straps sidewise or pushed back. Then after a while we said our prayers and went back up to bed.

"It was terrible and frightening. But then there were the roses.

"Surreal? Who could come up with such a combination, even if they tried?"

For Mrs. Lockspeiser too, leaving England was a rupture: "Terrible for Mary, to have been taken away from her people. And for myself, a whole section of my life was lost. I had left all my paintings in a house that was bombed, and I lost them all. Then when we came back to the States, I painted and painted. It was my salvation.

"We lived with my parents at first, but they treated me as if I were a child, so Mary and I moved to the Village. From the time she was five, she had danced. I would have wanted her to go to college, but when she was about sixteen she said, 'I want to be an artist.' Well, art was the only important thing in our household. And it had been in England too."

Eleanore Lockspeiser's own father had come from Russia and had become the first multilanguage printer in America. Her mother had come from St. Petersburg, and her talent was for sewing. "She had a marvelous sense of color, and her fingers were so delicate. She dressed us like princesses! When she was old and nearly blind, she picked up a shirt I was making for Mary—

who was just a little girl—and felt the material and said, 'You've put the sleeves on backward.' And there was only a half-inch difference between front and back on that pattern. It was her sense of form. Of line."

Music was Lockspeiser's first love; she played the piano and sang. Then one day she encountered the painter Pepino Mangravite and he agreed to give her some lessons. "I can't draw, but I love color," she warned him.

"He gave me paper and hard pencil, and he said, 'Draw fast—as I tell you.' And he said, 'Draw apple . . . pear'—whatever. It was as if he were a Svengali. Whatever he asked me to draw, I drew. He gave me no chance between words even to think or to see. I just drew. It was crazy.

"And then I went home and made a complicated drawing of the lake, the trees . . . And then I was drawing, just as if it came from the sky to me. I couldn't believe it—faces, people, everything.

"Then later I took my first painting class, with Max Weber, and did my first still life. I put *everything* in. Weber came into the room, and I was so frightened I hid. He looked at the picture and shrugged and asked who had done it. I said, 'Me.'

" 'It's terrible,' he said. 'But it's wonderful too!' And then he threw everything off the table, put down only an apple, a knife and some drapery, turned my canvas over, asked me for a palette knife and drew just a few edges. . . .''

Speed and edges: elements of an esthetic that may have been handed down from mother to daughter, though today Mary Frank is precise about their differences. As a child she was always turning out something with her hands, little paintings for Christmas cards, little figures. For her mother, "it was always the formal problems to be solved. She has a greater seriousness. For me, making art always has something of play about it. I do hundreds of different things—sketchbooks, drawings on birchbark, drawings on leaves, even on mushrooms. For me, making art seems to be just the normal thing. I can't imagine not working unless I were crazy or dying."

Lockspeiser's gift is for color. She paints tender roses, blue and green fields with vague hints of horizon, in which quizzical Miroesque shapes flutter and posture with a pressured animation. For a while she had a taste for hand-carved frames, like John Marin's, and it may have been to enlist Mary's help in making these that she gave her a first set of carving tools. Mary had then just gotten over her first enthusiasm: to join the circus.

For a while she tried out her new tools in the studio of a neighbor and sculptor, Alfred van Leon. He was not encouraging, and the wood figures she was trying to make were "awful." Their inspiration was Henry Moore, though bodies seen at the Graham studio may also have been an influence. That dancer was the most impressive figure in Mary's world at the time. "She was ferocious and overwhelming. She talked about Greek ideas I wasn't interested in at the time, and she talked about sculpture. Particularly Henry Moore, the first sculptor I felt connected to."

In 1950, still only sixteen, Mary graduated from the Children's Professional School in New York and went to Paris for the misencounter with her father and the encounter with her husband-to-be. A year later, she had her first child, Pablo. In '54, their daughter Andrea was born. It was a fast growing up. That early period of marriage and motherhood was, as far as Mary Frank is concerned today, an underground period of helpless disorganization.

"We lived such a bohemian life. I'm always amazed at people with kids making schedules for a work and so on. It seems to me I've had no plans at all. Robert got a Guggenheim Fellowship to photograph this country, and we just took off in a car. I thought we were going off on some sort of picnic. Two kids, one of them sick, no place to wash the diapers. I couldn't drive. We didn't know where we were going or where we'd stay. Along the way, Robert got put in jail for taking pictures and looking foreign.

"But I idolized him. He was committed, passionate and judgmental about his and other people's work. He had a strong, personal, nonintellectual eye, very fast. With him, I learned to see, work, draw fast. I loved his photos, but on the other hand I was never interested in the urban scene. He was. I walk, and I see, but I don't *use* the city."

Robert Frank's famous book *The Americans* was shot along the highways of that trackless trip West. His pictures of it are angled, grainy, fast: empty roads shafting back, oblique screens of billboards, half-caught faces of bewildered, hurt-looking women. The photos were random, desolate. They made his mark. He was the working artist in those days and she the mother, though she did begin to do some drawing when Pablo was a year old. "But at great expense all around. For the children. For me. There was always this pulling. I was very tenacious, but it was a terrific conflict. Every woman I know talks about it."

In 1950 and '51 the family lived in Paris, Spain and London. To Mary Frank it seems now that she spent her time in hotel rooms while Robert went out to work, though now and then he would baby-sit so that she could visit a museum. Wednesday evenings the Louvre was open. She would go, take a bench in the Egyptian wing among sphinxes and pharoahs, sit in the silence under pale electric light and listen to distant footsteps. It was the same in the Etruscan wing and the Asian galleries. For a while, she went once a week to the cellar studio of a forger of Chinese terra cottas. He cast his Tang horses and left them standing under pipes that dripped antiquing fluids. Literally underground, Mary Frank "carved a little" there. But her thinking about work was still vague.

Something she did not do was keep up with the contemporary art gallery scene. Nor does she today. "We were in Paris a year and a half, and I never saw anything contemporary. Years later I went to the Musée d'Art Moderne, and I was crazy about Matisse, Giacometti, Picasso. But even then I would also go back to the ancient things. Even today, I'll go to Asia House or the Met if I want to look at art."

Back in New York, Mary Frank began to take a few studio classes. She had worked a bit with the German Expressionist painter Max Beckmann. Now she attended Hans Hofmann's school for a time. The focus on Cubism was not for her, but she made a few friends, especially the young painter Jan Müller, whose Expressionist dream-forest scenes populated by ghost horses and masked figures were attracting attention. He was the victim of progressive heart disease, and it was his struggle to get his image down on canvas fast that affected many of his artist friends.

"Jan was a fantastic painter, extraordinary, very free, and so sick that he had an extraordinary intensity. He felt he hadn't much time but he was generous about looking at other people's work. And I was interested in the same imagery: horses, women, women falling off horses, landscape, figures that were part icons, women, lions—and horses again."

The Franks lived on Third Avenue near Tenth Street, a core artists' neighborhood in those days. Al Leslie lived next door, Milton Resnick lived nearby, and de Kooning's place was across the back yard. But in those early years of the '50s she felt cut off from the art world. "I was working in a very isolated way. I didn't even know the work. It may have been reverse snobbism, all those cult figures. Everybody was either working like them or thinking like them or talking like them. They had the quality of rock stars." [4] Later, when she would have found her own medium and imagery, there would be something of the Abstract Expressionist esthetic in her broken forms and the quick gestural sketch, especially something from de Kooning, whom she admired most.

By the mid-'50s, she began to carve in wood again, turning out ponderous, folded or globular forms. They looked abstract, pretty much pure wood, possibly related to works by the Rumanian Raoul Hague. His massive, barely carved log torsoes, carrying mute titles like Log Swamp Pepper Wood, were first shown in 1956 at the Museum of Modern Art. Mary Frank's had Surreal titles: Soul Catcher, Heart of Darkness, Bird Figure. To her, they seemed to be richly figurative.

"Friends came, saw the work, and they weren't so interested. It wasn't

*Drawing. Ink on paper. 20"
by 26". Zabriskie Gallery,
New York.*

very *different*. The wood pieces had the look of abstraction, I know, to other people. But for me they were based on human gestures. On a combination of images, like a bird-person." They were, as their material suggests, *root* figures, perhaps the expression of some private impulse to move. They strained to lift themselves up from the ground by a heavy contortion. Some had the posture of cumbersome never-to-fly arrows.

The forms became bigger. The family began to spend summers on Cape Cod, and she would have friends help her drag logs from the beaches back to her studio. Those same summers she began to draw a great deal, trying to find her own way of seeing a pitch of land, the ocean. To what was she coming closer? It seemed important to get down to the ground. Even get *into* the ground. She would find a path that led to the beach, climb the dunes, dig a hollow, lie down, eyes close to the sand, and watch the figures come and go.

"The light on the Cape . . . on the dunes . . . people destroyed by light. The nudes so beautiful. The sea. You can't see people like that anywhere else. You lie down with your head on the sand. Get your eye down on the level of the snake. I didn't care where I was, only that my eye would be on that level."

Her daughter Andrea would be at the water's edge, playing in sunlight, always the least static of models. Lying down, Mary Frank would see a foot or legs and between them, far down the beach, another figure very tiny, and, always behind, the sea. So much space and light—and relationships between separated people—could be noted on paper with the brush. "People were always coming and going on the beach. They follow the water's edge. I would draw the people as they would approach, recede, approach. Always these entrances and departures and changes of scale."

Now that old image of the bird-person she had once tried to do in wood— it was an Eskimo motif of a man with a bird on his back—came to mind, only now not as an idea, but as something seen, to be drawn from life. "When people are standing in water, they almost always raise their arms. I don't know

300

why. Everyone does. And they look like birds, elbows down, wrists up, hands down. There was that metamorphosis of figures into bird and then into light that took place as you watched from the dunes."[5]

Drawings like these were exhibited during the 1960s and caused a growing excitement. "She is so closely in touch with her own creative sources that even a dancer or a bather in a swift drawing can have the evocative and luminous presence of a Klee or a Rilke angel . . ." wrote a critic in *Art News*.[6] She had also begun to make small figures in wax to be cast in bronze. Freed by the material, she made dozens, hundreds, of little rearing horses, winged creatures now nearly airborne, buds unfolding, flowers and tree shapes. In 1963 she showed work in wood, ink and bronze, and *New York Times* critic Hilton Kramer discussed it at length.[7] He pointed out a contradiction between her handling of wood and of drawing and wax. The impression was that in some way the block of wood was a deadweight on her imagination. She was burdened by its impassivity. Mute and static, the block just sat there. But pen and ink, paper, wax between the fingers—these were something else.

Since the late '50s Frank had occasionally built a piece out of plaster, using wire or wood armatures. At the time, the sculptor Reuben Nakian, of Greek ancestry and spirit, was using that material in original ways, cutting and modeling free-form masses on which he incised quick drawings—nymphs and Pans, Europas and Neptunes—or else combining horizontal lumps and swags of plaster like far-flung hills or reclining bodies. There was a novel fascination, a permanence-in-flight to the substance. It could be poured and molded, cut and drawn upon with a stylus. The artist could make a shape, leave it for a year or fifty years, come back and work it again. One could combine a number of elements in one structure to create a scene with background and foreground, and figures in between. Some of Mary Frank's works of this kind took up the theme of the seashore. Heavy slabs were waves advancing, threatening to fall.

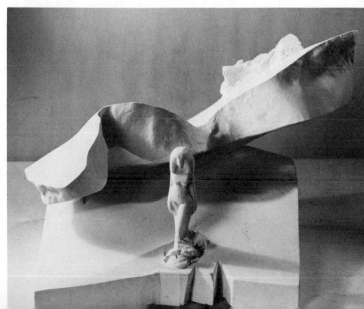

The Wave, 1967. Plaster. 15" by 24" by 17". Collection Virginia Zabriskie, New York.

Out of their way walked that self-impelled small figure with its self-identifying mane of hair. There were also figures of lion-women, crescent moons, lunar barques—portents of change if read that way. By 1968 Kramer noted she had got the message: "For years this thematic material has haunted her drawing . . . and now she has success in realizing these affecting images in a highly individual sculptural form . . ."[8]

In 1969 Frank and her husband separated. About the same time, she relinquished plaster as a material for sculpture. Dry, it was dead, gritty, got into the skin. She was tired of breathing it. "I wanted something else, but I didn't know what." A few artists were experimenting with clay, trying to find ways of using it that went beyond the standard forms. Her mother was familiar with the material: she had developed a method of repairing broken antique Chinese pots by coating the surfaces with milk and wiring them together. An aunt, Sylvia Weinstein, was a potter of distinction in the 1930s; one of her pieces was acquired by the Metropolitan Museum. The sculptor Margaret Israel was making intriguing anthropological images, half pottery, half figure, in unglazed clay; the potter-sculptor Jeff Schlanger taught Mary Frank what he knew about the technique. It was a material she had used only to make molds for the plasters. Now she tried working directly and found it a clean medium. It had interesting overtones of antiquity: the earliest shape made by man may have been a clay cup. There was character in its very commonness. Unlike bronze, it had no intrinsic value. It was dust; could be let go back to dust; in between, it could be given a form. "Some people felt I found myself with clay—the speed, the imagery—but I never felt I 'found myself' at any particular time. The earlier pieces were just different . . . heavy . . . dense."

In spite of her feeling that it marked no special breakthrough, Frank's adoption of clay led to an extraordinary series of inventions. It forced her to figure out new ways of proceeding, and these in turn engendered new images. Plaster can be molded and pressed onto an armature for a work that stands up. Clay longs to lie down. It sags and seeks a way back to the earth. The clay images eventually would be earth images, things that lie on the ground—water, bodies resting, bodies making love; things that fall to the ground—rain, leaves; things that brush the ground—wind, shadows of wings.

Practically speaking, clay will survive the kiln with no armature except another piece of itself. If big figures are wanted, they must be self-supporting or propped on rolls of paper that will burn out in the fire. "I had to work out a way for the large pieces to be armatures for themselves. The inner surface of a head, for instance, had to be actually the armature for the outer surface. Sometimes hidden, sometimes not." A complex of vertical piers might have to be erected. Between the upright supports and overlaid sections of skin, face, drapery, a counterpoint would be set up. Convex forms that lift from the ground were now also shelters for their own infrastructure. What a juggling act was then required to make a figure composed of many separate elements in which each non-flat-lying section would be held upon its own buttress, a bent leg bent according to nature but also into a massive triangle to hold itself up.

"Roll out slabs with the rolling pin . . . fold them . . . wait for it to dry just enough to be cut. Everything about clay is common. How hard, how dry, how soft. It's a matter of five minutes one way or the other. Wait too long, or don't wait long enough, the thing will collapse or become too rigid. If you had four large hands it would help . . . with quite long fingers!"[9]

Then how to get the figures to a kiln, since in the New York studio there was none? Why, make the components demountable, take them apart, carry them down one by one in the elevator, have them fired, bring them back, then reassemble. Such a long time would elapse between the idea and the realization! The artist's very intention might change along the way. The work would grow with time. It was the opposite beat of work from the quick sketches, the fast wax to catch the moment. Months went by before there was a full, fired complement of sections for the first big piece. This was a new nervous adventure as well as a formal one. "I felt it was a major change. It seemed a dangerous thing to do. It was exciting."[10]

In 1974 there were reports of the finding in China of a burial cache of over-life-size pottery figures of horses and soldiers. The scale of these reaf-

Lovers, 1973–74. Terracotta. 19" by 5'2" by 33". Collection Robert J.
Goldfein, New York.

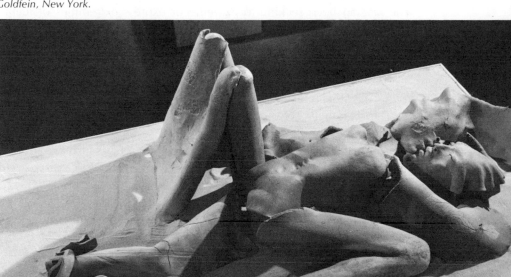

firmed Mary Frank in her own reach for bigger scale. The thought had been to show six of the new near-life-size pieces assembled, hanging on a wall. But the elements all together turned out to be too heavy and had to be laid on the grass if she was in the country or in sand beds in the city, for a show planned for early '75. Then the figures took on their most expanded appearance: now those hollow half-shells of body—upper halves of arms, of ribs, planes of faces—seemed to be literally in the process of being extruded from the ground, or sinking back into it. Hollow, all disconnections, empty space and imper- manent manifestations of matter, the figures hovered somewhere between worlds, as living people standing in sea water with their arms bent seem to belong wholly to neither the land nor the air.

Hollowness and disconnection: these esthetic characteristics might ex- press some aspects of contemporary life. So technique had bred forms that now reached out toward the world and a new content: the dismemberment endemic in our world. Some events hit Frank hard. Tortures in Vietnam: she had not ever found a way to put these facts into images. A local horror: a woman walking one night in a city in Massachusetts was set upon by hoodlums who poured gasoline over her and set her on fire. "It wasn't that she was a saint. She may have been out of contact, or stupid. It was the cloudy, intense impossibility of her life—wasted, in a particularly crazy way. I didn't set out to make a piece about her, but it seemed to have connections." [11]

Now those clay figures that seemed to combine innocence (unglazed clay now sometimes marked with ferns and grass burned into the surface during firing) with pain (those cut edges of clay left agape) appeared to be working on a new metaphoric level, probing general human themes of peril, suffering and fleeting transcendence.

The art had been seeking to examine or express extremities of feeling. Now there occurred a human event that overwhelmed the art, feeding back into these already broken figures a new rush of content that would render them nearly unbearably graphic. Only weeks before the big show, Frank's daughter was lost in a plane crash. At once, even if only to a knowledgeable audience, figures that until that moment had been readable as metaphors took on a fearful reality. The cross-over between ecstasy and anguish, that ancient theme of tragic drama, became the new theme here. Yet the focus as always was per- sonal, never rhetorical. The message of these new works was also a restatement and impassioned intensification of the familiar seaside dialectic: shore-water- air. Being-here, and being-nowhere.

"After the accident, I began to work again. I didn't even want to. It was just what happened. Sometimes I couldn't even look at the work when it was done. Working, I fell every time into an area that was so sensitized, into the very deep things that were there. Everything I would do would come back to that imagery.

"I couldn't get out of it, except by drawing. From life—from a model, a plant. Something that didn't feel so aware."[12]

There is a process of healing that the mind provides for itself in some cases, and the source of the gift is often the natural world.

For a long time, Frank had been working on monoprints. The process had fascinated her for its elusive effects. And then, too, working itself has its healing result. "Initially I did them on glass, painted by hand. Or you use metal. Then I began to look at the plate itself, after I'd taken the paper off. I got interested in using gold leaf, like the café signs in Paris."

The plate goes through dozens of stages of painting with etching inks. She changes the elements laid on it, bits of real petals or leaves, or torn paper—so that each new print is a little different, a bit more revealed, a bit more taken away. "Such mixtures! The underneath layers coming out as you print; the ghost of the very first figure you laid down reappearing again after several printings; figures seeming to move, animals running across—all determined by so many factors, like how much ink was on the brush or something as unexpected as that the day was sixty degrees and not eighty, or humid, or dry.

"It's like having your cake and eating it. You can make changes in a way you can't in sculpture or drawing. You have the first print, then you make changes on the same plate and have a second, and a third, and maybe up to

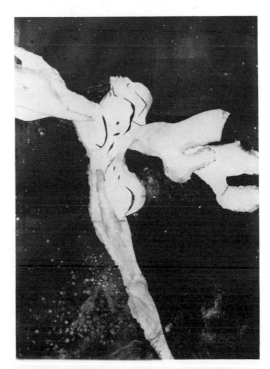

Daphne, 1976. Monoprint. 31" by 23". Collection Mr. and Mrs. William Silverstein.

seven as a series. The stages get paler and paler, or darker, and also iridescent. Anything can happen, like film. I don't know another medium where that is true.

"You can have your past and present and future in front of you."

In the past three years, Mary Frank has made hundreds of these prints showing figures flying and dancing, plants growing, animals running. There are the white birches of her mountainside, flowers from the garden, fish from the pond and human lovers in poses natural as leaves. An iconic figure many times repeated is Daphne with arms outstretched and fingers breaking into sprays of laurel—at last life-, not death-dealing. Another image is the amaryllis, the poppy or any stalky plant with a stem round and even all the way up, from ground to petal, like a pipe stem: the channel through which the living fluid flows. One of these was bought by the Metropolitan Museum in 1978.

Indeed, often in the monotypes these stalks or the reaching arms and wings of figures grow so long in the sheer process of printing that they stretch out across several sheets of paper joined together and overlayed, sheet after sheet, without squared-off edges as if it were the artist's business not to catch and center the image, to "make" art, but to pursue it, letting it grow according to its own time and impulse. "Because, as you're working, things often go beyond where you thought they were going—somehow the thing extends itself. I care where the form has to move to! I grab anything I can grab at that moment. I can't help it when the given space is gone beyond. It doesn't seem fragmented to me then; it seems whole.

"The square and the triangle are arbitrary shapes for art, after all. Prehistoric work was done on modulating, curved, corrugated surfaces, roofs and walls of caves. Things went in all directions, north, south, east, west, up, down, sideways, diagonally. I've never been in those caves, but I've read about them. That you lose whatever sense of direction you normally have there [under the rosebushes?].

"I feel art should—or could—be like that." [13]

What of Mary Frank's art for the future? Will there have to be a way beyond the enlarged figures in their extremity?

"Obviously, I'm still attached to the figure, but I feel I must begin to see it in some other way. I'm looking for something else.

"I've tried to think about combining glass with some sort of clay structure. Maybe a thick square of glass could lean against a clay support [like those trees up the hillside, where the quarriers left their rocks?]. Or maybe I could set mica into a tree with a lens in front of it, or even put some small sculptures in behind with gold leaf at the back, and you would look through the glass.

"O I love the idea of fire and water. But how to combine them?"

EM: "What about groups of figures in environments?"

MF: "I'm not sure I have the . . . the something that's often connected with male thinking—the power of seeing things in such large terms. I think about doing groups like that, but in vague terms. It takes tremendous courage. I lose heart and start doing the two-inch drawings."

Whatever new materials and images she takes to, there are two ways of perceiving the world so natural to Mary Frank it is hard to imagine her departing from them. One is the gift of empathy, the power of self-projection into the world or, to put it in the reverse way, an exquisite vulnerability to penetration by the world. Mary Frank remembers her experience with Martha Graham as awakening her to such fine details as being conscious of "what it is to move from a standing position—at what angle the body takes off or how a foot runs."

The other is an instinct for a natural dialectic that can be expressed in many ways. For Joan Mitchell the opposites are green and white, summer trees, winter-frozen lake. Frank talks about her two landscapes: the mountains with their impacted density of trees and foliage into which she has to make continual excursions to find the *edge,* and that place of archetypal edge, the seashore.

On another level, the alternation is, of course, between the object and infinite extension, love and loss, life and death.

The course of an artist's exploration of these things through the metamorphoses of her or his materials cannot be known in advance, though we know the terms and the landscape:

. . . the end of all our exploring
will be to arrive where we started . . .
[at] the children in the apple-tree,
Not known, because not looked for,
But heard, half-heard, in the stillness
Between two waves of the sea. . . .

Beyond that, the restlessness to which this kind of mind is subject was described long ago by that most metamorphic of artists, Leonardo: "Tell me, can anything ever be truly finished?"

Women of the
Third Wave:
Sisters of the
Crossroads

INCLUDING

ELISE ASHER AND

SHEILA DE BRETTEVILLE

In the decade of the '60s—without edges, without, to some extent, law, order or program—the arts like politics and the social system encountered confusing new potentials of freedom. As students milled from classrooms to gyre in college yards; as thousands marched on Washington to demand civil rights or protest the war; as assassins' bullets and murderously fast cars took their truly absurd flights; as Marshall McLuhan and Dr. Strangelove revealed more about the American mind of the time than one cared to contemplate; so in the visual arts, Assemblages, Environments, Happenings and the isms called Pop, Op, Minimal, Conceptual, mingled in a bewildering and also challenging eclecticism. But what dramatically characterized the cultural world of the '60s was economic boom. As she has explained it earlier, the artist-organizer June Wayne was well aware of the rising tide she was riding when, in '59, she launched her Tamarind Lithography Workshop with unprecedented funds from the Ford Foundation, then only beginning its interest in art projects. When, in '63, the international art corporation Marlborough Galleries installed itself in New York with a roster of top artists gathered by blandishments both legal and questionable, an expansionist mold was set to the art world not to be questioned until the middle of the next decade. Yet another development of the time, with special importance for women, was the production, in 1960, of the birth control pill. By '65, this means of self-liberation would have changed life fundamentally for all females.

Not coincidentally, these were also the years when, slowly and still from obscurity, women artists of various ages and styles began turning out works of strange-appearing prophetic character, nontrivial experiments not intended to "sell" the public but to expand each artist's perimeter of self-revelation. Of this sort were Lee Bontecou's steel-and-canvas structures; Eva Hesse's works in latex, rope, rubber, cloth; Lenore Tawney's semifigurative weavings. Similarly, it was 1961 when Anne Truitt sat on her bed "like a bullfrog" and conceived structures that would incarnate "my childhood." This was also the decade when Mary Frank turned to wax, plaster and clay; when sculptor Nancy Grossman stitched up, in plaster and leather, images of male figures of an unparalleled Surreal power; and when Sylvia Stone turned to Plexiglas en route to her *Crystal Palace*. It was also the decade when many artists long at work came to

311

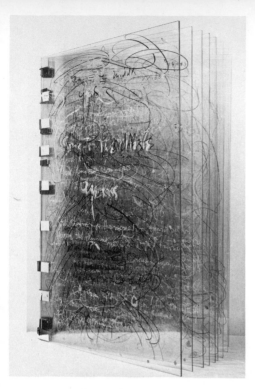

Elise Asher. Song for the Middle Years, *1973. Oil on Plexiglas. 30" by 16" by 12". Collection the artist.*

grips with new imagery particularly grounded in their own pasts, like Isabel Bishop's walking figures and Jeanne Reynal's *Ronde des Heures*. This was, for instance, the time when poet-painter Elise Asher began to merge her two talents in works of lyric, not-to-be-deciphered calligraphy on large book pages of acrylic. The material was of the moment, but the multilayered effect of light and vague drifts of color was a near-direct recovery of her childhood fascination with toys made of glass, especially the little glass balls filled with colored candies. "I'd spill out the candies, put in colored water and make believe they were lighted lamps," she recalls. In her most recent works Asher has foraged even further into fantasy, filling scenes, still on acrylic sheets, with curious seal-like figures that mock and pantomime the solemnities of male literary and political worlds (*At the Grave of Henry James, Listening to the Watergate Committee*). The oracular postures of these characters, too, come from things seen. For a while, Asher lived on the California coast atop "dismaying drops into that wild sea" where a colony of seals lived, fed, birthed and died in their own closed society.

This was also the era when art departments of universities began graduating women in great number. Sheila de Bretteville was one of these, finishing at Barnard College in 1961 and continuing to the Yale School of Art and Architecture for professional training in graphic design. During the rest of the decade, she worked in Europe and this country designing for various commercial enterprises including Olivetti International. By the time the '70s broke, with

312

the Feminist art movement in full swing, de Bretteville was in California ready to take a lead role designing, writing, lecturing, teaching. In '72 she set up a Feminist Studio Workshop at the Woman's Building in Los Angeles with artist Judy Chicago, art historian Arlene Raven and poet Deena Metzger. She is today an editor and the designer of *Chrysalis,* the important Feminist publication. Today de Bretteville talks with vivid personalization about Feminist esthetics and psychology. She projects exercises to develop in other women that capacity an artist like Mary Frank so instinctively exhibits: empathy, the consciousness of psychic bonds between the creator and her plastic materials. If the idea comes out of Zen and other sacramental religious procedures, the practice at the time was rooted in consciousness-raising theory.

De Bretteville is conscious of the interweaving, too, of her own personal history with the structures of her present beliefs. She was born in Brooklyn, daughter of Polish immigrants and factory workers. At home there were crowds of fellow-workers, fellow-immigrants, talkers, arguers, nurturers. For the child, there was no private space; everything was to be shared. Yet there came a painful experience of separation: when she was three, her father suffered a heart attack. A hospital bed was moved into the house and she, the child, told to stay away. Thereafter, there was, as de Bretteville so significantly says today, always a "feeling of distance I wanted to break through."

So, too, this was the decade when Alice Neel was "discovered" and Lee Krasner "rediscovered." It was the time when older and middle-generation artists Cecile Abish, Chryssa, Margaret Israel, Ruth Vollmer, Claire Zeisler and others moved into distinctly original new idioms, and when, at the decade's end, Nancy Graves invented her epochal *Camels.*

It was also a time when, as in years to come, among all the invention, obfuscation, flamboyance and fakery, there could also be seen artists pursuing, with quiet self-knowledge and freedom, ways that may not be epochally new but are still open to the most varied personal interpretation, like various-generation Abstract Expressionist painters Alice Baber, Natalie Edgar and Emily Mason.

Anne Truitt

BORN 1921, BALTIMORE, MARYLAND

[We] spent all that day looking at art. . . . I saw Ad Reinhardt's black canvases, the blacks and the blues. Then I went on down the ramp and rounded the corner and . . . saw the paintings of Barnett Newman.

I looked at them, and from that point on I was home free.

I had never realized you could do it in art. Have enough space. Enough color.

—ANNE TRUITT
Washington, D.C., 1977

Truitt's outer self mirrors one inner self. Her wide blue eyes, straight white-blond hair, voice fluty and precise, may be read as the external signs of a point of view: "I have total faith in who I am, and who is God in me. I don't ever worry about it. I always have had it, ever since I was born." An old-fashioned, mystical faith for a woman named by critic Clement Greenberg in 1968 as "one whose painted structures helped change the course of American sculpture"![1] Yet there are recesses of memory and experience here that neither the voice nor the claim to faith exhaust. She is also one who looks for her touchstones in the Lives of the Saints.

Likewise, Truitt's works are chapel-plain to the eye while like chapel walls also laid with shadows when seen from another point of view. They are carefully crafted wood boxes, pillars, mostly standing upright, exuding a cool yet unformidable presence that might be interpreted as *figure* if it were not for their milky, nature-colored surfaces so studied that it is clear that *color* is their reason for being. Truitt also makes paintings that combine two or more of her colors on a flat field, say an October-twilight-over-fields orange, underwritten

314

by a sullen purple ridge. In a still more puritanically reductive series of paintings called "Arundel," mere pencil lines and faint strokes of white pigment barely disturb dimensionless white fields that seem to "go on and on." Truitt has shown works of these kinds since 1963, had a retrospective at the Whitney in 1973 and has had major museum shows yearly since. Still, in spite of much written about her art, we turn in need to the artist herself to explain what she seeks, since she often states she is not simply making "ensembles of objects." [2]

"I want color in three dimensions," she begins. What she says she would like would be for the structures—the boxes and stretched canvases—to dissolve and color hang there disembodied, mere columns or passages of light like the shimmer of fields or the ocean. *Landfall* refers to an island seen from across water at dawn. Of *Spring Snow,* she once wrote, "icy green falls from the top of the sculpture through the tender air of early spring onto the warming earth below, which flattens itself to receive it." [3] *A Wall for Apricots* is a memorial icon to her close friend the painter Mary Pinchot Meyer, who lost her life in an episode of blind chance and to whom white walls and apricots had a special "radiance."

"Icon" is the word. These structures are objects for contemplation, philosophers' stones, the Chinese jade teardrop in which one sees the universe. Truitt explains how the pieces occur to her:

"I see them in my head. Then I bring them down, so I can see them here. I walk to the wall and make marks. I measure, and have wooden constructions made to my specifications. Then I develop the surface until I get as close as I can to what I've seen in my head."

Georgia O'Keeffe said it, too: that she carries ideas in her head until they jell and then works fast to get the concept down on canvas. [4]

In the sense of giving form to such primary visual and motor events, Truitt's works might be called classically Minimal. Yet they are, it seems to me, more than the term implies in deriving from feelings instead of intellectual categories: love of place, love of persons, barely glimpsed turns of events that may mirror deeper contradictions. Like Louise Bourgeois, Truitt will labor to resolve those contradictions in Euclidean abstractions. All the same, the sculptures, however abstract, unfold their meanings as icons do only to those who take pains to learn their iconography. As in so much of the art of our time, that iconography can be taught only by the artist in terms of her own life and ideas.

To hear Truitt talk about her life is to hear, at first, Minimal esthetics laid bare, as a Chinese painter's descriptions of walks, talks and meditations teach the Tao. To hear her talk is also to hear an echo of American Puritanism, and

315

Studio with standing sculptures, 1977. Painted wood.

then, later on, to remember how the dark woods of Hawthorne lay around the Pilgrim's house.

"My first memory: I was lying on a table and a light moved across the ceiling, right to left. I had a feeling of intense, total, undiluted surprise. I remember thinking: how odd, to be *me*, inside such a little pulpy body!

"I remember our first house. A beautiful eighteenth-century house in Easton, Maryland. I still go back sometimes just to walk around it. The doors, for example. Beautiful rectangular doors with rectangular panels. Handmade plain brass knobs, highly polished. My work still comes out of all this today. A feeling of amplitude and proportion. And a particular light, too, on the Eastern Shore of Maryland—Claude's light over a landscape, or Piero della Francesca's: daylight and, again, amplitude, that quality of a place where the water touches the land.

"Later on, we moved to still another eighteenth-century house. Two beautiful houses we lived in, until I was fourteen."

EM: "And your parents?"

AT: "Mother came from Boston; Father from St. Louis. He was warm-

316

hearted, eager, quick, instinctive. Mother was tall, reserved, from a long line of Boston bluestockings. Her mother, for instance, was in the first graduating class of Smith College, in 1878; she taught herself Spanish so she could read *Don Quixote* in the original. Mine went to Radcliffe and maintained an interior life much like a character in Jane Austen or George Eliot. Strict, Puritan. Self-centered but unselfish. Delicate, with high principles and an enormous respect for the integrity of people.

"Actually, my mother's self-centeredness was a boon to me, because it set me free. I knew, for example, that she was totally to be trusted. Therefore, if her mind was off me, I knew I was safe. Also, she was rather like Virginia Woolf's mother, who understood the 'final proportions of things.' Therefore there was never any frenzy around her, or rarely, at least. If something went wrong, she dealt with it, and that was that.

"In those days, everything was keyed to writing. Mother read the Brontës and Austen to me. And poetry—Matthew Arnold, Tennyson. When I wrote something, Mother would say, 'That's interesting, Annie dear,' and put the piece of paper into an inlaid Chinese box. I knew she wouldn't lie. She meant it if she said it was good. She never treated me like a child.

"It was her theory that children were like cabbages: give them sunshine and space and they will grow. So I wore loose cotton dresses, bloomers, shifts with little pockets but no sashes, washable and soft. For Sundays, smocking on the dress. I felt *comfortable* in my clothes and in my body—a feeling of being able to move around freely. And we had extremely good meals! Brown bread, apples, lamb chops. Nursery food—junkets, rice pudding, Indian pudding. Nothing extra. Plain clothes, plain meals. No special attention paid to the things that had to do with just living. I didn't expect happiness from people, for instance. I got my happiness from my freedom.

"When I was given a bicycle, I had a whole way of being for myself. I knew where everything was, all the back lots, the alleys, the flowers. I knew where the best white violets were—in an alley behind Judge Sheehan's house. I'd go and check them out in the spring. There were carpenters whose shops I used to haunt—go stand and watch. And a brick kiln. I had a sense of domain.

"I still go back to Easton when I'm in trouble. I stay in an inn and walk around. It's all gone now, though, and only in my head now, and the big house is divided into apartments. But I can go back in my memory and be there. The colors, sights, smells. What the air was like and the textures. Not so much the people. I remember them, but never so vividly as the colors, the textures, the light."

EM: "I suppose there had to come an end to this idyll. Because the troubled times too would have pushed you on."

317

AT: "Yes, the first crisis period was when I was about eighteen months old and my twin sisters were born. I had a period of weakness then and had to lie in the sun a lot. The house, for a while, seemed clotted and dark. Then as I recovered I was put out in the garden to play by myself, neglected—or set free.

"I suppose I got over the crisis because I adored being alone. I was in the garden, and no one paid any attention to me. A long, narrow garden, running east to west. Three quarters of the way down away from our house was a line of poplar trees, and I would go beyond them and look at everything.

"Next door was a chicken house. There I discovered death. There was a long whitewashed shed with the best violets in Easton. The biggest and most purple because of the chickenshit. I used to stand holding on to the wire fence and watch Mr. Phillips, the grocer, kill the chickens. Put their heads on a stump and chop them off with a hatchet. Violets on one side. On the other, the chickens. I would take some violets home to Mother and not tell her what I'd seen. She would not have been happy to know. And, besides, I felt that that experience belonged to me.

"Then, because I walked all the time and eventually bicycled around town and looked, I soon noticed that things outside were different. There were poor people. So I began to suffer guilt. I would say prayers every night for the poor people. I was always conscious of being privileged. That my privilege must be passed on, that life was given to me as a trust and that when I died it would be returned to some original source. That I was responsible for what I did with it. My mother put that burden on me.

"Then, too, very young, I decided that my father was silly. He drank. He could be frightening. I had to decide whether to love him or not. So I made a conscious decision. I remember distinctly that I decided to love him. And that became a pattern in my life: not to reject but to embrace.

"What saved me in the early days and all my life was that I was brought up with those sensible habits, so that there was exterior order that mirrored interior order. But within that order you could do exactly as you pleased. Therefore I became, externally, a 'good' child. Not naughty. It was a pragmatic decision, like the decision to love my father, to love the very person who made me feel insecure."

EM: "And then?"

AT: "In the winter of the year I was fourteen, everything changed. Mother got sick and went to Baltimore for treatment. Father was ill as well. The whole house fell in on me. I was the one who had to order the meals, take care of *his* nurses, everything. When I think about it now, it seems incredible that nobody stepped in. But I had only myself to rely on, because there was nobody else.

So I did my schoolwork and ran the house. I had to reassure everybody, make everybody feel that everything was holding together. The experience made a crack in me. The crack was here: I had to act as if I knew more than I did.

"And in those days I never had a feeling of being, or of wanting to be, an artist. I never thought about it. I only thought, This is the way I am."

EM: "There must have been moments when your thinking and sensing of life took shape. When you began taking note of things."

AT: "I remember vividly learning to read. The moment when I didn't have to say, 'The . . . boy . . . ran . . . with . . . the . . . ball.' When I could take it all in at once, the whole. When the separate words made a thought. From then on, I read everything. And I loved making relief maps with the governess. We'd make them of all the continents: South America, Europe, Asia. We used flour and water; no color.

"As for *things:* at home we had French furniture. In the front hall a round marble pedestal with a bust of Caesar Augustus. Another bust on top of an inlaid chest: Marie Antoinette, in blue cloissonné enamel and marble. Behind her a gilt Venetian mirror. And we had a lot of Canton china, because my mother's family had been clipper-ship owners. But there was no emphasis on these things. We just used them.

"The first distinguished work of art I saw was in the summer house of the famous collectors the Arensbergs. I was thirteen and my father took me there to swim. It was the age when I was embarrassed to be seen in a swimsuit. As I was leaving the house, my eye fell on a small painting by Renoir. I was so struck that I forgot my appearance and stopped and gathered my courage and asked Mrs. Arensberg what it was. It was the first time I realized it was possible to make something more beautiful than what *was.*

"I had been given glasses only in the fifth grade. I'd been astonished by what I saw! Buckminster Fuller had the same problem, only in reverse. He was farsighted. As a result—it is his *Weltanschauung*—he deals only with things belonging in the realm of vast distances. I, on the other hand, see things only close up. Beyond eight inches I see only a blur. I had lived the first nine years of my life in that blur.

"I had gone to a great extent on my intuition. I could feel people's fear, for instance, acutely. I had a strong sense for what was under my feet and under my hands—in my own circumference. That childhood condition made me a solipsist, I believe. I developed an instinct, a sort of kinesthetic sense. I feel shapes not with my eyes but with a kind of radar. I think it must have been because of this sense of my *body* that I began later on to place my sculptures so that they too *stand.*

319

"Also, the experience made me concentrate on color. I have vivid memories of color, of being up early and out in the garden looking at things—at dawn, in the twilight—times when the colors change the quickest."

Anne Truitt's first thought was to be a nurse. That was back in the childhood days in Easton. "All around me were people in pain," she says. "It was a little town and you could practically *see* everybody's pain. It was as if I were steeped in it. So when I went to college I thought I would devote myself to alleviating pain. I was set to save the world. Dead serious." At Bryn Mawr she enrolled as a psychology major. Her first year there, she nearly died of appendicitis. Later she would have trouble bearing children because of complications that followed. "And that was pure fate, because if I had had children early in my married life I might never have become an artist. As it turned out, I would have eight more years of growth, of apprenticeship to myself, before their births."

Two years after her own illness, her mother died. A summer some years before, the family had traveled together to England. One afternoon Anne Truitt and her mother made a visit to Westminster Abbey. "Mother and I went into the cloister. She explained the flying-buttress system.

"I was absolutely struck dumb by the fact that the interior and the exterior of the cathedral matched. From then on, I never stopped being aware that outsides and insides matched, and that they did the same with people. Even as a child I had known that I could sense the inner condition of people. Now I could double-check my intuitions by studying their exteriors. Maybe the reason the idea struck me so forcibly was because my mother herself was a Gothic person. At least when I was a child I had looked up at her and seen her as a tall slender shape.

"So it seems that in the end my sculptures are all somewhat Gothic, or perpendicular: they are, in that one sense, like my mother."

Her mother's death gave Anne Truitt financial security and the right to take her own life in hand. She applied to Yale for studies in psychology, and when the letter of acceptance came she took a walk, thought it over and decided that scholarship was not her bent. Instead she took a job as a researcher at Massachusetts General Hospital and soon realized she had made another wrong choice. "There I was in my starched coat behind the desk. It somehow seemed a lie. I was in the wrong place. So I left." She spent some time working on her writing and then met James Truitt, an engaging and literate journalist, married him and moved to Washington, D.C. And there, step by step, she began her education as an artist.

"Life is always surprising me. I will be going along, doing one thing on the surface, while underneath something else is brooding and preparing itself: the thing I am *going* to do.

"I had taken a night class in sculpture in Cambridge. I made one little figure there, of a woman, and I was surprised that it gave me no difficulty. But I didn't pay much attention, because I was writing poetry then. Gradually, however, I began to realize that I really was not interested in sequence of events in time, in narrative, the basis of literature. I had been steeped in Joyce and Woolf, but in my own writing I couldn't figure out how to break away from the confines of *time*.

"By then I was taking a sculpture class at the Institute of Contemporary Art in Washington with Alexander Giampietro, learning stonecutting, plaster, casting, clay: straight sculpture techniques. I didn't think very much about it. It was like breathing, or washing the sheets. I didn't think about results. Giampietro had, by the grace of God, no feeling about the art world—there was not a pretentious cell in his body—and I was without ambition in any terms except my own. I had not set out to be an artist. I was interested only, at that point, in certain concepts that involved the human body, such as, in what way does experience mark it? I was making Cubist-derived work in the style of Archipenko. Awful. I've done more rotten work than most people, and eventually I destroyed it all. All the work from 1948 to 1961, and all the sculpture I made when James and I lived in Japan from 1964 to '67. My eye was, I now consider, off then.

"And in 1950 we lived in Dallas for a year and I studied with Octavio Medillin, who taught me to make life-size figures out of clay."

Wherever the Truitts moved, from coast to coast and abroad, for James's work, Anne set up her studio and looked for teachers. That way she studied life drawing, casting cement and metal welding. After a trip to Yucatán, she began making small, horizontal, slablike clay structures rather imitative of Mayan architecture: a step toward pure geometry. Beyond that, "I kept the house, did what had to be done, put James first, and my three children. And only then I did what I wanted to do."

In 1960 the family moved back to Washington. Anne Truitt took up an old friendship with the painter Kenneth Noland, who was beginning to attract attention for his *Targets*. That year Clement Greenberg had made an attempt to launch Noland and his Washington fellow Color-Field pioneer Morris Louis in a show in New York, but the step was premature. Abstract Expressionism, Pop and the art of Assemblage—sculpture in the Dada-Surreal-Constructivist mode—were still on center stage.

A year later, Truitt made a trip to New York with Noland and Mary Meyer.

"I remember telling her when we set out that I felt like a *plowed field*. I'd had my three children. I knew I wouldn't have any more. I had James, whom I dearly loved. I had my studio. I had everything I thought I wanted. My life was in order. I felt fertile.

"Mary and I spent all that day looking at art. In my own work, I'd been making those clay block-sculptures moving toward geometry. But as I look back now I realize I had still been thinking of sculpture in terms of people. The forms had to be based on people, because I had only known emotion reflected through the human body. Now it was as if for the first time in my life I really saw what art could be. At the end of the day we went to the Guggenheim Museum. I saw Ad Reinhardt's black canvases, the blacks and the blues. Then I went on down the ramp and rounded the corner and then, right there before me, I saw the paintings of Barnett Newman.

"I looked at them, and from that point on I was *home free*.

"I had never realized you could do it in art. Have enough space. Enough color.

"When I saw the Newmans, they had exactly the feeling I had been groping to express. And they had nothing to do with people whatsoever. I was totally astonished.

"I went back to the apartment where I was staying, and I couldn't sleep. I suppose if I'd taken a sleeping pill that night, I wouldn't be here today. I just sat in the middle of the bed like a bullfrog, and gradually it all came together. I had what you might call a conversion. Or a vision.

"I thought, 'I will make exactly what I please. I will make trees and fences and fields. I will make my childhood. I will make what I know.'

"I had also seen in New York a small wood sculpture made of lathe-like elements. I had thought, Just like my old carpenter shops at home in Easton! It never occurred to me before that moment that I could make use of things I'd seen and known in my childhood. So I thought then, I'll use wood. Houses are wood. And fences.

"Back in Washington, I bought a roll of shelf paper and drew three full-scale forms like pickets, plus three connective pieces and a base. Then I went to a lumberyard and ordered the seven pieces of wood. I went back to the studio and glued the pieces together, bought some house paint and painted them white, and there was my fence.

"Then I went to the bank, took some money I had never touched and opened an Anne Truitt Special Account. From then on, I used my inheritance in wallops and invested in myself. I never looked back."

Truitt learned she could make scale drawings and have the lumberyard build

Catawba, 1962. Painted wood. 42½" by 60" by 60". Museum of Modern Art, New York.

the basic shapes, leaving only the application of color for her to do. She settled down to make her pieces and also to raise three children. Eventually her marriage failed, with all that that implies in pain, and she was left with financial burdens she could no longer handle with ease. Later she would teach, lecture, apply for grants. But now she rented Noland's studio building and set up a factory system, drawing the forms, ordering them, always in series of three, painting them and moving them straight into the next room for storage. "And I kept quiet. Nobody saw the things for quite a while. Then one day Ken asked to come and I showed him."

Clement Greenberg and David Smith were the next to see the work. Both praised it. In September 1962, Morris Louis died and a number of New York friends came down for the funeral. The dealer André Emmerich came and offered Truitt her first show. "So I never had to struggle, or even to think, about 'identity'—'Am I an artist?' I just kept working, and events happened to the work."

EM: "What about the future? Will you go on making the same forms? How does the process of change or growth make itself seen in works of such simplicity and repetitiveness?"

AT: "But the works are still always failures to me! Never right. When I get them down here, I never get the color right. And I'm in a process of change right now. I used to do everything in threes. I would feel an agony if I couldn't get them out—like those tortures where they tied the women's feet together during childbirth. But now I feel a little more free.

"I'm moving in the direction of more brilliant, variegated color. The sculptures were frontal before, like Egyptian works, with only a few changes of color across the planes. But these new columns have six or more colors that go around the corners. I mean them to record changes of light from second to second. In fact, I find I have nearly abandoned form: form doesn't interest me now. What I want is color in three dimensions, color set free, to a point where, theoretically, the support should dissolve into pure color.

"I used to work in bursts of intuition. Now I find that the very process of working step by step feeds my imagination. There is a metaphoric meaning to that: my painful recognition that life does not always come to you in one sudden vision but as a gradual process. It seems I have learned to bear the anxiety of uncertainty. Now I accept that one can't know ahead of time what is on the other side. You might say these new works project a greater degree of jeopardy.

"Events on the physical plane, I have come to see, do take place in time. My lifelong problem has been to reconcile myself to this fact and still embody in the physical works my intuition of timelessness. You remember I had thought first I was, then I was not, interested in the passage of time. I think I meant I lost interest in time as it is dealt with in literature, as narrative. As soon as I found a way to incarnate timelessness in a single, static work of sculpture, I found I could move forward and deal again with the idea of passage. So I have come full circle.

"People see only the standing column. The meaning escapes them because they fail to experience the passage of time that is implicit in the piece. The passage of light around the column of colors [across a ceiling, right to left?] is a metaphor for the way things are. The paradox: time in passage, caught and held still."

Lenore Tawney

BORN LORAIN, OHIO

. . . as I was weaving, the warp began to hang in places looser than the woven part. I thought to myself, It won't be any good. Then I thought, But I don't have to show it to anybody; it's just for myself. And I felt so free! I did as I wanted. And then when I took it off the loom and threw it on the floor I felt that tiny click near the heart that meant: It was not bad.

So I learned in that piece that I had freedom to do what I wanted. I didn't have to please anybody but myself.

—LENORE TAWNEY
Los Angeles, 1977

Lenore Tawney is, one feels, an artist on the threshold of enlarged public life. She first came to prominence in the '60s as a weaver who transcended the limits of those few struts of wood and thread called "loom" to make works of sculpture in a medium no more substantial than line-and-air. A group of these in black and white linen thread, created in an outpouring of invention during a mere six months' period, worked sources of memory and imagination more conventionally only tapped by painting or orthodox three-dimensional "hard" sculpture. She also excels in fields of Surreal assemblage, poetic writing and painting. In other words, her oeuvre is varied and mutating. Yet between her phases of phenomenal activity she disappears from sight, sinks like the sun or a bird behind clouds so that her public has yet to be assured of her continuing presence on the scene.

She is, in person, a tiny, dark-eyed presence who enters a room like an Indian dancer, shy yet possessed of the flame. She may be wearing white Indian trousers, and her hands may already be stirring the air as if she were plucking at strings. If she hears music, and people are dancing, her way of joining is to raise her arms up to shoulder height, hold her head back and turn around like a child before her elders. Her conversation moves around that way, too. She spins her words in spirals, now memories that still have power to wound her, now anecdotes of travels all over the world and lucky encounters. But what I, catching her in midpassage, wanted to follow was the thread of Lenore Tawney's finding her way to the position she holds as the pioneer inventor of the art of woven sculpture. It was, in her case, a rather long odyssey.

She was born into a Catholic household near Lorain, Ohio, between the shore of Lake Erie and a forest rich in wildflowers. "Blue" is the color that keeps coming up as she speaks. There were bluebells, spring beauties and jacks-in-the-pulpit in the fields where Tawney and her siblings picnicked with their mother, a farm girl from Ireland. At her side, too, Lenore learned to sew and embroider and became proficient enough to adorn the sleeves of her plain blue serge schooldress. But when she wore it to her convent school, the nuns disapproved. They preferred a modest conformity among their students, and Tawney thinks of that early flight of fancifulness as a first turn toward the life she would eventually make. The convent spirit oppressed her in other ways as well. When a ballet teacher came and got the girls going in pliés and arabesques and then dressed them up in tutus for a show, the sisters shut the door on that activity. Dancing too was a release not to be enjoyed for a long time.

Doors close as deliberately on the next passage of Tawney's life, though she may drop a few clues to the way she came. She left home, went to Chicago, was married and lost her husband, grieved a long time for him but by then without the solace of her Catholic faith. She had lost that in one tremendous moment of revulsion after reading Schopenhauer, much as Lee Krasner abandoned Orthodox Judaism. In the restlessness she then experienced, Tawney turned tentatively back to thoughts of the arts and enrolled, in 1946, in the Chicago Institute of Design, where a staff of emigré Bauhaus masters had been assembled by Moholy-Nagy. Tawney signed up for the whole course: drawing, painting, sculpture, photography, weaving and woodwork. According to Bauhaus theory, there was no distinction drawn between craft and fine art, none between craftsperson and "artist" and relatively little between male and female. Marli Ehrman taught her the rudiments of weaving, the American abstractionist Emerson Woelffer taught her watercolor painting, and "Moholy taught me to draw, when I thought I could not draw," said Tawney.

EM: "What was his magic formula?"

LT: "He came in and said, 'Now, everybody knows how to write his name.' We agreed. Then he said, 'Write your name up there in the corner of the paper.' And then he told us to *draw* our names. So we all drew our names, with great big lines on big sheets of paper, exactly the way we had signed them.

"The next time he came in, he had a piece of string. He held it up and dropped it, and we were to draw it just as it fell. Those exercises were very freeing to me."

Archipenko, pioneer Modernist sculptor whose influence had permeated American advanced circles since the Armory Show of thirty years earlier, taught drawing and sculpture at the Institute and also ran a summer school in the art colony of Woodstock, New York, to which, one year, he invited Tawney. "He was an earthy vital person, and he worked all the time. We all did. We were working in clay, modeling, making abstract forms. Everybody who was a student of Archipenko's worked the way he did. He wanted you to do that, and that's why eventually I had to leave him. But in the early days I did it his way, and I did one male figure for him and one female. Working all day on one of those sculptures, I had what I think of as my first *ecstatic* experience. It was reaching a state of being where there is nothing but the work.

"The feeling was so intense that when I got back to Chicago I felt I had to make a decision. I realized I couldn't continue working at that level in Chicago. I wanted to have a personal life, an emotional life, even a social life. I wasn't ready to give that up yet. And so, since it seemed to me I couldn't give all my energies to the sculpture, I'd have to renounce it. It had to be all or nothing. If I couldn't give everything to it, I wouldn't be capable of reaching that state again." If saintlike renunciation was called for to be a sculptor, Tawney was not ready. The breaking point came when she was remodeling a house in Chicago into apartments and had to decide whether to fit part of the space out for herself as a studio. Instead, "While the house was all torn up, I had a couple of wonderful parties with a famous jazz pianist. Everyone came and drank a lot. And I destroyed all my sculpture."

EM: "I can't believe that statement!"

LT: "It's true. There was a place where you'd open a door and there were no stairs. That's where I threw my sculpture. I threw it all down in the hole— just down into the cellar. I threw all my clay, everything. Out. I even destroyed the last sculpture I had made, a very strange one. One I couldn't understand. A figure, with a hawk's head—an Egyptian sort of head, with a large beak. I wasn't frightened by it. I just didn't understand. I was far then from knowing that something new can be marvelous. No. I just didn't want to face it."

So again Tawney's life digressed for a while, though she might not see it as a digression. She bought a secondhand loom, a small one, and decided to work "part time." "I thought it was something I could just do while I was living my life. I thought I might be able to get away with that." But she was too good

327

at it: her eyes and hands would not conform to the limitation of nonsuccess. The very first pieces she made—some black-and-white table mats of coarse jute and white horsehair—were chosen for a Museum of Modern Art Good Design show.

She fled (the hounds of heaven?) to Europe and lived there a year and a half, traveling and having her kind of quixotic adventures in France, Spain, North Africa. And then in '54, on the way home by ship, she heard that the famous Finnish weaver Martta Taipale was teaching in North Carolina. So she went down to learn what she could, and there, at last, whatever dark selves had harried her went off to sleep. "It was the beginning of my real weaving."

Tawney learned what Taipale had to teach, especially the use of color, and worked for a while from her cartoons. Then, at a point, she decided to make a piece of her own inspiration. She took some old warp threads she had used in Taipale's studio—"it seemed I had to take that in order to get myself started"—strung them on her own loom, made a quick sketch on a piece of brown paper with a pencil, and proceeded to weave a work called *Saint Francis and the Birds,* letting the colors work themselves out as she went. It was the first step toward letting herself go free, and she feels today in hindsight that in some way the figure referred to her father and certain forgivenesses that were called for before she could go further.

EM: "That was an oddly personal way to feel about a work of weaving. Did you have an inkling at that point that you would want to take the medium into new territories?"

LT: "No, I didn't think like that. I only felt I had got my hands on something I could work with, work with what I had inside me.

"In the end, after six weeks, I had to leave Taipale. She was like Archipenko: she wanted me to weave her designs; but by then I wanted to do my own. My work had to begin to come out of the depths of myself, or it wouldn't be worth doing. I couldn't work for someone else. What good would that do me?

"Soon after I left her, however, I became very sick. I nearly died. When I came out, it was like being newborn. And only a few months after that I did the first piece of what's now called open-warp tapestry."

EM: "How did that one come out?"

LT: "I was planning to do a piece six feet by three feet. I drew a design. But then when I began to weave, I filled in only the part where there was a form, and all around it I left the warp threads open. What happened was that, as I was weaving, the warp began to hang in places looser than the woven part. I thought to myself, It won't be any good. Then I thought, But I don't have to show it to anybody, it's just for myself. And I felt so free! I did as I wanted.

And then when I took it off the loom and threw it on the floor I felt that tiny click near the heart that meant: It was not bad.

"So I learned in that piece that I had freedom to do what I wanted. I didn't have to please anybody but myself."

EM: "What year was that?"

LT: "That was '55."

EM: "And did that piece have a name?"

LT: "It was called *Family Tree*. It was of two trees intertwined, black and white, and in the branches were nests, and some had birds. And I realized, again, it had to do with my childhood, only this time my brothers and sisters."

The real turning point in Tawney's work, however, would come only after these rite-of-passage images had been achieved. For *Family Tree* and other works of this transitional period—*Shorebird, Flowering Tree, Reflections,* etc.—showed novel weaving techniques and subject matter, but in shape and concept they were still relatively conventional. They are essentially paintings in thread. The style of "drawing" was Modernist-expressionistic; the colors were suffusions and heightenings of naturalistic hues—glowing sunsets, sky and foliage, sand and water dwindled to pale tones almost like washes on paper. Possibly a sign of new flights ahead was her occasional use, since *Family Tree,* of feathers woven into the threads.

In November of '57, the call of a professional art milieu in New York became overwhelming. She moved to the city into a loft on Coenties Slip, down by the old cobblestone Fulton Fish Market on the East River, where an artists' colony was gathering. Jack Youngerman was her landlord; Robert Indiana, Ellsworth Kelly and Chryssa were neighbors. Next door lived her close friend the Canadian-born painter Agnes Martin, who was experimenting with a number of Color Field–related modes. In this ambiance of light and weather, flowing river, tugboats, coiled ropes and fishboxes, lives and ideas were mingled and unmingled,[1] and, between 1960 and '62, Tawney's work would take off for far horizons.

She had a large show at the Staten Island Museum in '61, and while it was on the walls—that time of reassessment for many artists—she launched herself into the production of images of a wholly new order. "I began to order a great deal of black and white linen thread. I only knew I wanted to weave forms that would go *up*." By this time she had moved around the block to an even larger loft on South Street. A tall central shaft in the building with a pulley and hoist at the top offered her vertical space three stories high to think about. But apparently, if the forms were to grow so tall they must also acquire contours, break away from the square or rectangular to *become* what her earlier weav-

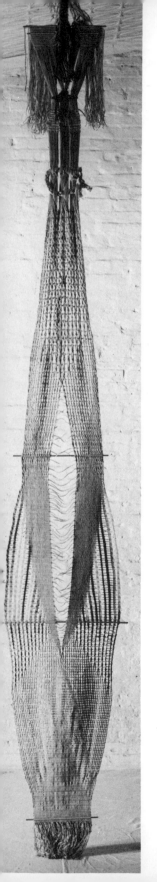

ings had only portrayed: figures. "But you can't weave forms like those on a conventional loom. I had to invent a new kind of reed—the device that holds the warp threads apart. I designed it. And I had it made. And then I set to work.

"The new pieces were *aspiring*. I thought at the time, they'll never be shown. They're too tall. But I kept on doing them. They came off the loom eleven . . . twelve . . . thirteen . . . sixteen feet tall. Then I made one twenty-seven feet tall [*Untaught Equation,* with knots huge as ships' bumpers]. Archipenko would have liked them! They were tall and thin and went up to a thin head, so they showed his influence. I was very sorry he died just before my first show in Manhattan [at the Museum of Contemporary Crafts in 1963]." With Agnes Martin's help, they were named: *The King, The Queen, The Virgin* and *The Bride.* There was the *Mourning Dove* too, and *Waterfall.* They were forms drawn out of themselves into elongated webs, shadows of tall, thin beings, wavering in space.

"They came into being as I did them. I did all that work in six months, working all the time, January until June.

"They just poured out like a fountain or a river. In fact, I did one piece called *Dark River*. And another called *Fountain*. And another *River*. The river was right out my window, and I looked at it every day. During that winter, Agnes Martin and I would talk on the phone, though we hardly ever saw each other. One day she said, 'I'm doing a river.' And I said, 'Oh, I'm doing a river, too!' She was painting a river, and there I was weaving a river. And mine was black."

EM: "I'm fascinated that you could work so spontaneously in a medium that involves as much mechanical setting-up as the loom."

LT: "I'd just put on a length of warp and begin. I had no sketches, nothing. I hadn't any idea what I was going to do when I sat down. But the curious thing was, there was some kind of knowledge here in my center, and in my fingers, of proportions and everything else. Because of course I could only see a bit of the work as I was doing it, no more than a foot or so and then it would roll under. But every time I took a whole finished piece off the loom, the proportions seemed right."

The Queen's Sister, *1962. Linen thread. 13½' high.*

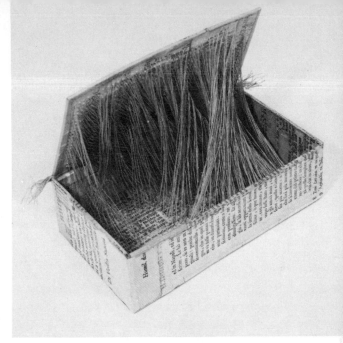

*Thread Box, 1968. Wood, collaged
book pages, thread. 7" by 8½" by 5".*

As her weavings grew larger, Tawney also began to explore the micro-cosm in a series of haunting and elegantly carpentered and furnished boxes, many of them juxtaposing images of birds, birds' feathers and bones (images of things in flight) against treetops, the sky, the whole earth, the cosmos (images of the field of flight). "Later on it occurred to me: here I am picking up these things that otherwise are ground into the earth. No one ever looks at them. But when I put the feathers into a work, they are looked at and they become beautiful. The same with the bones." The theme is, it seems, the one we have so often heard: retrieving what otherwise would be irrevocably lost and fixing it in a form.

In the years since then, Tawney has moved through far fields of inspiration. Her writings reveal a deepening mysticism fed by medieval, Asian, Jungian sources. Some of her latest woven works have returned to the square that now encompasses a circle: rising red suns and moons that seem to permeate or shine through the warp. It is these that bear the mystical titles like *The Waters Above the Firmament* ("The Firmament is the connecting link between time and eternity," wrote the sixteenth-century mystic Jacob Boehme, whom Taw-ney quotes in reference to these works.) Others stretch out rectangular wings like doves or eagles or even the Egyptian hawk Horus (resurrected from the cellar at last?). That impulse to bridge time and space must also be what keeps her sending her friends postcard collages of extraordinary intricacy and sub-stance (bearing tiny pasted-on pebbles, sticks, bones, shells) that wing their way from postbox to postbox like the truth-speaking nightingales of old China.

331

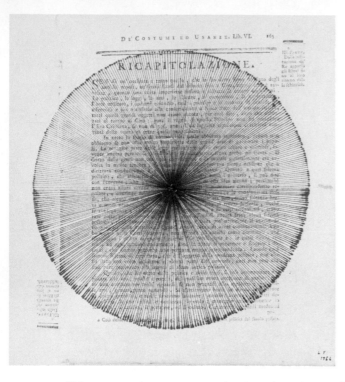

Diamond Sutra, 1966.
Collaged book page with ink drawing.

"My postcards are communications into the void. Thrown to the winds. Things I can't say in words."

After her years of searches and what she once referred to as "cringes," Tawney appears to be mustering herself again now. Important exhibitions in the Brookfield, Connecticut, Craft Center[2] and at the Hadler Gallery in New York in 1978 were milestones; a film on her work by Maryette Charlton has been completed; and she has finished a U.S. government commission for a federal building in Santa Rosa, California, that inspired her to a new scale of three-dimensional thread sculpture. All her life so far, she has paid for moves toward freedom and its concomitant—that ecstasy she spoke of—with counterplummets. One of these took place in a painfully literal way while she was working on the Santa Rosa piece. She broke her arm, as she had done the year before, jumping off a moving train in India. All the same, halfway along on the commission, she sent a hopeful word: "I went out to see the building. I saw great spaces, very high ceilings, a marvelous feeling of openness. Sometime later, I came to the idea of making a *Cloud* for the space. This idea may have developed out of the drought that Northern California and I were suffering at the time.

"I am working on this *Cloud* now. It is thirty by fifteen by five feet.

"It is blue."

332

In the catalogue for her Brookfield show was a picture of one of Tawney's notebook pages with the words "For Boehme, a high deep blue means 'Liberty,' the inner 'Kingdom of Glory' of the reborn soul." *Cloud* was inaugurated in the summer of 1978: two thousand white linen threads that spindle from a blue "sky." They hang down from a height of twenty-five feet to a level some three feet above the head of an observer. Looking up, one is within a tremulous field of gathered light that transmits the least disturbance in the environment but effectively creates a vision of permanent unobstructed upward dimension.

Sylvia Stone

BORN 1928, TORONTO, CANADA

Gradually I had become aware that I was now a so-called professional. That people were expecting things of me. . . . [There were] certain rules of the game. . . . I became depressed with what I seemed to lack. The problem was part technical, part emotional, part rhetorical. . . . I was essentially still working for myself. Still underneath was that old emotional thing of the high.

—SYLVIA STONE
Woodstock, New York, 1977

The trajectory from *there* to *here* for Sylvia Stone has been as single-intentioned as one of the arc-edges in her sculptures: a persistence through space and time. She describes here the world of losses and shifts from which she came. The titles of her works—*Another Place, Crystal Palace, Egyptian Gardens, The Only Entrance*—are titles of tales about that world to which she adds the poignant texts. It is left for us to describe the artifacts.

They are works of orthodox formalist pedigree and so are rightly admired in an era of formalist preoccupation. They come out of Cubism, Constructivism and the Bauhaus, as well as out of the materials-dazzled decade of the '60s when Stone broke through to her own original idiom. Meticulously engineered, the geometric forms out of which they are put together are joined into large, sweeping structures that make fit comments on qualities the material itself possesses: that smoky, light-reflecting, crystal-surfaced Plexiglas sometimes juxtaposed with planes of mirror or metal. Moreover, from an orthodox point of view, these sculptures "work." They lie on the floor "as sculpture should," offering their half-views of forms beyond, within, adjacent as one moves around them. Then various ambiguous messages of recesses and distant angles are received, a faint clear music like the chiming of Chinese bells in a garden.

334

But it seems to me Stone's works find their real depth when they are seen not merely in terms of form or even as literal illustrations of the experiences she relates here, but as poetic epiphanies of those experiences. The artist herself uses, apropos of her work, while apologizing for doing so, the term "glamour" so out of favor today. Yet one might well describe her art by that same phrase of Frank O'Hara's I quoted apropos of Frankenthaler: "an abyss of glamour encroached upon by a flood of innocence." The image is large enough to encompass both artists while not binding them together, for while the painter's works are all gesture, wrist, evanescence, Stone's palaces and gardens are no insubstantial pageant but the very crystallization of longing. From these greenish-gray perspectives, nothing will ever vanish. They are, while permeable, immutable. And the work of both these artists deals on a transparent level with the stuff of memories from both the abyss and the time of innocence, however much each artist might sometimes wish to be seen as merely a master of intellectual themes.

Born in Canada, Stone has been in New York since 1946. Since the early '60s she has exhibited widely, and she was included in the "Two Hundred Years of American Sculpture" exhibition at the Whitney Museum in 1975. Through her experience as a teacher of graduate and undergraduate courses at Brooklyn College and observing students of her husband, Al Held, head of the Yale School of Art and Architecture, she has had a chance to observe the changing patterns of the "professional" art world.

"It all began one night when I was under two. Mother packed us up, my sister eight years older helped dress me, and we ran away in the middle of the night. There had been a great deal of unhappiness in the house. From then on, it was downhill all the way. I only remember utter shabbiness.

"Mother had been brought up in a typical middle-class household in England, run away from her own family, married, come to Canada and had three girls. After she left our father she found herself unable to handle the situation, so for a few years I was sent to various Children's Aid homes and my sisters were separated and sent to farms where extra help was needed. When I was about six, we went back to live with her in a little English-type bungalow covered with roses. We all worked together and made a garden. I loved that house. It was the first time we all were together, and it was a kind of idyll for me. Always after it seemed I'd had that one ideal home, the one with the garden. The first home of my consciousness.

"Then the Depression grabbed us, Mother lost her job and everything went downhill again. She had been formed by a typical pre–World War I finishing-school education to fit her for the group she expected to grow up

335

with. She learned figure skating, tennis, horseback riding, and she had a distinct talent in art, though she never did anything with it. What she was really interested in was the good life. But all of that faded away for her, and we suffered a total decline. We moved and moved, always in the middle of the night, always owing the landlord rent. From one house, I remember, everything went. I remember sitting on a wooden crate and watching it all go out the door. The furniture was disappearing, Mother's china was disappearing, the silverware was disappearing, and what was left was a deep concern about how many meals a day we could have.

"It seems to me now that I reacted to the stress by developing this compulsion: I would draw an ugly house on a piece of paper, and then erase the house line by line and turn it into a beautiful one. I did that over and over. The same with people's faces. Draw, and erase. I think now I was trying to make something beautiful out of what was ugly.

"I was always drawing, not the way other children draw, but with a sense of compulsion. I think that saved my life. When I was about eight, for instance, I collected scraps of paper in an envelope and took it with me everywhere I went. I'd sit on the porch and draw, or sit on the lawn and draw, or sit in the living room and draw. People were always complaining about the mess, but drawing was my way of holding on to a reality. Mother encouraged me and identified with me. She thought perhaps I was the one who would be most like her, and I'm sure I absorbed that idea myself. In fact, in the end, my whole identity seemed to come from being able to draw and paint.

"In school I was always chosen to do special projects. That was what I was happiest doing. There was a program for talented kids in Toronto. One or two grade-school students were picked each year for special classes, and I was the one chosen all the way through. And then I went on to a high school that was rather like the High School of Music and Art in New York today, and that was where I found myself. The day I went to register and saw the drawings of the students on the walls, I thought it was the turning point of my life.

"One of the reasons that school was so important to me was the mix of students. There were talented musicians, talented painters, very bright kids with ethnic backgrounds different from mine. My own background was strongly Scots-English. I hadn't known a single 'foreign child' in my life. Even someone who was Irish was considered just a little exotic. But at that school I met every ethnic variety, and I loved it. I was going through an anti-English rebellion then anyway; I would tell any lie rather than be taken for English, and in the end I didn't want to have anything to do with anyone except the kids in that school. By then, my mother had left for the West Coast and my sisters were married, so I was living pretty much on my own. Mother sent me rent

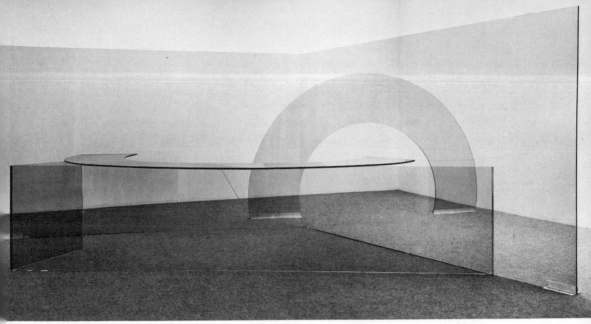

Crystal Palace, 1971–72. Plexiglas. 76½" by 18'6" by 11'8". Collection the artist.

money and I earned what else I needed by working after school at Woolworth's. I could get Charity Case allowance for books and art supplies, and I tried it one term, but I was so humiliated at having to present the vouchers and stand in line that I determined not to do it again. But those years at Central Tech changed my life. Here was a confirmation of my ability. There was an incredible amount of talent, many students on their way to becoming professional, and supportive teachers.

"There was a Mr. Goldhammer, for one, who taught lettering. I remember so vividly his dry subject and how I loved placing the letters—really a nervous, muscular thing. Today when I'm working in my studio I sometimes remember what a thrill it gave me just to work with those letters, moving them an inch one way or another, and the feeling that came over me when they were right. I call it magic. Or even ecstasy. When you say, 'That's it,' and you feel so *high*.

"There was another teacher, a woman, Marie MacCarthy, who said to me—I loved the way she said it—'Sylvia, you are going to have to make *your decision* earlier than the other girls.' She meant that I was precocious sexually too. And that was wonderful as well. Here was an artist and a woman understanding one of the basic problems of a creative woman.

"Then, when I was sixteen, there was no more support from the family. I had to go to work. That was a tragedy for me. I took various jobs, beginning by working in a war plant on the night shift so I could go back to school in the days. I couldn't always make it, but the teachers welcomed me no matter when I turned up, and allowed me to go into the classes and draw or paint as I

337

wished. One of the main helps in my life, in fact, was the teachers' seeing not only my problems but also what they considered my talents. And they weren't just educators, they were professional painters and sculptors; for them, it was the work that counted, and their value for me came from that.

"Eventually I landed a job doing display. It wasn't traditionally a woman's field, but it was wartime and there was a labor drain. I loved that work. I loved being surrounded by other artists. And I had a marvelous boss. And also I was a little bit of a crazy kid at the time: I had dreams of going to New York and studying and then going to Paris. Well, I never did get to Paris, but when I told my boss what I wanted to do he said he would sign the necessary emigration papers for me and back me up. So when the war ended and I was seventeen, I left Toronto with twenty-five dollars in my pocket for New York. At the border, I had to pay a head tax, and that left me twelve dollars.

"The first couple of years in New York were very difficult. Sometimes I've wanted to write about them, because it was so tough and I was so unprepared for that kind of struggle. I couldn't ask anyone even for money to go home."

EM: "Were you painting and drawing then?"

SS: "I tried to go to the Art Students League at night. Then for a while I even switched to working at night, taking photographs in a nightclub, so that I could spend days at the League, but I was scared to death in that kind of atmosphere and it didn't last very long. Also, it was hard getting into the League because many GI's were enrolled in those days and they had preference over others in the classes. So I would sneak in and out of the studios, listen to the criticisms and try to apply them to my own work. At a point, I talked my way into an excellent job and for a couple of years gave up thoughts of art altogether, but inside I experienced that tremendous longing.

"Then I married. I think I did so to find a family. I wanted that desperately. Inside of three weeks I was pregnant, and from that time on I became very bound up trying to make that marriage last because I didn't want to repeat the experiences of my own childhood. But within a year I was back at the League again, with much disapproval from my husband's family, studying again, feeling I had lost my way, that this was where I belonged. I was still young then, only twenty-two, but I had a child, and so I couldn't attend classes full time. I had to work at home on my own and bring my paintings in for crits. That was the best thing that could have happened to me, because there wasn't anyone to hold my hand or to help me develop. I learned to paint alone, and I also learned to submit to the criticism. I would receive one whopping crit a week and often it was a tough one, but at least it was clear and simple."

EM: "How did the work go during those years? It was still the late '40s. The scene was confused. Various idioms conflicting."

SS: "I studied with the Social Realist painter Harry Sternberg and got involved with his ideas. Then I lost interest in that. I began wandering into other classes and became aware of good abstract painting.

"In the end, I left Sternberg and went into Morris Kantor's class, and Vyclav Vytlacil's. He took an instant dislike to me. He rolled me over good, in loud tones. He said I painted a surface like linoleum. I came back for more. I took it and got better and better. He made me deal with ideas. He wasn't concerned with how good the painting was in terms of surface or articulation of form; he was concerned with the idea behind the work. The finesse would come later. He would give me a crit that made me feel I could paint for a month, because it was so concerned with ideas.

"At that point I knew that painting was the passion of my life, and I was ready to give up everything for it. My husband knew that. He found he couldn't tolerate living with a woman whose attention was divided, and so the marriage was terminated in spite of my fear that I was leading my children into the very life I'd experienced myself."

"At that point I set about to educate myself. I laid out a reading program. I even wrote a fan letter to Saul Bellow—I'd just read *Augie March*—and asked if he could recommend books. He wrote back giving me a nineteenth-century reading program. Read everything, he said, read Dostoyevsky, read Tolstoy, and don't read only what they've written, read everything you can find about them. So I did that, and it pushed me along the road. I began tussling with ideas and also with my identity. At one point I was reading David Riesman, and I came on the phrase 'minority groups like women and blacks.' It was the first time I'd

Shifting Greys, 1976–77. Gray Plexiglas and aluminum. 4' by 15'6" by 16'. Collection the artist.

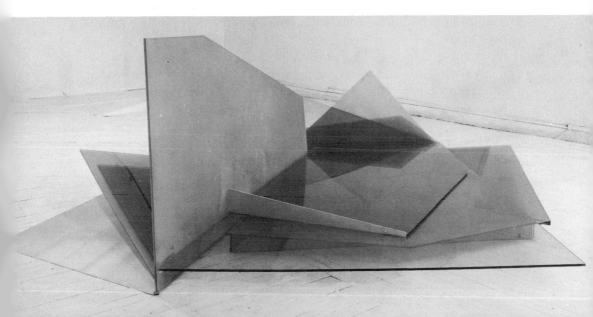

thought of women in that light. That was long before the Women's Movement, but I can still remember the shock and then the flash of recognition."

EM: "There was a decade of experiment in the '50s, I know, and then in the '60s you found your original idiom. How did you get to that point?"

SS: "I'd gone from figurative to abstract landscape and then Hard-Edge painting. I moved with the masses, and showed in a number of group exhibitions in New York. And then, in the '60s, the line began to dissolve between what was painting and what was sculpture. The attitude was, anything goes. Sculpture didn't have to be what Brancusi thought, or Henry Moore or David Smith thought. So a lot of us got into materials. You have an idea, and if it doesn't work in one medium you turn to another. It's on the wall, it's off the wall, it's hanging from the ceiling. It could be anything. Eva Hesse, for instance, began as a painter as I did. I knew her, and, like her, I was a product of the time, a hybrid; and there were many more.

"I became interested in stretched, shaped canvases, but I didn't want to send out for the prepared stretchers. So a friend taught me how to paint on Plexiglas. That material gave me everything the '60s were about: Hard-Edge finish, glossiness and intensified color because light passing through the edges of the Plexiglas enhances its intensity. You put color on a canvas, it sinks in. But the hard industrial surface that Plexiglas has and its easy cuttability were the most important things for me.

"At least I thought it was easy cuttability. Other artists, however, used it for a while and then abandoned it for technical reasons. I wasn't into the technical, physical side of dealing with it then. I simply borrowed a jigsaw from Alex Katz and began to cut it. And immediately the paintings—they were still paintings—with their cutouts became organically big and impressive. Some were twelve or fourteen feet wide and eight feet high. They were complicated to put together, and at the time I was naïve about how to do it. So I went to Robert Kulicke, who has been helpful to artists, and he showed me how to laminate the pieces, first onto rag paper and then onto Masonite. So the paintings went on getting very big and brilliant in color, with contradictory, illusionistic forms that twisted and turned. I had a show of them in March of '67 at the Tibor de Nagy Gallery, and the critic James Mellow put the work down then as hideous and bandwagony.

"Usually, I make a reassessment after a show. That time I discarded paint color. I went to a Plexiglas factory and looked over all the different transparencies available. I found I liked the bronzes and grays and particularly a green I've used ever since, that most people mistake for glass.

"And when I became interested in transparency, it was natural that the pieces should come down off the wall so that you could look through them.

Then the question was, how to energize the surfaces and also still keep that transparency? I cut out the forms and also introduced internal drawings with black acrylic paint, just enough to be visible within. Hence, the contradictory forms—the cutouts and the drawn forms—had to coexist. And, you know, it worked! Yay!

"And then, for the first time, I got some recognition. The scale had gone up right away, and I was learning to build, trying to make pieces that would stand by themselves. I fumbled along at first, learning to be a craftsperson. I'd hire someone to work along with me to teach me the techniques. Eventually I mastered them. It's funny, because I'd hated math as a kid, but now I have all these technical books, and I do joints and angles and so on. I had never expected to do that."

"Just about then, I fell into an almost incredible depression. Gradually I had become aware that I was now a so-called professional. That people were expecting things of me. There was pressure to produce, to get new pieces out to museums. And at the same time I was becoming aware of certain rules of the game. What you have to do, what you shouldn't do. I became depressed with what I seemed to lack. The problem was part technical, part emotional, and, I think, part rhetorical.

"To be a professional, for instance, you have to be prepared to install your work. I remember a piece for a major museum show that had to be cantilevered and suspended from the ceiling below a scrim to hide the apparatus that held it. I wanted no nuts or bolts to be visible. My wish for a feeling of magic. I had installed the piece in a crude way in my studio, but I had no idea how it should be done in the museum. The staff took over and did it for me, but later the director advised me to take a lesson from a certain other artist because he knew how to put up his work and take it down. I answered that that was true, but the other artist was doing the same piece over and over, while for me each work was different and required a different solution. But still I realized I was just muddling along, dealing with the problems as they came up, essentially still working for myself. Still underneath was that old emotional thing of the *high.*"

EM: "Say some more about professionalism. We know it's the premise and goal of most university graduate art departments nowadays."

SS: "The idea is you aren't supposed to get your graduate degree until you can define yourself in words. Explain what your work is about. The principle is that you are going to teach and make a living from your art, so you have to have a *rap,* be a mature artist by the time you graduate. That seems impossible when you consider that the average graduate student is no more than twenty-four.

"I got through in another way myself. Only a few people took me seriously for a long time, but I'm one of the survivors who managed it differently. In the old days Ad Reinhardt taught at Brooklyn College, and I replaced him in some classes when he was ill. He told me there were only two choices: join the system or teach. If you teach, you'll be an academic, he said, but your soul will be your own. He was right, right for then and right for now. The department at Brooklyn had faith in me. They recognized my art and my teaching ability. They appointed me an assistant professor before women's lib. Recently they made me a full professor in spite of no university credits and no rap.

"In fact, I once wrote that I've been helped along by men in my career as well as women. I was criticized by the Women's Movement for saying that, but I had to say it. Helped by the teachers back in Toronto who saw there was something with this dizzy kid who wanted to be something and possibly could; by my boss there who signed his name for me; by my teachers when I was a down-and-out kid with no aunts or uncles, only a split-up alienated family. And at Brooklyn by faculty that chose me on my merit, so that eventually I got ahead not because of degrees I'd earned but by what I'd accomplished as an artist.

"I've been at Brooklyn thirteen years now and my husband teaches at Yale, and I'm amazed to see the degree of professionalism in our students today. They might as well be carrying briefcases and be studying law. When they graduate, they have their transparencies in hand and plan on having their first show in a couple of years. In the '50s, an artist was fortunate to have a show in ten years. Showing was one of those marvelous things that might happen. But the basic drive was to make art and exchange ideas with friends.

"I often wonder, really, what it is that makes a painter. I think of all the students I saw at the League, the ones doing the flashiest paintings, the ones most admired. Where are they today? I don't see their work. I don't hear their names. So it can't be just talent alone that makes a painter survive. There has to be a tremendous need, a need that has to override everything else you want to do, everything you think you ought to do. One has not to be able to live without it. I wonder whether that need exists on the part of all these professionals."

EM: "What about the difference between men's and women's experiences in the arts these days?"

SS: "The greatest change I've seen since I've been an artist has been just this new professional attitude on the part of women. Growing up in the past, women were taught not to compete. Now they have been taught to do so. Women are coming along now with the idea that work can be the center of their lives, not peripheral to marriage. Much of this has come about because of the eradication of middle-class guilt after the war, the end of programming girls to go back into housework. I remember the deep guilt I felt when I was married and had small children and also wanted to work at the League. Now women have an assurance that they're entering a going profession. Since their youth, the art world has been expanding, prices going up, museums being built. That world isn't private anymore but careeristic. Big business. And the quota system in the galleries has about vanished. I can remember when you counted the women on a gallery's roster and if there were three you didn't apply, because that was the quota.

"It's taken me a long time to come to terms with this new world, and probably I never will fully. Not because I'm 'pure maiden' about it, but because the impulse behind my art has always been personal. I never expected to make a living with my art. And if you don't expect your work to become public, you never feel the pressure to build a rhetorical foundation for what you make."

EM: "There's an introspective character to your work that does go counter to what some of the high-powered male steel and cement workers of this day are doing. Has that hurt you?"

SS: "I know the plastic pieces look almost as if they'd floated in through

the door. They look delicate. That scares some people. Steel sculpture looks bolted together, and it is. The joints are naked. Because the structure and the bolts aren't apparent in my work, some people think it's not formed.

"But beyond that, my work is, you can imagine, very expensive to make, and that makes me think sometimes about giving up the material. It gets more costly every year. It's heavy to handle. Hard to take care of. Hard to ship. Or at least hard for me. But it continues to fascinate me, and I find new ways to use it. So I make the works and later cannibalize them to make new ones. It doesn't matter. Years later, I find I've gone back to the same motifs."

EM: "What are the motifs? And what is the drive?"

SS: "For me it was always that impulse from childhood. It had to do with fantasy, with what made me paint and draw so long ago. The material itself is a fantasy material, as well as being an industrial one. I've taken it and made excursions, seductive ones, into it. The best of the works are not only luxurious but also contemplative. Think of the titles. *Another Place:* another place to *be,* I was thinking when I made it. *Crystal Palace. The Only Entrance.* They are all house names. Environmental names. Places to enter into.

"I'm much the same way about the places where I live. When I move into a place, immediately I make a spot for myself. Just the opposite of that old house of my childhood: *in* comes the bed, in come the pictures, the chairs, the music. It becomes a comfortable place, apart from the studio. A refuge. In the studio, by contrast, I work like a factory worker. The place is run like a factory. My hair is short because of the dust. I use routers and saws. I wear work clothes, blue jeans, a face shield, goggles. But then when I get home I like to be someone else. It goes back to the idea of making a glamorous atmosphere.

"There are people who are suspicious of the idea of 'glamour.' But I think of that quality as poetic, shifting light, a metaphoric synthesis of many layers of experience, very much what, actually, my art is about. In fact, it may be that the works present themselves rather as I do—as being less than what they are. But inside, there is an intellectual rigor. The lines and edges are clearly visible from all sides, and their disposition is worked out according to a strict formal esthetic. To support an arc, for example, I might use a triangle, and that form would then echo a triangle somewhere else in the piece. It's all thought out and measured within a sixteenth of an inch. The piece may seem to be only surface. But underneath, it embodies an intelligence. Still, that I don't talk about my works exclusively in intellectual terms offends some people. I prefer to talk about how I came to make them . . . how I started as a painter . . . and how my mind moved."

Beverly Pepper

BORN 1924, NEW YORK CITY

I often think that all I want to do now is to avoid suicide, accidental or otherwise. Other than that, I think living on the edge is what drives my work and me beyond a certain point. The artist lives with anxiety. When you finally reach a plateau of achievement, there comes a new anxiety—the hunger to push on still further. That Angst *is what makes you go forward.*

—BEVERLY PEPPER
Todi, Italy, 1977

Pepper works in steel—cutting it, welding, rewelding. Concrete is a new material for her, one she likes for its paradoxical look of antiquity. Making, remaking, and setting the finished work into a space-time span determines her rhythm, and always has done so. She did that in another way in her youth, taking apart and remaking an important career that had lost meaning for her.

She took some years finding herself as a sculptor. Then a serendipitous meeting with some cut-down trees provoked her to begin to carve. From wood she moved to steel and found that it was her real medium. Finally, in the art boom of the '60s, she came into prominence making open, ribbonlike steel sculptures to be seen on pedestals against the sky. Later she made big, rough-edged or polished stainless box sculptures reflecting the shifting colors and shapes of landscape.

By the '70s she was turning out enormous architectural projects, jutting, angular steel constructions like *Sudden Presence,* for the city of Boston. At the same time, she began to design site pieces and concrete and steel environments like one for the AT&T Building in Bedminster, New Jersey, that seats a thousand people. Her esthetic roots as a steelworker are with Constructivism: Gonzales and Picasso, the Bauhaus and David Smith. But now more and more when she follows her own inclination she has been devising fantastical plans for the future. Some are extraordinary combinations of metal, concrete and nature; a necropolis atop the dormant crater of Mount Vesuvius for the city of Naples; sculptures for highway shoulders; sculptures to be set in sand and sculptures to change with the seasons. She even projects sculptures transformed by the wind, or by the overhead flight of airplanes, or to be seen through lenses and prisms.

In a way, all this widening of a vision is a response to what she knew as a child. When I asked her about her feeling for landscape, she said, "It's because of my Brooklyn childhood. You have another conception of sky in Brooklyn. You can be unaware for years that you never see it. The first time I saw sky unbroken by buildings I turned my head from side to side, to see it all around me. I had a feeling of absolute, incredible, extraordinary luxury."

EM: "Tell me about your family, who they were, what they did."

BP: "I was brought up in a world of freethinking women. My paternal grandmother left Russia with her hair bobbed, at seventeen. She was a Menshevik. My mother, like her, was an activist. She was committed to Roosevelt and the NAACP. She gave me a sense of commitment that became part of what I think of as professionalism: pride in what one does. My father was in the fur business and traveled when I was young, so I have few memories of him.

"Though all my grandparents were Russian, my mother's parents were unlike the others—religious, gentle, well-read. That grandmother kept rose gardens and made rose jelly. In front of their house in Brooklyn was a cast-iron horse used for hitching horses; one of my earliest memories is of that iron post. I also have two cast-bronze plaques of heads of Washington and Lincoln made by my paternal grandfather. Long after he died, I learned he had worked at a jeweler's trade. So he was my artistic heritage. I wish I'd known him better, because for a long time I felt hopelessly lost in a cultureless world. I was eighteen when I first walked into a museum. At the time, I felt angry and cheated. God, how much time I'd lost! But in another way it was a positive experience, because then the discovery was fresh and exciting.

"But I was always the artist. I can't remember not drawing, going to Saturday art classes, winning prizes. I was a crazy *Wunderkind,* decorating other people's rooms when I was ten, twelve, fourteen; doing my brother's and sister's art homework and geography maps. When their teachers finally got me as a student they wouldn't believe I was doing my own work. I have a painful memory of one art teacher who wouldn't accept my work as my own. In fact, I wasn't allowed to major in art in high school. It seems to me my whole history is one of having to fight to be allowed to become an artist."

EM: "How about after school?"

BP: "I wasn't quite sixteen when I went to Pratt Institute. I immediately became interested in industrial design. I loved that more than anything I'd ever done. I made my first sculptures, worked with plaster, really became involved with manual work. But, after a while, they refused to allow me to go on. They said I used the tools incorrectly. It was too dangerous. I might hurt myself. Lose a finger or even a hand. Yet today almost everything I do requires my using heavy machinery.

"In the end I studied advertising art. I was so behind that I worked doubly hard those years. I hardly slept except during Christmas and on weekends. I even went to Brooklyn College at night to take a course with the Bauhaus designer Georgy Kepes because I felt I wasn't learning enough at Pratt. In fact, however, Pratt was a good training ground for what came afterward, Site Works, photography, Conceptual pieces—even marriage. I married one of my classmates for a brief time."

EM: "How was the real world, when you found yourself part of it?"

BP: "When you're preparing to be part of a superstructure in American society like the advertising business, you learn to exploit your talents to the extreme. You think on your feet all day. It's a world of ideas, and I was good at it. I was also young and innovative. I did a lot of inventing in those days, from a tube cap for squeezing mayonnaise out in flutes to converting packages into toys. That was when I discovered that my grandfather too had invented things and patented them. And today I continue to invent and modify my own equipment.

"Then all this world collapsed when I was twenty-one. I began to show signs of a nervous breakdown. I'd try to open the doors of moving taxis to get out, mix up the food and my hat—put the hat in the refrigerator and the food in the closet. In deep trouble, I went into analysis. At the same time, I began going to the Art Students League at night. I had friends who were painters, and I gradually became involved. I was doing abstract painting in a Gorky-like mode then, though I didn't even know Gorky's work. It was 1946 and I was far from being in the mainstream of art. Yet it was plain to me I didn't want to be in advertising. So I left business, and in '48 I went to Paris."

EM: "How was life there just postwar?"

BP: "I went by ship, tourist class, because I wanted to feel like an art student; I was trying to live up to my fantasy of an artist. In Paris, I worked with the painters André L'Hôte and Léger—and also the Cubist sculptor Zadkine. Actually I didn't study with Zadkine, but his class was down the hall and I would go and stand and watch. I knew while I was watching that I wanted to be a sculptor. I had known it back at Pratt when they took the tools away from me. I knew then I wanted to work three-dimensionally. One of the reasons I love to cook nowadays is because you use your hands so much. Also, I discovered I could learn almost any craft by watching, that I had an instinct for engineering.

"Yet it was a frightening period. I had a sense of my abysmal ignorance and an awareness of what I had to learn. In a way I was a freer artist when I got to Europe than just afterward. Those first years nearly overwhelmed me. I needed to travel. I wanted to be understood. I wanted a knowledge of art history. Léger was a great help in all this. He gave me a sense of *how* to approach work."

EM: "How?"

BP: "If you're as ignorant as I was when I arrived in Paris, you accept the cliché about what an artist is: someone who meanders, who lives day by day waiting for inspiration. From Léger, L'Hôte and Zadkine I learned that making art is work. It was the beginning of a belligerent commitment. For instance, now I go to my studio every day. Some days the work comes easily. Other days nothing happens. Yet on the good days the inspiration is only an accumulation of all the other days, the nonproductive ones.

"Eventually I left Paris, and outside the city I gradually began seeing the poverty and social devastation throughout Europe. As a result, my commitment to the world around me began to strike me as shameful and irresponsible. My political mother!

"So I abandoned abstract art and began to do figurative work with social overtones 'for the people.' About that time I met Bill Pepper, and we were married in October 1949. I had twenty years' education in our first years together. We went to every museum, studied all of art history. My hunger was extraordinary. Bill had been an art-history major and that helped, of course, but the formation also involved some deformation too, because it was coming from a literary person. Eventually I had to empty my mind to become my own self."

EM: "Why don't you talk about that?"

BP: "Bill introduced me to the Renaissance, to the Sienese painter Duccio. Bill took me through the Uffizi. Bill was with me everywhere. Through him, I became involved with the literal content of the art. It took me many years to rid myself of that concern. Until one day I finally turned to him and said, 'I don't care who's cutting whose head off, I'm interested in the form—and shapes.' "

EM: "And the next step?"

BP: "Rome in the '50s was a learning period, a rehearsal. My two children were young. I was painting, and had some shows, and accumulated some reviews and sales. Yet I was dissatisfied. I think now my commitment to painting was a way of finding out about myself: a way of reaching a part of myself that I could accept—and then move on.

"In 1960 we traveled through the Far East—Japan, India and finally Cambodia. I visited the temples of Angkor. That trip had two effects on me. First, I saw appalling poverty. Then the thought that the caste system—a twelfth-century political invention designed to allow one group to control another by labeling it 'untouchable'—should still be in effect after eight centuries repelled me so violently that, somehow, I was released from the idea that I could save the world through art.

"When I got back to Rome, I found I was no longer interested in content or Social Realism. I stopped doing anything literary. Content as such didn't exist for me. I was obsessed by my memories of Angkor and the banyan trees growing over the stone statues, and suddenly I became recommitted to my first love—sculpture. From that moment, my emotional and intellectual drive was to that alone—to sculpt.

"Then there was a fortunate happening. Near our house a large number of elm trees had been felled. There were thirty-six tree trunks lying in the field before my eyes, waiting for me to set free whatever was locked inside them. The divine accident!"

EM: "That was the point when you were invited to show at the Italian Festival of Spoleto."

BP: "Again, an enormous piece of luck. I had finished quite a lot of work in those two years. When Giovanni Carrondente, organizer of the sculpture section of the festival, asked if I knew how to weld, I didn't say yes and I didn't say no. I asked why. He said David Smith and Calder were going to be there, and he would like to have another American welder, preferably a woman. The show was to be in April. It was then September. Yes, I said, I could weld. And immediately I went out and apprenticed myself to the nearest ironmonger.

"The Spoleto sculptors were invited to make their work in factories in various Italian cities. I was sent to Piombino, a Communist area where they thought a woman would be treated with more respect than, say, Naples. Piombino freed me in several ways. First, my family got used to my disappearing for long periods. They could come up weekends, or I could go home."

EM: "And you made enough welded-steel sculpture in six weeks to make a strong showing in Spoleto."

BP: "By working about ten hours a day. After Spoleto I stopped working in wood, clay, wax or any molded medium. I began working directly in metal."

EM: "You've said you 'joined the art world' at that point, that you were 'born in the '60s.' What changed your thinking then? You became a friend of

David Smith's through the Spoleto experience. Was he an influence?"

BP: "For the first time, I began meeting major artists as an equal. Until Spoleto, I'd never really talked about art. Then I met Chadwick, Calder and others. But most of all David Smith. It was amazing to find him confirming many of the things I had been thinking about. How much courage it took to go beyond the image one has lived with, to move on to the next concept. That the work is never finished, is always in transition, complete on its own but still part of another 'work-to-come.' Seeing what I'd been doing was one thing, but understanding it was something else. It was a great comfort to learn that other artists also have moments of paranoia.

"I realized also that the artist is always alone. Early in life I had thought I needed other people to confirm or approve what I was doing. I read criticism about my work as if it were a corrected class paper, expecting to learn what to keep and what to reject. You think, if you start from such ignorance as I had, that you are inadequate. It was important for me to learn that what I wanted was really no different from what other artists wanted: confidence that I could be my own censor, my own audience, my own competition.

"Failures too are important to an artist. Something to study. I had always felt I could create something beyond what I'd done to that point. In talking with David and others, I learned I wasn't alone either in my loneliness or in that sense I had of lagging behind my potential.

"In the end, I feel that one has to have a bit of neurosis to go on being an artist. A balanced human seldom produces art. It's that imbalance which impels us. I often think that all I want to do now is to avoid suicide, accidental or otherwise. Other than that, I think living on the edge is what drives my work and me beyond a certain point. The artist lives with anxiety. When you finally reach a plateau of achievement, there comes a new anxiety—the hunger to push on still further. That *Angst* is what makes you go forward."

EM: "How did you go forward?"

BP: "My next step was to find a gallery. Marlborough Gallery was forming in those days. I joined them, and the first years were fruitful. The gallery was growing. Not yet crassly exploitative.

"It was also a time of increased work in factories. I learned all about steel techniques, working with all types of metal, how to control every phase of work. Even today, when I'm dealing with large-scale monumental pieces I'm always there in person to intervene."

EM: "What about those pieces of the mid-'60s—those boxes of Cor-Ten or stainless-steel slabs, painted red inside and gashed so that drops of the melted steel hang there like teeth? They seem extraordinarily violent, or at least expressionistic, to me."

350

BP: "I wanted to humanize the steel. Instead of the mechanical cuts one usually gets with a shears or a guillotine cutter, I wanted to show the guts of the steel. I'm still involved with that idea today.

"I was working then at a U.S. Steel subsidiary in Newark, New Jersey, where there was sophisticated equipment. There I found out you could actually cut steel with carbon rods. Pure heat. That allowed me to manipulate the steel as easily as clay. The excitement was sensual. The technique was truly one of those divine accidents: suddenly learning you could cut two-inch stainless with huge shears."

EM: "What about the new work—the environmental pieces of the '70s? At Dartmouth, in New Hampshire, and Bedminster, New Jersey, for example?"

BP: "The site sculptures? They started in Dallas: a combination of landscape and time. So in a sense they still show the effects of my memory of Angkor. You walk in them. You drive around them. You sit on them. And still, if you can get far enough away, the work has an independent existence.

"The *Amphisculpture* in Bedminster can hold a thousand people, but it's not depersonalizing. The ground cover running in and out of it, completing the

Amphisculpture *(and detail), 1974–77. Poured concrete and ground cover. 200' diameter, plus 70' extension; 14' deep; 8' aboveground. American Telephone & Telegraph, Bedminster, New Jersey.*

forms, relates man to nature, like the trees that grow over the stones at Angkor.

"The Dartmouth sculpture has to do with the seasons. It's painted white because of the light in New England and because there's snow much of the year. But one hundred feet of it is below ground level, and at times the work disappears into the snow. In the winter it becomes white. Then, as the snow recedes, it becomes brown and white, then green and white. Eventually the full summer sculpture is visible with the ground in and around it. So time literally affects its form and color.

"For the Bedminster work, I used porous concrete. I like the effect of time on that material. It's like the Giotto frescoes at Assisi. I love those because they have a look of antiquity. There's something about the visible expression of the passage of time that I find moving. When you go to these monuments of the past, you have a sense of past, present and future coming together.

"I'm not interested in the negative aspects of the current scene: works of art that are monuments to destruction, that make use of explosions, that disintegrate. I believe in permanence, and what I'm trying to do in my work is to communicate my sense of that permanence. That's my responsibility: expressing confidence that there will be a future. When you sit in the Colosseum, you feel the past, and therefore you have a sense of continuum into the future. I cannot accept dire predictions. My mind conceives of a continuity. If the prophets of gloom prove right, I say we will see only changes. Not an end."

EM: "Do you think environmental sculpture, where work and nature intermingle, can be interpreted as a metaphoric attempt to hold on to the ground? To make time stop? History stay where it is?"

BP: "No. There is no stopping. There's merely the illusion that gives us time to catch our breath before plunging in again. We need this hiatus, however, to consider where we're going. We're living in a time when buildings no longer have the same modular relationship to the human being. Everything is outsized. We have no heroes, no monuments to heroes, and yet we are involved with monumental scale. A man goes to the moon. The moon is visible on TV. Everything seems possible. The old, conscious relationship between man's scale and his environment has been broken. But now we find new ways of expressing those relationships. My kind of sculpture has to do with that kind of continuity.

"What I am concerned with is working out a passage from one place, or one situation, to another. Final, ultimate questions don't interest me. It's like that old song, 'The bear went over the mountain . . . He saw another mountain.' I think final answers only suggest further questions. And one finished work is just a link to the next."

352

EM: "How about the present work? These new naked-rib structures that lean in different directions with a sense of accumulating movement?"

BP: "I'd been wanting to strip down what I was doing. To go beyond what I'd accomplished before. To take the internal areas of my movable sculptures— as opposed to the Site Works—and make them visible. To expose all the ribbing, the gussets and the welds by stripping off the skin.

"The essential remains. The emphasis on precarious falling, slipping in time, rising up (depending on how these works are viewed). In a way they refer back to the earlier ones. The difference is that now I don't want to hide my working methods, the craftsmanship. I come from a world where the artist was considered a product of tradition. As such, we worked *from* and *for* something; we were from somewhere and our works reflected our search. It was part of accumulated experience. That same vocabulary supports my work today."

EM: "Would you say something about the life of a female artist, and your own life in particular?"

BP: "Being a woman is important for me. But being an artist is more important. Any ghetto is an anathema, and counterproductive for the artist. I

The artist with works in progress, 1977. Welded steel.

support the battle for women's rights on most fronts. Yet I feel that the war is against the kind of discriminatory society we live in. My position is, I feel, a more global one.

"I come out of the time that formed me. During World War II, women were called on to replace men in management jobs, not just menial ones. After the war ended, Rosie the Riveter could be replaced, but women in authority were not easily disposed of. They were making money for the firm. True, they were probably paid less, but they were treated with a freedom and an equality that had no precedents. In my experience, many women of that war generation would not agree to taking secondary positions, to do menial household tasks not shared by our men. Nor did we question our new rights. They were ours.

"Even when the men came back, we held on to our independence. Many of us were fiercely political. We read Lenin on the women's question, we agreed with the idea of women's equality. But we didn't have to be Feminists to be radical, or to be able to recognize barriers against women.

"I've been very lucky. I never felt the need to work for a gender-free society. I like the difference between men and women, and I think that generally what's happened to women is that we've been set free by technology to go beyond the limits of our personal strength (as have men, for that matter). And we're taking advantage of that.

"Yet I've had my problems as a woman on the job. I've had to work twice as hard to get the riggers to follow my instructions, to gain my co-workers' respect, to stare down the insinuations. I even joined the boilermakers' union. At one time I was the only sister among the brothers!

"On the other hand, I've been privileged. I'm married to an unthreatened husband, with two supportive children. I had the satisfaction of painting maternal pictures when my children were young, satisfying a most genuine maternal need.

"Yet that doesn't mean I want to be a *woman* artist. The real privilege is to have been born an artist."

Betye
Saar

BORN 1926, LOS ANGELES

There was energy locked away in me, from anger, from sadness or just from doors being closed. . . . I was still, in a way, locked into that child who was six when her father died . . . that little girl was also a very imaginative and creative being . . .

—BETYE SAAR
Los Angeles, 1977

Betye Saar's work pays the most literal witness to the point I am arguing: that the artist moves in a circle to reclaim the past. The subject matter of her collages, assembled boxes and sculptures is taken directly from her life and her family's: days of old, relatives here and gone, the larger family of her race. The very mediums she works in—fragmentary, dispersible, tenuously held in a structure—can be seen as a metaphor for life interrupted by death and revived by the imagination.

Saar is a small, trim, curly-haired woman with a quick optimistic manner that must conceal a great power of concentration and also the memory of struggle. She works in a house halfway up a cliff in Hollywood, in her piled-up kitchen with children and cats underfoot, and she stores her three-dimensional and ritualistic rattan *Spirit Catchers* and *Altars* in a tiny adjoining room. "These have power," she explains. "I can't just turn them out quickly. They have to wait to be made."

New works in progress cover the walls. Rows of drawers hold material for future ones. This abundance and order is as she wants it. "Three years ago, I decided never again to do anything I didn't want to do. You have to live that way or it kills a part of you." And indeed, Saar's last decade of hard work has brought her considerable success. Her first show in California was in '65. In

1970, the Whitney Museum took one of her pieces for its Annual, and in '75 she was given a one-person show there.

Saar was born in the Los Angeles of another era, as Krasner, E de K, Pepper and others were born in another Brooklyn. She grew up in nearby Pasadena, but the place that stands out in her memory is Watts in the days when it too was country. It was there that her life as a noticer of things around her, a picker-upper and so an artist, began.

"It all began when I was a child, here in California. My mother and father would go on holiday, and I would spend that time with my grandmother in Watts. It was rural then, back in the early '30s: very country. I'd go out in the back yard and find bits of glass and stones in the dirt. Sometimes we'd go to the beach and I'd collect little shells and even bits of dirt. My grandmother didn't have a car and she lived half a block from a railroad track. Once a week, we'd walk down that track to Watts, to do the shopping, and I'd be picking up objects all the way. Then we'd pass the famous Watts towers. Simon Rhodia, who built them from scratch, would always be out there hard at work. I was fascinated. The place was magical and strange and curious. But it wasn't until I was grown and took my own children to see them that I spied bits of crockery and tiles and glass and all the other things he set into the concrete that had originally caught my eye.

"Then it happened that my father died. I was six then. His death marked my life.

"Mother had worked as a seamstress. After his death she took jobs as a receptionist and so on. Because she was always working, we had to amuse ourselves, and the big thing was to work with crafts. We went to all the summer classes at the parks, and sometimes she'd come along and take a class, too. So we'd be taking puppetry or clay, and she would be taking jewelry, and now and then we'd take one together. At Christmastime, we'd all be making things for each other. We all learned to sew, so we'd be making clothes for our dolls, and we'd paint their faces so they'd look new, but really they were the old ones, remade. And later as teenagers we'd make puppets and have shows, or begin our Christmas projects the summer before. So it was recycling and also making things for other people, to give them pleasure. I think that has a lot to do with why I make art."

EM: "How about that family of yours, and the early school years?"

BS: "I was the eldest of three, so my father spent a lot of time with me. He was creative too, in another way. He had written plays and poetry and was doing graduate work when he died. He was religious, many-faceted and creative. After he died, we settled in Pasadena, and I went on into the public-school system. This was the '30s. Depression time. Being in California during the Depression wasn't like being in the Midwest or the East, however. There wasn't the same hardship. We had an extended family. My grandmother and aunts and uncles sheltered us and encouraged us. Outside the family, though, there wasn't much of that. In those days it wasn't recommended for black students to be in the art program, for instance. The most you could hope for was to become a designer. That was conceivable. But I never got any particular praise. When I went to Pasadena City College, I was aware there was an art clique— an art club and an honorary art society. I had as good grades as anyone who belonged, but I was never asked. Every year, the class would design a float for the Tournament of Roses. My design was picked several times, but when they found I was black I would be given honorable mention or some consolation prize. I was angry, but what could a teenager do about it?

"Looking back, I don't think the experience was all bad. I've realized in the past few years that anger also helped drive me to make it. Wanting revenge is a good way out. It pushes you. When I look now to what the other students are doing, I see that most of them are teachers. Only one is a designer. The rest just aren't out there. And I am."

EM: "Go back to the house you lived in as a child."

BS: "It seemed mysterious, filled with psychic forces. It's the house I recall over and over in my dreams.

"I had my own room. One time I remember I had a temper tantrum. I screamed and went flying around that room. And I had clairvoyant powers at that age. I could see things. Some afternoons I would say, 'Oh-oh. Daddy's really mad. He missed his bus.' And just then the telephone would ring and it would be he saying, 'I'm really mad. I missed my bus.' That was unsettling for my family. And I had an imaginary playmate named Rosie who lived in a barn near our house. Those barns were being turned into garages when I was a child, because people were giving up their horses and beginning to buy cars. But in the old days they were filled with worn-out buggies and thrown-away paraphernalia. Dark and spooky. That was where Rosie lived.

"But after the death of my father, I changed. I was no longer psychic or clairvoyant. It was as if a door had shut. Now I don't see things anymore except in dreams. The gift comes out only in feelings or intuition. But I've kept my interest in the occult."

Saar graduated from college in 1949 and became a designer of costumes among other things. She also married another artist and spent the 1950s raising a family of two, then three, daughters. A decade later, a new charge of energy took hold and she set out to make art of her own free choice. She began with

357

prints. Printmaking led to boxes. Making boxes led to an obsession with things. Things led into the past as she went back into the cupboards of her family house and so backward into other recesses: dreams, personal memory and the history of her race. During the politicized '60s, she made works with bitter racial connotations, mixing pictures of Uncle Toms and Little Black Sambos with mammy dolls, toy guns and banshee warrior dolls. *Liberation of Aunt Jemima* and *Exploding the Myth* told the story of the times.

EM: "I know that one of the things that put you on your new track was seeing a show of Joseph Cornell's boxes, with their occult and astrological images. How did you begin on your own?"

BS: "I'd collected little bits of things all my life, as I said, but I was working with prints and drawings at the time I saw Cornell's pieces. I began framing some of them. Then I found an old leaded window in a shop down on Big Sur and used it as a frame for some prints and drawings. Later I made *Black Girl's Window* in that assembled idiom. Even at the time, I knew it was autobiographical. We'd had the Watts riots and the black revolution. Also, that was the year I got my divorce. So in addition to the occult subject matter there was political and also personal content. There's a black figure pressing its face to the glass, like a shadow. And two hands that represent my own fate. On the top are nine little boxes in rows of three marked by the crescent, the star and the sun. The next row has a vision of a little black couple dancing. But look what's in the center. A skeleton. Death is in the center. Everything revolves around death.

"In the bottom is a tintype of a woman. It's no one I know, just something I found. But she's white. My mother's mother was white, Irish and very beautiful. I have a photograph of her in a hat covered with roses. And there's the same mix on my father's side. I feel that duality, the black and the white."

EM: "How would you read this piece?"

BS: "About three years ago, I went to a psychic who reads your energy, and through her I began to understand the work. She explained how one's energy is locked away, and how certain words can be keys to unlock it. The body is a door, and the word is the key, and the opening of the door is accompanied by a release of energy.

"She explained to me that there was energy locked away in me, from anger, from sadness or just from doors being closed. As I worked with her, I came to see I was still, in a way, locked into that child who was six when her father died. From the time my father died, there was always the image of death somewhere in the corner. She urged me to push on through the death imagery, to meet it face to face. Because that little girl was also a very imaginative and creative being and could deal with it.

"I showed slides of all my work to her, and she pointed out the many death symbols. My work has a certain sophistication because I've had so much academic training, but there's still the naïve child behind it all.

"From that point, I began to look through my other work for the same meanings. And I discovered that each of my boxes carried the same kind of information. Some are called Mo-jo boxes. They refer to the Mo-jo women, to use the African word. They refer to voodoo. And they refer to our passage from Africa to, in my case, New Orleans. They tell the historical tale. Those pieces, especially the ones with feathers, have a feeling of the past, of lost and dead civilizations. One of them is called *Wizard*. I did all the early pieces without dwelling on the subject of death at a conscious level. Only later I realized the boxes are coffins. They're all coffins. They contain relics from the past.

"Just around that time, my great-aunt died. She had raised my mother, and she was as close to me as a grandmother. Her death stirred the old feelings about my father again. It was out of that experience that I began taking a workshop at UCLA called 'Intensive Journal,' based on the work of psychologist Ira Progoff in New York. There were procedures laid out for opening the imagination in order to do autobiographical writing, or to make art. One exercise was this: Close your eyes and go down into your deepest well, your deepest self. Whatever you meet there, write down. I had this vision. There was water and a figure swimming. I had a feeling of intense sadness. I started to weep right there in class. Later I realized that of course the figure was myself.

"Beginning then, I made a number of works dedicated to my aunt, using things I'd found in her house. Five are boxes of the old kind. *Record for Hattie*, for instance, has all the things I remember her using: a pincushion she had on her bureau, with pins and rings still on it. Her girlhood autobiography book. An egg timer. And a tiny black crucifix in a corner, and the skeleton—images of death again."

It is true that since the end of the '60s, with the passing of the active phase of the Black Movement, Betye Saar has found her own political interests subsiding into an introspective concern with her own life. Meanwhile, new formal and technical problems have drawn her into new waters. Raffia, feathers, bones, textiles, photos—all these are the standard stuff of collage and assemblage. But recently she has been making marvelous use of that new invention halfway between gimmick and ghost: color Xerox.

Those latest works are "the most painterly things I've done." The Xeroxes, in their floods of uncanny blues and greens, are pasted onto grounds of old etchings, and the whole is treated with latex. *Night Letters*, for example, is built up of Xeroxes of sea and marshland, where space flows and moves as if a plasm were actually shifting under the latex skin.

Saar is also now making collages of things like handkerchiefs, combined with cutout symbolic images: butterflies, for example—guardians of the grave—or, in many recent works, a single glove pressed to the glass or the frame of the work as much as to say, "I touched this; I am standing here in this moment, this place. The past may be there, but I am here."

EM: "How do you go about picking the objects?"

BS: "Sometimes for their symbolic value. And sometimes just by intuition. In this case, I began with color. The box is red. Everything I chose, I chose to go with that color. When I begin to work, I pull out all my drawers here in the kitchen and sift them. I have collections of little things, miniature skeletons, crucifixes and pins. All kinds of things. The objects are all symbolic. Here is one that has to do with the heavens. And there's a heart . . . and there's an eye . . . and a hand. Then there are the sparkly things, and the antique gold things.

"But the fact is I don't add to the collection of objects anymore. I've moved away from that kind of imagery. If all my dreams, and all my work, are telling me clearly what I am trying to express, it would be silly to go on making

Smiles We Left Behind, 1976. Assemblage: fabric, photo, feathers, glove, frame, ornament, butterfly. 13½" by 10" by ½". Monique Knowlton Gallery, New York.

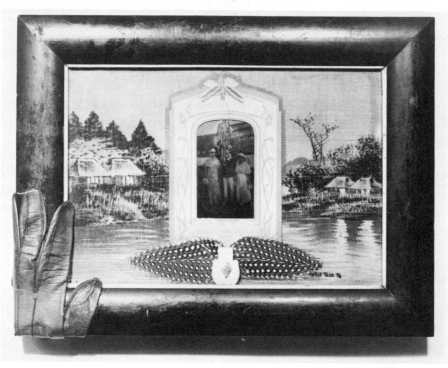

the same sort of work. The only way I can grow is to move away from it. Oh, it's still a kind of veil I put on every once in a while—making a box in the old way—but then I know I'm deliberately putting on a costume from an earlier time."

EM: "How about these marvelous flat collages you're doing now?"

BS: "The literal fact is I began simply by trying to use up the material I got from my aunt's estate instead of buying new materials. But all the same, those pieces are still mysterious to me. The meaning is still veiled. I do know they're still related directly to my aunt. She kept all her letters, for instance, so I've done a series of abstract works called Letters from Home. They're large, done in layers, and very dreamlike. They work on two levels. They deal with the past because the letters are old, and they come from a time when she too was growing old. But I'm also dealing with pure words here, taking the letters and tearing them into pieces and making forms out of the paper.

"My intention was to try to stay as conscious of what I was doing as I could at every step. The pieces came out with certain resemblances to earlier ones, but much more poetic, more mysterious. Larger. I don't understand them yet.

"There is only this idea that is beginning to surface in me. I've been working here with my aunt's materials for some time. And I've begun to be aware that all of that, all that material, all those images, including her herself, are part of the past. And that I, the artist, am now standing on the other side of it. The other side of the past."

Sheila
Hicks

BORN 1934, HASTINGS, NEBRASKA

*One day George Kubler... flashed on the
screen a whole series of pre-Columbian textiles.
I remember thinking they were the closest thing
to my dream world. One of them literally vibrated to me.... I thought I had found myself.*
—SHEILA HICKS
Paris, 1977

Sheila Hicks always wanted to get free of landlocked Nebraska.

If the threads of a conventional loom might be said to be a barrier to free
invention, then Hicks treated them with as little reverence as she did the
borders of her home state. Inspired by Bauhaus theory at the Yale School of Art
and Architecture, by courses there with designer-painter Josef Albers, weaver
Anni Albers and architect Louis Kahn and also, later, by pre-Columbian textiles
she found in South America, Hicks moved fast in the decade of the '60s to
break with convention and make the art of textile weaving a vehicle for her
own ideas.

In 1965 she settled in Paris, where she opened a big, soon thriving stu-
dio-workshop, the Atelier des Grands Augustins. Since then she has won and
completed major commissions for a number of international organizations
ranging from the Ford Foundation to the United Arab League (for its new
mosque in Riyadh, Saudi Arabia). In '69, she had a major exhibition at the
Stedelijk Museum in Amsterdam; in '74, she received the gold medal of the
American Institute of Architects, and the Stedelijk Museum showed her work
once more; in '76, she was made an honorary fellow of the Kunstakademie in
The Hague. Meanwhile, in 1973, she opened a second workshop in Paris, the
Atelier Bourdonnais. Meanwhile, too, she had married (now to a Chilean-in-
exile painter) and raised two children.

Her first original pieces, back in 1960, were small loomed works with

362

complex granular passages played against passages of open-warp wrapped and knotted threads. She describes their meaning in her own words below.

In subsequent commissions, Hicks has pushed the esthetic limits of her art as far as she can. She has wrapped threads around neon lights and created structures that produce sound when moved by the wind (a raffia *Wind Tapestry,* for a Carmelite convent in France). She has built three-dimensional structures like *Labyrinth,* a cage of enormous wrapped ropes; and she has made conceptual works—sewn, crumpled, pleated hangings of cotton, or stacks of folded goods—that pose basic questions about this esthetic medium that historically spans the gap between the useful and the intellectual. Her constructivist assemblages of wrapped and exposed threads with Surreal titles (*The Preferred Wife Occupies Her Nights*) clearly are meant to be taken as works of content-laden "art."

Hicks, in fact, is as much interested in theory as in practice. She explains that works of woven art fall into four classes: closed compositions like hanging prayer rugs; open compositions like her hanging-cord tapestry walls that are infinitely expandable, with Rapunzel-like falls of raw, unwoven stuffs wrapped in bright-colored silks; compositions based on small modules that can be multiplied to fill an architectural space; and "ephemeral compositions." It is in the last category that Hicks flies freest of tradition and also of the pragmatic confines of her craft. At present, among other projects, she is working on an altar tapestry for the main chamber of St. Peter's Lutheran Church in New York, for which Louise Nevelson designed the Good Shepherd Chapel. Hicks explains that her work, a series of layers woven of gold thread, is intended as a metaphor for the concept of infinity.

"I was born in Nebraska, a mythic place for me: the little town of Hastings. My maternal great-aunt Gertie was the first woman graduate of Hastings College, one of three old-maid sisters who lived in the family house where I spent summer vacations. It was a homesteading family, German–Lowland Dutch, thrifty, very much the Cather spirit. They had brought out with them from Boston the first piano seen in those parts, with melon-ball legs. There were ferns all over the house, and all-flax, hand-woven dish towels.

"There was a veranda around the house. I remember the great-aunts sitting there, sewing for all the nieces and nephews, great-nieces and -nephews and a few adopted orphans. Or rather, Emma sewed, Lizzie played piano, and Gertie drew and made us read. She taught us all to draw, and since I was the firstborn of the new generation, she spent special time with me. Partly because I was a girl, and eager, she identified with me.

"These were wonderful, invisible citizens of the Midwest, dreaming of

things happening in other places far away, for we were wholly landlocked. I never saw a body of water or ate a fish until I moved away."

EM: "How about your parents?"

SH: "Father was part Cherokee, but he didn't think much of that background, and he was orphaned at a young age. He had gone to work in the general store in town, met Mother, and they eloped. She was a strong person and gay, with that positive frontier spirit. They left Hastings as soon as they could, but then came the Depression. My father worked in about a dozen places from Nebraska to Texas, and from Michigan to Florida. We lived in twelve towns before I was fourteen. That's why going back to Hastings every summer was important.

"When you move around as a child, you get a helicopter view of life. No matter what situation you're in, you see it from a distance. You develop a sense of purpose not affected by the winds that blow. You move through environments and circumstances and economic levels. The penurious and then the glorious; great hotels, then ghetto schools. During the Detroit riots, I was about the only white student in my school. Looking back now, I think my mother and father were rather poetic in their life style. What they might say about those years would be: flurries of desperation and flurries of compensation.

"Eventually my father got ahead in the American Way. He became a prosperous stockbroker in ball and roller bearings. He calculated there was one thing that everyone needed in time of war or peace: ball bearings. For a watch, for a locomotive. By the time he reached his level, he began to feel that I too should figure out a format for my own life. He saw my imaginative powers and felt he had to help me set some boundaries. He began talking about my old doll house and how I shouldn't expect just to fold up my life periodically and move on. So I had a tug of war with him, and when I was seventeen or eighteen I left home and never went back except for vacations, though now we're very close friends."

EM: "Doll house?"

SH: "I loved doll houses, because I always wanted a place to live. They were all collapsible and mobile. I could take them apart, switch around all the furniture. The people were interchangeable, too. 'Mother' could be at home or

364

out working. 'Father' could be at home or working. That came from my feeling that everyone was really replaceable. My own mother and father had equal say, even equal personality, so they were interchangeable. My two younger brothers and I grew up with equivalent feelings, and we five people were a

The Communications Labyrinth, 1976. Tapestry bas-relief being mounted. 16' high. American Telephone & Telegraph, Basking Ridge, New Jersey.

nucleus always moving in space. In fact, traveling seemed the natural thing to me. When I was still in high school I wanted to go off to Brazil as an exchange student. But my father couldn't conceive of that far a trip, so I didn't go to Brazil. Instead, I went to Syracuse University for two years."

EM: "To study art?"

SH: "It didn't matter, because I didn't stay.

"I've always admired strong and bright women, and sought them out. At Syracuse I met the girl who was first in our class. She persuaded me to transfer to Yale with her. But the summer before we were to go, she killed herself. She wrote a letter to her family saying, 'I don't have the strength to go on and see the whole thing through.' She was only eighteen.

"What I did, in reaction, was to go to Mexico alone. I was eighteen myself. I wanted to prove that even alone and in alien circumstances I would make the opposite decision. That I would see things through. And I did. I wandered, read books. The experience helped me come to grips with a decision all young people have to make some time or other: to go ahead or to remain a victim of circumstances. That's the choice: to take an optimistic view and manage or to accept defeat. I took the resolution in Mexico. And then, in 1954, I went off alone to Yale. Josef Albers of the Bauhaus was in his last years at Yale then."

EM: "How did you like his Germanic view of life and art?"

SH: "First, he reinforced some ideas I already had about myself. I went knowing I had talent. I knew that other people had begun to seek me out. I had a sense of responsibility. And I also had that helicopter view of life. I resisted falling into the banality of cliques. I listen to what people say and then make my own decision. I think that's why I live in Europe today. I feel strongly about not wanting to be sucked into small talk, small intrigues. I want to be 'at large,' not to have to adapt myself to a small format. I envision limitless formats! *Malgré le papa*. Remember, it was the late '50s when I got my B.F.A. As I became aware of the art world there was more of an internationalist feeling than there had been for some years. Monet and the Abstract Impressionists were being talked about. Joan Mitchell had left New York, gone over the border as it were. It always seemed to me that to be a success you had to get over the border literally or figuratively.

"That was the point Albers reinforced. He kept pushing us forward all the time. If you had a piece of wood in your hand and you took it to a saw, you couldn't just demolish it. You had to do something articulate and clear, something you understood. You had to work with intelligent hands and also thoughts. If you were writing, you had to research your subject, to ground it in history. 'How can you expect someone to understand what you're trying to say if you can't express it yourself?' he'd say. When I graduated in '57, he was on the Fulbright Committee and knew I was dreaming of going somewhere. Perhaps Chile? So off I went."

EM: "Chile?"

SH: "One day George Kubler, the art historian, flashed on the screen a series of slides of pre-Columbian textiles. I remember thinking they were the closest thing to my dream world. One of them literally vibrated to me. So I decided to write my thesis on the subject and set out to find an adviser. I walked into the Museum of Natural History in New York to talk with Dr. Junius Bird, and there again I thought I had found myself. That place is mud-deep in other people's weird customs and cultures.

"When I decided to go to Chile, I went by land in small hops, by local buses and trains and small planes, following maps Dr. Bird had given me, all the way to Tierra del Fuego. Eventually I settled in Santiago, found an empty store, bought a bed, put nails in the walls and hung up my clothes. It was like having a family around me, all those clothes hanging around the room.

"I studied pre-Columbian textiles there until I understood where they fit in the cultural history of the area. That place and period has the largest vocabulary of textile *structures* in the world.

"I'd been doing some weaving of my own, too. I'd made my first loom at Yale. Then I began improvising little looms I could use while I was sitting around and talking—a sort of *passe-temps des dames*. I was painting in those days, as well. I'd worked with Rico Lebrun at Yale. But gradually the left hand came over and absorbed what the right had been doing. For the first ten years of my working life people would say, 'What a pity you're not painting!' They considered weaving a second-class artisanry. Also, I was married by then to a Mexican apiculturist and had two children, and one of my many rifts with my husband was that he thought it was a waste of time making 'potholders.'

"I finally decided to prove otherwise to him. I took a plane from Mexico to New York and simply called up the Museum of Modern Art. I said I was just off the plane and had some weavings with me. These early works were my own invention. I called them "Hieroglyphs" and "White Letters." They were structured in a secret monochrome alphabet spelled out in threads. In the end, members of the staff bought all I had with me and ordered more. Alfred Barr said he would take one for the museum's collection if I made it larger. So I went back to Mexico and set up a loom I thought was huge: two feet square. The museum took the three I made on that one, but again they said, 'Bigger!' So I went back down to Mexico, took my garden table, turned it upside down, strung a loom between its legs, and did two more. Thereafter, I worked larger and larger."

EM: "Where has the work come to today?"

SH: "I'm just getting into full sail. I have two studios running full time in Paris. Right now we're working on forty commissions at the same time. But, what's most important, I'm developing my personal handwriting, trying to compose textiles that stand as works of art. I have a project related to linguistics. The idea is to take a single pliable element—in this case, of course, a single thread, comparable to a thread of language—and to demonstrate, as you might weave ideas around a theme, the most that can be done with it from both the constructive and the sensuous sense. Because this is a medium where you can be both intellectual and sensuous at the same time.

"And I've programmed what I consider a Conceptual Happening in textile/art process, for a hospital in Lausanne, Switzerland. I took eight tons of clean hospital blouses neatly folded and massed them into an enormous avalanche in front of a vast linen backdrop. I call it *The Untangler*. The idea is to sort out the polemic that exists in the field of tapestry, to open the closets and take out all the ideas, technical, material and conceptual. When I was asked to describe that work, I said it was a 'field of meditation.'

"The point, of course, is to break the barrier between artisanry and art. Albers made no such distinction. Bauhaus theory made no distinction."

EM: "Isn't there a contradiction between the egocentric, self-expressive artist and the self-effacing craftsperson, usually crafts*woman,* mute and unremembered? Essentially, between the artist who works alone and the craftsperson who works with and always for others?"

SH: "But from the time that friend of mine committed suicide, I realized that I would be alone. So if I have gravitated to weaving as my form of art, I do it in my own way, from myself. What links us all is our need to express our intuition of continuity. I keep notebooks to provide that continuum for myself. I keep them all together, in one bookshelf. They reassure me that there is a continuous developing process going on beneath all the separate projects. Thanks to that, I have no fear about going here and there in the world. I accept the fact that I can go for days and days and nothing seems to have meaning or fall into a form. Then there comes one idea or insight that binds it all up.

"And then there's a continuity among the practitioners of an art themselves. When I first learned about the other two leading American weavers, Lenore Tawney and Claire Zeisler, before the first modern weaving show at the Museum of Contemporary Crafts in New York in 1962, I absolutely didn't want to be in it with them. I was young and arrogant. I wanted a one-person show. That's the artist's ego! The organizers of the show just went ahead and borrowed some of my work from the Museum of Modern Art, and later I met and loved both of those artists.

"When you're young, you think you're the cat's pajamas. But by now I've listened to the older generation and also I've tried to help younger people find their way. You have to do both, I feel.

"You have to find your place in the chain. When I was leaving Mexico the first time, the man who became my first husband said to me, and it persuaded me to marry him, 'Even a penguin needs a piece of iceberg to sit on.' "

With Gold Column, 1973. Polished
bronze, silk and wool. 9'9" tall.

Barbara Chase-Riboud

BORN 1939, PHILADELPHIA

*I grew up that year.... The blast of Egyptian
culture was irresistible.... From an artistic
point of view, that trip was historic for me.*
—BARBARA CHASE-RIBOUD
Paris, 1977

Chase-Riboud grew up in an American middle-class family in Philadelphia in
the era when cultural assimilation was the great goal. Her father was an aca-
demically trained painter; her mother, Canadian and convent-educated. Both
of them, as well as her grandparents, lavished on a talented Barbara all the
advantages they could muster. It must have been a troubling passage for them
later to watch their world tilt in another direction as the Civil-Rights Movement
impelled young American blacks away from the ideals of assimilation toward
their own ethnic roots. In the end, it took Chase-Riboud a long time to put
together an idiom of her own, neither ethnic nor Western, but a merging of the
two.

The *Ur*-image behind her extraordinary works that combine bronze and
textile ropes is the African tribal mask with its blind wood gaze and raffia skirts.
But Chase-Riboud's cast-metal forms, scored in pleats of gleaming light that
counterpoint cascades of silk and wool, show a high level of technical sophistication. She also makes drawings that combine a particular precision and a
loose linear grace, of rocks and other natural forms. She also writes poetry
(*From Memphis and Peking* was published in 1974) and in 1978 finished a
novel. Its theme is the love affair between Thomas Jefferson and Sally Hemings,
the slave who became mother of seven of his children. Chase-Riboud declares
that the contrast presented here in fictional form—between a male in power

370

and a submissive woman who, paradoxically, wields the power—is the same dialectic that drives her work in bronze and cloth.

"I was one of those theatrical brats, bred for the arts. Trained and trained for some unknown purpose. At seven I was going to the Fletcher Art School in Philadelphia for lessons and to the Philadelphia Museum for Saturday classes. At eight I won my first 'art prize.' I was also taking both piano and ballet seriously.

"My father was a frustrated painter and architect: There were stacks of his paintings in the basement, and I looked at them all the time. He should have been an architect, but because of his color he couldn't get accepted.

"My mother was raised in a convent in Montreal. She was a Canadian, the daughter of a jazz musician. She married at seventeen. It's interesting to me that she remained undeveloped until very late. She was in her forties before she made a statement on her own. At that point, she went back to school and got a technical degree in pathology. By then she had long since given me a happy childhood.

"We had a house with lots of books but not many art books. No paintings, except my father's. But one thing I remember about the house, when I was three or four years old, was the blackout curtains. My grandmother was afraid of the dark. We had air-raid warnings in those days. Instead of just turning out the lights, she had gigantic (at least to me) black curtains made for the windows. When the sirens blew she drew them. Ritually she then sent my grandfather out to see if there was light around the edges. Those black curtains impressed me. I imagined my grandfather under 'enemy' planes overhead while he checked the curtains.

"Eventually I got too tall for ballet, and I'd been badly trained at the piano. I had a lot of dash but little substance. Finally just the art remained. By the end of high school, I had won a *Seventeen* magazine art prize for a woodcut, sold my first prints to the Museum of Modern Art, and collected a fistful of scholastic awards.

"Remember, this was the time of Jim-Crowism: a gifted black youngster would be overwhelmed with benevolence. When I graduated, I had seven scholarships, several to black colleges, several for free-anywhere and several to state colleges. Eventually I went to a small art school connected with Temple University, where I was the only black student. And there I learned the basics: drawing, painting, sculpture, printmaking. At Temple we were required to take courses in the medical school: medical drawing, anatomy and dissection.

"And at that point I won the *Mademoiselle* guest-editorship award—the

371

first black girl to do so. I spent a month in New York working at the magazine. Then I was offered a job at *Charm* magazine, and that was a turning point. I could have stayed on in the fashion world, but the designer Leo Lionni urged me to go to Europe instead. He recommended me for a fellowship from the John Hay Whitney Foundation, and I took off for a year in Rome, staying part of the time at the American Academy.

"That was only the first step in my adventures. As a dare at a Christmas Eve party, I left on the spot with friends on a trip to Egypt. When we arrived in Alexandria, the couple I had embarked with decided they didn't want me to tag along, and dumped me on the dock. Where does a lost American go in Alexandria? To the Hilton Hotel, of course. And there I sat in the lobby, and by chance met the president of Coca-Cola in Egypt. He said, 'I'm going to put you on a plane to Cairo. And when you get there, go straight to the YWCA. And don't move.'

"So I did what he said. I went to the YWCA in Cairo. Then I went to the American cultural attaché, who turned out to be black and asked me what a nice Philadelphia girl like me was doing wandering around the Middle East in the midst of the Suez crisis. He took me home to his wife. I had come for three weeks and I stayed for three months.

"I grew up that year. It was the first time I realized there was such a thing as non-European art. For someone exposed only to the Greco-Roman tradition, it was a revelation. I suddenly saw how insular the Western world was vis-à-vis the nonwhite, non-Christian world. The blast of Egyptian culture was irresistible. The sheer magnificence of it. The elegance and perfection, the timelessness, the depth. After that, Greek and Roman art looked like pastry to me. From an artistic point of view, that trip was historic for me. Though I didn't know it at the time, my own transformation was part of the historical transformation of the blacks that began in the '60s.

"When I got back to Rome, someone suggested that I go to the Yale School of Art and Architecture. I was accepted and was helped financially, the only black woman in the school.

"Albers was nearing the end of his tenure as director then, but he was still the power. So my memories and impressions of Egypt were varnished with Bauhaus discipline. I fought it like hell, but it stood me in good stead later.

"At the end of my second year, I got a commission to do a fountain in Washington, D.C., and I decided to do it as my master's thesis. I began working in aluminum instead of cast bronze, but still I wanted to get as close as I could to organic, sensuous shapes. I'd done some bronze casting in Rome, of vaguely vegetal-humanistic forms, and this was a compromise. I began looking for a factory that could produce something along the line of a paper model I'd made.

I found an airplane factory that could stamp out seven basic shapes. With these seven shapes, I designed two screens from which jets of water came out. Later on, I realized I had also made a musical instrument, because the water striking the metal made a series of sounds.

"I spent six months on the project. It was an enormous project for a thesis. But at the last minute the faculty decided it wasn't acceptable because it hadn't been done under supervision, even though I'd proposed it, shown all the drawings, the plaster models, and offered them photos and casts. The compromise was that I could graduate if I did another thesis. So in four weeks I did a book of engravings from Rimbaud's *Season in Hell:* six engravings, all the typography and production. The situation had conventional sexist and racist overtones. The message was: I should have been grateful to be there in the first place—the only black, the only woman. Partly my problem was that I'd brought from Rome a kind of assurance and a Europeanization that shocked Yale. I had seen a bit of the world and I knew that New Haven wasn't the center of it.

"In the end, however, the Yale experience was superb training. It was *professional.* Albers himself had shaped the program. He was impossible and adorable, difficult, exigent, dogmatic, intimidating, brilliant and unforgiving. What he formulated was a methodology—a system. It involved a way of thinking about art. 'Professional' implied a certain attitude toward one's work: that one was committed to a career.

"The principle was: You can think any way you want, but your ideas must be clear. A logic has to be there as a grid to support your ideas. Your technical training has to be impeccable in regard to form, color, design and straight thinking. Engineers, doctors, scientists and lawyers think straight. Artists should, too. If you didn't master this idea, you would never do anything significant in your art, no matter how much talent you had or how hard you worked.

"Also, it's true, there was a focus on success. The atmosphere was competitive. And that idea of coming up with a single image—that put a lot of pressure on people who weren't formed by the time they came to Yale. Perhaps women are even more influenced by this kind of teaching than men, because they are not used to having such stringent discipline imposed on them.

"My own ideas, developed around this time, were these: I was not restricted to the Western mode of art. The Greco-Roman heritage was only a part of a vast reservoir. There were other ways as important for me, as valid intellectually, deeper, and as beautiful. I could turn to the non-Western arts for ideas without feeling I was working with folklore."

Barbara Chase graduated from Yale in 1960 and took off for Europe. She lived

373

in London for a while, and then on a trip to Paris she met the noted journalist-photographer Marc Riboud. She married him in '61, hyphenated her name, had two sons, traveled richly if frenetically until '67 and then decided she was going back to work.

"And I found that my work had changed radically. The change was due to many things. The impact of the Civil-Rights Movement in the States was one thing. My own travels in China, the East and Africa, culminating in a Pan-African festival in Algeria in '68, were others. That festival was the turning point.

"I felt a great pressure to fuse these influences with my Western heritage. I made sketches, especially of African masked dancers. An idea that fascinated me was the concealing of *structure,* as in the case of masks, so that objects would take on a magical presence.

"My work up to then always had a realistic, humanistic aspect. There were legs on the pieces, for instance. They were *figures.* Now I wanted to get rid of those legs. I didn't want to make organic monsters. But the problem was, I didn't know how to stand pieces up without legs. I made some sketches, and then I went to talk with Sheila Hicks, my classmate from Yale. She knew techniques of making ropes and wrapping them. I told her my problem. We sat down and tried to come up with something.

"Then it hit me. Like one of those light bulbs over your head. I had found a way to hide the legs! And that was it. And once I was rid of the legs, the rest just fell into place. I could do exactly what I wanted.

"Little by little I evolved and refined the technique. I veiled the structural components, the 'legs,' with curtains of rope. The figures stood, but were not exclusively 'human.' The first skirts were simple, then they became more complicated. The first works with the silk in '60 looked like hair. I got away from that as fast as possible. I wanted the curtain to look like water. I began to knot it, to try to move it away from the free-flowing; the knots gave it solidity. Then the silk began to imitate what was going on in sections of bronze. That effect was interesting and odd.

"In the early pieces, I had used bronze in a fluid, liquid way, while the wool was static. So there was a paradoxical transfer of power from the bronze to the silk or wool. It really looked as if the wool was holding up the bronze. The fiber became a column that literally seemed to hold up the bronze. So the wool became the strong element—let's call it, for argument's sake, the male element. And the bronze became the soft, or female, element. I liked the impossibility, the contradiction of that. It pleased me no end."

The first bronze and silk- or wool-rope pieces were exhibited in New York in

Cape, 1973. Cast bronze variously patinaed, with hemp cord; welded
aluminum support. 6' high. Collection the artist.

1970; included were four large pieces dedicated to Malcolm X. It was not
politics, however, that inspired Chase-Riboud to her most extraordinary work
but a confrontation of another kind. Suddenly, she was presented with an
example of historic art that synthesized those two qualities she had tried to
make work together: the hard and lasting and the soft, flowing-away. In '73, a
letter from her husband in China brought news of the magnificent all-jade
burial suit just unearthed there (it later toured the West in a show of Chinese
National Treasures). Here then was an image that stood at the crossroads of
civilizations and also esthetics: a work that presented itself as softly *sewn,* but
was actually made of immortal *stone.* Chase-Riboud's variant on that theme,

375

her Han Shroud, or *Cape,* shown in New York in '77, is an enormous work of sheer hand labor: thousands of bronze squares, each cast individually, with various glowing patinas, all joined by gold wire. The great cape was posed on an armature, gigantic and empty, as if its over-life-size owner—empress, emperor or shaman—had just shrugged it off and laid it there: a work of power, paradox and synthesis, in its metallic heaviness soft, and in its falling softness ponderous as history itself.

"For the future, I want to carry the sculpture into a new dimension. I want to do a series of pieces with silk or nylon, cut in basic geometric shapes, sewn onto metal parts, under tension but also slightly undulating, like sails. The idea comes out of my book. It will be a monument to the nine million African deportees who died in the Middle Passage. I'd like to do these pieces in black bronze and black nylon, and mount them outdoors in a seaside site, along the Hudson River or on Chesapeake Bay.

"As for my own life, in France, I have a country place in the Loire Valley, a big old restored farmhouse. I work well there. I wrote the first draft of the novel there, as well as my first book of poetry. When I began writing poetry, there was an enormous outpouring in an intuitive way. And then, as I acquired experience, I found that my training as a visual artist, a draftsman, helped me. One shapes one's life thus: biology or inheritance, history, training, intuition, luck and love."

Lee Bontecou

BORN 1931, PROVIDENCE, RHODE ISLAND

I had taken the drawing class, and then I took the painting. And then I thought, Well, I'll just go down and try sculpture. And that was that. I never came up afterward. I liked it. It was for me. I was happy there. It made sense somehow. So I said to myself, Okay, I want to keep pushing it as far as I can go.

—LEE BONTECOU
New York, 1977

Somewhere between decades and styles, Bontecou is beached temporarily, though she might not describe it that way. She is drawing a lot and working as she did long ago in clay, feeling it out, putting together small objects out of "tons of forms" that lie around her work space. Her life too has changed since the 1960s when with her grin and her bobbed hair and her powerful works in forged steel and canvas she was the best-known younger American sculptor in the world, shown and purchased from New York to Tokyo and between. Her last exhibit was in 1971; during the five years before that, she had shown vacuum-molded transparent plastic figures of fish, birds, flowers that presented a quite different aspect from her earlier works. In the meantime, she has been living out the transition in privacy. "I don't care about anything else [presumably sales, success, name] as long as I'm working." She has also married, had a daughter, lost her mother and is presently making a home for her aging father. In other words, Bontecou is a human being who in the middle of the way of her life has come to a place I am moved to describe, if I let my own imagination run, as surrounded by dark water where silver fish swim.

That past she is halfway beyond is the Constructivist/Surreal/Abstract Expressionist one, with its humanist baggage of power, protest, organicism. The world she has not yet moved into and may indeed eschew is that "cool,"

377

often called "dehumanized" one of the '60s and the '70s, with its contradictions hidden behind a mask face. Bontecou has been claimed by each. Indeed, her works of the early '60s were of such an awesome openness to interpretation that they caught the Zeitgeist by many sails. To people with archaeological, anthropological or art-historical sense, for instance, they had overtones of antiquity, calling to mind the skinned, flattened bird masks of Chinese bronzes. To others they seemed to be icons of industrialism, mechanical power, thrust, propulsion: snouts of planes, funnels of jets mounted bizarrely on skeletons of boats. To people still reacting with gut fear at the sight of snub ends of cannons, these forms were the totems of war. And to many, especially women newly tuned to Feminist preoccupations, these shapes were sexual apertures, the private parts of Moloch's mother herself, splayed on the marble examining tables of museum walls. And so it happened—Georgia O'Keeffe in the 1920s had the same story to tell—that whenever you stood before a work by Lee Bontecou, whatever your predilection, that black funnel spoke to you.

Meanwhile, by their unconventional process of manufacture—canvas, cut from the worn-out conveyer belts of a laundry, sewn onto steel frames—these works had a major influence on some later materials- and process-obsessed artists like Eva Hesse. So, in fact, did Bontecou's use of that worn, frayed canvas itself. And along the same line of rather wild experiment, Bontecou showed in the '60s a collection of Futuristic drawings done "in pencil and soot," or "carbon sprayed on muslin: I took great big pieces of paper, put them on the wall. Then if you eliminate the oxygen in a torch, it's black soot that comes out. If you move quickly enough, you won't burn the paper, but you have a velvety, deep residue, so black. Just what I wanted."

Indeed, in this sense of being in transit between periods, Bontecou's experience parallels Mary Cassatt's: conceptually held in a humanist past while pulling technically toward a strange future. But now psychosocial as well as esthetic evolutions have made it more likely she will survive such a transition, and also Bontecou has always been independent, not bound to art-world fashion or, even in the bonding days of Tenth Street, camaraderie. "I just wasn't there. I had no community spirit. I haven't that many friends in the art world. And I'm not really involved with the Women's Movement: it's nothing new to me. I mean, I've been doing it all my life.

"I don't even have a studio now. I just work where I can find a place to sit down. I don't care.

"I never imposed my life style on anybody. As a matter of fact, I think my husband and I are just getting used to being married. And now there are three, and that really floored both of us. But all through, I've been drawing and that's been helpful. And I just kept all my . . . my mess and my studio and my private life apart.''

EM: "You like to be free.''

LB: "Yeah. Be out on the old mud flat. When you go to Nova Scotia, get out and try it. It's . . . it's really nice. Get to see all those worms!''

"All I remember is the sea and walking barefoot around there—mud-flat walking. Ever mud-flat walked? It's great. Your parents don't know that the tide comes in so fast and deep. But we kids understood. We knew about the eel grass. How the tide comes in underneath so fast it could be dangerous. But the mud squishes through your toes when you're walking out there, and there are lots of animals. Crabs and fish. So we went ahead and did it, though we cleaned up before we went home—washed off those black stockings up to our thighs. That's how deep the mud was, sometimes.''

Those were the summers that Bontecou and her brother and parents spent in a cottage in Nova Scotia, not far from her mother's family place, near Yarmouth and the Bay of Fundy, halfway out toward the sea between those mud flats and a forest. The forest too made an impression on an impressionable child. There were tremendous storms once in a while, and trees would be knocked down to lie there with their great root pads lifted into the air staring you in the face. "It's very wild. I don't know why our house is still standing. All the trees—the roots of the trees would heave up. They're spruce, so the roots aren't deep. When you walk through the woods, the earth just goes up and down under your feet, and when the wind pushes, those roots begin to move underground, they're so shallow. Once in a storm, my grandmother ran out saying, 'Oh, our trees, our trees!' She took a big roller and put it next to one, thinking it was heavy enough to hold the roots in place, but it went bobbing around itself, so she propped a big stick on the other side of the tree to try to hold it down.''

It was a childhood among fishermen and fishermen's children, though Bontecou would escape sometimes to her own room and copy drawings out of bird books or any kind of book, and make things. "I'd whittle lots of things. Little ox carts—you make the yoke for the oxen—and little hay carts, and then I went into the pine-cone business, making animals out of them, reindeer and farm animals,'' while out in the marshes she and the other kids made "whole situations'' in between and with the running rivulets and the swaying grasses. And meanwhile there was her maternal grandmother, one of those admirable matriarchal figures so many of the artists here tell about, who, like many of them, "had a good pioneering spirit—boy, did we love her.'' She and her

British forebears had been in that location for a long time, and the big family home was stately, "the kind of musty place where you made calls and they came down in black rustly widow's weeds. We'd go through those formal calls and then escape to the Cape again."

But it was not really the traditional side of Nova Scotian life that Bontecou was impressed by. "I think I was lucky to have two perspectives on life: the American one, where I grew up winters, and the Canadian one where we were embraced around with people who were very international even though they were fishermen and had absolutely nothing. In America, everyone was loaded and had everything they wanted, while when I went to Canada you played with the land, you played with the sea, there was nothing given to you or bought. And this showed me you don't need all that. And it helped me, too, when I came to New York and got a loft. It didn't phase me one bit to put my own plumbing in, or to live with no heat, or not to have much food for a while. Because I'd seen that it could be done."

"When" was quite a while off, however. Bontecou was born in '31 in Providence, Rhode Island, and when school years came the family moved down to Westchester County, New York, where the public education system was a good one. During the war, her father worked as a salesman in the glider business, but he turned against the product because so many soldiers were killed shortly after landing in them. Eventually, however, he achieved something remarkable: with a relative by marriage, named Stumpy, he had the idea for and had a model made of the first all-aluminum canoe.

"That was his claim to fame. When I was a kid, I used to play in the first model. It was all full of bumps and stuff by then. You get up on the gunwales and you stand there and you can shift the canoe along through the water, race it up and down with your legs, or side to side. You just skim along. It's nice!" Besides that, he was an outdoorsman and had had a life of adventure before coming East and becoming domesticated. "He came from Kansas, went to college a couple of years and then had an incredible life of camping and hunting—something you can't do anymore today, just wandering around and taking jobs when he wanted to. The way he describes it, it sounds like a different country, with wild antelope and other animals running loose. What he was seeing was the end of the frontier.

"He tells about Kansas City, for instance, and how the sidewalks and roads were made. First of dirt. Then they took enormous logs and sank them into the ground upright so you had streets paved with these enormous circles. There were incredible visual things like that we'll never see. He saw the change come.

"He killed rattlesnakes and he'd shoot birds, and he would fish for hours, though he told me he wouldn't kill a deer. He loved fishing so much he never would find the time to teach us how to do it. Once, though, I went up the salmon streams in Nova Scotia with him. The fish were coming four, five feet long, slapping against the water as they jumped, like cannon fire. My knees were trembling. I thought, What if I get ahold of one with my rod! I could understand the fisherman's delight, just holding on to that rod."

Bontecou's mother was an independent, too, "merry and energetic," with the "brightest red cheeks" of a Britisher. Dutifully she did the domestic chores required, sewed and cooked, but didn't care for it much. What she had enjoyed was working in a wartime factory wiring submarine components. She performed that intricate manual task so well, in fact, that every one of her machines worked when it was tested, and she turned them out so fast that the union told her to slow down, a rather depressing advice for woman "so bubbly and enthusiastic" and feeling her oats. It may have been some of her own spirit and confidence that inspired Bontecou's first remembered impression that she too could become, and do, something particular in life. "That time, I must have been eight or nine, I was going down the stairs mooshing up some sand to try splattering it on a piece of wood to make a drawing, and I remember distinctly thinking, I can do anything in the world, if I only have the tools to do it with."

School years passed ("The elementary school had an old First World War airplane, and all I can remember is clambering over that thing, and that everyone would get in and pretend whatever they wanted") and then two years at Bradford Junior College in Massachusetts. "I'm glad I did that; it's one thing with the arts: you don't have to start young. Whenever you do, it's all right." It was her decision to go on to art school, and her parents agreed. "I was free. So when I went to New York and began working at the Art Students League, I became independent. From then on I worked my way through with part-time jobs." She began in a drawing class, then moved to painting, and then the intuitive machinery began taking over. "All these people were drawing up storms, and here I walked in from Canada or Westchester or somewhere and I got my stick figure down. But then it grew and grew. My parents began to be worried, because they didn't know where I was going. Obviously I wasn't interested then in getting married. I wanted to *do* something! So I kept telling them I was planning to be a commercial artist, so I wouldn't have to answer questions. It was sort of not nice, but it left me free.

"I had taken the drawing class, and then I took the painting. And then I thought, Well, I'll just go down and try sculpture. And that was that. I never came up afterward. I liked it. It was for me. I was happy there. It made sense

381

somehow. So I said to myself, Okay, I want to keep pushing it as far as I can go. But there never was any real specific moment of decision.

"Nowadays sometimes people come to me and ask, 'Well, am I an artist?' And I say, 'If you have to ask that question, it's dangerous. You can't be in art because your mind tells you to be. It has to be mind plus heart. It's too dangerous an area to enter unless you're willing not to get so much back.' When someone says, 'I'm going to get my Ph.D. in art, or my M.F.A.,' it's like a puzzle to me. 'What's that for?' I ask. Though I suppose things have changed and now it's the security that counts. And maybe in a way that was needed.

"I didn't want strings, however. That's one reason I couldn't have taken money from the family. I wanted to be free. I was entering such a different world and I couldn't talk about it with them. It was, really, the only area I missed with them, not being able to talk. That began when I was a teenager, because I had ideas that weren't . . . fitting."

At the League, Bontecou worked first in sculpture with William Zorach, the well-known figurative stonecutter. She did some pieces in terra cotta and then took off with plaster, making some rather far-out numbers. "I was a nuisance in class. 'Come on, let's have coffee instead of . . .'—you know. And I would do something incredibly stupid and bizarre, but he would just say, 'Go ahead—go ahead.' " One, six feet high, was "a mess. I made it in slabs and then put them together. An abstract thing. It was awful but good experience. When I came back after a couple of weeks and looked at it, I just knocked it down. Then I made a lot of small things, just putting them up and tearing them down. One summer I went to Skowhegan, and that was an incredible experience. And then I went to Italy, and there I began working as an ex-student. I mean, I was *out*."

Bontecou won a Fulbright Fellowship for her League work and went off to Rome, in '57, for two years. There it was that she began working fast toward the image that would coalesce when she got back to New York. The early steps were welding frames, with the idea of making wall pieces. At first, she filled the frames with metal pieces. These constructions were "a disaster. I pulled the whole wall out."

Next, she poured wax into thin sheets three or four feet wide, cut the wax into forms and seared them together into structures that were then cast directly into metal. And these exceedingly thin complexes turned out, to everyone's surprise including the foundry workers', "just incredible. No shrinkage or anything." The imagery in those days was principally birds. Semiabstract, rather heavy, expressionistic forms with pouter chests and splayed claws to grip the floor. "Some of the birds were grounded. In no way could they fly. If you

382

skinned them and laid them flat, the forms would be close to my later pieces. I also did some strange-looking people. I remember not wanting to do faces. I'd been so happy with Henry Moore because he simply eliminated the features and put in little dots for eyes.

"Then for a while I lived in a terra-cotta factory and used clay. I'd lay clay over the welded metal frames, let it dry, take it off, fire it and cement it back. It was almost like a mosaic, made in pieces. And I still work in pieces. That way, I can extend the surface way beyond what it naturally will do. I get involved with space.

"In fact, if you took those shapes I made back in Italy, they were rather like the ones I made when I came back home. Not far from them. In those days, I kept thinking how nice it was to be able to change, not to be stuck in a mold. But the strange thing is that even after you have changed, as you believe you have, and then look back, you see there is one thread through it all."

In 1959, Bontecou returned to New York and found herself a loft on Avenue C and Sixth Street, "in the lousiest area, because it was reasonable. And it was nice there, I enjoyed it. There was crime and that kind of thing on every other block, but this was before the drugs. It wasn't like now." It was there she built in the plumbing, and there she had no heat. Requirement impelled her to drill holes in the floor to enjoy some of the excess heat generated by her downstairs neighbor, the laundryman. Living so close atop him, she noticed that he discarded from time to time old canvas conveyer belts. She had by now tried all kinds of materials to bridge or span those welded steel frames: clay, heavy

Exhibition at Castelli Gallery, New York, 1960.

metal, thin metal sheets cast by the lost-wax technique. Now she made forays into the garbage disposal and began to make use of forms cut out of worn, stained gray canvas, sewn onto the frames with wire. Now and then she also filched an empty mail bag left against a mailbox until she learned that tampering with the post was a federal crime.

At first, she made a number of tries with small-scale boxes and geometric forms, combining the canvas with leather and metal. Then there came a moment when she saw the way to go. "I welded up a frame and realized I could hold everything together inside it. So I got to work. And the pieces opened up onto the wall. It was a nice freeing point. The pieces got larger and larger.

"And then there was something else, rather hard to explain. I was after a kind of illusion. With painting you have illusion. The surface is two-dimensional, so everything that happens on it is illusionary. I love that. But it seemed you couldn't have that in stone, wood, or most welded stuff because the material is so heavy; there's no illusionary depth. But this canvas was the answer. I could push a part of the structure way, way back. I could go way deep, and the blackness played its part in that, too. Or I could come up forward with lighter grays. Or even different colors. You were free to vary the values as you liked."

It was one of those remarkable and productive technical breakthroughs that engender conceptual and imagist breakthroughs to follow. Besides, there was an accumulation of feeling, those days, that was seeking outlet.

"I was angry. I used to work with the United Nations program on the short-wave radio in my studio. I used it like background music, and, in a way, the anger became part of the process. During World War II we'd been too young. But at that later time, all the feelings I'd had back then came to me again. Rockefeller was trying to push bomb shelters on us. Africa was in trouble and we were so negative. China was trying to make her thing and we were negative. Then I remembered the killings, the Holocaust. The political scene. And out of that came two kinds of feeling.

"In the first place, I'd get so depressed that I'd have to stop and turn to more open work, work that I felt was more optimistic—where, for example, there might be just one single opening, and the space beyond it was like opening up into the heavens, going up into space, feeling space. The other kind of work was like war equipment. With teeth. Not many people realized that. But the funny thing is that those canvases ended in German museums or Israeli ones. Just where they belonged, without my saying a thing. One of those pieces went to the Jewish Museum in New York. It was a sort of memorial of my feelings. I never titled any of these. Once I started to, and it seemed to limit people to a certain response, so I didn't continue. I hate the feeling of being

Untitled sculpture, 1962. Welded steel and canvas. 76" by 70½" by 27". Whitney Museum of American Art, New York.

put into a little pigeonhole. It's like fighting, to keep out of the pigeonholes"—
or, could one say, to stay loose as the scooping, swift machinery of a thin-
skinned aluminum canoe pumped by the bare legs of a small tomboy?

That impulse not to stay caught impelled Bontecou, around 1967, to give up
that most extraordinarily "successful" of images altogether. She began instead
to work with various plastics, turning out smaller pieces of vacuum-molding
and then combining them into complicated structures, in this case, a raft of
natural forms, especially fish and flowers, with trailing fronds and tubes, all
transparent and cartilaginous rather like the glass flowers at the Peabody Museum in Cambridge or models of sea flora at the American Museum of Natural
History in New York. It would be too easy to say that those organic forms
reflect merely certain turns in her private life. Bontecou meant a sharp political
statement with them as well. "Just as there were gas masks and Nazi helmets
involved in the steel-and-canvas sculpture, so the flowers in their way were
saying, 'Okay, we have to have plants. If you don't watch out, this is all we'll
have to remember what flowers used to look like, this kind of flower that is
made out of plastic.' My making them out of synthetics was a way of saying
what would happen if we keep gallivanting the way we are. But really, nothing
is so clear-cut, so black, white and gray.

"But I've just kept working, really, the way I did before. Partly through
dreams, even daydreams, partly through imagination. There's a certain technical part too. You get started on it and then you close your eyes and you walk
away from it. I used to go to museums a lot, the Museum of Natural History
and the Met. And galleries, some. But I'd still rather take from what's around
me. On the street, or on the seashore. There are things that excite me. Like
when you walk down the beach and the shadow hits the sand. Have you seen
that kind of thing? It's incredible. The ripple of sand is hit by the light, and
there you have your darks and lights.

"Or there's the jet power in the airplane. I used to like to sit over the wing
so you could see the propeller going as well as the jet part, and you could see
the wing area and how it was all riveted together. You felt that incredible force.
It would just about make my imagination go out of bounds.

"So you take from the world, but then it goes into the dream. Like when
you read a book and the man speaks to you and you feel Here's a friend. It's
the same when I look at a porpoise or when I see an airplane with a certain
design: There's a friend. I can understand you. I don't mean copying—there's
no way you can copy those things. I don't really even like to get too close to
something that moves me like that."

"Well, all those few years I worked with plastics and certain forms I was trying for, something I wanted, but I couldn't get it. The material just wouldn't give. So now I'm working back with clay, working with much the same shapes, however. Though it's more dream, more imaginary—like imaginary dream creatures or something. Small, yes. I've really finished only a couple so far, though I have tons of forms around, parts, elements, stuff like that.

"It's beginning to work out. I can see where it might grow and grow and grow. Anyway, I'm interested in it, and I'm happy with that. I don't really care about anything else, as long as I'm working."

Women
of the
Fourth Wave:
Humboldt's
Daughters[1]

INCLUDING
ATHENA TACHA,
MARY MISS,
ALICE AYCOCK

1970 was the turning point from "private to public" for women in the art world [2]—for the young with their appetite for success whetted by graduate studies at Yale, Rutgers and other universities, and for elders of previous waves who found inspiration in the political model. The Ad Hoc Women Artists' Committee, formed that year to harry the Whitney Museum on its sexist exhibition policies, led the way. Strikes, marches, speeches were effective in the art world as, at last in 1973, they would be vis-à-vis Vietnam. The Whitney Annual of 1970, then, included more women than ever before; more than one in this book showed in that place for the first time. And soon there existed a Women's Art Registry; the "East–West Bag"—a crosscountry network of women artists; women's centers in Los Angeles, New York, Chicago, etc.; and publications of Feminist news, art criticism and literature like the *Feminist Art Journal, Heresies, Chrysalis, Women Artists' Newsletter* (now *Women Artists' News*) and others. What was, in fact, surprising was that a centuries-old prejudice about the visual arts as male enclave should wither so fast. ERA might be in trouble across the land by 1978, but in no American museum, one suspected, would it be broached again that women, as artists, were collectively inadequate.

Meanwhile, from an economic inflation that had become international, the art world, now women included, took its own expansive momentum. As the Metropolitan Museum in New York enlarged into a $75-million plant; as works of art changed hands in flamboyantly publicized auctions and deals; as the National Endowments, private foundations, corporate tax-deductible accounts and community art groups vested more money in art projects [3] in which women now took part; so the scale and also the ideological reach of works made by those women grew. Was there ever more vivid proof of the interrelationship between the movements of a society and the forms of its art? To refute two old chauvinist saws, one might say that, indubitably, many creations of the 1970s—like Nancy Graves's 5,000-pound bronze *Ceridwen* in Dag Hammarskjold Plaza in New York; Anne Healy's 35-foot-high colored nylon *Cathedral;* Rosemary Mayer's 10-foot-high fabric-and-wood *Galla Placidia;* Louise Nevelson's 54-foot steel *Sky Tree* in San Francisco; Beverly Pepper's 200-

foot-diameter *Amphisculpture* in Bedminster, New Jersey; Miriam Schapiro's 50-foot-wide *Anatomy of a Kimono;* Sylvia Stone's 28-foot-long *Egyptian Gardens;* Lenore Tawney's 30-by-15-foot *Cloud* in Santa Rosa, California—were made by female artists "with wings" or other attributes.[4]

And those perpetuators, as I have said, of the romantic-scientific-universalist viewpoint: they have taken on themselves the task of flinging their net of form so wide it must encompass the whole seen and felt universe (Bartlett); the history of a race (Ringgold); the phantoms of the unconscious (Antin); all geological creation (Stuart); all biological life (Johanson). I see them participating in the most undisguised way in the fundamental creative exercise: the invention of mental structures that, projected outward (concretized in the work), serve to bind up past and present to render the figures, moods and moments of the past immortal. That the forms they have invented—and that they talk about here—are not the conventional ones in oil paint, acrylic, the "normal" materials of sculpture, does not make them any the less susceptible to interpretation in the way I have already proposed in this book. Raw hemp, pulverized rock, sifted sand have their tales to tell, if one wishes to read.

Those who speak in this section at length are far from alone. Works of a challenging diversity of look, medium and implication have been seen in public exhibition in the past half decade by, among some others not mentioned elsewhere in this book, Alice Adams, Hélène Aylon, Mary Bauermeister, Lynda Benglis, Rosemarie Castoro, Diana Chang, Sonia Chusit, Agnes Denes, Donna Dennis, Anne Dunn, Susan Eder, Jackie Ferrara, Suzi Gablik, Suzanne Harris, Nina Holton, Alison Knowles, Constance McMillan, Joan Miller, Elizabeth Murray, Ann Norton, Deborah Remington, Dorothea Rockburne, Susan Rothenberg, Ce Roser, Joan Semmel, Elisabeth Munro Smith, Shirlann Smith, Ann Sperry, Pat Steir, May Stevens, Nancy Webb, Hannah Wilke and Barbara Zucker.

There is also Athena Tacha, born in 1936 in the mountainous north of Greece, doctor of esthetics, sculptor and now professor and museum curator at Oberlin College in Ohio. "For my father," says Tacha, "I was to be both son and daughter. He was teaching me to be the goddess Athena. 'With that name, you have to be someone!' he said.

"He said, 'As Aristotle gave Alexander Achilles as his model, so I give you Athena as yours!' "

This Athena reincarnated builds Site Works. One is a sculpture park in Smithtown, Long Island, of concrete, pebbles, myrtle, water and a mural painting. Another is *Streams,* a series of sandstone-strip steps that ascend a gentle hill in Oberlin, while back down the hill, as the title suggests, cascades a

Athena Tacha. Streams, 1975–76. Sandstone, pumice rocks, pebbles. 10' by 30' by 20'. Oberlin College, Oberlin, Ohio.

graceful rubble-wash of pink pumice rocks and lake pebbles. And her inspiration? "Only after a month's seclusion in a village on Mount Pelion, the wildest mountain of Thessaly, did I find my own way. Achilles trained there. Whenever I need soul-searching, I go back. So I still have the mountains of Greece in my blood."

There is, also, Mary Miss, born in '44, daughter of an army engineer who moved from site to site setting up artillery installations. She makes viewing works in which one must find a place-to-stand in order to sight through the architectural structure. Of her work at Artpark in '76, Miss wrote as if she were describing the literal elevation of a missile in its silo: "Rising slowly, you pass the marked layers, bands of steel, as though coming-up through layers of the

393

Mary Miss. Battery Park (city landfill project), *1973. Wood. 5'6" by 12' sections at 50' intervals.   New York.*

earth—like rising out of the center of a crater . . . it is by sighting down the four troughs that the outside landscape is first revealed."[5]

Then there is Alice Aycock, who makes deliberate references back and forth between her works and her past life, dreams and reading. Her complex and fascinating wooden climbing, tunneling and wandering structures offer, as she explains, both claustrophobic experience and claustrophiliac, acrophobic and acrophiliac. But all these experiences are, as she also conveys, elaborations of primal experiences undergone in childhood homes: a grandmother's airless attic in the South; a grandfather's orchards planted upon mining-ravaged hills of Pennsylvania.

In one of those experiences she climbed into that attic and stood under its low rafters.[6] That was the paradigm: standing in that space. Later, she did so again in a tholos tomb in Greece; later still, apparently, in dreams where a girl child lay dead behind a screen. Constantly, the stairs or shafts of her wood structures lead her upward or down, acting out, as I see it, the drive Simone de Beauvoir described: "to find again the dead child within herself, even to revive it."[7]

The process of making the art, then, may be read, at least on this level, as a lifelong climbing of the stairs, a fabricating of the screen only so as to push it aside, a summoning up of the face that can never be seen again but which cannot be allowed to be forgotten.

Alice Aycock. Studies for a Town, 1977. Wood. 3' to 10' high, 11' to 12½' diameter. Executed for the Projects Room, The Museum of Modern Art, New York: "An elliptical wooden structure cut on a skew to provide a bird's-eye view of the whole and to reveal its interior components: steps, walls, doorways, windows, ladders, roofs, shafts, and alleys, some of which may be reached by the spectator; others, only seen, remain inaccessible. The work incorporates references to medieval walled towns, Roman amphitheaters, military bunkers, Egyptian shanty towns and desert citadels, and an eighteenth-century Indian observatory" (Aycock).

Jennifer Bartlett

BORN 1941, LONG BEACH, CALIFORNIA

I ask myself, Am I not trying hard enough? Or, Why am I not doing anything else? It's projecting yourself into the future—if you have a future. . . .

But I've always been able to go ahead. That's why I chose the plates—to set up a situation that would always be open.

—JENNIFER BARTLETT
New York, 1977

It is merely the universe that Bartlett wants to possess. To do that, she invented a device and a methodology, as those who wanted to file the world's knowledge in a box with buttons and blinkers had to invent—among other things—the method of linear programming. How frustrating it is, then, to find that just as ultimate answers keep receding from the computer's bank, so *totality* seems to keep blowing backward away from this artist's imagination in open pursuit.

Jennifer Bartlett's first long shot was with *Rhapsody,* an arrangement of 988 steel plates bearing painted notations, aligned along the walls of her New York gallery. It was hailed in 1976 by critics as a work of bravura complexity and originality. *Rhapsody* in fact made stunningly explicit a new consciousness in art that had been emerging from the late '50s on, under the influence of, among other things, those two basic devices of our time: film and the computer. Both, as we know, distribute experience along a serial plan. The mind, then, takes a walk. And since nothing is new under the sun, one can find plenty of historical precedents for that approach to content. All the paths of history down which Mind walked conveyed by Feet would fit the formula: Sacred *allées,* processional halls, aisles of churches were early devices for laying out experience for the brain which then might process the information by memory. Figures punched in clay tablets, letters on a page, sculptures in a frieze and "forms" in "space" were also commonly accepted devices for feeding infor-

396

mation seriatim into the head. Bartlett would strip the process and pare it down to the bone, as the computer does with, say, the stuff of Shakespeare or Romany songs. However, as happens in those cases too, "something"—which we think of as the essence—escapes through the grid and demands being dealt with in another way.

Rhapsody, then, began as a clear-cut perambulation around the Paula Cooper Gallery in SoHo, proceeding from left to right along those nearly one thousand separated steel and enamel plaques, each one a foot square, each one pre-etched with a grid providing 2,304 cells, within and across which the artist laid out a string of images. Theme facts were introduced, then pursued: House, Tree, Mountain, Ocean were world facts. Yellow, Red, Blue, Green, Black, White were hue facts. There were then "brush-stroke facts": short marks, dots, strokes, etc., made with various-sized Japanese brushes (more facts) in Testor enamel of the kind hobbyists find useful for painting in short spurts because the bottles can be emptied by a set number of brush dips. Brush-dip number, too, is fed into the workings of *Rhapsody.* Is there thematic progression toward a climax, that old predilection of human nature that negates, in principle, the concept of *merely* linear unwinding? There is. *Rhapsody* begins in a simple way with House, meanders through romantic images of green-blue Trees and snow-capped Mountains toward a final apotheosis: Ocean, a flattened, cresting wave of no fewer than fifty-four separate shades of blue.

"Yes," says the artist. "The blues were meant to convey transcendence." Moreover, she tapped a classic psychoesthetic intuition in creating the work by sensing its overall, organic configuration even while claiming to be concerned in an equivalent way with every detail.

Rhapsody, 1975–76 (detail). 988 plates, baked enamel and silkscreen grid on 16-gauge steel. Each plate 12" by 12". Installation 7'6" by 153'9". Collection Sidney Singer, Mamaroneck, New York.

"For *Rhapsody* I never measured the space. Along the way, I enlarged it in my studio to work out various themes. And then at the end, when I went to install it, I found it filled the whole gallery with just six feet to spare. *That shocked me.* Apparently I had some sort of intuition about the size of space and the size of a piece to fit into it. Now I have confidence these things will work out." A confession made by the artist in her cheerful, nonobfuscating way. The plates, then, reflect a psyche that seeks a holistic experience. With that vital information, we set out upon a walk through her life.

"I was born in Long Beach, California, by the ocean. Then the family moved inland; then after a while they made more money and moved back to the ocean. This was when I was about nine."

Her mother had been a fashion illustrator who gave up her work when she was pregnant with Jennifer, the first of four children. "I knew my mother was artistic, though I didn't see much of that side of her. I only knew she'd given it up when I was born, so naturally I thought I'd stopped her." Her father, born in Idaho Falls, was a contractor for pipeline and sewage systems and spent much of his working life, on the road, between California and Nevada and Arizona until he died in '76. His death was more painful for his family than he might have expected. It turned out he had lived several dimensions of other lives in the guise of living a linear one. What to all appearances life had put together, in actuality life had put asunder (see page 422 for more on this). The artist is still processing and suffering that information.

Still, in the early days, the family together was happy when they lived by the sea. "I adored that. We lived on a small peninsula with the bay on one side and the ocean on the other. Waves would dash across the boardwalk, and there were secret places to play underneath it. I still have a loathing for any kind of suburban situation with lawn and trees, the kind of place we lived in before we moved back to the ocean. I feel trapped in that kind of place."

Jennifer was "the best artist in kindergarten, the best artist in first grade. I always told everyone I wanted to be an artist. And I kept doing repetitive things. When I saw Disney's *Cinderella* I made about five hundred drawings of Cinderella with different trim on every one of her dresses. Or I'd buy lots of those fuzzy chickens you get on Easter, and divide them up by color and put them in pens according to their color. Once I made a series of pictures on brown paper of California missions: missions with Indians in the field; missions with priests; missions in fields; with cliffs; with oceans; with mountains; with boats. Once I drew a fair, with every single booth. Anything to do with organization. I once said if they held an Art Olympics in Madison Square Garden with all the materials laid out—paints, brushes, paper—I'd organize it all.

"And I loved *things*. I loved the place in Laura Ingalls Wilder where the children get their first orange and eat it. Or in *Swiss Family Robinson* where things are so precious. I'd ask myself, if I were a Chinese and came to earth here in America what would be the first *thing* I'd notice?

"Noticing things so much and having decided to be an artist gave me the feeling, early, of being special. Even of having a mission. I felt independent from an early age. I could take care of myself. I was aggressive and decisive. So much so that after the sixth grade I was always in trouble. I ran away from home, smoked, had fights with my parents. One time I was even arrested for shoplifting. It was Christmas. My mother and I were decorating the tree and I saw there weren't enough balls, so I went out and stole some. The police came and took me to a detention cell to scare me. I was fingerprinted and the police were very tough. Mother came and picked me up in the car, and cried. But we never talked about the episode. I never discussed it with either of my parents.

"I was having trouble in school then, a combination of isolation and exhibitionism, grandiosity and depression. I was involved with the idea of genius. I got that from reading. I read all the Oz books, for example. I would have wanted all power and all control. I'd have liked to be a witch. A Good Queen. A Sue Barton nurse.

"At a point, I lost about forty pounds and decided to be popular. I was writing poems in those days and dating a lot, but I felt I didn't really fit in anywhere. At the same time, I was picking up ideas about the kind of life I really wanted: as early as thirteen, I'd had some lessons in art from a woman who'd lived in New York. The idea of living in New York was wonderful! I'd wanted that since I was six, from seeing pictures in the movies and on TV.

"Then, three or four years ago on my birthday, that woman burned herself to death smoking in her bed." The American way of death: not on a pillow among gathered generations, but suddenly, alone, in a moment of violence. One who wants to possess the universe in the 1970s will have to mark a separate key for pain, because conflict of many kinds, as we well know, became common during the years young Jennifer Bartlett surfaced through a sky-blue California world.

"We had a black woman working for us, who had a child. One day we went to the beach and we were kicked off. I asked my mother to tell the lifeguard to let us stay. She wouldn't. I despised her for that. . . .

"During the Korean War, I wrote a letter to the Long Beach paper complaining about their running the Miss Universe pageant while the war was going on. My father was furious because he was negotiating a pipeline contract with the city. . . .

"Twice a man exposed himself to me. I took the license plate of his car and had to testify in court. Once my brother found a blood-stained wallet in our garden. It belonged to a war vet who had axed his wife to death and dropped it in our yard. My brother had to testify in court, too."

Mills College, where Bartlett went next, was, one might say, insulated from conflict by enclosing so much of it on equal terms for an eclecticism that probably characterized most American institutions of the time. Might one not expect young people to come out more distanced from political and social issues than involved? "Chiang Kai-shek's grandson was in our crowd. So were Hungarian freedom fighters. These were my first contact with foreigners. There were also two Japanese in our group, a black girl, the Spreckles sugar heiress and Pia Lindstrom. A political confusion!" But distancing does not mean that knowledge is nonexistent, merely recircuited or temporarily blocked.

At college, Bartlett ran the route of the gifted: good grades, high honors, prizes. Also nonconformism, some flaunted rebelliousness and also the beginning of motivation and a sense that one might find a way beyond being blocked. "I was always depressed as a child in California. Oppressed and depressed. Bored. But as soon as I got to college, I was highly motivated."

Part of the cause was the welter of (esthetically equivalent) ideas and images that marked California's McLuhanesque world in the late '50s.

"We saw our first big show of Rothko and Franz Kline and Pollock at the Palace of the Legion of Honor. I'd seen a Van Gogh show at home and wept, I was so moved. I saw John Gielgud in *The Ages of Man,* and when he did Lear's speech I was crying. . . . At Mills I heard my first concerto, by Cage, scored for fifty pianos. . . . I heard Berio, and Stravinsky.

"I saw my first Monet, brown, with an overturned boat—the same form as his haystacks, I later realized. I thought it was remarkable to take an image so dumb, so emotionally flat. Like a teacup. Later on, after the fact, his haystacks made me think of my House.

"We didn't make any distinctions between figurative and abstract in those days. Rauschenberg and Johns just seemed a continuation from de Kooning, etc. But Warhol came as a shock. The *Portraits.* Then the Minimal group. Stella, and Lichtenstein. That made me want even more to go to New York.

"Senior year, I met Elizabeth Murray, the first woman I'd met who I thought was superior to me. There we were, taking things so ponderously, talking about *The Brothers Karamazov* and so on, and she'd be reading *Ulysses*

400

and roaring with laughter, or sitting by herself listening to Verdi's *Requiem*. She worked constantly, wouldn't go to meals, lived on Grape Nuts. She was a real artist to me."

Abstract Expressionism with its romantic baggage of ego and swashbuckle was the academy now. One decade from invisibility to orthodoxy. "When I went to Mills, the people who taught me had studied with Clyfford Still. Sophomore year I discovered Gorky and Kandinsky. Even the figure classes were relatively abstract. We'd learn traditional perspective, color and so on, in two-week bursts, and then go right back to working in our own ways.

"[Again] I had a terrible painter's block at first. I just couldn't begin. I'd stand for hours in front of the easel. Then at a point I dropped creative writing— I'd been trying to carry both—and at once I started in painting and painted all the time. First a landscape, then a figure. Then I began on my own, concentrating on organic abstract shapes, working very large, with glazes. It was exciting. I was allowed to go my own way."

Graduating in '63, Bartlett took off for the Yale School of Art and Architecture, where the Abstract Expressionist painter Jack Tworkov was now in the head chair. Freedom was the rule. Some like Tworkov even felt the eclecticism bordered on incoherence. "There just wasn't a cohesive culture," he himself remembers of those days. Part of the esthetic of the Abstract Expressionists had involved gestural freedom, accident, as a method of dredging the deeps. There was an opportunistic element there, too: the artist hoped that fresh and personal forms would be dredged up by accident where logical, linear thinking would fail to evoke them. Now the artists were all exploring for themselves, finding identities for themselves.

"For myself," says Tworkov, "I found stimulus through geometry. I determined that if I could set up a geometric grid and limit myself only to forms within it, then I might find infinite possibilities there. Within the grid lines, I could take any shapes I needed . . . I could make a program, say, of triangles, or rectangles. I could take the movements of chessmen, say, and work by them, a Knight's approach, for instance. I could engage, or refuse to engage, the intersections. I could go on infinitely finding shapes within the grid."

Bartlett, after a West-to-East entry process that involved an episode of culture shock, began painting enormous quasi–Abstract Expressionist works, "with things breaking through, and very spastic drawing," some with attached panels and constructed elements like wooden struts. It was open field day for experimentation, though she recalls one teacher who clarified the issue of originality. He said, "All over the United States, in every town of ten thousand

401

people, there's one baritone. And every Saturday there's a talent show. And at each talent show is a baritone singing the same song in the same voice: 'Come Back to Sorrento.' And that's your painting, Jennifer."

That was somewhat the feeling she herself would take away from Yale two years later, the year of the bombing of North Vietnam and the beginning of a country-wide protest movement. Social and political traumas, however, would not find their way into the art of the '60s as Social Realism had expressed the disturbances of the '30s, and Abstract Expressionism the traumas related to war. Protest, this time, was taking other forms: pantomime (Happenings), mask (Pop Art), and that distancing again (Minimalism), that contemporary form of radicalism that may conceal trauma too deep for songs. Bartlett, for one, spent some three years getting her life together, marrying a medical student, setting up two living situations—a Connecticut apartment and a SoHo loft—teaching with her new M.F.A., and continuing to turn out the enormous canvases. One was thirty feet wide, done with spray paints; another was all black with a grid of glossy enamel car paint. "I was completely bored with myself then. I hated building those big stretchers. I hated having to make decisions about the size."

As far back as college, Bartlett had begun to be aware that the Abstract Expressionist idiom had lost its generative force for her. A vocabulary of only a few shapes kept on being born out of the void of possibilities. She would start with lines and end sooner than later with "real feet," "some dots," "organic body shapes." It was, she feels now, the all-is-possible, the *vastness* that appalled her.

"Picking colors revolted me. There never seemed to be any reason to make any special choice. It always ended up with my solving the problem in the same way. If you go to the grocery store every day with no more than a vague intention, you'll take the same route every day.

"That old way of painting could get me started, but it wasn't *efficient* afterward. I got bored. I needed a mental structuring to make everything clear to me. So I began to use grid paper. It was an organizational device.

"The problem I was facing was that I couldn't judge between alternatives. I'd do forty drawings for one painting. But then you have to pick. And I had the feeling my choices were structurally arbitrary. So I decided, instead of making choices, to try to do everything.

"In 1966 I did a painting, on canvas nine feet by eighteen, with two hundred fifty twelve-by-three-inch vertical rectangles, each one a different color. I mixed up two hundred fifty different colors. I entered a number for each color on a card, numbered the paint cups and drew a card for each rectangle. I started at the upper left and ended lower right. And then the process of decision, at last, was completely out of my control.

"It was kind of fun!"

With the art process now out of her control, she turned to get her life *under* control. Since graduating, she had split her life between those two establishments, domestically cooking dinner in New Haven, independently painting in New York. Other young woman of many eras have also felt, with Bartlett, "I had to be good at everything." In 1969 she went into analysis, divorced, sold the car she received in the divorce settlement back to her ex-husband for a thousand dollars to begin life anew and hit on the idea of the plates. She had noticed that the station signs in New York subways made use of steel plaques to spell out any known set of words. She ordered them for her own use. At the same time, she was moved to begin writing again. By the same method. "I began using the thesaurus, writing out all the words I could that began with *A*, then *B*, then *C*, then all the birds, the fish, the mammals—all the names in the world. Then I just started writing."

The writing expanded. "The linear-program idea could apply to writing too," as plates, cards and paint cups would let visual imagery expand.

"It was fun developing the idea of the plates because everybody thought I was nuts. But I wanted something flat to the wall, something that I could wipe down and make corrections. Something where the work would be absolutely explicit, with no layers."

"No layers" is a key to the nature of the transformation in the esthetic. Layers imply acceptance of simultaneity and uncertainty, the half-seen and not wholly comprehended. Since the fifteenth century when painters developed oil-based pigments, one of the marvels of the medium was the potential it offered for layering of colors and tones, for the enrichment of reflected light that, to the eye, conveys qualities the mind interprets as "life." Color-stain painters like Frankenthaler gave up the layering potential of oils but kept the "magic" by extending their control over gesture that, in its way, too, could convey an impression of the irresolution, the complexity, the impermanence of life. One might say that both these earlier medium techniques implied a vitalist psychoesthetic: humanity the unknown; nature the incalculable. *Life,* layered and whole.

There was a boldness to Bartlett's claim on simplicity in her painted works, but a radical cutting away of overtones. Her life moves, at the time, were as directed. She put her all into the effort of enlarging this new idiom. By the time *Rhapsody* was finished, she would be ten thousand dollars in debt to friends and doctors for equipment, materials and medical treatments.

Both: details from Rhapsody *(see page 397).*

Pre-*Rhapsody* plate works were formulations of black dots in series: original device but not yet original content. Similar works had been made by Constructivist and Bauhaus artists. In 1970, Bartlett had her first show of these abstract works.

"Then I thought, If a system is valid when it's presented abstractly, why can't it be as serious and effective in a figurative context?" And indeed, later that year, she laid out an original *Ur*-plate with a House on it, then elaborated in seventy-two plates that followed. Next she introduced landscape elements as counters in a bigger game. For these—significantly—she elected those features of the conventional American scene that filled her with boredom or loathing back in Long Beach.

"I decided to choose the most conventional possible landscape. I wanted a house anybody could aspire to; that anybody would have been in at least once. I wanted the kind of landscape anyone who lived in the East, Midwest or West would find in a painting for sale in any dime store. So I chose a red House, a Pond with a duck, a white Fence and three green Hills." These, with Sky, blue Water, green Grass would comprise all the elements of her future works as, for a composer of a rhapsody, middle C may have no more weight than D or E (though the notes in combination may break the heart).

There was a scheme for turning out the first variations. "I drew a card for each plate. In each plate, one element used in the previous plate drops out. Ducks drop out of one, Ponds drop out of the next and so on. So I proceeded until nothing was left.

"Another short run was 'Four Times of Day.' There were four colors, for noon, twilight, night, dawn. Another was 'Four Seasons.' I decided on the most typical possible days: dead of winter with a watery sun, no ducks; spring with cumulus clouds and ducks in a pond; summer with stratus-cirrus and fields in bloom; autumn with cumulus-nimbus clouds, ducks.

"For another, I squared each space, increasing the size of the image over the previous plate. And soon I observed that there's a point at which any system self-destructs. Look at a shoe, for instance. Enlarge it. Double the size again. Soon you'll lose sight of the fact it's a shoe."

Subpieces or spinoffs appear from time to time. Bartlett explains how they work: "*Parabola* goes on a numbering system. White is dominant. It's a thirty-six-plate piece with 2,304 dots per plate. The series goes: 123456, 112345, 111234 and so on. That piece took me six months to do. Nowadays, going at top speed with six years' experience, it takes me forty-five minutes to do each plate. And if I'm counting as I go—as I have to in these numerical ones—it takes forever."

392 Broadway works variations on the House, using four colors with black and white. At either end of this series is a smooth diagram of a house. Next group in on each side is a "free-hand" area where the house is blurred in a welter of expressionistic strokes. In the center area: demolition.

"The plates are all flying apart, rough and smooth. All the plates are trying to smash their way in. But obviously there's not enough room. That struck me as funny! Well, I try not to think too imagistically, but the fact is all the plates really are trying to smash their way in.

"All these plates are painted by formula. I count the strokes on each one. For the 'messy' plates, I use ten strokes of one color until I use up one bottle of paint. Then ten strokes of gray, then blacks and then one bottle of white if white is dominant. The 'rough, freehand' sections, on the other hand, have about ten bottles of paint of each color, forty bottles *in toto*. I use three different-size brushes, enlarging them in series.

"Freehand has to be painted standing up.

"By now the painting has *become method*."

Method does not necessarily lead to conclusion. As it prods forward, a line may lie shallow, not get under the surface. The evidence is distributed, but the conclusion escapes. The universe expands, but why? The atom has many parts, but how? Fossils describe life, but to what end?

Bartlett's ambitions were growing, however. She sought a new expressive channel, began now to enlarge her writings. Those dictionary words of the early essays now gave way to narration of packets of experience, also laid out along the line. *History of the Universe* stands today at one thousand pages. However, dealing with that layered matter, autobiography, it drives more into the shadows than the visual works do. If *Rhapsody* takes a daylit way toward Blue, reveals a mind reaching for transcendent universality, *Universe* shows us a mind veering toward demolition (that characteristic of these times revealed also in the book *Looking for Mr. Goodbar*):

. . . at thirty-one I'm scared of everything. Of fainting . . . of breathing deeply to avoid fainting, of remaining conscious during terror. I am scared of cars, people driving, me driving, big trucks. I am frightened of circumscribed existence and terrified by instability, of elevators stuck and falling. . . . I think of sinking ships, rapists, murderers, madmen, doors slamming shut or creaking open in the night, of being alone or being with someone. . . .

He put his hand on my buttocks. I said don't do that he said you're supposed to like it. I said well then you're doing it wrong. . . . he had to piss I said you can piss at the bar he said no I said you can piss in the street he said no I said OK you can come up but I'm going to act as though no one is there but me. . . .

. . . I don't like their parties, I don't want to go, don't like their guns, their warehouse, don't like their guru, their psychiatrist, don't want the free stuff, don't want to eat at the cafeteria. I hate the doctor, the men by the truck, don't trust the Japanese sorting with his gun, the poison meat. Don't want to grow a penis don't want to cooperate. I want to fix up my loft. They'll let it drop for a while. I'll go along, get things done, when I'm not suspecting it, on the street, at a restaurant, a party, on my couch, watching TV, painting, eating, in bed, anywhere, sometime, they'll kill me.

EM: "Jennifer, why do you paint?"

JB: "I want to move people. Yes. I'd like to be a strong, heartbreaking artist."

EM: "Well, tell me about *Rhapsody*. Did you mean it to elevate, to move, to convey ecstasy?"

JB: "I thought a lot while I was doing that piece. I was making a bid—for whatever. I was trying hard, full throttle. Then I finished it, but I didn't have a title. Or, I had humble titles. I was in favor of Gertrude Stein then: her grandiose ideas and simple titles. I talked to a friend. He said 'Music.' I thought right away *Fugue* or *Bach*. He said, 'No—*Rhapsody*.' I cringed in horror. It sounded romantic, soft, creepy. I hated it! I wouldn't be able to face anyone.

"I went to the dictionary and looked up every musical term. Last of all,

'rhapsody.' A synonym was 'bombastic.' Perfect! That title would force me to face my horror of the kind of feelings in it."

EM: "What do you mean? What's in it? What's it about?"

JM: (Pause.) "Don't you think the idea of Einstein is a little . . . heartbreaking? The degree of abstraction he proposed? His ideas? They seem a little sad. Because they're so large.

" 'Poignancy' is too mild a word. Sad. Like a Truffaut movie. Moments when you could weep. A sense of time. Of time running out. A feeling of inevitability, like that line of Hopkins—'Márgarét, are you gríeving . . . ?'[1]

"But this is the kind of stuff I loathe saying. Why? Because it's embarrassing. Why? Because I'm *an American!*"

EM: "Where is the work going? Where are *you?*"

JB: "Ah, if you arrested Cézanne at thirty-five, or had only one Cézanne, you wouldn't know what he was doing. If you looked at Picasso in 1903, you wouldn't know what he meant.

"I'm feeling very midthirties-crisis now. Not having got much work done. Many deaths in my family. I tend to get distracted. I ask myself, Am I not trying hard enough? Or, Why am I not doing anything else? It's projecting yourself into the future—if you have a future.

"But I've always been able to go ahead. That's why I chose the plates—to set up a situation that would always be open."

EM: "Children, Jennifer? How about that?"

JB: "When I was younger, I'd say I didn't want to. Or I said it to provoke my mother, or because she gave up her career to have me. Now I'd like to. I had an abortion once. A month after my father died, I got pregnant. For many reasons I acted right away. It was the most horrifying experience I've ever had. Utterly self-destructive. I'll never do it again.

"I used to have this idea of Art or a Child. I haven't had that conflict for a few years. There's a point you reach when you know you're going to do your work, no matter what.

"Anyway, I'm curious."

Walk back two squares to Gerard Manley Hopkins: ". . . nor mouth had, no nor mind expressed/What heart heard of, ghost guessed . . ."

The difficulty, one supposes, for a gifted and ambitious artist in her midthirties in the late 1970s is to put back together what these random-violent times have sundered. To find expression not only for what mouth, mind and eye can tally up in their linear machinations, but also for what heart and ghost crave to make known: that it is ". . . Márgarét you mourn for."

Faith
Ringgold

BORN 1930, NEW YORK CITY

*I began to see that I would have to do my work-
ing-out on my own. And that it would be a very
lonely life.*

—FAITH RINGGOLD
New York, 1977

Faith Ringgold was formed as an original in the politicized late '60s and '70s,
and her art today drives toward the single goal of moving and re-forming
people. Coming through a number of unresolved and unfulfilling experiments
with old-fashioned painting albeit filled with her own subject matter, she has
now put together an individual idiom that combines painting with sculpture
and theater. Meanwhile she is writing her autobiography and continuing to
make and exhibit African-inspired masks of velvet, lace, feathers, pearls and
colored thread, and over-life-size stuffed cloth figures based on heroes of her
people, like Adam Clayton Powell and Martin Luther King.

Meanwhile, too, Ringgold has raised two remarkable daughters—Mi-
chele Wallace, the author of *Black Macho and the Myth of the Superwoman*
(Dial Press, 1979), the other a graduate student in linguistics—has been married twice and divides her time between a living apartment and a studio apartment in Harlem. During the protests, marches and strikes of the 1970 art-world
crisis, she took an active, even fractious role in both the Women's and the
Black movements. She was, as she tells here, tested in the process, and when
the dust settled she determined that the job of remaking people's minds had
still to be done on a personal scale and so broadened her message to reach
students in colleges.

Ringgold is a short, impassioned, not unbitter woman in African dress with

409

a coif of tiny beads and quivering braids. She looks back to a childhood in a Harlem that few remember and where the feelings that imbue her work were born. "Mostly, I remember people. Faces of people. Everything about people. And then, early on, I got involved with the souls of people.

"I was born in Harlem in 1930, in the deep Depression. But that Harlem was different. It was a highly protective place. Almost an extended family. My father drove a truck for the Sanitation Department, a good job in those days. Then as people began to lose their jobs, cousins and other relatives came up from the South. So there were relatives around, and these gave us a feeling of community.

"My father taught my brother to protect my mother and us girls. He brought him up to understand that idea. That to him was being a man. Therefore though we've lived in Harlem all these years, the women in my family have no tales to tell of muggings or rapes. My mother too was consistently presenting a wholesome picture of life to us. She was what some would call a 'good Christian woman.' Today I'd shorten that to a 'good woman.' She was trained as a fashion designer and was always sewing. If I'd been left alone, I'd have done my own kind of thing earlier based on sewing. As it was, it wasn't until the Women's Movement that I got the go-ahead to do that kind of work.

"When I was about two, I got asthma, and this affected my life in many ways. The days when I lay in bed were the foundation of my life as an artist. It was just me and my mother in a nice quiet place. She was industrious, always doing things, and there I was, making things in my bed: drawings, watercolors, all kinds of things. When I look today at how I manipulate cloth to make sculptural forms, I know for a fact that I am doing what I wanted to do from early childhood when I was sitting in bed with asthma. And as I consider how I have moved and developed, I get another feeling: that what I am doing now is the completion of something, the solution to problems that began way back there. I was spoiled and pampered. And I got the impression that life should adjust to me. That I ought to enjoy life. There should be more enjoyment than pain. Then, when I was very young, Mother and Father separated, and he would come on his days off and get me and take me here and there to show me off, sit me on a bar and show how I could read off the signs. The bartender would keep my milk ready for me. My father was probably the first to teach me to read, from the signs in the bars.

"And Mother taught me at home; the teacher kept her informed. And all through school, though I never thought of art in a professional way, art was fun. It was something I could do alone, and I've always been a person who knows how to enjoy time spent alone.

"I didn't think of art as a profession until I graduated from high school and the question of a career came up. In 1948 I went to City College. There I copied Greek busts and got a sound background in Western art. Greek sculpture. Compositions after Degas. Then I began to feel that though I'd done the exercises fairly well, I wanted something more. But I didn't know how to get from Degas and the Greek busts . . . to Faith. That would take me considerable time."

EM: "You married a jazz musician in '50, had two children in '52 that one year (in January and December) and as you've often said, 'floated along' till you figured he was an unsteady bargain and went home to Mother. What then?"

FR: "The decision to become an artist had been made back when I graduated from high school in 1948. My idea was to teach. There were no women then in the School of Liberal Arts at City College, so I went to the School of Education. From 1955 on, I was teaching. That was in the family anyway. Mother's father was principal of a school; her mother was a teacher, and there were cousins too who taught. But after I got my M.A. in '59, I began to want to move toward becoming an artist.

"It was the Abstract Expressionist period; it seemed to me there was little doing, for me, in the gallery scene. So in 1961 I took the kids and my mother on a trip in Europe. We went to the galleries and museums in France and Italy, and I realized how much I love paintings. The images, the colors overwhelmed me. Magic, I said; I'm hooked!

"But when I got back home, I still had to find out whether I could do that sort of work myself. So I set up a studio in the dinette. And at that point I did something a lot of women do: I got married again. My new husband was encouraging for a couple of years, till he saw I was serious. And then he became *discouraging*. But I was on the way. I had to get from the Greek busts . . . to me.

"I had no background. No knowledge about the visual arts of black people. I appreciated the beauty of European art. The Rembrandts at the Uffizi anyone can appreciate. But I understood that that wasn't my heritage, the way you can enjoy a Chinese dinner and still not want to cook Chinese all the time.

"Most black people who are artists have the same problem. Even if you want to adopt a culture that isn't yours, you can't. The only way you can make works of art in another person's style is to copy, but then you have to keep on copying and going back for reference to things someone did in the past. It hampers your own development. It's making art from art instead of art from life.

"Here was a serious problem, for instance: what color are people supposed to be? I couldn't truthfully sit down and paint people without deciding what color they were. I was painting black people in the European, Impressionist way, with a thick palette knife. As a matter of fact, I thought it was coming along nicely. And so in 1962 I decided it was time to start showing. So I got some introductions to galleries and went on down.

"I showed one painting with flat posterish figures of white men in a strong Hard-Edge pattern, with blue-gray shadows on their faces, to a woman at the Contemporary Arts Gallery. She just laughed and said, 'What's this?'

"Then I went to the Ruth White Gallery. I took that same painting and some others, of trees and flowers. I showed them to her and she said, 'Do you know where you are?' I said yes. She said, 'Are you sure?' And I said, 'Yes. On East Fifty-seventh Street.' And she looked at me and said, 'You can't do this. *You can't do this!*' And she was being honest.

"I looked at her, and then I noticed Birdie, my husband, looking at the exhibition in her gallery. I saw there was every style of painting in there. But the idea was: This is not something *you* can do. This does not come out of *your* experience. You have to make your own contribution. We left, and my husband said to me, 'Now, don't get angry. But she said something very valuable in there. There's a lot of that kind of art in there already. But the point is, *you* can't do it.' Therefore I tried to develop a style of painting related to what I imagined to be the African idiom. I still painted figures, but without the use of chiaroscuro—realistic but flat—to lend a high degree of visibility to the image of the American black person. And as a matter of fact, African art achieves something of the same result. By its decorative, flat appearance, it helps project the real look of black people. If you have a dark form, and you modulate it with shadows, you have nothing. But if you flatten it out and indicate the shadows in flat, contrasting colors, you have a strong pattern.

"In 1967, I completed and exhibited a work in that genre titled *Die*, a twelve-foot-wide mural depicting a street riot. I carried the theme forward and three years later showed a group I called 'American Black.' One of these paintings was *Flag for the Moon, Die Nigger*. The Chase Manhattan Bank almost bought that one, until they noticed the words of the title worked into the design. Then they turned it down and bought another. Political art was taboo then as always. I was wasting my time trying to develop as an artist without an audience.

"I made some stylistic changes. I decided to take the white pigment out of my painting. When you use oils, you use a lot of white. After a while, you may lose your sensitivity to other colors. The white gathers all the light. And I wanted to paint dark tones like Ad Reinhardt. To create *black light*. He was dead by then, so I couldn't ask him how he did it. Finally I worked it out by using dry pigment with burnt umber and making my own oil base. Then, in

1971, I got a CAPS grant to do a mural for the Women's House of Detention on Rikers Island.

"The inmates wanted me to show women of all ages and all races, a parable about rehabilitation. One of them asked me to paint 'a long road leading out of here.' Another asked for 'all the children with God in the middle.' All of them agreed they wanted to see no crime, no ghetto, no poverty. So I gave them a Feminist composition: a woman as President, a policewoman, a sportswoman, a mother giving a bride away, a woman priest, a woman doctor, a white woman with a mixed-race child, and women musicians.

"That mural was well received, but I had had a terrible time walking it down fourteen flights of stairs. It was too large to fit into the elevator. So I decided, no more heavy pictures. There are enough roadblocks in front of a woman artist anyway. Thereafter, I made paintings matted upon lengths of cloth that could be rolled up—like Tibetan tankas."

The years 1970, '71 and '72 were years of militant, revolutionary action in the New York and California museum and gallery worlds as politicized artists' groups protested Vietnam and the lack of women in all parts of the art world. Ringgold puts it this way: "I became a Feminist in 1970. It happened the day I decided to launch a protest against an exhibit, to be held at the School of Visual Arts in New York, protesting the U.S. policy of war, repression, racism and sexism—an exhibit that itself was all male! I declared that if the organizers didn't include fifty percent women, there would be 'war.' Robert Morris, the organizer, agreed to open the show to women, and that was, so far as I'm concerned, the beginning of the Women's Movement in New York. Later there were demonstrations at the Whitney Museum and other places.

"Two years after that, I went to Europe for the Documenta Exhibition in Kassel, Germany. The theme was a political one that year, and I thought it would be good to see and be included in it. So I took some posters I'd made, called *U.S. of Attica,* and copies of the *Feminist Art Journal* and *Women's World* and simply entered them in the show. It seemed to me I was the only black person in the city. I decided I couldn't possibly be inconspicuous, so I just walked around in my bright colors and put my posters everywhere, on the floor, on the walls and in the bookstores.

"By '73, however, I was ready for a new focus on things. And now, some years later, my politics have changed a great deal. I'm into a new way of dealing with both art and life."

EM: "Tell me."

FR: "It began back around '72. I was doing a lot of traveling. And I began to see, truthfully, that black women were not working for their own liberation.

I saw that large groups of black women were not moving out together. I began to see that I would have to do my working-out on my own. And that it would be a very lonely life.

"I looked around and saw that our black families are crumbling. Our families, like yours, are breaking up today, and there's nothing to take their place. The push among blacks today is to gain political power. But that's no use unless the families are maintained. Anyone who wants power has to be supported. There's no better support than the family.

"In 1973, that year of change, I had a ten-year retrospective of my oil paintings at Rutgers University in New Brunswick, New Jersey. I'd been teaching African crafts at Bank Street College in New York, beadwork, appliqué, mask-making and so on. A student of mine saw the show and afterward wrote me that she was disappointed in it. 'I didn't see any of the techniques you teach us,' she wrote. 'Beading. Tie-dyeing. Why aren't you using the techniques of African women?'

"Around that time, too, there was a good deal of questioning whether there is such a thing as Feminist art. I concluded that there might be, but that we haven't been free to explore it. And so I decided to experiment. To stop denying the part of me that loves making things with cloth. But I still wanted my art to have a more human dimension than the flat tankas.

"As I set to work, I began to remember how, back in the 1930s when I was a child, people were close to other people. How Harlem then was a friendly beautiful place. I remembered there was a Mrs. Brown, who was like another mother to me. So I did Mrs. Brown in cloth, and sat her in a chair. Then I did Catherine, her child, and put her in her arms.

"Florence was a beautiful woman. When we were little we used to love to sit and watch her dress up for parties. I would kiss her, hug her, rub her hair. A beautiful black woman. I made a sculpture of her.

"All these black women had a sense of themselves. No shyness. No holding back. Doing the best they could with what they had.

"On a trip to Africa in '76, I would see the same qualities. I saw the black woman as she is in her own environment: unafraid. She can go anywhere. She can get into a crowded bus with her breasts uncovered to nurse her baby, and any man there will come to her aid if she needs it.

"Later, I did Wilt Chamberlain, seven foot three inches tall, just a natural-born sculpture. Rope inside for legs, loose long legs and high-heel white shoes. He even had a ding-dong. My husband said, 'Don't make him with nothing in his pants. If someone unzips him, they'll think you're trying to make some kind of statement.' All my people have their sexual parts, the women and the men.

414

Mrs. Brown and Catherine, *1973.*
Cloth, beads, thread, ribbon.
Life-size.

"Well, eventually I began taking these figures around to colleges, and the kids loved them. But people kept feeling the legs, and they were disappointed because there was only rope in there. So I decided to develop the bodies. I cut flat patterns in foam and sewed them to create forms, and then I sprayed the forms with paint. And so I began, with my mother, making a *Family of Woman.*

"I would make a needlepoint face, say a smiling woman with flowers on her face in tapestry stitching. We'd go shopping together for material for the dress. Then I'd create the body, make the hair, formulate the whole thing. The 'Couples' series is about the relationship between men and women, for instance. One of the pairs of figures is Zora, a bag lady, and Fish, a street drunk who takes care of her. They look like lonely bums, but they have their relationship just as other people do. Zora and Fish have been exhibited all over the country. People take nips from their wine bottle and leave money in Zora's cup. She's collected about $3.18 to date.

"Then I created an environment called *Windows of the Wedding,* with a series of abstract tankas hanging around the room where I displayed the couples. The tankas were based on designs of the Kuba tribe: eight triangles inside a rectangle. Originally those designs spelled out words. The language is lost now. What I was doing was trying to devise a language meaningful to me."

In recent years, Faith Ringgold has moved into new fields with her sculpture

415

figures. She has developed, for example, a performance with masks and soft sculptures, based on the experiences of a couple, Bina and Bubba, who have died. Bubba died of an overdose of drugs, and Bina died of grief. The figures are laid out on a "cooling pad," surrounded by mourning women. In the course of the performance, a great mourning event takes place, culminating in their resurrection. Ringgold directs this event in colleges across the country, using student performers and playing recorded church music from the Abyssinian Baptist Church in Harlem.

FR: "At first, I used only masks for Bina and Bubba. Then I found I had to make bodies for them. People will come from miles around to see a body. Death is the ultimate Art Piece.

"We do the performance differently in each place. Sometimes they give me a chapel, sometimes an art gallery or a theater. I tell the story to the kids, play the tape, and then they perform it. I don't tell them what to do. I just let them experience it.

"I explain that Bina did what a lot of women do: she died of grief over Bubba. Women in all nations have this same role: to stay there and to weep. In one performance, a girl began screaming while the wake was going on. A woman screaming in a church is a whole history of suffering. That woman just walked in and fell down on her knees.

"I call the piece *The Wake and Resurrection of the Bicentennial Negro.* There are no spoken words; the characters dance and the music speaks.

"It's the first time, in a work of art or theater, there has been this focus on the black woman's drive to liberate herself. You see, the resurrection of Bubba has to do with his redefining his manhood and rehabilitating himself from drugs. But Bina's task is more abstract. She has to become a free woman. Not many of us know yet what that means."

The artist as the Ballerina.

Eleanor Antin

BORN 1935, NEW YORK CITY

. . . I stopped smoking two months ago because I'm taking ballet lessons and voice lessons. That's because two years from now I want to do a performance with splits and pirouettes and everything else to freak them out. Be a great ballerina. And I'm also singing, because I would like to burst into Brechtian song during the performance. When I was smoking I couldn't do it. So I stopped. For art, you see. For art I could lose weight. For art I could do anything.

—ELEANOR ANTIN
Del Mar, California, 1977

Eleanor Antin disposes of the human personality as Jennifer Bartlett does the visible world; she splits it into its component parts, each of which is then set off upon its own linear narrative track. Scientists and other artists have done the same in this era, naming fragments of the psyche. Oedipus and Electra are the two we are most familiar with, of course; Carl Jung's animus, anima and Old Man of the Sea might come next; then Marcel Duchamp's Dandy, Mutt and Rrose Sélavy. Duchamp's young follower Alan Kaprow, one of the inventors of Happenings in the 1960s, teaches now in San Diego and is a close associate of Eleanor Antin's. So her preoccupation with role-defining, with characters, contours and props is experiment in a high tradition. She also makes reference, with that ambitious eclecticism characteristic of her generation, to the Commedia dell' Arte, Brecht, Pirandello, Cocteau and Charles Chaplin—a lofty pedigree for any art.

At the same time, her art, like Bartlett's, might be read as metaphor for a self-dissecting, compartmentalized yet integration-hungry age. What is "the real me"? she poignantly inquires. At the far end of the question she has sought

417

and even once, she suspects, encountered that elusive figment: an Integrated Self. At another borderline, the past, she cannot help but encounter her grandfather, who plied his trade as an exorciser of dybbuks in old Poland. Her mother has a place in the solar system which is "Eleanor," too, for she acted in the Yiddish theater and played with cardboard kings and queens when she was a child.

A number of women have used the theater recently to exercise potential alternate identities, often male. Carolee Schneeman, Laurie Anderson, Adrien Piper are three. Of them all, however, Antin is the most antic, conceptual and in her far-out moments, even perhaps daemonic. After some years of meandering through unfulfilled episodes of life and work, she broke through to her own style with the famous photo narrative *Adventures of 100 Boots,* in which she set those hundred soles free to find their own way across fields, ditches, army bivouacs, all the way into the Museum of Modern Art for an exhibition. Over the next few years, she evolved her self-dissecting system of four characters— the King of Solana Beach, the Ballerina, the Nurse and the Black Movie Star. Her "art" consists of scenes, some improvised, some written, involving these aspects-of-herself as lead characters. Antin also turns out videotapes and photo narratives using puppets, some small, some life-size, which she moves and speaks for in a voice tinged with the oracular, rather—she likes to think—like that of a Kabuki actor. In these scenes, too, fragmentary subvoices exchange words on topics like the economy, politics and love. Viz.:

LE GRAND SKIEUR: To me, snow is like a woman—beautiful, sensual. Ever she calls me. Ever she eludes me. She is my lifelong mistress.
NURSE: O how poetic.
[*Tenderly, Antin picks up two paper dolls, moves them through the air, lays them on bits of paper: snow.*]
LE SKIEUR: I am at peace.
NURSE: I too am at peace.
LE SKIEUR: I make a nest for you. . . . We cover ourselves with a blanket of snow. . . .
[*Break*]
I arise as the Black Match Girl!
Now I am never hungry, never thirsty, as I command the stage. Not too correctly as to be boring, not too askew as to be peculiar—just a little off in order to be intriguing. . . .

I visited Antin in the house upon a bluff overlooking the Pacific where she lives with her husband, poet David Antin, and their son Blaise Cendrars, or, as he would rather be called, Blaze. Both Antins are tenured professors in the Visual Arts Department of the University of California at San Diego. She is a short, voluble individual possessed by ardor and gifted, in life, with that integrative power she plays games with in her art.

"Memories of childhood? My first is a sad one. It was in our apartment in the Bronx. It must have been summer. I was sitting on my mother's lap. I had the feeling it was around five in the afternoon, because I heard boys playing stickball outside: the crack of the ball. There was no sun coming in. It was light outside the window, but dark inside. My mother was crying, and I was sad because of that. I felt helpless. Strange.

"In school, later on, I used to tell stories in assembly and scare people. Some kids were screaming, 'Stop it! I can't stand it!' I was pleased. Not because I wanted them to be miserable. I didn't stop.

"Earlier than that I remember the paper dolls. That began when I wanted to be religious. Oh, I love thinking of these things. I'm grateful you're asking me. I'm such a work fiend these days I never have time to think for pleasure. I think only for work."

EM: "But remembering is part of your work, isn't it? Bringing out what's in the memory?"

EA: "Yes, but until I need something, I don't think of it."

EM: "Well, tell me about your parents in the days when they were king and queen for you."

EA: "Mother was the most important person in my life. She and my father immigrated from Poland and eventually divorced. She was a Marxist. He was apolitical. He told me this story: In his little town in Poland it was very hard for Jews, but they let him into the *Gymnasium* because it seemed he was a mathematical genius. They even invited the great mathematicians of Warsaw down to show him off. But when the mathematicians asked him questions, he was struck dumb. His mouth wouldn't open. He tried to write the answers with chalk on the board, but he couldn't press down on the chalk. So in America he worked as a cutter in the dress business. I always think of him as two little eyes sticking out from the wall. Like the little holes in knotty pine. Two little eyes looking out from the woodwork.

"My mother had been an actress in the Yiddish theater. When she came here she kept house for my father's mother, Selfish Dubka, and her seven sons. Her Marxist phase lasted many years. She used to take me out of kindergarten to sell *Daily Workers* with her on the subway platform. She said she sold more papers when I was around because I smiled at people. I had big blue eyes and long braids, and men used to pinch my cheeks, sometimes savagely. Then they would buy the paper. But she had too many personal loyalties, too much passion, to be a Marxist forever. Eventually she became a businesswoman. She

419

was into bankrupt hotels. But she wasn't really in it for the money. I know that now. She was in it to entertain her guests in a high-class cultural manner: Yiddish intellectuals, Stalinists not Trotskyites, fanciful artists who folk-danced and whittled little figures of old Jews with long coats. And they were entertained in the evenings by musicians from Juilliard who switched to being waiters by day.

"I got my energy from my mother. She always thought best on her feet. If the cook quit during Sunday dinner, she rolled up her sleeves and dished out a seven-course meal. She could charm a loan out of anyone!

"She told me stories, endlessly, over and over, and I would beg her to repeat them. About pogroms. Disasters. Living on potatoes and onions. When she was four—it was the First World War—the rivers ran with blood! The Germans came. Then the White Russians came. Then the Red Russians came. Trotsky came. Lenin came. She remembered their speeches: Trotsky was fiery. He banged his fists on the podium and shouted 'Tovarich!' Lenin was kind, a gentle father. Little father! Russians love czars. And Polish Jews, they love to be Russians.

"My grandfather was a Hassidic scholar, Reb Shmul Mekhem. Once my mother peeked through a window and saw him trying to get a dybbuk to come out of a woman's fingernail. But it came out through her throat instead, and she choked to death.

"She told me of her brother who became a Bolshevik and ran away to Russia to make his fortune. He was a gambler anyway, a card player, a wastrel, a *shteckel dreher*. He was a dead man. They said prayers for the prodigal son. Before he left he gave his little sister a deck of cards, and she used to sit in a corner playing with them for hours, gazing at the kings and queens, making up stories about them. One day her grandfather looked up from his prayers and saw her. A disgrace! 'Look what the child is playing with!' He tore them into little pieces. She gathered them up, screaming, 'Zade, zade, the *menshelekh*— why are you doing that to my *menshelekh?*'

"Another time, much later, she was reading *Anna Karenina* in secret. Her mother found it and showed it to her father. 'Look, look, how terrible!' A few days later, she saw the book hidden under the Torah. He was reading it. He would discover the bad things in it, and she would be lost. A week later the book was returned to her, without a word. Whenever she told me that story, she would cry. Now I cry when I tell the story, but I used to make her repeat it over and over."

EM: "How about your religious period? Your own paper dolls?"

EA: "It must have been around the time my sister was born that I became religious, when I was five or six. We didn't have a Bible, but we had a dictionary. I walked around my room carrying the dictionary under my arm, smiling sweetly to the right and the left of me. I looked up the definitions of religious words and read them aloud in a gentle voice. I'd look up 'Jesus' and read about 'Jesus.' Then I'd look up 'priest' and read about 'priest.' These were my sermons to my congregation. Then I blessed them, and the sun came in the windows. I held church only on Sunday mornings, of course. It was very holy."

EM: "Were your parents amused by this?"

EA: "They didn't know. I closed the door.

"It was about this time that I began Cutout Land. My paper dolls. There were lots of paper-doll books in those days. The dolls were on the covers and you punched them out. Inside were paper pages with clothes of all kinds to cut out. There were movie-star cutouts like Esther Williams, Rhonda Fleming, Rita Hayworth. Some of them had men. I threw all my dolls together and made them citizens of Cutout Land. It was a continuous world which I played with every day for many years, a complicated copy of the real one that adults lived in. Life there was continuous and motivated. Even time was subject to natural laws, not alterable as it is in the theater. Say my mother would take me to see *Carmen*. We would bring home the libretto. Some of the paper dolls would become singers and we'd do *Carmen* with me singing each word, making up the melodies. My idea of music was passion, not pitch. The performance might take several hours, until my voice was almost gone. Then at the end they would all applaud.

"Afterward the artist doll might make a portrait of the star on a little piece of paper. She paid him for it. The newspaper reporter reviewed the show in the newspaper, and I had to write the whole edition. The reporter and the artist were in love with the star. A triangle. Meanwhile other characters were living out their entanglements. I was even then an uncompromising representationalist. If anyone committed a crime of passion it would be reported in the newspaper. Say there was a murder. The person who had been killed was cut in half and buried in the national graveyard, a cheesebox that rested on my windowsill. The trial would be held, with a judge, lawyers and impassioned speeches. The guilty one would be convicted and executed. His head would be cut off. Flushed down the toilet. His corpse was not allowed to rest with the good citizens in the cheesebox. People normally didn't die until their heads fell off or they tore in half. If they got holes in their bodies they were dead, too. That came from making love. I would draw genitals on their bathing suits and then press them together and go 'Ohhhhhhh . . .' Afterward I erased the marks. But those who were very romantic eventually died. It was dangerous to be a romantic."

EM: "In those days, what did you want to be when you grew up?"

EA: "Great. I always wanted to be great. My mother used to think I was already. My father, however, would have thought it was poor judgment to be excessively great.

"But I always knew I would be an artist. I was in IGC classes for gifted kids, and a teacher in sixth grade even wrote in my autograph book that my talent for art, writing and dramatics would assure a successful future. At what? I went to the High School of Music and Art, where I was no better and no worse than the others in painting impassioned impasto purple and brown oils, but I was terrible at anything involving skills. I nearly flunked a watercolor class because I couldn't make the wash run in the right direction. But I did well enough in fashion design, because I came up with ideas like burlap and chiffon wedding gowns. The teacher said I could make a fortune spouting ideas, as long as I didn't lay my hands on any materials. But now I can make watercolors as well as anyone. My King of Solana Beach paints in a style somewhere between Tiepolo, Canaletto and Fragonard. He can do anything with a flick of bravura and a touch of wash, for only one reason: he has a reason for doing it, while I never had one.

"After that I went to City College, and I was majoring in writing when I got a job as an actress in a road company and quit."

EM: "What made you go into the theater?"

EA: "Honesty. I remember the decision clearly. It was a moral one. For years I had been haunted by the idea that I had no self. Or rather, that I had an endless supply of selves—an embarrassing state not experienced as prodigality but as absence. So I deliberately chose a profession where I could borrow other people's selves. I didn't know yet how boring most theater selves are, at least the ones they were willing to let me be. I wanted to do Miss Julie, for one, and they wanted me to do *Our Town* or *This Property Is Condemned*. Those were the days of the Actors Studio and Stanislavski emigrés. The directors were dark little people freaked out on blond women with Southern drawls who played Tennessee Williams nymphomaniacs. They were all Russians, you see, and they were in love with America. They didn't know what America was, so they had a dream of it.

"I was in analysis in those years, and my analyst was just the same, only Hungarian. She tried to save me from myself and turn me into a suburban matron. I say today that what she wanted was for me to marry a lawn mower. For a girl without a self I was pretty stubborn. I held out against her. But I suffered and had many misfortunes. I was very unhappy."

EM: "How about a success? There must have been one, at least."

EA: "There was one great one. It was at the first national NAACP convention held at the New York Trade Center in the '50s. Ossie Davis put together a show, and I improvised a scene that brought the house down. The Montgomery bus strike was on. I played the part of a white woman whose black maid refused to come clean her house because she didn't want to ride on the segregated buses. I wore a white dress and a big pink hat like a Southern belle, and I came on stage as if I were entering the maid's house and invented a very funny set of actions depicting what such a woman would do. Would I sit down? Maybe the chair had fleas. But my high heels do hurt so . . . maybe I can sit down just a wee bit on the very edge of the seat . . . oh, dear, is that a flea on my ankle? . . . I simply must scratch, but that's impolite . . . she might notice and get revenge and not come home with me . . . I've got to scratch just a little . . . oh, how come she doesn't see how sensitive I am to such appalling surroundings, after all my skin is delicate, et cetera, et cetera. At the end I was on my knees kissing the maid's hands and begging her to come home with me. The audience freaked out—it brought down the house, and Ossie Davis hugged me afterward, and that made me feel great.

"Then the Living Theatre asked me to join. But I couldn't because I belonged to Actors Equity, and the Living Theatre was just starting up and was nonunion. They said it didn't matter, that I could use another name. But I was already using another name. I had been born Eleanor Fineman and was now unionized as Eleanor Barrett after Elizabeth Barrett Browning. Now I think I just didn't want to commit myself to the theater. I did the same number with dance."

EM: "Dance?"

EA: "I used to dance around the house when I was a kid. Ballet was my great love. I used to sail around on tiptoes to Tchaikovsky music. My image of glamour has always been ballet. Ballet is one of the handful of professions where when they talk about the artist they automatically say 'she.'

"Later I studied at Martha Graham's studio on Twelfth Street until I couldn't afford it anymore. So they offered me a scholarship, and a month later I developed heart trouble. So I quit dancing, and the heart trouble went away. That was the message all right, but what was it saying? Everybody thought I was a coward. For a long time I considered myself chicken, too. But now I'm kinder to myself. Now I see that art is invention, not just the practice of a narrow craft, and I think I was simply bored doing what everyone else was doing. Thanks! It wasn't worth giving up my free Saturdays for.

"So I spent quite a bit of time just living in the Village, playing chess, going to the movies and being miserable. I was modeling for some painters. Isabel Bishop, Ruth Gikow, Jack Levine, Moses Soyer. The Levines were fine people. I loved them. But I had no image of myself then. I didn't even look up from my cappuccino at Rienzi's to see what was going on around me."

423

EM: "And then?"

EA: "And then I saw David again.

"I had met him at City College and we were friends for ten years before we became lovers. I didn't think then that you could like someone and love them. When we met again, I hadn't gone into a museum for what seemed like ten years. I had a feeling that if I did, I would cry. Don't ask me why. It was just that literally I would cry if I went in.

"The first show I saw after those ten years I went to with David. It was Abstract Expressionism, and Abstract Expressionism was already over the hill. It was Fourth Generation. I mean it was really old. I took one look at it and burst into tears. Don't ask me what all that meant. I don't know.

"From then on, I kept going to shows. I remember the Larry Rivers show, which I loved, and the Rauschenberg and the Johns. Then Pop came, and I really liked Pop a lot.

"I moved in with David and married him because he brought reality into my life, which is the one thing I never had. A sense of the real. By that I don't mean a low idea of practicality. He's more in tune with the real than anybody else I've ever met. He always says he married me because I made him laugh, which is very funny. Because when I moved in it was like I was a crippled person, a wretched, distressed person. And somehow it worked. I don't think marriage works for most people, but he and I work together.

"Now I live the only life I could, given the kind of work I do. I know there are people who live like *La Bohème*. I suppose I did, too, when I was younger. But that was before I was an artist. It seems to me you have to have your personal life organized so that it takes as little of your time as possible. Otherwise you can't make your art. And if you're an artist, I don't care what they say, you should be married to an artist. If not, forget it. If you aren't married to an artist, what would you talk about?"

EM: "So then the domestic side of life was set. How about the art?"

EA: "I began to write. Poetry. John Ashbery was the first editor to publish me—my 'Painter Poems' in *Art and Literature*. And I began to paint again, kind of Dada paintings, large Hard-Edge valentines with big shoulders like zoot suits. Then I spent several years making collages out of pieces of old art, fragments from books, magazines.

"My *Blood of a Poet's Box* was what I think of as my first developed work. I took blood specimens from the fingers of a hundred poets and filed them in a green slide box. It took several years, from about '65 to '68. In that period I had my first show at Long Island University, and I was also teaching full time. But gradually the Minimal scene in New York became a bore. The war had been on for years, and those guys hadn't even heard of it yet. So when Paul

424

Brach offered David a job in California, I said, 'Let's get out of here.' We packed my son Blaise, who had been born a year before, our books and ourselves into an ancient Chrysler Imperial and went on the road like a couple of Okies.

"What happened in California was that I discovered the Sears catalogue. It seemed incredible to an urban refugee that you could order everything from a refrigerator to a box of Kleenex from a book. So I got the idea of choosing several of these items and placing them together so that a reading could be made from them as a group. I ordered directly from the catalogue so that the objects would be new and untouched by extraneous history, and the groups became portraits: *California Lives* and *Portraits of Eight New York Women.* I showed both of these in New York.

"But coming back to California on the plane after the last show, I said to myself, 'No way.' It was costing me a fortune to traipse back and forth coast to coast. So I invented the *Adventures of 100 Boots* to make use of a less exhausting distribution system. I decided I could send that one all over the world without budging from the beach. So I sent the work out as postcards, fifty-one mailings. At the end, the boots walked into the Museum of Modern Art."

EM: "Who were the boots, really?"

EA: "They were my picaresque novel. Heroes. Adventurers.

"They began life quietly enough in the suburbs. Then they committed crimes, worked in oil fields and in a circus, cheated at cards, joined the Army, fought a battle, had dozens of other escapades and finally went to New York.

"John Perrault reviewed it for the *Village Voice* and said, 'Well, guys, she made it. There she is in the Museum of Modern Art.' But I was freaked that it was only the political implications of the distribution system that interested him. He was right in a way. The *100 Boots* was a political landmark. But I always thought it was more than that. To me it was a photo novel, a narrative work that was meant to be read in spite of time disjunctions on the receiving end."

EM: "What could follow *Boots?*"

EA: "I was doing other works all the time the *Boots* were being sent out. I was trying to discover myself, as I put it now, using the subject matter of everyday life: reminiscences, stories, drawings, photos. Even body alterations, like a series of photos taken of me in the course of dropping off ten pounds.

"But I soon saw that my *self*—if I had one!—wasn't waiting out there like America waiting for Columbus, for me to come along and identify it. I had to set up some inventive 'as-ifs.'

"So I asked myself, for instance, If I were a man, what sort of man would I be? I decided to apply hair to my face and find out. I learned I was not an

425

100 Boots out of a Job. *Terminal Island, California, February 15, 1972, 4:45* P.M.

100 Boots in a Field. *Route 101, California, February 9, 1971, 3:30* P.M.

explorer—a grizzled Hemingway. My small chin couldn't make it. I found I was not a fierce patriarch, nor Jesus. Only when I trimmed my beard into an elegant courtier style did I know I had found him/me. Later I learned I was a courtier king, since my image bore such an uncanny relation to Van Dyke's *Charles I.* When I read about that romantic, stubborn Hamlet figure, I knew I was right.

"Then I got the idea I had to go out and talk to my people. Ask how things were going. I was very nervous about that step myself. Well, I gritted my teeth and went out into the streets of Solana Beach, and they loved me! People asked me who I was, and I said, 'I'm the King of Solana Beach. I think Solana Beach deserves a king, don't you?' and most people agreed."

EM: "Did they recognize you?"

EA: "Only the librarian at the Solana Beach Library recognized me. Mrs. Voss. She looked real hard and I think it was my small size that gave me away to her. She asked, uncertainly, 'Eleanor?' I kissed her hand and we improvised a little minuet together. Every time I went out among my people, I stopped off at the library to kiss her hand. Until she retired.

"I did my first performance before an art-world audience at the Woman's Building in L.A. in '73. Since then, I always do several performances as part of my exhibitions. These used to be improvisations, but since last year I have

The artist as King of Solana Beach.

been writing scripts. I have too much material I want to get into each performance by now, and in an improvisation you lose a lot.''

One evening in 1974, in a performance at the Woman's Building in Los Angeles, Eleanor Antin attempted something extreme. She and David Antin tried to tell me what happened.

EA: ''I did that piece in '74, and it was about the Eleanor of '54. I sat in a chair and talked, and made confessions about things that had happened twenty years earlier. What I was trying to do was to find out if there was anything *real* left of that self. I tried to shame her out. The supposition was that if 'she' were ashamed of what happened back in the past, then obviously 'she' still exists somewhere.''

EM: ''Was it pretense, or for real? How did you deliver the confessions—in your natural voice?''

EA: ''I improvised the whole thing.''

EM: ''Then it was made up—fabricated.''

EA: ''No. The confessions were real.''

EM: ''But then why do you say you had to improvise?''

EA: ''It was an improvisation. A performance. But the assumption was that underneath my present performing self there was another, the *real*, me. So I told shameful stories. And as it turned out, I [or she?] was not in the least ashamed. Now, either that meant that one learns, as one grows older, to take everything with equanimity or that intervening events, all that happened in the meantime, had killed the old me.''

DA: ''No. Sorry. That isn't what happened. You didn't go up there with a clear program to drive her out. You went with the intention of answering questions about that possible self. Or trying to arrive at an idea of what that self was, if indeed it existed. To try to effect a rapprochement with a past you felt was gone simply because you are always so busy inventing yourself in the present.''

EA: ''Yes. I have always claimed and believed that I have no history. I can't remember the past. But that evening I was remembering childish things from far away. As I have done today, talking.''

DA: ''You went there with the intention of trying to find her by remembering her. You even had some props: some old photos of yourself way back. But you weren't making any headway. You felt very remote. You said, 'I don't feel it.' So at that point you stumbled on the idea of trying to shame her, as a last resort.''

EM: ''There are analytic techniques for getting 'back' to old selves. Have

428

you tried those? Of course, it would involve accepting the analyst's own projections or 'art'—Jung's, for instance.''

DA: ''As you say, that is his art. Eleanor Antin was doing her own. I tend not to believe anybody about final answers to investigations of reality, because everyone is his own artist. Eleanor Antin believes the same thing.''

EA: ''I invented my own psychological machine. I discovered myself. I don't use someone else's armature. I've got the King, the Ballerina, the Nurse and the Black Movie Star to discover and invent myself. Others do this through their traditional analyses. I use art.''

DA: ''You started that night in a straightforward way. You began by trying to remember. You tried to 'flush her out' by telling a story that would be so painful she would still feel it. If she felt it, then you could consider you had bridged the gap of years.

''The audience was very sad. The audience was weeping, except for the few of us who were, you know, in odd relationships to the truth. You had the audience freaked out with compassion and sympathy.

''Then you started to defend her. But the question was, would she answer you back, speak up for herself, defend herself? Because you were taking advantage of her. You were standing there in her place giving her no stage.

''We were all there watching. We were watching it open up. You weren't sure what you were going to do, nor were we. Everybody was surprised at what you did. You took more and more extreme measures, as it were. You didn't say you were going to speak in voices, but apparently you did take on several other ones.

''Then you let her speak. Her speech was like a not quite fully realized shamanism. She appeared, so to speak. When she disappeared, afterward, you conceded you had been unfair to her. But then you tended to revert and say she was trivial and no more real than anything else. But she was not less real either. You had let something come through to say, *You* are not being fair to me.''

EA: ''Then I was defending someone. There *was* someone before!''

EM: ''Is she a *her?*''

DA: ''She is a her. It's Eleanor before she becomes a full adult. At nineteen you didn't regard yourself as fully yourself.''

EM: ''Who was that ancestor who exorcised dybbuks?''

EA: ''My grandfather! That's wonderful to think of!''

DA: ''If I may say so, that's a hilarious oversimplification of what you did. One of the most interesting aspects of the thing was how hard it was to determine who was telling the truth: this one, or that one? Even the performers themselves were in disagreement about who *you* were."

EM: "To get back to the other characters—the King and so on. How much of *you* is involved when you're being them? Do you have stage fright before you do the improvisations?"

EA: "The King always takes a shot of Scotch. The Ballerina is fine. The Nurse is always on video, and there's no problem there."

EM: "No. Do *you* have stage fright?"

EA: "That's what I'm saying. The King is nervous."

EM: "Well, who is the one living in the house here?"

DA: "They all live here."

EM: "Have the characters completely taken over? Who washes the dishes here? Who takes care of Blaise, makes love, writes the script? Those aren't collaborative committee operations."

DA: "You could say that what life has put together life also puts asunder."

EA: "I just keep going back and forth. Writing the scripts, preparing the actors—the painted figures. Staging and memorizing. So most of my time is spent making true art. A lot is spent teaching, besides. And there's some left over for life (I've always defined an artist as someone who never takes a vacation).

"For instance, I stopped smoking two months ago because I'm taking ballet lessons and voice lessons. That's because two years from now I want to do a performance with splits and pirouettes and everything else to freak them out. Be a great ballerina. And I'm also singing, because I would like to burst into Brechtian song during the performance. When I was smoking I couldn't do it. So I stopped. For art, you see. For art I could lose weight. For art I could do anything.

"I'm doing very well. I make a lot of money. And that's essentially it.

"It's all very simple!"

Jackie Winsor

BORN 1941, NEWFOUNDLAND

. . . I began to encounter some people whose lives struck me as being defined in a new way. . . . It had to do with a quality of internal energy: the potential for growth. There was a struggle for the right words; the ideas were not just spilling out. . . .

So gradually I began to have a sense that there was something out there I could become involved with . . . a glimpse of what I might do with my life. . . .

—JACKIE WINSOR
New York, 1977

In a decade since graduating from Rutgers University, Canadian-born Jackie Winsor has invented a distinctive and moving body of work—large-scale wood, rope and wire constructions, owned by museums including the Whitney and the Museum of Modern Art. They fall into two main classes, both under the rubric of Minimalism: works of raw log members wrapped in hemp or wire; and carpentered wood box forms that appear solid but have grilled openings and peep holes. In objects of the first class, the wrapping is a theme in itself, wound and wound about to hold, say, true old grandfathers of the forest in bonds as solacing and tender as the arms of a Cassatt midwife. The lattice boxes with their chambers within also offer peace and security. Wrapping and joining these works involves that process elevated to an act of conscious statement in the '60s: repeating. If Gertrude Stein's diction and rhythm were the immediate model, people all over the world have attested to the quieting effect of repeated hand or body movements in the arts of weaving, carving, carpentering, not to speak of music and dance. Winsor put it this way:

431

Bound Square, *1972.*
Wood and hemp. 77" by
78" by 14½". The
Museum of Modern Art,
New York.

"When you repeat an action again and again, you produce an effect of certainty or security in the viewer's mind. You're not trying to discover something, or to convince yourself of something. You're dealing with certainty, then, as a formal concern. And that soothes the viewer."

Interior space, carpentered construction, actions like wrapping and joining that bring feelings of safety and peace: these are psychoesthetic elements in Winsor's work. What do they come from and what signify?

"House, to me, means something all torn up. My mother and father building and rebuilding houses. Again and again they tore them to pieces, reconstructed them. It would take them forever to finish one, then they would start another. All my childhood, it was walking over boards through one kitchen or another. Chaos! And yet I remember one of the more beautiful experiences of my childhood. They had torn the whole back end of a house away. There was no roof on the kitchen. We were sleeping in what had been the dining room. I was only about six then. I woke up one night, opened my eyes and saw stars shining through the kitchen walls.

"I remember, too, hearing that before I was born, my father ordered lumber from Labrador and spent all one winter measuring, cutting and marking it. Then when summer came and he was at his usual job, Mother built the house. It turned out to be the first house I lived in.

"I was my father's special helper. I think he had wanted a son, and I

432

wasn't it, but I would do, seeing that there weren't to be any more than us three girls. A summer when I was about eight, he tore down a barn to put up a garage and it was my job to straighten the old nails and then hammer them down after he started them. The rest of the time I was always outdoors, biking, climbing trees, playing by the ocean on rocks and sand, and playing in the woods behind the house.

"Mother was the daughter of a farmer-fisherman and was born in a tiny village in Newfoundland on the top of a high cliff overlooking the sea. When I was little, we lived about ninety miles away and went back often to visit. Then there was no electricity in the village, no telephone. Later on they ran a single electrical line into the place and installed one telephone. The people there were self-sustaining. They lumbered their wood, kept cattle, grew their own vegetables, stored their food in underground cellars. They gathered their own firewood, fished and hunted. My grandfather, like the other men of the village, crocheted his nets in the winter months, and in the spring he went out on the icefields to hunt seals.

"When I was an adolescent and living, by then, in the States, I went back one first time alone, and after that I went again and again. It's I, of the children, who keeps the flame burning. I love watching the village people. I like watching how they run their days. They have to get up in the morning and decide what to do; there aren't jobs already laid out for them. When you're a generalist, you might say, you have to use your mind, use ingenuity. There's a similarity between that life style and the so-called 'alternative life style' I've made for

Fifty-fifty, 1975. Wood and nails. 40" by 40" by 40". Private collection, New York.

myself. Observing them, I learn how to run my day. And in turn I suppose I provide a certain entertainment for them.

"There was one thing I remember from the old days. Between the cottages were elaborate wooden structures called 'flakes,' for drying fish, made out of fir poles. The men would cut off the branches, then erect whole forests of those scaffolds with nailed joints, rows upon rows of poles with little ladders and tar-papered roofs every now and then—all for drying the fish stacked up in pyramids. I remember crawling up the steps to play, sitting and looking out through the poles between the fish.

"None of that exists anymore. The fishing industry took another turn. The big American and Russian factory fisheries took over the Grand Banks, and the island fishermen were out of luck."

The family moved to Boston, and Winsor went through school, taking art as an elective and working hard on the side baby-sitting, running a summer camp, doing settlement work and saving her money to go back, summers, to Newfoundland, sometimes with an aunt, or a sister, but most often alone, "the best thing that ever happened to me." Aside from that, like other talented youngsters, she went to Saturday-morning art classes at the Boston Museum of Fine Arts and was picked for an advanced class. But, for practical reasons, she majored in secretarial work at high school—how many girls did—and after graduation took an office job.

"There was very little thought about 'what to do in life' for women in those days and that place. What would one do? Most of the women thought about being mothers. I guess what our father wanted for my sisters and me was that we would be with someone, so life wouldn't be too difficult. Aside from that, one might be a schoolteacher, or a nurse, or a clerk in a department store. For my sisters and me, the idea of doing something else never existed."

Office work, however, turned out not to suit her. She had had reading and spelling difficulties and was a left-hander, and when it came to transcribing shorthand she was at a loss. "I spent the whole first day on my first job trying to transcribe one single letter. I lasted a month and lost ten pounds from anxiety. I applied to another company. They gave me an aptitude test and said they'd send me to art school at night if I worked in their art department in the daytime. But I figured if they felt I was worth investing in, I could do the same for myself. So I quit the first job and went back up to Newfoundland to think it over. That was my crisis period.

"I thought it over and over, and in the end decided to go to college and major in art. I felt good about the decision. It seemed to me I had found a direction. It's hard to describe. It's rather like dressing. You just get dressed.

You can button buttons easily. It's just something *you do*. I didn't know there was such a thing as a 'professional artist.' I'd never met one! All I knew was that it was possible to *make art,* and that that was what I wanted to do.

"There'd been some energetic students at the Museum School, but they didn't register with me as 'artists.' But when I went to the Massachusetts College of Art, and Yale School of Art and Architecture one summer, I began to encounter some people whose lives struck me as being defined in a new way. I'd go to a concert and see someone—maybe the conductor—who seemed to me to be 'doing something' with his life. At Yale, I met Al Held; Richard Stankiewicz lectured at Boston University. There was something about both these men that I identified with. It had to do with a quality of internal energy: the potential for growth. There was a struggle for the right words; the ideas were not just spilling out. An art teacher once had taken me to a concert given by an aged pianist. I'd been deeply moved and I thought, *There* is a beautiful spirit. I hadn't encountered it again before Held and Stankiewicz, but those two had it.

"So gradually I began to have a sense that there was something out there I could become involved with . . . a glimpse of what I might do with my life. I thought if I went on to graduate school, I might get a clearer idea. So I went to Rutgers and there was a nucleus of students with that same sense of identity. That sense of themselves, that they were going to 'do something with their lives.' "

During her college years, Winsor went through a fast-paced evolution. She began painting and drawing figuratively; a year later she had abandoned the figure. By the time she reached Rutgers, though she was officially a painting major, she had pretty much given up that medium and begun experiments with collage and graphics. Then she took off for three dimensions, first in that popular '60s material, cast polyester resin, making "gray-surfaced pieces with the texture of rocks that lay on the floor or were sometimes waist-high. And the teachers left me alone. The painting teacher let me make graphics. The graphics teacher let me make sculpture. They didn't bother me, and I showed all my work to all of them. I was working hard, and it seemed important to me to be left alone.

"I'd paid my own way, went to Rutgers with three hundred dollars in my pocket. I got loans, got scholarships, then assistantships. But all those years I hadn't the money to go back to Newfoundland, and I yearned for it, for six years."

In the spring of '67, she received her M.F.A. and moved into a New York loft on Canal Street. She and the man she was living with, also a sculptor, were broke and beginners. They took jobs where they could. When Winsor began to be promoted in one of them, she quit. She wasn't in the market for a job that would take her mind off the real thing.

"I worked and changed a lot that year. At first I used the polyester resin, and then I became frightened of it. Once in graduate school I'd sanded a piece of solid resin for fifteen minutes, felt exhausted, went home and slept for thirteen hours. I had huge fans working in the Canal Street loft, but I still realized how dangerous it was.[1] I began using latex until I found out it was just another form of plastic. So I began shopping for a material that wouldn't do me in. Eventually I found a place under the Brooklyn Bridge where they sold all sorts of leftover materials, and there I bought some little ends of mountain-climbing rope [four ropes coiled around a straight center rope, for extra security], some blue-dyed rope and some enormously thick rope—four inches in diameter. They lay around the studio for a year or so until I decided how to tackle them."

In '68, Winsor began working with the ropes. The mountain-climbing lengths she wound around armatures in rigid upright forms that made reference to Brancusi's *Endless Column.* The blue-dyed rope ended in coiled, lying-down pieces. And the biggest rope, four inches across, turned into great, wrapped balls or thick rings that might weigh as much as six hundred pounds. "My intention was to make you realize, just by looking at the piece or perhaps touching it, that it was a solid—all rope, even in the interior. The piece was about knowing what is inside from outside. The form was created by wrapping." By the early '70s, she was working with wood as a countertheme to the rope, turning out the lattice structures, or empty boxes of lattice fencing. Next she took rough-hewn saplings and bound them into the lattices. The wrapping of the joints—with rope or copper wire—became the process theme. Step by step, those knobbed joints became larger until they became the focus. Joints and wrappings: fishermen's nets crocheted on winter nights, and "flakes," those space-filling structures that once were functional, then in the course of time became functionless, only memory structures—were these sources of the imagery?

In '74, Winsor turned to the solid, blocklike box structures crafted with great care and precision, with very small apertures: windows, peepholes. "The windows are like tunnels, sometimes penetrating twenty layers of sheet rock on your way to the space in the interior. That interior space is illuminated by these tiny windows, so after all that density there's a tiny light. The interior is soundproof. You get a feeling of its *dead deadness.* Nothing there.

Double Bound Circle, 1971. Hemp. 16" by 61". Paula Cooper Gallery, New York.

"I have thought of this image for years and dreamed about it. I have architectural dreams—finding spaces that have been hidden. They become accessible to you and are quiet.

"Your physical body is about outward movement. I wanted the interior of these structures to be about quieting. Reflecting. Perhaps, also, about finding new recesses within yourself."

Michelle Stuart

BORN LOS ANGELES

. . . as a child, I was looking for models, wanting to know what women could become; in school, I was interested in the stories of queens, because they were the only women I could find who moved history. I was trying to find a place for myself in the scheme of things.

—MICHELLE STUART
New York, 1977

To take her place in a universe barely tapped by moon shots and computer records, on the crust of time deep as the deepest strata of rocks and charted by males alone—priest, tale-teller, explorer, scientist: here stands an American woman of the late 1970s, ambitious to embrace it all. That her reach must exceed her grasp by light-years is plain to see, but in her mind she edges toward boundaries where she might, in Merleau-Ponty's words, "possess the voluminosity of the world." Those reaches are not mystical ones to be penetrated by Tao, Zen or Christian sudden shafts of light, though the landscape to be won is the same ("the simple ground, the still desert, the simple silence"—Meister Eckhart). There is work enough to be done in the real for these essentially materialist granddaughters of real pioneers.

Like Jennifer Bartlett in her way, Michelle Stuart lays claim to dominion over the vast: "I see forever . . . hundreds of miles into the mountains across a plain [where] generations struggle [and where] the universe twenty-six billion light-years in diameter pulsates in a period of eighty-two billion years . . ."[1] Poignant, innocent, this artist's *cri de coeur* may be the same one the great American actor Joseph Jefferson spoke from the stages of cities and frontier hamlets at the turn of the century: old Rip van Winkle's *"How came I here?"* And in the next breath, from deeper down still, *"Where is the world I knew?"* Few artists in this book link up worlds known, lost and then intuited with procedures in the world of here-and-now for as haunting a symbolic answer as Michelle Stuart.

Her works are large, monotone (umber, crystal- or leaden-gray, ocher) wall hangings with a curious mineral glow, whose texture, puzzling to the eye, faintly pocked but sleek to the touch, reveals itself as literally compacted of earth and granulated stone rubbed in and polished. She also binds packets of those earth-saturated papers into books loosely tied with raw leather or hemp stuck with feathers and bits of bone. There is no writing on the pages. Perhaps there is no language besides this one of the artist's handwork to tell of the transmutation of time and ground into form that might be held on the open palms of a reader. Like Rothko's paintings, these empty pages speak of images lost from or not yet come into sight, of lore forgotten or still unknown, dust returning to or just barely raised up from the dust.

How comes Michelle Stuart here?

Her paternal grandfather was a Scots Highland mining engineer who emigrated to Australia in the nineteenth century. There his son, Stuart's father, met a Swiss woman whose mother had run her own lace-making factory back home and whose father was an inventor of, among other things, an apparatus to roll cigarette papers. Kindred adventurers, they migrated to the American South-

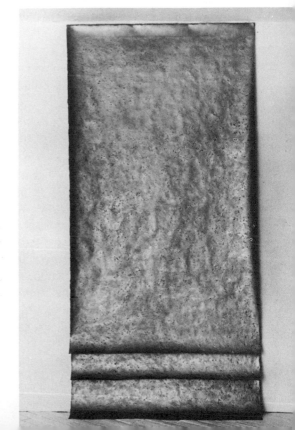

#50—High Falls, New York, *1975–76. Earth from High Falls, rock indentations, graphite silver on muslin-mounted rag paper. 131" by 61". Private collection, Dusseldorf, Germany.*

west, where Stuart's father became an engineer, mapping watercourses in their natural meanderings in advance of the building of dams to contain them. He was "a volatile, strange man, a lover and collector of old books, maps, charts, a teller of extravagant tales and a tireless explorer. I rode with him early. He taught me how to hold a .45 and how to shoot it when I was so small it nearly knocked me over. He loved me, but I was afraid of him for years."

The land the Stuarts inhabited as a family made its binding but uneasy impression. "California is vulnerable country. You're aware of that when you travel. In places, the land has shifted ten, fifteen feet. The presence of earthquakes changes people. Their eccentricity comes from their awareness of instability underfoot, and the cataclysm that seems inevitable. There are the small quakes, that seem to mark time, and along the coast, the falling precipices that mark space."

Wherever they went, young Michelle played in the earth, collected rocks, listened to tales of the old days and far-off places, dreamed of becoming an explorer herself one day ("up the Orinoco River—across the Hindu Kush") and wrote in her journals. And if there was instability in one quarter, there was security in another. "I have an even, strong and loving mother. I took my manual ability from her, and my esthetics. Everything she touched became beautiful. She took me to the ballet and the opera. She loved to sew, and her paraphernalia filled the house: bolts of cloth, paper patterns, sketches. She introduced me to form and color; my father, to the intellect and to risk. He gave me a love of books. They were both, in their own ways, traditional role models."

Stuart was a gifted child and was put into special classes at school. She studied languages, piano, dancing, minored in art and leaned first to an academic career while her own impulse was quietly shaping itself: ". . . as a child I was looking for models, wanting to know what women could become; in school, I was interested in the stories of queens, because they were the only women I could find who moved history. I was trying to find a place for myself in the scheme of things.

"I can't remember ever wanting to be anything except an artist. I accumulated notebooks and pads of drawings and watercolors. I built model planes, made sculptures and sand castings." When she opted for art school instead of college, her parents were disappointed, but not to the point of opposing her wishes. And since then she has read on her own, "about everything—literature, history, anthropology, archaeology . . ." In addition to taking classes and workshops at Chouinard Art Institute in Los Angeles, for a while she worked also as a cartographer and topographical draftswoman. "I told them I could do it, walked in and did it. You had to be almost perfect on the lines and symbols. It was rigorous and exacting." There were days when she had classes nights and worked days; other times, she went to school in the days and worked in the print shop at night running the presses until 2 A.M. Her fascination with maps grew. She thinks of them now as presenting "memory connections—abstract time bridges." At the time, she realized that traveling as a life endeavor was more important to her than going to art school. So she left California and went elsewhere to study and work.

Elsewhere was, first, south of the border. There Stuart lived with a Mexican family, learned Spanish by reading García Lorca and landed a job as one of Diego Rivera's assistants on his last mural project. "I was seventeen or eighteen. He took my hands and kissed them and said, 'You want to work? Fine! We can use an assistant!' He did everything with grace. He was amazing, a huge man but delicate on the scaffold. Very gentle." Meanwhile, she underwent the traditional culture shock, distilling thoughts through the grid of a foreign grammar, immersing herself in new colors and fragrances and meeting a new political spectrum. "There was the Catholic ambiance, so sensuous; the rich fabric of village life in Cayoacán with shadows of wild dogs crossing the white walls at night. Later I moved into a building with art galleries and studios of Mexicans, Russians and Spanish refugees, anarchists, poets and artists." The connection took, she married a Spanish artist and sailed to Europe for two years of painting, writing, traveling and studying Romanesque and Gothic architecture.

By the mid-'60s she was in New York, alone, and living in a studio on the Upper West Side. It would take several years of evolution to move Stuart to the original idiom that would speak to the Zeitgeist and so bring her to prominence.

The surface of her paintings grew heavier and thicker as she let materials have their way in the '60s mode. She began dipping the canvas into plaster, then making plaster reliefs, heads or full figures that were displayed mounted in black box constructions. The figures were monochrome, white or black, silver or gray. There were obvious connections with boxes of Cornell and some figures of Segal, but for Stuart the works were exclusively autobiographical and hermetic. One showed a head breaking through its cover in a welter of broken-glass shards, literally "coming through." Another showed a female bound down with strips of plaster-soaked cloth that wrapped and double-wrapped the body. Faces of these figures were literally modeled from the artist's own. Now that she has moved on to new fields, Stuart is reluctant to show or even talk about these works. "I'm not interested in that part of the past. It was a reclusive time. The work was private."

One can speculate that the change in Stuart's thinking during the years of the '60s came about, at least partly, when old fascinations of hers were revived by the Gemini and Apollo flights and when certain memories of the past were revived by the death of her father. There came a point when she returned to her love for mapping and began a series of renderings, made after NASA photographs, of the surface of the moon. She mounted these in two-foot square boxes that she aligned in series extending some twelve or sixteen feet across. From some boxes, little trailing strings extended, representing currents of wind or water. The intention was for the viewer to walk along the piece, passing from section to section, surveying the "land" and passing through time. Each work was, as Stuart explains today, "an open-ended continuum that described change."

She was, it seems, seeking a way of delivering this gradually clarifying new subject matter: the process of change in matter and time. "My art until then had been concerned with forms as containers of personal memory. The 'moon' pieces with their serial repetition explored literal and geological time. But then I wanted to deepen my involvement with the changes that time effects in matter. I wanted to find a way that was more personal. To involve myself physically in the process."

The last of the serial drawings were combined with sections of rubbings made from the ground near an old country house she was at that point living in. "I laid the paper on top of the earth and rocks and used graphite as a tool to record the changes worked by the passage of time."

Even that procedure soon failed to bring her close enough to the material at hand. The sheets of paper themselves had become very large, and now she decided to dispense with the boxes and let the papers find their own limitations. "That was important. A big leap ahead. When I broke away from the units, it released me from the boundaries I had imposed myself.

"And I remember exactly how the next step in my working-process took place. Every day, I had been photographing the changes and configurations that certain rocks and samples of earth revealed when I laid them on top of a paper. That way, I logged the rain, wind and even animal tracks that marked this new 'surface.' Then I made a decision literally to indent those geological events into the paper—in other words, to stop the flow of natural events and render it permanent. That was an important moment for me, and the ritual of this new way of working inevitably led me to the invention of new forms." The first of Michelle Stuart's new papers, then, were made in that hilly plain by a stream, in a setting of flat rocks and a fissure in the earth that led to an old quarry, worked long before. It was, one imagines, the gradation and contrast in the ground that appealed to her, as she set about spreading out her paper, piling rocks and earth upon it and then rubbing them into its fibers instead of the other way around.

And the technical breakthrough also led to the exploration of deeper strata of feeling and memory. At just about the same juncture, Stuart began to gather into scrapbooks all the notes, old photos, maps and snatches of texts she had been amassing for years. "I was living near Woodstock, New York, then, but I was remembering California. These new scrapbooks had to do with the past. With places I'd visited as a child. With the California desert, Baja, Nevada and Arizona." By now, those collections of memory-jogs and mementoes of the past have become a massive set of volumes with the inclusive title *Return to the Silent Garden*. "I think of nature as the silent garden," says the artist.

By now, too, the technical turn of a moment, repeated and defined, has become a ritualistic event. The very process sheds its own historic and mythic ramifications back onto the work. The artist collects shovelfuls of earth and rocks from various sites and pounds them to powder with the biggest rock, all the time bending over the work like a tribal woman kneading bread, planting seeds or washing clothes. So she goes on transferring, pressing and packing the earth into the fibers of the paper ground until it is loaded and scarred. From these mineral earths, the papers take their extraordinary dull shimmer like the

The artist at work in the field, with local earths and rocks laid upon paper.

walls of a cave seen by daylight. *Sayreville Strata,* of 1976, is a quartet of golden-brown papers from a site in New Jersey. Others were made in New Hampshire, New York State and westward, in tones of clay, shale, Plumbago carbon. "Give me some mud off a city crossing," she quotes John Ruskin, "some ocher out of a gravel pit, a little whitening, and some coal dust, and I will paint you a luminous picture . . . "

The scale of the new works probes its own near-infinite. Some are human size; others may reach twelve feet high and lap in a relaxed way forward upon the floor. Her biggest work was *Niagara Gorge Path Relocated,* made for Artpark, in Lewiston, New York, in 1975. It was 450 feet in height and was unfurled down the face of the same cliff where, eighteen thousand years ago, the falls actually ran. Again, she was mapping geological changes, isolating the colors and configurations of the various strata of the gorge wall. And in "relocating" the falls from its present to its original site, she was, in essence, recapitulating a passage of time in terms of her own idiom.

Stuart's most ambitious work in terms of schedule is going on now and will be for a decade to come in an abandoned rock quarry at Tomkins Cove, New York. For *Color/Time/Landform/Transformations,* she laid three rolls of paper—ninety, sixty and thirty feet long—on three different rock elevations at three escarpment levels where the earth changes from red to ocher to raw

Niagara Gorge Path Relocated, 1975. Project for Artpark, Lewiston, New York. Rock indentations and earth from the Niagara Gorge escarpment: muslin-mounted rag paper. 420' by 62".

The Pen Argyl Myth, *1977. Muslin-mounted rag paper impacted with earth from Pen Argyl, Pennsylvania, quarry: pheasant feather also from Pen Argyl; woven string. Collection the artist.*

sienna. "By marking the strata from different eras, you evoke the memory that lies buried in the earth. And then, too, the ecology of the site is changing. Slowly, now that all blasting and pumping have ceased, this area is returning to its natural state. Plant growth and animal life are reappearing. I want to record the past, as before, but now I will also incorporate present and future cycles of nature." The program will be carried on by still photography and also by Videotape, on foot and from a helicopter each spring for the next ten years. Packed and rubbed papers annually will collect the literal ground.

Since she set upon her own way of working and conceptualizing that work, Stuart has earned considerable recognition. She says she can almost date the time when she moved "from private to public." It was 1970, when the Women's Movement began to affect the art world and she made certain decisions about her personal life, taking on a new independence. In '72, she began to exhibit. She had her first one-person show in New York in '74 and has since showed at the Museum of Modern Art as well as in Europe. In 1977, a three-section wall piece, *Breezy Point,* was bought by the National Collection of Australia in Canberra, and the Museum of Modern Art in Teheran purchased the hanging *#46: Niagara.* Nowadays, Stuart travels constantly, tirelessly—as she once said of her father—especially toward remote sites that tempt her more and more for their cultural history. She confesses a growing interest in the "spiritual involvement of people with land, in the fact that people have been in the place, chosen it for a particular reason: Mesa Verde, Tikal, the serpent mounds in Ohio . . . "

445

Though she teaches and lectures, Stuart is a maker and doer, not a theoretician. She is not much interested in examining her work for art-historical influences. She admires Robert Smithson but feels their work is not related. Of Max Ernst's famous *frottages,* or rubbings, she says only that hers were done for entirely different reasons. Some critics have mentioned Zen, but that too seems only an informal eclecticism on this artist's part, though inevitably she knows something about Buddhist time cycles and Zen "intentionless intentions." Japanese art, on the other hand, especially the gardens of Ryoanji, is an affinity she acknowledges. But apart from that, the simplest statement is perhaps the most accurate: "The work progressed from a personal, psychological journey to a search for new meanings in marks and forms."

Out of the constantly enlarging *Silent Garden,* Stuart has put together a short, loose but thematic cluster of episodes she calls *The Fall.* Here she tells the story of an Indian maiden, Red Poppy, whose fate it was to be "sewn into the still-warm skin of a dead calf," locked up, dragged and finally delivered for deliverance to "a silver fish, who came from Monterey." The artist means this tale to be read partly as autobiography: "Red Poppy and I are the same person. She is a mediator, a partner in exploration. The story is about California, and its disenfranchised peoples, the Indians and later the Mexicans. I mean to imply, too, the rape of California itself. For nature itself is one of those without power or protection, and the land out there has been laid bare in the pursuit of gold and, later, real estate."

Stuart's incantatory prose unwinds encrusted with facts like fossils in matrix: ". . . the red clay bed . . . : a pile of white quartz . . . fish silver with meteoric dust . . . sharp crystals, stickery weeds and digger pine . . . a cruciform cluster of nebulae . . . a greenish fan-shaped mass . . . a mackerel sky." *The Fall* includes an historical tale about a woman abandoned on an island, who dressed herself in skins of birds and was so long lost that no one remembered her language. Behind these granulations of word and image, Stuart's diction sinks back to a vagueness, one might say to a *ground:* "scrolls of silence . . . maps of the void . . . questions without answers . . . extensions of our mortality." Indeed, at a point, history itself as collated by scribes is a thing come apart and reduced to dust: ". . . this enormous history book was useless and they abandoned it. . . . In the deserts of the West some torn and fragmented pages of the book remained. . . ." There is, in the end, no book left on earth to tell what really took place but "a string of shells that records the spiral sea . . ."

Stuart's writing, like the process of making the papers, is simple, primitive, full of impulse. A running river of intention and also, in the sense I have already described, possibly an example of early work in a vein that has not yet been plundered.

446

Connie Zehr

BORN 1938, EVANSTON, ILLINOIS

It wasn't until I . . . began taking a ceramics class that I made up my mind. I went into the work-shop and sank my hands into that clay. And I had found myself.

—CONNIE ZEHR
Los Angeles, 1977

The transitory, that shifts, flows, appears in dreams and vanishes: This is the raw material of Connie Zehr's curious, uncategorizable art. She works with sand, light, a hint of a sound, the mark of a tear. She also has built a number of Surreal dream environments, with life-size unfired clay objects and pieces of clothing, that evoke American Indian legends and scenes from her own dreams. These, like the sand works, are one-time events set up, filmed or photographed, then disassembled. *Crystal Carpet,* for example, told the tale of a journey: a carpet of white sand embedded with glass shards, their network of shadows and light projections cast on the smooth surface. The enlarged shadow of a canoe was cast on the black wall behind it, and a pair of carved white porcelain toe shoes were placed in front. The pelt of a wild rabbit hung at the side; two holes, cut out, transformed it into a mask. Surrealism and Joseph Cornell, the art of Happenings and Lenore Tawney all might have had an influence upon Zehr's work, except for its apparent innocence of art history. In fact, her art seems almost painfully personal, extruded from a mind in a kind of isolation. If she has an ancestor, it might be the abstract painter Arthur G. Dove, who wrote:

We have not yet made shoes that fit like sand,
Nor clothes that fit like water—
Nor thoughts that fit like air.[1]

But Zehr, in a sense, has done these things.

She caught the end of a thread as a child in a small Ohio town, held on to it while her family moved and moved again. Held it during two years' residence in India, held it during years of burdensome young motherhood, when she had no time for work. "At one time I felt very angry about my life from a Feminist point of view. My husband's colleagues, all of them artists, simply weren't interested in my work. They'd come to our house and walk right through my studio on the way to his. I realize now they simply didn't see my work. It didn't enter their consciousness. The kind of thing I was doing, for them, wasn't even art." In the end, however, memories of childhood days on her Amish grandfather's dusty farm mingled with those of a dry, dun India and its little clay lamps, and with present feelings for a monochrome California landscape, to provide the ground for creations that have earned Zehr considerable success and been exhibited in major U.S. museums.

She lives in the horse country north of Los Angeles today in a house she and her sculptor-teacher husband built for themselves and two sons. Low jagged mountains cut the sky beyond it; neighbors have corrals, but this family has sold its horses. "Our financial situation is not good. On the other hand, I don't want to work full time teaching." Zehr's own development, at last, is the important thing. Therefore she's not too interested in more acclaim for the moment but in staying flexible, open, to let the art grow.

"My father's family were Amish, the Plain People. My great-grandmother wore a long dark dress, long black stockings and a little white hat. I sometimes stayed overnight with her when I was a child. I'd braid her hair, and she'd share her hot-water-and-lemon-juice toddy with me before she went to bed. I remember a huge Bible in her house. My earliest experience with 'art' was that Bible. It was filled with prints, and I'd look through it for my entertainment. One engraving was fascinating: a crowd of people on a huge rock, the flood waters coming up around the rock.

"My grandfather was progressive, and he contributed to improving livestock in the region. And my father had a college education. But there were no conveniences on the farm. It was very, very plain. I remember playing in the dirt a lot, an incredible amount of imaginary play, filling bottles with water, making little objects out of mud. I had a bakery; some things would be round, some like doughnuts, some flat like little cakes. I'd pick berries and green leaves and decorate them. Colors mattered, too. Later when we moved to town, I remember buying candies wrapped in cellophane. I wasn't half so interested in eating the candies as in taking the colored cellophanes and wrapping up objects I had made out of the dirt."

EM: "And others in your family?"

CZ: "Mother came from a large Catholic family; twelve children. But she left all that and found herself totally involved in my father's life. She wasn't career-oriented, and she didn't encourage me that way. But she thought a great deal about our home. My father was a dairy farmer and is now an agricultural economist. For his work, we moved around a great deal—twenty-two times so far in my own life! In the end, one takes on a strange feeling of transiency. On the other hand, the moving when I was younger forced me to develop a sense of myself. I was, in a way, my only point of stability. In any case, as a child, I felt *different*."

EM: "Was that feeling related to an artistic talent as well as to the moves?"

CZ: "Yes, I remember one day in the fourth grade we were sitting at our desks in school, drawing, and suddenly everyone wanted me to draw something for them. And about that same time something happened that I've never forgotten and that has a connection with the way I feel about my art today. I had long braids, but one day I talked Mother into letting me wear my hair loose. I went off to school feeling absolutely beautiful. There was a swing in the schoolyard, and I remember putting my head way back, swinging, letting the air flow through my hair. It felt wonderful. Floating.

"Then I must have fallen. I woke up, dazed but quite calm, in a room in the school. Nowadays sometimes when I'm working in my studio and completely wrapped up in what I'm doing, doing whatever comes into my head, working without any interference but in complete control of myself, that feeling of swinging comes back to me. Swinging, and feeling air and space, and being in a sort of state. I have a place in my mind always, it seems, that I can escape to and be completely free.

"I even think that inner freedom I feel is what allows me to reject a good deal of conventional art thinking: the idea of making objects to show in galleries. One might imagine I am simply indifferent to success, or unable to discipline myself. But there is literally something about being assigned a date for an exhibition, or presented with a price list, that stops me cold. I don't want those considerations to enter my work at the moment. I back off."

EM: "What about encouragement from outside?"

CZ: "My parents had a relaxed attitude about bringing up an only girl. They weren't intellectual; we didn't have many books in the house. When I was in fifth grade my ideal was to be a beauty operator. Then one day the art teacher from school called on my parents and told them they were making a mistake with me. That I was talented and ought to be encouraged. We lived in a very small town where there wasn't a museum, so there just weren't any models for me there. Later, of course, I've seen that I needed other things in my life. But at the time, the only encouragement came from that teacher's telling me I was silly to think about fixing people's hair. That I could do more.

"And then, when I was fourteen, my father was asked to spend two years in India as an agricultural adviser. In Delhi I went to a Catholic girls' school, made some Indian friends and also met an American woman, a commercial artist. She and I would take drawing paper and drive out to various parts of the city and work. She gave me the feeling 'if you're going to be an artist, you just do it; that's what you do.' She told how she organized her time, spending her mornings in her studio undisturbed. Gradually I began to feel there might be something ahead for me, a way of expressing myself. In India that feeling became a lifesaver, and in the end I became rather bound up in the idea as a sense of my identity."

EM: "How about the Indian landscape?"

CZ: "My memories of the country are sensuous. The landscape is dry, arid, monotone. The houses are earth-colored. And against that dun background the people stand out, the colors of their costumes and their skin. The village men wore white; the women were the colorful ones. The utensils they used were brightly polished. And of course their skins were rich and dark.

"In fact, a strange thing happened to me one day after being out in the marketplace. I looked into the mirror and was shocked to see how light my skin was. You come to think of yourself as like the people around you, but of course you're not. That feeling of being isolated, or different, again, affected me strongly in India.

"It wasn't until much later, when I married and moved out here to California, that I found a place I felt I was coming home to. I love the dryness here, the sparseness, the space. I also love the fact that the landscape is all of one color, like India, so that no one feature of it jumps out at you."

EM: "Were there festivals, pageants, rituals?"

CZ: "Oh, I remember best the spring Festival of Lights. We were invited to a private home. The women of the house were in charge of the decorations. They had drawn patterns on the floor with colored rice and set little clay oil lamps around. In one spot was the figure of a goddess, holding another lamp. The low illumination fascinated me. I'd forgotten about that until you asked.

"In the end, I'd absorbed so much of that Indian atmosphere that coming home was hard. I was more aware than ever of that feeling of being different, even in some way threatening to my old friends. My first idea was to get away, get somewhere where I could do something of my own. I tried music, playing the violin, met a number of professional artists and decided to go to Michigan State. It wasn't until I had arrived there and taking a class in ceramics that I made up my mind what it would be. I went into the workshop and sank my hands into that clay. And I had found myself.

"The teacher left me alone that year, and I used up a lot of clay! The next year I went to Ohio State as a sculpture major, and before I graduated I also got into working in plaster. I never enjoyed working with the technical processes of sculpture—carving, making molds and casts. I wanted to work directly, laying on the plaster with a spatula, filing it off."

EM: "And then?"

CZ: "I met David Elder, also a sculptor. We were married and eventually moved to Southern California, where he had taken a job, but it didn't work out. So David was without a job, our first son was born and President Kennedy was assassinated, all in one year. I grew up a lot that year. As it turned out, our baby had something wrong with his eyes. I had come to California thinking life was new and exciting and we had lots of time, but I realized there were numerous alternative possibilities. Finally we moved to L.A. David got another teaching job and was involved with his work. I was involved with a sick baby. My career had to be simply put aside. As David said, 'We can afford only one habit.'

"Then we bought a house with a space for a studio—for David. I got pregnant again. And finally one day I realized I had bought a ticket in terms of being a wife and mother that just wasn't enough for me."

EM: "How did you cope?"

CZ: "We divided up the studio space, and I moved into part of it. I wrote my grandfather saying I knew I had some inheritance coming and asked if I could have it. There was no way I could afford supplies otherwise. And he sent the money.

"And then I began working again. I started back with the plaster, making large abstract pieces and painting them. I liked the effect of color on top of the white plaster. It made a separate form, and I became interested in the relationship between these two fields of energy. Eventually the works got so big and heavy I couldn't move them, and David said, 'Look. If you're going to make something, you have to be able to move it,' and he was right.

"I was interested in Claes Oldenburg's work. So I got myself an old sewing machine. I thought that might be something I could do with one kid on my hip and one tagging along behind: wander through fabric and upholstery shops. So pretty soon I was making sewn sculptures.

"I became interested in things that weren't completely filled. I would make them so that the filling—I was using little plastic beads—would shift into

451

The artist, forming conical sand-shapes for an installation.

certain parts of the shape when you picked it up, so that some parts would be full, some flat and empty. Then I began working with sand as a filler. I'd make large cloth objects, floor pieces, like still lifes, several together, some covered in fur, some in vinyl. Something about the shifting of these hard and soft pieces, their relationships and the power of gravity acting on them interested me.

"Then one day I made a still-life group on a sheet of vinyl and added two cones of poured sand. When I lifted the vinyl up later to pour off the sand, it shifted into a pattern that struck me as wonderful.

"From then on I worked that way deliberately. I laid down vinyl, poured sand cones, then shifted the sand in various ways. What I had done was to throw away the cover. Really, it had always been the changing quality of the sand that interested me. And If you look at forms made out of that shifted sand, you'll see they're organic, related to the human body. I'm so aware of the earth out here in the West as a massive body, exposed, without grass or trees as clothing."

EM: "Your first show was at Mount San Antonio College near Los Angeles. How did that work out?"

CZ: "I was invited to use two gallery rooms there. I had never done anything so large, and I was nervous! I made two mound fields, as I called them, one in each room, by pouring the sand through a grid structure I built over the floor. The action of the sand as it diminished at the top, pouring through the holes and piling into mounds at the bottom, fascinated me. Then I arranged lights to illuminate the mounds but without casting any shadows. It

452

wasn't until I came into the room later and saw it all together that I grasped what I'd done. The silica had picked up the light and begun to glow. It radiated light through the whole room. It was like walking into another space warp [or a house readied for the goddess of the Festival of Lights?].

"After that, I only did room installations. The Women's Movement gave many of us a new visibility. At the Pasadena Museum and again at the Wadsworth Atheneum in Hartford, Connecticut, I filled part of a curved room with mounds of white sand in grid alignment and set a brown egg in each one. Nineteen dozen eggs. To me it represented a sea of infinite possibilities. At the art gallery of the California State University at Los Angeles, I rolled a granite boulder between two flat mounds of sand. The stone and its imprint were contained mysteriously in the center. The other piece in that show was gold sand (from Baja, California) and a rope that I had woven in order to control its color and tension. The rope was lifted, leaving a diagonal scar across an irregular group of large mounds. One end was suspended from the ceiling so its shadow cut across the cluster of mounds."

Red Carpet (detail), 1975. Sand and unfired terra-cotta objects. 8" by 120" by 144". Installation at the Whitney Museum of American Art Biennial, New York.

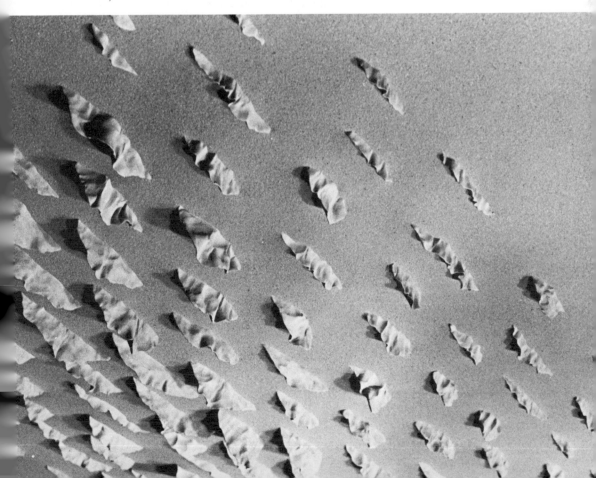

EM: "Recently you've made environments with small clay pieces set in sand. What about these?"

CZ: "For the first one, at the Museum of Contemporary Crafts in Chicago in '74, I used hundreds of little hand-formed unfired porcelain pieces. We had just finished building a new house in LA. It had rained a lot that year, and I was experimenting with the wet adobe we were building the house on. That spring, the place went from a sea of mud to a meadow of grass. The rhythm of rolling bits of clay into balls, then into snakes and then into flattened shapes and cups seemed like the process of growing itself. So I called the work *The Place Between Two Waters,* from an American Indian legend. The story was that every seven years the elders of the tribe would go to a place with that name and see how the water had overflowed, then receded, how plants had grown, how rocks had been moved. They called it 'reading the sand' and made prophecies from what they saw. *Red Carpet,* done for the Whitney Annual in 1975, included pieces of unfired terra-cotta in red sand from the Valley of Fire in Nevada. David and I have traveled in many of the Indian countries of the Southwest, and wherever we've gone I've collected sands.

"But it wasn't until I was invited to Artpark in upstate New York in 1976 that I ever actually worked outdoors. I used the silver-gray shale from the Niagara River Gorge, sifting it and carrying it by wheelbarrow to the site above the river. It rained heavily that summer, and everything I accomplished one day was washed aside the next. The shifting forms I had planned to do couldn't be accomplished in the wet shale. It sagged, but it wouldn't shift. I sagged, too. It was the culmination of a series of frustrations that made me decide to withdraw into my studio for a while. Traveling around and doing the installations had eroded both my work and my life. There was little money involved for me, if any. There were weeks of research and preparation and then often uncontrolled situations that affected the results. My family seemed to be managing without me, but I wasn't managing. I wasn't sure why. The fact that the shifting process which had been so essential in the Artpark work had been aborted was a clue.

"Unfinished clay, shifting sand, dream images were no longer sufficient, it seemed. I got an NEA grant to explore my ideas on film. I'd never been free enough for long enough to do that. The time had come! In a way, it's been like the childhood experience on the swing. For some time, it had been right to explore ideas as they came, deal with opportunities as they came up, and just let the results fall out. But then it was I who fell out. I spent that year in limbo, muddled and miserable. My last show summed it up.

"It was called *tears.* There were eight "water on silk" prints I made by pressing water-soaked handkerchiefs into silk. There were also twelve prints of tearstains on silk. In the same room, a tape recorder played a constant sound. One day I'd been alone in my studio and I heard that sound. It was sad but regenerative, like a child getting over tears. Self-comforting in a way. It turned out the sound was my own voice. Many people at the show didn't even want to listen, but later they said they found it comforting, like a low, repeated chant.

"Now I'm excited about my new work. There is technology involved. I'm learning. I'm using photography to capture the process of change. Exploring ideas in a new way. Swinging again!"

Betty Klavun

BORN 1916, BOSTON

Suddenly I was thrust into that world. I hadn't known a thing about contemporary painting . . . But the very concept was exciting. I'd drive in from Connecticut and drive back out so excited. I didn't really even know what I was excited about. I couldn't put it into words. And then, gradually, I could.

—Betty Klavun
New York, 1977

Chronology is no factor in the arrival of some artists at the threshold of the advance guard. Betty Klavun graduated from Bennington College in 1938, spent years in a demanding motherhood, returned in the '50s to the practice of art she had begun in college, and only in the late '60s began to exhibit her drawings and then her sculpture professionally in New York. It is in this decade of the '70s, however, that she has come into her own as one of that group of sculptor-architect-fantasists who make outdoor works that deliberately invite the perambulation of onlookers. In this way it can be suggested that she is exploring with a touching directness aspects of the life she led as a child.

From age four, Klavun spent her summers with her Old New England family in New Hampshire on land once owned by the State Poor Farm which, by that time, had long since abandoned it. There, meadows gave way to cellar holes and cows ambled at will through falling-down barns. There was everything here for a mother to do and make, and Klavun's was an example of the old-fashioned matriarch, daughter herself of an immigrant Scots cabinetmaker who rose in life to a prominent business career. She milked the cows, made butter, collected berries, raised bees. She crossed flowers, grafted trees and grew mushrooms in what had been the Poor Farm morgue. She trundled up a mammoth chickenhouse from somewhere else, set it atop some cellar or other,

456

bought a set of old paneling decorated with paintings of George Washington, designed her own pine trestle table, refinished secondhand pieces and made there a sometime home. Nearby was a bigger, permanent, beautiful old home as well, always light and airy. You looked through the rooms toward the windows as extensions of the inner space, on out to the outdoors.

"And my father was terribly proud of her, only his pride didn't go so far as for him to help her. Only when they went fishing did they go as companions. Men were not brought up to think of women as 'free' in those days." No more perhaps than the women did themselves. Later, in fact, though Klavun's parents accepted her becoming an artist, they both deplored what she describes as her "curiosity and so-called liberal attitude."

There were models of independence and an artistic life however: three artist-couples who lived nearby and acted as caretakers. Every good day they went out with young Betty, each with his or her twelve proper pencils, six hard and six soft, to sketch among the rambles. Or they went into town to draw the old houses, the ponds and trees. "Whenever anything was wrong, I'd go out and draw. They were my schooling, till I went away to college."

At Bennington, Klavun majored in theater design, ran her own costume shop and designed sets. After a postgraduation trip to Europe, where she recalls being impressed by the power of Socialist peoples' theater to draw crowds off the street and offer them socially consolidating entertainment, she came home and married. Over the next decade and a half she raised her four children, one of whom had to be shepherded through years of corrective surgery. "I lived her life, it was so all-absorbing. But it's true that every minute I had to myself, I lapsed back to working. And then it was very simple: as I got time and needed money because I was going to get a divorce, I decided to go out and do commercial art. But I got stuck there. I couldn't do that kind of work! An agent said I should go to the Famous Artists' School and become a *real* artist, so I ordered a full set of their books. They're still moldering in my basement."

Klavun's opening came when she joined a painting class in Manhattan taught by the then head of the Yale School of Art and Architecture, Abstract Expressionist Jack Tworkov. "Suddenly I was thrust into that world. I hadn't known a thing about contemporary painting at that point. But the very concept was exciting. I'd drive in from Connecticut and drive back out so excited. I didn't really even know what I was excited about. I couldn't put it into words. And then, gradually, I could."

She was painting in those days, but the flat canvas was a frustration. Her mind needed space to move; the three dimensions of an open stage had been more congenial. "I came to a barrier. I didn't know which way to go. Then one day I began working out the same ideas in clay, and immediately the

Head, 1968. Papier-mâché. 10" by 8".
Collection the artist.

barrier fell away." From that point on, it was steady progress. Klavun's first participation in a group show was in '61. Her first decisively personal works were made in the early '60s—scenes in relief constructed of corrugated cardboard cut into Cubist forms. They were small theatrical montages, one might say, showing rural groups of trees and farms. Next, she passed through one of those near-ritual autobiographical phases one often witnesses in artists' lives, making a series of moving expressionistic studies of heads modeled directly in papier-mâché from her children. Around 1970, she found the direction in which she would continue, making Constructivist-style models for city parks and also now frankly for theater sets, some of which became fantasies of mesh scrims, columns and panels that could be drawn upward or let down on pulleys. She liked the idea, at that time, of engaging people in the work. "I began parks because I wanted people in my designs. A park has to do with making people comfortable, having them sit and talk as if they were on their own stoops, having a good time, not pushing or getting in each other's way." And as her own mother had in creating an environment for her family to be "comfortable" in, Klavun reached out to all possible sources of material to make these models: paper, wire, fishing line, various types of mesh and plastic, and Fiberglas. With such a pragmatic medley of natural and man-made stuff, she put together, in 1976, a *Treehouse* on the roof of her own house in Manhattan. It still stands there, a permanent structure of angled, sail-like forms hinged to a scaffold of metal uprights, with flights of stairs both functional and fantasy that lead to doors both false and real. The next year she received her first important public grant, to build an environment at Artpark on the upper banks of the Niagara Gorge in New York State, where other artists working the same vein of form and imagination have been represented. Her piece there was a wood-and-plastic sitting place of Constructivist heritage, a sort of gentle ghost of a Moholy-Nagy or a Johannes Itten in a site of wild American grandeur. And the summer after that, Klavun mounted a number of her constructions in wire, wood, steel, nylon filament and again mesh on the grounds of a private estate in Southampton, Long Island, where, in a scene of windy bay water and gray-green beach grass, it was possible to imagine how such sculpture-sketches—for such is what most of them essentially were—might look erected full scale.

It is both the thrust of forms in space (that truly sculptural capacity) and their capacity to attract and contain light (as a stage might do) that seem

Treehouse, 1976. Corian and aluminum. 7' by 10' by 10'. Collection the artist.

The Columns, 1974. Wire mesh, aluminum, conduit wood. 8' by 30' by 20'. Installed at Water Mill, Long Island, 1978.

alternately to interest Klavun as she progresses in her opening career. As she moves between sculptor and environmentalist, it might be simplest to relate her present work to structures first encountered on the idyllic farm: frameworks for spaces, meant to be both looked at and used. A wire-mesh frame, for instance, will bend upon itself to contain a trembling skein of white nylon threads that, from a distance, seems to be a cloud of phosphorescence; this is Dream Exit, both a place of passage and a condition of mind and mood of one held captive in its luminous ambiance. Such a work, too, is Loom, a standing narrow enclosure containing several mesh and Fiberglas panels, transparent and trembling in the wind, that seem to exist for the purpose of accumulating a dusty light across their surfaces. Other works, like Banners, a flying covey of bright streamers flung back in the wind from a metal scaffold, are concerned with pure movement, while Wave is a projected dream city unto itself, a series of piers designed to jut from a shallow seashore or basin of water, each one bearing a miniature environment of walls, doors, benches, sunshades.

It is all once again, as Camus intimated, that long wandering back to the place where originally sunlight played upon meadows and reflected off the walls of a "light and airy" old home. "Yes, it's true," says this artist. "I think of walking in the fields, back when I was a child. Walking around things to draw them. I find now that all my drawings go back to those early days, interpreting and reinterpreting them. Even *Treehouse*. It reminds me that one wanted privacy in those early days. A place to go. I feel children need a place to go. I make a home for them out of materials that come to my hand. Magic! What a child might like.

"And at the end . . . I put in the windows."

Loom, 1974. Steel, nylon filament, Fiberglas and mesh. 6'2" by 3'10" by 7'4". Installed at Water Mill, Long Island, 1978.

Patricia Johanson

BORN 1940, NEW YORK CITY

The world as a work of art is an idea that has been with me for a long time, the idea of the vast configuration, art that could never be seen all at once, and that would be understood only by very sensitive, intelligent people with good memories and a good sense of history, geography and so on . . .

—PATRICIA JOHANSON
Bennington, Vermont,[1] *1960*

The theme, once more, is walking through time and space toward meaning.

Parks and woods were where this family walked together, four or more in a row, Sunday after Sunday, exploring their city: "*All* the parks, Central Park, Prospect Park, Bronx Park, the Brooklyn Botanical Gardens. We left no stone unturned! All of us together, with our grandparents, picnicking, rowing on the lakes, riding ponies, but mostly walking, without any definite goals. Just finding our way and meeting up with things. I remember every nineteenth-century cast-bronze statue we ever met.

"Nowadays, when someone asks me how I expect to enrich people's lives by making my kind of city projects, I answer, 'In ways I can't imagine.' "

Before the parks, there were other trajectories. Patricia Johanson's father, for example, was an engineer for celestial guidance systems. When she was a child in the '50s, they lived in Cape Canaveral hard by the testing field for the Polaris missiles. The glowing arc-paths of rockets through the sky, momentous rumblings of air and ground: these were the background for a fascinated child who was "absolutely my father's buddy."

"Nights, we could see the wake kicking up, the lights of things being fired. One time the building shook and we all rushed outside. It was like daylight. The sky was red. Something had exploded on the pad by mistake."

Probably years before Canaveral, there were other excursions by imagination. Stories and fairy stories, family stories and personal stories. Johanson's mother was an artistic, aspiring woman whose hopes for college were dashed during the Depression when, like many girls, she had to give up her right to an education because her parents believed that "women should marry." That Feminist issue was something Johanson early caught on to. "In my family the women were the strong ones. They all ran things. But there were still several generations of frustration behind me. My Norwegian great-grandmother got the highest score in all of Norway on a school entry test, and still she couldn't go, because she had to take care of her brothers. It was obvious to me these women were strong and intelligent, and the fact that they hadn't done things was due to circumstances beyond their control."

Johanson's own mother became a Powers model and a guide to all the arts for her two daughters. "She took us to everything, every ballet, every symphony, all the museums. I can't remember her ever doing anything for herself: it was all for us. Ballet and acrobatics for my sister; music for me. I played the clarinet and the tenor sax well enough to be in a dance band. And I always made things—drawings, paintings, boxes and boxes of things.

"In the end, there was a conflict that worked to my advantage: my father's technical mind, and my mother's sense for poetry and culture. I made a big effort to acquire both."

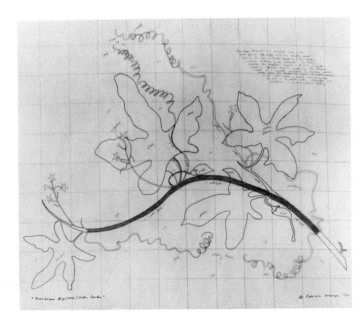

(Opposite) *The artist installing* Mask-Park, *Cleveland, 1977.*

(Right) Brandegea Biglovii/ Water Garden, *1974. Ink and charcoal. 30" by 36".*

463

Johanson auditioned to enter Bennington College as a music major until a clarinet teacher told her she already played with professional proficiency. "I had always envisioned climbing the mountains. He made it seem so easy, only a matter of technique. So I stopped music." Instead she majored in art, as Frankenthaler had some years before and Klavun a bit before that. Her magnum opus there was something she calls *Color Rooms* and talks about rather protectively. The project involved filling painting teacher Paul Feeley's office with a forestial tangle of orange paper surrounding a green-black paper structure at the heart. It was a Happening, a Site, an Environment. It was a Hans Andersen forest through which princesses might go, breaking off golden leaves. It was also a fire hazard and had to be taken down over Johanson's protesting body. "I've always been determined to build what I wanted."

A more permanent benefit of those years was Johanson's meeting, through the network long set up by Frankenthaler et al, with the New York art world. In 1960 she spent her off-campus session at the Art Students League and also working in a studio lent her by Frederick Kiesler, that visionary, elfin architect-sculptor who figures encouragingly in so many artists' biographies. Of all his many inventions, those that most influenced Johanson may have been his model for *Inside the Endless House* (1959–61) of wire mesh, or the portentous *Galaxies*—sprawling, open structures of raw wood that meandered through space, cutting new ground for what one might call expressionistic walk-works.

Leaving Bennington in '62 but not forever—she had formed a close friendship with art historian Eugene Goossen, who lived in a nearby valley offering promising forest-fields for future projects—Johanson took two fast degrees, a master's degree in eighteenth-century American art history and an architectural degree afterward, "because I was already tired of structural engineers telling me I couldn't do what I knew I could do." She was also painting, in those days, very wide canvases—many twenty-eight feet across—somewhat Barney Newman–like, with a single line of color spanning a neutral ground. In '67 she had her first one-person show at the Tibor de Nagy Gallery. But the gallery scene with its apparatus of flattery and pragmatism "never interested me." Over the next few years, instead, she turned out a number of site pieces exploring ramifications of the *line,* forcing what had been only a visual image into structures of such immensity that they became (like Jennifer Bartlett's expanded shoe) subject to new laws—in this case, of perspective and atmospheric effect. *William Rush,* celebrating the nineteenth-century American carver, was a 200-foot-long steel I beam, ordered from a factory, cut in half, painted red and laid down on supports in a mowed strip of upper New York State woodland. Another was *Stephen Long,* after the vanquisher of Pike's Peak: 1,600 feet of plywood painted red, yellow and blue, laid this time on the Boston and Maine

Cyrus Field *(two views)*, 1971. Cement blocks in natural woodland. 8" by 3200' by 4". Buskirk, New York.

Railroad bed. To walk the length of these pieces was to experience an inexplicably piercing sense of passage of time, like that single plucked note at the end of *The Cherry Orchard.* Johanson herself made another connection. "I remember my father reading to me about Einstein, the railroad engine coming, the pitch of the whistle rising, then falling as it moves away." Whatever the overtones, it was visually striking to watch the passage of clouds and hours change the colors of this strange object that ran beyond eyesight into the green of the trees, like the track of an arrow or a rocket.

At about the same time, *House and Garden* magazine commissioned Johanson to design and describe a series of fantasy gardens. The shape these took again assumed the shape of linear walk-tracks. There was a proposed *Road Garden—* with scholarly bows to Pliny, Lenôtre and Capability Brown: five thousand miles of planting in changing color clusters to line a highway. There was also, frankly, starkly, a *Line Garden,* an unwinding of metamorphosizing materials: now water, then brick; now bluestone, then mosaic, aluminum and mirror; now maze, then waterway; now path, then bridge. There were also, to spin on, *Out of Sight Gardens* and *Vanishing Point Gardens, Artificial Gardens* and *Water Gardens.* The last began to finger a new thread: nature itself, induced to masquerade as art. The *Water Garden,* as proposed, would begin with a natural fountainhead somewhere in the hills and follow a natural course to the sea.

Meanwhile, Johanson was beginning to take on commissions for civic Site Works. For a high school in Columbus, Indiana, she designed three sculptured forms, of grass, earth and stone, to push out the school space into open-air classrooms and seating areas. For the Consolidated Edison Indian Point Visitors' Center in New York State, she created an eighty-acre park with path, terrace, overlook and sculpture areas. Each of these combinations of meander and sitting place was also bound into a holistic image: from the air, the Columbus space had the shape of a bird, related to the form of some nearby Indian mounds. From the air, the Indian Point plan was a snake. In '77, Johanson went to Cleveland, Ohio, as one of four site artists each given a plot of land in the inner city to do with as they liked. Johanson hired a backhoe-loader and created a small amphitheater-park out of rubble and trash from a demolished building. Again, an aerial view would have revealed the ground plan as, in this case, an African mask. The total cost of the project: $466.

In the early '70s Johanson married Goossen, had a son and was homebound for a while and to a degree, she was delighted by the event. "For the last five years I've literally lived in the woods, with Alvar on my back. There were children on both sides of my family, and I was so happy to have him.

466

And I have no regrets for the domestic changes. I've tried to be a super-mom.'' What she has done is to strap the baby on her back or into the car and go out hauling planks and chunks of marble or cement, and foraging for fieldstones with which she has built parts of an extraordinary Site Work that extends into the Green Mountain woodland behind their house.

The structure is called *Cyrus Field,* for the man who laid down the first transatlantic cable. Its first "movement" involves a mile and a half of cement-block, marble and redwood-plank footpaths that turn back and forth through changing stands of birch, red maple and pine. Now the path lies ahead, now it turns, doubles back on itself, draws itself even into double or triple width as if a hand were gathering up ribbons. It proceeds through a pine grove where the wind makes a weaving sound in the branches and the redwood is rough underfoot with fallen needles. It reaches a clearing where the trees part like the eye of the roof of the Roman Pantheon and a shaft of light falls through. It proceeds. Fallen leaves lie upon it. The wind casts branches and twigs where it will, and in the distance the walker sees, always changing, the white verticals of birch against the darker green of the grove. The sense of smell (of pine and wet leaves or fragrant wind), the sense of touch (of wood or stone underfoot) and the imagination are all affected, while the eye continually seeks the path as it threads ahead to lie around the roots of trees, splaying into many directions like a spill of brooks.

The second "movement" of *Cyrus Field* is a ramble of rough rocks, laid in the grass, that one discovers mostly with the eyes and, at first, a fairly perplexed mind.

"I became interested in plants after Alvar was born. I turned into a botanist that year. I made hundreds of drawings and became interested in Darwin's 'form classes.' I focused on bacteria and began making drawings of various ones.

"There was a place in the woods that used to be a series of cleared fields; now they are grown with trees but still have a rough shape of rooms. I couldn't work with steel at that time, or even marble. But I could put the baby in the car and go off to collect rocks! They were free, too—a good medium. So I began to gather them and lay them down in the grass in the shapes of the bacteria I'd drawn.

"First I did gonorrhea. Then diphtheria. Then other bacteria, 'round,' 'rod' and 'spirilla.' Everything was there: my interest in Darwin, plants, rocks. I began to add some elemental plant forms. The land, I observed, seemed to be moving in three dimensions, so some of the forms I'd laid down appeared to be moving, crawling up the slope.

"Now, this isn't the same as an esthetic Japanese garden. It has another kind of order. There is information behind these rough forms, though you don't recognize what it is."

This Humboldtean interest in formal correspondences, between biological forms and the projected forms of the human imagination like language and art, has continued to absorb Johanson, as has her intermeshing of creative work and childbearing. In the spring of '78, on the brink of delivering her second son, she had a one-person exhibition at the Rosa Esmond Gallery in New York of "Plant Drawings for Architectural Projects." These were simple line drawings of botanical specimens that, laid out flat on grid paper, might suggest such promenade fantasies as *Stepping Stone Path Across Water (Brake Fern)* or *Summer House—Winter House (Mahoe Blossom).*

Would one treading that path across water know that she/he was also following the path of the plasm that, over millennia, formed itself into the fern? Here, then, is the dynamics of this pantomime of Johanson's, as of other artists of this genre: they are laying down structures comprehensible on one level as "art," with another level of obscure "scientific" meaning. Working, the artist "knows." By the time the work is done and given to the world, the key to understanding it is gone. Back and forth between knowledge and unknowledge the artist goes, the very personification of time and memory. And always she returns like the princess after her night of fabulous dance, to find in her hand, from some forgotten forest, a leaf of gold ("I was more convinced than ever that that image of the trees hung with gold, then silver, then diamonds, must be the secret source of works like the redwood piece," Johanson said). So with this new woman artist in all her mysterious occupations: laying rocks in the grass to spell out "bacteria"; kneeling in the soil to scrub particles of it into sheets of paper; drawing—by means of her structuring of walls, tunnels, ladders—an uncomprehending but willing audience into the recesses of her own imagination. Is she a herald, as I asked before, of a form of imaginative investigation that, as Alice said of Gertrude, "will take her years to understand"? The very dimensions of her expectations for herself, we know at least, are awesome: "The world as a work of art is an idea that has been with me for a long time," wrote Johanson when she was only twenty, back in 1960, "the idea of the vast configuration, art that could never be seen all at once, and that would be understood only by very sensitive, intelligent people with good memories and a good sense of history, geography and so on . . ."

Afterword

The most, it seems, that one can say about such a future mode of art is that it would involve a more open embrace of a role not in recent years always considered relevant for "art": investigation both of the artist's personal roots and also of our common roots in the natural world.

Where the natural world is subject, there *time* must be subject, too. Already we see new forms of the arts literally embodying time, the perennial. In our cities, the Cor-Ten sculptures slowly rust on their bases, turning the brown-umber of redwood trees. Grass grows and withers, to be replaced by snow on sculptures half buried in the earth. An artist kneels and takes a handful of earth. An artist walks down paths that lead back through the forest of Grimm. Like the heroine of Margaret Atwood's much discussed Feminist novel *Surfacing,* who seeks holistic immersion in the Canadian wilderness, Humboldt's daughters and many of their mothers are seeking, in pantomime and through the structures into which they project themselves, to claim their dominion over the nature-ground.

And how many "wonders of nature" reside in that ground to be drawn, as I said before, through the meshes of their minds if this should in fact turn out to be the direction? It seems that the natural sciences have opened a cornucopia of possibilities for an art that probes deeper resources than the objectless Conceptualism of the 1960s. For here is the conceptually mysterious bedded in the amazing real: the dark of the moon, Mars red behind its clouds, black holes, the deep seas, bacteria in their plenitude just beyond the limits of our optical power. Fortunate those communities of a disjointed world rooted enough in a believing past to possess, in addition to the art museum, that other trove, the natural-history museum, where so many women in this book told me they spend hours among the cycloramas, dioramas, cases of stuffed animals, walls painted with the descent of all forms of life, models of crystals and plants, fish and anemones, together with sleds from the Eskimos, huts from the Bushmen, fetishes from the Philippines, tiny shoes from the Chinese concubine! How our forebears, the nineteenth-century science-enlightened liberals I spoke of earlier, dreamed of passing on such natural proofs of continuity: to "foreigners" to be bound into One World by knowledge of our common origin; to artists, to learn from correspondences in nature what form is; to the young, to be given a sense of form, but in this order—*first* in its incarnation in life and *then* in its reincarnation in art.

That binding up of a life into the forms of art that Camus spoke of and that we have traced through all the pioneer artists in this book, the youngest of them seem in fact to seek to do in so undisguised a way that I have stopped short of claiming they make their work out of the very stuff of their forebears' lives only by my fear of proposing such a simplicist idea. But Erik Erickson has made the same claim in reverse about political revolutionaries. He proposes they structure their lives and work at least partly out of rage against those from whom they come. Is it less credible to say these women artists are motivated, at some level, by the sense of human concern, not superficial sentiment but the later distorted, disappointed or forgotten attachments that, for the child, spelled survival itself?

Is it not possible that, if revolutionaries act from motives of destructiveness against the past, and if some artists, as we have seen, are impelled to maintain continuity with it as well as with the future, this is a reason why "art," however devoid of easy subject matter it may passingly appear to be, still exerts its power over people, drawing thousands in our unworshipful times just as once people paid their respects to icons in their niches? Does the public hunger to share in this type of human initiative mask the intuition that, dehumanized as the work may appear, in some way it carries forward the germ of human consideration—our only hope, in the end, for survival?

Then, too, it might be clear why this behavior has been visible in the lives of these *women* artists: because they were insulated, like revolutionaries by their anger and religious devouts by their sense of grace, from distorting an instinctual need for calculated reasons of economics or power.[1] Imprisoned in their formative years in isolation, they were forced (or freed) to go through those primal procedures that, once accomplished, continue to align all their later work (as long as they keep true) with what almost every artist I spoke with referred to at some point, without embarrassment, in some such words as the "rhythm of nature."

On the other hand, these women have also, it is only too clear, been shielded from the other side of the facts of life in this era: violence, war, poverty.[2] In this era of global political anguish, many are apolitical, even solipsistic, and most are astonishingly hopeful. Sometimes, when one stops to consider, it seems frighteningly possible that their precious vision of life as a

472

web of interconnections and interrelationships—that creative vision nurtured in insulation from a world seemingly bent on destruction—could be with a sweep of events simply swept away.

What I mean to say is that whether the male-directed world society of the next decades will provide the peace required for the kind of exploration these women are making is a whole other question.

Chapter Notes

ACKNOWLEDGMENTS

1. Details of the Women's Movement in the art world are available in Lucy Lippard, *Changing: Essays in Art Criticism,* and her *From the Center.* For the West Coast, see Faith Wilding, *By Our Own Hands.* Also, issue No. 1 of the Feminist publication *Heresies* carried a large bibliography on Feminism, Art and Politics. A report of the events of autumn 1970 when Feminist and other protest groups attacked New York Establishment institutions is in Elizabeth C. Baker, "Pickets on Parnassus," *Art News,* September 1970, p. 31. When the Movement reached scholarly circles, it inspired, among other Feminist studies, Linda Nochlin's "Why Have There Been No Great Women Artists?," *Art News,* January 1971, p. 23, and then the momentous exhibition with its catalogue by Ann Sutherland Harris and Linda Nochlin, *Women Artists: 1550– 1950.* Meanwhile, Cindy Nemser's *Art Talk* introduced a general audience to women artists as thinking, conversational beings, not just faces in magazines or names on (a few) labels. Meanwhile, too, the Movement had found tangible expression in women's centers, sometimes including exhibition space, in many cities. The most famous are the Women's Interart Center, 549 W. 52nd St., New York, and the Woman's Building, 1727 N. Spring St., Los Angeles.

Methods and Matriarchs

PROCEDURAL NOTES

EPIGRAPH

1. Quoted by John U. Nef in Owen Gingerich (ed.), *The Nature of Scientific Discovery,* p. 501.

2. Cf. ". . . the artist's devotion, which forbids us to know anything about their life and places their work beyond private or public history and outside the world like a miracle, hides their true greatness from us" (Maurice Merleau-Ponty, *Signs* [Northwestern Univ. Press., 1964], p. 64). Among present exceptions are Harold Rosenberg's *Saul Steinberg* (New York: Knopf with the Whitney Museum of American Art, 1978), a biography of Frieda Kahlo by Hayden Herrera in the works and, reportedly, one on Louise Nevelson by Hilton Kramer. Artists' memoirs today are as rare, but when they

do appear the books may even convey a sense of greater "greatness" than some of the art. Consider Robert Motherwell's searching and prolific writings and, though on another level, *Diary of an Artist,* by Raphael Soyer. However, there is this, difficult to phrase: more than other kinds of art criticism, psychological biography has to be done "right." Painters call that unnameable quality "light" (see note 9, page 482). Writers might call it "taste" or "judgment"—the avoidance of the banal, meretricious, prying. Not to be Pop. So self-warned, I proceed.

3. "Formalism," an approach to the study of the visual arts based exclusively on data available to the seeing organ, is rooted in nineteenth-century German tradition. Roger Fry and Clive Bell followed the "formalist" line in British esthetics, and among advocates in this country was Thomas Munro, who reflected the ideals of his teacher John Dewey and the American pragmatic preference for objective analyses of phenomena. During the '30s and '40s, the group the American Abstract Artists advanced formalistic theories to support its concentration on non-nature-based abstract art. Partly in reaction to that "European" esthetic but partly also inspired by another European one—Surrealism—the movement called Abstract Expressionism would coalesce in the mid- to late '40s. But none of these schools was "pure." Subject and form were both always present, as they are in all the arts. It was only in the late '40s to '50s, when Clement Greenberg sharpened what had been primarily a mode of description and analysis into one of Marxist-type criticism, assigning historic inevitability to certain mannerisms, especially in painting, that the word "formalist" came into popular use and then soon became a term of opprobrium when the fashion in art and artspeak changed again in the 1960s.

4. Barbara Rose, "ABC Art," in *Art in America,* October/November 1965, reprinted in Gregory Battcock (ed.), *Minimal Art,* p. 274.

5. Harold Schonberg, "Maazel Conducts Druckman's 'Chiaroscuro,' " *New York Times,* Nov. 4, 1977, refers to the "Great Schism" of 1950–70, "when the [musical] avant garde did little else but write for one another."

6. Harold Rosenberg, *The Anxious Object,* p. 42.

7. A point of view encountered more than once is that if some make it, others can if they have what it takes. "I say, hang up the pictures on the wall!" said one woman. "Let's see the *work!* By blacks, Jews, male, female, monkeys, college-educated, non-college-educated. Give me the goods!" Not tactful, but a measure of truth.

8. Lucy Lippard, *From the Center,* p. 238. With apologies to this otherwise canny and far-seeing critic.

9. George Steiner, "The Lollipopping of the West" *New York Times,* Dec. 9, 1977, p. A 27.

10. Albert Camus, *L'Envers et l'endroit.* Testimonies to the validity of this insight are available on all sides. Albert Einstein, for example, in his autobiography written at age sixty-seven, recalls the "wonder" he felt at age four when he first saw a compass: ". . . this experience made a deep and lasting impression on me. *Something deeply hidden had to be behind things."* In other words, the childhood event became a paradigm from which the very form of his adult intuitions evolved. As Einstein scholar Gerald Holton says ("On Trying to Understand Scientific Genius," *The American Scholar,* Winter 1971–72, p. 95), "the episode is an allegory of the formation of the playground of his basic imagination," and, in a footnote, "the significance and validity

of childhood experiences of this sort among scientists and inventors [or presumably artists] have not been sufficiently studied." The most famous pronouncement is of course Proust's "The past is hidden somewhere outside the realm, beyond the reach of intellect, in some material object (in the sensation which that material object will give us) which we do not suspect . . ." (Swann's Way). Vladimir Nabokov, in Speak, Memory (New York: Putnam, 1966), p. 130, contributes ". . . the odd fact that whenever possible the scenery of our infancy is used by an economically minded producer as a ready-made setting for our adult dreams." It seems reasonable that the same image-producing mechanism as operates in the sleeping fantasies of all people does so also in the waking visions of artists, scientists, etc. On the other hand, there is this observation of Simone de Beauvoir's: ". . . let the future be opened to her and she will no longer cling so desperately to the past" (The Second Sex). How much of the modern woman artist's embeddedness in her past and so in nature is a common human trait and how much a social maneuver is not clear, except to say that the young I interviewed expressed the same attachments in, if anything, even less disguised imagery.

11. Cf. New York painter Ethel Schwabacher's childhood memory, "I was in a garden in Pelham, New York. I looked up and saw a red bird, a tanager, flying across space. Tones came up in its wake. The bird moved, and tones moved around it. It was a question of progression and movement in space. If I moved my head and moved the image myself, it became even more complex. . . . That is why I became an artist. Because I could not tell anyone what I had seen." For a discussion of "epistemic abstraction," Robert Pincus-Witten's opposing idea of what some art in these days is about, see his "The Neustein Papers," Arts, October, 1977, p. 102.

12. Otto Rank, Art and Artist, p. 383.

13. O'Keeffe, Georgia O'Keeffe, unpaged.

14. Cindy Nemser, "A Conversation with Lee Krasner," Arts, April 1973, p. 48.

15. Helen Frankenthaler in Avenue, June 1977, p. 40.

16. Barbara Haskell, Arthur Dove, p. 8.

17. Katherine Kuh, The Artist's Eye, p. 119.

18. Ibid., p. 131.

19. Ibid., p. 116.

20. Simone de Beauvoir, The Prime of Life, p. 7. Or, even more pointedly, "The woman she has become regrets the human being she was, and she seeks to find again the dead child within herself, even to revive it" (The Second Sex, p. 633). For an undisguised pantomime-art-work on this theme, see p. 394.

21. Virginia Woolf, Moments of Being, p. 64.

22. To carry the argument on, then "authenticity" would become as valid a test for the importance of an artist as "originality," which is after all only a function of the coincidence of an artist's location a little ahead of the ever-advancing frontier. The critic's job would then be not only the judgment of works by formalist criteria but also by whether the motivating drive was authentic or counterfeit. In this way, today's critic would not, for one thing, face the dilemma she or he does in judging socially exploitative works like pornography or mass-audience art that incites to violence. The critic would also then be granted a largess in determining who "is" and who "is not" an artist. I am aware the good critic takes this approach instinctively, but in these days of irrational inflation of the value of some art (and artists) it might not be useless to put the

idea into words. One does not hear scientists, for instance, however deep their disagreements, making statements like "So-and-so is not a scientist [compared with So-and-so who is]," whereas that is common parlay in the art world.

23. This is of course related to the process Claude Lévi-Strauss describes in his discussion of the methods of geology, psychoanalysis and Marxist history, *Tristes Tropiques* (New York: Criterion Books, 1961).

24. June Wayne, "The Creative Process," *Craft Horizons,* October 1976, p. 67.

25. Rothko had been trained as a scene painter, and there was something of the concealing scrim to his stains or veils, through which light diffused almost as if a cataract had formed over the eye of the canvas. That light filled the artist himself with "poignancy," as he said, and there was, it seems to me, something wistful, some sense of regret for what might-have-been-seen in these canvases he so arduously labored with glazes and films. In this regard, the eventual biographer of Rothko will, I believe, have to take into account his early abandonment by his father and then, shortly after the family was reunited in Seattle, his father's death.

26. . . . Don Flavin's white-light sculptures . . . : Barbara Rose, "ABC Art," in Gregory Battcock (ed.), *Minimal Art,* p. 296.

27. The interesting question is whether there are general patterns that determine the disposition and character of forms and images in the mature work. But they are surely not to be sought for in the work of art as a phenomenon in isolation but in the process of transformation in the artist's mind. Here is where a biographer fortunate enough to be able to work over a long period with a living and willing subject could make a contribution. I consider that the artists who cooperated with me in this book have opened the door.

28. See the letter by Lawrence Campbell to *Art News,* February 1971, on this issue as it was raised by Linda Nochlin, "Why Have There Been No Great Women Artists?," *Art News,* January 1971. Lawrence explains that from 1875 women worked from the nude model at the Art Students League of New York and that "it is a matter of record that there were women's life classes at the [Pennsylvania] Academy" in the 1880s. That these classes were segregated was a social fact but had nothing to do with the women's ability to study the nude.

29. Much of the gist of professionalism involves making the object functional so it can be transported, installed, etc. For this, public commissions are a goad—one reason why young Site artists quickly take on a markedly professional attitude and their work develops rapidly.

30. Then in Los Angeles; now Tamarind Institute–University of New Mexico, Albuquerque, N.M.

31. The fashionable late-19th/early-20th-century American portraitist Cecilia Beaux met in Paris, at the Académie Julien, a girl from California with an "incredible" gift for drawing. She vanished utterly. Beaux later wrote, "She was one of the gifted who have no sense of their own value . . . So the rarest appears and floats away . . ." In Winthrop and Frances Nielson, *Seven Women: Great Painters* (Radnor, Pa.: Chilton Book Co., 1969).

32. Clement Greenberg, *Art and Culture,* p. 218.

33. Karl Lunde, *Isabel Bishop,* p. 25.

34. Thomas Hess, "Editorial: Barnett Newman," *Art News,* September 1970, p. 29.

35. See Johannes A. Gaertner, "Myth and Pattern in the Lives of Artists," *Art Journal,* Fall 1970, p. 7.

36. In "The Male Artist as Stereotypical Female," *Art Journal,* Summer 1973, p. 414, artist June Wayne says: ". . . the ancient demonic myth prepares us to accept the warped and bizarre personality . . . as proof of genius." She argues that this character type is attributed willy-nilly to women, that therefore male artists and all women are considered to be trapped in a condition of biological abnormality.

37. One of many famous examples was Susan MacDowell, who married the Philadelphia painter Thomas Eakins. She had been one of the most gifted students at the Pennsylvania Academy. A friend later wrote: "Mrs. Eakins was kinda killed when she married. . . . She was a great help to him, though, a sustaining influence." Winthrop and Frances Nielson, *Op. cit.* Another case was Helen Torr, wife of Arthur G. Dove, who gave up her painting entirely during the last few years of his life to care for him. Another, who was subjected to constant caustic disinterest, was Josephine Verstille Nivison, wife of Edward Hopper. His famously morose manner was judged by many of his male admirers to be the result of his wife's acerbative and obstructing (sic) personality. She worked in a studio as large as his, with its own skylight, in their Cape Cod house, now a local monument to the austere, lonely "Hopper spirit." Her own works, however, were of "her small, crammed world, of Truro, flower pieces, interiors of her room and pictures of cats and pot-bellied stoves." The visitor who saw these works was also "daintily" served sandwiches and "tea fragrant with a clove in each cup." Nivison died a year after Hopper, in 1968, suffering from near blindness and almost total isolation. Raphael Soyer, *Diary of an Artist,* p. 250.

38. Edward Butscher, *Method and Madness* (New York: Pocket Books, 1977).

39. "Every subject plays his [sic] part as such specifically through exploits or projects that serve as a mode of transcendence; he achieves liberty only through a continual reaching out toward other liberties" (Simone de Beauvoir, *The Second Sex,* p. xxviii).

40. Cf. ". . . the old roles, even when they are breaking down, make nonconformist behavior and attitudes a liability; a liability that hurts and limits the nonconformist not only publicly but within him- or herself. It is the questioning of one's own goals and actions within one's own mind that is most hurtful, for it saps the confidence one must bring to sustained and purposeful action. It invites distraction and the waste of guilt-feelings over failing to meet conventional standards." (Elizabeth Janeway, *New York Times Book Review,* Nov. 28, 1971, p. 35, reviewing *Out of My Time,* by Marya Mannes.)

41. Several women reported feeling different from and superior to their siblings, whose childish enjoyments they found boring. Jeanne Reynal (p. 180) allowed her remarks to be used.

42. The combination of will and endurance of pain is obviously no prerogative of artists. But artists and religious devotees perhaps differ from other "called" individuals in the apparent irrationality of their hoped-for ends. Here is young Protestant missionary Emily Blatchley, who sailed to China in 1866, fell in love with her pastor and, when he wed another, wrote in her journal: "And so it is in love and mercy my God cut off my flowing stream at which He perhaps saw I should drink too deeply. Therefore such great blessing must await me for Jesus to bear to see me have so much pain." (Pat Barr,

To China with Love [London: Secker & Warburg, 1972].) If it were not the style for artists *not* to reveal their inner struggles we might have as eloquent lines, in a language we understand, from them. Again, gratitude to the women who let themselves be recorded here, but also especially to Louise Nevelson, who has openly been quoted before.

43. Compare Jane Freilicher's "something was creative *in* me" (page 205).

44. Ann Sutherland Harris and Linda Nochlin, *op. cit.*

45. This matter of recombination of factors and breakthrough has parallels in other fields. Harvard geologist Stephen Jay Gould, in "Evolution: Explosion, Not Ascent," *New York Times,* Jan. 22, 1978, argues for a replacement of Darwinian theory of evolutionary "gradualism" by what he calls "Punctuated equilibria," or sudden, episodic change in species as in geological phenomena. He notes that this reading of events has appeal for "an intellectual climate bursting with interest and recognition for punctuational change in discipline after discipline."

46. Georgia O'Keeffe, *op. cit.*

47. Quoted in Adelyn D. Breeskin, *The Graphic Work of Mary Cassatt,* p. 12.

48. Specific influences between males and females living in close relationships or not are interesting but uncomfortable to pursue. What, for instance, is the relationship between the famous photo by Inge Morath of Saul Steinberg in a paper bag mask, standing before a wall of such masks (1958), and Hedda Sterne's remarkable exhibit of faces on unstretched, unframed canvases crowded row upon row on the walls of the Betty Parsons Gallery in 1970? What of influences back and forth between Helen Frankenthaler and Robert Motherwell, especially during their shared summers in Provincetown when he was experimenting with hurled and spattered paint for his *Beside the Sea* series (1962)? What is the relationship between Ronald Bladen's enormous (26-foot-wide) Minimalist structure *X*, at the Corcoran Gallery of Art in 1967, and Miriam Schapiro's *OX* of 1967 (acrylic, 9 feet wide)? Clearly women and men have the same roving imaginations. The time is not yet historically ripe, however, to go into the subject. This is the only point on which nearly all the women drew back, and the most obvious sources of influence (as for example a husband's scholarly interest) were not to be explored.

49. In spite of my support for free abortion, I am not one who feels we gain this freedom at no cost. Women now take on themselves the burden of becoming, like males, humans who willfully destroy. For the relevance of this issue to esthetics, see pp. 40 and 42.

50. This theme was pursued throughout 1973 in issues of *Womanspace Journal* (published in Los Angeles), especially in articles by Miriam Schapiro and Judy Chicago. The next year, it was taken up in *New York* magazine by Barbara Rose, "Vaginal Iconography," and Dorothy Seiberling, "The Female View of Erotica" (both, issue of Feb. 11, 1974). Rose's important essay related the new ideas about female sexuality to the concept of Negritude, the conscious self-savoring by black peoples of their own essential nature, fostered originally by the poet-politician Léopold Senghor of Senégal. Pop manifestations of vaginal esthetics began in 1971 with Judy Chicago's print *Red Flag,* showing a hand withdrawing a tampon. The genre came to a crisis with sculptor Lynda Benglis' famously scandalous and much-discussed full-color photo, inserted in *Art-forum,* November 1974, of herself holding a dildo.

51. Eleanor Antin's Performance Art differs: she wears clothes, indeed costumes,

and she often tries to come to grips with nonsexist human longings as for love, fame and power (see p. 417 and passim).

A CENTURY OF HISTORY AND THE
NEW WOMAN ARTIST

1. If inclusion in the self-electing National Institute of Arts and Letters (founded 1898; 250 members) and American Academy (founded 1905; 50 members) is to be taken as a measure of acceptance by the elite Establishment in American art, literature and music, women have fared poorly. There was no woman Institute member until 1907, when Julia Ward Howe ("The Battle Hymn of the Republic") was elected. It took the membership nineteen years to elect another, writer Mary Deland. Bishop was not admitted to the Institute until 1944; she has had the longest tenure, however, of any of the twelve living women artist members (there are seven deceased women artist members, none of them admitted until 1927). She and Georgia O'Keeffe are the only two living women artists elevated to sit with the august Academicians. She is presently vice-chancellor for art of the Academy and the only woman artist officer ever. Other Institute members in this book are Frankenthaler (admitted 1974), Neel ('76), Nevelson ('68) and O'Keeffe ('49). Thanks to Institute librarian Hortense Zera for this information.

2. John Cage on Robert Rauschenberg, from his "On Rauschenberg, Artist, and His Work," *Metro*, Vol. I (1961), No. 2, p. 50, reprinted in William C. Seitz, *The Art of Assemblage*, p. 116.

3. Simone de Beauvoir has fully argued this point vis-à-vis women writers, except that she communicates a deep anti-Feminist bias and sense of cynical superiority over women "shut up in immanence," as she puts it. See her chapter "The Independent Woman," in *The Second Sex*, especially p. 711: "Women do not contest the human situation because they have hardly begun to assume it. This explains why their works for the most part lack metaphysical resonances [etc.]."

4. Titled *The Dinnerparty*, this multimedia project includes a stage setting of a table with thirty-nine place settings, each with porcelain plate, knife, fork, spoon, goblet and placemat all decorated in individualized vaginal imagery and manufactured under Chicago's direction in her Santa Monica studio. The table awaits Feminist heroines of myth and history from Earth Mother Gaea to Georgia O'Keeffe and including party-shy Emily Dickinson and Neo-Platonic philosopher Hypatia. The table rests on a platform of white porcelain tiles inscribed with 999 other role-model names. It was Chicago's plan to attract female helpers and so set in motion again the lost arts of china painting and stitching, but when I visited the operation in '77 there was only a sprinkle of devotees at work and those arts, far from being economically revived, were being inexplicably shored up by a five-figure matching grant from the National Endowment for the Arts. Undeniably, however, Chicago played a major role in bringing Feminist awareness to California (see her *Through the Flower: My Struggle as a Woman Artist*), and has been in her time a true original, if one most comfortable in the company of women who, as she puts it, "did not become frightened by my strength, my courage, my determination" (p. 200). For another Feminist project including a stage setting designed, as *The Dinnerparty* is, to travel, see Gloria Feman Orenstein's "The Sister

Chapel, a Traveling Homage to Heroines," *Womanart,* Winter/Spring 1977, p. 12.

5. Herbert Spencer, *Literary Style and Music* (New York: Philosophical Library, 1951), p. 76.

6. Quoted in Barbara Haskell, *Arthur Dove,* p. 33.

7. Wassily Kandinsky, *On the Spiritual in Art,* p. 43. This, one of the fundamental texts of Modernism and then Abstract Expressionism, was published first in 1911, translated into English and published simultaneously in London and Boston in 1914 titled *The Art of Spiritual Harmony,* and republished in '46 by Hilla Rebay for the Museum of Non-Objective Art, of which she was director.

8. Barnett Newman, unpublished reply to Clement Greenberg's Dec. 6, 1947, review in *The Nation,* printed in Thomas B. Hess, *Barnett Newman,* p. 37.

9. The tradition is of course very ancient and must stem from the earliest phases of human consciousness. Egyptian, Hebrew and Zoroastrian texts treat of Light as symbol of Good, Life, even Immortality (*"While ye have light, believe in the light, that ye may be the children of light"*: John 12:36). Medieval goldsmiths and poets like Dante spoke of the tangible (gold) and intangible (golden light) as divine. Renaissance painters, transferring their interest to the real world, crowned their saints with luminous nimbuses but also painted into their backgrounds summer landscapes, light-shot, to show how gentle a place the world could be. And: "It was this mystical sense of the unity of creation expressed by light and atmosphere which, however unconsciously, provided a basis of pictorial unity for the Impressionists; and the claims to science, which they sometimes felt called on to make in defense of their intuitions were only a nineteenth-century way of stating the same belief [in] some underlying natural order . . . in the nineteenth century when more orthodox and systematic beliefs were declining, faith in nature became a form of religion." (Kenneth Clark, *Landscape into Art,* p. 33 and *passim.*) The concept has never lost its power. Arthur G. Dove wrote, "There was a long period of searching for something in color which I then called 'condition of light.' It applied to all objects in nature . . . all have their certain condition of light . . . to understand that clearly, go to nature, or to the Museum of Natural History and see the butterflies. Each has its own orange, blue, black . . . all carefully chosen to fit the character of the life going on in that individual entity." (In Barbara Haskell, *Arthur Dove,* p. 1.)

So "light," that once represented the unifying principle in all nature, for Dove has come to represent the essential identifying characteristic of an individual *thing.* For Joan Mitchell, the focus has narrowed down again: it is the quality of "virtue" or failure in the individual thing, an otherwise inexplicable quality that some works of art have, others lack. "Light is something special. It has nothing to do with *white.* Either you see it or you don't. Matisse, Goya, Chardin, van Gogh, Sam Francis, Kline have it for me. But it has nothing to do with being the best painter." For Helen Frankenthaler, see page 220. An artist who made a conscious theme of it is Loren MacIver, whose famous painting *Vigil Lights* (at the Museum of Modern Art) might even be read as a symbol for the life spirit banked yet burning (a hidden or unconscious Feminist message?). Among many studies, see Barbara Novak, *American Painting of the Nineteenth Century,* and Willoughby Sharp, "Luminism and Kineticism," in Gregory Battcock (ed.), *Minimal Art.*

10. Cf. Henry James, "The only obligation to which in advance we may hold a novel, without incurring the accusation of being arbitrary, is that it be interesting" (*The Art of Fiction*). Thanks to Carol Shookhoff for this.

11. Cf this policy statement written for the famous 1920s Modernism magazine *The Dial:* "*The Dial* is not interested in making money (it only desires to be self-supporting) and the only idea it is interested in propagating is that the source of the greatest happiness in life is a sincere and acute appreciation of the beautiful." (Quoted in Daniel Catton Rich, *The Dial and the Dial Collection,* exhibition catalogue for the Worcester Art Museum, 1959.) To this passage Rich appends: "By a strange confusion, the esthetic has taken on the qualities of the ethical . . ." His remark shows how far the American temper had, by then, departed from Modernist values. There was nothing "strange" or "confused" about a concept as old as Pythagoras, Confucius and Plato and as modern as Santayana. *The Dial,* incidentally, reproduced the first work by Georgia O'Keeffe ever published: *The Black Spot,* 1919 (issue of December 1921).

12. Those of us who missed knowing Gorky missed one of the great romantic figures in American art, whose influence was felt by many artists and friends especially, in this study, Jeanne Reynal and Elaine de Kooning. The painter Ethel Schwabacher studied with him and wrote an account of his life and personality that sheds light on his art: *Arshile Gorky* (New York: Macmillan, 1957). In particular, she quotes from his conversation and writings passages that speak to a mood of today: "What I miss most are the songs in the fields. No one sings them any more . . . and there are no more ploughs. I love a plough more than anything else on a farm" (p. 128). Or ". . . often I had seen my mother and other village women opening their bosoms and taking their soft and dependent breasts in their hands to rub them on the rock. Above all this stood an enormous tree all bleached under the sun, the rain, the cold and deprived of leaves. This was the Holy Tree . . ." (p. 66). His suicide in 1948, Reynal later wrote, "served to galvanize the instincts we all had in the early '50s about the seriousness of the new art and of our own role as individual artists." See *The Mosaics of Jeanne Reynal,* text by Ashton, Campbell, Tyler, de Kooning, Pfriem, Reynal, p. 101.

13. The history of this club, a nearly exclusively male organization set up for instruction and fun, parallels the fortunes of the Abstract Expressionist artists who belonged. It began in 1948 as a small cooperative school, The Subjects of the Artists, started by Motherwell, Baziotes, Hare and Rothko, to teach the principles of abstract art; Still had talked about the idea but never joined; Newman was an early member. Some fifteen artists came regularly and presented their ideas. It lasted only a short time, folded for lack of funds and reappeared as The Club in the fall of '49 on Eighth Street in Greenwich Village. From time to time, favored women artists were "invited" to attend: Elaine de Kooning, Mercedes Matter, Nell Blaine and a few others. By the time The Club moved to its larger quarters on Tenth Street, the mold of Abstract Expressionism had been set, that rather ragged movement given its unifying and binding title, forays against the museum Establishment launched, and women—though some of them were by then beginning to exhibit their "Second Generation" works—were even less central to the politics of the group than before (see Blaine, p. 269). An early and guiding member was sculptor Philip Pavia, now married to the abstract painter and art historian Natalie Edgar.

14. Statement by Adolph Gottlieb and Mark Rothko, published in art critic Edward Alden Jewell's column, *New York Times,* June 13, 1943, in response to denigrating comments about their work by Jewell.

15. *The Dream of Reason Produces Monsters* is the title of Goya's etching from the *Capricios,* 1797.

16. Barbara Rose writes that Lee Krasner considers that the pose of machismo was imported and due to the "misogyny of the Surrealists, who both idealized and denigrated women" ("Lee Krasner and the Origins of Abstract Expressionism," *Arts,* February 1977, p. 100). Whatever its source, machismo was part and parcel of a psycho-esthetic that cast male artists as sublime-tongued and -fingered prophets in touch with "the chaos of ecstasy" (Newman, *op. cit.*). Nevelson, somewhere, reports her fury on being informed by a male that one had to have balls to be a sculptor. Similarly, Lila Katzen reports a dinner toast at her home by Hans Hofmann, " 'To art . . . only the men have the wings,' Of course I was outraged" (in Cindy Nemser, *Art Talk,* p. 238). An enlightening exchange is this, spanning three issues of *Art News,* launched by critic Hubert Crehan in 1959; in December he accurately wrote (p. 32) apropos of Clyfford Still: "The celestial world of light is the domain of God who has all masculine attributes. . . . The kingdom of darkness . . . has no God at its head. This world has only a feminine personification . . . Still seems to have a preternatural affinity for the continuation of [the Manichean] myth, which reduced to its simplest terms means that man is a superior being and more spiritual than woman . . ." Before then (April 1959, p. 12), Crehan had baited Barnett Newman on his *Vir Heroicus Sublimis:* "It is a proud and inflexible archaic male sensibility, lifted from the Old Testament. But we live in another world really, one certainly that is in need of the phallic charge, although the new man, I imagine, will be aware that we should have more music with the dancing. It takes two to tango." Newman, stung, replied in the June issue (p. 6): "What is to be pitied is [Crehan's] love of impotence, his stupid fear of the creative man—man spelled masculine. . . . Mr. Crehan attacks my steadfastness, my 'masculine' strength, by saying that it takes two to tango . . . Someday Mr. Crehan may learn that no matter how many it takes to tango, it takes only *one real man* [his italics] to create a work of art." Editors Frankfurter and Hess gave Crehan the last word: "As far as Mr. Newman's paintings are concerned, I understand their impudence more clearly than their impotence, which is not my issue but one which Mr. Newman drags in . . . [etc.]." My point is not who won this juvenile exchange but that it took place in a context of art criticism. Machismo was in the winds then, and the art world was not the only place it was heard. That same year, Norman Mailer published his diatribe against "talented women who write," calling them "fey, old-hat, Quaintsy Goysy, tiny, too dykily psychotic . . . etc." and ending with the bad news that "a good novelist can do without everything but the remnant of his balls" (*Advertisements for Myself*). That "museum piece," as Tillie Olsen calls it, was resurrected in her *Silences,* p. 238.

17. For these and other such details of the time see Calvin Tomkins' profile of dealer Betty Parsons in *The New Yorker,* June 9, 1975, p. 44.

18. *Clyfford Still,* exhibition catalogue for the Institute of Contemporary Art, University of Pennsylvania, October/November 1963, p. 9.

19. Quoted in John Tancock, "The Oscillating Influence of Marcel Duchamp," *Art News,* September 1973, p. 29.

20. Donald Judd, quoted in Gregory Battcock (ed.), *Minimal Art,* p. 154.

21. Or consider also Andy Warhol's famous pronouncement, "I want to be a machine. I think everybody should be a machine. Liking things is being a machine because you do the same thing every time. You do it over and over again." ("What is Pop Art? A Symposium," *Art News,* November 1963.)

22. Latter-day Existentialism was no passing zephyr in the Zeitgeist. Thirteen years

after John Cage wrote his bit of nonsense about Rauschenberg (see page 40), Allen Leepa, professor of art in the Department of Graduate Painting at Michigan State University, wrote this ("Anti-art and Criticism," in Gregory Battcock [ed.], *The New Art*, p. 136). The idea, of course, has deep roots in European philosophy, but delivered in the context of a piece of comfortable American pedantry it has a hollow sound. Cage at least preserves the wit of his Zen instructors: ". . . the grand thing about the human mind is that it can turn its own tables and see meaninglessness as ultimate meaning" (Cage, *Silences* [Boston, M.I.T. Press, 1966]).

23. Rose's voice has been a strong and often solitary one in behalf of sense in criticism and the wider human domain. Consider "The advantage of the Duchampian position that 'there is no solution because there is no problem' is that it permits art to be as value-free an activity as science. Ironically its current popularity among thinkers . . . who ignore questions of meaning and value, coincided precisely with that moment when scientists are being forced to consider questions of morality and ethics—the value systems that were once the province of the humanities." (In her "Yes, but Is It Art?," a review of Suzi Gablik's *Progress in Art* in *New York Times Book Review*, June 26, 1977, p. 26.)

24. Some of the younger artists shared this skeptical view of this and other Christo projects. Patricia Johanson writes of another, "Wrapping three miles of Australian cliffs is so ecologically irresponsible as to obviate any possible esthetic merit" ("Value and Meaning in Women's Art as Opposed to Handiwork," unpublished ms., 1977).

25. Here is Harold Rosenberg apropos of the swooning acclaim given Robert Rauschenberg's retrospective at the Whitney Museum in 1977: "Joy and exuberance provide an alternative to ideas; in literary circles this set of values is known as anti-intellectualism. One is urged to believe that the art world has been overburdened with thought, and that Rauschenberg has come as an embodiment of inarticulate energy—a kind of Mynheer Peeperkorn or Harpo Marx—to liberate art and the art public from excessively precise thinking." (*The New Yorker*, May 16, 1977, p. 123.)

26. Art historian Joan Lukach is preparing a biography of Rebay for the Guggenheim Museum. The full story will document not only her achievements as a patron of advanced European art at a time when it was unknown or excoriated in this country but also her patronage of at least three generations of artists: Kandinsky, etc.; Pollock, etc. (whom she employed at her museum when they were broke); Noland, etc. Alice Trumbull Mason and I. Rice Pereira were two of many women she helped. After the war, she sent monthly gifts to some three hundred European artists in straits, including Delaunay and Gleizes. Her ouster in '52 from the museum she had founded in 1939 and directed thereafter was a product of postwar anti-German sentiment as well as conflicting ambitions in the art world.

27. Cooper, who came onto the New York scene in 1959 and opened her SoHo gallery in '68, notes that at that time there were no women coming into the gallery to show their work. She would visit a studio to see a male artist and not be aware his wife was "also a painter." But around that time, Cooper told me, Eva Hesse began to be talked about and "then all of a sudden there were all these young women emerging. From zero to this: now sixty percent of the people who come in to show their work are women. Now I find the women's work *more* interesting than the men's. They're more in touch with their work. Men are more aloof and formal in their way of approaching art. The women are more in process of exploring themselves and being independent.

There still isn't as much pressure on them to be successful. Of course, whether the work is ultimately 'better' I don't know. . . ."

28. Cf. "Human society is . . . a moral order in which redemption is the discharge of obligations to those who came before us—obligations of nurturance, obligations of faith, obligations of tradition" (Daniel Bell in *New York Times Book Review,* March 14, 1976, p. 24). Some of the young are to be heard talking this way. Patricia Johanson, for instance, in 1977 wrote that "the one important thing an artist can do is establish values. There has been a great deal of selling and trend-setting in recent art, but relatively little responsibility or morality. I find it interesting that all the 'great' women of the past—those who managed to reach out to the larger world, deal with real issues and effect change—were acutely aware of the 'meaning' of their work. They got beyond the 'busy hands' syndrome because they understood that 'content' is as important as 'form.' " This manuscript, titled "Women's Traditional Arts: Organizing the Scraps," was commissioned by *Heresies* but rejected, possibly because the editors considered her use of "busy hands" as a denigration of traditional women's art.

29. This is the Berkshire Museum in Pittsfield, founded in 1903 by Zenas Crane. "Here He Still Liveth" reads a plaque beneath his portrait, as if to underline the relationship between religion and science we spoke of. The collection includes relics of Peary's trek to the Pole, stuffed birds of many kinds, stuffed animals including a moose head nicknamed "Old Bill" after a local gamewarden, fossils and models. The murals are by Helen Damarosh Tee-Van and were painted in 1937–38. They represent "A Picture Book of Life": insects, mammals, birds, reptiles, mollusks and plants in their phyla and classes. Tee-Van, a member of the noted musical family and wife of a director of the New York Zoological Society, also painted renditions of William Beebe's undersea observations.

In the Museum there is also a case of relics of Cyrus W. Field, (1819–92), who laid the first Atlantic Cable. His first try failed; after the Civil War he tried again and succeeded. He provided a model and title for one of Patricia Johanson's works (see page 467). Thus serendipitously did I fall upon first evidences of the loose conceptual sisterhood I call "Humboldt's Daughters" (see note 33, below, and page 389 and *passim*).

30. Nancy Graves in the catalogue for her exhibition at the Whitney Museum, March 1969. She continues, ". . . the work refers only to itself [!] . . . I cannot imagine or perceive a camel until it is completed."

31. Alfred Frankenstein in the San Francisco *Sunday Examiner and Chronicle,* April 6, 1969.

32. Marcia Tucker, "Nancy Graves," exhibition catalogue, Whitney Museum, March 1969.

33. The two brothers von Humboldt were, with Goethe, the greatest men of their age, whose explorations, studies and writings laid the foundation for much scientific and philosophical work today. Alexander (1769–1859) was a naturalist and traveler. As a boy, he collected plants, shells and insects and studied foreign languages, anatomy and astronomy in addition to the rich complex of sciences and humanities that was standard fare in German universities then. During a five-year trip through South America he spent four months exploring the Orinoco and, among other things, observed meteor showers, volcanoes, changes in the magnetic pole. The last decades of his life were occupied with writing his colossal work of natural philosophy, *Kosmos,* that in its far-

flung organicism plowed territory Darwin and Spencer would work from their more meticulous British points of view. His brother Wilhelm (1767–1835) focused on literature and language, laying the foundations for structural linguistics in his essay "On the Heterogeneity of Language and Its Influence on the Intellectual Development of Mankind." Here he proposed the fruitful idea that the character and structure of language—meanings in words and the ways they are combined into sentences—embodies the thoughts of a community. Both brothers were, in the style of the times, universal men, scientists and philosophers, friends of the great and powerful, part-time diplomats and lions in the courts, salons and academies. That the young women artists of whom I speak seem to me to aspire to pack a Humboldtean measure of intuitions about the world into simple, even primitivistic artworks is a phenomenon I find awesomely innocent, interesting and also symptomatic of the laying of groundwork in "a mode of art that may have a long way to go" (see also page 57 and *passim*).

34. Kenneth Clark, *op. cit.,* p. 241.

35. Here is another correspondence between what I would call the authentic artist and the scientist (and the religious believer). Despite the fact that knowledge may increase through quantum leaps, it is not so certain that the flow of understanding, in this case in the arts, is marked by discontinuities. In this regard, Gerald Holton remarks, again of Einstein, that, despite his radical intuitive leaps, he was "a conservative who stressed the continuity of physics" (Holton, "On Trying to Understand Scientific Genius," *The American Scholar,* Winter 1971–72, p. 95).

MARY CASSATT

Cassatt–Spartain correspondence courtesy the Archives of the Pennsylvania Academy of the Fine Arts, Philadelphia. Cassatt–Havemeyer correspondence courtesy the National Gallery of Art, Washington D.C.

1. The first statement was made by Cassatt to publisher-writer A. F. Jaccaci, in her old age, when he asked whether she would marry if she had her life to live over. The second statement was made to Forbes Watson, also in her old age. Both quoted in Nancy Hale, p. 150. See also Cassatt's letter to Havemeyer, C 65 November 1910, Thanksgiving Day: ". . . there is the stumbling block to much in women's lives and yet the great interest in the world, a child or children to bring into the world and bring up."

2. I realize that in focusing on this feature of Cassatt's work, I am going against a current. In the Harris-Nochlin exhibition catalogue *Women Artists: 1550–1950* (p. 240), Nochlin says that "modern art historians are slightly embarrassed by Mary Cassatt's interest in painting children," and goes on with the not very encouraging explanation that "the fact is that children were such a popular subject in the late nineteenth century that we are still in a period of reaction to it."

3. Cassatt's French biographer Achille Ségard went into this issue in his *Un Peintre des enfants et des mères,* pp. 120–27.

4. Ellen Moers, *Literary Women,* p. 233.

5. "You are the only Mother I have known who had not a marked preference for her boys over girls. My Mother's pride was in her boys. I think sometimes a girl's first duty is to be handsome and parents feel it when she isn't. I am sure my Father did, it

wasn't my fault though . . ." (Mary Cassatt to Louisine Havemeyer, Letter B 171, Nov. 29, 1907.)

6. That their Protestantism was important to the Cassatts' psychosocially if not theologically is proved by their industry in finding themselves a circle of fellow non-Catholics whom they saw exclusively in Paris. See also Cassatt–Havemeyer Letter B 173, Dec. 18, 1906, in which Cassatt advocates Protestantism as the "only salvation" for France and asks Mrs. Havemeyer to contribute to Protestant missions there.

7. See page 26 and note 28, p. 470.

8. Quoted in Frederick A. Sweet, *Miss Mary Cassatt,* p. 23, among other places.

9. See Mary Cassatt's letters to Emily Spartain during her enforced sojourn in Hollidaysburgh, Pa., after this European tour, especially that of June 9, 1872.

10. *Ibid.,* May 22, 1872.

11. *Ibid.,* July 10, 1872.

12. *Ibid.,* June 9, 1872.

13. *Ibid.,* Oct. 27, 1872.

14. *Ibid.,* Oct. 21, 1872.

15. Cassatt to Spartain, from Seville, "New Year's Evening, 1873."

16. *Ibid.,* from Madrid, Oct. 5, 1873.

17. *Ibid.*

18. *Ibid.,* from Seville, Oct. 27, 1873.

19. This, perhaps Cassatt's most famous reflection, made to her friend Mrs. Havemeyer, was first published in that lady's memoir of the painter in *The Pennsylvania Museum Bulletin,* May 1927, p. 377.

20. Quoted in Adelyn Breeskin, *The Graphic Work of Mary Cassatt,* 1948, p. 12.

21. Degas quoted in Barbara S. Shapiro, "Edgar Degas: The Reluctant Impressionist," exhibition catalogue for the Museum of Fine Arts, Boston, 1974.

22. *Ibid.*

23. See Frederick A. Sweet, *op. cit.,* p. 25 and *passim.*

24. *Ibid.,* p. 42.

25. Quoted in slightly different form in Nancy Hale, p. 103, among other places.

26. Ségard *op. cit.,* p. 67 and *passim,* discusses this issue.

27. Mary Cassatt to Mrs. Havemeyer, Letter C 59 A, Feb. 22, 1910.

28. Cassatt to Havemeyer, Letter B 97 AB, Nov. 13, 1910, in which she also speaks of Cézanne's "figures really dreadful neither drawing nor color" and Matisse's recent exhibition "that looks as if the pictures were painted by negroes from the Congo. They, poor souls, are at least naive and sincere, but Matisse is neither and there is a public ready to swallow anything . . ."

29. *Ibid.*

30. Indicative of Mary Cassatt's Feminism is her work for the World's Columbian Exposition in Chicago, 1892. Her friend Mrs. Potter Palmer toured Europe the previous summer drumming up interest and talking a number of expatriate American women artists into contributing. Cassatt labored over a mural painting, even constructing a special work space at her château with a glass-covered excavation into which the enormous canvas could be lowered while she painted the upper part. She never dared show the work to Degas, fearful that he might criticize it and so "demolish me completely." Apparently she knew that the Italianate finish and decorative effect of this narrative, didactic work rendered it *retardataire.* But the theme she picked was Feminist:

"Young women plucking the fruits of Knowledge and Science." Pissarro and Degas talked about the work and agreed that a "decorative picture is an absurdity," though in its use of elements of Japanese and Kate Greenaway–type design, it may have been more interesting even than she thought. The American audience was not impressed: some of the "Lady Managers" of the Exposition considered her presentation of modern woman "somewhat inaccurate." The work disappeared, and in 1894 Cassatt wrote a friend: "After all, give me France. Women do not have to fight for recognition here if they do serious work. I suppose it is Mrs. Palmer's French blood which gives her organizing powers and her determination that women should be *someone* and not *something*." (Sweet, *op. cit.,* p. 130 and *passim.*)

31. Mary Cassatt to Colonel Paine, Cassatt–Havemeyer correspondence, Letter C 116, Feb. 28, 1915.

32. Cassatt to Havemeyer, Letter B 26 A, March 24, 1917.

33. *Ibid.,* Letter C 153, June 26, 1916.

34. *Ibid.,* Letter B 124 AB, March 8, 1911.

35. *Ibid.,* Letter B 135, March 17, 1911.

GEORGIA O'KEEFFE

1. This colossal work, which some have called a proto conceptual work, was an assemblage of photos, in three- to four-minute poses, of her body, nude and clothed, from every possible angle. Later in the '30s, Stieglitz made yet another "biography in photographs" of the sensitive future writer, then patron of An American Place, Dorothy Norman. But the concept had been foreshadowed back in 1889 by his photo *Sun Rays—Paula—Berlin,* a study of a young girl in a room surrounded by pictures of her own face, asleep, awake, in many poses. If this was the paradigm, and all the works part of an overriding concept, it was indeed "Woman" in all her incarnations Stieglitz was seeking.

2. Another reason why she went on doing them: they were an instant success and sold better than anything else in Stieglitz' stable except works by Marin. She sold her first one for $1,200, and Stieglitz "was impressed, I can tell you." (Leo Janos, "Georgia O'Keeffe at 84," *The Atlantic,* December 1971.)

3. The passage by Hartley from his *Adventures in the Arts,* 1920, reprinted in the Anderson Galleries catalogue of O'Keeffe's first show in 1923, was the quintessential piece of this kind of writing.

4. Barbara Rose, "O'Keeffe's Trail," *New York Review of Books,* March 31, 1977, p. 29. The question of whether O'Keeffe is a mystic is perennial, but what is certain is that her ethics were close to the Transcendentalist code. Emerson's exhortation in *Self-Reliance* might have been her own: "There is a time in every man's education when he arrives at the conviction that imitation is suicide, that he must take himself for better or worse as his portion." Transcendentalism derived that view in turn from German Romanticism, which had its final flowering in twentieth-century Expressionism: "Every artist as a creator has to express his own personality . . ." (Kandinsky). The other Romantic-Transcendental concept that both Stieglitz and O'Keeffe echoed was the theory of correspondences: the idea that nature presents the mind with a number of symbolic

expressions of an inner reality; that these various forms are related to one another; and that between them all and that inner essence a clear correspondence exists. A young Georgia O'Keeffe first was awakened to the concept in the experience she has often described in Amon Bement's classroom in 1912 (see page 83).

5. In her painting of the '60s and '70s, O'Keeffe did obliterate the identification of objects and, by enlarging some beyond recognition, turn them into flat fields of color, and she says she feels a closeness to the work of Kelly et al. Goossen ("O'Keeffe," in Vogue, March 1, 1967, p. 174) says she "has absolutely no sentiment whatsoever for the objects when she paints objects. She treats them as coldly as she does her abstracted shapes. She is an existentialist and so are her objects. Her paintings have no 'content' in the European sense of the word." I agree with Goossen's recognition of the directness in her portrayal of objects—their nonsymbolic character—but I also feel that she is being correctly read by her enormous audience today for the content I describe.

6. See Mary Lynn Kotz, "Georgia O'Keeffe," in Eastern Airlines' Review, May 1978, p. 50, for color reproductions of these new paintings.

7. "It's a curse, the way I feel I must continually go on with that door. . . ." (O'Keeffe to Katharine Kuh, in Kuh, The Artist's Eye, p. 190).

8. Again, the question is of O'Keeffe as a mystic. Though she maintains she is not, she gives some credence to the idea by occasional remarks about things like "power spots" in the landscape where she likes to paint. Moreover, the all-pervasive, apparently sourceless light in her works speaks to our ancient intuition of "infinity" (see note 9 page 482). Still I maintain she gives us the natural world as it is: a correlative to our own bodies, therefore mysterious, but not a vessel of mystical spirit. A fascinating event apropos this point was the view provided in the fall of 1978 of two early figure studies by O'Keeffe (in the show "The Eye of Stieglitz" at the Hirschl-Adler Gallery, New York). These little works were said to have been done in 1917 and were, indeed, close in form and handling to her abstractions of the time. The nude bodies were rendered in warm umber tones; featureless, they were not unrelated in their simplicity to Rodin water-colors seen at 291 as early as 1908, but were more earthy. O'Keeffe has managed cannily to keep her figure paintings off the market to enhance her "single image" as a nature painter. How tempting it is to suppose her private stores may be full of such works which would illustrate the point I make here: that she gradually focused her search upon the "body" in the landscape.

9. Katherine Kuh, op. cit.

10. There was another factor: the new esthetics relating the practice of art to mental elevation fit nicely with progressive Western education theory that had been evolving away from the stiff pedagogical goals of the past century toward an ideal of nurturing the "whole child." The idea promulgated by Pestalozzi and others in Europe that a free spirit could create works of art of special quality and that the process itself would have a liberating effect and, not incidentally, build healthier, happier citizens, fell on fertile ground in an America already conditioned by a half-century of educators in the Horace Mann tradition. At Teachers College of Columbia University, Dow and Bement of course worked in the aura of John Dewey, advocate of learning through experience.

11. A thirty-six-year-old O'Keeffe wrote this on the occasion of her first one-person show at Stieglitz' Anderson Galleries. Exhibition catalogue, January 1923. Among many other places, the quote is reprinted in Art News, March 1958.

490

12. Cf. "The words, or the language, as they are written or spoken, do not seem to play any role in my mechanism of thought. The psychical entities which seem to serve as elements in thought are certain signs and more or less clear images which can be 'voluntarily' reproduced and combined . . ." (Albert Einstein, quoted in Holton, "On Trying to Understand Scientific Genius," *The American Scholar*, Winter 1971–72.

13. Pollitzer herself told the story using the famous phrase in "That's Georgia," in *The Saturday Review*, Nov. 4, 1950, p. 41. But in her handwritten letter in the Bienecke Rare Book Library, Yale University, the words are inserted in another script. In her article, she also says Stieglitz decided that same day to show them. But in fact Stieglitz returned the drawings to Pollitzer, who gave some of them to Bement. He irritated her by showing them around, ostensibly to find them another show spot, since he mistrusted Stieglitz. Later, when Stieglitz again had the drawings in hand, he showed them to a number of his associates including Steichen and Katherine Rhodes, a poet-artist whom he had exhibited. Neither of these was as enthusiastic as he, though Rhodes eventually warmed to them. As for O'Keeffe's famous but puzzling "anger" when she heard that Stieglitz had put the drawings on view, future researchers should find documentation for the suggestion that what she really objected to was having her painfully achieved work bandied about in public for free. She was young, on the brink of wanting to give up her teaching métier; sales would be helpful. Simple praise would not. A clear Feminist case. (Private communications to author.)

14. O'Keeffe to Calvin Tomkins, in "The Rose in the Eye Looked Pretty Fine," *The New Yorker*, March 4, 1974, p. 66.

15. See Therese Thau Heyman, *Anne Brigman, Pictorial Photographer/Pagan/Member of the Photo-Secession*, exhibition catalogue for the Oakland Museum, 1974. An early Feminist ("Why should I seek the artificial atmosphere of a court to secure a legal freedom from my husband when my soul is free without that relief?"), she was also a harbinger of the nature cult of today. "One day," she wrote, "during the gathering of a thunder storm when the air was hot and still and a strange yellow light was over everything, something happened almost too deep for me to be able to relate. New dimensions revealed themselves in the visualization of the human form as part of tree and rock rhythms." In 1910, she abandoned her sea captain husband and came East to meet Stieglitz; later she wrote that the encounter had revealed to her "the deeps within the deeps." Käsebier was called "beyond dispute the leading portrait photographer in the country" by Stieglitz as early as 1898. She was a founder of the Photo-Secession and had her first one-person show at 291 in 1906; after she broke with Stieglitz, partly because of his waning interest in romantic-style photography and his new enthusiasm for the more "American" style of Paul Strand (that coincided with his espousal of that perfect American, O'Keeffe), she joined with Clarence H. White and Alvin Coburn in founding an anti-Stieglitz group, the Pictorial Photographers of America. See Mary Ann Tighe, "Gertrude Käsebier Lost and Found," *Art in America*, March/April 1977, p. 94.

16. The Suffragette cause had triumphed only in 1919 when the 19th Amendment was passed.

17. See Dorothy Gees Seckler's *Provincetown Painters* for a discussion of artists' colonies. See also van Deren Coke, "Why Artists Came to New Mexico," *Art News*, January 1974, p. 22.

18. Dove himself, in 1913, told Stieglitz that his recent excursion into pure abstract painting in the European mode had drained him of his sense of life and that he was

going back to nature to revive himself, a procedure that Hans Hofmann later recommended to Jackson Pollock (see note 4, p. 492 below). (Barbara Haskell, *Arthur Dove,* p. 20.)

19. Cf. "The sky was as full of motion and change as the desert beneath it was monotonous and still—and there was so much sky, more than at sea, more than anywhere else in the world . . . a blue night set with stars, the bulk of the solitary mesas cutting into the firmament" (Willa Cather, *Death Comes for the Archbishop,* p. 92).

20. See O'Keeffe, *Georgia O'Keeffe.* See also critic Henry McBride's wry but intuitive piece on her crosses in *The New York Sun,* Feb. 8, 1930, reprinted in the catalogue for the Georgia O'Keeffe exhibition at the Amon Carter Museum of Western Art, Fort Worth, Texas, 1966, p. 13. He describes her as saying that anyone who doesn't feel the crosses doesn't comprehend that country. She is clearly talking about the crosses as having personal meaning for her, not just as "cold" abstract form. For more on O'Keeffe's use of "black," see note 22, page 486.

21. Leo Janos, *op. cit.*

22. Cf., again, Willa Cather's counterpoint between "the sky full of motion and change" and "the desert beneath it monotonous and still." Again, that depiction of the duality that the imagination intuits in nature takes us back to the Platonic core that is in Emerson: "All over the wide fields of earth grows the prunella or self-heal . . . and though we are always engaged with particulars, and often enslaved to them, we bring with us to every experiment the innate universal laws. These, while they exist in the mind as ideas, stand around us in nature forever embodied, a present sanity to cure and expose the insanity of men." (Emerson, *Nature.*) The artist may be an individual more enslaved than most by the particulars that keep so vivid an appearance in the memory and eventually merge into semblances of those "universal ideas." The drive is to make structures combining the two symbolically dichotomous elements—line and "light"—that assuage the feeling of intolerable restlessness that the sense of this disharmony in nature induces. There is nothing mystical about the condition or the response, though there is plenty that is mysterious. As the naturalist Thomas Huxley wrote a quarter century after Emerson's poetic *Nature:* "The question of all questions for humanity, the problem which lies behind all others and is more interesting than any of them is that of the determination of man's place in Nature and his relation to the Cosmos." I think most of the women artists with whom I spoke would agree, despite the quaint use of the possessive pronoun.

Women of the First Wave

LEE KRASNER

1. Louise Varèse, preface to Arthur Rimbaud, *Illuminations* (New York: New Directions Paperback, 1946), p. xvi.

2. *Ibid.*

3. Lee Krasner, in *Science and Technology,* September 1969.

4. When Krasner first took Hofmann to see Pollock's paintings, in Provincetown one summer, Hofmann told the younger man that he must always go back to work from nature or be condemned to repeat himself.

5. First published in *Art News,* December 1952, reprinted in John W. McCoubrey, *American Art 1700–1960.* A decade later, Rosenberg took up the theme again in "Action Painting: A Decade of Distortion," *Art News,* December 1962, in which he called that idiom "the last serious 'moment' in art." He found by then the "consciousness of the crisis has been further dulled," and that "the tension of the painter's lonely and perilous balance on the rim of absurdity is dissolved into the popular melodrama of technical breakthrough, comparable to the invention of the transistor."

ALICE NEEL

1. The painting is Kline's interpretation and heightening of a famous photo of the dancer as Petrouchka by Elliot & Fry, London, 1911, reproduced in George Amberg, *Ballet* (New York: Duell, Sloan and Pearce, 1949).

LOUISE NEVELSON

1. Louise Nevelson, *Dawns + Dusks,* taped conversations with Diana MacKown, p. 123 and *passim.*
2. Nevelson to interviewer, television film produced and directed by Jill Godmilo and Susan Fanshel for Station WNET–Channel 13, New York, 1977.
3. Nevelson in *Art News,* November 1972, p. 67; reprinted from Arnold Glimcher, *Louise Nevelson,* 1972 ed., with prologue by the artist.
4. Nevelson, *Dawns + Dusks,* p. 148.
5. Nevelson in *Art News,* p. 67.
6. WNET television film, 1977.
7. Nevelson, *Dawns + Dusks,* p. 1.
8. *Ibid.,* p. 27.
9. *Ibid.,* p. 43.
10. *Ibid.,* p. 46.
11. *Ibid.,* p. 76.
12. *Ibid.,* p. 154.
13. The great dream in middle-class America before the Women's Movement gave girls other goals: to be Queen of something or other—the May, the Orange Bowl, Roses, Peaches, etc. Betye Saar (see page 355) was another artist excluded from this exercise because of her race.
14. Nevelson, *Dawns + Dusks,* p. 87.
15. A point not necessarily related to quality of the works but of interest to art history may be who first came onto the scene with a sculptural wood "environment." Nevelson claims the point with her 1955 show at Grand Central Moderns: "Since I claim that I was the first American to arrest environment, enclosures, and so forth . . ." (Arnold Glimcher, *Louise Nevelson,* 1976 ed., p. 188.) But in fact Louise Bourgeois presented such a concept in her show at the Peridot Gallery in 1949 (see page 163).
16. Hilton Kramer in *Arts,* special sculpture number, June 1958, quoted in Arnold Glimcher, *Louise Nevelson* 1976 ed., p. 84.

17. Nevelson, *Dawns + Dusks,* p. 144.

18. *Ibid.,* p. 144.

19. *Ibid.,* p. 115.

20. *Ibid.*

21. WNET television film, 1977.

22. Traces of this once-living Manichean symbology are all around us, from the traditional bride's costume to the traditional habit of the nun who takes on herself the sins of the world. Nevelson is obviously acutely sensitive to the different effects on the viewer of a white or a black environment: my point is that for a rich experience of Christian theology, both elements must be present. It is interesting to consider Georgia O'Keeffe's attitude toward those two noncolors. She has often insisted that she finds them morally neutral, of equal emotional weight. Yet one who wanted to write a thesis on her use of "black"—black doors, black skyscrapers at night, Black Iris, Black Cross, etc.—might turn up the opposite psychoesthetic attitude. The fact that she was educated as a child in a Dominican convent, where the traditional habit consists of white dress with black over-robe, may figure. Carl Sagan, in *The Dragons of Eden* (New York: Ballantine ed., 1977), p. 185, explains that both words seem to have the same origin in Anglo-Saxon, in a term meaning absence of color. O'Keeffe's *wish* for neutrality, then, may be another example of her intuitive focus on the natural and her wish to get back behind imposed cultural biases.

ISABEL BISHOP

1. T. S. Eliot, "The Waste Land," *Collected Poems,* New York: Harcourt Brace, 1963.

2. These famous photo studies by Edward J. Muybridge, made in the 1880s of humans and horses in stopped motion, have interested many artists, beginning with Thomas Eakins.

3. In Karl Lunde, *Isabel Bishop,* p. 71.

LOUISE BOURGEOIS

1. Marius Bewley in his introduction to Louise Bourgeois's *He Disappeared into Complete Silence,* a suite of nine engravings.

2. See note 15, page 493.

HELEN LUNDEBERG

1. The first showing of the French Surrealists took place in Paris in 1925, under the leadership of Andrew Breton, who wrote the group's first manifesto. It took six years for the idea to cross the ocean, and in December '31 the Wadsworth Atheneum in Hartford, Conn., exhibited the European masters including Dali, de Chirico, Man Ray, etc. Later the collection traveled to the Julien Levy Gallery in New York, which there-

after was a focus for the movement here and gave one-person shows to the major European and, eventually, East Coast American artists. He showed Dorothea Tanning (coincidentally, born in Lundeberg's home town) in '45. By '34 the idiom had traveled to the West Coast: that year saw the first Post-Surrealist show, with Lundeberg and Feitelson, at the Centaur Gallery in Hollywood. In 1936, the Museum of Modern Art in New York put on an epochal international show, "Fantastic Art, Dada and Surrealism." That catalogue and also Julien Levy's book *Surrealism* that came out the same year became standard texts. Then when between 1941 and '46 the French Surrealists came in person, New York became the international center. Peggy Guggenheim's Art of This Century Gallery, opening in '42, was one of the main watering places. That all this international Modernist embroilment was going on in America during years conventionally thought of as devoted to Social Realist and Regional esthetics is another of the facts of life that certain Abstract Expressionists forgot later when it seemed advantageous to deny the French foundation of that movement. See Jeffrey Wechsler's exhibition catalogue *Surrealism and American Art: 1931–1947* for Rutgers University Art Gallery, March 5–April 24, 1977 (copyright 1976), which includes a section on Los Angeles Post-Surrealism and the work of Helen Lundeberg (p. 43 and *passim*).

2. "I am apparently," wrote Lundeberg in 1942, "a classicist by nature as well as conviction. By classicism I mean . . . a highly conscious concern with aesthetic structure, which is the antithesis of intuitive, romantic or realistic approaches to painting. My aim is to calculate and reconsider every element in a painting with regard to its function in the whole organization." (Wechsler, *op. cit.*, p. 45.)

JEANNE REYNAL

1. Quoted in Ashton *et al.*, *The Mosaics of Jeanne Reynal*, p. 29.
2. This way of working would be the link between Reynal and the Abstract Expressionists. Compare Jackson Pollock on painting upon the floor as "akin to the method of the Indian sand painters of the West" (in *Possibilities* Number 1, Winter 1947–48.)
3. Cf. Nevelson's famous remark about her husband's family, which was "terribly refined. Within their circle you could know Beethoven, but God forbid if you *were* Beethoven." (From Arnold Glimcher, *Louise Nevelson*, 1972 ed., quoted in *Art News*, November 1972, p. 67.)
2. Can Feminists congratulate themselves on a revolution won when four major, mature artists from this collection have never shown solo at the Whitney Museum of American Art: Nell Blaine, Helen Lundeberg, Jeanne Reynal and Lenore Tawney?

Women of the Second Wave

HELEN FRANKENTHALER

1. Frank O'Hara, *Jackson Pollock*.
2. See note 9, page 482.

3. Harold Rosenberg, "The American Action Painters," *Art News,* December 1952, p. 22.

4. Clement Greenberg in *Partisan Review,* 1949, quoted in Jack Kroll, "Some Greenberg Circles," *Art News,* March 1962, p. 35.

5. Clement Greenberg, *Art and Culture,* p. 155.

6. *Ibid.,* p. 181.

7. *Ibid.,* p. 152.

8. *Ibid.,* p. 199.

9. See note 9, page 482.

10. "Winds of remembering/Of the ancient being blow,/And seeming-solid walls of use/Open and flow. . . . (Emerson, *Bacchus*).

11. All, quoted in Frank O'Hara, *Robert Motherwell,* pp. 58–67.

12. Quoted in John Gruen, *The Party's Over Now,* p. 194.

13. Quoted in *New Works in Clay by Contemporary Painters and Sculptors,* exhibition catalogue of the Everson Museum of Art, Syracuse, N.Y., Jan. 23–April 4, 1976, p. 34.

14. Helen Frankenthaler, "The Romance of Learning a New Medium for an Artist," *The Print Collector's Newsletter,* July/August 1977, p. 67.

15. Quoted in Judith Goldman, "Painting in Another Language," *Art News,* September 1975, p. 28.

16. *Ibid.,* p. 31.

17. These ecstatic expressions of a felt connection between the artist's mind, body and nature (see also Joan Mitchell, p. 246) state in poetic and conceptual form the principle from which, it seems to me, the young nature or Site artists of today are working in their less metaphoric, more direct way (see p. 392 and *passim*). It was a rhetoric, but perhaps the fundamental and most persuasive teaching in Abstract Expressionism, other pronouncements notwithstanding.

18. Greenberg, *Art and Culture,* p. 157.

JOAN MITCHELL

1. See note 16, page 484.

2. See note 13, page 483.

3. See note 17, above.

ELAINE DE KOONING

1. Elaine de Kooning, "Reynal Makes a Mosaic," *Art News,* December 1953, p. 34.

NELL BLAINE

1. Joan Mitchell, Nell Blaine, June Wayne and Anne Truitt wear glasses today and talked about the shock of receiving them as children and how the event focused their attention on the world in a new way.

2. Blaine's major work from this period, *Lester Leaps,* 1944, was one of the last paintings purchased by Thomas Hess for the Twentieth Century Department at the Metropolitan Museum before his death in '78.

MIRIAM SCHAPIRO

1. Quoted in Pamela Daniels and Sara Ruddick, *Working It Out,* p. 284.
2. See note 4, page 481.
3. *Anonymous Was a Woman,* copyright Miriam Schapiro for the Feminist Art Program, California Institute of the Arts, 1974; *Art: A Woman's Sensibility, ibid.,* 1975.

JUNE WAYNE

1. June Wayne, "The Creative Process," *Craft Horizons,* October 1976, p. 67.
2. *Ibid.*

MARY FRANK

1. In the spring of '77, before I began working on this project, Hayden Herrera, who was preparing an important retrospective exhibition of Mary Frank's work, spent several hours interviewing the artist. Since I followed shortly on her heels and did not wish to ask the artist to repeat herself, both the artist and Herrera kindly gave me permission to work from the transcript of their talk. Some of Mary Frank's statements that follow, therefore, come not from conversation with me but with Herrera. I indicate them with gratitude below. See Hayden Herrera, *Mary Frank: Sculpture/Drawings/Prints,* exhibition catalogue for the Neuberger Museum, State University of New York, Purchase, N.Y., June 4–Sept. 10, 1978.
2. *Ibid.*
3. This was not always considered an outlandish treatment for girls' insubordination. Kate Millet, the writer, has described a similar event and so does Jeanne Reynal (page 182).
4. Frank to Herrera.
5. *Ibid.*
6. "She is so closely in touch . . ." S. B. in *Art News,* May 1966.
7. The several articles Kramer devoted to Mary Frank's work were a remarkable display of constructive criticism from which this artist profited. See his "The Possibilities of Mary Frank, *Arts,* March 1963; "The Sculpture of Mary Frank: Poetical, Metaphorical, Interior," *New York Times,* Feb. 22, 1970; "Art: Sensual Serene Sculpture," *New York Times,* Jan. 25, 1975.
8. Kramer, *New York Times,* Feb. 10, 1968.
9. Frank to Herrera.
10. *Ibid.*
11. *Ibid.*

12. *Ibid.*

13. *Ibid.*

14. T. S. Eliot, *Four Quartets* (New York: Harcourt Brace, 1943).

Women of the Third Wave

ANNE TRUITT

1. Clement Greenberg, "Changer: Anne Truitt," *Vogue,* May 1968, p. 212.

2. Clement Greenberg, quoted by Michael Fried, "Object and Objecthood," in Gregory Battcock (ed.), *Minimal Art,* p. 120.

3. *Anne Truitt: Sculpture and Painting,* exhibition folder for the University of Virginia Art Museum, Oct. 17–Nov. 19, 1976, p. 6.

4. Georgia O'Keeffe, quoted in Leo Janos, "Georgia O'Keeffe at 84," *The Atlantic,* December 1971.

LENORE TAWNEY

1. It is historically the case that at exactly the same time painter Agnes Martin was crystallizing her style or "image" into the "grid works" that have brought her enormous fame. The question can be asked who influenced whom? What is certain is that Martin's first grid works, like *The Ages* ('59–'60), *Islands No. 1* ('60), *Starlight* ('62), *Whispering* ('63), were all near-literal renditions of woven textiles with warp and woof clearly delineated. Martin of course went on refining this single image in obsessively repeated, delicately mutating surfaces that have offered only the most minute variations of line and color. Tawney might be said to have dissipated the relative impact of her extraordinary inventions of that time by her frequent dips out of sight but also by the very richness and variety of her oeuvre.

2. See *Lenore Tawney: A Personal World,* exhibition catalogue for the Brookfield Craft Center, Brookfield, Conn., June 18–Sept. 4, 1978.

Women of the Fourth Wave

1. See note 33, page 486.

2. See note 1, page 475, top.

3. Grant monies for artists are available through the National Endowments for the Arts and Humanities in Washington, D.C., through states' Arts Councils, CAPs, the John Simon Guggenheim Foundation, the American Council of Learned Societies and numerous local, private foundations. A number of these organizations invite the Site Workers to come and build structures on land that will be later returned to its original condition. Of these, the most famous is Artpark, which opened in July of '74 on a wild stretch of landfill atop the Niagara River Gorge outside Lewiston, N.Y. Several artists

included here have spent time at Artpark, where they can build, dig, erect as they wish; their structures are afterward removed to make room for the next season's roster. There is the frustration of knowing one's work is transitory but also the encouragement to experiment with plans that are ephemeral or far-out.

    4. See note 16, page 484.

    5. Mary Miss, quoted in *Artpark: The Program in Visual Arts,* p. 160.

    6. See Alice Aycock, "Work: 1972–1974," in Alan Sondheim (ed.), *Individuals: Post Movement Art in America,* p. 110.

    7. *The Second Sex,* p. 633.

JENNIFER BARTLETT

    1. Gerard Manley Hopkins, "Spring and Fall: to a young child."

JACKIE WINSOR

    1. Sculptors today know the dangers to the health of breathing fumes from plastics. Eva Hesse did not, and some people attribute her early death from brain cancer to her unprotected use of the resins. That Winsor's builder father also suffered from a materials-induced ailment made her doubly wary.

MICHELLE STUART

    1. Michelle Stuart, in *Return to the Silent Garden,* journal in progress since 1970. Compare Georgia O'Keeffe's description of a walk during which she climbed a green hill, looked out at red, yellow and purple features of the landscape, the hues intensified by the pale gray-green underfoot (see the quotation in Daniel Catton Rich, exhibition catalogue for the Art Institute of Chicago, 1943, p. 35.) O'Keeffe releases the tension of her awe through a summation of colors; Stuart, through numbers. Both artists are attempting to come to grips with what their forefathers rapturously described and painted as "the sublime," in terms that remain down-to-earth, naturalistic, simple, even primitive: the mind of the '70s.

CONNIE ZEHR

    1. "A Way to Look at Things," in the exhibition catalogue *Seven Americans,* Anderson Galleries, 1925, reprinted in Barbara Haskell, *Arthur Dove,* p. 136.

PATRICIA JOHANSON

1. Unpublished manuscript, 1960.

AFTERWORD

1. Cf. "The longing to behold that pre-established harmony is the source of the inexhaustible perseverance and patience with which [Max] Planck has given himself over to the most general problems of our science, not letting himself be diverted to more profitable and more easily attained ends. I have often heard colleagues trying to trace this attitude to extraordinary will power and discipline—in my opinion, wrongly. The state of feeling which makes one capable of such achievements is akin to that of the religious worshipper or of one who is in love; his daily striving arises from no deliberate decision or program, but out of immediate necessity." (Albert Einstein, 1918, quoted in Gerald Holton, "On Trying to Understand Scientific Genius," *The American Scholar,* Winter 1971–72, p. 109.)

2. Some women understand this point very well. Gloria Emerson has written: "True equality is a fearful thing. If women really want to be equal, let them carry their own things in a knapsack going through the jungle, let them go out with nineteen year olds carrying their own mortars. For me, it was very nice that a principled lady reporter could refuse to carry a forty-five. By refusing, I kept my principles. But it meant some draftee half my age with an M-16 would have to fire twice as often to protect me. So much for principles." Quoted in "Men, Women and Violence: Some Reflections on Equality," by Natalie Zemon Davis, *Smith College Alumnae Bulletin,* Winter 1977, p. 12.

A Selected
General Bibliography

America and Alfred Stieglitz: A Collective Portrait. New York: Doubleday, Doran, 1934.

Anonymous Was a Woman. Valencia, Calif.: California Institute of the Arts, 1974.

Art: A Woman's Sensibility. Valencia, Calif.: California Institute of the Arts, 1975.

Artpark: The Program in Visual Arts, catalogue for Artpark, Lewiston, N.Y., 1976.

Ashton, Dore, *The New York School: A Cultural Reckoning.* New York: Viking, 1972.

Battcock, Gregory (ed.), *Minimal Art.* New York: Dutton Paperback, 1968.

————, *The New Art.* New York: Dutton Paperback, 1973.

Beauvoir, Simone de, *The Prime of Life.* Penguin edition, 1962.

————, *The Second Sex.* New York: Knopf, 1953.

Brooks, Van Wyck, *Fenollosa and His Circle.* New York: Dutton, 1962.

Brown, Milton, *American Painting from the Armory Show to the Depression.* Princeton, N.J.: Princeton University Press, 1955.

Cather, Willa, *Death Comes for the Archbishop.* New York: Random House, Vintage Books, 1971.

Clark, Kenneth, *Landscape into Art.* New York: Harper & Row, 1976.

Daniels, Pamela, and Sara Ruddick, *Working It Out.* New York: Pantheon, 1977.

Dewey, John, *Art as Experience.* New York: Capricorn Books, 1934, 1958.

Frankenstein, Alfred, "Arthur Dove: Abstraction at Will," *Art in America,* March/April 1975.

Friedan, Betty, *The Feminine Mystique.* New York: W. W. Norton, 1963.

Friedman, B. H., *Jackson Pollock.* New York: McGraw-Hill, 1972.

————, *Gertrude Vanderbilt Whitney.* New York: Doubleday, 1978.

Funding a Future for Women in the Humanities (booklet). Bethesda, Md.: Vandegriff Research, 5209 Bradley Blvd., 1976.

Gaertner, Johannes A., "Myth and Pattern in the Lives of Artists," *Art Journal,* Fall 1970.

Gingerich, Owen (ed.), *The Nature of Scientific Discovery: A Symposium.* Washington, D.C.: Smithsonian Institution, 1975.

Greenberg, Clement, *Art and Culture.* Boston: Beacon, 1961.

Gruen, John, *The Party's Over Now: Reminiscences of the Fifties.* New York: Viking, 1972.

Harris, Ann Sutherland, and Linda Nochlin, *Women Artists: 1550–1950.* New York: Knopf, with the Los Angeles County Museum, 1976.

Haskell, Barbara, *Arthur Dove,* exhibition catalogue for the San Francisco Museum of Art. Greenwich, Conn.: New York Graphic Society, 1974.

Hess, Thomas B., *Abstract Painting: Background and American Phase.* New York: Viking, 1951.

———, *Barnett Newman.* New York: Walker, 1967.

Hills, Patricia, *The Painter's America: Rural and Urban Life: 1810–1910,* exhibition catalogue for the Whitney Museum of American Art. New York: Praeger, 1974.

Holton, Gerald, "On Trying to Understand Scientific Genius," *The American Scholar,* Winter 1971–72.

Hunter, Sam, *American Art of the Twentieth Century.* New York: Abrams, 1973.

Johnson, Ellen H., *Modern Art and the Object.* New York: Harper & Row, 1976.

Kandinsky, Wassily, *On the Spiritual in Art.* New York: Solomon R. Guggenheim Foundation for the Museum of Non-Objective Painting, 1946.

Kingsley, April, "Six Women at Work in the Landscape." *Arts,* April, 1978.

Kuh, Katherine, *The Artist's Eye.* New York: Harper & Row, 1962.

Levy, Julien, *Surrealism.* New York: Black Sun Press, 1936.

Lippard, Lucy, *Changing: Essays in Art Criticism.* New York: Dutton Paperback, 1971.

———, *Eva Hesse.* New York: New York University Press, 1976.

———, *From the Center.* New York: Dutton Paperback, 1976.

McCoubrey, John W., *American Art, 1700–1960,* Courses and Documents in the History of Art series, ed. H. W. Janson. Englewood Cliffs, N.J.: Prentice-Hall, 1965.

McShine, Kynaston, *The Natural Paradise: Painting in America, 1800–1950.* New York: Museum of Modern Art, 1976.

Moers, Ellen, *Literary Women.* New York: Doubleday, 1976.

Munro, Thomas, *Art Education: Its Philosophy and Psychology.* New York: Liberal Arts Press, 1956.

———, *Evolution in the Arts.* Cleveland, Ohio: Cleveland Museum of Art, 1963.

Nemser, Cindy, *Art Talk.* New York: Scribner's, 1975.

New York City: WPA Art, exhibition catalogue for the Parsons School of Design, New York, November 1977.

Norman, Dorothy, *Alfred Stieglitz: An American Seer.* New York: Duell, Sloan and Pearce, 1960; Random House, 1973.

Novak, Barbara, *American Painting of the Nineteenth Century.* New York: Praeger, 1969.

O'Hara, Frank, *Robert Motherwell.* New York: Museum of Modern Art, 1965.

———, *Jackson Pollock, The Great American Artists series.* New York: Braziller, 1959.

Olsen, Tillie, *Silences.* New York: Delacorte, 1978.

Rank, Otto, *Art and Artist.* New York: Knopf, 1932.

Rodman, Selden, *Conversations with Artists.* New York: Devin-Adair, 1957.

Rose, Barbara, "ABC Art," *Art in America,* October/November 1965. Reprinted in Gregory Battcock, (ed.), *Minimal Art* (New York: Dutton Paperback, 1968).

———, "America as Paradise," *Partisan Review,*

———, *American Painting: The 20th Century.* New York: Skira, 1973.

———, "Twilight of the Superstars," *Partisan Review,* 1974, No. 4.

502

————, "Vaginal Iconography," *New York* magazine, Feb. 11, 1974.

Rosenberg, Harold, "Action Painting: A Decade of Distortion," *Art News,* December 1962.

————, "The American Action Painters," *Art News,* December 1952.

————, *The Anxious Object.* New York: Horizon, 1964.

Rosenblum, Robert, *Modern Painting and the Northern Romantic Tradition.* New York: Harper & Row, 1975.

Seckler, Dorothy Gees, *Provincetown Painters,* exhibition catalogue for the Everson Art Museum, Syracuse, N.Y., 1977.

Seiberling, Dorothy, "The Female View of Erotica," *New York* magazine, Feb. 11, 1974.

Seitz, William C., *The Art of Assemblage.* New York: Museum of Modern Art, 1961.

Sex Differences in Art Exhibition Reviews. Albuquerque, N.M.: Tamarind Institute– University of New Mexico, 1972.

Sondheim, Alan (ed.), *Individuals: Post-Movement Art in America.* New York: Dutton Paperback, 1977.

Soyer, Rafael, *Diary of an Artist.* New York: New Republic Books, 1977.

Steinberg, Leo, *Other Criteria: Confrontations with 20th Century Art.* New York: Oxford University Press, 1972.

Tomkins, Calvin, *The Bride and the Bachelors.* New York: Viking, 1965.

200 Years of American Sculpture, exhibition catalogue for the Whitney Museum of American Art, New York, 1976.

Warhol, Andy, *The Philosophy of Andy Warhol.* New York: Harcourt Brace Jovanovich, 1975.

Wechsler, Jeffrey, *Surrealism and American Art: 1931–1947,* exhibition catalogue for Rutgers University Art Gallery, March–April 1977, copyright 1976.

Wilding, Faith, *By Our Own Hands.* Santa Monica, Calif.: Double X Publishers, 1977.

Woolf, Virginia, *Moments of Being.* New York: Harcourt Brace Jovanovich, 1976.

A Selected
Artists' Bibliography

In the section that follows, I have tried to provide merely toeholds for readers who want more information about some artists mentioned in this book. In no case is the listing complete. Most galleries will provide bibliographies. Where there is no gallery affiliation, I have listed an institution where the artist is known or, if possible, the artist's studio address. Current art magazines—*Arts, Art in America, Artforum, Art News*—run exhibition reviews (as do newspapers). The *Art Index* is a standard reference catalogue to these sources. The Archives of American Art, The Smithsonian Institution, Washington, D.C., has material on individuals in the art world living and dead. Local museums, libraries and women's centers have the same. I have listed no films or taped interviews, but many have been made. Inquire at Archives of American Art and major museums.

ANTIN, ELEANOR
Catalogue: *The Angel of Mercy,* for the La Jolla Museum of Contemporary Art, La Jolla, Calif., September–October 1977.
Interview: Nemser, Cindy, *Art Talk.* New York: Scribner's, 1975.
Statements: *Anonymous Was a Woman* (1974) and *Art: A Woman's Sensibility* (1975). Feldman Gallery, New York.

ASHER, ELISE
Statement: *Art: A Woman's Sensibility.* Valencia, Calif.: California Institute of the Arts. Ingber Gallery, New York.

AYCOCK, ALICE
Book: Sondheim, Alan (ed.), *Individuals: Post-Movement Art in America.* New York: Dutton Paperback, 1977.
Catalogue: *Projects in Nature: Eleven Environmental Works Executed at Merriewold West, Far Hills, N.J.,* September–October 1975.
John Weber Gallery, New York.

BABER, ALICE
Catalogue: *Alice Baber: Color, Light and Image,* for St. Mary's College of Maryland Gallery, St. Mary's City, Maryland. February–March 1977.
Statements: *Anonymous Was a Woman* (1974) and *Art: A Woman's Sensibility* (1975).

504

BARTLETT, JENNIFER

Articles: Hess, Thomas, "Ceremonies of Measurement," *New York* magazine, March 21, 1977.

Russell, John, "Finding a Bold New Work," *New York Times,* May 16, 1976.

Book: Bartlett, *History of the Universe,* unpublished ms.

Paula Cooper Gallery, New York.

BISHOP, ISABEL

Book: Lunde, Karl, *Isabel Bishop.* New York: Abrams, 1975.

Midtown Galleries, New York.

BLAINE, NELL

Statement: *Art: A Woman's Sensibility.* Valencia, Calif.: California Institute of the Arts.

Fischbach Gallery, New York.

BONTECOU, LEE

Leo Castelli Gallery, New York.

BOURGEOIS, LOUISE

Books: Bourgeois, *He Disappeared into Complete Silence,* suite of nine engravings, introd. by Marius Bewley (Gemor Press, 1947).

Lippard, Lucy, *From the Center.* New York: Dutton Paperback, 1976.

Catalogue: *200 Years of American Sculpture,* for the Whitney Museum of American Art.

Xavier Fourcade Gallery, New York.

CASSATT, MARY

Books: Breeskin, Adelyn D., *The Graphic Work of Mary Cassatt.* New York: H. Bittner & Co., 1948.

Hale, Nancy, *Mary Cassatt.* New York: Doubleday, 1975.

Havemeyer, Louisine, *Sixteen to Sixty: Memoirs of a Collector.* New York: Metropolitan Museum of Art, 1930.

Ségard, Achille, *Un Peintre des enfants et des mères: Mary Cassatt.* Paris: P. Ollendorff, 1913.

Sweet, Frederick A., *Miss Mary Cassatt: Impressionist from Philadelphia.* Norman, Okla.: University of Oklahoma Press, 1966.

Watson, Forbes, *Mary Cassatt.* New York: Whitney Museum, 1932.

CHASE-RIBOUD, BARBARA

Article: Nora, Françoise, "From Another Country," *Art News,* March 1972.

Book: Chase-Riboud, *From Memphis and Peking.* New York: Random House, 1974.

Catalogue: *Chase-Riboud,* for the University Art Museum, Berkeley, Calif., January– February 1973.

The artist, 3 rue Auguste Comte, Paris.

CHICAGO, JUDY

Books: Chicago, *Through the Flower: My Struggle as a Woman Artist,* with introd. by Anaïs Nin. New York: Doubleday, 1973.

Lippard, Lucy, *From the Center.* New York: Dutton Paperback, 1976.

Statement: *Anonymous Was a Woman* (1974) and *Art: A Woman's Sensibility* (1975).

The Woman's Building, 1727 North Spring Street, Los Angeles.

DENNIS, DONNA
Catalogue: *The 1979 Biennial Exhibition,* for the Whitney Museum of American Art.
Holly Solomon Gallery, New York.

DIENES, SARI
A. I. R. Gallery, New York.

DE BRETTEVILLE, SHEILA
Articles and typography in the Feminist magazine *Chrysalis,* 1976 to date.
Statement: *Art: A Woman's Sensibility.* Valencia, Calif.: California Institute of the Arts.
The Woman's Building, 1727 North Spring Street, Los Angeles.

FRANK, MARY
Articles: Kingsley, April, "Mary Frank: A Sense of Timelessness," *Art News,* Summer
         1973.
   Kramer, Hilton, "Art: Sensual Serene Sculpture," *New York Times,* Jan. 25, 1975.
   ———, "The Possibilities of Mary Frank," *Arts,* March 1963.
   ———, "The Sculpture of Mary Frank: Poetical, Metaphorical, Interior," *New York
         Times,* Feb. 22, 1970.
   ———, *New York Times,* Feb. 10, 1968.
Catalogue: Herrera, Hayden, *Mary Frank: Sculpture/Drawings/Prints,* for the Neuberger
         Museum, State University of New York, Purchase, N.Y.

FRANKENTHALER, HELEN
Book: Rose, Barbara, *Helen Frankenthaler.* New York: Abrams, 1971.
Catalogue: Goossen, Eugene C., *Helen Frankenthaler,* for the Whitney Museum of
         American Art, New York, 1969.
André Emmerich Gallery, New York.

GRAVES, NANCY
Book: Lippard, Lucy, *From the Center.* New York: Dutton Paperback, 1976.
Catalogues: For the Whitney Museum, March 1969.
   For the La Jolla Museum of Contemporary Art, La Jolla, Calif., August–October 1973.
   200 Years of American Sculpture, for the Whitney Museum of American Art.
Interview: Wasserman, E. "A Conversation with Nancy Graves," *Artforum,* October
         1970.
M. Knoedler and Co., New York.

FREILICHER, JANE
Article: Schjeldahl, Peter. "Urban Pastorals," *Art News,* February 1971.
Statements: *Anonymous Was a Woman* (1974) and *Art: A Woman's Sensibility* (1975).
Fischbach Gallery, New York.

GRIGORIADIS, MARY
A. I. R. Gallery, New York.

GROSSMAN, NANCY
Interview: Nemser, Cindy, *Art Talk,* New York: Scribner's, 1975.
Cordier & Eckstrom Gallery, New York.

506

HARTIGAN, GRACE
Interview: Nemser, Cindy, *Art Talk,* New York: Scribner's, 1975.
Genesis Galleries, Ltd., New York.

HEALY, ANNE
Zabriskie Gallery, New York.

HICKS, SHEILA
Book: Lévi-Strauss, Monique, *Sheila Hicks.* Paris: Pierre Horay & Suzy Langlois, 1973;
        London: Studio Vista, 1974.
Atelier Sheila Hicks, 3 Cour de Rohan, Paris.

HOLT, NANCY
Article: "Sun Tunnels," *Artforum,* April 1977.

ISRAEL, MARGARET
Article: Kramer, Hilton, *New York Times,* April 3, 1976.
Cordier & Eckstrom Gallery, New York.

JOHANSON, PATRICIA
Book: Battcock, Gregory (ed.)., *Minimal Art.* New York: Dutton Paperback, 1968.
Catalogue: *Plant Drawings for Projects,* for the Rosa Esman Gallery, March/April 1978.
Rosa Esman Gallery, New York.

KATZEN, LILA
Interview: Nemser, Cindy, *Art Talk.* New York: Scribner's, 1975.
Statement: *Art: A Woman's Sensibility.* Valencia, Calif.: California Institute of the Arts.
Gloria Cortella Gallery, New York.

KENT, CORITA
Botolph Gallery, Cambridge, Massachusetts.
Corita Prints Gallery, 5126 Vineland Ave., N. Hollywood, California.

KLAVUN, BETTY
Article: Edgar, N., "The Dream Space of Betty Klavun," *Craft Horizons,* February 1973.
The artist, 313 West Twentieth Street, New York.

KOONING, ELAINE DE
Articles: Campbell, L., "Elaine de Kooning Paints a Picture," *Art News,* December 1960.
Articles by E de K in *Art News* regularly, 1949–50.
Interview: Taylor, John, "An Interview with Elaine de Kooning in Athens," *Contemporary Arts Southeast,* April/May 1977.
Graham Gallery, New York.

KOZLOFF, JOYCE
Catalogue: *The 1979 Biennial Exhibition,* for the Whitney Museum of American Art.
Tibor de Nagy Gallery, New York.

KRASNER, LEE
Articles: Rose, Barbara, "Lee Krasner and the Origins of Abstract Expressionism," *Arts,*
        February 1977.

Robertson, Brian, "The Nature of Lee Krasner," *Art in America,* November/December 1973.
Catalogue: *Lee Krasner: Paintings, Drawings and Collages,* for the Whitechapel Gallery, London, 1965.
Interviews: Nemser, Cindy, *Art Talk.* New York: Scribner's, 1975.
 Rose, Barbara, "American Great: Lee Krasner," *Vogue,* June 1972.
Statements: *Anonymous Was a Woman* (1974) and *Art: A Woman's Sensibility* (1975).
Pace Gallery, New York.

LANSNER, FAY
Book: *Fay Lansner, Conversation with Irving Sandler,* Swarthmore, Pa.: Ava Books, 1976.
Statements: *Anonymous Was a Woman* (1974) and *Art: A Woman's Sensibility* (1975).
Marlborough-Graphics Gallery, New York.

LUNDEBERG, HELEN
Catalogue: Wechsler, Jeffrey, "Surrealism and American Art: 1931–1947," for the Rutgers University Art Gallery, March–April 1977.
Statement: in *Sourcebook for Interior Design,* November/December 1974.
Article: Kramer, Hilton, "A Survey of California Art," *New York Times,* June 19, 1977.
The artist, 8307 West 3rd Street, Los Angeles.

MARISOL
Interview: Nemser, Cindy, *Art Talk.* New York: Scribner's, 1975.
Janis Gallery, New York.

MARTIN, AGNES
Catalogue: *Agnes Martin,* for the Institute of Contemporary Art, University of Pennsylvania, Philadelphia, Pa., January–March 1973.
Pace Gallery, New York.

MISS, MARY
Article: Onorato, Ronald J., "Illusive Spaces: The Art of Mary Miss," *Artforum,* December 1978.
Book: Lippard, Lucy, *From the Center.* New York: Dutton Paperback, 1976.
Catalogue: *Artpark: The Program in Visual Arts,* for Artpark, Lewiston, N.Y., 1976.
Max Protetch Gallery, New York.

MITCHELL, JOAN
Book: Lippard, Lucy, *From the Center.* New York: Dutton Paperback, 1976.
Article: Rosenberg, Harold, "Artist Against Background," *The New Yorker,* April 29, 1974.
Catalogue: *My Five Years in the Country: An Exhibition of Forty-nine Paintings,* for the Everson Museum of Art, Syracuse, N.Y., March–April 1972.
 Tucker, Marcia, *Joan Mitchell,* for the Whitney Museum of American Art, New York, 1974.
Xavier Fourcade Gallery, New York.

NEEL, ALICE
Article: Hess, Thomas, "Sitting Prettier," *New York* magazine, Feb. 23, 1976.

Catalogues: *Alice Neel,* for the Whitney Museum of American Art, New York, 1974.
   Alice Neel: The Woman and her Work, for the Georgia Museum of Art, University of
         Georgia, Athens, Ga., 1975.
Interview: Nemser, Cindy, *Art Talk.* New York: Scribner's, 1975.
Statement: *Art: A Woman's Sensibility.* Valencia, Calif.: California Institute of the Arts.
Graham Gallery, New York.

NEVELSON, LOUISE
Books: Glimcher, Arnold, *Louise Nevelson.* New York: Praeger, 1972; Dutton, 1976.
   Nevelson, Louise, *Dawns + Dusks.* New York: Scribner's, 1976.
Catalogue: *200 Years of American Sculpture,* for the Whitney Museum of American Art.
Interview: Nemser, Cindy, *Art Talk.* New York: Scribner's, 1975.
Pace Gallery, New York.

O'KEEFFE, GEORGIA
Articles: Goossen, Eugene C., "O'Keeffe," *Vogue,* March 1, 1967.
   Janos, Leo, "Georgia O'Keeffe at 84," *The Atlantic,* December 1971.
   Kotz, Mary Lynn, "Georgia O'Keeffe," *Eastern Airlines' Review,* May 1978.
   Pollitzer, Anita, "That's Georgia," *The Saturday Review,* Nov. 4, 1950.
   Rose, Barbara, "O'Keeffe's Trail," *The New York Review of Books,* Mar. 31, 1977.
   Tomkins, Calvin, "The Rose in the Eye Looked Pretty Fine," *The New Yorker,* March
         4, 1974.
Books: O'Keeffe, *Georgia O'Keeffe.* New York: Viking, 1976.
   Kuh, Katherine, *The Artist's Eye.* New York: Harper & Row, 1962.
Catalogues: *Georgia O'Keeffe,* for the Amon Carter Museum of Western Art, Fort Worth,
         Texas, 1966.
   Goodrich, Lloyd, *Georgia O'Keeffe,* for the Whitney Museum of American Art, New
         York, 1970.
   Rich, Daniel Catton, *Georgia O'Keeffe,* for the Art Institute of Chicago, 1943.

PEPPER, BEVERLY
Catalogues: *Beverly Pepper: Sculpture 1971–75,* for the San Francisco Museum of Art,
         October 1975.
   Beverly Pepper: Sculpture 1960–73, for the Tyler School of Art in Rome, Temple
         University, Philadelphia, Pa., March–April 1973.
André Emmerich Gallery, New York.

REYNAL, JEANNE
Articles: de Kooning, Elaine, "Jeanne Reynal," *Craft Horizons,* 1976.
   Guest, Barbara, "Jeanne Reynal," *Craft Horizons,* 1971.
Book: Ashton, Dore, Lawrence Campbell, Parker Tyler, Elaine de Kooning, Bernard
         Pfriem, and Jeanne Reynal, *The Mosaics of Jeanne Reynal.* New York:
         October House, 1969.
Statements: *Anonymous Was a Woman* (1974) and *Art: A Woman's Sensibility* (1975).
Bodley Gallery, New York.

RINGGOLD, FAITH
Book: Lippard, Lucy, *From the Center.* New York: Dutton Paperback, 1976.
The artist, 345 West 145th Street, New York.

ROCKBURNE, DOROTHEA

Articles: Bochner, Mel, "Dorothea Rockburne," *Artforum,* March 1972.
   Pincus-Witten, Robert, "Mel & Dorothea," *Arts,* November 1978.
Catalogue: *The 1979 Biennial Exhibition,* for the Whitney Museum of American Art.
John Weber Gallery, New York.

ROTHENBERG, SUSAN

Article: Rosenthal, Mark, "From Primary Structures to Primary Imagery," *Arts,* October
            1978.
Catalogue: *The 1979 Biennial Exhibition,* for the Whitney Museum of American Art.
Willard Gallery, New York.

SAAR, BETYE

Catalogue: "Betye Saar, Selected Works 1964–1973," for the Fine Arts Gallery, Cali-
            fornia State University, Los Angeles, October 1973.
Interview: Nemser, Cindy, "Conversation with Betye Saar," *The Feminist Art Journal,*
            Winter 1975–76.
Statements: *Anonymous Was a Woman* (1974) and *Art: A Woman's Sensibility* (1975).
Monique Knowlton Gallery, New York.

SCHAPIRO, MIRIAM

Book: Daniels, Pamela, and Sara Ruddick, *Working It Out.* New York: Pantheon, 1977.
Articles: Seiberling, Dorothy, "Lacy Fare," *New York* magazine, July 12, 1976.
Statements: *Anonymous Was a Woman* (1974) and *Art: A Woman's Sensibility* (1975).
Lerner-Heller Gallery, New York.

SCHWABACHER, ETHEL

Article: "Formal Definitions and Myths in My Paintings," *Leonardo,* Vol. VI (1973).
Book: Schwabacher, *Arshile Gorky* (New York: Macmillan, 1957).

STERNE, HEDDA

Catalogue: "Hedda Sterne: Retrospective," for the Montclair Art Museum, Montclair,
            N.J., April/June 1977.
Betty Parsons Gallery, New York.

STONE, SYLVIA

Article: Sandler, Irving. "Sylvia Stone's Egyptian Stones," *Arts,* April 1977.
Catalogue: "Sylvia Stone," for Bennington College, Bennington, Vt., 1978.
   200 Years of American Sculpture, for the Whitney Museum of American Art.
André Emmerich Gallery, New York.

STUART, MICHELLE

Article: Hobbs, Robert, "Michelle Stuart: Atavism, Geomythology and Zen,"
            WomanArt magazine, Spring/Summer 1977.
Books: Stuart, *The Fall.* New York: Printed Matter, Inc., 1976.
   Lippard, Lucy, *From the Center.* New York: Dutton Paperback, 1976.
Statements: *Anonymous Was a Woman* (1974) and *Art: A Woman's Sensibility* (1975).
Droll-Kolbert Gallery, New York.

510

TACHA, ATHENA

Article: Howett, Catherine, "New Directions in Environmental Art," *Landscape Architecture,* January 1977.

Books: Lippard, Lucy, *From the Center.* New York: Dutton Paperback, 1976.

Johnson, Ellen H., *Modern Art and the Object.* London: Thames and Hudson, 1976.

Allen Art Museum, Oberlin College, Oberlin, Ohio.

TAWNEY, LENORE

Catalogues: *Lenore Tawney: Weaving, Collage, Assemblage,* for the Art Gallery, California State University, Fullerton, Calif., November–December 1975.

Lenore Tawney: A Personal World, for the Brookfield Craft Center, Brookfield, Conn., June–September 1978.

Hadler-Rodriguez Galleries, New York.

THOMAS, ALMA W.

Catalogues: *Alma W. Thomas: Retrospective Exhibition,* for the Corcoran Gallery of Art, Washington, D.C., September–October 1972.

Alma W. Thomas: Recent Paintings, for Howard University Gallery of Art, Washington, D.C., October–November 1975.

Alma W. Thomas, for the Whitney Museum, New York, April–May 1972.

Martha Jackson Gallery, New York.

TRUITT, ANNE

Article: Greenberg, Clement, "Changer: Anne Truitt, American Artist Whose Painted Structures Helped to Change the Course of American Sculpture," *Vogue,* May 1968.

Book: Battcock, Gregory (ed.), *Minimal Art.* New York: Dutton Paperback, 1968.

Catalogues: *Anne Truitt: Sculpture and Drawings 1961–1973,* for the Corcoran Gallery of Art, Washington, D.C.

Anne Truitt: Sculpture and Painting, for the University of Virginia Art Museum, Charlottesville, Va., October–November 1976.

200 Years of American Sculpture, for the Whitney Museum of American Art.

André Emmerich Gallery, New York.

WAYNE, JUNE

Articles: Wayne, "The Creative Process," *Craft Horizons,* October 1976.

Wayne, "The Male Artist as a Stereotypical Female," *Art News,* December 1973.

Tabak, May Natalie, "Tamarind Lithography Workshop," three-part article, *Craft Horizons,* October/December 1970; February 1971.

Book: Basket, Mary W., *The Art of June Wayne.* New York: Abrams, 1969.

Statements: *Anonymous Was a Woman* (1974) and *Art: A Woman's Sensibility* (1975).

The artist, 1108 North Tamarind Avenue, Los Angeles.

VOLLMER, RUTH

Articles: Friedman, B. H., "The Quiet World of Ruth Vollmer," *Art International,* March 12, 1965.

Smithson, Robert, "Quasi-Infinities and the Waning Space," *Arts,* 1966, No. 1.

Books: Ashton, Dore, *Modern American Sculpture.* New York: Abrams, 1967.

511

Catalogue: *Ruth Vollmer, Sculpture and Painting: 1962–1974,* for the Everson Museum
of Art, Syracuse, N.Y., 1974.
Betty Parsons Gallery, New York.

VON WIEGAND, CHARMION
André Zarre Gallery, New York

WILSON, JANE
Book: Gruen, John, *The Party's Over Now: Reminiscences of the Fifties.* New York:
Viking, 1972.
Fischbach Gallery, New York.

WINSOR, JACKIE
Articles: Smith, Roberta, "Winsor Built," *Art in America,* January/February 1977.
Book: Lippard, Lucy, *From the Center.* New York: Dutton Paperback, 1976.
Catalogue: *Jackie Winsor: Sculpture,* for the Contemporary Arts Center, Cincinnati,
Ohio, October–November 1976.
The Paula Cooper Gallery, New York.

ZEHR, CONNIE
Articles: Golden, Amy, "The New Whitney Biennial: Patterns Emerging?," *Art in Amer-
ica,* May/June 1975.
Catalogues: *Attitudes Towards Space: Environmental Art,* for Mount St. Mary's College
Art Gallery, Los Angeles, Calif., January–February 1977.
Artpark: The Program in Visual Arts, for Artpark, Lewiston, N.Y., 1976.
Visual Arts Center, California State University, Fullerton, Calif.

ZEISLER, CLAIRE
Catalogue: A Retrospective, for the Art Institute of Chicago, 1979.
Hadler-Rodriguez Galleries, New York.

Index

Italic page numbers refer to illustrations.
Works in the Portfolios of Color are located as PCI, PCII, PCIII, PCIV.

Mannerist art, 64, 177
Marc, Franz, 44
March, Avery, 34
Marcus, Marcia, 202
Marin, John, 87–88, 217, 218,
    222, 297
Marisol, 41, 202
    *Women (self-portraits) and
    Dog, 41*
market, and art, 29, 49, 53
marriage and similar
    relationships, 32, 35, 277,
    343, 479n, 480n, 485n
    see also childbearing; name of
    artist, marriage
Marsh, Reginald, 151
Martin, Agnes, 95, 329, 330,
    498n
    Whispering, PCIV
Mason, Alice T., 108, 110, 485n
Mason, Emily, 34, 313
Masson, André, 162, 163
materials and processes, 39, 52–
    53, 97–98, 311, 378, 382,
    392, 499n, PCI
    see also names of artists
mathematics, and art, 22, 25,
    405
    see also geometry
Matisse, 45, 73, 81, 106–7, 112,
    140, 143, 219, 250, 266,
    290, 299, 482n, 488n
Matta, 162
Matter, Mercedes, 202, 245,
    483n
Matthiasdottir, Louise, 202
Maurer, Alfred, 81
Mayer, Rosemary, 391–92
McBride, Henry, 491n
McCarthy era, 48, 94, 156, 163
McLaughlin, John, 174
McMahon, Audrey, 108
McMillan, Constance, 392
meaning, search for, 43–45
    rejection of, 49–51
mechanism, 484n
media, influence of, 48
Medillin, Octavio, 321
Mellow, James, 340
Melville, 115, 238–39
memory, and creative
    mechanism, *see* childhood;
    experience, and art
Merleau-Ponty, Maurice, 57,
    438, 475n
Metaphysical artists, 172
Metzger, Deena, 313
Meyer, Mary P., 315, 321–22
Meyer, Melissa, 281
Michelangelo, 250

Mies van der Rohe, 238
Miller, Brenda, 7
Miller, Dorothy, 51–52
Miller, Joan, 392
Miller, Kenneth, H. 140, 148–51
Miller, Lee, 281
Millet, Kate, 494n
Mills College, 400–1
Minimalism, 50, 187, 315, 402,
    424, 431
Miro, 216, 297
Miss, Mary, 29, 393–94
    *Battery Park (city landfill
    project), 394*
    *Perimeters/Pavilions/Decoys,
    PCII*
Mitchell, Joan, 41, 48, 53, 201,
    214, 233–47, 307, 366
    Abstract Expressionism, 201,
        233, 234, 246
    art influences on, 234, 240,
        244–45
    childhood, 233, 238–43
    education and training, 240,
        242–43
    experience, and art, 24, 25
    eyesight, 496n
    isolation, 235–36, 240, 241–
        242, 247
    landscape, 232, 238–40, 246,
        PCIII
    "light," 44, 52, 482n
    marriage and similiar
        relationships, 237, 244, 247
    white, use of, 233, 234–35,
        239
    WORKS
    Bridge, 245
    Canada, 246–47
    Posted, PCIII, 236
    Quatuor II, 234, 235, 238
MKR's Art Outlook, 214
Modernism, 38, 40, 42–49, 78,
    82, 83, 109, 172, 329,
    482n, 490n
Moers, Ellen, 60–61
Moholy-Nagy, 238, 326–27,
    459
Mondrian, 28, 47, 103, 110,
    265, 266, 268
Monet, 66, 72, 73, 236, 238,
    400
Mongen, Angus, 51–52
Monroe, Harriet, 241
Moore, Henry, 60, 297, 298,
    340, 383
Moore, Marianne, 289
Morath, Inge, 480n
Moreau, 250
Morgan, Maud, 95

Morisot, Berthe, 60, 67, 70
Morley, Grace Mc., 51–52
Morris, Robert, 413
mosaics, 178–79
    Reynal, Jeanne, 178ff., 495n
mothers
    characteristic, 56, 60
    empathy for, 53
    as theme, 59, 60–61
    see also name of artist,
        childhood
Motherwell, Robert, 24–25, 44,
    45, 47, 220–22, 476n,
    480n, 483n
Mt. San Antonio College, 452
movements, artistic, 40–42
    see also names
Müller, Jan, 201–2, 299
Murillo, 64
Murphy, Virginia, 250
Murray, Elizabeth, 29, 392,
    400–1
museums, 20, 42, 46, 151–52,
    413
    Berkshire, 486n
    Boston, of Fine Arts, 434, 435
    Brooklyn (N.Y.), 250
    Carter (Amon), of Western Art,
        495n
    Contemporary Crafts
        (Chicago), 454
    Contemporary Crafts (New
        York), 330, 368
    Field, of Natural History, 241
    Guggenheim, 322, 485n
    Jewish (New York), 221, 384
    Los Angeles Municipal Art
        Gallery, 170
    Louvre, 298
    Metropolitan, 250, 253, 299,
        306, 386, 391, 497n
    Modern Art (New York),.50,
        51, 96, 106, 141, 163, 164,
        251, 254, 275, 299, 328,
        367, 368, 418, 425, 431,
        445; shows, notable, 115,
        201, 217, 495n
    Modern Art (San Francisco),
        170
    Modern Art (Teheran), 445
    Musée d'Art Moderne (Paris),
        299
    National Collection
        (Australia), 445
    National Collection of the
        Fine Arts, 173
    National Gallery (London),
        182
    National Gallery of Art
        (Washington), 228

Photograph Credits

I was asked while working on this book why I was not including photographers. There was, first, the question of space. But also there was my expectation that, because of the direct fix of the photographer on the real object, the transmutation of that real into forms of art would proceed differently than in the other mediums. Clearly, however, women have excelled in this métier since early days, as Alfred Steiglitz may have been first to acknowledge (see note 15, page 491). While I am grateful to all listed here regardless of gender, Ellie Thompson and Gwen Metz worked for me on assignment and deserve special notice. Works below are listed by artists' names. Special thanks too, to Anita Duquette of the Whitney Museum Department of Rights and Reproductions.